Springer Proceedings in Business and Economics

Springer Proceedings in Business and Economics brings the most current research presented at conferences and workshops to a global readership. The series features volumes (in electronic and print formats) of selected contributions from conferences in all areas of economics, business, management, and finance. In addition to an overall evaluation by the publisher of the topical interest, scientific quality, and timeliness of each volume, each contribution is refereed to standards comparable to those of leading journals, resulting in authoritative contributions to the respective fields. Springer's production and distribution infrastructure ensures rapid publication and wide circulation of the latest developments in the most compelling and promising areas of research today.

The editorial development of volumes may be managed using Springer Nature's innovative EquinOCS, a proven online conference proceedings submission, management and review system. This system is designed to ensure an efficient timeline for your publication, making Springer Proceedings in Business and Economics the premier series to publish your workshop or conference volume.

This book series is indexed in SCOPUS.

Luminita Chivu • Valeriu Ioan-Franc
George Georgescu
Ignacio De Los Ríos Carmenado
Jean Vasile Andrei
Editors

Constraints and Opportunities in Shaping the Future: New Approaches to Economics and Policy Making

ESPERA 2022, Bucharest, Romania, November 24-25, 2022

Editors
Luminita Chivu
National Institute for Economic Research
Romanian Academy
Bucuresti, Romania

George Georgescu
National Institute for Economic Research
Romanian Academy
Bucuresti, Romania

Jean Vasile Andrei
Business Administration
Petroleum & Gas University of Ploieşti
Ploiesti, Prahova, Romania

Valeriu Ioan-Franc
National Institute for Economic Research
Romanian Academy
Bucuresti, Bucuresti, Romania

Ignacio De Los Ríos Carmenado
GESPLAN Research Group
Technical University of Madrid
Madrid, Spain

ISSN 2198-7246　　　　　　ISSN 2198-7254　(electronic)
Springer Proceedings in Business and Economics
ISBN 978-3-031-47924-3　　　ISBN 978-3-031-47925-0　(eBook)
https://doi.org/10.1007/978-3-031-47925-0

© The Editor(s) (if applicable) and The Author(s), under exclusive license to Springer Nature Switzerland AG 2024

This work is subject to copyright. All rights are solely and exclusively licensed by the Publisher, whether the whole or part of the material is concerned, specifically the rights of translation, reprinting, reuse of illustrations, recitation, broadcasting, reproduction on microfilms or in any other physical way, and transmission or information storage and retrieval, electronic adaptation, computer software, or by similar or dissimilar methodology now known or hereafter developed.

The use of general descriptive names, registered names, trademarks, service marks, etc. in this publication does not imply, even in the absence of a specific statement, that such names are exempt from the relevant protective laws and regulations and therefore free for general use.

The publisher, the authors, and the editors are safe to assume that the advice and information in this book are believed to be true and accurate at the date of publication. Neither the publisher nor the authors or the editors give a warranty, expressed or implied, with respect to the material contained herein or for any errors or omissions that may have been made. The publisher remains neutral with regard to jurisdictional claims in published maps and institutional affiliations.

This Springer imprint is published by the registered company Springer Nature Switzerland AG
The registered company address is: Gewerbestrasse 11, 6330 Cham, Switzerland

Paper in this product is recyclable.

Contents

1 Foreword: Excellence in Scientific Economic Research in the Romanian Academy 1
   Valeriu Ioan-Franc

2 On Morality in Economy and Scientific Research 7
   Valeriu Ioan-Franc and Andrei Marius Diamescu

3 Towards Ethics-Driven Public Organisations 17
   Mauro Romanelli

4 Employees' Trust as the Hard Core of Success to Business Integrity 23
   Adriana Grigorescu, Cristina Lincaru, and Speranta Pirciog

5 The Role of Humans as Key Enablers of Industry 5.0 39
   Elda Dollija and Kriselda Gura

6 Determinants of Organisations' Decisions Regarding Investments in Human Resource Development 57
   Alic Bîrcă, Luminița Chivu, and Christiana Brigitte Sandu

7 Examining the Empirical Relationship Between Happiness and Human Development in Emerging Economies 71
   Md Ataul Gani Osmani, Laeeq Razzak Janjua, Mirela Panait, and Vikas Kumar Singh Tomar

8 The Impact of Large Families on Demographic Evolution 83
   Mihaela Hrisanta Mosora, Irina Granzulea, and Cosmin Mosora

9 Dynamics of the School Population, Differences Between Emigrants and Immigrants in Romania: Comparative Analysis 99
   Mihaela-Georgiana Oprea, Mihaela-Irma Vlădescu, and Carmen Gheorghe

10	**Employee Resourcing Strategies in Tight Labour Market**........ Alic Bîrcă and Christiana Brigitte Sandu	109
11	**Estimation of Disembodied Technical Change During the Kuznets Cycles of Romania's First Transition to Market Economy**... Florin Marius Pavelescu	123
12	**R&D Expenditure – Conditioning Factor of Increasing Competitiveness – Indicators and Trends**.................... Alexandra-Ioana Lazăr and Adela-Simona Vlășceanu	139
13	**The Impact of Digitalization on the NUTS-2 Regions in Romania**.. Daniela Antonescu and Ioana Cristina Florescu	147
14	**Citizen Participation, Good Governance, and ICT Nexus for the Sustainability of Smart Cities**....................... Kriselda Sulcaj Gura, Fatmir Guri, Servet Gura, and Elda Dollija	155
15	**Digital Finance Is a Key of European and Global Integration**..... Otilia Manta	171
16	**Modeling the Perception of the Business Environment Through the Analysis of Entrepreneurial Opportunities**......... Ionela Gavrila-Paven and Ruxandra Lazea	187
17	**Circular Economy Performance at Regional Level in European Union**....................................... Victor Platon, Simona Frone, Andreea Constantinescu, and Sorina Jurist	199
18	**Bibliometric Analysis of the Evaluation of Interest in Urban Regeneration**...................................... Anna-Maria Vasile, Carmen Ghimus, and Mihaela-Georgiana Oprea	213
19	**Investigating the Impact of COVID-19 Policy Decisions on Economic Growth: Evidence from EU Countries**............. Cosmin-Octavian Cepoi, Bogdan Andrei Dumitrescu, and Ionel Leonida	241
20	**The Impact of Pandemic Crisis on Fiscal Sustainability**.......... Ada Cristina Albu	249
21	**Stock Market Reactions to ESG Dynamics: A European Banking Perspective**....................................... Iulia Lupu and Adina Criste	259
22	**The Efficiency of Futures Markets on Cryptocurrencies**......... Radu Lupu and Catalina Maria Popa	271

23	**The Impact of Climate Change on Revenues from Environmental Taxes and Expenses for Environmental Protection in the EU for 2010–2020**............................ Alina Georgeta Ailincă and Gabriela Cornelia Piciu	283
24	**Recovery of Critical Metals from Mine Tailings**................. Alina Butu, Paula V. Morais, Marian Butu, Sorin Avram, and Steliana Rodino	293
25	**The Geopolitics of Resources: The Critical Minerals**............. Cristian Marius Moisoiu	301
26	**The Critical Mineral Rush: Lithium and Cobalt – A Canadian Perspective**... Daniel Bulin	315
27	**How Romania May Benefit from the Natural Gas Resources' Offshore Exploitation of the Black Sea Romanian Continental Shelf?**... Marius Bulearcă	329
28	**Application of Machine Learning Techniques in Natural Gas Price Modeling. Analyses, Comparisons, and Predictions for Romania**... Stelian Stancu, Alexandru Isaic-Maniu, Constanța-Nicoleta Bodea, Mihai Sabin Muscalu, and Denisa Elena Bălă	343
29	**Recent Developments of Medium Technology Activities Specific to the Romanian Manufacturing Industry in the Context of the COVID-19 Pandemic and the War in Ukraine**............ Andrei Silviu Dospinescu	357
30	**Characterization of the Main Changes in the Natural Gas Market in Romania on the Context of Current Energy Crisis**...... Alexandru Isaic-Maniu, Stelian Stancu, Constanța-Nicoleta Bodea, Mihai Sabin Muscalu, and Denisa Elena Bălă	367
31	**Solutions for the Adoption of a Real Sustainable Mobility System**... Frantz Daniel Fistung	379
32	**Industrial Policies Regarding R&D Activities and Their Effects on Economic Performance**.................... Alexandra-Ioana Lazăr	391
33	**Study Regarding the Use of Mobile Phones in Romania**.......... Vanesa Madalina Vargas and Cosmin Alexandru Teodorescu	397

34	**The Impact of Energy Crisis on the Vegetable Sector in Romania**.. Cornelia Alboiu	407
35	**Assessment of Pesticide and Fertilizer Consumption and Its Effects on Agricultural Output in Romanian Farms**....... Cecilia Alexandri, Bianca Pauna, Corina Saman, and Lucian Luca	421
36	**Identifying the Determining Factors of the Adoption of Ecological Practices by Dairy Farms in Suceava County, Romania**........... Mihai Alexandru Chiţea, Marioara Rusu, Violeta Florian, Lorena Florentina Chiţea, Elisabeta Roşu, Monica Mihaela Tudor, Sorinel Ionel Bucur, Lucian Luca, Iuliana Ionel, Ioan Sebastian Brumă, Lucian Tanasă, Codrin Dinu Vasiliu, and Gabriel Simion	433
37	**Pollution and Value Added in Agriculture: Evidence from the Biggest Agricultural Producers in the European Union**...................................... Mihaela Simionescu	445
38	**Strategies for Bioeconomy in Central and Eastern Europe: BIOEAST Initiative and BIOEASTsUP Project**................ Dan-Marius Voicilas	457
39	**Are Census Socioeconomic Variables a Consistent Tool for Analyzing Human Resources Sustainability on Romania's Labor Market?**............................... Raluca Mazilescu, Valentina Vasile, Ana-Maria Ciuhu, and Marius-Răzvan Surugiu	471
40	**Montanology and Current Challenges at European and Global Level**.. Radu Rey and Otilia Manta	491
41	**Relevant Methods for Reducing the Phenomenon of Food Waste in the HORECA Sector in the Romanian Mountain Regions**....... Daniela Antonescu and Ioan Surdu	507
42	**Study on Demographics and Tourism as the Main Economic Activity in the Dornelor Country** .... Niculina Onesifereanu, Dănuţ Gîţan, and Mioara Bocanici	517
43	**Conclusions and Follow-Ups** .... Luminiţa Chivu, George Georgescu, and Jean Vasile Andrei	527

Index... 533

Chapter 1
Foreword: Excellence in Scientific Economic Research in the Romanian Academy

Valeriu Ioan-Franc

Conceived by its founders not only as a forum of consecration but also as an active body of scientific research, in 2022, the Romanian Academy celebrated its 156 years of fruitfulness, reaffirming, on this occasion, the mission of serving the interests of the Romanian nation and, at the same time, of being a fair mediator between the globalisation and integration tendencies and preserving the national identity.

According to its status, the Romanian Academy, relentless and everlasting, is currently operating on three coordinates: (1) it is a forum of consecration and recognition of outstanding merits of the country's scientists, scholars and writers; (2) it is the most important pillar of fundamental research in Romania, being also active in applied research and (3) it is an active participant in the life of Romanian society, asserting its point of view on important issues for the country, such as education, national heritage, Romanian identity, European integration and life quality of the citizens.

Involved in a series of programmes of particular importance for the evolution of Romanian society, the Romanian Academy proved to be the link and the guarantor of promoting Romania's new path after 1989, with the accomplished stages for a European destiny, namely the transition to a market economy, the pre-accessions and accession to the EU, sustainable development and establishment of the new normal.

The "Costin C. Kiritescu" National Institute for Economic Research (INCE), established from the recomposition of Romanian economic research with roots in the beginning of the twentieth century, is a public law scientific organisation of national interest with a vocation for fundamental research in the field of economic

---

V. Ioan-Franc (✉)
National Institute for Economic Research "Costin C. Kirițescu" Romanian Academy, Bucharest, Romania

© The Author(s), under exclusive license to Springer Nature Switzerland AG 2024
L. Chivu et al. (eds.), *Constraints and Opportunities in Shaping the Future: New Approaches to Economics and Policy Making*, Springer Proceedings in Business and Economics, https://doi.org/10.1007/978-3-031-47925-0_1

science which also develops applied research for real economy and external partnerships, being part of the Romanian academic research network.

INCE correlates its own research strategy with the vocation of the Romanian Academy, with the strategic areas and priority directions of research included in the Strategy for Scientific Research in the Romanian Academy, upgraded for the next stages with the national and European strategies and policies in the field of science and research, also taking up a role for the development and preservation of the scientific patrimony, of institutions and national identity, not only in the field of economic sciences, but also in the other fields of national culture and science, by undertaking and promoting projects of major interest.

INCE aims to develop and strengthen scientific competition, knowledge and expertise in the field of economic research in Romania, wherever it takes place, in agreement with the objectives of the national and European development strategies.

Coordinated into a coherent program, the Institute's competencies and capabilities, projects and research themes aim: globally – the national economy in its full complexity, economic forecasting over different horizons and the macro modelling of the national economy, the global economy and international economic relations of Romania, quality of life and fighting poverty, promoting consensus in economy and society; and sectorial – the economy of industry and services, the agricultural economy including the mountain economy and agri-food biodiversity, financial and monetary issues, demographic and demo-economic aspects, energy security and safety, IT applications in research and the complexity of economic and social processes.

The range of the Institute's concerns is complemented by the permanent efforts to capitalise research results through publication and dissemination, with its own publishing programme including both periodicals and non-periodicals as well as, in editorial form, books by researchers of the Institute or by national economic thinkers confronting world's economic ideas.

The priority research directions coordinated by INCE and the units in its networks are as follows: The sustainable economic development of Romania. Models, scenarios, assessments; Efficient capitalisation of the natural resources national heritage; Human capital. Economic development based on knowledge, innovation and intelligence; Analysis of national economy dynamics. Directions of improvement of economic structures in conditions of increased competitiveness; New conditions of European integration and globalisation. Real and nominal convergence; Economic instability and stabilisation policies in conditions of financialisation of economies and increasing complexity and vulnerability of economic and social processes and institutional system; Development of economic and social forecasting tools. Models, scenarios and numeric and quantitative analyses; Economic and social criteria of regionalisation and local development in Romania; Retrospective research regarding the evaluation of experiences and economical-social and political thinking; Quality of life and evaluation of social policies; Demo-economic research. Population balance in Romania; The New Encyclopaedia of Romania; Development and creation of working tools – dictionaries, data bases, bibliographic repositories, archives, etc.

Increasing international visibility of academic economic research

In October 2022, the "Costin C. Kiritescu" National Institute of Economic Research secured the top 3% position according to the international RePEc database, the most representative in the field of economics (4.2 million indexed papers and over 65,000 authors cited), i.e. it was ranked 190th out of over 8,200 economics institutes and universities/departments worldwide. Compared to its 380th position in January 2015, in October 2022, INCE advanced to the 190th position, a remarkable improvement in the context of intense scientific competition worldwide, which contributes significantly to the prestige of Romanian Academy.

For the correct assessment of the scientific relevance of this position, one must highlight that the following are in the top positions in the world ranking: (1) National Bureau of Economic Research (Cambridge, Massachusetts, USA); (2) Department of Economics – Harvard University; (3) London School of Economics; (4) Economics Department – Massachusetts Institute of Technology (MIT); (5) World Bank Group.

It is important to mention that among the 34 criteria (indicators) according to which the general index of the position in this ranking is established, in the number of „Abstract views" and „Downloads" weighted by the number of authors over the last 12 months, INCE ranked higher positions worldwide, i.e. 48 and 44, respectively, in October 22, 2022.

Of the 2600 economic institutes and universities/departments in the European Union, according to RePEc international database, in October 2022, INCE secured the 69th position.

According to the national ranking established by RePEc, INCE (with 169 cited authors) holds the second place, the quality of its human resources being revealed by the fact that 21 researchers from its network of institutes and centres are in the top 5% of the total of 1167 listed authors in Romania.

It is important to mention that in the October 2022 national ranking of publications over the last 10 years, selecting the top 10 ranked authors from each institution, one finds INCE on the first position, significantly ahead the second place occupant.

An important effort to be taken to increase the visibility and the national and international prestige of economic scientific research and researchers alike is strengthening the partnership role of INCE at national and international levels and also integrating in new similar actions that provide the basis for future scientific cooperations. Only in the year 2022 the following became operational: (1) Memorandum of Understanding (October 2022) with the Lab for Entrepreneurship and Development (LEAD), Cambridge (Massachusetts, USA), with the main objective of developing bilateral relations, the mutual promotion of the actions organised by each partner and to exchange experience. The general forms of collaboration generally agreed are as follows: joined research publication and conferences, colloquia and lectures, scientific research databases exchanges as well as other mutually agreed activities; (2) Memorandum of Understanding (January 2022) with the European Marketing and Management Association (EUMMAS) under which the signatory institutions mainly aim to collaborate through research activities in the field of marketing, management and related disciplines; to contribute through the results of joint research to the enhancement of the quality of management, marketing, policies and decision and to the awareness of the importance of both public and private efficient and effective management for local, regional and global prosperity; to contribute to the development of a professional and academic network aimed for the exchange of expertise and knowledge under the aegis of EUMMAS; to jointly organise and mutually participate in various scientific events, i.e. conferences, training courses, seminars, workshops, round tables, consultancy activities, projects; (3) European Community of Practice in Partnership (January 2022) (ECOPP), a body of the European Commission, joining 150 organisations and authorities from the European Union, established to improve the partnership for the implementation of European funds and which has as an objective of exchanging best practices and bottom-up approach in the field of implementation of European funds; (4) Continuation of the joint approach with the Association of Faculties of Economics in Romania (AFER), with INCE having been present for years in the first line of major decisions for the enhancement of higher economic education at excellence level and of high academic research institutions with permanent representatives in the Academic Council of the Association.

Under the sign of excellence.

The researchers in the "Costin C. Kiritescu" INCE network play an important part in all the priority projects of the Romanian Academy: "Romania's development strategy in the next 20 years"; "Principles, criteria, issues and challenges of the update of the National Strategy of Sustainable Development of Romania 2013-2020-2030"; "National Energy Strategy for the period 2017-2030 and time horizon 2050"; Establishing the GIS database of degraded ecosystems at national level and related maps; Implementation of a monitoring procedure of the projects of restoration of degraded ecosystems at national level and of inclusion of this information in the GIS database; Mapping of degraded natural and semi-natural ecosystems at a national level; Modernisation and simplification of the Common Agricultural Policy in the Technical Working Group for the preparation of the Romanian agricultural sector in the context of the modernisation and simplification of the common agricultural policy (CAP); "The social state of Romania. Quality of life: current situation and prospects for 2038"; Report "Natural and man-made disasters platform"; "Rodna and Retezat Biosphere Reserves compliance programme to the provisions of the statutory program of BIOSPHERE Reserves"; Multiannual strategy for the protection and sustainable development of mountain areas in Romania; Poverty assessment methodology, national and local databases and mapping of poverty indicators (ongoing); Methodology for estimating existing and needed social services, national and local databases and mapping ongoing; Methodology of assessment of the existing and needed social infrastructure, national and local databases and mapping (ongoing), etc.

The conferment by the Romanian Academy, in the last years, of the highest distinction – "the Academic Merit" – to the "Costin C. Kiritescu" National Institute of Economic Research for its 25 years of fruitful and efficient activity in the field of economic and social sciences; to the Institute of Economic Forecasting for its

45 years of academic scientific research in the field of economic forecasting; and to the Institute of World Economics for its contribution to fundamental economic research and the argumentation of major domestic and foreign policy decisions for the integration of the national economy into the world economy, through highly prestigious specialists who worked in the institute, are, without a doubt, expressions of the recognition of the value of Romanian economic research.

The institute had at the same time secured a well-regarded place in the international academic meetings calendar through its annual conference. INCE international scientific conference "Economic Scientific Research – Theoretical, Empirical and Practical Approaches" – ESPERA, having as an objective the presentation and assessment of the portfolio of academic scientific research in the field of economic sciences, aimed at arguing and substantiating, inclusively through European and global best practices, the strategies of economic and social development of Romania, reached, in 2022, its ninth edition, establishing itself as an important event in the calendar of international scientific meetings. Making ESPERA permanent speaks of the organisers' confidence that Romania needs its own economic research, its own scientific interpretations and arguments to assert its national interests.

The ninth edition of the ESPERA international conference took place on November 24 and 25, 2022, on the theme "Constraints and opportunities in shaping the future. New approaches to economics and policy making". ESPERA 2022 has benefited, from one year to another, from a high-quality national and international partnership, joining over 120 participants in the plenary session and approximately 140 papers presented in the 15 parallel sessions. We cannot end these lines of a report, as we are already thinking about the preparation of the tenth edition of the ESPERA Conference in 2023, without paying tribute, yearly and not only, to the initiators of this project – the late former deputy general director, Ph.D., Constantin Ciutacu, and to our Director, Professor Luminita Chivu, Ph.D., who continues his bright initiative.

Chapter 2
On Morality in Economy and Scientific Research

Valeriu Ioan-Franc ⓘ and Andrei Marius Diamescu ⓘ

Abstract The call to morals in economics and scientific research hasn't been completely missing during the last two centuries. However, it was rather secondary to the Smithsonian "invisible hand".

The engine and, at the same time, the central concept of the economic activity since the dawn of the industrial age until today has been and still is "the greatness of profit" without which the contemporary economic thinking seems not to be able to evolve. Reflecting on the last two decades successive economic crises and, especially, on the powerful polarization in the global distribution of wealth, the discussion of this very inequality becomes topical again, making it hard for us to account for the "stubborness" with which the real economy fights the direction of this evolution. The main opponents of moral economics – which we are going to name "the economics of social welfare" – are the big end capital holders and their companies. The economic-financial crisis of 2008 made it clear – if still needed and for how many times yet – that in crisis situations it is still "the many and, sometimes, the needy" who are called to help "the few and the rich".

It is not even 15 years since the heads of the American economy and finance – H. M. Paulson și B. Bernanke – asked for and saved with "the state's money", i.e. of the many, not only the American economy but also the great banks and credit institutions which "ultimately" had generated the crisis.

These topics, and not only, framed within the principles of the humanist economy school of Barcelona that our Institute also joined, are the focus of our speech.

Keywords Moral · Economics · Research · Science

V. Ioan-Franc (✉) · A. M. Diamescu
National Institute for Economic Research "Costin C. Kirițescu", Bucharest, Romania

© The Author(s), under exclusive license to Springer Nature Switzerland AG 2024
L. Chivu et al. (eds.), *Constraints and Opportunities in Shaping the Future: New Approaches to Economics and Policy Making*, Springer Proceedings in Business and Economics, https://doi.org/10.1007/978-3-031-47925-0_2

2.1 Introduction

Maybe more than ever in the history of mankind, the beginning of the current century has brought to the attention of science people the issue of morality in economy and the contemporary economic research.

Paradoxically, or maybe not, Adam Smith, the one who, following his famous study dedicated to Economics – *An Inquiry into the Nature and Causes of the Wealth of Nations*, was to become known throughout the world as the "*the father of capitalism*" and a leading promoter of selfishness, supported in the paper "*The Theory of Moral Sentiments*" ideas of altruism and justice in business and politics, pleading for *social responsibility and empathy.*

Referring to this almost forgotten book, Russ Roberts (2015), a reputed contemporary economist, a researcher at Hoover Institution at Stanford University and president of Shalem College in Jerusalem, states that "The Theory of Moral Sentiments changed the way in which I was looking at people and, maybe the most important thing, the way I looked at myself. Smith made me aware of how people interact in ways I hadn't noticed before. He gives timeless advice on how to relate to money, ambition, fame and morality. He teaches the reader how to find happiness, how to manage material success and failure. He describes the path towards virtue and goodness and the reasons this path is worth following".[1]

Although the appeal to morality in Economics and economic research hasn't completely been missing in the last two centuries, it was rather secondary to the Smithsonian's "invisible hand". The engine and, at the same time, the central concept of the economic activity since the dawn of the industrial age until today has been and still is "the greatness of profit" without which the contemporary economic thinking seems not to be able to evolve.

Reflecting on the last two decades successive economic crises and, especially, on the powerful polarization in the global distribution of wealth, the discussion of this very inequality becomes topical again, making it hard for us to account for the "stubbornness" with which the real economy fights the direction of this evolution.

To simplify, perhaps unduly, one may say that the main opponents of moral economics, which we would name "the economics of social welfare", are the big end capital holders and their companies, in other words, the 1% who hold the 90% of the world's wealth.

This reasoning isn't, for sure, lacking grounds, but to limit ourselves to it is as if we would that the one responsible for the acute soil drought that we are going through is... rain alone! What is actually really surprising is the fact that we think about and sometimes even find ways to influence nature and stimulate the rainfall, while we are incapable of generating solutions, public regulations/policies ultimately that "tame" the greed and selfishness of the big capital owners!

Moreover, the serious economic-financial crisis of 2008 made it clear – if still needed and for how many times yet – that in crisis situations it is still "the many and,

---

[1] Roberts (2015, p. 14).

sometimes, the needy" who are called to help "the few and the rich". It is not even 15 years since the heads of the American economy and finance – H. M. Paulson și B. Bernanke – asked for and saved with "the state's money", i.e. of the many, not only the American economy but also the great banks and credit institutions which "ultimately" had generated the crisis.

While for the actors responsible for the crisis, banks and credit institutions, the consequences of the incessant rush for profit were *difficult*, for a lot of "*the many*", they were *dramatic*. Let's not forget what it meant for many of the employees in our country the overnight reduction of 25% of their earnings!

Situations like these face us with an extremely difficult question which, we believe, are far from having reached an answer: in 2008, as well as in other similar situations too, did the American state, and, in general, the state, actually protect its own population or the main corporations and their main stakeholders?

As expected, the unanimous answer of the decision-makers to this question was one of this kind: by saving the big banks and financial institutions the economy in general was saved and, thus, the citizens/the population! This is an answer which, to a certain extent, can be considered correct, yet it doesn't clarify maybe the most important two aspects: the first one – who paid the price for the "salvation" of the economy and, the second one, were the decisions taken in order to save the economy moral in relation to the contemporary goals of the states?

While, as far as the first aspect is regarded the "silence of the politicians" is "understandable", *the price being almost completely paid by the population*, a point of view regarding the second aspect is, as expected, much more debatable and difficult to formulate.

While from an economic point of view and, especially, from the normative economics point of view, the decisions taken to overcome the crisis are justificd, leaving only the possible alternatives to be discussed, from a moral point of view the approach of the measures taken requires a predominantly political or political-economic perspective, or, more specifically, of the relationship between the state and the citizens/population.

We believe that, in order to formulate a point of view regarding this aspect, the answers to the following questions are of the most importance:

1. Was the population consulted on the measures to be taken?
2. Was the damage caused by the crisis recovered from the ones responsible for it?
3. Were the citizens/population paid compensations after the crisis had been overcome and the macroeconomic indicators restored?

The answers, obviously negative for any informed reader show us, without any doubt, *that the majority of the decisions taken by the state authorities to overcome the crisis had nothing to do with the will/wish/acceptance of the citizens*, some of them seeming to be taken even in contempt of the citizen! Thus, in the respective context, a discussion about morality in Economics, more specifically, in economic policy-making, becomes obsolete today.

Our reference to the economic-financial crisis of 2008, maybe too extensive for some of the readers, was meant to point out, by means of an exceptional situation, widely publicized and analysed, a series of aspects which tend to become a constant of state activity in the economic field.

2.2 The Gap Between Economic Policy Decisions and the Will of the Citizens

The gap between *economic policy decisions and the will of the citizens* ultimately of the electorate *is clearly detrimental not only to the moral dimension of the economy but to democracy itself,* in the broad sense of the concept. For that matter, this very rift between the elected representatives and the electorate, periodically visible in several states, some with great democratic tradition even, generated the concept of *"illiberal democracy"*, about which the academician Daniel Daianu (2019) said in his reception speech at the Romanian Academy: *"Just as one can talk about «illiberal democracy», one can also talk about «undemocratic liberalism», when people feel they no longer have control over their own lives, when they have less and less trust in the ones governing them, when they accuse the power of money over the decision-making process (the capturing of the government by interest groups seen as illegitimate"*.[2]

I pointed out in another article that I have published this year (Pop & Ioan-Franc, 2022) that, when "we speak about economics or politics, in any order they may come, we speak about people"[3]! But how much truth is there today in the concrete, pragmatic, dimension of this statement?

Theoretically, the previous statement remains, obviously, perfectly valid, representing, ultimately, a part of the essence of democracy. In practice, we observe that, in many countries of the world and, especially in borderline situations, the national budgets and used/abused discretionary by the political actors in disagreement with the views of the economists and, very seriously, *"by changing the role of the political class from promoting national interests to promoting group interests!"* (Pop & Ioan-Franc, 2022).[4]

This mutation, generically called corruption, too easily stated to be found everywhere in the world, is the one that "cancels out" and form of morality in economics. The generalization of corruption is truly discouraging, but it should not, under any circumstance, make us stop fighting it.

"Traditionally", we may say, the fight against corruption is fought by legal means and, unfortunately, the results are often unsatisfying, as political people have the possibility and also the capacity to "dress" various interests contrary to the public good in legal "clothes". For this reason, we believe that, by perpetuating the current

---

[2] Daianu (2019, p. 31).
[3] Pop and Ioan-Franc (2022, p. 23).
[4] Idem, p. 88.

divorce between politicians and economists, the results in fighting corruption, will stay, for a long period of time, limited.

Legal norm alone doesn't have the capacity to eradicate the promotion of interests contrary to the public good, assumed as an essential goal of the state, and this happens because the scourge called corruption carries in itself a strong amoral connotation.

Even though *"the influence of morality, the conventional one and the one found in the ideals of a society, on the law is unquestionable [...], it doesn't follow from this that, in order to be legally valid, the laws need to reflect moral principles"*,[5] the philosopher and legal theory professor H.L.A. Hart would point out in perhaps the most important paper on the subject written in the twentieth century, *The Concept of Law*.

For this reason, the author (Treta, 2020) of Hart's book review continues, *"no matter how strong the aura of public authority, the laws in a society should be subject to scrutiny to avoid the use of law as a domination instrument by the people in power. From here starts yet another discussion about the amorality of a law, which has to be separated from its lack of validity"*.[6]

It is obvious that such an approach to the legislative process is virtually impossible, the only law approved by universal scrutiny being the fundamental law – the Constitution and, for this reason, contemporary politicians, the legitimate representatives of the citizens, opened the path to the "undemocratic illiberalism/liberalism" whereby the public good, the social state can be avoided/delayed/ dodged/ignored in favour of group interests.

Although the "moral sanitation" of contemporary leading elites may seem like a "mission impossible", we believe that the solution lies, as in many other situations we have been referring to over time, in the return to the "old normal" (Pop ct al., 2021) by re-establishing the connection (marriage) between politicians and economists![7]

1. We have been often asking ourselves in the last years whether dropping the phrase "political economy" (including in the names of institutions or subjects of study) has had beneficial consequences for economic science in general.

From a purely theoretical point of view, we understood the desire of the scientific community to become autonomous and to distance itself from the strong ideological imprint that political economy taught in the political economy faculties in the communist countries before 1989 used to have. We have also become aware of the potential benefits that giving up "political economy" could bring in framing a maybe more objective epistemological field for the scientific subject called economy

---

[5] Treta (2020).
[6] Idem 5.
[7] Pop et al. (2021, pp. 179–214).

(Ioan-Franc & Pop, 2021).[8] Last but not least, we agree that, by this decision, we have better delimited economic science in the area of "economics"!

Yet, what makes us doubt at times the opportunity and benefits of this giving up is whether, by doing so, we may have fully contributed to the current "divorce" between economists and politicians.

By strictly separating the two essential domains of human action, economics and politics, we might have offered the economists the quietness of the libraries and the politicians total freedom, not even scientifically censored, of the decisions in the economic field.

We do not dispute the possibility that the current status quo is convenient to both social-professional categories, considering that in Romania too we can speak about a professional political class, but, just like many times the "victims" of the dissolution of a marriage are the children, in our case, the ones who pay the price of the consequences of the divorce are the citizens.

To establish whether the divorce, in general, is or is not a moral action is not the purpose of our intervention, but, for sure, *depriving the economic policy decision of the scientific validation makes it seriously vulnerable from a moral point of view!* However, *the scientific contribution to the economic policy* shouldn't be seen as the sole and sufficient condition to *ensure the morality of the decision*.

It is true that there are contemporary studies which maintain that as long as science is the best able to establish facts, it also has the duty to establish truths and moral values. The philosopher and neuroscientist Sam Harris even argues that it is past time for science to only describe human behaviours and not intervene in the controversies over moral values and, from this perspective, he conceives morality as an underdeveloped branch of science[9] (Harris, 2013).

Nevertheless, there is enough evidence, well known in the history of science, that renowned researchers/scientists have been deeply disappointed with the way their discoveries were exploited/used. Nobel, Einstein and Oppenheimer are only a few of the world's famous scientists whose discoveries have seriously questioned morality in scientific research.

Most probably, none of these scientists were aware, at the time of their research, of all the fields in which their discoveries could be used, but this only exonerates them as researchers from the catastrophic consequences for humanity, we may say, and it doesn't solve the problem of morality in scientific research, ultimately in knowledge.

---

[8] Ioan-Franc and Pop (2021, pp. 98–108).
[9] Harris (2013).

2.3 How New is the Knowledge-Based Economy?

For a few decades there has been a lively discussion among economists, about the "knowledge-based economy" most often with the adjective "new" (Hoffman & Glodeanu, 2006).[10]

Our observation in direct connection to what we have previously stated refers to: *How new exactly is the knowledge-based economy?*

We can easily notice that all the examples I have just referred to represented at the same time small revolutions in economic development, be it the use of dynamite in mining or the production of electricity through nuclear power plants. Before these discoveries, the invention of the steam engine opened up a new era in the world's economic development.

Also, in all these great discoveries, knowledge has been, maybe, one of the most important resources for maximizing profits: technologization/re-technologization, robotization and automation are, after all, expressions of the knowledge-based economy which had appeared long before economists theoretically, systematically, developed this "new" concept.

In our country since the initial period of conceptual clarification of the "new economy", knowledge has been described (Caragea et al., 2003) either as "predominant in the creation of value added",[11] or "the main resource in the creation of national wealth, power, prestige, population welfare and competitiveness",[12] synthetically, in our understanding, as *the main source of profit maximization.*

This is why we maintain that, *as long as we continue to view the benefits of a knowledge-based economy primarily through the contribution of knowledge to profit, this is neither "new" nor, we dare say, "moral" or, at least, "closer to morality" than all the other economies!* "*Ipsa scientia potestas est*", the famous aphorism attributed to Francis Bacon is already over four centuries old!

2. It is undeniable that the knowledge-based economy reconsiders and brings increased values to research, innovation, learning, teaching and dissemination of knowledge/information, but one needs to admit that all these come as a natural consequence of technological development, especially in the IT field and the dissemination of knowledge/information.

If the ultimate goal of the economy, stripped of any ideological or other connotations – and we mean profit, especially the "profit by all means" – isn't going to change, we believe that it is difficult, if not incorrect, to speak of "new economies".

At the opposite end, *shall we have the knowledge and the ability to use both knowledge and new technologies to build a sustainable, ecological, economy finally meant to bring well-being for everybody and social peace, then we have the right to*

---

[10] "Speaking of the *new economy*, we are using a metaphor that can only be explained through the synthetic term of *knowledge-based economy*", acc. Hoffman and Glodeanu (2006, p. 73).
[11] Caragea et al. (2003, p. 1).
[12] Hoffman and Glodeanu (2006, p. 77)

characterize this economy by the adjective "new" and consider it "closer to morality"!

3. To some readers, such a goal might seem too far, if not utopian. To us, it is a realistic, feasible one, provided we have the determination to meet two consecutive conditions:

   (1) *"Rehumanization"* of knowledge
   (2) *"Resetting"* the current goal of the economy – profit making – and its turning around *towards "shared welfare"*

Hard to accomplish as well, the first condition is not only necessary but also compulsory in order to meet the second one and it necessitates, nowadays, an action sustained and coordinated through public policies promoted both at the level of states as well as international bodies. A mere investigation of the data referring to contemporary scientific research shows that the latter is focused on technology and engineering sciences, followed by exact sciences and, at a distance, on humanities.

In Romania, for example, *only 4.1% of the total of the so few researchers, work in the field of humanities*, while 49.3% of the total are in the engineering and technological sciences and 17% in natural and exact sciences.[13]

Far from the wish to get into polemics with our colleagues in the other scientific fields, but in order to achieve a real paradigm shift in the current economic, as well as social and administrative thinking, we think that we need, in the first place, philosophy and political economy.

It is time, we believe, that, just like the Ancients, such as Plato, but also Pythagoras, Aristotle, Socrates and many others, or the classics Adam Smith, Francis Bacon, Thomas Hobbes, etc., or Constantin Noica and his correspondence with the economist Gheorghe Staicu,[14] today's researchers/scientists get down in the agora, debate and look for solutions to the problems that the market economy and, implicitly, capitalism and democracy are facing.

Actually, this kind of approach is may be the only solution that would make possible the "rewriting of economics textbooks, their interpretation having remained too dogmatic, in many aspects, with respect to the world's economic realities", as we pointed out in a previous article.[15]

2.4 Conclusions

Last, but not least, through the "humanization of knowledge" science would truly gain moral features. For centuries, science, including economic science, has been put "at the service of man", generically, thus making possible the invention of

---

[13] National Institute of Statistics (2020, p. 11).
[14] Noica (1997).
[15] Pop and Ioan-Franc (2022, p. 99).

dynamite, atomic bomb or economic crisis. Through "humanization", science will have as a purpose to bring "benefits to humanity" and thus to provide the framework for the fulfilment of the second condition: *resetting of the current economic system.*

We are fully aware of the difficulty of such a process. At the same time though, we are convinced of its necessity. We are therefore joining the efforts of the Barcelona School of Humanistic Economics, made up of leading figures of the world of research gathered at the Academy of Economic and Financial Sciences (RACEF) of the Spanish Institute, to shape and develop the necessary epistemological frame for this truly "new" type of economy, which is certainly the only one able to cancel the polarization/disparities generated by the current free market economy, but also of *giving the economy a new moral dimension.*

In the end, we feel the need to make the following remark: by changing the main goal of the economic activity from "maximization of profit" – ultimately, the acquisition of wealth – to the acquisition of "welfare" we by no means understand "egalitarianism", "common property" or other concepts that proved in the recent past their inconsistency.

What we mean by "shared welfare" is the access of as many people as possible to the results of economic activity, the reduction of the existent gap in the distribution of wealth and of the existent disparities in the retribution/appreciation of the work value depending ultimately of the geographical area, country, economy in which each is born and lives.

References

Caragea, A., Gheorghiu, R., & Țurlea, G. (2003, November). *Economia bazată pe cunoaștere în România. Evaluarea progreselor recente; Blocaje*; *Recomandări de politică economică* (Knowledge-based economy in Romania. Assessment of recent progress; Bottlenecks; Economic policy recommendations). https://www.scribd.com/doc/252650083/raport-ke

Daianu, D. (2019, November 5). *Drumul spre cunoaștere. Facerea unui economist* (The road to knowledge, the making of an economist). Reception speech, Aula of the Romanian Academy, in Revista Academica, no. 12/2019.

Harris, S. (2013). *Cum poate determina știința valorile umane* (How science can determine human values). Paralela 45 Publishing House.

Hoffman, O., & Glodeanu, I. (2006). *Cunoașterea – noua resursa a puterii* (Knowledge the new resource of power). Tipografia Intact Publishing House.

Ioan-Franc, V., & Pop, N. (2021). Încotro, gândirea economică? (Economic thinking, where to?). *Caiete Critice magazine,* no. 3–4.

National Institute of Statistics. (2020). *Activitatea de cercetare-dezvoltare în anul 2020* (Research-development activity in 2020). At https://insse.ro/cms/sites/default/files/field/publicatii/activitatea_de_cercetare_dezvoltare_8.pdf

Noica, C. (1997). *Manuscrisele de la Câmpulung. Reflecții despre țărănime și burghezie* (The campulung manuscripts, reflections on the peasantry and the bourgeoisie). Humanitas Publishing House.

Pop, N., & Ioan-Franc, V. (2022). Un divorț prelungit între economiști și politicieni (A prolonged divorce between economists and politicians). *Caiete Critice Magazine,* no. 3–4. Expert Publishing House.

Pop, N., Ioan-Franc, V., Diamescu, A. M. (2021). România în confruntare cu pandemia Covid-19. Gestiunea riscurilor versus asumarea oportunităților (Romania facing Covid 19 pandemic. Management of risks versus taking opportunities) In *Pandemia – Constrângeri și oportunități economice* (The pandemic – Economic constraints and opportunities).

Roberts, R. (2015) *Cum poate Adam Smith să vă schimbe viața. Un ghid inedit despre natura umană și fericire* (How Adam Smith can change your life. An unexpected guide to human nature and happiness). Publica Publishing House.

Treta, D. (2020, August 11). Legea și Moralitatea, o relație complicată: The concept of law autor H. L. A. Hart (Law and morality, a complicated relationship: The concept of law, author H.L.A Hart). *Revista de Științe Juridice*. https://www.juridice.ro/692741/legea-si-moralitatea-o-relatie-complicata-the-concept-of- law-de-h-l-a-hart.html

Chapter 3
Towards Ethics-Driven Public Organisations

Mauro Romanelli

Abstract Rediscovering the ethical dimension within public administration supports the managerial role as a key driver of organisational effectiveness and service motivation. Acknowledging ethics enables public organisations to construct processes of social and public value creation with communities. This study refers to the role of public management as a driver of public service motivation that supports ethical behaviours within public organisations. Rediscovering the managerial dimension and public service motivation enables ethics-driven and responsive public organisations that contribute to social innovation. Public managers play a key role in driving ethical and organisational effectiveness within public administration, supporting the commitment and public service motivation of the employees to organisational goals and public values.

Keywords Ethics · Public organisations · Public management · Public service motivation

3.1 Introduction

Rediscovering the importance of ethics within public organisations drives managerial practices that enable wealthy administrative action (Macaulay, 2020; Svara, 2022). Ethics refers to a set of principles that enables individuals to opt for the correct action (Lawton et al., 2013). Organisation is essential to ethics (Rhodes, 2023). Organisations enhance ethics supporting managers as agents of employee empowerment (Grigorescu et al., 2020). Responsive public organisations rely on the

---

M. Romanelli (✉)
Department of Business and Economics, University of Naples Parthenope, Naples, Italy
e-mail: mauro.romanelli@uniparthenope.it

quality of human resources and human capital (Vigoda, 2000). Rediscovering public service motivation supports employees' ethical behaviour and commitment (Moynihan & Pandey, 2007).

Public organisations are rediscovering a pathway to ethics as an asset for change and value creation, relying on public managers who can engage citizens and communities (Moore, 1995), strengthening collaborative responsiveness (Bryer, 2007), searching for a dialogue with communities within society and following an ecosystem view (Dumay et al., 2010). As accountable institutions that serve the public interest and support democratic life (Parker & Gould, 1999), public organisations encourage employees to build partnerships with citizens (Denhardt & Denhardt, 2001).

Rediscovering that the office is a vocation (Du Gay, 2005) empowers administrative officials who drive responsive public administration in the relationships with the community and support public service motivation of employees at work. As agents of organisational change, public managers enable employees to assume ethics-driven behaviours and inspire collaborative processes that involve communities.

While many studies focus on public management and public service motivation, few investigate how public management and public service motivation may affect ethical behaviours and address organisational choices. The research question relies on understanding how public organisations develop ethics in administrative practices and actions, promoting managerial and behavioural dimensions, enhancing the role of public management and supporting public service motivation. This study relies on rediscovering how the managerial role supports public service motivation and ethical leadership, cultvating ethics-driven behaviours and actions within public administration. Public organisations have to empower public management as a driver of employee empowerment and human capital enhancement, supporting public service motivation and commitment of employees at work. The aim of public management is to drive ethics-led and value-oriented public organisations. Hence, rediscovering the role of public service motivation enables ethics-driven public organisations and supports the commitment of employees to the organisational mission and goals of public administration.

3.2 Literature Review

Ethics is a driver of managerial practices and supports the behavioural dimension within public administration. Employees and administrators are ethical agents in their work settings (Stewart, 1985). Advancing ethics within public organisations relies on citizens and employees who contribute to public value. Public administrators drive ethics, acting as accountable managers while public servants serve the public interest and contribute to wealthy communities (Denhardt & Denhardt, 2001).

Public management and organisation contribute to shaping ethical behaviours and supporting public values and democratic life within communities (Dobel,

1988). The aim of public administration is to support public values (Van Wart, 1998) and promote the ethical commitments of public managers (Dobel, 2006). Ethics is incorporated into employees' everyday behaviour (Svara, 2022). Ethics-oriented public organisations enable managers to rediscover both the workplace and the office as a vocation (Du Gay, 2005) and ethics management supports accountable administrators in front of the citizens (Maesschalck, 2004). Ethics guides the attitudes and behaviours of public management working for healthy communities, and shaping managerial responsibility and autonomy (Pandey & Wright, 2006).

3.3 Methodology

The study analyses some contributions that investigate the role of public management regarding support to public service motivation and leadership roles, leading to new perspectives (Denyer & Tranfield, 2006). Public management is a driver of ethics within public organisations. Public managers promote the organisational dimension, thereby and sustaining public service motivation.

The approach is descriptive. The relationship between ethics and public organisations is presented in the introduction and methodological section. The section elucidates that public managers are viewed as key agents of ethical behaviours and supporters of public service motivation.

3.3.1 Driving Ethics within Public Organisations Through Public Management for Leadership and Public Service Motivation

Public management contributes to ensuring a better quality of life, thus supporting public values. Crucially, public administration should be a vehicle to express the values and preferences of citizens and communities (Bourgon, 2007). Public organisations have to restore trust and re-establish legitimacy (Holzer, 2022), dealing with uncertainty, complexity and goal ambiguity (Rainey & Bozeman, 2000), and adopting outcome-oriented and ethical behaviours in their decision-making styles (Brereton & Temple, 1998).

Public organisations contribute to public value-creation processes, searching for a shared dialogue with communities (Moore, 1995). As ethics-led and responsive institutions that are open and willing to respond (Stivers, 1994), public organisations facilitate public managers to search for collaboration with citizens as partners for value creation processes (Bryer, 2007; Osborne, 2018; Denhardt & Denhardt, 2001).

Consequently, public organisations must support the ethical behaviours of public managers and employees in order to benefit the community and contribute to public value (Macaulay, 2020). Public managers conduct effective public administration

(Moore, 1995) and contribute to addressing the determinants of performance (Boyne, 2002) to restore or strengthen legitimacy (Verhoest et al., 2007).

Driving managerial roles and supporting public service motivation helps to shape ethics-driven public organisations, initiating leadership for public value (Goldfinch & Wallis, 2010). Organisations that achieve good practices have leaders who foster ethical behaviours (Downe et al., 2016). In particular, ethical leadership exerts a positive influence on employees' organisation-related attitudes (Thaler & Helmig, 2016) and helps to support ethical organisational climate and culture. Ethical leaders focus on the relationships between organisational members and develop the ethical behaviour of employees (Arar & Saiti, 2022). Ethical leadership and high intrinsic motivation support organisational commitment (Potipiroon & Ford, 2017). As leaders, public managers support public service and value motivation and employees' ethical behaviours, thereby promoting responsive public organisations (Hassan et al., 2014). Importantly, public managers improve human capital, supporting commitment and service motivation in order to support organisational changes (Wright et al., 2013).

Public service motivation drives employees to select public administration in order to act to meet the needs of a community (Rainey & Steinbauer, 1999; Vandenabeele, 2008), refers to the relationship between public management and administration, and enables employees to contribute to the public benefit (Kim & Vandenabeele, 2010). Rediscovering the importance of public service motivation assists in overcoming declining motivation and work satisfaction as the issues of the dark side of managerial visions (Diefenbach, 2009). Public organisations enable public managers as supporters of public service motivation, commitment and loyalty of employees (Moynihan & Pandey, 2007). Public organisations are investing in the quality of human capital, attracting people with high public service motivation as an organisational source that helps to support public employment performances and benefit the community (Vandenabeele, 2008). Furthermore, public organisations enhance leadership and managerial capabilities, aligning employees' behaviour to public service as a vocation in the interest of citizens (Christensen et al., 2017; Du Gay, 2005). Public service motivation and transformational leadership positively affect the performances and evaluations of employees with high mission and public service motivation (Caillier, 2014).

3.4 Conclusions

Rediscovering the behavioural and organisational dimensions within the public administration field supports ethics-driven public organisations. Employees contribute to ethical administrative action by promoting coherent behaviours with public values and virtues and supporting processes that motivate public value creation and lead to organisational innovation. Rediscovering the organisational dimension of public administration enhances the ethical aspects of administrative action. Equally, rediscovering the importance of public management as an engine for leadership and public service-oriented motivation shapes organisational innovation, and empowers administrators, officials, employees, citizens and communities to identify innovative solutions for the common benefit.

Public organisations are rediscovering the ethical attributes of administrative action by investing in the quality of human resources, empowering employees at work and enhancing managerial capabilities. The successful and ethical pathway of public organisations develops by supporting public managers as effective agents of change and drivers of employees' ethical behaviours and attitudes, guiding driving ethics-driven public organisations that contribute to developing the human capital and the organisational dimension of public administration. Rediscovering the leadership role supports ethics-driven organisational change and innovation within public administration. Future research perspectives will refer to how local autonomies are redesigning practices for managing human resources frameworks and choices, following an ethics-led view of public service motivation and organisational changes.

References

Arar, K., & Saiti, A. (2022). Ethical leadership, ethical dilemmas and decision making among school administrators. *Equity in Education & Society, 1*(1), 126–141.

Bourgon, J. (2007). Responsive, responsible and respected government: Towards a new public administration theory. *International Review of Administrative Sciences, 73*(1), 7–26.

Boyne, G. A. (2002). Public and private management: What's the difference? *Journal of Management Studies, 39*(1), 97–122.

Brereton, M., & Temple, M. (1998). The new public service ethos: An ethical environment for governance. *Public Administration, 77*(3), 455–474.

Bryer, T. A. (2007). Toward a relevant agenda for a responsive public administration. *Journal of Public Administration Research and Theory, 17*(3), 479–500.

Caillier, J. G. (2014). Toward a better understanding of the relationship between transformational leadership, public service motivation, mission valence, and employee performance: A preliminary study. *Public Personnel Management, 43*(2), 218–239.

Christensen, R. K., Paarlberg, L., & Perry, J. L. (2017). Public service motivation research: Lessons for practice. *Public Administration Review, 77*(4), 529–542.

Denhardt, R. B., & Denhardt, J. V. (2001). The new public service: Putting democracy first. *National Civic Review, 90*(4), 391–400.

Denyer, D., & Tranfield, D. (2006). Using qualitative research synthesis to build an actionable knowledge base. *Management Decision, 44*(2), 213–227.

Diefenbach, T. (2009). New public management in public sector organizations: The dark sides of managerialistic 'enlightenment'. *Public Administration, 87*(4), 892–909.

Dobel, J. P. (1988). Personal responsibility and public integrity. *Michigan Law Review, 86*(6), 1450–1465.

Dobel, J. P. (2006). Public management as ethics. In E. Ferlie & L. E. Lynn (Eds.), *The Oxford handbook of public management* (pp. 156–181). Oxford University Press.

Downe, J., Cowell, R., & Morgan, K. (2016). What determines ethical behavior in public organizations: Is it rules or leadership? *Public Administration Review, 76*(6), 898–909.

Du Gay, P. (2005). *The values of bureaucracy*. Oxford University Press.

Dumay, J., Guthrie, J., & Farneti, F. (2010). GRI sustainability reporting guidelines for public and third sector organizations: A critical review. *Public Management Review, 12*(4), 531–548.

Goldfinch, S., & Wallis, J. (2010). The Myths of convergence in public management reform. *Public Administration Review, 88*(4), 1099–1115.

Grigorescu, A., Lincaru, C., & Pîrciog, S. (2020). Ethic leadership trigger for talents. In A. Grigorescu & V. Radu (Eds.), *Lumen proceedings: Vol. 11. 1st international conference Global Ethics – Key of Sustainability (GEKoS)* (pp. 32–44). LUMEN Publishing House.

Hassan, S., Wright, B. E., & Yukl, G. (2014). Does ethical leadership matter in government? Effects on organizational commitment, absenteeism, and willingness to report ethical problems. *Public Administration Review, 74*(3), 333–343.

Holzer, M. (2022). The future of public administration. *Public Integrity, 24*, 102–109.

Kim, S., & Vandenabeele, W. (2010). A strategy for building public service motivation research internationally. *Public Administration Review, 70*(5), 701–709.

Lawton, A., Rayner, J., & Lasthuizen, K. (2013). *Ethics and management in the public sector*. Routledge.

Macaulay, M. (2020). Towards a new public ethics. *Policy Quarterly, 16*(1).

Maesschalck, J. (2004). The impact of new public management reforms on public servants' ethics: Towards a theory. *Public Administration, 85*(2), 465–489.

Moore, M. H. (1995). *Creating public value*. Harvard University Press.

Moynihan, D. P., & Pandey, S. K. (2007). The role of organisations in fostering public service motivation. *Public Administration Review, 67*(1), 40–53.

Osborne, S. P. (2018). From public service-dominant logic to public service logic: Are public service organizations capable of co-production and value co-creation? *Public Management Review, 20*(2), 225–231.

Pandey, S. K., & Wright, B. E. (2006). Connecting the dots in public management: Political environment, organizational goal ambiguity, and the public manager's role ambiguity. *Journal of Public Administration Research and Theory, 16*(4), 511–532.

Parker, L., & Gould, G. (1999). Changing public sector accountability: Critiquing new directions. *Accounting Forum, 23*(2), 109–135. Taylor & Francis.

Potipiroon, W., & Ford, M. T. (2017). Does public service motivation always lead to organizational commitment? examining the moderating roles of intrinsic motivation and ethical leadership. *Public Personnel Management, 46*(3), 211–238.

Rainey, H. G., & Bozeman, B. (2000). Comparing public and private organizations: Empirical research and the power of the a priori. *Journal of Public Administration Research and Theory, 10*(2), 447–469.

Rainey, H. G., & Steinbauer, P. (1999). Galloping elephants: Developing elements of a theory of effective government organizations. *Journal of Public Administration Research and Theory, 9*(1), 1–32.

Rhodes, C. (2023). The ethics of organizational ethics. *Organization Studies, 44*(3), 497–514.

Stewart, D. (1985). Ethics and the profession of public administration: The moral responsibility of individuals in public sector organizations. *Public Administration Quarterly*, 487–495.

Stivers, C. (1994). The listening Bureaucrat: Responsiveness in public administration. *Public Administration Review, 54*(4), 364–369.

Svara, J. H. (2022). *The ethics primer for public administrators in government and nonprofit organizations*. Jones & Bartlett Publishers.

Thaler, J., & Helmig, B. (2016). Do codes of conduct and ethical leadership influence public employees' attitudes and behaviours? An experimental analysis. *Public Management Review, 18*(9), 1365–1399.

Van Wart, M. (1998). *Changing public sector values*. Routledge.

Vandenabeele, W. (2008). Government calling: Public service motivation as an element in selecting government as an employer of choice. *Public Administration, 86*(4), 1089–1105.

Verhoest, K., Verschuere, B., & Bouckaert, G. (2007). Pressure, legitimacy, and innovative behavior by public organizations. *Governance, 20*(3), 469–497.

Vigoda, E. (2000). Are you being served? The responsiveness of public administration to citizens' demands: An empirical examination in Israel. *Public Administration, 78*(1), 165–191.

Wright, B. E., Christensen, R. K., & Isett, K. R. (2013). Motivated to adapt? The role of public service motivation as employees face organizational change. *Public Administration Review, 73*(5), 738–747.

Chapter 4
Employees' Trust as the Hard Core of Success to Business Integrity

Adriana Grigorescu ⓘ, **Cristina Lincaru** ⓘ, **and Speranta Pirciog** ⓘ

Abstract In a globally competitive economy, business integrity emerges as key to building a leadership role and attracting and retaining employees in a trusted environment for business. The literature argues positive relationships between team trust and performance, sales, profits, employee turnover, leader empowering behavior, job crafting, work engagement, ethical leaders, employment engagement, management, interpersonal justice, commitment, satisfaction, intent to stay, and so on. To respond to the research question "Across EU 27 countries are there any relationships between employee's trust reflected in job tenure and business integrity expressed by training in 2015 compared with 2020?," we apply Kendall's tau-b correlation. Variables failed the normality and linearity assumption for Pearson correlation. The main conclusion of this chapter is that across the EU 26 countries studied, there is an increase in employee retention in the medium term, at the same time with increasing enterprises that provide management training stronger in 2015 than in 2020. Training in IT, either general or professional, does not have any relevance in retaining employees. We emphasize the importance of training in management as a direct measure of integrity even though our assumption was designed as an indirect measure. Our main contribution is to measure, in a quantitative manner, integrity by training in management using official statistics. Also, integrity is a dynamic value that is more important and has to be defined, formalized, and implemented inside the organization.

Keywords Employee trust · Business integrity · Job duration · Training · Skills · Digitalization · Kendall's tau-b correlation

---

A. Grigorescu (✉)
National University of Political Studies and Public Administration, Academy of Romanian Scientists, Romania, National Institute for Economic Research "Costin C.Kiritescu" – Romanian Academy, Bucharest, Romania
e-mail: adriana.grigorescu@snspa.ro

C. Lincaru · S. Pirciog
National Scientific Research Institute for Labor and Social Protection, Bucharest, Romania

© The Author(s), under exclusive license to Springer Nature Switzerland AG 2024
L. Chivu et al. (eds.), *Constraints and Opportunities in Shaping the Future: New Approaches to Economics and Policy Making*, Springer Proceedings in Business and Economics, https://doi.org/10.1007/978-3-031-47925-0_4

4.1 Introduction

Business integrity is a value that defines business success. Organizations' Code of Ethics and Conduct (CEC) regulates leadership behavior in internal and external dimensions in all decisions and actions. A CEC is considered successful if it is a source of trust. This management tool is a bridge to ensure the ethical involvement of employees in the organization, co-creating a long-term sustainable business.

4.1.1 The Importance of Integrity for Business Success

Pirson and Malhotra (2008) find that employees who are loyal, motivated, or productive do not trust the organization's management or the leadership.

Silva et al. (2021) emphasize two plans resulting from integrity commitment behavior, internal regulation, and the decision decentralization process. The first plan is the Ethical Code formal organization's definition and employee adoption in terms of good/bad behaviors in a formal way. The second plan sets up the rules and norms of the decision-making process (Silva et al., 2021). Matthew (2020) affirms that integrity is critical for a business; to have sustainable growth, innovative climate, customer loyalty, well-being culture, etc., in the long term, one should do the right think. Olsen (n.d.) states that "if you want your business to be successful, you need to make sure that integrity is at the core of everything you do."

Purshotam (2019) presents that cases of success based on integrity, considered a key issue to build a solid relation between employers and employ-ees, generates stability, higher job satisfaction, better performance, high productivity; summarized as a healthy organization culture on the benefit of all stakeholders.

4.1.2 The Importance of Integrity for Employees' Trust

Olsen (n.d.) argues that an upright leader promotes integrity in business and in the company, creating an environment of trust and honesty between the employees and between the managers and their teams. This is reflected in job satisfaction and performance, building a long-term business, loyal customers and suppliers, sustainable and creative company.

Honesty and integrity are the most valuable moral characteristics for a leader who expects the same from the staff. Creating a trustful climate in the company and inculcating the values of integrity are the main attributes of a leader (Purshotam, 2019; Grigorescu et al., 2020). Restructuring leadership in terms of integrity and trust will permit the co-creation of social innovation and will support the sustainable development of the companies in the long term instead of collapsing due to individualism, corruption, and disjointness (Schwella, 2021; Abou-Ali and Abdelfattah, 2013).

The same conclusions were found for public institutions based on the reports and nonconformities (Florea Munteanu et al., 2020). Establishing a climate of trust in an organization, Schwella (2021) considers integrity as a measure of coherence and consistency. Shahid and Azhar (2013) find out that the followers look to the leader as truthful, moral, and a person of integrity and expect him to behave accordingly to motivate them to do so.

Our approach is based on two components:

(a) The formal training offered by the organization as indirect measure for Integrity – Starting from the question formulated by (cfoselections.com) How Do We Measure the Integrity of Our Business? We propose an indirect measurement for Business Integrity: the Share of companies provid-ing CVT courses by tree types of skills: IT general and professional skills and management skills. The presence of the Code of Conduct implies formal training provided by companies. This is a management type of training provided usually in situations such as recruitment of new employees, internal job rotation, and technological innovation adoption.

(b) The job tenure as a measure of trust is in line with Shahid and Azhar (2013, p. 70) who express the trust of employees to follow and connect individually if the leader creates the environment to generate personal commitment and emotional engagement in the long term. A brief job tenure could signal the absence of trust. Shahid and Azhar (2013, p. 69) define the absence of trust as the inaccessibility of the leaders and managers for the staff and the behavior that creates the perception of a non-important presence or contribution. In this conditions the employees are caution in devoting, spending more time or energy, involving over the minimum needed. More than this, they will retreat, isolate, and look for opportunities outside the organization. Employees' mistrust generates a lack of interest, sarcasm, criticism, low productivity, and recklessness (Shahid & Azhar, 2013).

The research question we address in the present study is "Across EU 27 countries are there any relationships between employees' trust and business integrity in 2015 compared with 2020?"

We applied Kendall's tau-b correlation for 2015 and 2020 and found that the variables Integrity/Training and Trust/Job Tenure failed the normality and linearity assumption for Pearson correlation. The relatively small sample size of 26 terms (for 26 countries, no data for the Czech Republic for 2015) eliminates the alternative to using the nonparametric Spearman rank-order correlation coefficient. For the two-tailed null hypothesis H0: $\tau = 0$, Integrity/Training and Trust/Job Tenure are not monotonously related. The alternative hypothesis Ha: $\tau \neq 0$, is susceptible to have a positive monotonous relationship for both variables, the same tendency to increase was registered simultaneously.

There are two assumptions for Kendall's tau-b: (H1) both variables are measured on a continuous scale and (H2) there is a monotonic relationship between analyzed variables checked by the Spearman rank-order correlation test. The variable categories with monotonic relationships are discussed.

4.2 Literature Review

4.2.1 Integrity in Business and Employee Trust

Palanski and Yammarino (2009, p. 201) found that transparency among the team is positively related to integrity and helps to create team trust. They also found evidence that trust positively influences productivity and performance.

The trust in the general director was studied by Davis (2012, p. 563) for the restaurant industry in relation to the organization's performance. The findings highlighted a significant relationship between sales, profit, and employee turnover.

Scientists studied various variables in relationship with the trust in leaders as managers: job creation, work engagement, and employee and leader empowerment. Kim and Tak (2015) find a positive relation between them. Engelbrecht et al. (2017) put together a strategic management approach and found that ethical leaders play a key role in creating a climate of trust and engagement among employees.

T. L. Simons et al. (2007) found that black employees rated their managers by race, with a stronger "trickle-down effect for black managers." More than this, these differences in perceived behavioral integrity cross-race differences have a significant impact on employees' trust toward management, job satisfaction, commitment, and tenure.

A better understanding of the topic starts with working definitions, the main ideas, models, or theories found in the literature related to the present research.

Integrity is defined as "the consistency of an acting entity's team virtues words and actions" (Palanski & Yammarino, 2007), expanded in a multilevel theory on the integrity of teams (Palanski & Yammarino, 2009).

Behavioral integrity is a coherent language expression with a manager's behavior (Simons, 2002). The behavioral integrity of leaders generates followers' trust, both in theory (Simons, 2002) and in practice (Simons et al., 2007). Business integrity is considered ethical and honest behavior all the time, no matter if the financial benefit is lower (CFO Selection Team, 2021).

According to Matthew (2020), the key elements of behavioral integrity are trust, honor, and respect. The trustworthiness, reliability, and respect shown to the customers are the base of business integrity. Matthew (2020) considers that integrity is critical for business, make it better in good times and help it to survive in bad time. Neither customers nor business partners are willing to deal with an unethical company or managed by cheating, lying, or faking leaders. Attributes such as deceitful, insincere, fraudulent, or unaccountable are transferred from leaders to organizations, and no one wants to work for or with these kinds of people. Business integrity has been considered recently as a measure of success and has become more important (CFO Selection Team, 2021).

A comprehensive and complex image and role of the Code of Conduct training is pictured by Traliant (2021), who considers it as the first brick of the ethics and compliance program. This code has the role of stating and communicating the mission, vision, and core values that govern the organization's activities and has the role of inspiring the employees that they are a team that works as a body for the benefit of all. The implementation and transposition of it in reality belong to leaders, and if they break the roles, the entire construct falls down.

One kind of specific management training is compliance training, and we consider it a key issue in building the employee's trust. Malik (2021) defines compliance training as a specific tool used for new employees, mandatory in accordance with the laws or regulations for specific domains or positions. The main role is to assure the employees' safety and diminish the risks of work accidents if we refer mainly to industrial areas. The overall role in all areas is to facilitate the fast integration of the new entry and to plant the safety and team acceptance seeds.

Palanski and Yammarino (2009) differentiate transparency and consider a collective organizational construct from behavioral integrity and trust, both constructs at the individual level. They can be in synergy or can ruin each other. Pirson and Malhotra (2008) warn that transparency is overrated and integrity is not given enough importance. In their opinion, the right competence and the value congruence matter. Another finding is related to keeping the balance of build-destroy groups' trust.

4.2.2 How to Measure Business Integrity

Engelbrecht et al. (2017) formulate the core research question to measure business integrity: the frequency the team keeps promises and the frequency of the team acting under these values. Engelbrecht et al. (2017) applied an electronic web-based questionnaire to 204 employees. The respondents come from various business organizations.

Other approaches to the corporation ethics are given in Table 4.1.

The study of organizational citizenship behavior (OCB) developed by Mayer and Gavin (2005) has developed a trust scale to reflect the measurement of integrity as the shared principle by the managers and their team members. They used the ability, benevolence, and integrity of company management and team management, and the relationship with the ability to focus reflected on in-role performance, OCB individual, and organizational.

Table 4.1 Organizational ethics and compliance

Corporate best practices and rules	Areas to be measured
Written Standards	Existence of a formal and written Code of Conduct
Program Responsibility, Structure, and Resources	Conflict of interest disclosures or certifications from senior managers and non-employee directors
Communications and Training	Employees percentage that gets formal training on the Code of Conduct
Program Auditing and Monitoring	Background checks on all employees and new vendors
Discipline and Enforcement	Formal process of reporting, tracking, and investigating

Source: Authors' selection (CFO selection Team, 2021)

Traliant (2021) decouples professionalism from integrity. He considers that the employees' handbook should include five principles: integrity, objectivity, competence, confidentiality, and professionalism.

Simons et al. (2007) found that there is a hypersensitivity of behavioral integrity for black managers. The conclusions show that black employees were more critical than non-black employees.

Table 4.2 presents three solutions for building integrity in firms.

Appel (2022) stated that in the past, compliance training was optional; however, now organizations are forced to do it by the laws or regulations formalized in a specific Code of Conduct (respectively for Training).

It could be seen that the literature review reveals the constant concern about business integrity and employees' trust, how to build and maintain them, the shift process from managers to team and vice versa. One of the most important aspects less approached is how we can measure them. This chapter proposes a model to measure business integrity expressed by training. The culture of integrity results from the "regular compliance training, based on the company's Code of Conduct." Our approach links the right behavior delimited by the "very alive" right or wrong frontier described by the Code of Conduct with its effective implementation on a daily basis. But it is impossible to update this Code of Conduct in a highly dynamic environment if there is no transparency and participatory involvement, which creates "an ethical work culture as a priority and everyone's responsibility" (Traliant, 2021).

Table 4.2 Solutions to build integrity in firms

7 tips to nurture a culture of integrity at your workplace (Matthew, 2020)	6 Common Types of Employee Compliance Training Programs in 2021 (Malik, 2021)	Solutions provided by Traliant
1. Define integrity 2. Role model integrity 3. Clearly explain the consequences for inappropriate actions/define unacceptable actions and their consequences. 4. Document the standards of ethics and integrity you expect of teams, such as in a Code of Conduct manual. 5. Regular compliance training based on the company's Code of Conduct. 6. Employee engagement. … Employee engagement programs are an ideal platform to nourish engagement. 7. Slow change of behaviors.	1. "Occupational Safety and Health Administration" – or OSHA. 2. Cybersecurity Training 3. Ethics Training 4. Diversity Training 5. Anti-Harassment Training 6. Anger Management Training	1. Preventing Discrimination and Harassment 2. Building a Culture of Diversity, Equity and Inclusion 3. Promoting Ethical Practices in the Workplace 4. Cultivating an Environmental, Social, and Governance (ESG) Mindset 5. Preventing and Responding to Workplace Threats 6. Creating Positive and Healthy Workplaces 7. Complying with Labor and Employment Laws 8. Cybersecurity and Data Privacy

Source: Authors selection from the literature: Matthew (2020), Malik (2021), Traliant (2021)

From this perspective, the Effective Code of Conduct Training becomes a valuable tool to define in a more profound way the singularity of the organization, its values, and its adaptable mechanisms.

4.3 Methodology

4.3.1 Data Collection

We use the Eurostat data for trust and integrity, which are detailed in Tables 4.3 and 4.4.

Engelbrecht et al. (2017) use item analysis and confirmatory factor analysis conducted via a structural equation to model the variables "integrity, ethical leadership, trust, and work engagement." Palanski and Yammarino (2009) apply standard deviations, correlations, and discriminant validity for all the variables.

We apply Kendall's tau-b correlation for 2015 and 2020. The variables Integrity/Training and Trust/Job Tenure failed the normality (Table 4.5) and linearity assumption for Pearson correlation (Figs. 4.1 and 4.2).

The relatively small sample size of 26 terms (for 26 countries, no data for the Czech Republic and no data for 2015) eliminates the alternative to use the nonparametric Spearman rank-order correlation coefficient. The two-tailed null hypothesis is H0: $\tau = 0$. The Integrity/Training and Trust/Job Tenure are not monotonously related. Alternative hypothesis Ha: $\tau \neq 0$ is likely to have a positive/negative monotonous relation, respectively, both variables' sizes increase/decrease. The monotonic relationship's existence and its power are checked by the Spearman rank-order correlation test or Spearman rank correlation test (Thankachan, 2022).

ρ measures the strength of association between analyzed variables. According to Dancey and Reidy (2007), this association could be described as

- Very weak if ρ [0–0.19]
- Weak if $\rho \in$ [0.2–0.39]
- Moderate if $\rho \in$ [0.4–0.59]
- Strong if $\rho \in$ [0.6–0.79]
- Very strong if $\rho \in$ [0.8–1]

Table 4.3 Trust: job duration measured by four categories

Variable code	Variable name	Category (months)
JT1y	Employment for persons aged 15 years or over by job tenure	0–11
JT1_2y		12–23
JT2_5		24–59
JT5y		≥ 60

Source: Eurostat indicator "Employment for persons aged 15 years or over by job tenure" [LFSA_EGAD__custom_4366702]

Table 4.4 Integrity: training measured by employers that provide continuous vocational training measured by three categories

Variable code	Variable name	Category (skills)
IT_GEN	Share of enterprises providing CVT courses in skill:	General IT
IT_PROF		Professional IT
MGMT		Management

Source: Eurostat indicator [TRNG_CVT_29N2$DEFAULTVIEW]

Table 4.5 Checking the normality by the Shapiro–Wilk test of normality for small sets of data (<50 cases)

	Shapiro–Wilk			
	Statistic	df	Sig.	Decision
JT1y2015	.982	26	.914	Normal distribution
JT1_2y2015	.964	26	.466	Normal distribution
JT2_5y2015	.966	26	.518	Normal distribution
JT5y2015	.969	26	.602	Normal distribution
IT_GEN2015	.920	26	.044	Not normal distribution
IT_PROF2015	.946	26	.189	Normal distribution
MGMT2015	.961	26	.413	Normal distribution
JT1y2020	.974	26	.741	Normal distribution
JT1_2y2020	.985	26	.955	Normal distribution
JT2_5y2020	.982	26	.920	Normal distribution
JT5y2020	.963	26	.450	Normal distribution
IT_GEN2020	.945	26	.181	Normal distribution
IT_PROF2020	.953	26	.273	Normal distribution
MGMT2020	.915	26	.035	Not normal distribution

Source: Author's computation
Note: If Sig > 0.05, data are normally distributed (Danea, 2016)

Kendall's tau-b (τb) correlation coefficient is a hypothesis test: (H1) both variables are measured on a continuous scale and (H2) there is a monotonic relationship between analyzed variables checked by the Spearman rank-order correlation test (Laerd statistics, n.d.). τb assesses the strength and direction of association that exists between two ordinal measured quantities.

We apply the following for interpreting τb as an effect size proposed by Geert van den Berg (n.d.)

$|\tau b| = 0.07$ weak association
$|\tau b| = 0.21$ medium association
$|\tau b| = 0.35$ strong association

Also, Geert van den Berg (n.d.) points out that Kendall's tau has better known statistical properties than Spearman correlations, coupled with more reliable confidence intervals, smaller absolute values, and smaller standard errors.

We use Kendall's tau-b to calculate the strength and direction of the relationship between job tenure as a measure of trust and training for integrity. Job tenure is split

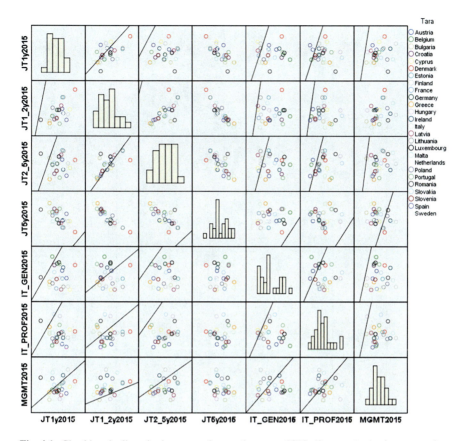

Fig. 4.1 Checking the linearity by scatterplot graphs – year 2015. (Source: Author's computation with the SPSS Scatter Plot Matrix)

into four categories, see Table 4.3, and training is split into three categories, see Table 4.4.

4.4 Analysis/Results Interpretation

We calculated Pearson coefficients for the linear variables, but these were not significant (Tables 4.6 and 4.7).

Laerd statistics (n.d.) modeled τb correlation between trust as *job tenure* and integrity among 26 countries. We reject the H0, and there were identified six correlation significant ant 0.05 level, only for the variable Integrity/Training measures as the share of enterprises providing CVT courses in Management Skills appeal in short Integrity, iterated by increasing Trust:

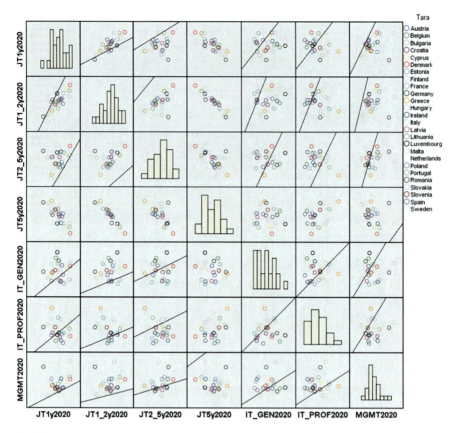

Fig. 4.2 Checking the linearity by scatterplot graphs – year 2020. (Source: Author's computation with the SPSS Scatter Plot Matrix)

(a) One strong, negative correlation between Trust/Job Duration 60 months or over in 2015 and Integrity 2015, which was statistically significant ($\tau b = -.282^*$, $p = .045$)
(b) Some strong, positive correlation between Trust/Job Duration from 12 to 23 months regardless of the time in short *Job Duration from 1 to 2 years*:
   (1) Trust in 2015 and Integrity in 2015, which was statistically significant ($\tau b = .323^*$, $p = .022$)
   (2) Trust in 2020 and integrity in 2015, which was statistically significant ($\tau b = .288^*$, $p = .040$)
   (3) Trust in 2020 and integrity in 2020, which was statistically significant ($\tau b = .276^*$, $p = .050$)
(c) Some strong, positive correlation between Trust/Job Duration from 24 to 59 months and short *Job Duration from 2 to 5 years*:

4 Employees' Trust as the Hard Core of Success to Business Integrity

Table 4.6 How strong is the monotonic relationship between the data of the pairs of variables illustrated by the Spearman rank-order correlation test

Variables		IT_GEN2015	IT_PROF2015	MGMT2015	IT_GEN2020	IT_PROF2020	MGMT2020	Spearman's rho
JT1y2015	Correlation Coefficient	−.105	−.147	.257	−.025	−.299	.259	
	Sig. (2-tailed)	.608	.473	.206	.905	.138	.202	
JT1_2y2015	Correlation Coefficient	−.086	−.010	.414*	−.213	−.262	.276	moderate
	Sig. (2-tailed)	.675	.963	.036	.296	.195	.172	
JT2_5y2015	Correlation Coefficient	−.014	.250	.272	−.114	.033	.136	
	Sig. (2-tailed)	.944	.218	.180	.580	.872	.506	
JT5y2015	Correlation Coefficient	.121	−.035	−.381	.135	.234	−.285	
	Sig. (2-tailed)	.555	.864	.055	.509	.250	.158	
JT1y2020	Correlation Coefficient	–	–	.262	–	–	.255	
		.170	.185		.061	.325		
	Sig. (2-tailed)	.408	.365	.196	.768	.105	.208	
JT1_2y2020	Correlation Coefficient	−.049	−.065	.390*	−.073	−.205	.353	weak
	Sig. (2-tailed)	.812	.752	.049	.724	.315	.077	
JT2_5y2020	Correlation Coefficient	.110	.294	.474*	−.171	−.050	.464*	moderate
	Sig. (2-tailed)	.591	.145	.014	.403	.809	.017	
JT5y2020	Correlation Coefficient	.069	.096	−.380	.104	.284	−.357	
	Sig. (2-tailed)	.739	.640	.055	.612	.160	.073	

Correlation significance level for $N = 26$:
*At the 0.05 level (2-tailed)

(1) Trust in 2020 and integrity in 2015, which was statistically significant ($\tau b = .350*$, $p = .013$)
(2) Trust in 2020 and integrity in 2020, which was statistically significant ($\tau b = .319*$, $p = .023$)

Table 4.7 A Kendall's tau-b correlation

		IT_GEN2015	IT_PROF2015	MGMT2015	IT_GEN2020	IT_PROF2020	MGMT2020
JT1y2015	Correlation Coefficient	−.077	−.090	.198	−.015	−.211	.211
	Sig. (2-tailed)	.581	.522	.158	.912	.133	.133
JT1_2y2015	Correlation Coefficient	−.047	.034	.323*	.096	−.180	.193
	Sig. (2-tailed)	.741	.808	.022	.494	.200	.171
JT2_5y2015	Correlation Coefficient	−.037	.198	.201	−.086	.040	.096
	Sig. (2-tailed)	.791	.158	.152	.537	.774	.494
JT5y2015	Correlation Coefficient	.099	−.050	−.282*	.080	.158	−.207
	Sig. (2-tailed)	.480	.724	.045	.566	.260	.139
JT1y2020	Correlation Coefficient	−.117	−.130	.213	−.043	−.207	.225
	Sig. (2-tailed)	.402	.354	.128	.758	.140	.107
JT1_2y2020	Correlation Coefficient	−.056	.031	.288*	−.043	−.102	.276*
	Sig. (2-tailed)	.691	.825	.040	.757	.467	.050
JT2_5y2020	Correlation Coefficient	.062	.217	.350*	−.124	−.034	.319*
	Sig. (2-tailed)	.659	.122	.013	.378	.808	.023
JT5y2020	Correlation Coefficient	.052	.022	−.241	.071	.210	−.266
	Sig. (2-tailed)	.708	.877	.085	.612	.134	.058

Correlation significance level for $N = 26$:
*At the 0.05 level (2-tailed)

(b) an (c) cases indicate a positive monotonic[1] increasing relationship between trust and integrity whereas case (a) indicates a negative monotonic[2] relationship. Even if the τb relationship is not a causal one, it gives us "hints" about possible causal links.

---

[1] *Positive Monotonic:* Both variables present the same tendency to increase.

[2] *Negative Monotonic:* Each variable presents opposite tendencies, one increases and the other decreases. https://www.statology.org/monotonic-relationship/

Even if the relationship is not causal, "correlations can tell us interesting things and can help us understand possible causal links."

There is a monotonic relationship between trust measured as job duration from 1 to 2 years and integrity measured as the share of enterprises providing CVT courses in management skills in 2015 and 2020 for 26 EU countries. The correlation between formal training in management skills and job duration between 1 year and 2 years indicates that the Code of Ethics and Conduct is updated on average in this time interval.

4.5 Conclusions

The main conclusion of this chapter is that across EU 26 countries studied, employee retention increased at the same time with increasing enterprises that provided management training more accentuated in 2015 than in 2020. Also, in general, it looks like there is no relationship between training in IT, either general or professional, and trust in retaining the employees.

We emphasize the importance of training in management as a direct measure of integrity; although in our assumption it was designed as an indirect measure.

Our main contribution is to enrich the sense and importance of management training in any kind of organization. We propose to measure in a quantitative manner integrity using official statistics. Also, integrity is an important dynamic value that has to be defined, formalized, and implemented inside the organization. Our modeling approach of integrity through the lens of training catches the dynamic of building ethic and integrity, especially in a highly dynamic environment driven by changes like science and technological progress, various global shocks (Pandemics, Wars), and different simultaneous transitions (Digital Transition, Green Deal, Demo-graphic Transition, Climate Neutrality, etc.). Beyond the AI adoption and agile transformation of the organization, a perennial human dimension is the business integrity regulated by the CEC.

We identify a monotonous correlation relationship between trust and integrity as a starting point for further causal analysis. We match the job duration with trust and management training with integrity as measures of behavior compliance with CEC in the medium term. Also, our analysis reveals that there is no correlation between trust and general IT or professional IT training regardless of the time horizon (from 0 to over 5 years of the job tenure).

We suggest, as possible applications and extensions of the research, the study of the causality between trust and integrity on the econometrical side. Also, at present, the types and content of the training programs funded from public budgets, especially for management skills, mainly focus on updating each organization's CEC as a tool to increase the adaptability of organizations.

Among some major limitations of the present research, we iterate the following:

- We evaluate the presence of correlation between the variables trust and integrity, but do not explain causality.
- Both characteristics of business integrity and employee trust are:
- Multidimensional, and we model in partial and indirect measures. Integrity is a multidimensional qualitative asset of a business, difficult to measure in a quantitative manner.
- Difficult to measure in a quantitative manner using official statistics indicators. Our approach assumes that any upgrading of the CEC is correlated with management training. The training data do not provide these details yet.

Acknowledgments This work was supported by a grant from the Romanian Ministry of Research and Innovation in the Project Functional perspectives of local labor markets in Romania, in the context of smart and innovative economy, PN 19130101, coordinator Dr. Speranța Pîrciog.

References

Abou-Ali, H., & Abdelfattah, M. Y. (2013). Integrated paradigm for sustainable development: A panel data study. *Economic Modelling, 30*, 334–342. https://doi.org/10.1016/j.econmod.2012.09.016

Appel, A. (2022). *Survey: Measuring the impact of code of conduct training.* https://www.complianceweek.com/surveys-and-benchmarking/survey-measuring-the-impact-of-code-of-conduct-training/32437.article

CFO selection Team. (2021). How do we measure the integrity of our business? *THE CFO'S PERSPECTIVE.* https://www.cfoselections.com/perspective/how-do-we-measure-the-integrity-of-our-business

Dancey, C. P., & Reidy, J. (2007). *Statistics without maths for psychology.* Pearson education. https://www.abebooks.com/9780132051606/Statistics-Maths-Psychology-Using-Spss-0132051605/plp

Danea, G. (2016). Testarea normalității distribuției datelor. *Analize Statistice.* http://analize-statistice.eu/testarea-normalitatii-distributiei-datelor/

Davis, J. (2012). Prosuming identity: The production and consumption of transableism on Transabled.org. *American Behavioral Scientist, 56*(4), 596–617. https://doi.org/10.1177/0002764211429361

Engelbrecht, A. S., Heine, G., & Mahembe, B. (2017). Integrity, ethical leadership, trust and work engagement. *Leadership & Organization Development Journal, 38*(3), 368–379. https://doi.org/10.1108/LODJ-11-2015-0237

Florea Munteanu, I., Grigorescu, A., Condrea, E., & Pelinescu, E. (2020). Convergent insights for sustainable development and ethical cohesion: An empirical study on corporate governance in Romanian public entities. *Sustainability, 12*(7), 2990. https://doi.org/10.3390/su12072990; https://www.mdpi.com/2071-1050/12/7/2990

Geert van den Berg, R. (n.d.). *Kendall's Tau – Simple introduction.* SPSS Tutorials. Retrieved 1 April 2023, from https://www.spss-tutorials.com/kendalls-tau/#:~:text=Kendall's%20Tau%20%2D%20Interpretation,-%CF%84b%20%3D%20%2D1&text=%CF%84b%20%3D%200%20indicates%20no,lower%20score%20on%20variable%20B

Grigorescu, A., Lincaru, C., & Pîrciog, S. (2020). Ethic leadership trigger for talents. In A. Grigorescu & V. Radu (Eds.), *Lumen proceedings: Vol. 11. 1st international conference*

Global Ethics – Key of Sustainability (GEKoS) (pp. 32–44). LUMEN Publishing House. https://doi.org/10.18662/lumproc/gekos2020/05

Kim, H., & Tak, J. (2015). The effect of leader empowering behavior on work engagement. *Korean Journal of Industrial and Organizational Psychology, 28*, 275–299. https://doi.org/10.24230/kjiop.v28i2.275-299

Laerd statistics. (n.d.). *Kendall's Tau-b using SPSS statistics.* https://statistics.laerd.com/spss-tutorials/kendalls-tau-b-using-spss-statistics.php#assumptions

Malik, P. (2021). What is compliance training? +Examples, challenges & tips. *Whatfix.* https://whatfix.com/blog/compliance-training/

Matthew, H. (2020). Why integrity in the workplace is important for business growth and success. *Pulse.* https://www.linkedin.com/pulse/why-integrity-workplace-important-business-growth-success-hanmer/

Mayer, R. C., & Gavin, M. B. (2005). Trust in management and performance: Who minds the shop while the employees watch the boss? *Academy of Management Journal, 48*(5), 874–888. https://doi.org/10.5465/AMJ.2005.18803928

Olsen, A. (n.d.). *Why integrity is key for success in business. GROCO advisors to the ultra-affluent.* https://groco.com/article/why-integrity-is-key-for-success-in-business/

Palanski, M., & Yammarino, F. (2007). Integrity and leadership: Clearing the conceptual confusion. *European Management Journal, 25*, 171–184. https://doi.org/10.1016/j.emj.2007.04.006

Palanski, M., & Yammarino, F. (2009). Integrity and leadership: A multi-level conceptual framework. *Leadership Quarterly, 20*, 405–420. https://doi.org/10.1016/j.leaqua.2009.03.008

Pirson, M. A., & Malhotra, D. (2008). Unconventional insights for managing stakeholder trust. *MIT Sloan Management Review, 49*, 43–50.

Purshotam. (2019). *Why is integrity important in business?* https://www.purshotam.com/why-is-integrity-important-in-business/

Schwella, E. (2021). *Leadership for the greater good: Reflections on today's challenges from around the globeleadership as integrity and trust.* ILA International Leadership Association. https://ilaglobalnetwork.org/leadership-as-integrity-and-trust/?gclid=CjwKCAiAkrWdBhBkEiwAZ9cdcDc_3SW00XPuOCdLCI9qDtoDpGDxQYdTxbwkUQvrLQ7tPByfzhWm7BoCFXkQAvD_BwE

Shahid, A., & Azhar, S. (2013). Integrity & trust. The defining principles of great workplaces. *Journal of Management Research, 5*, 64. https://doi.org/10.5296/jmr.v5i4.3739

Silva, R., Santos, R. C., Rodrigues Sousa, A., Orso, L., & Khatib, S. (2021). Code of ethics and conduct in the light of corporate governance: The stakeholders' perspective. *Revista de Administração Da UFSM, 14*, 405–422. https://doi.org/10.5902/1983465954702

Simons, T. (2002). Behavioral integrity: The perceived alignment between managers' words and deeds as a research focus. *Organization Science, 13*(1), 18–35. JSTOR. http://www.jstor.org/stable/3086064

Simons, T. L., Friedman, R., Liu, L., & Parks, J. M. (2007). Racial differences in sensitivity to behavioral integrity: Attitudinal consequences, in-group effects, and 'trickle down' among Black and non-Black employees. *The Journal of Applied Psychology, 92*(3), 650–665.

Thankachan, K. (2022). Every statistical test to check feature dependence: Correlation and hypothesis tests for different datatypes and assumptions. *Towards Data Science.* https://towardsdatascience.com/every-statistical-test-to-check-feature-dependence-773a21cd6722

Traliant. (2021). *Code of conduct training: What is it and why is it important? Online compliance training for employees - helping employees make the right decisions at the right moments.* https://www.traliant.com/blog/code-of-conduct-training-what-is-it-and-why-is-it-important/#:~:text=Code%20of%20conduct%20training%20increases, inclusion%20and%20social%20media%20use

Chapter 5
The Role of Humans as Key Enablers of Industry 5.0

Elda Dollija and Kriselda Gura

Abstract In 2011, the German government introduced Industry 4.0. A decade later, the European Commission initiated a new area of revolution named Industry 5.0. Based on the latest studies, this article explains the reasons behind the introduction of this new industry. It confirms the idea that I5.0 is a revolution rather than the evolution of I4.0. The Fifth Industrial Revolution, 5.0, aims to improve on the drawbacks of the previous one. Previous researchers have stated that, despite its benefits, I4.0 has lost its human and environmental dimension. Furthermore, during the COVID-19 pandemic, I4.0 did not prove resilient enough to withstand the disruption and be recovered later. Therefore, Industry 5.0 supplements I4.0's focus on three core values: human centricity, sustainability, and resilience. I5.0 will address the fundamental issue of the loss of human employees in the industry and the promotion of skills and diversities through innovative ways such as Operator 5.0 or Co-bots. Additionally, tighter cooperation between people, machines, and digital technologies is required in order to achieve mass personalisation. Mass personalisation helps achieve environmental and economic sustainability as well as industry resilience. Recent studies have shown that, despite Industry 5.0's contribution to the world economy, ecology, and society, we will face many challenges during its implementation. The first challenge is developing the soft and practical skills of the workforce and other necessary abilities to execute Industry 5.0 as a whole. Specialised training programs, instructors, and other actors are necessary to offer training sessions for the development of these new soft and practical skills. On the other hand, strict privacy, security, and ethical concerns are necessary for the adoption of disruptive technology applications used in Industry 5.0.

Keywords Industrial revolution, Industry 4.0 · Industry 5.0 · Sustainability · Resilience · Human-centric

---

E. Dollija (✉) · K. Gura
Beder University College, Tirana, Albania
e-mail: edollija@beder.edu.al; kgura@beder.edu.al

5.1 Introduction

The world has always been in continuous progress. As we know from history, it took thousands of years to pass from the stone age to the bronze age and then to the iron age. When we refer to the industrial revolutions, we realise that it took nearly a century to pass from the first Industrial Revolution (Industry 1.0) to the second (Industry 2.0) and the third (Industry 3.0), but we are impressed to confess that it took only decades to pass from the third to the fourth (Industry 4.0). Recently, as we were getting used to the fourth industrial revolution, we started talking about the fifth industrial revolution (Industry 5.0) (Fig. 5.1). We are facing the highest level of dynamism ever, as some generations have faced three industrial revolutions during their lives (I3.0, I4.0, and I5.0).

The First Industrial Revolution (Industry 1.0) originated in England around 1760 and spread to the United States by the end of the eighteenth century. It was characterised by a transition from human manufacturing processes to machinery driven by steam or water. Therefore, the products were manufactured using techniques and methods developed and empowered to be produced by machines. Industry 1.0 was a revolution that made the disruption and the shift from the traditional economy to a technology-intensive one for the majority of sectors (Mourtzis et al., 2022; Vinitha et al., 2020). Between 1871 and 1914, the industrial sector underwent a transformation recognised as Industry 2.0, which allowed for faster mobility of people and new ideas. The second revolution introduced new technology such as electricity, telecommunications, combustion engines, railway networks, fossil fuels, cable, sewerage, and water delivery. This revolution is characterised by economic development, increased company productivity, and an increase in unemployment as machines replace manufacturing workers (Adel, 2022; Mourtzis et al., 2022; Vinitha et al., 2020). The digital revolution, which began in the 1970s with the automation of memory-programmable controllers and computers, is referred to as Industry 3.0. This phase's focal point was mass production and the usage of digital systems, and integrated computer chips (Adel, 2022; Mourtzis et al., 2022; Vinitha et al., 2020). Technology advances are altering traditional items as well as corporate practices. One of the main advancements of the last revolution was the shift towards digitalisation. Industry 4.0 was initiated in the twenty-first century (2011) as the convergence of physical assets and modern technologies such as Artificial Intelligence (AI), the Internet of Things (IoT), robotics, 3D printing, and cloud computing. Organisations that have implemented I4.0 are integrative and functional to any decision-making process reliable on big data (Adel, 2022; Mourtzis et al., 2022; Vinitha et al., 2020).

Fig. 5.1 Industrial revolutions (From Industry 1.0 to Industry 5.0). (Source: the author)

"Industry 5.0 provides a distinct approach and emphasises the significance of research and innovation to assist the industry in its long-term service to humanity within the bounds of the planet" (Breque et al., 2021). I5.0 is the next generation of technology developed for intelligent and cost-effective machinery (Adel, 2022; Wang, 2022).

Through a deep analysis of the latest research papers on the Fourth and Fifth Industrial Revolutions, this research paper attempts to respond to these Research Questions:

1. RQ1. Why, despite the fact that Industry 4.0 has not yet been adopted globally, many organisations and academic researchers have started introducing a new era of the revolution known as Industry 5.0?
2. RQ2. Is Industry 5.0 a continuation or a substitute for Industry 4.0?
3. RQ3. What is the role and importance of humans, as key enablers of the next paradigm, on the three core values of Industry 5.0: Human-Centricity, Sustainability, and Resilience?

5.2 Literature Review

In 2011, the German government's high-tech strategy launched a program that initiated the Fourth Industrial Revolution. It is defined as a collection of technologies that can establish cyber-physical systems within organisations and in production processes (Kagermann, 2015). There are some obvious advantages to implementing Industry 4.0, which enables companies to reduce costs, enhance quality standards, increase flexibility, and customise their products. This would enable widespread customisation, which would allow businesses to meet customers demands as well as generate profit by introducing new goods and services to the economy (Guo et al., 2021; Tjahjono et al., 2017; Jain et al., 2021; Nahavandi, 2019). According to Boston Consulting Group, "The nine technologies that enabled the transformation of Industrial production on behalf of I4.0 are big data and analytics, autonomous robots, simulation, horizontal and vertical system integration, the Internet of Things, cybersecurity, cloud computing, additive manufacturing, and augmented reality" (Fig. 5.2).

The introduction of the new industrial revolution (I5.0) is based on solving three main disadvantages related to Industry 4.0. Firstly, while I4.0 was being developed and implemented with a greater focus on cost reduction, standard quality enhancement, flexibility increase, and product customisation, it has lost its human/value-centred dimension (Aheleroff et al., 2022; Nahavandi, 2019; Xu et al., 2021). Secondly, I4.0 is not concerned with protecting the environment, and it has not invested in technologies in order to improve their impact on the Earth (Aheleroff et al., 2022; Breque et al., 2021; Longo et al., 2020; Nahavandi, 2019). Thirdly, the COVID-19 pandemic has demonstrated the emergency for resilience in industrial production, which has transmitted its problems to individual workers and the whole

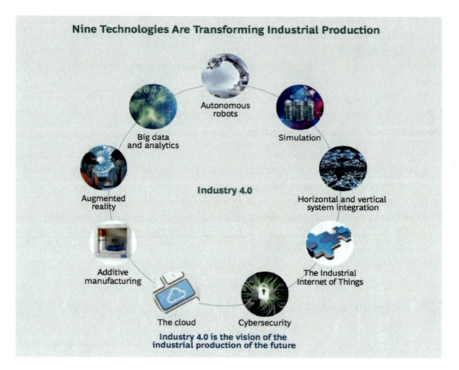

Fig. 5.2 The nine technologies of Industry 4.0. (Source: Boston Consulting Group (2015))

society as well as to businesses worldwide because they are not as robust as expected (Grabowska et al., 2022; Kusiak, 2020; Romero & Stahre, 2021).

As a result, even though it has not yet been fully implemented globally, many actors have initiated the introduction of a new era of revolution called Industry 5.0 (Demir et al., 2019; Nahavandi, 2019; Longo et al., 2020). On the 2nd and 9th of July 2020, there were two virtual workshops by the "Directorate Prosperity" of the General Directorate for Research and Innovation in the European Commission, with the participation of research and technology organisations and funding agencies across Europe. The workshops were designed to gather input on the overall concept of I5.0 and to address enabling technology and potential challenges. The discussions concluded with the introduction of the Fifth Industrial Revolution through the publication of the document entitled "Industry 5.0: Towards a Sustainable, Human-centric, and Resilient European Industry" on the 4th of January 2021 (Breque et al., 2021). Industry 5.0 was developed in response to a trade-off between social progress and economic expansion (Aheleroff et al., 2022).

The European Commission, "emphasizes the fact that the main development when it comes to the shift towards I5.0 is that it is not derivative of I4.0, but rather expands and complements it by adding socio-environmental elements" (Breque et al., 2021). Other studies confirm the fact that the Industry 5.0 paradigm is not a historical continuation of Industry 4.0 (Carayannis & Morawska-Jancelewicz, 2022;

Ghobakhloo et al., 2022). The outcome of a forward-looking activity, Industry 5.0, frames the coexistence of industry with new societal trends and requirements. As a result, Industry 5.0 expands upon the distinguishing characteristics of Industry 4.0. The necessity to reveal man's contribution to cyber-physical systems is what essentially drives the transition of industrialisation from Industry 4.0 to Industry 5.0 (Grabowska et al., 2022). As a result, the notion of Industry 5.0 is centred on values rather than technology, such as human-centricity and environmental or social advantages.

5.3 Methodology

This is a qualitative study based on the literature review of the previous research in Industry 5.0. It aims at explaining the aforementioned research questions by analysing the recent studies on the core values of I5.0 and its advantages and challenges.

The true potential for Industry 5.0 development rests in maximising technological, mechanical, and human cooperation. It involves a partnership between the ever-powerful and precise technologies, such as Smart Computerised Numerical Control (CNC) and Collaborative-Robots (Co-bots), cutting-edge technologies like IoT, and the distinctive creative potential of people (Aheleroff et al., 2022). I5.0 supplements the previous I4.0 framework by emphasising that there are three important basic features of I5.0: an intensive approach to humans, resilient, and sustainable industries, which are interconnected with each other (Fig. 5.2) (Mourtzis et al., 2022). The social, environmental, and economic aspects are acknowledged by the Industry 5.0 reference model. This approach goes beyond Industry 4.0's purely technological focus by integrating social and environmental dimensions of sustainability with organisational practices with the extensive support of technology in this regard (Ivanov, 2022) (Fig. 5.3).

5.3.1 Human Centricity

Despite its advances and opportunities, I4.0 unavoidably ignores the human cost of process optimisation. The main disadvantage of I4.0 is the lack of human perspective (Breque et al., 2021). Choi et al. (2022) emphasise "worker welfare, health problems, and worker satisfaction as consequences of disruptive technology implementation". It is the most significant challenge that will emerge very soon when the full impact of Industry 4.0 is realised. As a result, criticism from labour unions and politicians will arise. Since the role of present employees is hardly emphasised, numerous scientific studies emphasise the need to include people's critical role in future industrial development assumptions (Romero et al., 2016). When it comes to using advanced technology to improve process efficiency, it is not necessary to be on the defensive. Once the backward push begins, we will require Industry 5.0 to do

Fig. 5.3 The three core values of Industry 5.0. (Source: "European Commission. Directorate General for Research and Innovation" (2020))

this (Nahavandi, 2019). Furthermore, narrow, profit-driven thinking ignores the costs and benefits to society and the environment. In order to grow into a real supplier of progress, the industry's actual mission should be focused on society and the planet. It includes sustainable innovation focused on boosting more savings or profits by enhancing wealth for all stakeholders: shareholders, employees, customers, society, and the environment (Breque et al., 2021).

Industry 5.0 will resolve the reduction of human workers in the industry

Advanced and intelligent technological enablers of Industry 4.0 (and previous industries) substituted human workers in manufacturing. According to Aheleroff et al. (2022), "many smart technologies of Industry 4.0 have improved production, but fall short when it comes to the sustainability, resilience, and labour productivity needed in times of world emergencies like the pandemic". Due to the COVID-19 pandemic, whole industrial lines worldwide came to a halt in March and April 2020. Why could not the machineries continue to function if the virus impacted only people? This experience emphasised the role and significance of humans in the labour market. We understand that, even though machines and equipment may automate processes, all sectors will still need humans. People require sufficient space to enhance their abilities and utilise their personal imagination on the one hand and technology on the other, solely as an assistance to peaceful cooperation instead of a means of substitution for their labour. The emphasis on human-centricity is being addressed to every employee. "In a workplace that promotes safe work and technical assistance in the functions the operator needs, Operator 5.0 has to cooperate well with the machinery through leveraging one's own sensory, physical, and cognitive capacities while technologies give real-time information for making prompt judgments" (Zizic et al., 2022).

There is a risk of job loss once technology changes, since there may be instances in which automation through robotic systems might substitute skilled workers, but there are also many newly generated occupations that make it possible for the introduction of automatisation processes. It seems obvious that certain occupations would vanish as new advancements in technology occur, so it makes sense that some professions will no longer exist when new technologies are introduced. Nevertheless, several newly generated occupations support the aforementioned automatisation process (Frey & Osborne, 2017). Industry 4.0's main problem is automation, whereas Industry 5.0 will feature collaboration between intelligent machines and people. Human resources make the difference, and robots can replace practical tasks but not cognitive and creative thinking (Breque et al., 2021). Wang et al. (2021) suggest that automated systems can collaborate with humans rather than substitute them. The autonomous workforce will be aware of human intentions and aspirations. "The human kinds will coexist peacefully with robots at work, resulting in an effective and efficient collaboration between parties". The final outcome of such incorporations is going to be an improved manufacturing process and a believed independent functioning, which decreases wastes and related expenses" (Nahavandi, 2019, p. 10).

Industry 5.0, through adaptive robotics, Cognitive Cyber-Physical Systems (CCPS), and solutions for interpersonal interactions as well as identification, produces a human-centric approach that prioritises fundamental workforce demands while preserving or enhancing production efficiency. For instance, adaptive robots can overcome the drawbacks of classical robots and collaborative robots, enabling qualitative production while preserving the high comfort of the participating human workers (Ghobakhloo et al., 2022). Furthermore, by re-centering human beings in industrial production, people will focus on innovation and effective business solutions while collaborative robots will execute monotonous and risky tasks (Adel, 2022). Therefore, Industry 5.0 encourages businesses to install Co-bots that need a huge staff and allow individuals to achieve fundamental human aspirations. This way, Co-bots will assist businesses in achieving a distinctive value offer rather than replacing employees (Aheleroff et al., 2022). Nahavandi (2019), in contrast to common assumptions, asserts that I5.0 can actually create more jobs than it removes. Numerous employment opportunities will probably be generated in specific fields of advanced technologies, management, retraining, organising, and so on. Additionally, as there is no necessity for monotonous tasks to be carried out by a human worker, encouraging everyone to employ various types of robots in the workplace creatively would be very effective.

Industry 5.0 will "promote talents, diversity, and empowerment"

Industry 5.0 aims for life quality enhancement and a balanced society for all, not just those people participating in industrial activities. "With its flexible and adaptive technology, I5.0 is rapid to act, resilient, and respectful of the planet's constraints while nurturing talent, diversity, and empowerment" (Mourtzis et al., 2022, p. 6). Moving away from development based solely on technology and embracing an approach that truly prioritises humans and society means that the essential needs and desires of people are now the central focus of the manufacturing processes. As the perception of people shifts from being seen as a "cost" to an "investment", industrial workers will be assigned new responsibilities (Xu et al., 2021).

To compete in an increasingly competitive market, businesses want individuals who can manage changes and transition to new information and procedures, which demands diverse skill sets (Zizic et al., 2022). Knowledge and skills in big data analytics, advanced analytics, and artificial intelligence are really beneficial for potential professions (Frey & Osborne, 2017). Among these professions, we may mention programming, organising and planning, training, maintenance, etc. In these conditions, in many businesses and countries, finding, serving, and retaining talent is becoming far more difficult than attracting, offering, and keeping clients. As the tendency still persists, the business's approach must adapt to accommodate it. In this regard, for example, Battini et al. (2022, p. 12) add the inclusive dimension in terms of labour market and job opportunity creation with the entrance of Industry 5.0. Companies have a lot of difficulty in the manufacturing industry because of the variability of workers' experience, productivity, and physical capabilities. The proposed model attempts to address these issues by simultaneously taking into account a variety of socio-technical factors, including the experience of the workers, their physical capabilities and restrictions, their health, their exposure to pollution and stress, and their level of monotony. Furthermore, according to Nahavandi (2019), Industry 5.0 will improve operational effectiveness and productivity, be more environmentally friendly, decrease workplace accidents, and minimise manufacturing cycle times.

5.3.2 Sustainability

The industry must be sustainable by respecting the limits of the planet. "It must create circular processes that reuse, recycle, and repurpose natural resources, reduce energy consumption, reduce CO_2 output, lessen waste generation, protect the environment, and eventually create a circular economy" (Breque et al., 2021). Every day, we are developing greater awareness that despite the benefits of technological breakthroughs, humanity is now confronted with the drawbacks and hazards that they represent, such as threats to our environment. Global environmental pollution significantly increased after the Second Industrial Revolution. Nowadays, in addition to the human aspect, many authors have identified research needs in the Industry 4.0 concept related to sustainability, accountability, safety, and other topics (Longo et al., 2020).

Unfortunately, despite the fact that many various AI algorithms have been employed to study sustainability in the past decade, I4.0 does not consider environmental preservation. Besides this, there has not been any specific technology developed to increase the Earth's ecological sustainability. As a technology-driven approach, the Industry's 4.0 goal is oriented towards achieving efficiency. However, unlike in previous times, the industrial sector is concerned with various areas of pollution creation and disposal as well as eliminating negative environmental consequences from its operations (Nahavandi, 2019). The human-centric approach in Industry 5.0 is driving economic development to a great standard of sustainability.

According to Ghobakhloo et al. (2022, p. 729), Industry 5.0 improves the production and consumption processes transforming them into more sustainable processes that create economic, social, and environmental values for current and future generations. Additionally, it is believed to be the main revolution that fosters a circular economic model for a resilient and climate neutral society (Breque et al., 2021). Therefore, I5.0 is going to encourage industry demands for greater resilience and long-term sustainability (Aheleroff et al., 2022). I5.0 prioritises environmental protection, which has sparked the development of sustainability and resilience as new trends converge with consumer preferences, the majority of governmental regulations, and international organisations like the United Nations' Sustainable Development Goals (SDGs).

The SDG agenda includes 17 goals and 169 targets related to environmental, social, and human developmental objectives. In a systematic analysis of 70 peer-reviewed articles studying SDG interactions, Kasinathan et al. (2022) considered the technology-driven approach as the most adequate one to hasten the progress of the SDGs. In their study, they concluded that disruptive technologies are among the most ground-breaking, have the most potential to propel mankind toward sustainable development in the future, and could help SDGs be achieved more quickly. Furthermore, for each SDG, they identified the support provided by disruptive technologies, which drive significant changes in the entrepreneurship environment and sustainable society (Kasinathan et al., 2022, p. 8).

Nahavandi (2019) goes further, proposing a new manufacturing role: "Chief Robotics Officer (CRO), a person who has knowledge about robotics and how they interact with people. CROs will gain experience in a variety of fields, including robotics, artificial intelligence, human factors modelling, and human–machine interaction". Because of the CROs' superior collaborative robotic technologies and their ability to harness the power of recent advances in computation, environmental management will also be improved. Lowering pollution and waste production and protecting the environment will eventually boost the sustainability of human society.

From an economic point of view, the Circular Economy can protect the environment. Geissdoerfer et al. (2017, p. 766) define the circular economy as a closed-loop system designed to be regenerative. All products will be designed to have an extended or a second life to protect the environment through recycled products yielding lower waste and natural resources conservation. The use of intelligent products further facilitates the role of humans in achieving net zero production through their enhanced comprehension and decision-making authority. The achievement of circular economy objectives through intelligent products offers a convincing case for the combination of human expertise and knowledge with automation technology to achieve ambitious recycling goals, particularly in light of the growing need to reduce carbon emissions in the industry. Turner et al. (2022) show how mass personalisation also tries to address sustainability issues by lowering the amount of trash and resources used during production. According to Aheleroff et al. (2022), Industry 4.0 provides the necessary technologies for mass personalisation, while Industry 5.0 requires even more collaboration between people, machines, and digital technologies to achieve mass personalisation for sustainability and resilience. To achieve resilience for mass personalisation, which could cater to consumers' needs and give them a sense of ownership and loyalty to products, both humans and technology are essential.

5.3.3 Resilience

The third core element of Industry 5.0 is Resilience. According to Madni and Jackson (2009), resilience is a complex systemic characteristic that includes the possibility to prevent, tolerate, reconfigure, and restore from predicted and unforeseen shocks. The resiliency of our society and economy has been tested by the pandemic situation. The COVID-19 pandemic has demonstrated to businesses worldwide that many of their present production processes failed because they were not as robust as expected (Romero & Stahre, 2021). The situation emphasised the emergency for resilience in industrial production, which transmitted its problems to individual workers and the whole society. The future of the sector depends on its ability to adapt quickly to dynamic political developments and natural disasters (Breque et al., 2021).

Manufacturing resilience is crucial because major disruptions of all kinds, from pandemics to man-made and natural disasters, will continue to occur (Kusiak, 2020). How can Industry 5.0 increase resilience? Technology-smart machines–human interaction is the key to resilience. Through the cooperation between humans and machines, the responsibilities and work division can be easily changed to respond to shifting circumstances (Kaasinen et al., 2022). By enhancing human skills in addition to automation's speed, accuracy, scalability, predictive capacities, and repeatability, Industry 5.0 switched from automation-focused robotics (of I4.0) to collaborative robots (Aheleroff et al., 2022). By maximising the interaction between technology, robotics, and the human mind, Co-bot is growing into a sustainable source of revenue. The next generation of Co-bots can provide a speedier, more approachable, and highly adjustable interface between humans and robots in order to fulfil customisation at scale. Co-bots, which serve as partners rather than competitors, are used increasingly often to load and unload machines and to produce highly personalised 3D-printed parts (Kaasinen et al., 2022).

A system would be more resilient if worker diversity were carefully taken into account while formulating work policies. A worker whose particular abilities and circumstances have continually been matched with job demands and task schedules would be a better and more resilient performer when compared to performances created by a random or uniform distribution of tasks to workers (Battini et al., 2022).

Romero and Stahre (2021) propose a vision for the "Resilient Operator 5.0" that is human-centred, inclusive, and integrative for every one and sustainable for current and future generations supported by appropriate technologies. According to the "human-automation symbiosis" theory, a Next-Generation Operator seeks to establish trusting relationships (based on interaction) between people and technologies. This will ensure technological advancement and a sustainable digitalised manufacturing system to fully take advantage of the opportunities being created by Industry 4.0 technology while also equipping with proper capacities, abilities, and tools.

Industry 5.0 is driving the transformation of supply and production chains into intelligent, adaptive, and programmable systems that are adjusted continuously and integrate market dynamics. In reaction to changes caused by supply and demand curves, Industry 5.0 allows innovative, dynamic, and systemic adaptive production processes to instantly rearrange and reallocate their elements and skills. When used effectively, Industry 5.0 may boost productivity and efficiency while boosting the industrial and supply networks' resilience, sustainability, and viability. Kusiak (2020) proposes an architecture for a sustainable strategy that can upgrade the market to face challenges. In order to achieve many goals, such as the incorporation of analytic skills and simplicity elements, which are in line with the sustainability criteria, he suggests that open manufacturing systems need to be set up and reconfigured. Strategy centric rather than operations are provided by digitisation, more transparency, and a rising focus on customer service in production. He proposes a method for simplifying digital models. The complexity reduction method breaks down complicated systems and makes their constituent parts more comprehensible and visible. Other well-known notions promoting adaptability, such as the complexity of goods and operations and postponed product diversification, might be served by the same algorithm and its variations and are explained by an example (Kusiak, 2020).

On manufacturing floors, teams of people and robots are frequently needed to work together to accomplish a similar goal. The ultimate goal is to effectively maximise collaboration between people and robots in factories that are durable and sustainable in the future. In the future, robust smart factories can be sustained with empowered humans in charge of robotics and machinery, making it feasible for super operators with improved abilities to complete currently impossible tasks (Wang, 2022).

5.3.3.1 Barriers and Challenges of Industry 5.0

Across its great expectations about the future of smart-technological, human, social, environmental, and sustainability levels, Industry 5.0 will face many barriers and challenges (Tavares et al., 2022). Even though it is well deserved and beneficial to the global economy, nature, and community, the implementation of Industry 5.0 is going to face many barriers and challenges. First of all, we have to raise awareness about the main concepts, functioning, benefits, and limits of Industry 5.0, as they are understudied (Ghobakhloo et al., 2022). After that, we must be aware of the soft and practical skills required by the workforce. To fulfil the criteria of I5.0, employers, managers, and leaders need to adapt and develop their competencies and abilities. According to the 2019 World Manufacturing Forum, future manufacturers will need ten important skills (Fig. 5.4).

Mitchell and Guile (2022), based on the work of Wilson and Daugherty (2018), go further, calling for "Fusion skills", which are a combination of human and computer skills. By analysing current human–machine contact and distinguishing between human-only and machine-only talents, they were able to determine the novel types of interactions that humans and machines would engage in in the context of work in the future.

The new soft and practical skills need training programs, educators, and experts who are using the new technologies (Feng et al., 2020). The adoption of new, cutting-edge technology calls for capable change managers. Additionally, companies and managers will need to put in more time and effort. The need for a competent workforce and new technologies will increase by the time Industry 5.0 is completely implemented, necessitating proper training for both the trainees and the future instructors. The biggest challenge in the skill space is that individuals who work with co-bots find it challenging to get the necessary training due to a lack of qualified trainers and financial constraints. Additionally, some businesses might not have the necessary infrastructure to support the recent technological advances (Maddikunta et al., 2022).

Fig. 5.4 The WMF's Top Ten Skills for the Future of Manufacturing. (Source: World Manufacturing Forum (2019))

Because Industry 5.0 applications are based on ICT systems, rigid privacy and security requirements are indispensable in order to prevent privacy and security concerns (Ayan et al., 2022). With the increasing digitisation of computing, it is essential to ensure the security of heterogeneous data handling and the use of cloud services for managing various types of user and industrial data. As a result, Industry 5.0 may encounter significant security challenges. According to Abdel Hakeem et al. (2022), I5.0 will have to meet related to safety credibility, accessibility, identification, and auditing, similar to conventional CPSs. Privacy is also a critical concern as the whole infrastructure depends on valuable trademarks, costly raw materials for manufacturing, and membership management (Maddikunta et al., 2022). To connect people, machines, designers, and other collaborators, and to transmit monitoring and control information, data are sent over the Internet in Industry 5.0. Keeping the trustworthiness of the infrastructure for cloud-based manufacturing is vital to prevent hostile Internet users from accessing such data (Esposito et al., 2016). Human data protection rights, or the idea that persons have ownership over their data, are one of the privacy concerns. They are entitled to compensation for any data theft that affects their personal or sensitive data. In order to protect data privacy, user data must be protected (Maddikunta et al., 2022). When offering personalised and anticipatory services to customers, it is crucial to address ethical issues, conduct transactions that protect privacy, and ensure that data collection does not compromise privacy. Additionally, ethical design decisions must be made so that human–machine collaboration can be successfully designed. When deciding how to divide up jobs between humans and machines, how to use the capabilities of both humans and machines, and how to establish work practices where humans and computers complement one another, privacy and integrity are crucial principles to keep in mind (Kaasinen et al., 2022).

Laws and regulations are a key prerequisite for each industrial revolution's complete acceptance. Although there are generally accessible standards for automation, innovation policy, and industrial rules, the more particular norm for this new period has to be enforced. Different rules related to both the human and co-bot are required to develop as Industry 5.0 intends to revitalise humans to collaborate with co-bots and smart robots. For more accurate forecasts and sophisticated co-production, regulations that encourage the employment of AI, co-bots, and other robots in the manufacturing business should be developed. Adoption will be quicker, more complete, and easier to manage with improved rules, legislation, guidelines, and standards (Adel, 2022; Maddikunta et al., 2022).

The aforementioned challenges all involve additional expenses. Costly investments are needed to support advanced technology. It costs money to adopt Industry 5.0 since it necessitates sophisticated machinery and highly trained workers to boost output and efficiency. An additional expense is the cost of training human workers for new occupations (Adel, 2022). Therefore, significant funding from government organisations will be required in order to enhance the implementation of Industry 5.0 (Xu et al., 2021).

5.4 Results and Discussions

This paper is a review of the studies on the latest industrial revolution, called Industry 5.0. Initially, the paper is focused on explaining the reasons why, less than a decade after the implementation of Industry 4.0, the European Commission (Breque et al., 2021) introduced the new era of I5.0. The reasons lie behind the disadvantages of Industry 4.0 in three main pillars: Human centricity, Sustainability, and Resilience. First of all, I4.0 has lost its human-centred dimension as a result of its development and implementation, which have focused more on cost reduction, improved quality standards, greater flexibility, and product customisation (Aheleroff et al., 2022; Nahavandi, 2019; Xu et al., 2021). Additionally, neither an emphasis on environmental protection nor a focus on technology to increase the Earth's environmental sustainability can be found in Industry 4.0 (Aheleroff et al., 2022; Longo et al., 2020; Nahavandi, 2019). Finally, the COVID-19 pandemic has enforced the need for industrial production to be resilient. During the pandemic, the enterprises resulted to be not as resilient as predicted, which resulted in difficulties for specific employees and the entire society (Grabowska et al., 2022; Kusiak, 2020; Romero & Stahre, 2021).

Therefore, the Directorate-General for Research and Innovation in the European Commission, on January 4, 2021, introduced the Fifth Industrial Revolution by publishing the document entitled "Industry 5.0: Towards a Sustainable, Human-centric, and Resilient European Industry" (Breque et al., 2021). The European Commission and further researchers do not consider Industry 5.0 as a chronological continuation or alternative to I4.0 (Carayannis & Morawska-Jancelewicz, 2022; Ghobakhloo et al., 2022; Grabowska et al., 2022; Xu et al., 2021).

Therefore, Industry 5.0 supports the previous industry, based on three core principles: Human centricity, Sustainability, and Resilience (Breque et al., 2021; Mourtzis et al., 2022). The present study is based on the results of various research papers that argue for the substantial role of humans as key enablers of Industry 5.0. Many previous studies have argued on how Industry 5.0 will make people the pillar of the whole industry, considering them as an investment rather than a cost (Xu et al., 2021). These studies explain how I5.0 will resolve the actual problem of the reduction of human workers in the industry, for example, through Operator 5.0 (Zizic et al., 2022) or Co-bots (Aheleroff et al., 2022), as well as promoting talents and diversities (Battini et al., 2022). Furthermore, closer collaboration between people, machines, and digital technologies is required in order to achieve mass personalisation. Mass personalisation helps achieve environmental and economic sustainability and industry resilience (Battini et al., 2022; Kaasinen et al., 2022; Kusiak, 2020; Romero & Stahre, 2021; Turner et al., 2022).

Recent research confirms the statement that, despite its benefits to the global economy, ecology, and society, the implementation of Industry 5.0 will face many challenges and barriers. The first challenge is related to the soft and practical skills required to develop the workforce in order to implement Industry 5.0 (Adel, 2022; Liu et al., 2020; Mourtzis et al., 2022; Wang, 2022). Additionally, these new soft and practical skills need to be developed through training programs and by educators and experts who are using the new tech technologies (Feng et al., 2020). On the other hand, the implementation of disruptive technological applications used in Industry 5.0 requires rigid privacy, security, and ethical considerations (Ayan et al., 2022; Abdel Hakeem et al., 2022; Kaasinen et al., 2022; Maddikunta et al., 2022).

5.4.1 Limitations and Future Research

This research paper gives a general overview of the literature review on Industry 5.0 focussing on its three core values: human centricity, sustainability, and resilience. Being a very new concept initiated only in 2021, it is difficult to conduct a deep empirical analysis about the concrete and tangible dimensions of its advantages and challenges. It sounds to be a more academical than a practical concept. Therefore, future research is suggested to study concrete details of its implementation in different sectors: breaking through the challenges and benefiting from the opportunities. Additionally, detailed studies about the benefits and challenges of other aspects of Industry 5.0, such as Society 5.0, Government 5.0, and Education 5.0 are suggested, too. Further studies could explore effective practical, political, governmental, organisational, and societal aspects of implementing Industry 5.0 in all its dimensions and aspects. The concrete role of humans as key enablers of I5.0 should be studied in specific fields.

References

Abdel Hakeem, S. A., Hussein, H. H., & Kim, H. (2022). Security requirements and challenges of 6G technologies and applications. *Sensors, 22*(5), 1969. https://doi.org/10.3390/s22051969

Adel, A. (2022). Future of Industry 5.0 in society: Human-centric solutions, challenges and prospective research areas. *Journal of Cloud Computing, 11*(1), 40. https://doi.org/10.1186/s13677-022-00314-5

Aheleroff, S., Huang, H., Xu, X., & Zhong, R. Y. (2022). Toward sustainability and resilience with Industry 4.0 and Industry 5.0. *Frontiers in Manufacturing Technology, 2*, 951643. https://doi.org/10.3389/fmtec.2022.951643

Ayan, B., Güner, E., & Son-Turan, S. (2022). Blockchain Technology and Sustainability in Supply Chains and a Closer Look at Different Industries: A Mixed Method Approach. *Logistics, 6(4)*, 85. https://doi.org/10.3390/logistics6040085

Battini, D., Berti, N., Finco, S., Zennaro, I., & Das, A. (2022). Towards Industry 5.0: A multi-objective job rotation model for an inclusive workforce. *International Journal of Production Economics, 250*, 108619. https://doi.org/10.1016/j.ijpe.2022.108619

Breque, M., et al. (2021). *Industry 5.0: Towards a sustainable, human centric and resilient European industry*. Publications Office. https://data.europa.eu/doi/10.2777/308407

Carayannis, E. G., & Morawska-Jancelewicz, J. (2022). The futures of Europe: Society 5.0 and Industry 5.0 as driving forces of future universities. *Journal of the Knowledge Economy, 13*(4), 3445–3471. https://doi.org/10.1007/s13132-021-00854-2

Choi, T., Kumar, S., Yue, X., & Chan, H. (2022). Disruptive technologies and operations management in the Industry 4.0 era and beyond. *Production and Operations Management, 31*(1), 9–31. https://doi.org/10.1111/poms.13622

Demir, K. A., Döven, G., & Sezen, B. (2019). Industry 5.0 and human-robot co-working. *Procedia Computer Science, 158*, 688–695. https://doi.org/10.1016/j.procs.2019.09.104

Esposito, C., Castiglione, A., Martini, B., & Choo, K.-K. R. (2016). Cloud manufacturing: Security, privacy, and forensic concerns. *IEEE Cloud Computing, 3*(4), 16–22. https://doi.org/10.1109/MCC.2016.79

European Commission. Directorate General for Research and Innovation. (2020). *Industry 5.0: Human centric, sustainable and resilient*. Publications Office. https://data.europa.eu/doi/10.2777/073781

Feng, H., Wang, X., Duan, Y., Zhang, J., & Zhang, X. (2020). Applying blockchain technology to improve agri-food traceability: A review of development methods, benefits and challenges. *Journal of Cleaner Production, 260*, 121031. https://doi.org/10.1016/j.jclepro.2020.121031

Frey, C. B., & Osborne, M. A. (2017). The future of employment: How susceptible are jobs to computerisation?. *Technological Forecasting and Social Change, 114*, 254–280. https://doi.org/10.1016/j.techfore.2016.08.019

Geissdoerfer, M., Savaget, P., Bocken, N. M. P., & Hultink, E. J. (2017). The circular economy – A new sustainability paradigm? *Journal of Cleaner Production, 143*, 757–768. https://doi.org/10.1016/j.jclepro.2016.12.048

Ghobakhloo, M., Iranmanesh, M., Mubarak, M. F., Mubarik, M., Rejeb, A., & Nilashi, M. (2022). Identifying industry 5.0 contributions to sustainable development: A strategy roadmap for delivering sustainability values. *Sustainable Production and Consumption, 33*, 716–737. https://doi.org/10.1016/j.spc.2022.08.003

Grabowska, S., Saniuk, S., & Gajdzik, B. (2022). Industry 5.0: Improving humanization and sustainability of Industry 4.0. *Scientometrics, 127*(6), 3117–3144. https://doi.org/10.1007/s11192-022-04370-1

Guo, D., Li, M., Lyu, Z., Kang, K., Wu, W., Zhong, R. Y., & Huang, G. Q. (2021). Synchroperation in Industry 4.0 manufacturing. *International Journal of Production Economics, 238*, 108171. https://doi.org/10.1016/j.ijpe.2021.108171

Ivanov, D. (2022). The Industry 5.0 framework: Viability-based integration of the resilience, sustainability, and human-centricity perspectives. *International Journal of Production Research*, 1–13. https://doi.org/10.1080/00207543.2022.2118892

Jain, V., Ajmera, P., & Davim, J. P. (2021). SWOT analysis of Industry 4.0 variables using AHP methodology and structural equation modelling. *Benchmarking: An International Journal, 29*(7), 2147–2176. https://doi.org/10.1108/BIJ-10-2020-0546

Kaasinen, E., Anttila, A.-H., Heikkilä, P., Laarni, J., Koskinen, H., & Väätänen, A. (2022). Smooth and resilient human–machine teamwork as an Industry 5.0 design challenge. *Sustainability, 14*(5), 2773. https://doi.org/10.3390/su14052773

Kagermann, H. (2015). Change through digitization—Value creation in the age of Industry 4.0. In H. Albach, H. Meffert, A. Pinkwart, & R. Reichwald (Eds.), *Management of permanent change* (pp. 23–45). Springer Fachmedien Wiesbaden. https://doi.org/10.1007/978-3-658-05014-6_2

Kasinathan, P., Pugazhendhi, R., Elavarasan, R. M., Ramachandaramurthy, V. K., Ramanathan, V., Subramanian, S., Kumar, S., Nandhagopal, K., Raghavan, R. R. V., Rangasamy, S., Devendiran, R., & Alsharif, M. H. (2022). Realization of sustainable development goals with disruptive technologies by integrating Industry 5.0, Society 5.0, smart cities and villages. *Sustainability, 14*(22), 15258. https://doi.org/10.3390/su142215258

Kusiak, A. (2020). Open manufacturing: A design-for-resilience approach. *International Journal of Production Research, 58*(15), 4647–4658. https://doi.org/10.1080/00207543.2020.1770894

Liu, Y., Yuan, X., Xiong, Z., Kang, J., Wang, X., & Niyato, D. (2020). Federated learning for 6G communications: Challenges, methods, and future directions. *China Communications, 17*(9), 105–118. https://doi.org/10.23919/JCC.2020.09.009

Longo, F., Padovano, A., & Umbrello, S. (2020). Value-oriented and ethical technology engineering in Industry 5.0: A human-centric perspective for the design of the factory of the future. *Applied Sciences, 10*(12). https://doi.org/10.3390/app10124182

Maddikunta, P. K. R., Pham, Q.-V., Prabadevi, B., Deepa, N., Dev, K., Gadekallu, T. R., Ruby, R., & Liyanage, M. (2022). Industry 5.0: A survey on enabling technologies and potential applications. *Journal of Industrial Information Integration, 26*, 100257. https://doi.org/10.1016/j.jii.2021.100257

Madni, A. M., & Jackson, S. (2009). Towards a conceptual framework for resilience engineering. *IEEE Systems Journal, 3*(2), 181–191. https://doi.org/10.1109/JSYST.2009.2017397

Mitchell, J., & Guile, D. (2022). Fusion skills and Industry 5.0: Conceptions and challenges. In M. Bouezzeddine (Ed.), *Insights into global engineering education after the birth of industry 5.0*. IntechOpen. https://doi.org/10.5772/intechopen.100096

Mourtzis, D., Angelopoulos, J., & Panopoulos, N. (2022). A literature review of the challenges and opportunities of the transition from Industry 4.0 to Society 5.0. *Energies, 15*(17), 6276. https://doi.org/10.3390/en15176276

Nahavandi, S. (2019). Industry 5.0—A human-centric solution. *Sustainability, 11*(16). https://doi.org/10.3390/su11164371

Romero, D., & Stahre, J. (2021). Towards the resilient operator 5.0: The future of work in smart resilient manufacturing systems. *Procedia CIRP, 104*, 1089–1094. https://doi.org/10.1016/j.procir.2021.11.183

Romero, D., Bernus, P., Noran, O., Stahre, J., & Fast-Berglund, Å. (2016). The operator 4.0: Human cyber-physical systems & adaptive automation towards human-automation symbiosis work systems. In I. Nääs, O. Vendrametto, J. Mendes Reis, R. F. Gonçalves, M. T. Silva, G. von Cieminski, & D. Kiritsis (Eds.), *Advances in production management systems. Initiatives for a sustainable world* (pp. 677–686). Springer International Publishing. https://doi.org/10.1007/978-3-319-51133-7_80

Tavares, M. C., Azevedo, G., & Marques, R. P. (2022). The challenges and opportunities of era 5.0 for a more humanistic and sustainable society—A literature review. *Societies, 12*(6), 149. https://doi.org/10.3390/soc12060149

Tjahjono, B., Esplugues, C., Ares, E., & Pelaez, G. (2017). What does Industry 4.0 mean to supply chain? *Procedia Manufacturing, 13*, 1175–1182. https://doi.org/10.1016/j.promfg.2017.09.191

Turner, C., Oyekan, J., Garn, W., Duggan, C., & Abdou, K. (2022). Industry 5.0 and the circular economy: Utilizing LCA with intelligent products. *Sustainability, 14*(22), 14847. https://doi.org/10.3390/su142214847

Vinitha, K., Ambrose Prabhu, R., Bhaskar, R., & Hariharan, R. (2020). Review on industrial mathematics and materials at Industry 1.0 to Industry 4.0. *Materials Today: Proceedings, 33*, 3956–3960. https://doi.org/10.1016/j.matpr.2020.06.331

Wang, L. (2022). A futuristic perspective on human-centric assembly. *Journal of Manufacturing Systems, 62*, 199–201. https://doi.org/10.1016/j.jmsy.2021.11.001

Wang, B., Tao, F., Fang, X., Liu, C., Liu, Y., & Freiheit, T. (2021). Smart manufacturing and intelligent manufacturing: A comparative review. *Engineering, 7*(6), 738–757. https://doi.org/10.1016/j.eng.2020.07.017

Wilson, H. J., & Daugherty, P. R. (2018). *Human + machine: Reimagining work in the age of AI*. Harvard Business Review Press.

World Manufacturing Forum, W. M. Forum. R. (2019, Report). *Skills for the future of manufacturing*. https://worldmanufacturing.org/report/report-2019/

Xu, X., Lu, Y., Vogel-Heuser, B., & Wang, L. (2021). Industry 4.0 and Industry 5.0—Inception, conception and perception. *Journal of Manufacturing Systems, 61*, 530–535. https://doi.org/10.1016/j.jmsy.2021.10.006

Zizic, M. C., Mladineo, M., Gjeldum, N., & Celent, L. (2022). From Industry 4.0 towards Industry 5.0: A review and analysis of paradigm shift for the people, organization and technology. *Energies, 15*(14), 5221. https://doi.org/10.3390/en15145221

Chapter 6
Determinants of Organisations' Decisions Regarding Investments in Human Resource Development

Alic Bîrcă ⓘ, Luminița Chivu ⓘ, and Christiana Brigitte Sandu ⓘ

Abstract The study analyses the determinants influencing the decisions of organisations to invest in human resource development. The researchers in the field have been particularly interested in investments in human resources, having analysed various aspects of such investments. At the same time, it should be noted that most research in this field investigated the impact of human resource development investments on organisational performance as it could influence future decisions on the amount of investments. We also found that there is insufficient research on the perception of specific determinants of managerial decisions on human resource development investments. In this context, we have identified several determinants that, depending on the way they are perceived and valued by organisations, could influence managerial decisions regarding investments in human resource development. We also believe that the existence of a human resource development policy at the organisational level can have an impact on the assessment of the determinants that influence the level of investment for employee training. Based on the aforementioned, we formulated the following research question: Could an assessment of determinants influence the organisations' decisions regarding investment in human resource development? For this purpose, we have developed a survey comprising several determinants that can more or less influence investments in human resource development. The Likert scale from "1" to "5" was used to evaluate the determinants. The study results show that the determinants with a higher score give greater responsiveness to organisations in terms of human resource development investments.

A. Bîrcă · C. B. Sandu (✉)
Academy of Economic Studies of Moldova, Kishinev, Republic of Moldova

Alexandru Ioan Cuza University, Iasi, Romania
e-mail: brc.alic@ase.md; christiana.balan@uaic.ro

L. Chivu
National Institute for Economic Research "Costin C. Kirițescu", Romanian Academy, Bucharest, Romania
e-mail: chivu@ince.ro

© The Author(s), under exclusive license to Springer Nature Switzerland AG 2024
L. Chivu et al. (eds.), *Constraints and Opportunities in Shaping the Future: New Approaches to Economics and Policy Making*, Springer Proceedings in Business and Economics, https://doi.org/10.1007/978-3-031-47925-0_6

Keywords Human resource · Human resource development · Human resource investment · Training · Vocational training

6.1 Introduction

Human resources are a significant variable contributing to reaching organisational performance. Also, employee development influences organisational results by modelling the behaviour and attitudes of employees (Huselid, 1995; Whitener, 2001). When discussing human capital, Carnevalle et al. (1990) position human resource development (HRD) at a strategic level in an organisation. They see employees as a resource requiring continuous training in order to maintain organisation's competitive advantage and grow its value. From this perspective, the authors see HRD activities, especially professional training, as being utilitarian in an organisational strategy.

In knowledge-based society, investments in human resource development have become more important for decision-makers in organisations. Therefore, Samson and Bhanugopan (2022) analysed the implications of strategic human capital and organisational performance on managerial decisions. To cope with new challenges generated by a turbulent environment and high uncertainty, top management of organisations has been more aware that more financial resources should be allocated for employee training. In this context, Luthans and Yousse (2004) discuss the need for treating human resources as a capital investment as being more vital than ever before, considering that restructuring, outsourcing and other approaches to human resource downsizing have become almost a standard in coping with today's economic challenges. Moreover, Salas et al. (2012) argue that in order to remain competitive, organisations should make sure that their work force learns and develops continuously. Also, Lewis (2014) believes that the modern economy tends to see the decisions of employers regarding the supply of training programs through human capital theory, which sees training as an investment asking for sacrifice in current income in exchange for higher future revenue.

Several authors in the field have lately studied the response of organisations to such emerging challenges as the knowledge economy, globalisation, competitiveness and performance pressure need to stimulate organisational flexibility through employment and life-long learning policies (Nijhof, 2005; Murphy & Garavan, 2009).

Several researchers see investment in human resource development as an element of work flexicurity, largely implemented in the EU member states. Many EU decision-makers have been concerned about human resource development investments out of a desire to transform Europe into a competitive knowledge-based economy (Kornelakis, 2014). The author also argues that in order to promote employability, competencies should not be defined narrowly using organisation's current needs but rather the future ones. In turn, employees should always be aware of training and learning opportunities provided by several suppliers and organisations granting their access to learning through funding. Similarly, human resource development practices could contribute to growing organisational creativity (Hirudayaraj & Matić, 2021).

At organisational and national levels, professional training is an important element of HRD. Professional training of employees depends on the organisation's financial capability expressed as the amount of financial resources allocated for employees' professional training as well as the perception of top managers of return on investments. In turn, governmental organisations could provide investment and tax incentives to organisations so that they could actively get involved in the process of employee development (Zidan, 2001). Professional training provides individuals the opportunities to improve their abilities, relationships, attitudes, and mentality as well as grow organisation's efficiency (Aguinis & Kraiger, 2009; Bell et al., 2017). Also, professional training contributes to employee retention in an organisation and therefore ensures a high degree of workforce employment in the country.

The decision to invest in human resource development depends on the efficiency of training programs that could be reflected in the added value of employees and the organisation overall. Besides this, there are other factors forcing top managers invest in employee training, such as the degree of development of the continuous professional training market, quality of continuous professional training programs, and professionalism of trainers. Starting from what has been discussed so far, we aim in this study to analyse how specific determinant factors described above could influence the decisions of organisations regarding investments in employee development. For this purpose, we have formulated the following research question: Could the assessment of specific determinant factors influence the decisions of organisations regarding investments in human resource development?

6.2 Literature Review

6.2.1 HRD Concept

The HRD concept was first introduced by Leonard Nadler in 1969 by the American Society for Training and Development and renamed in 2015 into the Society for Talent Development (Han et al., 2017).

There are various interpretations of the HRD concept in the literature in the field. Some authors in their definitions underline the impact of HRD on employees and organisations (Armstrong, 2003; Swanson & Holton, 2001), while others extend its impact to the national level (McLean & McLean, 2001). Therefore, Armstrong (2003) views HRD as ensuring the provision of learning, development and training opportunities for employees aiming at improving their individual, team and organisational performance. McLean & McLean (2001) argue that HRD is any short- or long-term process and activity with a potential of developing competencies, expertise, and productivity of adults at the workplace, whether for their personal or team gain, or for the benefit of the organisation, community, nation, or even nation or humanity. HRD has been studied in terms of inclusion and diversity.

The aim of HRD is to improve learning activities, human potential and performance related to work systems (Ruona & Lynham, 2004); grow long-term strategic and immediate performance at organisational level (Yorks, 2005); provide employees the opportunities to develop the skills needed to fill the present and future requirements at the workplace (Werner & DeSimone, 2006); and improve the organisational system, work process and individual and group performance (Swanson & Holton, 2001).

6.2.2 Investment in HRD

Studies on human capital at the national level were conducted by economists who analysed the effect of instruction initiatives on national economic performance (Aguinis & Kraiger, 2009). The authors investigated the role of investments in human capital for making decisions regarding company localisation (Matouschek & Robert-Nicoud, 2004); the relationship between investments in human capital and the perception of automation risks that could influence the decisions of employers regarding investments in professional development outside the workplace (Innocenti & Golin, 2022); and the link between labour safety and efficiency of investments in workforce (Jing et al., 2021).

At organisational level, investments in HRD are a high commitment strategy affecting employee involvement and motivation (Ichniowski et al., 1997; Youndt et al., 1996). Investments in employee development provide a competitive advantage to an organisation as its employees are engaged in a process of continuous learning to develop their current skills and acquire new ones to be applied in their professional work (London, 1989).

Considering that investment in employee development involves specific costs, several authors analysed the relationship between investments in human resource training and organisational performance (Garavan et al., 2019; Kwon, 2019; Seeg et al., 2021). Acquiring tangible results could force top management to continue investments in training employees, even by increasing the amount of investments. The financial impact of training is an important variable due to its impact on organisational performance (Sitzmann & Weinhardt, 2019). Also, organisational performance is affected by a wide range of policies, procedures and contextual factors going beyond professional training, which may exclude a big influence of the effect (Ployhart & Hale, 2014). Still, professional training could be costly for an organisation, affecting positively its profit (Kim & Ployhart, 2014). That is why Sitzmann and Weinhardt (2019) believe that the calculation of return on investment is important for justifying the financial resources allocated for professional training.

Also, the decision of top managers on investments in human resources may be influenced by such other factors as efficiency of professional training programs, quality of professional training, professionalism of trainers, etc. However, the demand for a qualified workforce in a constantly evolving global economy has made professional training programs to become a priority for organisations

(McNamara et al., 2010). Organisations have been assessing the efficiency of professional training programs by the degree to which they reach their goals (Noe, 2010). Taking into account the importance of professional training programs, there is a high pressure that they were assessed and provided with a high degree of success (Curado & Bernardino, 2018). It is difficult to assess the efficiency of training as it may be influenced by the choices of managers, trainee persistence, organisational features and environmental factors (Bernardino & Curado, 2020).

The efficiency of professional training programs also depends on the quality of their content. Several researchers focused on analysing the quality of professional training programs (Seyfried, 1998; Blom & Meyers, 2000; Snell & Hart, 2007). The level of quality of professional training programs may be measured by formative and summative assessment (Noe, 2010). The formative assessment shows how well is organised a training program, as well as the degree of trainee learning and satisfaction (Bernardino & Curado, 2020). In turn, summative assessment measures to which degree a trainee's behaviour has changed after attending training programs as well as their effect on performance (Sitzmann & Weinhardt, 2019). The outcome of instruction also depends on the professionalism and competencies of trainers, and how they manage to share knowledge and competencies by using various methods and techniques.

Organisational instructional policy focuses on ensuring the compatibility between professional training and other activities of human resources. Big organisations operate using customised human resource practices, made specifically to maximise employee motivation, loyalty and productivity (Lewis, 2014). An organisational instructional policy describes the implementation methods of instructional activities, which could force top management allocate more financial resources to employee instruction. Also, an instructional policy makes the instruction as such become more visible for employees (Ostroff & Bowen, 2000). Also, it should be noted that the relationship between the instructional policy and factors determining investments in human resource development has been less analysed by the literature in the field.

6.3 Methodology

Human resource development at organisational level, including the investments made for this purpose, may be influenced by how specific determinant factors are perceived by the top management. Leaving this, we have formulated several hypotheses.

H1: Determinant factors that may influence investments in human resource development are perceived differently by top managers of organisations.
H2: Each determinant factor is perceived differently depending on the size of an organisation.
H3: The existence of a human resource development policy determines higher results of the determining factors.

To test and validate the research hypotheses, a questionnaire was developed and targeted at local employers. The questionnaire was applied to 350 respondents (employers). There were formulated five determinant factors describing investments in human resource development:

A. Amount of financial resources allocated to employee training
B. Efficiency of training programs taken by organisation's employees
C. Level of development of the educational market in the field of continuous professional development
D. Quality of continuous professional training programs provided by specialised centres
E. Level of professionalism of trainers involved in the training process

The respondents assessed each determinant factor using the Likert scale from "1" to "5", where "1" is the highest, and "5" is the weakest. Also, it should be noted that the assessment of determinant factors of investments in human resource development was done only by the respondent organisations which in the previous 3 years had provided training programs to their employees. Therefore, out of 350 respondents taking part in the survey, only 278 assessed the determinant factors of investments in human resource development.

6.4 Analysis/Results Interpretation

Statistically, the validation of the H1 hypothesis involves testing the level of appreciation of the determinant factors' intensity, which impacts the management's decisions on investments in human resource development. The distribution of responses of the organisations included in the study for the five determinant factors of investments in human resource development (A → E) is presented separately for the five levels of intensity of assessment (Table 6.1).

By analysing the overall data of the set of items defining the determinant factors of investments in human resource development, we may see that most responses include the rating *"strong"*, while the least of them is the rating *"very weak"*. Regarding each determinant factor, we note that the determinant factors B and E are the most appreciated, having the highest mean scores (Fig. 6.1). For these two factors, we note the highest weights of responses for *"very strong"* and *"strong"*, and the lowest weights for *"very weak"* and *"weak"*. Also, we may observe that the determinant factor A has the lowest weight of cumulated responses *"very strong"* and *"strong"*, and the highest weight of cumulated responses *"very weak"* and *"weak"*; therefore, its mean score is the lowest (3. 439) compared to other determinant factors (Fig. 6.1).

To study the correlation between the scores given to the determinant factor A and the scores given to other determinant factors, we used the Pearson bivariate correlation coefficient. Also, we applied the Paired-Samples *t* Test (Table 6.2) to test the differences between the mean scores for factor A and the other factors.

6 Determinants of Organisations' Decisions Regarding Investments in Human...

Table 6.1 Response distribution for determinant factors of investments in human resource development

Determinant factors	No. responses (%)					Total %
	(5) Very strong	(4) Strong	(3) Medium	(2) Weak	(1) Very weak	
(A) Amount of financial resources allocated to employee training	24.1	25.2	29.1	13.7	7.9	100
(B) Efficiency of training programs taken by organisation's employees	24.8	37.4	25.5	9.4	2.9	100
(C) Level of development of the educational market in the field of continuous professional development	19.4	30.9	30.9	14.0	4.8	100
(D) Quality of continuous professional training programs provided by specialised centres	22.3	30.2	33.4	10.5	3.6	100
(E) Level of professionalism of trainers involved in the training process	29.5	34.5	28.1	6.1	1.8	100

Source: Own calculations in SPSS 22.0

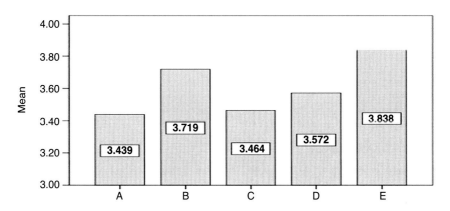

Fig. 6.1 Means for five determinant factors of investments in human resource development (A →E). (Source: Own calculations in SPSS 22.0)

We tested the null hypothesis that the mean of differences between A and determinants B/C/D/E equals 0. The determinant factor A is positively correlated and displays a statistically significant correlation with all other determinant factors at a level of significance of 1%. The strongest correlation is noted with the determinant factor B, and the weakest with the determinant factor D. Also, there are big significant differences between the means of the determinant factor A and the determinant factors B and E at a level of significance of 1%, as well as between the means of determinant factor A and D at a level of significance of 5%. At the same time, there are no significant differences between the determinant factors A and C.

To validate the second hypothesis H2, we applied the Fisher Test in the ANOVA procedure. We tested the null hypothesis that the differences in the

Table 6.2 Results for testing correlation and the differences between the determinant factors

Determinant factors	(A) Amount of financial resources allocated to employee training		
	Pearson correlation	Paired-samples t test	Decision
(B) Efficiency of training programs taken by organisation's employees	0.694***	−5.224***	Reject the null hypothesis
(C) Level of development of the educational market in the field of continuous professional development	0.599***	−0.403	Retain the null hypothesis
(D) Quality of continuous professional training programs provided by specialised centres	0.519***	−1.974**	Reject the null hypothesis
(E) Level of professionalism of trainers involved in the training process	0.578***	−6.455***	Reject the null hypothesis

Source: Own calculations in SPSS 22.0
Note: ***indicates significance at 0.01 level; **indicates significance at 0.05 level

Table 6.3 Results of testing the influence of the size of an organisation on the determinant factors

Determinants	Fisher test	Decision
(A) Amount of financial resources allocated to employee training	3.224**	Reject the null hypothesis
(B) Efficiency of training programs taken by organisation's employees	4.273***	Reject the null hypothesis
(C) Level of development of the educational market in the field of continuous professional development	2.523*	Reject the null hypothesis
(D) Quality of continuous professional training programs provided by specialised centres	3.053**	Reject the null hypothesis
(E) Level of professionalism of trainers involved in the training process	1.445	Retain the null hypothesis.

Source: Own calculations in SPSS 22.0
Note: ***indicates significance at 0.01 level; **indicates significance at 0.05 level; *indicates significance at 0.1 level

mean scores of each factor among the subgroups of organisations distinguished according to their size (Table 6.3).

The results show that four out of five determinant factors are assessed differently by small organisations compared to the big ones (Appendix). The most important differences are seen between the organisations with over 250 employees that gave high scores and other types of organisations with lower scores. The highest difference by type of organisation is noted in the case of determinant factor V, being followed by the determinant factor A. *Level of professionalism of trainers involved in the training process* is the only determinant factor that was assessed similarly by all the respondent organisations irrespective of their size. Both small and big organisations gave a relatively high score to the *level of professionalism of trainers involved in the training process*.

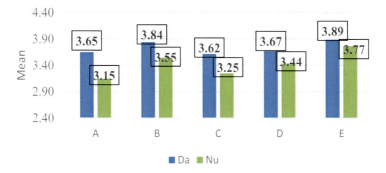

Fig. 6.2 Mean scores of the determinant factors of investment in human resource development. (Source: Processed by authors)

To test the H3 hypothesis, we first analysed whether the organisations included in the study have a human resource development policy. The results show that 50.6% of the organisations have a human resource development policy. The organisations that have implemented human resource development policies assessed better the determinant factors describing investments in human resource development (Fig. 6.2).

To test the differences between the scores given to the determinant factors A → E by type of organisation, differentiated by the existence of human resource development policy, we applied the Independent-Samples t Test. We tested the null hypothesis that the differences in the mean scores of each factor between the companies that have and those that do not have a policy in the field of HRD equal 0 (Tables 6.4).

The highest difference between the two types of organisations is seen in the amount of financial resources allocated to employee training: 3.65 in the organisations having implemented human resource development policies and 3.15 in the organisations not having done that. On average, the difference between the two types of organisations is 0.5. The next determinant factor displaying an evident difference between the two types of organisations is the *level of development of the educational market in the field of continuous professional development* (0.37). The lowest difference is noted in the level of professionalism of trainers involved in the training process (0.12).

6.5 Conclusions

In a knowledge-based economy to survive, develop and cope with competition, organisations should continuously invest in human resource development. Now, knowledge has become a strategic resource, becoming a higher concern for the management of organisations.

Table 6.4 Results of testing the influence of human resource development policies on the determinant factors

Determinants	Mean difference	Independent-Samples t test	Decision
(A) Amount of financial resources allocated to employee training	0.507	3.496***	Reject the null hypothesis
(B) Efficiency of training programs taken by organisation's employees	0.298	2.357**	Reject the null hypothesis
(C) Level of development of the educational market in the field of continuous professional development	0.373	2.837***	Reject the null hypothesis
(D) Quality of continuous professional training programs provided by specialised centres	0.235	1.835*	Retain the null hypothesis
(E) Level of professionalism of trainers involved in the training process	0.119	1.000	Retain the null hypothesis

Source: Own calculations in SPSS 22.0
Note: ***indicates significance at 0.01 level; ** indicates significance at 0.05 level; * indicates significance at 0.1 level

A study of determining factors for HRD has proven that many organisations are reluctant in allocating financial resources for this purpose. Specifically, this factor was given the lowest score by the organisations comprised in this study, with a score of 3439 out of five possible points. Still, it should be noted that the amount of investments in human resource development depends on other determining factors that create a specific perception among decision-makers inside organisations.

The educational market in the field of continuous professional training is a relevant determinant factor and is important in decisions affecting human resource development. The overall perception of the management of organisations towards the educational market may influence the decisions related to the allocation of financial resources to human resource development. The results have shown that this determinant factor was on average less appreciated (3464), so it could influence the decisions on investments in human resource development.

Also, investments in human resource development may be influenced by the quality and efficacy of professional training programs. These two determinant factors, as well as the professionalism of trainers, were better appreciated, so they could influence less the decisions of organisations on investments in HRD.

Small organisations compared to the big ones appreciated less the determinant factors of investments in HRD. It could be explained by the fact that managers of small organisations as respondents are less involved in this area, the assessment of determinant factors being made based on a created perception. In case of big organisations, the determinant factors of investment in HRD were assessed by human resource managers, who are more aware of the field and it allowed them to have a more objective view on the issue.

Also, it should be noted that a human resource development policy enables organisations to set precise goals regarding the qualitative evolution of their employees, understand the needs related to professional knowledge and competencies, and in line with this, select the most appropriate training programs. The study results show that the organisations that have implemented a human resource policy assessed better the determinant factors on investments in human resource development.

The main limitation of the study lies in the fact that the determinant factors of investments in human resource development were assessed only by employers, who are in charge of making decisions on investments in human resource development. In a future study, it would be important to evaluate the determinant factors of investment in HRD from the prespective of employees in order to understand the impact of professional development on the growth of their added value.

Acknowledgement This paper was developed within the research project "Development of labour market policies to increase employment", code: 20.80009. 1606.09, provided under the State program for 2020–2023 and funded by the Government of the Republic of Moldova.

Appendix: Results of Assessing the Determinant Factors By the Size of an Organisation

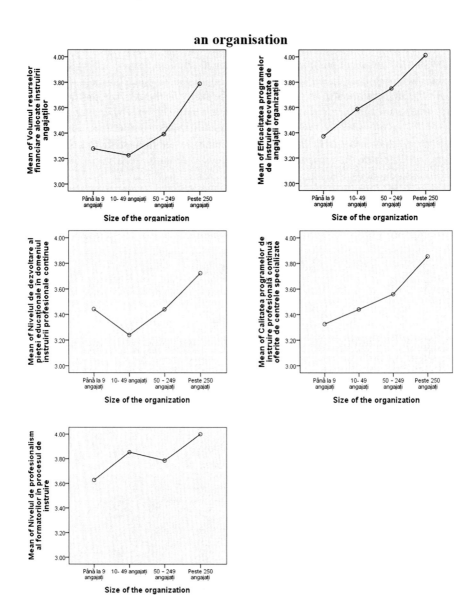

References

Aguinis, H., & Kraiger, K. (2009). Benefits of training and development for individuals and teams, organizations, and society. *Annual Review of Psychology, 60*, 451–474.

Armstrong, M. (2003). *Managementul resurselor umane. Manual de practică* (p. 872). Editura CODECS.

Bell, B. S., Tannenbaum, S. I., Ford, K. J., Noe, R. A., & Kraiger, K. (2017). 100 years of training and development research: What we know and where we should go. *Journal of Applied Psychology, 102*(3), 305.

Bernardino, G., & Curado, C. (2020). Training evaluation: A configurational analysis of success and failure of trainers and trainees. *European Journal of Training and Development, 44*(4/5), 531–546.

Blom, K., & Meyers, D. (2000). *Quality indicators in vocaţional education and training. International perspectives*. Retrieved from: https://www.ncver.edu.au/_data/assets/file/0015/5118/nr0026.pdf

Carnevalle, A., Gainer, L., & Villet, J. (1990). *Training in America: The organization and strategic role of training*. Jossey-Bass.

Curado, C., & Bernardino, G. (2018). Training programs' return on investment in the Portuguese railway company: A fuzzy-set qualitative comparative analysis. *International Journal of Training and Development, 22*(4), 239–255.

Garavan, T., et al. (2019). Measuring the organizational impact of training: The need for greater methodological rigor. *Human Resource Development Quarterly, 30*(2), 291–309.

Han, S.-H., Chae, C., Han, S.-J., & Yoon, S.-W. (2017). Conceptual organization and identity of HRD: Analyses of evolving definitions, influence and connections. *Human Resource Development Review, 16*(3), 294–319.

Hirudayaraj, M., & Matić, J. (2021). Leveraging human resource development practice to enhance organizational creativity: A multilevel conceptual model. *Human Resource Development Review, 20*(2), 172–206.

Huselid, M. A. (1995). The impact of human resource management practices on turnover, productivity, and corporate financial performance. *Academy of Management Journal, 38*, 635–672.

Ichniowski, C., Shaw, K., & Prennushi, G. (1997). The effects of human resource management practices on productivity. *American Economic Review, 87*, 291–313.

Innocenti, S., & Golin, M. (2022). Human capital investment and perceived automation risks: Evidence from 16 countries. *Journal of Economic Behavior and Organization, 195*, 27–41.

Jing, G., Qi, T., & Guangzju, J. (2021). Labour protection and the efficiency of human capital investment. *Economic Analysis and Policy, 69*, 195–207.

Kim, Y., & Ployhart, R. (2014). The effects of staffing and training on firm productivity and profit growth before, during, and after the great recession. *Journal of Applied Psychology, 99*(3), 361–389.

Kornelakis, A. (2014). Balancing flexibility with security in organizations? Exploring the links between flexicurity and human resource development. *Human Resource Development Review, 13*(4), 398–412.

Kwon, K. (2019). The long-term effect of training and development investment on financial performance in Korean companies. *International Journal of Manpower, 40*(6), 1092–1109.

Lewis, P. (2014). The over-training of apprentices by employers in advanced manufacturing: A theoretical and policy analysis. *Human Resource Management Journal, 24*(4), 496–513.

London, M. (1989). *Managing the training enterprise*. Jossey-Bass.

Luthans, F., & Yousse, C. M. (2004). Human, social, and now positive psychological capital management: Investing in people for competitive advantage. *Organizational Dynamics, 33*(2), 143–160.

Matouschek, N., & Robert-Nicoud, F. (2004). The role of human capital investments in the location decision of firms. *Regional Science and Urban Economics, 35*, 570–583.

McLean, G. N., & McLean, L. (2001). If we can't define HRD in one country, how can we define it in an international context? *Human Resource Development International, 4*(3), 313–326.

McNamara, G., Joyce, P., & O'Hara, J. (2010). Evaluation of adult education and training programs. *International Encyclopedia of Education, 3*, 548–554.

Murphy, A., & Garavan, T. (2009). The adoption and diffusion of an NHRD standard: A conceptual framework. *Human Resource Development Review, 8*, 3–21.

Nijhof, W. (2005). Lifelong learning as a European skill formation policy. *Human Resource Development Review, 4*, 401–417.

Noe, R. A. (2010). *Employee training and development* (5th ed.). McGraw-Hill.

Ostroff, C., & Bowen, D. E. (2000). *Moving HR to a higher level: HR practices and organizational effectiveness*. Retrieved from: https://www.researchgate.net/publication/232465645_Moving_HR_to_a_higher_level_HR_practices_and_organizational_effectiveness

Ployhart, R. E., & Hale, D. (2014). The fascinating psychological microfoundations of strategy and competitive advantage. *Annual Review of Organizational Psychology and Organizational Behavior, 1*, 14.1–14.28.

Ruona, W. E. A., & Lynham, S. (2004). A philosophical framework for thought and practice in human resource development. *Human Resource Development International, 7*(2), 151–164.

Salas, E., et al. (2012). The science of training and development in organizations: What matters in practice. *Psychological Science în the Public Interest, 13*(2), 74–101.

Samson, K., & Bhanugopan, R. (2022). Strategic human capital analytics and organisation performance: The mediating effects of managerial decision-making. *Journal of Business Research, 144*, 637–649. Retrieved from: https://doi.org/10.1016/j.jbusres.2022.01.044

Seeg, B., Gauglitz, I. K., & Schütz, A. (2021). Explaining and enhancing training transfer: A consumer-centric evaluation of a leadership training. *Human Resource Development International, 25*(5), 506–526.

Seyfried, E. (1998). *Evaluation of quality aspects in vocational training programs, CEDEFOP*. Retrieved from: https://op.europa.eu/en/publication-detail/-/publication/642dd390-58be-422e-bf0d-7d4f5b034044

Sitzmann, T., & Weinhardt, J. M. (2019). Approaching evaluation from a multilevel perspective: A comprehensive analysis of the indicators of training effectiveness. *Human Resource Management Review, 29*(2), 253–269.

Snell, D., & Hart, A. (2007). Vocational training in Australia: Is there a link between attrition and quality? *Education + Training, 49*(6), 500–512.

Swanson, R. A., & Holton, E. F., III. (2001). *Foundations of human resource development*. Berret-Koehler.

Werner, J. M., & DeSimone, R. L. (2006). *Human resource development* (4th ed.). Thomson South-Western.

Whitener, E. M. (2001). Do "High commitment" human resource practices affect employee commitment? A cross-level analysis using hierarchical linear modeling. *Journal of Management, 27*, 515–535.

Yorks, L. (2005). *Strategic human resource development*. Thomson South-Western.

Youndt, M., Snell, S., Dean, J., & Lepak, D. (1996). Human resource management, manufacturing strategy, and firm performance. *Academy of Management Journal, 39*, 836–866.

Zidan, S. S. (2001). The role of HRD in economic development. *Human Resource Development Quarterly, 12*(4), 437–443.

Chapter 7
Examining the Empirical Relationship Between Happiness and Human Development in Emerging Economies

Md Ataul Gani Osmani ⓘ, **Laeeq Razzak Janjua** ⓘ, **Mirela Panait** ⓘ, and **Vikas Kumar Singh Tomar** ⓘ

Abstract This study explores the empirical relationship between happiness and human development in seven emerging economies. The sample emerging economies are selected from the World Bank list, such as China, Russia, India, Indonesia, Brazil, Mexico, and Turkey. by using panel data from UNDP and our world in data from 2005 to 2020, this study first applies the panel cointegration test to determine whether there is a long-run relationship or not and to find that no long-run relationship between happiness and human development in emerging economies is manifested. Second, the ultimate application of panel VAR modeling entails that a one-way short-run causal relationship running from human development to happiness in emerging economies exists. This means that in the short-run, in emerging economies, human development causes happiness but not vice versa. Therefore, for building significant long-run relationships, those economies should focus on long-term strategies of economic freedom and mental health development.

Keywords Happiness · Human development · Emerging economies

M. A. G. Osmani
Department of Economics, Varendra University, Rajshahi, Bangladesh
e-mail: ataul@vu.edu.bd

L. R. Janjua
Faculty of Applied Sciences, WSB University, Dąbrowa Górnicza, Poland
e-mail: laeeq.janjua@wsb.edu.pl

M. Panait (✉)
Petroleum-Gas University of Ploiesti, Ploieşti, Romania

Institute of National Economy, Bucharest, Romania
e-mail: mirela.matei@upg-ploiesti.ro

V. K. S. Tomar
Alma Mater Studiorum – Università di Bologna, Rimini, Italy
e-mail: vikaskumar.tomar@studio.unibo.it

© The Author(s), under exclusive license to Springer Nature Switzerland AG 2024
L. Chivu et al. (eds.), *Constraints and Opportunities in Shaping the Future: New Approaches to Economics and Policy Making*, Springer Proceedings in Business and Economics, https://doi.org/10.1007/978-3-031-47925-0_7

7.1 Introduction

Happiness and human development are closely interlinked. By improving access to education, health care, and personal freedom, human development policies can help to ensure that individuals are able to lead fulfilling lives and experience higher levels of happiness. To promote both happiness and human development, it is essential to focus on factors that support personal growth, social integration, and economic prosperity. Because of this, the public authorities should prioritize long-term policies of economic independence along with mental health development if they want to build meaningful long-term relationships. These are significant contributions to the happiness human development literature, which provide justification for engaging in this study – especially from the cross-country perspective (Vasile et al., 2013; Cordero et al. 2017; Jain et al., 2019).

Happiness and human development are two interconnected aspects of human life that have been widely studied and debated by scholars, researchers, and policymakers (Diener, 2000; Hirai et al., 2016; Georgescu et al., 2020; Lushch-Purii, 2021; Layard, 2005; World Happiness Report, 2021). Happiness is often described as a subjective experience of well-being, contentment, and satisfaction with life, while human development is a broader concept that refers to the expansion of human capabilities and freedoms, including economic, social, and personal growth (Vikash, 2019).

Studies on happiness and human development have shown that there is a positive correlation between the two concepts (Sen, 1999, Diener & Seligman, 2002; Helliwell, 2006). Higher levels of human development are connected with better levels of happiness. The developed countries that have higher levels of income and life expectancy tend to have populations with better well-being levels. In addition, people who have more opportunities to pursue their goals and aspirations better access to health care and education, and greater social support tend to experience higher levels of happiness (Leigh & Wolfers, 2006). However, the relationship between happiness and human development is not always straightforward. While greater human development can lead to higher levels of happiness, happiness can also influence human development. The research has shown that happy people tend to be more productive, motivated, and engaged in their work, which can contribute to development. In addition, happiness can play a role in promoting better health and well-being, which in turn can contribute to human development (Saida et al., 2021). Despite the strong correlation between income and happiness, it is important to specify that financial issues like income are not the main determinant of happiness. A number of other factors, including social relationships, health, and personal freedom, are also important contributors to happiness (Diener & Biswas-Diener, 2002).

Human development can contribute to happiness by fostering a sense of personal freedom and autonomy (Abdur Rahman & Veenhoven, 2018). Personal freedom and autonomy are important determinants of happiness, with scientific studies showing that persons who report high levels of freedom are more likely to have better life satisfaction (Diener & Biswas-Diener, 2002). Human development policies that focus on empowering individuals and promoting personal freedom can help to ensure that individuals are able to lead lives that are meaningful and fulfilling, which can in turn lead to increased happiness.

To probe the discourse, a panel of emerging economies is selected from the World Bank list, such as China, Russia, India, Indonesia, Brazil, Mexico, and Turkey over the period 2005–2020. The sample variables are used in this study, such as the Life Satisfaction index (LS) as happiness indicator and human development index (HDI) for representing human development. In order to find any long-run and short-run relationships between happiness and human development, the study adopts a Pedroni Residual Co-integration test along with VAR modeling approach. This article is structured in as follows: the results of the previous studies are presented in the literature review section. The methodology is detailed in the next section, and in the final part, the authors present results, discussion, and conclusions.

7.2 Literature Review

There are scientific studies that have been conducted on the effect of economic development in determining well-being and quality of living for different countries and regions (Li, 2020). The pursuit of well-being is an important goal for society. It leads to happiness for the whole of society. It is crucial to understand which factors are most critical in determining happiness. These factors can be correlated with socio-economic factors like income level, job and residential stability, and quality of life (Lopez-Ruiz et al., 2021). It is widely believed that improving the nation's happiness is the primary goal of economic growth (Li & Xie, 2020). The analysis and measurement of happiness are growing in importance in the field of social sciences (Yang et al., 2018). There have been many efforts to identify, quantify, and evaluate the subjective measure of happiness from the viewpoint of various academic disciplines, from psychology and neuroscience to economics and philosophy (Ballas, 2013). Yin et al. (2023) investigated the relationship between subjective well-being and the Human Development Index (HDI). The HDI is closely linked to affective than cognitive well-being. They examined the connections between the HDI components like health, education, income, and well-being. They also found that these three HDI components are equally crucial in Western and wealthy countries.

Veenhoven (2005), Diener and Seligman (2004) considered that happiness is an individual's opinion of different aspects of life and circumstances as well as the degree to which an individual is satisfied with their own life. The central notion of being happy is the subjective evaluation of one's own life or satisfaction with life (Diener et al., 1985). Also, Arechavala et al. (2015) considered that happiness can be measured using "Satisfaction with life in this city." The method used to measure happiness is supported by the research of Diener et al. (2013), Diener (2013), and

Veenhoven (2014). Additionally, Moeinaddini et al. (2020) believe that happiness is satisfaction as a feeling that can be found in everything around an individual.

Blanchflower and Oswald (2005) discovered a paradox in their discussion on the relationship between happiness and human development in Australia. They looked at economic research on happiness and explored the implications for policymakers. Roka (2020) used income, economic freedom, and economic growth as control variables to determine the human development effects of happiness. The study found a negative relationship between happiness and life expectancy. It also noticed positive associations between income and economic growth with happiness. The scientific studies confirmed the positive correlation between government health expenditures, food, and happiness. Murat and Gursakal (2015), using an analysis of canonical correlation (an approach to multivariate statistics), studied the relationship between HDI and Happy Planet Index (HPI) for 150 nations. The results of the study show that there is a solid connection to HDI as well as HPI. Stewart et al. (2018) analyzed the emphasis on happiness as the overriding aim of development.

One of the key factors that affect both happiness and human development is the presence of social support and a sense of community. Studies have shown that people who have strong social relationships and a sense of belonging tend to be happier and experience higher levels of human development (Doh & Chung, 2020; Sjåstad et al., 2021). Social support provides a sense of security, helps people overcome challenges and obstacles, and can lead to greater opportunities for personal and professional growth. Despite the well-established relationship between happiness and human development, there are still many questions and challenges that need to be addressed. For example, there is a debate about the most effective way to measure happiness, and there is also a need for more research on the causal mechanisms that link happiness and human development. One of the key findings in the literature on happiness and human development is that there is a strong correlation between income and happiness. According to a meta-analysis of over 150 studies, income is one of the strongest predictors of life satisfaction and happiness (Easterlin, 1974). However, this relationship is not always linear, and at high levels of income, the correlation between income and happiness tends to diminish (Easterlin, 1995).

One of the ways in which human development can contribute to happiness is by improving access to education. The scientific studies confirmed that education is positively correlated with happiness, and more educated individuals have higher levels of life satisfaction. Education can also play a role in improving access to employment, which can in turn lead to increased income and improved financial security, both of which are important contributors to happiness. Another way in which human development can contribute to happiness is by improving access to health care. Good health is an important determinant of happiness, with studies showing that individuals who report good health have better levels of life satisfaction (Schimmack et al., 2005). Improved access to health care ensures that individuals have access to the medical treatment and services they need to maintain good health, which can in turn lead to increased happiness.

Human development can contribute to happiness by fostering a sense of personal freedom and autonomy. Personal freedom and autonomy are important contributors to happiness, with relevant studies showing that individuals who report high levels of personal freedom are more likely to have higher levels of life satisfaction (Diener & Biswas-Diener, 2002). Human development policies that focus on empowering individuals and promoting personal freedom can help to ensure that individuals are able to lead lives that are meaningful and fulfilling, which can in turn lead to increased happiness. As it is well established in scientific literature, human development and happiness are interrelated and interdependent. However, in the field of empirical studies, there are still gaps in investigating the association and interdependence by comprehensive empirical methods. Based on the discussion and debate of measurement and connection between human development and happiness, the study finds a unique method to investigate the connection. The present study has used life satisfaction as a happiness indicator and the human development index by the UN as a human development indicator. The study is adopting new approaches, such as panel cointegration and Vector Autoregressive approach of causality for ensuring any short-run or long-run connection between human development and happiness. As far as our knowledge is concerned, there is no such type of previous studies conducted in emerging countries.

7.3 Methodology

7.3.1 Data Sources

The study is based on panel data from UNDP and Our World in Data for the period of 2005–2020, and the sample countries are emerging seven (E7) countries, such as China, Russia, India, Indonesia, Brazil, Mexico, and Turkey. The emerging seven countries were chosen following the study of Huidrom et al. (2017). The Life Satisfaction index (LS) as happiness indicator and the human development index (HDI) for representing human development were used as variables in this study.

7.3.2 Empirical Models

The undertaken variables are life satisfaction scores (LS) and human development index (HDI). To find out the empirical relationship, the study runs panel model. Thus, the first step is to check whether the data series are stationary or not. Therefore, the study used a panel unit root test. In the second step, the study applies the Pedroni Residual Cointegration Test to check the long-run relationship between the interested variables. Finally, a panel VAR modeling approach is adopted to find any short-run causality. The following two panel VAR models are estimated.

$$\text{HDI}_{it} = \sum_{j=1}^{2} \alpha_{ij} \text{HDI}_{i,t-j} + \sum_{j=0}^{2} \gamma_{ij} \text{LS}_{i,t-j} + u_i + \varepsilon_{it}$$

$$LS_{it} = \sum_{j=1}^{2} \beta_{ij} LS_{i,t-j} + \sum_{j=0}^{2} \delta_{ij} HDI_{i,t-j} + u_i + \varepsilon_{it}$$

where $i = 1, 2, 3, ...7$, there are two variables HDI and LS, u_i error term for fixed effects and ε_{it} are random error terms.

7.4 Analysis/Results Interpretation

In presenting and discussing the results of the study, first for panel data modeling, it is required to check the panel unit root test. Tables 7.1 and 7.2 present the results of the panel unit root test of variables. Table 7.1 presents the results of the panel unit root test of the variable "*human development index (HDI)*." It is found that HDI is not stationary at level but it is stationary at first difference for all tests performed under the panel unit root test.

In Table 7.2, the results of the panel unit root test of the variable "*Life Satisfaction (LS)*" are presented. It is found that the results are similar to HDI. LS is also not stationary at level but stationary at first difference.

The above results confirm that both interested variables, HDI and LS, are stationary at first difference. Therefore, they have integration of order one I (1). It ultimately leads us to test the long-run relationship between the interested variables by the cointegration test. In the present study, the Pedroni Residual Cointegration test is performed to find out the long-run relationship between human development and happiness. The test results are presented in Table 7.3.

The cointegration test reveals that the null hypothesis of no cointegration cannot be rejected as the majority test statistics of the Pedroni residual cointegration test

Table 7.1 Panel unit root test of HDI

At level		
Method	Statistic	Prob.
Null: Unit root (assumes common unit root process)		
Levin, Lin & Chu t	3.48947	0.9998
Null: Unit root (assumes individual unit root process)		
ADF – Fisher Chi-square	2.19689	0.9999
PP – Fisher Chi-square	0.13469	1.0000
At first difference		
Method	Statistic	Prob.
Null: Unit root (assumes common unit root process)		
Levin, Lin & Chu t	−3.83642	0.0001
Null: Unit root (assumes individual unit root process)		
ADF – Fisher Chi-square	29.2955	0.0095
PP – Fisher Chi-square	41.3181	0.0002

Source: Authors' own research

Table 7.2 Panel unit root test of LS

At level		
Method	Statistic	Prob.
Null: Unit root (assumes common unit root process)		
Levin, Lin & Chu t	−0.61358	0.2697
Null: Unit root (assumes individual unit root process)		
ADF – Fisher Chi-square	11.6590	0.6337
PP – Fisher Chi-square	15.9143	0.3186
At first difference		
Method	Statistic	Prob.
Null: Unit root (assumes common unit root process)		
Levin, Lin & Chu t	−9.05509	0.0000
Null: Unit root (assumes individual unit root process)		
ADF – Fisher Chi-square	82.8564	0.0000
PP – Fisher Chi-square	148.915	0.0000

Source: Authors' own research

Table 7.3 Pedroni residual cointegration test

Series: LS HDI				
Null Hypothesis: No cointegration				
Alternative hypothesis: common AR coefficients (within-dimension)				
	Statistic	Prob.	Weighted statistic	Prob.
Panel v-Statistic	−0.238921	0.5944	−0.860773	0.8053
Panel rho-Statistic	−0.517310	0.3025	−0.366675	0.3569
Panel PP-Statistic	−1.046396	0.1477	−1.098614	0.1360
Panel ADF-Statistic	−0.340284	0.3668	−0.615432	0.2691
Alternative hypothesis: individual AR coefficients. (between-dimension)				
	Statistic	Prob.		
Group rho-Statistic	0.208751	0.5827		
Group PP-Statistic	−1.641041	0.0504		
Group ADF-Statistic	−0.239521	0.4054		

Source: Authors' own research

are not significant. Thus, there is no long-run relationship between HDI and happiness in the sample of emerging countries.

Finally, the Panel VAR modeling approach entails whether there is any short-run causal relationship between the interested variables or not. In estimating the panel VAR model, we first specify the Var lag order selection criteria in Table 7.4 to determine the optimal lags to use in the estimation.

According to the obtained results in Table 7.4, we determine 2 lags according to all criteria except LR criteria. There are two models for estimating panel VAR. First, we estimate the fixed effect (FE) model and random effect (RE) model. Second, we perform the Hausman Test to choose between FE and RE. When running a regression, we reject the null hypothesis of the Hausman test that the random effect model is the appropriate model (Table 7.5).

Table 7.4 VAR lag order selection criteria

Lag	LogL	LR	FPE	AIC	SC	HQ
0	19.68392	NA	0.001823	−0.631569	−0.559235	−0.603525
1	191.5750	325.3653	4.54e−06	−6.627679	−6.410677	−6.543548
2	199.6661	14.73743	3.92e−06[a]	−6.773791[a]	−6.412121[a]	−6.633572[a]
3	202.2561	4.532367	4.13e−06	−6.723431	−6.217093	−6.527125
4	203.0741	1.373103	4.64e−06	−6.609789	−5.958783	−6.357395
5	205.8624	4.481250	4.87e-06	−6.566515	−5.770841	−6.258034
6	212.1096	9.593895[a]	4.53e−06	−6.646772	−5.706430	−6.282203
7	213.1855	1.575445	5.07e−06	−6.542340	−5.457330	−6.121684
8	215.8671	3.735046	5.39e−06	−6.495253	−5.265576	−6.018510

Source: Authors' own research
LR sequential modified LR test statistic (each test at 5% level), *FPE* Final prediction error, *AIC* Akaike information criterion, *SC* Schwarz information criterion, *HQ* Hannan–Quinn information criterion
[a]Indicates lag order selected by the criterion

Table 7.5 Correlated random effects – Hausman test

Test summary	Chi-Sq. Statistic	d.f.	Prob.
Cross-sectional random	26.562483	5	0.0001

Source: Authors' own research

Therefore, the estimated fixed effect equation running from LS to HDI is as follows:

$$hdi = 0.0234787734641 + 0.962601010774 \times hdi(-1) - 0.0177495826499 \times hdi(-2) - 0.00274431959971 \times ls + 0.00451576084252 \times ls(-1) + 0.00216066748134 \times ls(-2) + eqn\_01\_efct$$

The estimated regression results are presented in Table 7.6.

In order to see if there is any short-run causality from life satisfaction (LS) to human development (HDI) in emerging economies, we perform the Granger-Causality test. The results of causality analysis are presented in Table 7.7 when the target variable is HDI.

Table 7.7 reveals that we cannot reject the null hypothesis that life satisfaction does not Granger cause human development in emerging countries.

We perform a Hausman test for selecting an appropriate model when the target variable is life satisfaction (LS). The test result in the following table shows that fixed effect (FE) model is the appropriate model (Table 7.8).

The estimated fixed effect regression model is as follows when the target variable is LS.

7 Examining the Empirical Relationship Between Happiness and Human...

Table 7.6 The results of fixed effect model; target variable: HDI

Variable	Coefficient	Std. Error	t-Statistic	Prob.
C	0.023479	0.021548	1.089615	0.2789
HDI(−1)	0.962601	0.124302	7.744065	0.0000
HDI(−2)	−0.017750	0.120455	−0.147354	0.8832
LS	−0.002744	0.002164	−1.268207	0.2081
LS(−1)	0.004516	0.002186	2.065388	0.0419
LS(−2)	0.002161	0.002125	1.016919	0.3120
	Effects specification			
Cross-sectional fixed (dummy variables)				
R-squared	0.994262	Mean dependent var		0.727908
Adjusted R-squared	0.993528	S.D. dependent var		0.066839
S.E. of regression	0.005377	Akaike info criterion		−7.499113
Sum squared resid	0.002486	Schwarz criterion		−7.182586
Log-likelihood	379.4565	Hannan–Quinn criterion		−7.371084
F-statistic	1354.775	Durbin-Watson statistic		1.922751
Prob(F-statistic)	0.000000			

Source: Authors' own research

Table 7.7 Wald test for short-run causal effect of LS on HDI

Dependent variable: HDI
Null hypothesis: LS (life-satisfaction) does not Granger cause HDI (human development index)

Test statistic	Value	Df	Probability
F-statistic	2.699751	(3, 86)	0.0507
Chi-square	8.099254	3	0.0440

Source: Authors' own research

Table 7.8 Correlated random effects – Hausman test

Test summary	Chi-Sq. Statistic	Chi-Sq. d.f.	Prob.
Cross-sectional random	18.663122	5	0.0022

Source: Authors' own research

$$ls = 3.7694434167 + 0.381445281637 \times ls(-1) + 0.279290200237 \times ls(-2) - 6.68959469523 \times hdi - 4.60415613569 \times hdi(-1) + 8.78212930305 \times hdi(-2) + eqn\_01\_efct$$

The estimated regression results are presented in Table 7.9.

In order to observe if there is any short-run causality from human development (HDI) to life satisfaction (LS) in emerging countries, we perform again the Granger-Causality test. The results of causality analysis are presented in Table 7.10 when the target variable is LS.

Table 7.9 The results of the fixed effect model; target variable: LS

Variable	Coefficient	Std. Error	t-Statistic	Prob.
C	3.769443	0.991064	3.803431	0.0003
LS(−1)	0.381445	0.102658	3.715673	0.0004
LS(−2)	0.279290	0.101142	2.761361	0.0070
HDI	−6.689595	5.274846	−1.268207	0.2081
HDI(−1)	−4.604156	7.980027	−0.576960	0.5655
HDI(−2)	8.782129	5.872019	1.495589	0.1384
	Effects specification			
Cross-section fixed (dummy variables)				
R-squared	0.914931	Mean dependent var		5.528775
Adjusted R-squared	0.904050	S.D. dependent var		0.857028
S.E. of regression	0.265472	Akaike info criterion		0.299663
Sum squared resid	6.060881	Schwarz criterion		0.616189
Log-likelihood	−2.683470	Hannan–Quinn criterion		0.427691
F-statistic	84.08533	Durbin-Watson statistic		2.004427
Prob(F-statistic)	0.000000			

Source: Authors' own research

Table 7.10 Wald test for short-run causal effect of HDI on LS

Dependent variable: LS
Null hypothesis: HDI does not Granger cause LS

Test statistic	**Value**	**Df**	**Probability**
F-statistic	2.909679	(3, 86)	0.0334
Chi-square	8.729037	3	0.0331

Source: Authors' own research

It is found from the results of Table 7.10 that we can reject the null hypotheses, indicating short-run Granger-Causality. That is, human development (HDI) Granger causes life satisfaction (LS) in the short run in seven emerging countries.

7.5 Conclusions

This paper questions the happiness and human development dilemma by presenting empirical discoveries that are a lacuna in the existing literature. This empirical finding takes a new perspective and highlights whether happiness or human development impacts each other or not. The conclusion reveals that no long-run associations exist between happiness and human development; however, in the short-run human development causes happiness but not vice versa in emerging economies. This study first applies the panel cointegration test to find out whether there is any long-run relationship or not and finds no long-run relationship between the happiness indicator and human development indicator in the emerging seven economies. Second, the ultimate application of panel VAR modeling entails that there is a one-way causal relationship between human development and happiness in the emerging seven economies. This means that in short-run human development, granger causes happiness in emerging economies. Therefore, for building significant long-run relationships, those economies should focus on long-term strategies of economic freedom and mental health development. The limits of the research carried out are given by the choice of the period, indicator, and sample of countries. Motivated by the identification of these limits, the authors have in mind the expansion of research in the future and the concentration of studies on the analysis of the human development relationship for the countries of the European Union, taking into account the common concerns of the member countries regarding the increase in the well-being of the population.

References

Abdur Rahman, A., & Veenhoven, R. (2018). Freedom and happiness in nations: A research synthesis. *Applied Research in Quality of Life, 13*(2), 435–456.

Arechavala, N. S., Espina, P. Z., & Trapero, B. P. (2015). The economic crisis and its effects on the quality of life in the European Union. *Social Indicators Research, 120*(2), 323–343.

Ballas, D. (2013). What makes a 'happy city'? *Cities, 32*, S39–S50.

Blanchflower, D. G., & Oswald, A. J. (2005). Happiness and the human development index: The paradox of Australia. *Australian Economic Review, 38*, 307–318. https://doi.org/10.1111/j.1467-8462.2005.00377.x

Cordero, J. M., Salinas-Jiménez, J., & Salinas-Jiménez, M. M. (2017). Exploring factors affecting the level of happiness across countries: A conditional robust nonparametric frontier analysis. *European Journal of Operational Research, 256*(2), 663–672.

Diener, E. (2000). Subjective well-being: The science of happiness and a proposal for a national index. *American Psychologist, 55*(1), 34–43.

Diener, E. (2013). The remarkable changes in the science of subjective well-being. *Perspectives on Psychological Science, 8*(6), 663–666.

Diener, E., & Biswas-Diener, R. (2002). Will money increase subjective well-being? A literature review and guide to needed research. *Social Indicators Research, 57*(2), 119–169.

Diener, E., & Seligman, M. E. P. (2002). Very happy people. *Psychological Science, 13*(1), 81–84.

Diener, E., & Seligman, M. E. P. (2004). Beyond money: Toward an economy of well-being. *Psychological Science in the Public Interest, 5*(1), 1–31.

Diener, E. D., et al. (1985). The satisfaction with life scale. *Journal of Personality Assessment, 49*(1), 71–75.

Diener, E., Inglehart, R., & Tay, L. (2013). Theory and validity of life satisfaction scales. *Social Indicators Research, 112*(3), 497–527.

Doh, Y. Y., & Chung, J. B. (2020). What types of happiness do Korean adults pursue?—Comparison of seven happiness types. *International Journal of Environmental Research and Public Health, 17*(5), 1502.

Easterlin, R. A. (1974). Does economic growth improve the human lot? Some empirical evidence. In *Nations and households in economic growth: Essays in honor of Moses Abramovitz* (pp. 89–125). Academic.

Easterlin, R. A. (1995). Will raising the incomes of all increase the happiness of all? *Journal of Economic Behavior & Organization, 27*(1), 35–47.

Georgescu, I., Kinnunen, J., Androniceanu, A., & Androniceanu, A. M. (2020). A computational approach to economic inequality, happiness and human development. *Informatica Economica, 24*(4), 16–28.

Helliwell, J. F. (2006). Well-being, social capital and public policy: What's new? *The Economic Journal, 116*(510), C34–C45.

Hirai, T., Comim, F., & Ikemoto, Y. (2016). Happiness and human development: A capability perspective. *Journal of International Development, 28*(7), 1155–1169.

Huidrom, R., Kose, M. A., & Ohnsorge, F. L. (2017). *How important are spillovers from major emerging markets?* (Policy Research Working Paper; No. 8093). World Bank.

Jain, M., Sharma, G. D., & Mahendru, M. (2019). Can I sustain my happiness? A review, critique and research agenda for economics of happiness. *Sustainability, 11*(22), 6375.

Layard, R. (2005). *Happiness: Lessons from a new science*. Penguin Press.

Leigh, A., & Wolfers, J. (2006). Happiness and the human development index: Australia is not a paradox. *Australian Economic Review, 39*(2), 176–184.

Li, C. L. (2020). Quality of life: The perspective of urban park recreation in three Asian cities. *Journal of Outdoor Recreation and Tourism, 29*, 100260.

Li, Z., & Xie, Z. (2020). The impact of income inequality and the use of information media on happiness. *Open Journal of Social Sciences, 08*(02), 128–142.

López-Ruiz, V. R., Huete-Alcocer, N., Alfaro-Navarro, J. L., & Nevado-Peña, D. (2021). The relationship between happiness and quality of life: A model for Spanish society. *PLoS One, 16*(11), e0259528. https://doi.org/10.1371/journal.pone.0259528

Lushch-Purii, U. I. (2021). From homo economicus to homo eudaimonicus: Anthropological and axiological transformations of the concept of happiness in a secular age. *Anthropological Measurements of Philosophical Research, 19*, 61–74.

Moeinaddini, M., et al. (2020). Proposing a new score to measure personal happiness by identifying the contributing factors. *Measurement, 151*, 107115.

Murat, D., & Gürsakal, S. (2015). Determining the relationship between happiness and human development: Multivariate statistical approach. *Alphanumeric Journal, Bahadir Fatih Yildirim, 3*(1), 67–80.

Roka, D. (2020). The effect of human development on happiness: A comparative study of UN member states. *International Journal of Science and Business, IJSAB International, 4*(4), 61–78.

Saida, Z., Amalia, S., Darma, D. C., & Azis, M. (2021). Spurring economic growth in terms of happiness, human development, competitiveness and global innovation: The ASEAN case. *ASEAN Journal on Science and Technology for Development, 38*(1), 1–6.

Schimmack, U., Diener, E., & Oishi, S. (2005). Individualism: A valid and important dimension of cultural differences between nations. *Journal of Cross-Cultural Psychology, 36*(5), 563–582.

Sen, A. (1999). *Development as freedom*. Knopf.

Sjåstad, H., Zhang, M., Masvie, A. E., & Baumeister, R. (2021). Social exclusion reduces happiness by creating expectations of future rejection. *Self and Identity, 20*(1), 116–125.

Stewart, F., Ranis, G., & Samman, E. (2018). *Should happiness or human development be the main development objective? Advancing human development: Theory and practice* (Oxford, online ed.). Oxford Academic.

Vasile, V., Stănescu, S., & Bălan, M. (2013). Promoting the quality of life: Challenges of innovative models versus payment policies. In *The European culture for human rights the right to happiness*. Cambridge Scholars Publishing.

Veenhoven, R. (2005). Inequality of happiness in nations. *Journal of Happiness Studies, 6*(4), 351–355.

Veenhoven, R. (2014). Informed pursuit of happiness: What we should know, do know and can get to know. *Journal of Happiness Studies, 16*(4), 1035–1071.

Vikash, V. (2019). Human development index and gross national happiness indices: A conceptual study. *Advances in Management, 12*(1), 62–63.

World Happiness Report. (2021). *World happiness report 2021*. United Nations Sustainable Development Solutions Network.

Yang, J., Liu, K., & Zhang, Y. (2018). Happiness inequality in China. *Journal of Happiness Studies, 20*(8), 2747–2771.

Yin, R., Lepinteur, A., Clark, A. E., & D'Ambrosio, C. (2023). Life satisfaction and the human development index across the world. *Journal of Cross-Cultural Psychology, 54*(2), 269–282. https://doi.org/10.1177/00220221211044784

Chapter 8
The Impact of Large Families on Demographic Evolution

Mihaela Hrisanta Mosora, Irina Granzulea, and Cosmin Mosora

Abstract The demographic evolution is one of the greatest challenges of our century. Undoubtedly, the dramatic decline of the birth rate is an important structural problem that countries must face all over the globe. This problem finds its cause in the decreased number of children born by women of childbearing age, which leads to the impossibility of ensuring the generation replacement index. The specialized literature indicates that the improvement of the level of education among women is perhaps the main cause of the decrease in fertility (Kravdal, Demography 39:233–250, 2002; Lloyd, Education. Encyclopedia of population. Macmillan, 278–283, 2003; Lutz & Skirbekk, World population and human capital in the twenty-first century. Oxford University Press, 14–38, 2014; May & Rotenberg, Studies in Family Planning 51:193–204, 2020). This evolution in women's lives led to an increase in the cost of opportunity for women when they put on hold their careers in favor of birth. Unemployment, degradation of living standards, stress, and uncertainty (Ghetau, Sociologie Românească 2:5–41, 2004) are also important factors that influence the level of fertility in a country.

This paper aims to analyze the main demographic indicators for Romania and the impact of large families on demographic evolution. In order to understand the typology of the family with three or more children, we conducted a quantitative analysis (questionnaire) which showed some essential aspects about large families: the social structure of the family, living conditions, occupation, and education. According to Eurostat, in Romania, there were approximately 226,400 large families in 2021, but at the same time, 70% of households had no children. Moreover, for the period 2015–2022, families with three or more children replaced the lack of children in childless households (3.5%).

M. H. Mosora (✉) · C. Mosora
Bucharest University of Economic Studies, Bucharest, Romania
e-mail: mihaela.mosora@economie.ase.ro; cosmin.mosora@economie.ase.ro

I. Granzulea
ASFANU – Large Families Association, Bucharest, Romania
e-mail: info@asfanu.ro

© The Author(s), under exclusive license to Springer Nature Switzerland AG 2024
L. Chivu et al. (eds.), *Constraints and Opportunities in Shaping the Future: New Approaches to Economics and Policy Making*, Springer Proceedings in Business and Economics, https://doi.org/10.1007/978-3-031-47925-0_8

This chapter contributes to the improvement of specialized literature by analyzing an important segment of the population, namely, families with three or more children.

Keywords Demography · Birth rate · Large family · Fertility · Children

8.1 Introduction

In 2020, the Lancet conducted a study on the evolution of the global population until 2100. According to this analysis, the population growth trend will reach its peak in 2060, and then we will witness a demographic decline. Thus, it is predicted that in 2100, the population of the globe will reach 8.8 billion people. Among the causes that will lead to this evolution, the authors of this study list the following reasons: the increase in women's educational attainment, greater access to different methods of contraception, and the fertility rate decline (total fertility rate). In 2011, the world population reached 7 billion, and in 2023 (January), approximately will reach 8,013,049,760 persons (World Population Clock: 8 Billion People).

Population growth depends directly on the fertility rate, which is on a downward trend. According to the data provided by the United Nations – World Population Prospects, the current fertility rate in 2023 (January) is 2,418 births per woman, and it is predicted that in 2050 it will be 2,196 birth per woman, respectively 1,929 births per woman in 2100. If we look at the previous values, in 1950 this indicator was equal to five, and in 1990 it was 3.26 births per woman (World Fertility Rate 1950–2023 | MacroTrends). Longevity also influences the global population. The data provided by the UN show that the average life expectancy at birth will increase from 72.7 years in 2019 to 77.2 in 2050. However, there are quite large discrepancies between developed and least developed countries, the gap being approximately 7 years between areas.

Global data show us that the elderly population has increased from 6.88% in 2000 to 9.63% in 2021. This means that the elderly population represents approximately 10% of the working-age (15–64 years) population. Japan and Italy recorded the highest percentages of elderly population in 2021, 28.86% and 23.67%, respectively. On the other hand, Saudi Arabia (3.49%) and India (6.8%) recorded the lowest values according to the OECD. Romania recorded a high value of 19.39% in 2021 compared to 13.32% in 2000. These demographic developments have a strong impact on the pension and medical care system, with direct implications for economic growth, the wellbeing of the population, and last but not least the increase in the birth rate (Bloom & Canning, 2008; Nerlich & Schroth, 2018; Stamoulis & Lambro, 2021).

The results published by Lancet contradict the forecasts on the total population made by the UN for 2100, that is, 10.4 billion people on the planet compared to 8 billion predicted by the UN. These figures correspond to the following hypotheses:

the decrease in fertility in countries where large families are predominant (e.g., African countries) and the increase in fertility in countries with less than two children on average at the current time. In other words, the figures correspond to the middle scenario in terms of the projection of population evolution at the global level. If Africa still offers greater resistance to fertility decline, European countries are below the necessary limit for the complete replacement of the population in the long term (the fertility rate is approximately 2.1 births per woman). In countries such as Bulgaria, Croatia, Hungary, Japan, Latvia, Romania, and Moldova, the UN anticipates that the population will decrease by at least 15% by 2050.

Usually, specialized studies analyze the dramatic drop in the birth rate from different perspectives but do not study enough from the point of view of the intention of families to expand the number of members. This chapter aims to analyze the demographic evolution from the perspective of the rate of families with one, two children versus demographic trends of families with three or more children.

Families with three or more children play an important role from a demographic point of view because they cover part of the overall balance of the number of children for couples with fewer or no children.

8.2 Literature Review

Suciu et al. (2012) specify that, in recent years, demographic transition implies a decrease in the fertility rate and an increase in health. This fact led to a reduction in the weight of newborns and an increase in life expectancy at birth, especially in developed countries. Chesnais (1986) defined the demographic transition as the transition from a traditional regime with many children and a high fertility and mortality rate to a balanced regime, characterized by a low level of fertility and mortality.

The decrease in the birth rate can be explained both by traditional factors, such as unemployment, degradation of living standards, stress, and uncertainty (Ghetau, 2004), as well as by factors related to individualism, behavioral changes in marriage, contraception, and sexuality (Van de Kaa, 1987). The high standard of living in developed countries does not seem to positively influence demographic growth, the relationship being even negative in the second half of the last century (Ghetau, 2004).

In the specialized literature, there are many causes that have led over time to a decrease in the birth rate. Among these, the development of society (Davis, 1967; Kirk, 1996; Notestein, 1945) and especially the improvement of the level of education among women appear as dominant (Kravdal, 2002; Lloyd, 2003; Lutz & Skirbekk, 2014; May & Rotenberg, 2020). Breierova and Duran (2004) studied the relationship between women's education and the number of children in Indonesia between 1973 and 1978 and concluded that the birth rate decreases as the level of education among women increases. Osili and Long (2008) calculated the hypothesis in which an additional school year is added and the results showed a decrease in the birth rate by 0.26 births (by 0.26 births) in Nigeria. Murtin (2013) showed that schooling has a greater effect on fertility than the size of the population's income or infant mortality.

A high level of education also leads to a high participation rate of women in the labor market. Becker (1960) explains in terms of relative cost why educated and active women on the labor market do not want children. The reason is related to the increase in opportunity cost for each child born.

The "Unified Growth Theory" explains the relationship between the increase in the demand for female labor, which determines an increase in wages, and implicitly an increase in the opportunity cost in the case of giving up an hour of work. All these issues ultimately lead to a decrease in the birth rate because the opportunity cost is very high. Roser (2014) emphasizes the fact that education and increased opportunities for women have led to a change in the social status of women in society. Having more external options, women gave up having more children in favor of the opportunities offered by society and, therefore, the fertility rate decreased.

Race, religion, and living environment are important factors that can influence the birth rate in a country (Mosher & Bachrach, 1996; Martinez et al., 2012) as follows: among Catholic women, of Jewish origin and those without religion, we can meet fewer children, whereas among Hispanic families and Mormons, fertility is higher, regardless of race. There are also discrepancies between white, dark-skinned, and Hispanic women. Among white women, a smaller number of children were recorded, and the age of the mother at the first child is higher compared to the other two categories (Martinez et al., 2012).

Regarding education, studies have shown that men and women with a lower level of education could have a larger number of children (Martinez et al., 2012). The age of the adults in a family has a strong impact on the size of the family, that is, the number of children. Studies have shown that, in general, young, educated people living in urban areas prefer small families with fewer children (Ding & Hesketh, 2006; Matsumoto & Yamake, 2013). On the other hand, the fertility level increases among large families living in the countryside.

Large families represent a powerful catalyst that can replace families without children, thus contributing to the increase in the birth rate. Considering that more than two children are needed in a family to replace their parents, a large family leads to the constant maintenance of the population, respectively, to an increase in the number of the population (Stamoulis & Lambrou, 2021). According to INSEE (Institut National de la Statistique et des Etudes Economiques, France), a large family is defined as having at least three children. According to the National Institute of Statistics of Spain, a family unit is considered a large family if the couple, or the father or mother in single-parent units, lives with three or more common or exclusive children who meet specific conditions for participation in educational institutions.

According to Eurostat in 2021, 49% of households had one child, 39% had two children, 12% had three or more children, and 13% children had only one parent. From the data provided by Eurostat, most large families (three children+) are found in order in France (1,273,400 households), Germany (984,100 households), Poland (451,700 households), Spain (441,300 households), and Italy (441,800 households) in 2021. Romania ranks seventh in the EU with 226,400 households with three or more children.

The studies carried out in Europe among the female population of different ages and social categories showed us that in general, the desired number of children is two (United Nations Economic Commission for Europe; Șerbănescu et al., 2001), but this can't lead to a demographic increase, it can at most keep the population constant, if all families able to have children do so.

8.3 Methodology

In this research, we used both a descriptive analysis and a quantitative analysis, a questionnaire conducted among large families in Romania between May and June 2022 regarding the typology of a large family.

8.3.1 Descriptive Analysis

In this part of the research, we will present the evolution of the main demographic indicators, namely: population evolution, fertility rate, average life expectancy at birth, mortality rate, and structure of households in Romania in relation to the number of children.

8.3.1.1 Population

The highest level of the number of inhabitants was recorded by Romania in 1991 when the level of 22,842,482 inhabitants was reached through a progressive increase. Starting from 1992, the population of Romania began to decrease gradually, arriving in 2021 to a decrease of approximately 14% compared to the year 1991. The year 2022 is the first year in which a new cycle of growth in the number of inhabitants is initiated in Romania and continues with a growth forecast for the year 2023 when a number of 19,892,812 inhabitants are anticipated.

If we take 2022 as the reference year (19,659,267 people), according to the information provided by the UN – World Population Prospects, the country's population will decrease by 11% until the year 2050, reaching 17,457,213 people, respectively, and by 33.33% in the year 2100 (13,105,206 inhabitants) (Graph 8.1).

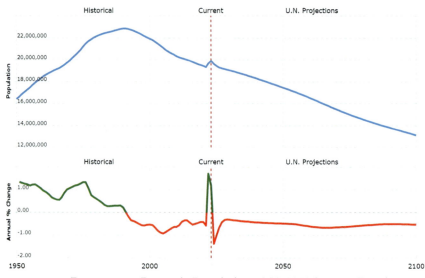

Data source: Romania Population 1950-2023 | MacroTrends

Graph 8.1 Evolution of the Romanian population for the period 1950–2100

8.3.1.2 Fertility Rate

Until 1989, the fertility rate (2.14) in Romania exceeded the level of two children born to a woman, which ensured a balanced level of population renewal. Starting with the year 1990, the fertility rate in Romania no longer reached the level necessary for the renewal of the population and recorded in 2022 the level of 1.64. The forecast for the year 2100 made by the UN – World Population Prospects shows an increase in the fertility rate in Romania to the level of 1.76, however, insufficient to ensure the stability of the population (Graph 8.2).

8.3.1.3 Life Expectancy at Birth

In 2020, life expectancy in Romania reached 74.4 years according to Word Bank and 74.2 years according to Eurostat. In practice, life expectancy increased by approximately 7% compared to 1990. From the data provided by Eurostat, for 2021, the value of the life expectancy indicator was 74.2 years (estimated value). There is a rather large discrepancy between life expectancy for men (69.4 years for 2021) and for women (76.7 years), the difference being approximately 7.3 years.

From the data provided by the UN – World Population Prospects, the life expectancy trend in Romania will remain on the rise position, so it will increase by 80.46 years in 2050 and 86.51 years in 2100 (Graph 8.3).

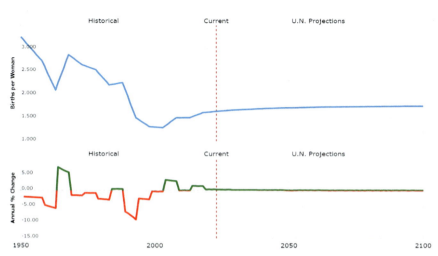

Graph 8.2 Evolution of the fertility rate in Romania for the period 1950–2100

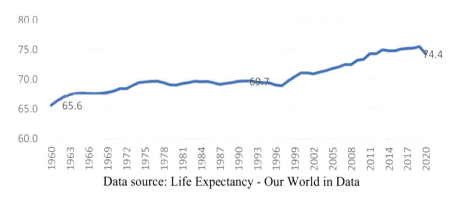

Graph 8.3 Life expectancy, 1960–2020. (Data source: Life Expectancy – Our World in Data)

8.3.1.4 Mortality Rate

If in the hierarchy of birth and fertility indices, Romania is in an average position at the global level, in terms of the mortality rate, Romania ranks second place after Bulgaria in its segment of reference states. In 2022, Romania recorded a mortality rate of 13.32. It should be noted that in the following 20 years, it will increase to the level of 15.77, and then it will be followed by a slight decline (Graph 8.4).

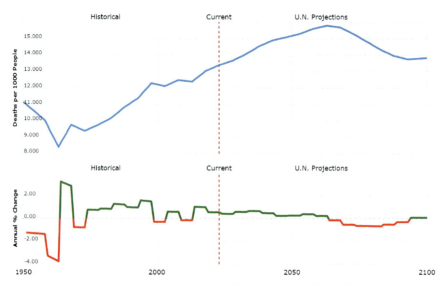

Data source: Romania Death Rate 1950-2023 | MacroTrends

Graph 8.4 Death rate

8.3.1.5 The Structure of Households in Romania in Relation to the Number of Children

From Graph 8.4, we can see that for the period 2015–2021, almost 70% of households in Romania have no children and approximately 17% of all households have only one child. If we analyze the dynamics for the period 2012–2021, we notice that there are no big fluctuations between the four categories of households (as a percentage of the total households).

Large families (with three or more children) represent 10% of all families with children in Romania (Graphs 8.5 and 8.6), respectively, 3% of all households in Romania.

In Romania in 2021, there were approximately 226,400 large families with three or more children, according to Eurostat data. In order to know the dynamics of families with children in Romania, we will make a correlation between births in Romania with the rank of newborns in the family (Graph 8.7).

Analyzing the data regarding the rank of newborns in the family for the period 2015–2021, we can observe that over 50% of the newborns have the rank of "first child." The second child born slightly exceeds 50% of the number of newborns who have the rank of "first child." As for families with three or more children, they represented 17.8% of the total number of newborns in Romania in 2021.

What is interesting to note is the fact that since 2018, the births of children with the rank of the first and second child have been decreasing, and the births of children with the rank of third and more have been on an upward trend.

Data source: own calculations based on INSSE data

Graph 8.5 The share of households with and without children in total households for the period 2012–2021

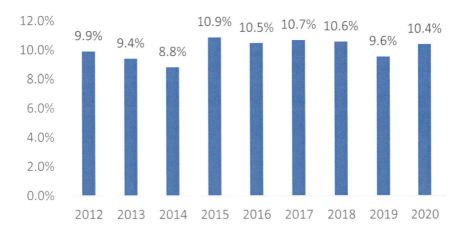

Data source: own calculations according to Eurostat data

Graph 8.6 The percentage of large families in Romania in total households with children

Following the statistical data presented previously, it is clear that families without children and families with one child are predominant in Romania. Given that the average number of births for a woman is less than two children, there is a need to balance the population pyramid, and this balance is achieved by large families who compensate the low fertility rate.

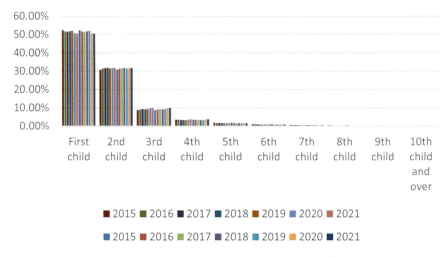

Data source: own calculations based on INSSE data

Graph 8.7 Share of newborns residing in Romania in total births, according to the rank of the newborn in the family 2015–2021

8.3.1.6 The Impact of Large Families on Demographic

To understand the impact of large families on the demographic evolution in Romania, we conducted a questionnaire between May 15 and June 15, 2022, among 300 large families, in order to make a portrait of the typology of the family with three or more children. The survey followed some essential aspects: the social structure of the family, living conditions, occupation, and education of large families in Romania.

According to our research, large families in Romania belong to all social categories, only a few families benefit from government support measures granted in favor of the family, and preconceptions and stereotypes related to the number of children represent a pressing problem for these families. Some conclusions that emerge from this study are presented in Graph 8.8.

In a family, more than two children are needed to replace their parents, but following the family typology in Romania, we will limit ourselves to reaching a standard of two children for each family. To ensure this standard, we consider that the third child in a large family balances the number of children for a family with one child, and the third and fourth children in a family with four children replace the lack of children in families without children. Basically, it can have the following structure:

- Family with three children – balances the number of children for families with one child.
- Family with four children – balances the number of children for the family without children.

8 The Impact of Large Families on Demographic Evolution

Data source: own study based on a quantitative analysis (questionnaire)

Graph 8.8 The typology of large families highlighted in the ASFANU study

- Family with five children – balances the number of children for families with one child, without children, or with three children.

Given the data provided by INSSE, we were able to calculate the compensation for the lack of children in childless households achieved by large families. Graph 8.9 shows that large families could replace more than 3.5% of households without children in the period 2015–2020.

8.4 Analysis/Results Interpretation

The decision of having children, regardless of their number, is a free one and involves multiple responsibilities related to their growth, care, and education. What we know for sure is the fact that every decision to give birth to a child represents a contribution to the overall development of society which offers benefits to all citizens.

The role of large families in society is essential from a demographic point of view because they contribute with human capital, that is, citizens who will be part of the active population and contributors to support the economic development of the country.

Given the fact that in Romania the fertility rate is at a level that cannot ensure the stability of the population (1.64), large families are the ones that compensate for the

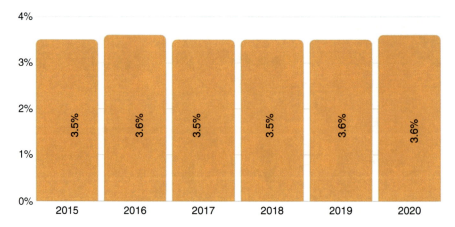

Data source: own calcultions based on INSSE data

Graph 8.9 Compensation for the lack of children in childless households by large families

low fertility index and balance the birth rate through their contribution of at least three children.

In Romania, families with three or more children represent a large and heterogeneous group, consisting of 226,400 large families in 2021, which have in common the fact that they have more children than the average of families in Romania. Large families represent over a million adults and children, which do not represent a single reality, but thousands of realities because there are families with three children and families with eight children, families with high or low socio-economic status, poor families, from the middle or upper class, rural or urban families, religious families, and others without any faith.

What unites large families are the common needs that derive from the size of the households, the time given to caring for children, the compromises related to the parents' workplace, or the cost of the bills that they have to bear.

8.5 Conclusions

The research on the realities of life, ways of having children, and why most parents only have one or two children is still very limited. What we know for sure is that families with children are essential for the demographic evolution, but also for the economic and social development of any country.

The factors that led to the worldwide decrease in the birth rate from 5 births per woman in 1950 to 2.4 in January 2023 are numerous: development of society, unemployment, uncertainty, individualism, behavioral changes on marriage or the improvement of education among women.

That is why in order to ensure the recovery of the birth rate, given that the average number of children born to a woman of childbearing age is far from what society needs (at least 2 children per woman), concrete measures and awareness steps are needed.

Romania, like other European countries, is not doing well at all in terms of birth rate. If we refer to the year 2022 (19,659,267 people), according to the information provided by the UN – World Population Prospects, we find out that the country's population will decrease by 11% by 2050, reaching 17,457,213 people. The mortality rate in 2022 was 13.32, and it is expected that in the next 20 years, it will increase to the level of 15.77. Our country is currently dealing with an aging population. The level of aging (elderly population) increased from 13.31% in 2000 to 19.39% in 2021, and this will put pressure on the pension and medical care system.

If we analyze the structure of households in Romania in relation to the number of children, we notice that for the period 2015–2021, almost 70% of households in Romania have no children, and approximately 17% of all households have only one child. Large families (with three or more children) represent 10% of all families with children in Romania, and this is a strong enough reason to be at the attention of social and family policymakers. Moreover, families with more children cover the lack of children determined by those who, for various reasons, do not have children. Practically, these families have replaced more than 3.5% of childless households for the period 2015–2020.

The quantitative analysis carried out in this chapter showed us that families with three or more children in Romania belong to all social categories, only a few families benefit from government support measures granted in favor of the family, and preconceptions and stereotypes related to the number of children represent a pressing problem for these families.

First, we feel it is necessary to raise awareness of the young generation about the responsibility they have toward the future development of society: adults are the ones who ensure the well-being of young people and children, but in fair compensation, when they become adults, they are the ones who have the responsibility to provide well-being to those who have already aged. The lack of children, or a small number of children born into the family, reduces in the short term the financial costs of maintenance a child by adults but reduces in the long term the number of employed people who can support the maintenance of these retiring adults.

Second, the family with children must be positioned at the center of a gradual system of investments and public support based on the number of children and consolidated with work-life measures. Even if this goal may be considered ambitious or perhaps impossible, we have to look at the effects of declining birth rates if family-centered measures are absent. This situation will lead to a shortage of skilled labor and increased pressure on social security budgets.

Third, the development of a national strategy that encourages demographic growth is essential for Romania. The experience of some countries similar to Romania from the point of view of economic development, but also from the perspective of belonging to the former communist bloc, such as Hungary or Poland, is relevant. These two countries show significant changes in the demographic evolution after the adoption of long-term measures to stimulate the birth rate. It is absolutely necessary for Romania to adopt a demographic strategy based on important aspects: stimulation, economic development, orientation toward the child, the mother, and the young family (Ghețău Correction of the demographic situation).

Last but not least, it is very important to be aware of the role in society of families with three or more children. On one hand, large families support the demographic evolution with human capital, and on the other hand, if large families are recognized as a value of the entire society, this new status may lead in the medium and long term, to the desire of other families to expand the number of children.

Note: STUDY ON LARGE FAMILIES IN ROMANIA – independent study carried out through ASFANU – Association of Large Families from Romania.

References

Becker, G. S. (1960). An economic analysis of fertility. NBER chapters. In *Demographic and economic change in developed countries* (pp. 209–240). National Bureau of Economic Research.

Bloom, D. E., & Canning, D. (2008). Global demographic change: Dimensions and economic significance, population and development review. *Population Aging, Human Capital Accumulation, and Productivity Growth, 4*, 17–51.

Breierova, L., & Duflo, E. (2004). *The impact of education on fertility and child mortality: Do fathers really matter less than mothers?* (NBER Working Paper No.10513). Online here: http://www.nber.org/papers/w10513

Chesnais, J. C. (1986). *La transition démographique. Etapes, formes, implications économiques. Etude de series temporelles relatives a 67 pays.* Press Universitaire de France.

Database – Eurostat (europa.eu).

Davis, K. (1967). Population policy: Will current programs succeed? *Science, 158*(3802), 730–739.

Ding, Q., & Hesketh, T. (2006). Family size, fertility preferences, and sex ratio in China in the era of the one child family policy: Results from national family planning and reproductive health survey. *BMJ, 333*(7564), 371–373.

Ghetau, V. (2004). Declinul demografic al României: ce perspective ? *Sociologie Românească, 2*(2), 5–41.

INSSE – Baze de date statistice – TEMPO-Online serii de timp.

Kirk, D. (1996). Demographic transition theory. *Population Studies, 50*(3), 361–387.

Kravdal, O. (2002). Education and fertility in Sub-Saharan Africa: Individual and community effects. *Demography, 39*(2), 233–250.

Lloyd, C. (2003). *Education. Encyclopedia of population* (pp. 278–283). Macmillan.

Lutz, W., & Skirbekk, V. (2014). How education drives demography and knowledge informs projections. In W. Lutz, W. Butz, & K. Samir (Eds.), *World population and human capital in the twenty-first century* (pp. 14–38). Oxford University Press.

Martinez, G., Daniel K., & Chandra, A. (2012). *Fertility of men and women aged 15–44 years in the United States: National survey of family growth.* National Health Statistics Reports, Number 51.

Matsumoto, Y., & Yamabe, S. (2013). Family size preference and factors affecting the fertility rate in Hyogo, Japan. *Reproductive Health, 10*, 6.

May, J., & Rotenberg, S. (2020). A call for better integrated policies to accelerate the fertility decline in sub-Saharan Africa. *Studies in Family Planning, 51*(2), 193–204.

Mosher, W. D., & Bachrach, C. A. (1996). Understanding U.S. fertility: Continuity and change in the national survey of family growth, 1988–1995. *Family Planning Perspectives, 28*(1), 4–12.

Murtin, F. (2013). Long-term determinants of the demographic transition,1870–2000. *The Review of Economics and Statistics, 95*(2), 617–631.

Nerlich, C., & Schroth, J. (2018). The economic impact of population ageing and pension reforms. *ECB Economic Bulletin, 2*.

Notestein, F. (1945). Population: The long view. In T. Schultz (Ed.), *Food for the world* (pp. 36–57). University of Chicago Press.

OECD Data.

Osili, U. O., & Long, B. T. (2008). Does female schooling reduce fertility? Evidence from Nigeria. *Journal of Development Economics, 87*(1), 57–75.

Roser, M. (2014). *Fertility rate*. Published online at OurWorldInData.org. Retrieved from: https://ourworldindata.org/fertility-rate [Online Resource].

Serbanescu, F., Morris, L. & Marin M. (2001). *Reproductive health survey Romania, 1999: Final report*. https://www.rhsupplies.org/uploads/tx_rhscpublications/ROMANIA-1999%20

Stamoulis, D. S., & Lambrou, D. N. (2021). Demographic policies for large families in Greece: An opinion survey and implications for the social administration. *Advances in Social Sciences Research Journal, 8*(4), 709–722.

Suciu, M. C., Aceleanu, M., Mosora, M., & Papuc, M. (2012). *Current demands and perspectives on the social and economic development of Romania*. Editura Printech. ISBN 978-606521-885-7.

Van de Kaa, D. J. (1987). Europe's second demographic transition. *Population Bulletin, 42*(1), Population Reference Bureau.

World Fertility Rate 1950–2023 | MacroTrends.

Chapter 9
Dynamics of the School Population, Differences Between Emigrants and Immigrants in Romania: Comparative Analysis

Mihaela-Georgiana Oprea, Mihaela-Irma Vlădescu, and Carmen Gheorghe

Abstract In the last two decades, the migration of people who aim to follow a higher education program has increased significantly, becoming an important subject that is dealt with from a political, social, and economic point of view. In this sense, the study tries to highlight the differences registered among Romanian emigrants and immigrants aged between 0 and 19 years and, respectively, among people who are pursuing bachelor's, master's, or doctorate university studies. The importance of this study derives from the amount and level of education of both immigrants and emigrants, because children and young people today represent, among other things, the source of labor in the near or more distant future, which contributes to supporting the social insurance system and more. Considering that the number of emigrants is considerably higher than that of immigrants and that the main motivations of young people in the analyzed categories are generally structured on jobs and well-being, it is necessary to fulfill objective no. 10 of the 2030 Agenda, which refers to the reduction of inequalities.

Keywords Student migration · School population · Demography · Education · Labor force · Inequalities

---

M.-G. Oprea · M.-I. Vlădescu · C. Gheorghe (✉)
National Institute of Economic Research "Costin C. Kirițescu", School of Advanced Studies of the Romanian Academy (SCOSAAR), Bucharest, Romania
e-mail: oprea@ince.ro; carmen.adriana@ince.ro

9.1 Introduction

The ever-wider and deeper movements taking place in the world economy have created new directions of development and interest. Within the European space, collaboration between the member states of the European Union is encouraged in order to build resilient and inclusive national education and training systems. Through the introduction of the European Transferable Credit System (ETCS) to the European Higher Education Area, academic qualifications and periods of study followed abroad are recognized.

Considering the demographic changes and the labor shortage, which can affect, among others, the social insurance system, it is necessary to implement policies that support and attract students from and in Romania, because they represent the labor force qualified in the near future (Vass, 2007).

Mobility for educational purposes is characteristic of younger people who have followed or want to follow a level of higher education (Sandu et al., 2018). Over time, the presence of foreign students from less developed countries has become a ubiquitous phenomenon in higher education in European countries.

In recent years, educational centers around the world have experienced a new reality generated by the presence of an increasing number of immigrant students, becoming much more heterogeneous in terms of origins. In the first stage, we mention the arrival of immigrant families with school-aged children who had access over time to all cycles of studies, and then the birth of children from immigrant parents – the second generation (Aparicio & Portes, 2014).

Although numerous researches in the field have emphasized to a greater extent the economic and material impact of immigration, the socio-cultural impact continues to be one of the great unknowns. In one study, the authors state that all the contributions of immigrants also have their projection on the other side of the border, in the direction of the countries of origin of the immigrants themselves, so that any contribution in the country of adoption is also reflected in the country of origin (Del Castillo, 2019). It happens not only with monetary remittances but also with any other change induced by immigrants to the extent that they remain connected to the country of origin (social, cultural, or political remittances).

Overall, we can talk about a contribution that is more difficult to quantify than the economic one, but undoubtedly a contribution with a fundamental component of enriching society in the context of globalization.

9.2 Literature Review

Pupils and students are an essential part of the educational system. They are the ones in whom society invests knowledge and the ones who can later contribute to a prosperous future for everyone. A significant portion of the Romanian Olympic students tend to choose to continue their studies (generally undergraduate studies) outside the country.

According to INS data, in the period 2008–2021, more than 540,000 people between the ages of 0 and 19 emigrated temporarily outside the country (Fig. 9.1).

One year after Romania's entry into the European Union, the highest value of the analyzed period was recorded. In the same year (2008), the global market crisis started, which affected the economy of our country to a greater extent than the economies of Western European countries, for example, and which, according to studies, influenced people's decision to emigrate. Another determining factor of the volume of migration was, as can be seen, the crisis caused by the COVID-19 pandemic which led to a significant decrease in the number of emigrants, primarily at the level of 2020, due to severe movement restrictions implemented by state governments in order to reduce the number of infected persons. The year 2021 is marked by an increase in the number of emigrants due to the temporary lifting of restrictions around the world.

In order to highlight the discrepancy between the entries and exits of Romanian people aged between 0 and 19, we will analyze in Fig. 9.2 the number of temporary immigrants.

Often, studies have focused on highlighting educational inequalities or distinct situations faced by students of immigrant origin (Carrasco et al., 2018), without paying attention to their possible contributions to the educational process such as the role of diversity as a factor of creativity and facilitator of innovation within the school institution (Garreta & Calvet, 2001).

Such an increase in academic interest toward the role of this category is mainly observed in the evolution of the word "clusters" over time. Carrying out the

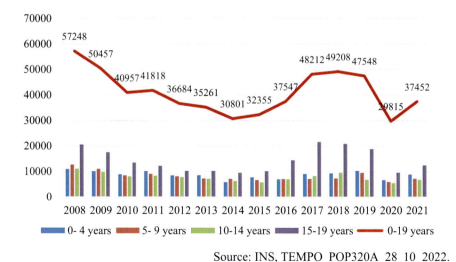

Source: INS, TEMPO_POP320A_28_10_2022.

Fig. 9.1 Number of temporary emigrants aged between 0 and 19 years in the period 2008–2021 (people)

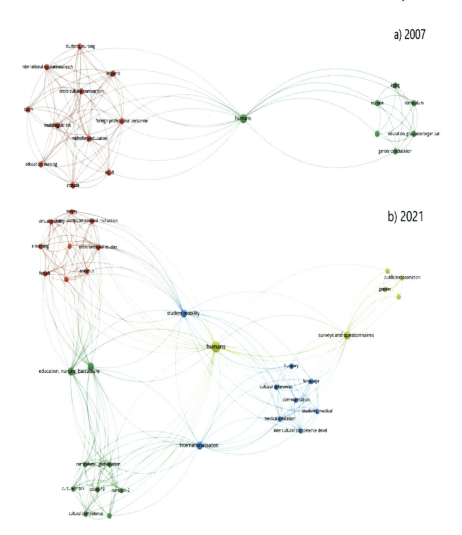

Fig. 9.2 Map of recurrent words corresponding to articles from the year 2007 (**a**), respectively 2021 (**b**) related to student mobility. (Source: Information processed from lens.org)

bibliometric analysis, we want to highlight how the academic landscapes related to the subject of this study have evolved and, especially, if there are notable differences between the years 2007 (a) and 2021 (b).

Although both figures above reveal links between people and education, we notice that these relationships have diversified considerably in the second analyzed figure, where we find elements such as internationalization, globalization, curriculum, cultural differences, public transport, and Erasmus, which show the multiplicity of work directions and continuous development of this phenomenon.

Gifted young people are looking for an environment that offers them the guarantee of the quality of the training and education process with the international recognition of the obtained qualifications. The perspective of superior material incentives and the possibility of promoting the most competent in educational research institutions or within powerful transnational companies should not be neglected. The receiving countries benefit from the effect of capitalizing on the intelligence of other countries, a phenomenon known as "brain-drain." If the specialists do not return to their country of origin, the brain-drain leads to a waste of the added value potential (Zaman & Vasile, 2003) that they could have generated for the development of society. The emigration of this segment of the population increasingly affects Romania, which is part of the group of donor countries. Whole sectors of the economy are affected due to the lack of specialists and the chasm is deepening every moment.

The "brain-drain" phenomenon has been intensely debated over time, often focusing on the loss of specialized human capital from less developed countries, as a rule, in favor of more economically developed countries. Although many researchers have emphasized the negative effect of this phenomenon (Grubel & Scott, 1966; Bhagwati, 1976), brain migration can also have a positive side (Beine et al., 2008; Batista et al., 2007), if the young people who left and have accumulated knowledge and experience choose to return in time to their country of birth and apply everything they have learned over time, in the country of origin (Mayr-Dorn & Peri, 2019), but in this sense, destination countries should make significant efforts to be able to generate return migration (Vlase, 2011).

Two characteristics of brain migration can be presented as indisputable:

1. The exodus is voluntary with the specification that it is encouraged by the receiving countries, while the countries of origin try to reduce it.
2. The investment in the education of the people who leave is often lost, because they choose not to return to their country of origin. From here comes the association with the term capital flight, which refers to the capital that is no longer invested in the country that created it and is forced to migrate in different directions due to multiple causes such as poverty, conflicts, lack of jobs, and low salary level compared to those existing in more developed countries.

According to studies, many migrants go abroad for opportunities to improve their skills, but some migrants return to their country of origin (Mayr-Dorn & Peri, 2019). In this regard, a clear example is the migration of high school or college graduates, who wish to participate in training programs.

An increased mobility of the labor force coming from among students from different countries directly influences the labor market, if they have employment opportunities during or after the completion of their studies (Government of Romania, 2015).

According to EUROSTAT data, annually, more than 20,000 students of Romanian origin follow university studies for bachelor's, master's, doctorate, or their equivalent outside the country. Among the preferred countries, we mention Denmark, Spain, Italy, France, Austria, and the UK (Fig. 9.3).

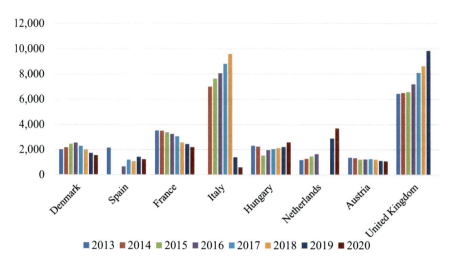

Fig. 9.3 Mobile students from abroad enrolled in bachelor's, master's, doctorate, or equivalent university studies – country of origin Romania (2013–2020). (Source: EUROSTAT, EDUC_UOE_MOBS02_31_10_2022. Notes: At the level of 2013, we do not have data available for Italy, respectively in 2020 we do not have data for the United Kingdom)

Throughout the studied period, the influence of the COVID-19 pandemic on this indicator can be observed in most countries. It is interesting to note that since 2016, the UK has been registering successive annual increases in the number of students, probably due to the announcement regarding the exit from the EU. In the period 2014–2018, Italy recorded the highest values of this indicator, values correlated with the large number of Romanian immigrants during that period.

Although many compatriots go to study abroad, our country has also become an option for foreign students over time (Fig. 9.4).

The highest percentage of foreign students is found in master's university studies, while the highest values in terms of continent of origin are recorded in Asia. In 2013, approximately 433,000 students were enrolled in undergraduate university studies in Romania, of which 9000 were foreign students. Although in 2020, according to INS data, a little over 418,000 students were enrolled in university undergraduate studies, the number of foreign students was higher compared to the value recorded in 2013 (over 14,000 people).

In general, the transition from student life to working life is often a challenge, but this stage is even more difficult for an immigrant. In this sense, the European Commission has undertaken numerous actions, programs, partnerships, and networks such as EURES to help facilitate the free movement of workers on the labor market, which aims to ensure that European citizens can benefit from the same opportunities, despite language barriers, cultural differences, bureaucratic challenges, and last but not least different employment legislation.

With the incorporation of migrants into the labor market, the economic effects of immigration on society become particularly important. As the International

9 Dynamics of the School Population, Differences Between Emigrants ... 105

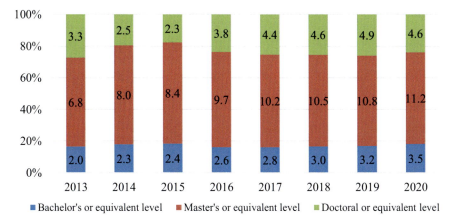

Fig. 9.4 Share of mobile students from the entire world enrolled by education level in Romania 2013–2020 (%). (Source: Eurostat data)

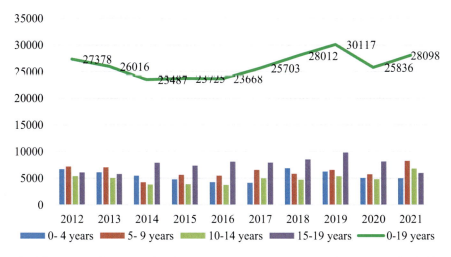

Fig. 9.5 Number of temporary immigrants aged between 0 and 19 years in the period 20,122,021 (people). (Source: INS, TEMPO_POP321C_1_11_2022)

Organization for Migration points out, the benefits of immigration materialize through greater labor availability, greater occupational mobility, and the reduction of wage and inflationary pressures, leading among other things to economic growth (IOM, 2005). Thus, the receiving countries considered the work of immigrants as a solution, although their insertion on the labor market often occurs under less favorable conditions for them (Fig. 9.5).

Although the number of immigrants from Romania aged between 0 and 19 years is much lower than that of Romanian emigrants, the two indicators have similar developments.

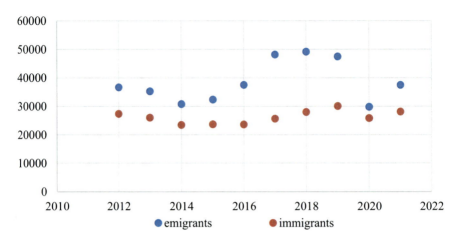

Fig. 9.6 The correlation between the number of temporary emigrants/immigrants aged between 0 and 19 years in 2012–2021. (Source: INS data)

The Pearson correlation coefficient is positive ($r = 0.61$) and indicates a direct correlation between the two variables (the number of emigrants and immigrants in and from Romania aged 0–19) for the analyzed period (Fig. 9.6).

By analyzing Fig. 9.6, we can conclude that global events such as the health and socio-economic crisis caused by coronavirus influenced the movement of the analyzed population. However, the differences recorded from 1 year to the next among emigrants are much higher than in the other indicator; the annual differences in the number of immigrants are much smaller. It is possible that the much higher values recorded in the period 2016–2019 among Romanian emigrants are due, among other things, to the withdrawal of the United Kingdom from the European Union.

9.3 Conclusions

Following the analysis of the data sets above, we can conclude that in the case of Romania, the number of immigrants between the ages of 0 and 19 years, respectively of students pursuing bachelor's, master's, or doctoral studies, is much lower than that of emigrants. Students with very good results often choose to study abroad, which is a loss in the opinion of some researchers. However, if Romania would build the necessary levers to encourage and support the return of Romanian graduates to the country, the whole society would benefit from the experiences and knowledge gained by them.

On the other hand, the other analyzed group of people migrates in most cases for the purpose of family reunification. Although the reasons for which people choose to migrate have diversified over time, the main reasons for Romanian emigration are based on economic reasons. Among the EU member states, Romania registers the second lowest value, ahead of Bulgaria, for numerous indicators such as average monthly earnings, annual net earnings for a single person without children, and minimum monthly salary.

In this sense, one of the seventeen objectives of the 2030 Agenda for Sustainable Development refers to the reduction of inequalities (Objective no. 10) both within countries and between EU member states.

References

Aparicio, R., & Portes, A. (2014). *Crecer en España: La integración de los hijos de immigrantes.* Social Work "La Caixa".
Batista, C., Lacuesta, A., & Vicente, P. C. (2007). *Brain drain or brain gain? Micro evidence from an African success story.*
Beine, M., Docquier, F., & Rapoport, H. (2008). Brain drain and human capital formation in developing countries: Winners and losers. *The Economic Journal, 118*(528), 631–652.
Bhagwati, J. N. (Ed.). (1976). *The brain drain and taxation: Theory and empirical analysis* (Vol. 2). Elsevier Science & Technology.
Carrasco, S., Pàmies, J., & Narciso, L. (2018). Abandono escolar prematuro y alumado de origen extranjero en España:¿ un problema invisible? In *Anuario CIDOB de la Inmigración* (pp. 212–236).
Garreta, J., & Calvet, N. (2001). *El espejismo intercultural: La escuela de Cataluña before cultural diversity.*
Government of Romania. (2015). *National immigration strategy for the period 2015–2018 "Migration is a process that must be managed and not a problem that must be solved".*
Grubel, H. B., & Scott, A. D. (1966). The international flow of human capital. *The American Economic Review, 56*(1/2), 268–274.
International Organization for Migration. (2005). *World Migration Report.* IOM Publications.
Mayr-Dorn, K., & Peri, G. (2019). Brain drain and brain return: Theory and application to Eastern-Western Europe. *The BE Journal of Economic Analysis and Policy, 9*(1), 1935–1682.
Sandu, D., Toth, G., & Tudor, E. (2018). The nexus of motivation–experience in the migration process of young Romanians. *Population, Space and Place, 24*(1), e2114.
Vass, A. (2007). The migration of Romanian brains between risk and opportunity. *OEconomica magazine, 03.*
Del Castillo, C., Blanco-González, A., & González-Vázquez, E. (2019). Influence of Attitudes Toward Immigration on State Legitimacy. *American Behavioral Scientist, 63*(7), 955–70. https://doi.org/10.1177/0002764218759575
Vázquez, J. L., Doménech, C. B., & Lozano, A. C. (2021). *The contribution of immigration to the Spanish society.*
Vlase, I. (2011). Return migration of Romanians from Italy. Case study in Vulturu, Vrancea. *Quality of Life, 22*(2), 155–176.
Zaman, G. H., & Vasile, V. (coord.) (2003) *Structural evolution of exports in Romania.* Expert Publishing House.

Chapter 10
Employee Resourcing Strategies in Tight Labour Market

Alic Bîrcă and Christiana Brigitte Sandu

Abstract This scientific endeavour addresses the problem of employee resourcing strategies in a tight labour market. Taking into account that employee resourcing is a complex activity, this study aims to analyse recruitment as its core element. Although the literature on this topic is rich, the analysis of options that organisations have at their disposal for attracting a workforce in a tight labour market has not been sufficiently explored. In this context, we have analysed several recruitment methods, traditional and via the Internet, used by organisations to attract different categories of workforce when there is a labour shortage in the labour market. The study focused on six traditional and three e-recruitment methods. Starting from this, the following research question was formulated: What are the recruitment methods most frequently used by organisations in attracting the workforce in a tight labour market? To answer the research question, a questionnaire was created which was applied to 350 organisations. Managers were used as respondents in case of small-sized organisations and human resource managers as the respondents of medium-sized and large-sized organisations. The research results show that organisations tend to use as many recruitment methods as possible to ensure the success of attracting the needed quantity and quality of the workforce.

Keywords Employee resourcing · Labour force · Labour market · Recruiting · Recruitment methods

---

A. Bîrcă
Academy of Economic Studies of Moldova, Kishinev, Republic of Moldova
e-mail: brc.alic@ase.md

C. B. Sandu (✉)
Alexandru Ioan Cuza University, Iasi, Romania
e-mail: christiana.balan@uaic.ro

© The Author(s), under exclusive license to Springer Nature Switzerland AG 2024
L. Chivu et al. (eds.), *Constraints and Opportunities in Shaping the Future: New Approaches to Economics and Policy Making*, Springer Proceedings in Business and Economics, https://doi.org/10.1007/978-3-031-47925-0_10

10.1 Introduction

Past negative demographic processes, high international migration and structural economic changes led to a high shortage of labour force, in terms of its quality and quantity. In the context of a tight labour market, employee resourcing is very important in the managerial activity of organisations, becoming a strategic function of human resource management. Apart from this, management wishes to solve through employee resourcing a set of issues related to the behaviour, values and attitudes of employees, as well as problems linked to new forms of work, work-life balance, employee commitment, etc.

Employee resourcing is a rather complex organisational function comprising provision of human resources, and personnel development and retention in an organisation. The goals of employee resourcing are to provide an adequate number of employees with the appropriate professional skills and knowledge, making sure that they are available at the right place and time. Recruitment is that element of employee resourcing that may ensure the needed human resources to solve both operational and strategic problems of an organisation (Beardwell et al., 2004).

In a labour shortage market, the activities of resourcing the needed specialists have become real challenges when it comes to attracting the labour force that an organisation needs in a specific period of time. It leads to higher competition among employers in terms of human resource attraction, the lack of which in some cases makes it impossible to reach organisational goals. Under these conditions, the analysis of labour market evolution becomes essential for organisations (Taylor, 2005), and its results will be used to apply different strategies of human resource attraction. Labour shortages and higher competition among companies for attracting new employees made several researchers in the field talk about a "war of talents" (Hiltrop, 1999; Cappelli, 2000). In this context, organisations use various recruitment methods and strategies depending on the categories of people they wish to attract to an organisation. In the case of workers and supporting staff, organisations may apply some recruitment methods, and others for specialists and managers. Depending on the target group towards which an organisation orients itself, and in line with its line of business, recruiters decide on the strategies that will be applied to attract the required labour force. When there is a labour shortage, organisations apply several recruitment strategies to make sure they will attract their short- and long-term goals. The rapid growth of the Internet made social networks websites as new recruitment methods to be applied more than such traditional methods as advertising, network of acquaintances, recruitment agencies, job fares, etc. At the same time, Acikgoz (2019) believes that traditional methods of recruiting candidates include advertisements, recruitment agencies and direct marketing.

Taking into account that employee resourcing is a complex function, we will analyse recruitment as one of the key elements of this function. Over the years, recruitment has remained a concern for researchers showing its importance for reaching organisational goals (Pilbeam & Corbridge, 2010; Breaugh, 2013; Rosario et al., 2019; Gilch & Sieweke, 2021; Krys & Konsadt, 2022), as well as underlining the future risks (Sobocka-Szczapa, 2021) and challenges for the organisation (Potočnik et al., 2021). On a labour shortage market, as that of the Republic of Moldova, recruitment plays an essential role in providing the needed human resources for organisations. Considering what has been mentioned so far, we have formulated the following research question: What are the most common recruitment methods used by organisations to attract human resources in a tight labour market?

Based on the above, we set ourselves as an objective the application of traditional recruitment methods for different categories of human resources – posting recruitment adverts in newspapers and magazines, a network of contacts, private recruitment agencies, agreements concluded with educational institutions, head-hunting companies and job fairs, and also e-recruitment made by posts on specialised websites, posts on company websites and employment posts on social networks. Also, we should mention that e-recruitment has lately been widely researched by more and more researchers (Chowdhury, 2022; Nicolaou, 2021; Waples & Brachle, 2020).

10.2 Literature Review

10.2.1 *Employee Resourcing Concept*

Employee resourcing involves matching the workforce with the organisation's strategic and operational needs, as well as their appropriate use. Also, Iles (2009) argues that employee resourcing covers the employment activities through which an organisation makes sure it has the needed human resources, also paying attention to staff fluctuation and retention. Also, Boxall and Purcell (2011) believe that employee resourcing aims at attracting and retaining the people that the organisation needs by their efficient employment.

As an HRM function, employee resourcing is also strategic as it aims not only at employee attraction and retention in terms of its quantity and quality but also at promoting people who match organisation's culture and strategic requirements (Armstrong and Taylor, 2014). And, human resource promotion is seen as an internal recruitment source of employees. According to Armstrong and Taylor (2014), strategic resourcing involves the integration of business and employee resourcing strategies, and the latter contributes to the realisation of the former.

Effective employee resourcing is based on the fact that human resource specialists have the needed knowledge and competence to manage the process efficiently (Dainty et al., 2009). The way an organisation opts for employee resourcing strategies and human resource flow strategies depends on the stakeholders assessing the process, and on other contextual features, such as the nature of the labour force, management's philosophy, technologies and business strategies. Armstrong and Taylor (2014) argue that the main goal of employee resourcing strategy is to obtain the needed resources as the workforce with the qualities, abilities, knowledge and potential matching of the organisation's future needs. In this context, the authors believe that recruitment of the most appropriate employees meeting the organisation's needs should be the main activity, around which, most HRM policies could be developed.

10.2.2 Recruitment: Core Activity in Employee Resourcing

As we have mentioned earlier, recruitment is the core element of employee resourcing which identifies and provides the employees needed for the organisation's short and mid-term survival and success (Armstrong & Baron, 2002). Also, Huselid (1995) believes that recruitment procedures providing a high number of qualified candidates could have a solid influence on the quality and type of skills that new employees show at the new workplace. In another approach, recruitment may be defined as the process of attracting the most appropriate candidates for an organisation's vacancies, based on their individual features (Melanthiou et al., 2015).

Recruitment is an activity of human resources management that consists of attracting the highest number of candidates, out of which, should be selected the individuals matching vacancies in the best way. According to Breaugh and Starke (2000), recruitment includes practices and activities conducted by an organisation and oriented towards identifying and attracting potential employees. Another study states that recruitment aims to attract candidates with the required qualifications and maintain their interest in the organisation so that they can accept a job offer (Barber, 1998).

The aim of recruitment is to identify the proper candidates to meet the organisational needs in a cost-efficient way (Tyson, 2005). The purpose of the recruitment activity is to create a pool of qualified candidates that allows the selection of the best candidates to achieve the organisation's objectives (Gamage, 2014). Also, recruitment is the point of workforce entrance into an organisation and the path an organisation should follow to make sure it attracts the right people for its culture and vibe so that its general strategic goals are achieved (Henry & Temtime, 2009).

Most studies on personnel recruitment refer to recruitment methods, as well as the effects of recruitment for an organisation (Rynes et al., 1991; Barber, 1998). On the same topic, Taylor and Schmidt (1983) found that recruitment methods vary by the category of people that are going to be recruited. The authors argue that recruitment methods could reach the most suitable people from an organisation, so they are more likely to be offered a job. To attract potential employees, organisations could apply different methods: newspaper ads, public and private recruitment agencies, Internet job forums, career websites, corporate websites, employer recommendations, university career centres, intermediary consultancies and job fairs (Ployhart, 2006). Recruitment agencies are a sort of intermediaries between the organisations looking for identifying and attracting new employees and the workforce searching for a job, or for another professional opportunity (Marchal et al., 2007). Job portals, recruitment agencies and newspaper ads are considered to be formal recruitment strategies, while employer recommendations are informal strategies (Taylor, 2005). Many organisations use such online platforms in their recruitment process as job boards, corporate websites and social media (Allen et al., 2007). E-recruitment refers to an umbrella term that involves recruitment activities carried out through the use of various electronic means and the Internet (Holm, 2010). Some researchers analysed the impact of recruitment methods on the behaviour of candidates (Bay et al., 2020).

Various factors may affect the job search decisions of the job seekers. Therefore, Ma and Allen (2009) analysed the influence of organisational cultural values on recruitment activities, as well as their relationship to the results of recruitment efforts. In this context, Phillips and Gully (2002) consider that the specific reactions of candidates are systematically linked to cultural values. According to Henkens et al. (2005), an important factor refers to the difficulties perceived by organisations regarding finding the desired personnel for filling the vacancies. The authors argue that the bigger the perceived difficulties, the higher the likelihood that the organisations will take specific measures for attracting a higher number of employees by applying formal and informal methods. Also, some authors analysed the elements of discrimination and diversity on the labour market that affect the recruitment of candidates (Adamovic, 2020; Golubovich and Ryan, 2022).

Labour force shortage and difficulties in attracting the candidates led to higher competitiveness in staff recruitment. Even more, Lievens et al. (2002) argue that "the war for talents" led to the shifting of the accent from candidate selection to attraction. Despite the fact that we live in the digital age when e-recruitment is widely used in organisations for cost-saving reasons and is becoming more and more popular in the process of candidate attraction, organisations have not abandoned the traditional methods that have been used over the years. In this context, Anderson (2003) argues that the use of Internet-based recruitment tools could be seen more and more in today's business. Parry and Tyson (2008) argue that online recruitment methods are more appropriate for middle managers and specialists, and less adequate for top managers. Thus, Internet recruiting, the use of web tools, including social networks, online job forums and corporate websites are used by organisations to differentiate the job offer from potential candidates (Alamro et al., 2018; Williams et al., 2021).

10.3 Methodology

This study starts from the research question formulated in the introductory section. The activity of organisations in a tight labour market requires an additional effort for attracting new employees. It first includes the diversification of recruitment methods increasing the chances of organisations in identifying and attracting the human resources they need. In this context, the following hypotheses were formulated.

H1: A tight labour market forces organisations to apply several workforce recruitment methods to reach their goals.

A tight labour market makes organisations be more concerned about the attraction of new employees. In this sense, organisations are "forced" to use many recruitment methods, irrespective of the category of human resources they are searching to employ. There is a higher likelihood for organisations to attract the needed workforce if several recruitment methods are used.

H2: The frequency of recruitment methods in organisations is higher in urban than in rural areas.

Considering that there is a higher conglomerate of workforce in urban areas, even on a tight market, organisations use more recruitment methods and with a higher frequency, so that the delivered message could reach any interested person.

H3: Recruitment methods are applied differently by workforce category and organisation size.

To attract a workforce, organisations apply different recruitment methods depending on their size. Similarly, organisations decide which recruitment methods should be used in order to ensure the categories of force work they need.

To validate the formulated hypotheses, we built a questionnaire which was applied to 350 respondents (employers). In the case of small employers, the questionnaire was targeted at managers, and for medium and big organisations at human resource managers. The questionnaire included new recruitment methods, out of which six were traditional methods and three were Internet-based methods. The respondents had to choose the recruitment methods applied in their organisations for different categories of employees. The results were processed using SPSS 22.

10.4 Analysis/Results Interpretation

The study results show that out of 350 organisations participating in the survey, only one mentioned not facing problems in attracting new employees while the other 349 organisations having difficulties in attracting new employees. The success of organisations in attracting new employees depends on the applied recruitment methods. To validate the first hypothesis H1, the respondents mentioned the applied recruitment methods for different categories of employees (Table 10.1).

As shown in Table 10.1, organisations apply a variety of methods for attracting new employees. The application of recruitment methods depends on the category of workforce to be employed. We should note that out of the variety of recruitment methods, the network of acquaintances remains a practice largely used in local organisations. The phenomenon of "nepotism" affected the entire society, determining its intense use even in the professional area, including employment, even if it does not generate the best results. Also, we use a reluctant use of recruitment methods generating costs (private recruitment agencies and head-hunting companies).

Testing the association between the applied recruitment methods and the categories of personnel was made using the Chi-square test as shown in Table 10.2.

Table 10.1 Distribution of responses of sample organisations on the applied recruitment methods by category or personnel (%)

Applied recruitment methods	Support staff	Workers	Specialists	Managers
Posting recruitment ads in newspapers and magazines	13.06	11.17	7.34	6.55
Posting ads on the specialised recruitment websites	16.26	15.57	17.47	17.43
Posting ads on corporate websites	11.47	12.14	14.18	16.25
Network of acquaintances	15.53	14.89	13.92	14.42
Agreements concluded with the educational institutions	3.92	7.05	7.85	4.33
Private recruitment agencies	5.22	4.60	6.50	8.78
Head-hunting agencies	3.63	3.33	4.98	5.64
Job fairs	9.29	10.58	9.54	7.47
Posting job ads on social networks	14.08	14.50	14.01	14.42
Other (National Employment Agency)	7.55	6.17	4.22	4.72
Total	100	100	100	100

Source: Processed by authors

Table 10.2 Results for the association analysis between the applied recruitment methods and the categories of personnel

Chi-square tests	Value	df	Asymp. sig. (2-sided)
Pearson Chi-square	88.391[a]	27	0.000
Likelihood ratio	88.362	27	0.000
No. of valid cases	3658		

Source: Own calculations in SPSS 22.0
Note: [a] 0 cells (0.0%) have expected count less than 5. The minimum expected count is 30.33

The results highlight that there is a statistically significant association between the applied method and the category of targeted personnel (Pearson Chi-square test = 88.391 with a P-value = 0.000).

To test the second hypothesis H2, we analysed the application of recruitment methods by the location of the organisation included in the study (urban, rural). The results prove that both the frequency and the diversity of recruitment methods are higher in urban than in rural areas. Both for urban and rural areas, the frequency of responses on the applied recruitment methods is shown by the main categories of workforce (Tables 10.3 and 10.4).

Tables 10.3 and 10.4 show that organisations located in urban areas apply recruitment methods more often than rural organisations. Also, we observe that some recruitment methods are used more often both in urban and rural areas (network of acquaintances, posting ads on websites and posts on social networks) targeting all categories of force work included in the study.

For the second hypothesis, the Chi-square test was used for testing the association between the applied recruitment methods and the category of workforce by the category of organisation defined by place where the organisation is located (see Table 10.5).

Table 10.3 Distribution of urban area organisation's responses on the applied recruitment methods by the category of workforce

Applied recruitment methods	Support staff	Workers	Specialists	Managers
Posting recruitment ads in newspapers and magazines	75	96	72	42
Posting ads on the specialised recruitment websites	88	127	170	107
Posting ads on corporate websites	72	102	142	101
Network of acquaintances	86	118	130	87
Agreements concluded with the educational institutions	24	60	78	26
Private recruitment agencies	29	36	60	51
Head-hunting agencies	21	28	48	36
Job fairs	55	87	94	45
Posting job ads on social networks	81	123	137	85
Other (National Employment Agency)	43	50	41	29
Total	574	827	972	609

Source: Processed by authors

Table 10.4 Distribution of rural area organisation responses on applied recruitment methods by the category of workforce

Applied recruitment methods	Support staff	Workers	Specialists	Managers
Posting recruitment ads in newspapers and magazines	15	18	15	8
Posting ads on the specialised recruitment websites	24	32	37	26
Posting ads on corporate websites	7	22	26	23
Network of acquaintances	21	34	35	23
Agreements concluded with the educational institutions	3	12	15	7
Private recruitment agencies	7	11	17	16
Head-hunting agencies	4	6	11	7
Job fairs	9	21	19	12
Posting job ads on social networks	16	25	29	25
Other (National Employment Agency)	9	13	9	7
Total	115	194	213	154

Source: Processed by authors

Therefore, we find a statistically significant association between the applied recruitment methods and the category of targeted workforce in the case of urban organisations (Pearson Chi-square test = 71.680 with a P-value = 0.000). For rural organisations, there is no statistically significant association between the applied recruitment methods and the categories of personnel.

Table 10.5 Results of the association between the recruitment methods and the category of workforce by organisation's location

Location	Chi-square tests	Value	df	Asymp. sig. (2-sided)
Rural	Pearson Chi-square	23.172[a]	27	0.676
	Likelihood ratio	23.657	27	0.649
	No. of valid cases	676		
Urban	Pearson Chi-square	71.680[b]	27	*0.000*
	Likelihood ratio	71.731	27	*0.000*
	No. of valid cases	2982		

Source: Own calculations in SPSS 22.0
Note: [a] 1 cells (2.5%) have expected count less than 5. The minimum expected count is 4.76
[b] 0 cells (0.0%) have expected count less than 5. The minimum expected count is 25.60

Table 10.6 Results of the association between the recruitment methods and the category of workforce by organisation's size

Size of organisation	*Chi-square tests*	Value	df	Asymp. sig. (2-sided)
Up to 9 employees	Pearson Chi-square	19.543[a]	27	0.849
	Likelihood ratio	18.871	27	0.875
	No. of valid cases	624		
10–49 employees	Pearson Chi-square	28.015[b]	27	0.410
	Likelihood ratio	28.483	27	0.386
	No. of valid cases	1101		
50–249 employees	Pearson Chi-square	59.945[c]	27	*0.000*
	Likelihood ratio	60.081	27	*0.000*
	No. of valid cases	990		
Over 250 employees	Pearson Chi square	23.866[d]	27	0.638
	Likelihood ratio	24.136	27	0.623
	No. of valid cases	943		

Source: Own calculations in SPSS 22.0
Note: [a] 0 cells (0.0%) have expected count less than 5. The minimum expected count is 30.33
[b] 0 cells (0.0%) have expected count less than 5. The minimum expected count is 6.13
[c] 0 cells (0.0%) have expected count less than 5. The minimum expected count is 9.07
[d] 0 cells (0.0%) have expected count less than 5. The minimum expected count is 7.50

H3 hypothesis was tested after the analysis of the applied recruitment methods by different categories of personnel by organisation's size. It should be noted that out of 350 organisations comprised in the study, 62 micro-enterprises (up to 9 employees), 100 – small enterprises (10–49 employees), 105 – medium-sized enterprises (50–249 employees) and 82 – big enterprises (over 250 employees) (Annex 10.1). Annex 10.1 results were calculated by relating the responses about each method of recruitment to the number of respondent enterprises by each category. Similarly, the association analysis was applied to test the relationship between the applied recruitment methods and the categories of targeted personnel by the category of organisation differentiated by size (see Table 10.6).

Table 10.6 shows a statistically significant association between applied recruitment methods and categories of targeted personnel for organisations having over 50–249 employees (Pearson Chi-square test = 59.945 with a P-value = 0.000).

The results (Annex 10.1) allow us to see that the most applied recruitment methods are those for attracting workers and specialists on all categories of enterprises. E-recruitment is often used by all categories of enterprises and for all types of jobs. The three e-recruitment methods used most often, irrespective of their size include posting *ads on the specialised recruitment websites, posting ads on corporate websites and posting ads on social networks*. Posting ads in newspapers and magazines as a recruitment method is used mostly for executive and management jobs. The study results show that it is true for all categories of enterprises. Attraction of new employees using private recruitment agencies is more often used for specialists and managers but less compared to other mentioned methods. It could be due to recruitment costs of services provided by private agencies.

10.5 Conclusions

Employers are forced by a tight labour market to make additional efforts to attract new employees. Diversification of methods used for attracting the workforce is a solution for organisations. Workforce shortage is felt by all categories of organisations, irrespective of their location – urban or rural. Also, both workers and specialists and managers are of shortage.

This is the reason why the implementation of a human resource strategy by using simultaneously several recruitment methods is also a solution that should be implemented by organisations. Study results prove that organisations not only implement specific recruitment methods but also try to benefit from each method that could supply the needed personnel.

In contrast with the traditional recruitment methods, e-recruitment methods are used more often in organisations, showing their advantages in reaching the set goals. Therefore, out of the three e-recruitment methods shown in our study, frequency of use ranges from 21% to 56%, depending on organisation size and the category of searched workforce.

Paradoxically or not, the network of acquaintances is still a recruitment method used frequently in local organisations. More than that, it is used for attracting all categories of personnel. Nepotism being a tradition in the Republic of Moldova covers various areas of life, turning into a recruitment method, although not being the most efficient when it comes to expectations from new employees.

There have been lately concluded several collaboration agreements on the labour market between organisations and educational institutions. Therefore, organisations try to deal with the labour shortage by attracting the young to do an internship followed which could later lead to employment. Although this method is less used, its frequency could grow in the future, especially with the development of joint programs.

Although head-hunting companies target a specific market segment, the study found that organisations use this method to attract all categories of personnel, more commonly applied for recruiting specialists and managers.

The limitation of this study is given by the fact that its results could not be compared to see the evolution over time in the application of recruitment methods. In a future study, we aim to research further this issue in order to discover the trends in the application of recruitment methods.

Acknowledgement The paper was written in the research project "Development of labour market policies to increase employment". The project is included in the State Register of Projects in the field of Science and Innovation and is funded from the state budget of the Republic of Moldova through the National Agency for Research and Development.

Annex 10.1: Application of Recruitment Methods by the Category of Employees

250 employees and more (83 organisations)	Job fairs	13.3	25.7	24.8	15.2
	Posting job ads on social networks	24.8	39.0	41.9	32.4
	Other	16.2	17.1	12.4	10.5
	Posting recruitment ads in newspapers and magazines	30.1	39.8	26.5	13.2
	Posting ads on the specialised recruitment websites	38.6	55.4	65.1	44.6
	Posting ads on corporate websites	25.3	39.8	49.4	34.9
	Network of acquaintances	31.3	42.2	53.0	26.5
	Agreements concluded with the educational institutions	8.4	19.3	28.9	12.0
	Private recruitment agencies	9.6	19.3	24.1	19.3
	Head-hunting agencies	9.6	12.0	15.7	9.6
	Job fairs	21.7	41.0	38.6	14.4
	Posting job ads on social networks	32.5	50.6	47.0	33.7
	Other	12.0	16.9	14.4	9.6

Source: Processed by authors

Annex 10.2: Organisation's Size

Size of organisation	Recruitment method	Category of employees			
		Support staff	Workers	Specialists	Managers
Up to 9 employees (62 organisations)	Posting recruitment ads in newspapers and magazines	24.2	38.7	30.6	21.0
	Posting ads on the specialised recruitment websites	27.4	46.8	53.2	30.6
	Posting ads on corporate websites	24.2	40.3	38.7	25.8
	Network of acquaintances	25.8	46.0	35.5	21.0
	Agreements concluded with the educational institutions	8.1	32.2	21.0	8.1
	Private recruitment agencies	11.3	16.1	14.5	19.3
	Head-hunting agencies	6.4	16.1	21.0	9.7
	Job fairs	24.2	32.2	30.6	12.9
	Posting job ads on social networks	21.0	37.1	43.5	29.0
	Other	17.7	11.0	16.1	9.7
10–49 employees (100 organisations)	Posting recruitment ads in newspapers and magazines	24.0	30.0	33.0	21.0
	Posting ads on the specialised recruitment websites	35.0	45.0	61.0	41.0
	Posting ads on corporate websites	22.0	32.0	54.0	43.0
	Network of acquaintances	38.0	45.0	46.0	35.0
	Agreements concluded with the educational institutions	7.0	17.0	27.0	9.0
	Private recruitment agencies	12.0	11.0	26.0	19.0
	Head-hunting agencies	8.0	8.0	18.0	14.0
	Job fairs	17.0	27.0	36.0	21.0
	Posting job ads on social networks	31.0	42.0	56.0	30.0
	Other	14.0	20.0	15.0	11.0
50–249 employees (105 organisations)	Posting recruitment ads in newspapers and magazines	24.8	25.7	12.4	4.8
	Posting ads on the specialised recruitment websites	26.7	37.1	56.2	34.3
	Posting ads on corporate websites	20.0	32.4	46.7	34.3
	Network of acquaintances	25.7	41.0	50.5	38.1
	Agreements concluded with the educational institutions	7.6	18.1	27.6	8.6
	Private recruitment agencies	8.6	9.5	21.0	19.0
	Head-hunting agencies	4.8	5.7	14.3	14.3

References

Acikgoz, Y. (2019). Employee recruitment and job search: Towards a multi-level integration. *Human Resource Management Review, 29*(1), 1–13.

Adamovic, M. (2020). Analyzing discrimination in recruitment: A guide and best practices for resume studies. *International Journal of Selection and Assessment, 28*(4), 445–464.

Alamro, S., Dogan, H., Cetinkaya, D., Jiang, N., & Phalp, K. (2018). Conceptualising and modelling E-recruitment process for enterprises through a problem oriented approach. *Information, 9*(11), 269.

Allen, D. G., Mahto, R. V., & Otondo, R. F. (2007). Web-based recruitment: Effects of information, organizational brand, and attitudes toward a web site on applicant attraction. *The Journal of Applied Psychology, 92*(6), 1696–1708.

Anderson, N. (2003). Applicant and recruiter reactions to new technology in selection: A critical review and agenda for future research. *International Journal for Selection and Assessment, 11*(2–3), 121–136.

Armstrong, M., & Baron, A. (2002). *Strategic HRM: The key to improved business performance*. Chartered Institute of Personnel and Development.

Armstrong, M., & Taylor, S. (2014). *Armstrong's handbook of human resource management practice* (13th ed.). Chartered Institute of Personnel and Development.

Barber, A. E. (1998). *Recruiting employees*. Sage Publications.

Bay, D., Cook, G. L., & Yeboah, D. (2020). Recruiting method and its impact on participant behavior. *Advances in Accounting Behavioral Research, 23*, 1–19.

Beardwell, I., Holden, L., & Claydon, T. (2004). *Human resource management: A contemporary perspective*. Prentice Hall, Financial Times.

Boxall, P., & Purcell, J. (2011). *Strategy and human resource management* (3rd ed.). Palgrave Macmillan PwC.

Breaugh, J. A. (2013). Employee recruitment. *Annual Review of Psychology, 64*, 389–416.

Breaugh, J. A., & Starke, M. (2000). Research on employee recruitment: So many remaining questions. *Journal of Management, 26*, 405–434.

Cappelli, P. (2000). A market-driven approach to retaining talent. *Harvard Business Review, 78*(1), 103–111.

Chowdhury, S. (2022). Recruiting on the NET: Insights for employers from prospective employees. *PSU Research Review*. Retrieved from: https://doi.org/10.1108/PRR-09-2021-0051

Dainty, A. R. J., Raiden, A. B., & Neale, R. H. (2009). Incorporating employee resourcing requirements into deployment decision making. *Project Management Journal, 40*(2), 7–18.

Gamage, A. S. (2014). Recruitment practices in manufacturing SMEs in Japan: An analysis of the link with business performance. *Ruhuna Journal of Management and Finance, 1*(1), 37–52.

Gilch, P. M., & Sieweke, J. (2021). Recruiting digital talent: The strategic role of recruitment in organisation' digital transformation. *German Journal of Human Resource Management, 35*(1), 53–82.

Golubovich, J., & Ryan, A. M. (2022). Implications of diversity cues in recruitment and assessment materials: Reactions and performance. *International Journal of Selection and Assessment, 30*(4), 467–485.

Henkens, K., Remery, C., & Schippers, J. (2005). Recruiting personnel in a tight labour market: An analysis of employers' behaviour. *International Journal of Manpower, 26*(5), 421–433.

Henry, O., & Temtime, Z. (2009). Recruitment and selection practices in SMEs: Empirical evidence from a developing country perspective. *Advances in Management, 3*(2), 52–58.

Hiltrop, J.-M. (1999). The quest for the best: Human resource practices to attract and retain talent. *European Management Journal, 17*(4), 422–430.

Holm, A. (2010). *The effect of e-recruitment on the recruitment process: Evidence from case studies of three Danish MNCs*. Retrieved from: https://ceur-ws.org/Vol-570/paper007.pdf

Huselid, A. M. (1995). The impact of human resource management practices on turnover, productivity, and corporate financial performance. *Academy of Management Journal, 38*(3), 635–672.

Iles, P. (2009). *Employee resourcing*. Edinburgh Business School, Heriot-Watt University. Retrieved from: https://ebs.online.hw.Ac.uk/EBS/media/EBS/PDFs/Employee-Resourcing-Course-Taster.pdf

Krys, S., & Konradt, U. (2022). Losing and regaining organizational attractiveness during the recruitment process: A multiple-segment factorial vignette study. *Journal of Work and Organizational Psychology, 38*(1), 43–58.

Lievens, F., van Dam, K., & Anderson, N. (2002). Recent trends and challenges in personnel selection. *Personnel Review, 31*(5), 580–601.

Ma, R., & Allen, D. G. (2009). Recruiting across cultures: A value-based model of recruitment. *Human Resource Management Review, 19*, 334–346.

Marchal, E., Mellet, K., & Rieucau, G. (2007). The use of technologies in the recruiting, screening, and selection processes for job candidates. *Human Relations, 60*(7), 1091–1113.

Melanthiou, Y., Pavlou, F., & Constantinou, E. (2015). The use of social network sites as an e-recruitment tool. *Journal of Transnational Management, 20*(1), 31–49.

Nicolaou, I. (2021). What is the role of technology in recruitment and selection? *The Spanish Journal of Psychology*. Retrieved from: https://www.cambridge.org/core/journals/spanish-journal-of-psychology/article/what-is-the-role-of-technology-in-recruitment-and-selection/451DF5C763B110A845EEAD50F5BAF851

Parry, E., & Tyson, S. (2008). An analysis of the use and success of online recruitment methods in the UK. *Human Resource Management Journal, 18*(3), 257–274.

Phillips, J. M., & Gully, S. M. (2002). Fairness reactions to personnel selection techniques in Singapore and the United States. *International Journal of Human Resource Management, 13*(8), 1186–1205.

Pilbeam, S., & Corbridge, M. (2010). *People resourcing and talent planning. HRM practice* (4th ed.). Pearson Education.

Ployhart, R. E. (2006). Staffing in the 21st century: New challenges and strategic opportunities. *Journal of Management, 32*(6), 868–897.

Potočnik, K., et al. (2021). Paving the way for research in recruitment and selection: Recent developments, challenges and future opportunities. *European Journal of Work and Organizational Psychology, 30*(2), 159–174.

Rosario, S. D., Venkatraman, S., & Abbas, A. (2019). Challenges in recruitment and selection process: An empirical study. *Challenges, 10*(2), 35. Retrieved from: https://doi.org/10.3390/challe10020035

Rynes, S. L., Bretz, R. D., & Gerhart, B. (1991). The importance of recruitment in job choice: A different way of looking. *Personnel Psychology, 44*, 487–521.

Sobocka-Szczapa, H. (2021). Recruitment of employees assumptions of the risk model. *Risks, 9*(3), 55. Retrieved from: https://doi.org/10.3390/risks9030055

Taylor, S. (2005). *People resourcing* (3th ed.). Chartered Institute of Personnel and Development.

Taylor, M. S., & Schmidt, D. W. (1983). A process oriented investigation of recruitment source effectiveness. *Personnel Psychology, 36*, 343–354.

Tyson, S. (2005). *Essentials of human resource management* (5th ed). Linacre House, Jordan Hill, Oxford.

Waples, C. J., & Brachle, B. J. (2020). Recruiting millennials: Exploring the impact of CSR involvement and pay signaling on organizational attractiveness. *Corporate Social Responsibility and Environmental Management, 27*(2), 870–880.

Williams, P., McDonald, P., & Mayes, R. (2021). Recruitment in the gig economy: Attraction and selection on digital platforms. *The International Journal of Human Resource Management, 32*(19), 1–27.

Chapter 11
Estimation of Disembodied Technical Change During the Kuznets Cycles of Romania's First Transition to Market Economy

Florin Marius Pavelescu ⓘ

Abstract Romania's first transition to market economy lasted more than six decades (from the establishment of the Romanian modern state in 1859 till the Land Reform adopted in 1921). This transformation of the economy can be viewed in the context of three Kuznets cycles, defined by the fluctuations of the gross domestic product, institutional changes and two major external shocks – the 1877–1878 War of Independence and the 1899 international economic and financial crisis. This paper identifies not only the Kuznets cycles but also the Kitchin and Juglar cycles of Romania's economy, estimates the rate of disembodied technical change and reveals the economic growth trajectory during each of the three Kuznets cycles during the 1863–1914 period. It concludes that the feature of economic growth has changed from one cycle to another and that the sensible fluctuations of the rate of growth were mainly caused by the blockages maintained in the agricultural activities.

Keywords Short economic cycles · External shocks · Primary sector · Economic growth trajectory

11.1 Introduction

From 1862, when the official statistics was established, to 1914, when WWI broke out, Romania registered a significant increase in its gross domestic product (GDP). According to Axenciuc & Georgescu (2017), in 1914, the respective indicator was more than 3.61 times higher compared to 1862, and the average yearly rate was

---

F. M. Pavelescu (✉)
Institute of National Economy, Romanian Academy, Bucharest, Romania

2.50%. This moderate rate of growth was unstable in time, being obtained in the context of cyclical fluctuations, caused by the actions of various factors. In this context, the study of the features of economic growth has to consider the short economic cycles and the changes in the institutional framework. We have not ignored that during the above-mentioned time interval, Romania experienced the first transition to market economy and this process was a complex one, with several stages, defined both by quantitative and qualitative changes.

11.2 Literature Review

The idea that Romania have experienced two transitions to market economy occurred in Postolache (1991). In the particular context of the early 1990s, the Romanian economist mentioned that the reforms initiated in Central and Eastern countries, which experienced the command economy, represented, in fact, a new transition to a market economy. The above-mentioned countries, including Romania, have passed a first transition to market economy, which began in the second half of the eighteenth century and lasted during the nineteenth century and the first two decades of the twentieth century. The respective transition process can be also observed in Western Europe and North America. But its time length and economic and social consequences varied from country to country. The first transition to market economy was the transition from an economy based on agricultural and handicraft activities to an economy orientated toward the market and where industry plays an essential role (Stokes & Conway, 1996). This transformation of the economy was earlier and shorter in Western Europe and North America. In the case of the United States, the respective transformation of the economy was analysed and defined as a "market revolution" by Sellers (1991). The above-mentioned author revealed that market revolution occurred in the early 1800s and was clearly manifested during 1820s and 1830s and has to be viewed in conjunction with the industrial revolution, the transportation development, the enlargement of the internal market through the Westward expansion and increase the openness to international trade. This market revolution has an impact not only on the economic dynamics but also on the social, cultural and political evolution.

In the case of Romania, the first transition to market lasted for an excessive period. Zeletin (1925) revealed the important impact of the openness to foreign trade and the implementation of Organic Reglement, as one of the provisions of the 1829 Treaty of Adrianople for the Romanian principalities of Walachia and Moldovia, to the occurrence and early development of market mechanisms and capital accumulation.

Pătrășcanu (1969) and Constantinescu (1991) remarked that the Treaty of Adrianople provisions, regarding the Romanian principalities were an occasion for the extension of the role of market mechanisms in the coordination of economic activities and capital accumulation but not the origin of a transformation process of the economy. The above-mentioned economists considered that the first challenges of the order of the feudal economy were represented by the fiscal reforms implemented in the middle of the eighteenth century both in Walachia and Moldavia.

S. Zeletin and L. Pătrășcanu considered that the adoption of the 1921 Land Reform practically represented the end of the first transition to market economy.

Having in view the above-mentioned opinions, Pavelescu (2013) considered that the first transition to market economy was a very complex process with several stages caused both by domestic and external factors. We can speak about a pre-transition and a transition to market economy proper. The pre-transition can be viewed in a narrow and large sense. In a large sense, the pre-transition includes the period from the fiscal reforms implemented in the middle of the eighteenth century to the 1859 Union of Walachia and Moldavia. In a narrow sense, the pre-transition began in the early 1830s in the context of the implementation of the provisions of the 1829 Treaty of Adrianopole and lasted till the late 1850s.

The first transition to a market economy proper was also a prolonged process, compared with the experiences of developed states, because its length of time was about six decades (from the establishment of a modern state in 1859 to the 1921 Land Reform). Also, we can identify some stages of the respective economic transformation. Like in the cases of the other states, the respective transition was correlated with the industrial revolution and the start-up of the industrialization process. For these reasons, there were created conditions for economic growth. The rate of growth was unstable and we deal with short economic cycles. In this context, if we analyse the features of economic growth, it is recommended to identify the different types of short economic cycles and to estimate the rate of disembodied technical change.

11.3 Methodology

The methodology used in this paper to identify the economic cycles, reveal the features of economic growth and estimate the rate of disembodied technical change includes in the following:

(a) *Emphasis on the features of recessions, revealed by the yearly decrease of the gross domestic product in real terms, and of economic relaunch, revealed by the yearly increase of the gross domestic product in real terms, during the 1863–1914 period.* We will highlight the role played by the fluctuations of the primary sector production in the occurrence of the recessions and relaunch of economic activity.

If we note that dPS is the yearly relative modification of the value-added created by the primary sector and dGDP is the yearly relative modification of the gross domestic product.

We deal with six cases:

1. dPS < 0, dGDP < 0 and dGDP-dPS < 0, recessionist situation caused both by the primary sector and the other non-agricultural activities
2. dPS < 0, dGDP < 0 and dGDP-dPS > 0, recessionist situation essentially caused by the primary sector
3. dPS > 0 and dGDP < 0, recessionist situation essentially caused by the other non-agricultural activities
4. dPS < 0 and dGDP > 0, economic relaunch situation in the context of the decrease of the gross value-added created by the primary sector.
5. dPS > 0 and dGDP > 0, economic relaunch situation in the context of the increase of the gross value-added created both by the primary sector and the other non-agricultural activities
6. dPS > 0, dGDP > 0 and dGDP-dPS < 0, economic growth essentially generated by the primary sector

Thus, we can reveal three types of recessionist situations and three types of economic relaunch situations, considering a dual structure of the economy, the primary sector and the other non-agricultural activities.

(b) *Identification of the Kitchin cycles, having in view both the definition given in Kitchin* (1923), which assumed that the respective cycles lasted 3–5 years and were caused by the fluctuations in the size of the stocks of raw materials and products to sale. We take into account also the dominant role played by the primary sector in Romania's economy during the analysed period. In this context, we assume that a Kitchin economic cycle began not only when the GDP decreased but also when the value-added created by the primary sector diminished. We also consider that the respective short economic cycle has included at least one economic relaunch year and its time length was at least 2 years. Hence, we deal with two types of Kitchin cycles: Kitchin cycles of type I, which began with a diminish of GDP and Kitchin cycles of type II, which began with a diminish of the value-added by the primary sector in the context of GDP growth.

(c) *Revealing the Juglar cycles, by taking into account Juglar* (1862), which considered that the respective cycle was determined by the renewing of the fixed capital and lasted 8–12 years. We consider that, as a rule, the Juglar cycles include two or three and exceptionally four Kitchin cycles. The inclusion of the Kitchin cycles in a Juglar cycle takes account of both the time length of the Juglar Cycle, the deepness of the recessions and the occurrence of major social-political events.

Also, we will reveal the economic growth trajectory by comparing the absolute values of the expressions $\ln(1 + Rav)$ and $\ln(1 + Rr)$, where ln is the natural logarithm, Rav is the yearly average rate and Rr is the representative rate[1] of the gross domestic product.

---

[1] The representative rate was first defined by Pavelescu (1986) as the constant rate which would ensure to obtain the geometrical mean of the fixed base indices of the analysed indicator.

If the gross domestic product tends to grow, we have rav > 0. If we consider the statements made by Pavelescu (2016), we may assume the following:

1. If rav$_{GDP}$ > rr$_{GDP}$ > 0, we deal with conventional convex (accelerated) economic growth.
2. If rr$_{GDP}$ > rav$_{GDP}$ > 0, we deal with conventional concave (slowed) economic growth.
3. If rav$_{GDP}$ > 0 > rr$_{GDP}$, we deal with unstable economic growth.

(d) *Identification of the Kuznets cycles.* Kuznets (1973), assumed that these cycles are the results of the actions of demographic factors, the fluctuations of the construction activities and the development stages of infrastructure. Conventionally, they last 15–25 years. In this paper, we assume that the above-mentioned cycle merged two Juglar cycles. We also review the most important changes in the institutional-legislative framework during each Kuznets cycle.

(e) *Estimation of the rate of disembodied technical change proper in the context of Kuznets cycles*, considering the behavioural equation:

$$\ln \text{IGDP} = a_1 + b_1 * t \qquad (11.1)$$

where ln GDP is the natural logarithm of the fixed base indices of the gross domestic product, a_1 is the intercept, b_1 is the rate of the disembodied technical change proper and t is the time factor.

The significance of the estimated parameter of the behavioural Eq. (11.1) will be revealed, considering the methodology presented in Pavelescu (2016).

Hence, if we have in view the algebraical properties of the parameters estimated by OLS, we are able to write as

$$a_1 = \ln(1 + \text{rr}_{GDP}) * (1 - s)$$

$$b_1 = \ln(1 + \text{rr}_{GDP}) * s$$

$s = \text{cov}(\ln Y, t)/\text{var}(t)$, where rr is the representative rate of the output, Cov $(\ln Y, t)$ is the covariance between the natural logarithms of fixed base indices of the gross domestic product and time factor and Var (t) is the variance of the time factor.

Having in view the above-mentioned relationship between Rav and Rr and the size of the factor *s*, we are able to deepen the analysis related to the features of economic growth during the considered periods.

Therefore, the size of *s* is dependent on the economic growth trajectory. We can consider that the standard situation is when *s* varies between 0 and 1.

The other situations can be considered as exceptions and reveal unstable or accelerated economic growth.

If $s < 0$, we deal with unstable economic growth.

Table 11.1 The possible cases of economic growth trajectory revealed by the behavioural equation ln GDP = $a_1 + b_1 \times t$

Nr. crt.	Relationship between Rr and Rav	Size of factor s	Feature of economic growth trajectory
1	ln(1 + Rr) > ln(1 + Rav)	0 < 1	Conventional concave
2	ln (1 + Rr) < ln(1 + Rav)	0 < 1	Moderate convex
3	ln(1 + Rr) > ln(1 + Rav)	>1	Unstable concave
4	ln (1 + Rr) < ln(1 + Rav)	>1	Conventional convex

If $s > 1$ we deal with accelerated economic growth or with unstable economic growth, depending on the relationship between Rr and Rav. We detect four cases of economic growth trajectory, which are shown in Table 11.1.

(f) *Estimation of the rate of disembodied technical change*, in the context of adding dummy variables related to the years when Romania's economy entered recessions, by using a second behavioural equation:

$$\ln \text{IGDP} = a_2 + b_2 * t + \text{Dummy recess} \quad (11.2)$$

where Dummy recess is the dummy variable for recessionist years from the point of view of the GDP dynamics.

We use the behavioural Eq. (11.2) if we consider that the coefficient of determination computed in the case of Eq. (11.1) is too low. If the adjusted coefficient of determination related to the behavioural Eq. (11.2) is higher than the above-mentioned coefficient computed in the case of the behavioural Eq. (11.1) we can conclude that the adding of the dummy variable is effective. Therefore, we can reveal some interesting features concerning the economic growth during Romania's first transition to market economy. If we are in a situation where the adding of the dummy variable is effective, we may conclude that the fluctuations of the economic activity have played an important role in explaining the behaviour of the gross domestic product dynamics.

Also, we have to compare the estimated values of the parameters b_2 and b_1. We note that behavioural Eq. (11.2) is a multiple linear regression. In this case, the size of the estimated parameter b_2 is given by the formula:

$$b_2 = b_1 * T_{2t,}$$

where T_{2t} is the coefficient of collinear refraction.[2]

Consequently, we can consider that the parameter b_1 is the estimated rate of disembodied technical change proper.

If the coefficient of collinear refraction varies between 0.95 and 1.05, we assume that the addition of the dummy variable has no significant impact on the estimated

---

[2] The coefficient of collinear refraction in the case of linear regression with two explanatory variables was first defined and named the coefficient of alignment by Pavelescu (1986).

rate of disembodied technical change. In other words, the rate of disembodied technical change was not sensibly influenced by the important fluctuations of GDP.

11.4 Analysis/Results Interpretation

11.4.1 *Fluctuations of the Value-Added of the Primary Sector and Kitchin Cycles of Romania's Economy During 1862–1914*

Axenciuc & Georgescu (2017) present data regarding the dynamics of Romania's GDP during the period 1862–1914. Based on these data, we identified 19 recessionist years, when the GDP decreased (Table 11.2). We deal with only two of the three possible types of recessions, which were previously defined. The recessions, which were essentially caused by the decrease of the gross value-added created by the primary sector, have occurred in 11 years. As a rule, during the respective years, Romania's economy was confronted with unfavourable weather conditions.

The recessions caused by the decrease of the gross value-added created in both the primary sector and the other non-agricultural activities have manifested in 8 years. Even in these cases, the unfavourable weather conditions were the main causes of the decrease of the gross value-added created by the primary sector, and implicitly of the recessions. But we have not neglected that other internal or external factors have contributed to the worsening of the economic and financial situation.

Table 11.2 Features of the recessions and economic relaunch situations in Romania during the period 1863–1914%

Case	Relationship between dPs and dGDP	Number of years	Years
Types of recessionist situations			
1	dPS < 0, dGDP < 0, dGDP-dPS > 0	11	1866, 1874, 1876, 1881, 1883, 1887, 1893, 1902, 1907, 1909, 1911
2	dPS < 0, dGDP < 0, dGDP-dPS < 0,	8	1865, 1869, 1884, 1893, 1897, 1899, 1904, 1914
3	dPS > 0, dGDP < 0	0	
Types of economic relaunch situations			
4	dPS < 0, dGDP > 0	9	1871, 1872, 1877, 1879, 1889, 1890, 1891, 1896, 1912
5	dPS > 0, dGDP > 0	19	1864, 1868, 1873, 1875, 1878, 1880, 1882, 1885, 1886, 1892, 1894, 1895, 1898, 1900, 1903, 1905, 1906, 1908, 1913
6	dPS > 0, dGDP > 0, dGDP-dPS < 0	4	1863, 1867, 1870, 1888

Own estimation based on the data from Axenciuc & Georgescu (2017)

We deal with all three economic relaunch situations, which are previously defined. The most frequent case of economic growth, which was manifested in 19 years, is when the increase of the GDP is obtained in the context of an increase of the gross value-added both in the primary sector and the other non-agricultural activities.

The second type of economic relaunch, which has occurred in the context of the expansion of the other non-agricultural activities and the diminishing of the value-added created by the activities grouped in the primary sector, can be identified in 9 years.

The third type of economic relaunch, generated by the increase of the gross value-added of the primary sector in the context of a recessionist situation experienced by the other non-agricultural activities, can be identified only during 4 years. We note that the respective type of economic growth occurred in the first half of the analysed period when industry and trade were at the beginning of their development.

We have identified 28 years when the value-added created by the primary sector has diminished. We note that the respective diminish was followed by a relaunch in 21 cases and by a consecutive diminish in seven cases.

Considering the methodological assumptions, mentioned above, we define the Kitchin cycles related to the 1862–1913 period. Because we have no available data for the 1859–1861 and 1915–1918 time intervals, we make qualitative judgements for the definition of the respective short economic cycles. Therefore, we consider the 1859–1861 time interval as a Kitchin cycle. During this period, the official statistical data were lacking because a unified statistical institution had not yet been established by the public authorities. The official statistical data were not available for 1915–1918, as a consequence of the chaos provoked by WWI. In this context, we consider two Kitchin cycles for the 1914–1918 period, i.e. (a) 1914–1915, period of neutrality and (b) 1916–1918, period of Romania's participation in WWI. Therefore, we identified 22 Kitchin cycles during the 1859–1918 period (Table 11.3).

We note that there are nine cycles, which lasted 2 years, 11 cycles, which lasted 3 years and 2 cycles which lasted 4 years. The average time length of the above-mentioned cycles was 2.72 years, while the median was 2.18 years as a consequence of the relatively high number of the 2-year cycles.

Table 11.3 Features of the Kitchin cycles of Romania's economy during the 1859–1918 period

Case	Time length of the cycle	Number of cases	Cycles
1	2 years	9	1869–1870, 1874–1875, 1879–1880, 1881–1882, 1887–1888, 1902–1903, 1907–1908, 1909–1910, 1914–1915
2	3 years	11	1859–1861, 1862–1864, 1871–1873, 1876–1878, 1883–1886, 1893–1895, 1896–1898, 1899–1901, 1904–1906, 1911–1913, 1916–1918
3	4 years	2	1865–1868, 1889–1892

Own estimation based on the data from Axenciuc & Georgescu (2017)

The unstable dynamics of GDP was a consequence of the dependence of the macroeconomic activity on the primary sector. During the analysed period, the value-added created by the primary sector was sensibly influenced by the weather conditions and also by unresolved problems concerning the agrarian relationships, which blocked the rise of the technological level and, implicitly the occurrence of favouring conditions for the stability of production. The sensible fluctuation of economic activity and the alternation of boom and bust time intervals can be found not only in Romania but also in other European countries and the United States. Grigoraș and Orzan (2020) have computed a concordance index of fluctuation of economic activity between Romania and other countries. Based on the respective indicator for the period 1862–1914, it is possible to show that Romania's short economic cycles appeared to be more correlated with those of the United States, France or Italy and less correlated with those of Germany, Spain or Greece.

11.4.2 The Economic Growth Trajectories During the Juglar Cycles

We can identify the Juglar cycles by merging the Kitchin cycles, previously defined, considering that their time length varied between 8 and 12 years. Under these conditions, we may speak about six Juglar cycles: (a) 1859–1868, (b) 1869–1878, (c) 1879–1886, (d) 1887–1898, (e) 1899–1906 and (f) 1907–1918. We deal with 2 eight-year cycles, with 2 ten-year cycles and 2 twelve-year cycles. Thus, the theoretical assumptions concerning the length of the Juglar cycles are met.

When we have defined the above-mentioned cycles, we have considered not only their time length but also some economic or social events which happened during the analysed period. Therefore, the first Juglar cycle (1859–1868) lasted 10 years. The respective cycle met the methodological requirements for its definition. The second cycle (1869–1878) also lasted 10 years. The finish of this cycle was marked by the 1877–1878 War of Independence.

The third Juglar cycle (1879–1887) began with a Kitchin cycle of type II., immediatly after state independence winning. Thus, the economic and social conditions and various aspects of Romania's international relations significantly changed. The beginning of the fourth Juglar cycle is in 1887, being related to the occurrence of a recessionist situation.

For the identification of the start year of the fifth Juglar cycle, we compared the deepness of the 1897 and 1899 recessions. We found that the relative GDP decline was −15.79% in 1897 year and −29.34% in 1899.[3] In this context, we assumed that

---

[3] The 1899 recession was the deepest of the 1862–1914 period. According to Axenciuc & Georgescu (2017), the gross value-added created by the primary sector decreased by 52.7%. In this context, the budgetary revenues collapsed and the budgetary deficit sharply increased. The difficult economic situation was manifest not only in Romania but also in other countries from Europe and Northern America. But, the deepness of the recession sensibly varied among the states, depending

Table 11.4 Indicators of the economic growth trajectory in Romania in the context of Juglar cycles during the period 1863–1914%

Period	Average rate	Representative rate	Economic growth trajectory
1863–1868	0.99	0.38	Convex
1869–1878	2.31	1.41	Convex
1879–1886	4.73	3.42	Convex
1887–1898	2.15	1.61	Convex
1899–1906	2.89	−0.31	Unstable
1907–1914	0.59	0.51	Convex

Own calculations based on the data from V. Axenciuc & G. Georgescu (2017)

the above-mentioned economic cycle began in 1899. Thus, its time length was 12 years and met the methodological requirements.

The sixth Juglar cycle began with the recession caused by the 1907 peasants' revolt when the GDP diminished by 21.8% and lasted till the end of WWI. We note that the fifth Juglar cycle lasted 8 years, while the sixth one lasted 12 years.[4]

The rate of economic growth has sensibly varied during the Juglar cycles of the analysed period. For the first three cycles, the economic growth trajectory was convex and both the average and representative rates increased from one cycle to another (Table 11.4). We note that the rate of economic growth was slow during the 1863–1868 period, at the beginning of the first transition to market economy, moderate during the 1869–1878 period when some European states (France, Austro-Hungary) and the United States were facing the 1873–1879 long depression, (Fels, 1949) and quite high, during the 1879–1886 period, after the State Independence Wining (1879–1886).

The GDP dynamics decreased during the last three Juglar cycles, as a consequence of the maintenance of blockages in the agrarian relations and implicitly of the important impact of the weather conditions. The economic growth trajectory was convex during 1887–1898 and 1907–1914 time intervals. During 1899–1906,

---

on the economic structure and the degree of development. For example, Bordo and Haubrich (2012) mentioned that in the case of the United States, the respective recession was mild, while Lychachov (2021) revealed that Russia faced a prolonged economic and financial crisis during the 1899–1902 period. Also, a very poor harvest caused a great famine in India during the 1899–1900 time interval (Wakimura, 1996).

[4] The definition of Juglar cycles presented in this paper is different from the definition shown in Pavelescu (2013, 2016), due to different methodological assumptions. In the above-mentioned papers, the analysed period is 1862–1918, and the author considered that a Juglar cycle began with the year when an increase in GDP was registered after a recession. Thus, the following Juglar cycles were identified: (a) 1862–1866, (b) 1867–1876, (c) 1877–1887, (d) 1888–1897, (e) 1898–1907 and (f) 1907–1914–1918 and also the following Kuznets cycles: (a) 1862–1876, (b) 1877–1897 and (c) 1898–1914–1918. The above-mentioned periodization of Romania's economic history during the second part of the nineteenth century has the advantage of correlating some of the Juglar cycles with some social and political events, such as the ample economic and social reforms implemented during the A. I. Cuza's reign (1862–1866) or the great liberal governance (1876–1888). The disadvantage of this periodization is that it was admitted a Juglar cycle which lasted only 5 years.

the respective trajectory was unstable, essentially caused by the ample fluctuations of gross value-added created by the primary sector.

11.4.3 The Estimated Rate of Disembodied Technical Change and the Feature of Economic Growth During the Kuznets Cycles

By merging two Juglar cycles, we can define three Kuznets cycles: (a) 1859–1878, (b) 1879–1898 and (c) 1899–1918. We note that each of the respective cycles lasted 20 years.

Each Kuznets cycle represents a stage of the first Romania's transition to a market economy. Therefore, during the 1859–1878 period, important economic and social reforms and other institutional changes were implemented. We mention as most important the normative acts for the land reform (1864), the education reform (1864), the state general administration (1872), the law for the cancellation of the guides (1873), agricultural credit (1873) and public health (1874). The respective normative acts created conditions for the economic and social modernization in line with the contemporary evolutions from developed European states. At the same time, they have practically broken the ties with the legacy of the Organic Reglement and other types of pre-market economy institutions in the important fields of economic and social activities such as the judicial system, education, administration, public health and organization of the labour market. The reform of land property was limited due to objective and subjective factors. The foreign trade policy was inspired by the free trade doctrine.

During the 1879–1898 Kuznets cycle, the institutional changes aimed to consolidate the institutions and practices designed to sustain the actions of market mechanisms, especially in the framework of non-agricultural activities. Also, the respective changes favoured the modernization of some social services, essential in a modern state (public health, administration, labour law). Therefore, Axenciuc (2005) mentioned that the Parliament adopted acts regarding trade marks (1879), establishment of the National Bank of Romania (1880), commodities and stock exchanges (1881), encouraging the paper industry (1881), forestry code (1881), registration of the firms (1884), encouraging the local entrepreneurs (1887), public accounting (1893), health protection of the unsanitary industries workers (1894), mining activities and especially the oil exploitation (1895), diminish of the patent tax on the professions (1896) and Sunday rest (1897).

In 1886, the government adopted new protectionist customs tariffs. The respective change in the foreign trade policy was generated both by the growing deficit of the foreign trade balance and by the need to create favourable conditions for the activities of local entrepreneurs and the industry development.

Thus, at the end of the nineteenth century, the institutional framework related to non-agricultural activities was compatible with the situation which was operating in the European developed countries. In agriculture, the reminiscences of feudal relations of production were mentioned, for multiple reasons, related to both the political system and the structure of foreign trade. In this context, Romania's economy had many features of a dual economy, in the sense defined by Lewis (1954). The primary sector represented the "traditional sector", which employed about 80% of the active population, while the non-agricultural activities acted as the "modern sector".

The dual economy was also perpetuated during the 1899–1918 Kuznets cycle, in spite of some changes in the normative framework aimed to resolve the social tensions and the blockages in the agriculture development. In 1903 and 1906, the Parliament adopted two acts which established the so-called People's Banks and amended the Rural Credit Act. The respective legislative changes were not effective and could not prevent the extended 1907 peasants' revolt. In April 1908, the Parliament voted the law for the establishment of the Rural House and the law for the diminishing of the size of agricultural land areas, which could be rented out. The respective normative acts aimed to decrease the social tensions in the rural areas.

Other legislative changes have in view the improvement of the economic and social situation of the craftsmen. In 1902 and 1912, the Parliament adopted two laws on organizing the handicrafts, i.e. the credit and the social insurances for the respective category of the employed population.

In 1912, under a conservative government, a new law for the encouragement of the national industry was implemented. The law-makers considered that it was necessary to support not only the manufacturing industry but also the activities which used the agricultural raw materials and those extracted from the national subsoil.

During the three Kuznets cycles of the first Romania's transition to a market economy, the average yearly rate of GDP has sensibly varied. The respective indicator was 2.4% between 1862 and 1878, 3.1% between 1878 and 1898 and 1.4% between 1898 and 1914. The estimation of the behavioural Eq. (11.1) reveals that the economic growth trajectory has changed from one Kuznets cycle to another, being conventional convex, during the 1863–1878 period, conventional concave during the 1897–1898 period and unstable during the 1899–1914 period. The estimated rate of disembodied technical change increases from 0.0268 to 0.0313 and is significant from the Student test point of view in the case of all the considered cycles (Table 11.5). We note that the coefficient of determination size varies considerably, from 0.5180, in the case of the 1899–1914 period, to 0.8108, in the case of the 1879–1898 period.

The addition of a dummy variable related to the recessionist years proved to be effective in explaining the GDP dynamics. The coefficient of determination size has considerably increased and varied from 0.7466, in the case of the 1899–1914 period to 0.8939 in the case of the 1879–1898 period (Table 11.6). In all three cases, the adjusted coefficient of determination in the case of behavioural Eq. (11.2) is higher than in the case of the behavioural Eq. (11.1).

The coefficient of collinear refraction related to the estimated rate of disembodied technical change varied between 0.9634 and 1.0091. Hence, the recessionist situations were a significant factor in explaining the GDP dynamics but they did not

Table 11.5 Indicators of the form of economic growth trajectory and the estimated parameters of the behavioural equation ln GDP = $a_2 + b_2/ \times t$ during the Kuznets cycles of the 1863–1914 period

Indicator	1863–1878	1879–1898	1899–1914
ln (1 + Rav)	0.0241	0.0312	0.0140
ln (1 + Rr)	0.0187	0.0335	0.0121
a_1	−0.0693 (−1.5255)	0.0442 (1.1061)	−0.1633 (−2.094)
b_1	0.0268 (5.7145)	0.0293 (8.7818)	0.0313 (3.8992)
R^2_1	0.6999	0.8108	0.5180
R^2_1adj	0.6785	0.8003	0.4836
Economic growth trajectory	Conventional convex	Conventional concave	Unstable

N. B. The statistics of the Student test are presented in brackets. R^2_1 is the coefficient of determination, R^2_1adj is the adjusted coefficient of determination

Table 11.6 Estimated parameters of the behavioural equation ln GDP = $a_2 + b_2/ \times t$ + Dummy during the Kuznets cycles during the 1863–1914 period

Indicator	1863–1878	1879–1898	1899–1914
a_2	−0.0274 (−0.7036)	0.0911 (2.7295)	−0.08120 (−1.2809)
b_2	0.0187 (6.9083)	0.0335 (10.9074)	0.0121 (5.2014)
Dummy	−0.1118 (2.9814)	−0.1188 (−3.6479)	−0.1931 (−3.4239)
R^2_2	0.8218	0.8939	0.7466
R^2_2adj	0.7944	0.8814	0.7076
dRadj	0.0945	0.0811	0.2240
T_{2t}	0.9694	0.9634	1.0091

N. B. dR^2adj = R^2_2adj−R^2_1adj, T_{2t} is the coefficient of collinear refraction related to the time factor

significantly influence the rate of disembodied technical change. Also, the addition of the dummy variable does not modify the economic growth trajectories initially identified by the behavioural Eq. (11.1).

11.5 Conclusions

The first transition to market was an economic transformation process experienced both by developed countries from Western Europe and North America and from Eastern and Central countries. There were similarities and differences between the two groups of countries. Among the similarities, we remark on the correlation between the above-mentioned transition and the industrial revolution and the extension of the transportation network. The differences are mainly related to the time length of the transition, the intensity and sense of institutional changes and the role of agricultural activities in sustaining economic growth. In the case of Romania, the persistence of feudal reminiscence in the agrarian relationships has a negative impact on the GDP dynamics. The primary sector was the cause of the great majority of the recessions. In this context, the weather conditions continued to have a high impact on the stability of economic growth, even when the non-agricultural activities registered significant development. Also, the features of economic growth changed during the three Kuznets cycles of the analysed period. Therefore, the economic growth trajectory was conventional convex, during the first cycle, conventional concave, during the second cycle, and unstable, during the third cycle. This evolution reveals the erosion of the premises of sustainable economic growth as a consequence of the failure to solve some of the structural economic and social problems, especially the blockages in the agrarian relations. Also, the dual economy was maintained, in spite of the notable development of industry, constructions, infrastructure and commercial services.

References

Axenciuc, V. (coord.). (2005). *Legiferarea si instituționalizarea economiei moderne în România (1856–1914) (Enactment and institutionalization of modern economy in Romania)*. Editura Expert (Expert publishing house).

Axenciuc, V., & Georgescu, G. (2017). *Romania's gross domestic product and national income 1862–2010. Secular statistical series and methodological foundations*. Editura Academiei Române (Romanian Academy Publishing House).

Bordo, M., & Haubrich, J. (2012). *Deep recessions, fast recoveries and financial crises: Evidence from the American record*. Working Paper no. 18194, National Bureau of Economic Research.

Constantinescu, N. N. (1991). *Acumularea primitivă a capitalului în România (The primitive capital accumulation in Romania)*. Editura Academiei Române (Romanian Academy Publishing House).

Fels, R. (1949). The long-wave depression, 1873-97. *The Review of Economics and Statistics, 31*(1).

Grigoraș, V., & Orțan, D. (2020). *Romania in the loop: An analysis of 155 years of business cycles in historical perspective*. Occasional Papers no. 30, National Bank of Romania.

Juglar, C. (1862). *Des crises commerciales et leurs retours en France*. Angleterre et aux Etat Unies, Gullamain, Paris.

Kitchin, J. (1923). Cycles and trends in economic factors. *Review of Economics and Statistics, 5*(1).

Kuznets, S. (1973). Modern economic growth: Findings and reflections. *The American Economic Review, 63*(3).

Lewis, A. W. (1954). Economic development with unlimited supply of labour. *Manchester School of Economic and Social Studies, 22*, 139–199.

Lychakov, N. (2021). The distributional effect of a financial crisis: Russia 1899–1905. *Scandinavian Economic History Review, 69*, 2.

Pătrășcanu, L. (1969). *Un veac de frământări sociale, 1821–1907 (A century of social unrest, 1821–1907)*. Editura Politică (Political Publishing House).

Pavelescu, F. M. (1986). *Considerations regarding the significance of Cobb-Douglas estimated parameters. A new approach*. Revue Roumaine des Sciences Sociales, Series Sciences Economiques no. 1-2.

Pavelescu, F. M. (2013). Some considerations regarding the economic cycles in Romania during the 1859-2010 period. *Romanian Journal of Economics, 36*(1), 45.

Pavelescu, F. M. (2016). Dinamica macroeconomică a României în cursul celor două tranziții la economia de piață (Romania's macroeconomic dynamics during the two transitions to market economy). In *Studii de istorie economică și istorie a gândirii economice (Studies of economic history and of history of economic thinking), Volume XVIII*. Editura Academiei Române (Romanian Academy Printing House).

Postolache, T. (1991). *Pentru elaborarea teoretică a tranziției la economia de piață în context est- și general European (For the theoretical elaboration of the transition to market economy in east- and general European context)*. Conferința Tranziția la economia de piață și cercetarea economică (Conference Transition tos market economy and economic research). Analele Institutului Național de Cercetări Economice (Annals of National Institute for Economic Research) no. 4–5.

Sellers, C. (1991). *The market revolution: Jacksonian America, 1815–1846*. Oxford University Press.

Stokes, M., & Conway, S. (Eds.). (1996). *The market revolution in America. Social, political and religious expressions 1800-1880*. University of Virginia.

Wakimura, K. (1996). Famines, epidemics and mortality in Northern India, 1870-1921. In P. Robb, K. Sugihara, & H. Yanagisawa (Eds.), *Local agrarian societies in colonial India: Japanese perspectives*. Routledge.

Zeletin, S. (1925). *Burghezia română. Originea și rolul ei istoric (Romanian bourgeois. Its origin and historical role)*. Editura Cultura Națională (National Culture Publishing House).

Chapter 12
R&D Expenditure – Conditioning Factor of Increasing Competitiveness – Indicators and Trends

Alexandra-Ioana Lazăr and Adela-Simona Vlășceanu

Abstract The availability of the financial resources necessary for intensive and lasting support of the innovation process is one of the indispensable conditions for increasing competitiveness. Considering the high technical progress, a high level of R&D expenditures must also be taken into account because only with such a level can the maintenance of technological competitiveness be ensured, a reality confirmed by the electronic and electrotechnical industry.

The existence of strong request directs R&D activities toward the realization of the innovations, necessary to satisfy it. In this context, the innovation process becomes only the technology bearer and the allocation of resources becomes a sine qua noncondition for the application of the most efficient technologies.

Keywords R&D sector · Expenditures · Competitiveness

12.1 Introduction

Currently, economic science attaches great importance to the R&D sector considered to be the main motor of competitiveness and economic growth.

In a highly competitive economy where maintaining and increasing competitiveness are imperative, it is worth emphasizing the idea that the impact of R&D activities on the future development of the economy is essential, which will encourage the development of innovative products and services. The ability to adapt to the new

A.-I. Lazăr (✉)
National Institute for Economic Research "Costin C. Kirițescu", Bucharest, Romania
e-mail: alexandra.lazar@ince.ro

A.-S. Vlășceanu
School of Advanced Studies of the Romanian Academy, Bucharest, Romania
e-mail: simona@acad.ro

© The Author(s), under exclusive license to Springer Nature Switzerland AG 2024
L. Chivu et al. (eds.), *Constraints and Opportunities in Shaping the Future: New Approaches to Economics and Policy Making*, Springer Proceedings in Business and Economics, https://doi.org/10.1007/978-3-031-47925-0_12

realities depends, to a decisive extent, on investments in R&D, which play a decisive role in this context.

In addition to the benefits brought to consumers, innovation also plays a key role in creating jobs, an ecological society, and improving the quality of life.

Against the background of these ideas, the main objectives pursued were highlighting the contribution of R&D investments to increasing competitiveness and reviewing the main research and development indicators and their trends.

The growing importance of R&D activities, an essential pillar of the development and increase in the competitiveness of an economy in the contemporary world, is convincingly illustrated by the fact that a good part of the world's countries, especially the developed ones, have made the intense stimulation of these activities a primary coordinate of their development strategy.

12.2 Literature Review

Numerous papers highlight the key role of R&D in increasing productivity as a measure of competitiveness (Fernando, 2020). Although there are notable differences between European countries, R&D expenditures seem to be the key factor that determines their innovation potential and performance (Hunady et al., 2017).

The most affected countries were those that are among the new members of the European community, especially the countries of central and eastern Europe (Filippetti & Achibugi, 2011).

R&D activities are fundamental to the competitiveness of knowledge-based economies, and investment in them must be a policy measure (Szarowska, 2017). A precise view of the importance of R&D can be rendered by addressing the main indicators – R&D expenditure, employees with higher education, ICT expenditure, innovative products sold, etc., which will provide a real assessment and a better understanding of the existing constraints (Taques et al., 2021).

12.3 Analysis of R&D Activities

The study of the European Commission European Innovation Scoreboard 2021 (European Commission, 2021) highlights that the share in GDP of expenses for R&D activities registered in the public sector in the European Union and China was increasing in 2021, compared to 2020, while in the public sector in the USA and Australia, the same share was recorded, a situation represented graphically in the following figure.

R&D expenditure recorded in the European public sector increased, as a share of GDP, from 2019 to 2021, by 0.04 and 0.02% points, and in the business sector by 0.01 and 0.006.

In both the EU and Australia, the share of GDP spent on R&D activities in the public sector is greater than that of business sector expenditure. Although, in the Australian public sector, the share of R&D expenditure in GDP recorded the same value in the period 2020–2021, Fig. 12.1 reveals the existence of differences of 0.21% points in 2020 and 0.19% points in 2021, compared to the European public sector, which in the same period registered an increase in expenses.

A possible explanation for the lower share would be the reduced investments from some member countries, the method of allocating them, but also the lack of a reform aimed at increasing the quality of the public sector through a rigorous evaluation.

It can also be observed that in 2021, in China and the USA, R&D expenditures recorded in the business environment sector, as a share of GDP, were 0.10 and 0.26% points higher, respectively, than those recorded in sector of the European business environment, which could provide an explanation for the reduced capacity of the European Union to develop enterprises with intensive R&D activity based on technological and scientific advances. In this context, conducting an elaborate analysis of the evolution of R&D expenditures recorded in the two sectors is imperatively necessary. The statistical data presented refer to a sample of 22 European countries, according to the following two figures:

According to Fig. 12.2, in 2021, the highest shares in GDP of R&D expenses in the business environment sector were recorded in Sweden, Austria, and Germany, 8.71, 7.96 and 7.82 times more higher than the share achieved by Romania, which registered a decrease of 0.02% points compared to 2020 and ranked penultimate among the countries presented.

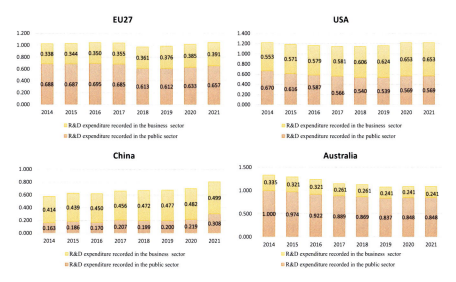

Fig. 12.1 R&D expenditure by EU, USA, China, and Australia funding sources, 2014–2021 (% of GDP). (Source: European Innovation Scoreboard 2021, https://ec.europa.eu/docsroom/documents/46013)

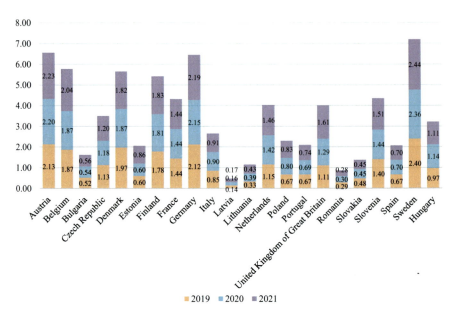

Fig. 12.2 R&D expenditure recorded in the business sector, from some European countries, 2019–2021 (% of GDP). (Source: Eurostat, https://ec.europa.eu/eurostat/databrowser/view/tsc00001/default/table?lang=en)

Regarding the share of the public sector in the financing of R&D activities, according to Fig. 12.3, Romania ranks last, recording the same value as in 2020 and 5.35 times lower than the share recorded by Denmark, which ranks first place among the countries presented.

In conclusion, we can say that in Romania the financing provided by the business and public sector has remained derisory, at half of that achieved by Bulgaria and Slovakia, respectively, which has determined a reduced innovative capacity and modest results. Given the existence of an economic environment that is not favorable for R&D activities and the limited availability of resources allocated to these activities, the prospects for reducing the gaps compared to the developed countries of the European Union are bleak.

An important aspect regarding R&D activities is the high share of highly qualified and educated workforce. The statistical data refer to the number of people with tertiary training and doctoral studies in Science, Technology, Engineering and Mathematics – STEM (see the following figures).

According to the data in Fig. 12.4, the share of the number of graduates of doctoral studies increased in the USA and Japan, in 2021, by 0.01% points, compared to 2020, and in the EU and Russia, it decreased by 0.10 and 0.22% points, while in Australia the share remained the same. A possible explanation for the weight that has fallen in the EU would be the lack of professional opportunities in some member countries, the inadequate salary in the R&D sector, and the lack of other funding

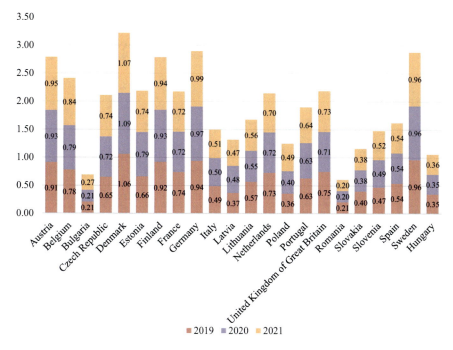

Fig. 12.3 R&D expenditure recorded in the public sector, from some European countries, 2019–2021 (% of GDP). (Source: Eurostat, https://ec.europa.eu/eurostat/databrowser/view/tsc00001/default/table?lang=en)

resources that lead them to go to fields other than those for which they are prepared or to emigrate to other countries (Fig. 12.5).

In 2021, the lowest share of the number of doctoral graduates was registered in Latvia, Poland, and Romania, ranking last among the European countries presented (Fig. 12.6).

The United Kingdom and Spain took the first place, which recorded a weight eight times and 6.5 times higher than that recorded by Romania, respectively.

Regarding the share of the number of people with tertiary education, according to Fig 12.5, in 2021, the largest shares were registered in Russia, Japan, and Australia.

An important effect of R&D activities is that of obtaining patents for inventions. Inventions are protected in Europe by national patents granted by the competent national authorities or by the EPO at the European level.

Patent applications at the European Patent Office (EPO) refer to those for the protection of an invention addressed directly to the European Patent Office (EPO) or filed in accordance with the Treaty on Cooperation in the Field of Patents and the Designation of the EPO (Euro-PCT).

In the European Union, according to the European Innovation Scoreboard 2021, the share of the number of patent applications was, in 2021, 2.96% in GDP/

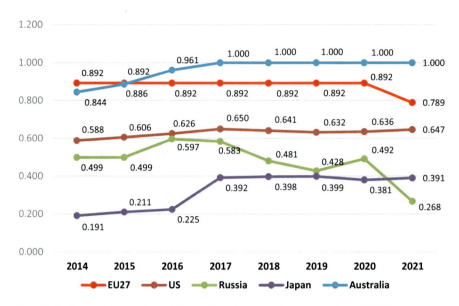

Fig. 12.4 Share of the number of doctoral graduates in the total number of R&D employees, 2014–2021 (%). (Source: European Innovation Scoreboard 2021, https://ec.europa.eu/docsroom/documents/46013)

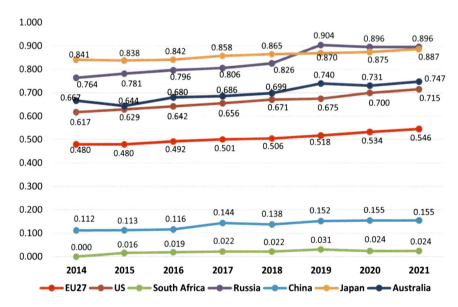

Fig. 12.5 Share of the number of graduates of the tertiary education system, in the total number of people between 25 and 34 years old, 2014–2021 (%). (Source: European Innovation Scoreboard 2021, https://ec.europa.eu/docsroom/documents/46013)

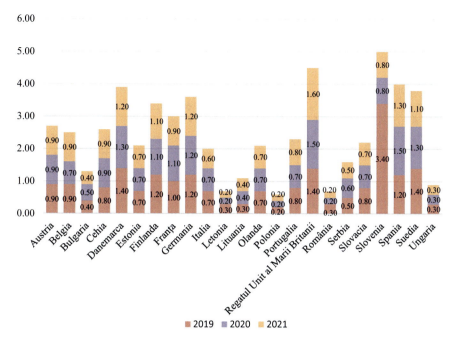

Fig. 12.6 Share of the number of graduates with doctoral studies, in the total number of R&D employees, in some European countries 2019–2021 (%). (Source: European Innovation Scoreboard 2021, https://ec.europa.eu/docsroom/documents/46013)

inhabitant. Among the member countries, Sweden had the highest share of the number of requests (8.92), followed by Finland (7.55), Germany (6.18), and Denmark (5.84). Romania is in last place, registering in 2021 (0.19), with 0.05% points less than in 2020.

As far as Romania is concerned, possible explanations for the low percentage would be the precarious managerial framework, the lack of strategic visions, indispensable for the development and application of modernization/re-technological programs, and the lack of capacity to identify and follow the most effective ways to stimulate creativity.

Currently, companies cannot successfully face the economic competition if they do not provide the necessary managerial framework for the operative adaptation of production to the constantly changing demands of the market. Also, they must consider the modernization and development of their product portfolio and the introduction of advanced technological processes and efficient management systems.

12.4 Analysis/Result Interpretation

The significant differences existing between the performances of the R&D system in Romania and the situation at the level of the European Union average underline the imperative requirement of revitalizing the system and the establishment of a coherent policy should take into account the following: the very low share of expenses for R&D, which requires the intensification of access to European structural funds and of investments; the excessive fragmentation of the system, in relation to the obtained performances, prevents reaching the critical mass necessary to achieve higher performances; the lack of long-term strategic vision significantly diminishes the role of R&D activities in creating high added value; the poor performance of the system in terms of the number of patent applications, granted patents, scientific publications abroad, and patent applications; the exodus of researchers abroad to other activities; the lack of prioritization in R&D activities of projects that can be financed by the business environment, more precisely those projects that correspond to its real needs; the extremely low funding of R&D activities by the business environment; and the lack of industrial policy to ensure the connection of scientific research, technological development, innovation, and industrial activity, and to strengthen cooperation between institutions and companies.

In the context of the developments of the R&D system in our country and the conclusions drawn, we appreciate that the orientation of the policy should be based on the following coordinates: the establishment of a strategy that outlines the priority directions for the concentration of efforts and conditions for achievement (allocated resources, expected results, responsibilities, deadlines) followed consistently over a long period of time, regardless of the alternations in government and intensifying the integration of universities and research institutions in scientific and technological collaboration projects.

References

European Commission (2021). European Innovation Scoreboard. Retrieved from https://op.europa.eu/en

Fernando, I. N. (2020). Tourism competitiveness by shift-share analysis to way-forward destination management: A case study for Sri Lanka. *Journal of Tourism and Services, 21*(11), 88–102. Retrieved from https://doi.org/10.29036/jots.v11i21.139

Filippetti, A., & Archibugi, D. (2011). Innovation in times of crisis: National systems of innovation, structure, and demand. *Research Policy, 40*(2), 179–192.

Hunady, J., Pisar, P., Musa, H., & Musova, Z. (2017). Innovation support and economic development at the regional level: Panel data evidence from Visegrad countries. *Journal of International Studies, 10*(3), 147–160. Retrieved from https://doi.org/10.14254/2071-8330.2017/10-3/11

Szarowska, I. (2017). Does public R&D expenditure matter for economic growth? GMM approach. *Journal of International Studies, 10*(2), 90–103. Retrieved from https://doi.org/10.14254/2071-8330.2017/10-2/6

Taques, F. H., López, G. M., Bassoc, F. L., & Areal, N. (2021). Indicators used to measure service innovation and manufacturing innovation. *Journal of Innovation & Knowledge, 6*(2021), 11–26.

Chapter 13
The Impact of Digitalization on the NUTS-2 Regions in Romania

Daniela Antonescu and **Ioana Cristina Florescu**

Abstract Digitalization represents a key element for the development of today's society. After the COVID-19 pandemic, it has become one of the community priorities that open up new opportunities for businesses and consumers, new horizons for relations with other economic areas worldwide, supporting the green transition and climate neutrality until 2050. Romania's National Recovery and Resilience Plan (NRRP) aims to ensure an optimal balance between national and European Union priorities in the context of recovery after this crisis. Regarding the regional approach, it can help increase the level of economic and social development and reduce territorial inequalities.

The article's main objective is to identify the relationship between e-commerce and broadband infrastructure, both indicators specific to the digitalization process, and regional GDP, using as an instrument of analysis econometric modeling through a panel model. All of the indicators contain data for the eight development regions in Romania.

The results of the research showed that chosen independent variables have a significant impact upon the dependent in Romania, for the 2010–2021 timeframe.

Keywords Recovery and resilience facility · COVID-19 pandemic · Digitalization · GDP per capita · e-commerce · Broadband infrastructure

13.1 Introduction

Each major crisis, such as the coronavirus pandemic (COVID-19), offers opportunities for rethinking national systems, resilience, and recovery. To support these opportunities, an instrument called the Recovery and Resilience Facility was

---

D. Antonescu (✉) · I. C. Florescu
Institute of National Economy, Romanian Academy, Bucharest, Romania

© The Author(s), under exclusive license to Springer Nature Switzerland AG 2024
L. Chivu et al. (eds.), *Constraints and Opportunities in Shaping the Future: New Approaches to Economics and Policy Making*, Springer Proceedings in Business and Economics, https://doi.org/10.1007/978-3-031-47925-0_13

devised at the EU level, which aims to support the economies of member states affected by the health crisis and to support the reforms and investments they propose. In this respect, 723.8 billion euro (current prices) (385.8 billion euro in loans and 338 billion euro in grants) have been allocated to mitigate the economic and social impact of the coronavirus pandemic, to make them more sustainable and resilient to the challenges and opportunities resulting from the green and digital transition.

The mechanism of this facility contributes to the sustainable recovery of member states that went through the COVID-19 pandemic crisis.

The Resilience and Recovery Facility (RRF) launched by the European Commission promotes the economic, social, and territorial cohesion of the union through the following actions:

1. Improving resilience, preparedness for crisis situations
2. Increasing the adaptation capacity and growth potential of the member states by mitigating the social and economic impact of the crisis in question, in particular on women (EUR-Lex, 2022a, b)
3. Implementing the European Pillar of Social Rights by supporting the green transition and digital transformation
4. Restoring and promoting sustainable growth and integrating the union's economies by creating high-quality jobs, contributing to strategic autonomy, and creating new added value

In Romania, the strategic aim of NRRP is to represent economic and social development through the implementation of essential programs and projects, which support resilience and prevent crisis situations, adaptation capacity, and growth potential, through major reforms and key investments from the funds allocated through the RRF.

Smart specialization (European Commission, 2022d) is a unique opportunity in developing contemporary innovation policies and supporting territorial development. European Commission supports the amplification of smart specialization process at the level of the member states, including at the regional level, through the funds for Facility of Recovery and Resilience.

For the 2021–2027 programming period, the financial instruments regarding recovery and resilience sustain important fields in actual context and provide the funds for five main policy areas: more smart, green, social, connected, and closer to citizens. Also, the smart specialization will play an important and strategic role for the regional development process and long-term adaptation. In this context, the smart specialization also offers huge potential for developing eco-innovation processes to meet challenges at the global environmental level.

13.2 Literature Review

The public investment included in the National Recovery and Resilience Facility has the potential to generate new jobs and ensure economic recovery in the current global context. This potential is closely linked to the strategic importance of the funded infrastructure and to the development of other adjacent sectors. This includes investments in public infrastructure, transport, energy, water management, social, and educational infrastructure. Also, supporting businesses and fostering their development in conjunction with the climate and digital transition and getting closer to the research environment are another dimension that gives potential for strengthening economic resilience.

Investments must be accompanied by reforms that can generate significant systemic and institutional changes at the national level. Thus, the reforms on the digitalization of public services, the implementation of the government cloud, monitoring the impact of legislative and budgetary changes and preventing and combating fraud, reforming the pension system in order to ensure its sustainability, minimum income, legislative systematization in the field of construction and urban mobility, and the principles of corporate governance are elements that give potential for structural changes and modernization of the state and public services offered, focusing on digitalization, simplification, and predictability in processes.

The investments and reforms financed by National and Recovery Resilience Facility funds must achieve 20% of the digitalization and 37% of the climate change pillars. The digital component of the facility represents opportunities for the projects formulated in the urban development strategies.

The digital transition represents an essential part of the Facility of Recovery and Resilience, at EU level, with proposed budget approximatively of 8.2 billion euro.

Actual Digital Agenda (European Commission, 2022a, b, c) aims to reform and reconstruct the strategic capacities and facilitate the development of digital technologies (e.g., AI-based applications and cybersecurity tools). The overall objective of the program is to grow the performance and the competitiveness at EU level through the resilience and recovery. Also, it will provide funds for projects in key areas such as supercomputing (2.4 billion euro), artificial intelligence (2.2 billion euro), cybersecurity (1.8 billion euro), and advanced digital skills (600 million euro) and promote a wide use of digital technologies at all levels of the economy and society (1.2 billion). From this perspective, the funds will target the health services, security, environmental protection, training in advanced digital skills for the workforce and students, SME-s, and public administrations.

The European Digital Innovation Hubs (European Commission, 2022b) will play a central role in the actual programming period. The centers will be a crossroads where industry, businesses, and administrations looking for new technology solutions will meet on the one hand and companies that can offer ready-to-market solutions on the other hand. Being spread over a wide geographical area in Europe, the centers will play a key role in the implementation of the program.

After the sanitary crisis, Europe will be greener, more resilient, and better prepared to face current and future challenges. Furthermore, the Recovery and Resilience Facility will support Romania's fulfillment of the enabling conditions "good governance of the national or regional smart specialization strategy" (The Ministry of Research, Innovation and Digitalization, 2022). Also, it will support strengthening the CDI capacities and the new and advanced technologies, the digitalization processes for citizens/companies and public administration, competitiveness of SMEs, digitalization, and so on.

The Recovery and Resilience Facility represents an important part NextGenerationEU instrument (total funds—672.5 billion of loans and grants—destined to sustain the investments and reforms. The main objective is to diminish the pandemic crisis' impact on a socio-economic development level at member state level. Also, it will contribute to resilience and recovery process and prepare for the new opportunity results from the Green transition and the Digital transformation and journal articles. Most of the sources should be provided from scientific articles.

13.3 Methodology

The panel analysis used in the article is based on a multifactorial regression model in which broadband infrastructure (%) and e-commerce (%) represent independent variables and the GDP value per capita (euro/inhabitant), the dependent one, aiming to estimate the impact of endogenous variables on exogenous at the level of the NUTS 2 regions in Romania, for the programming period 2010–2021. The data were taken from Eurostat. The dependency modeling is presented in the following equation:

$$yt = c + a_1 \times x_1 t + a_2 \times x_2 t + \varepsilon t,$$

where

yt = the endogenous variable Y, in our case GDP per capita chosen for the model.
$a_1, a_2,$ = the coefficients of the exogenous variables chosen for the model.
c = the constant of the regression equation.
$x_1 t, x_2 t,$ = independent variables X_1 and X_2, in our case broadband and online commerce.
$t = 2010, ..., 2021.$
εt = the residual variable.

For a better identification of the most appropriate regression analysis method, the OLS, OLS fixed-effects (FE), and OLS random-effects (RE) models were compared using the Akaike information criterion (AIC), the coefficient of determination, R_2, root-mean-square error (RMSE), and the Hausman test.

Following the selection of the optimal model, the results were discussed and the heterogeneity at regional level was analyzed, and the conclusions derived from this analysis will be presented.

13.4 Analysis/Result Interpretation

Following the application of the OLS method, the validity of the regression model is indicated by the probability (f-statistical) that has the value of 0.0000. This means that the model is valid and has coefficients other than zero.

According to R_2, the influence of endogenous variables on the exogenous one is only 42%, the probability of the e-commerce index is below the 5% threshold, and the broadband indicator is 0.24 > 0.05. In this context, this model does not explain well the correlation between variables. Next, we try to use the different types of econometric models:

(a) Random-effects panel (RE)
(b) Fixed-effects panel (FE)

The equation for the OLS model is:

$$GDP\_PER\_CAPITA = 64,00942 \times BROADBAND + 377,7075 \times E-COMMERCE + 6485,240 + \varepsilon_i$$

In the case of the random-effects OLS model, the estimation identifies e-commerce as having a significant positive effect on GDP per capita, as the Student t-test value is higher than 3 ($p = 0.00000$), thus demonstrating a direct and positive relationship between GDP per capita and online commerce (a 1% increase in e-commerce influenced growth of GDP per capita with 247.13 euros). The probabilities of the indicator coefficients are all below the threshold of 0.05, the model is statistically valid, and the value of the significance test F is 0.00.

The influence of broadband Internet infrastructure is positive and worth 32.567 euros per capita. The R_2 has a value of 0.761754, which is almost double the value of the OLS.

The equation of the random-effects model is:

$$GDP\_PER\_CAPITA = 32,5671650702 \times BROADBAND + 247,134798226 \times E-COMMERCE + 10589,9047142$$

It was then tested whether the random-effects panel model was appropriate using the Hausman test and determined the H0 assumptions: The model with RE is appropriate and H1: The model with FE is appropriate. Because the probability of the Chi-sq (46.87) statistics was zero, the alternative hypothesis H1 was accepted.

In the case of the panel model with EF, the broadband Internet infrastructure and e-commerce, as in the previous case, have a significant positive effect on GDP per capita. At a 1% increase in online trade, GDP per capita will increase by 192.76 euros per inhabitant.

Broadband Internet infrastructure also has a significantly positive relationship with GDP per capita, with a positive impact of EUR 39.04 per capita and EUR 39.04 per capita.

All estimates are statistically significant at threshold levels of 0.1, 0.05, and 0.01, with the probability of broadband coefficients, online commerce, and constant c being 0.0000.

The overall result of the FE model was very good, with independent variables explaining a significant part of the dependent variable variance (as corrected R_2 shows (0.96). The statistical F-test showed that the model is valid and statistically significant (Prob (F-statistic) = 0.0000). The coefficient of determination R_2 has the value of 0.9644 for the fixed-effect models, which indicates that the variation of the dependent variable is expressed by the two repressors at a rate of 96.44%.

The final equation of the model with FE is as follows:

$$GDP\_PER\_CAPITA = 39,0437564071 \times BROADBAND + 192,762233534 \times E-COMMERCE + 11048,9379175$$

The results show a direct correlation between the variables of digitalization process at the development level of the regions, and the important influence of broadband Internet infrastructure and e-commerce on GDP per capita. The result shows that any increase in the exogenous variables will conduct to an increase in the endogenous one.

The fixed-effects model allowed the identification of regional heterogeneity; thus, by calculating longitudinal effects, the free terms for the eight development regions considered. Could be determined, taking into account that the slope is the same.

Thus, from the point of view of the free term, the Bucharest-Ilfov region ranked first, the free term being 29,594 euro per capita, because this region is the most developed of Romania.

The second place went to the West Region, which registered the fastest growth in the period 2010–2021 with a free term of 11,459 euros per capita. The third place was the Central region, the third region of the country in terms of development, which is also reflected in the free term, 9727 euros per capita. This is followed by the Northwest regions with 8690 euros per capita, Southeast with 8830 euros per capita, South Muntenia with 7859 euros per capita, Southwest with 7013 euros per capita, and the last, Northeast, with 5218 euros per capita.

The coefficient of variation of the eight free regional terms is 69.84%, which led to the idea that there is a high regional heterogeneity.

In case of the elimination of Bucharest-Ilfov region, a lower coefficient of variation was obtained, with a value of 23.7%. This demonstrated that between the development regions in Romania, relatively low inequalities in digitalization were maintained during the analyzed period, the situation changing significantly when the Bucharest-Ilfov region is taken into account.

13.5 Conclusions

From the analysis of the developments in the pre-pandemic period, but also those during the pandemic period, we find that although Romania is still in the last places regarding the evolution of the selected indicators (broadband connectivity) both at the level of enterprises and at the level of households, the trend is of constant growth, and the new framework established by the National Recovery and Resilience Plan contains a rather solid component in terms of capitalizing on the financing sources specified by it, although the selected objectives are relatively modest compared to those in the other member states (European Union, 2022).

National strategies aimed at digitalization have attracted increased interest both from public and private stakeholders, but also from the general public, which has led to an activation of companies by showing an increased interest in introducing digital solutions. The analysis conducted by the Digital Future Index (Microsoft) showed that there are competitive advantages, such as the high number of young people with skills for developing solutions in the digital field, but which it is necessary to develop new policies to preserve these talents in the country, if we take into account that a considerable part of them choose to carry out their career abroad.

The acceleration in the IT services industry is currently 6.2% of GDP, outpacing developments in the national economy, and the interest is increasing, including at the level of development regions. An eloquent example, an argument for the dynamics and potential of implementing digital, innovative solutions is also the fact that one of the most disadvantaged regions, the North-East Region, has been involved in a bottom-up initiative, with the support of the North-East Regional Development Agency since 2019, through which a hub called Digital Innovation Zone was established by involving interested actors from the public and private sphere. The stated goals are to provide integrated digital services for SMEs and public institutions of digital, financial type, including advanced technological products, such as AI with particular application in the production of goods and for the provision of health services such as telemedicine and e-health. The econometric analysis shows a direct correlation of the specific variables. The equations of the model showed the direct and positive link between broadband infrastructure and online trade with GDP per capita, proving that any growth among independent variables will lead to growth among dependent variables, thus indicating a strong influence on the implementation of digitalization at regional level. The value of the coefficients thus demonstrates that with the increase in online trade by one percentage point, GDP per capita will increase by 192.76 euro/inhabitant. Also, the infrastructure of the broadband has a significant and positive relationship with regional GDP per capita and the influence is also positive (39.04 euro per capita). The high value of R_2 (0.96) shows a very strong influence on the two endogenous variables on the exogenous.

These findings have led to the inclusion in the Romanian Resilience and Recovery Facility of some provisions for the implementation of reforms and investments for the training of advanced digital skills for public sector employees, but also for the grant schemes for employees in enterprises that need improvement or retraining. In parallel, other schemes are foreseen for training new cybersecurity skills or for transforming libraries into training centers (hubs) for basic skills.

References

EUR-lex. (2022a). *EU recovery and resilience facility*. Retrieved from https://eur-lex.europa.eu/EN/legal-content/summary/eu-recovery-and-resilience-facility.html

EUR-lex. (2022b). *Opinion of the European Committee of the regions on 'European regional development fund and cohesion fund*. Retrieved from https://eur-lex.europa.eu/legal-content/EN/TXT/?uri=CELEX%3A52018AR3594&qid=1648377169475

European Commission. (2022a). *The digital Europe programme*. Retrieved from https://digital-strategy.ec.europa.eu/en/activities/digital-programme

European Commission. (2022b). *European digital innovation hubs*. Retrieved from https://digital-strategy.ec.europa.eu/en/activities/edihs

European Commission. (2022c). *Recovery and resilience facility*. Retrieved from https://economy-finance.ec.europa.eu/eueconomyexplained/recovery-and-resilience-facility_en

European Commission. (2022d). *What is smart specialization?*. Retrieved from https://s3platform.jrc.ec.europa.eu/what-we-do

European Union. (2022). *NextGenerationEU*. Retrieved from https://next-generation-eu.europa.eu/index_en

The Ministry of Research, Innovation and Digitalization. (2022). *Strategia Națională de Cercetare, Inovare și Specializare Inteligentă 2022–2027*. Retrieved from https://www.poc.research.gov.ro/uploads/2021-2027/conditie-favorizanta/sncisi_19-iulie.pdf

Chapter 14
Citizen Participation, Good Governance, and ICT Nexus for the Sustainability of Smart Cities

Kriselda Sulcaj Gura ⓘ, Fatmir Guri ⓘ, Servet Gura ⓘ, and Elda Dollija ⓘ

Abstract Smart cities use information and information technology to optimize the decision-making process for the enhancement of life quality. In the concept of smart cities, the sustainability approach for the sake of better citizen participation and effective governance has been incorporated. The contextualized framework is a synthesis of the debate, which relies on the integrated data exchange of the interplay between the following relationships: Smart cities need good governance to be sustainable, good governance needs citizen engagement to be effective, and Information and Communication Technology (ICT) is the main mediator of this nexus. Based on the systematic literature review, the main solution to the debate has been placed the digital citizen participation. Based on this, the focus of this work is to see how government uses its mechanisms to create value for citizens taking into consideration the fact that nowadays technological advancement is being a priority. To elaborate this, it raises questions like what kind of relationship fosters the sustainability of smart cities and how can technology contribute to that; how government deploys ICT to create and/or constrain opportunities for citizens in the decision-making processes; what are the similarities and/or difference in participation between urban and rural areas; and finally, what is the difference in the planning and implementation process. The main result of the research is that the sustainability of smart cities requires accountability measures by the governance and not necessarily to become active themselves. It is derived from the special importance of the clear participatory frame for the citizen, and the main recommendation derived is the special consideration to the context-dependent factors in the smart city.

K. S. Gura (✉) · E. Dollija
Beder University College, Tirana, Albania
e-mail: kgura@beder.edu.al; edollija@beder.edu.al

F. Guri
Agricultural University of Tirana, Tirana, Albania
e-mail: fatmirguri@ubt.edu.al

S. Gura
University of Tirana, Tirana, Albania
e-mail: Servet.Gura@kshk.gov.al

© The Author(s), under exclusive license to Springer Nature Switzerland AG 2024
L. Chivu et al. (eds.), *Constraints and Opportunities in Shaping the Future: New Approaches to Economics and Policy Making,* Springer Proceedings in Business and Economics, https://doi.org/10.1007/978-3-031-47925-0_14

Keywords Smart city · Good governance · Citizen participation · ICT · Sustainability

14.1 Introduction

In the last two decades, technology-based solutions to urban challenges have become one of the most popular strategies used by municipal administrations around the world (Allen et al., 2020). In this context, the concept of a smart city serves as inspiration for the creation of policies that enhance society and, as a result, the quality of life for inhabitants (Meijer et al., 2016). Since 2010, the idea of the "smart city" has repeatedly appeared in various studies, and despite having various definitions, the most frequently used definition in the studies goes under the scope to describe a city's technological prowess (Han & Kim, 2021).

The main result of ongoing urbanization efforts and the burgeoning urban population has been the evolvement of smart cities (Chourabi et al., 2012). In concent most of the works refer to the foundation of smart cities as a mix of data and human behavior which supported by proper technological infrastructure, result in an economic growth lowered inequality and raised living standard for the citizens (Capdevila & Zarlenga, 2015).

Before discussing how citizens might be involved in smart cities, it is important to comprehend several factors that directly affect the evolution of smart city concept. Among these factors, we want to emphasize how the simple "governance" has changed through time to become that of "Smart Governance". Lynn et al. (2000) proclaim that traditionally, governance has been thought of as the intersection of set of laws, administrative procedures and regulations, and judicial bodies that make up the framework for the authorized governmental practices. Odendaal (2003) relates "governance" mostly with the local authorities and describes how they manage territories to promote expansion, resource allocation, and efficient management in relation to stakeholders involved in it. It somehow limits the function of the governance of public institutions to properly operate and comply with the rules, which obviously does not integrate the technological infrastructure and most importantly public involvement. From its origin, the term "smart" is used to describe these two sizable groups' incorporation of it. When society participates and uses technology to its advantage, a higher standard of living is achievable because the needs come from society rather than from governing structures. Razagui and Finger (2018) present as the main solution the use of information and communication technologies (ICTs) for the implementation of smart governance in its proper conceptualization form.

To address this challenge, smart city appears as e-conglomerate of stakeholders starting from individual, civil society, businesses, organizations, associations, and public administration cooperating with each other for sustainable development goals fulfillment and increase in standard of living, which is considered nowadays as the best form of governance models. This development tends to combine citizens' wants and needs with digital solutions (Abella et al., 2017). In this scope, the body of literature is folded into two main channels. There is a group of research that approaches the smart cities from technological point of view. Jin et al. (2014) and Zanella (2014) present the enhanced service provision and quality management of resources where both managerial parties and citizens actively access the real-time data available through the technological improvements. Perera (2014) adds to the context of the private sector improvements, and Hienerth et al. (2011) explore the ways how citizens may be engaged in business practices and processes.

From the other side, research highlights other dimensions of the smart cities. Abella et al. (2015) emphasize the contribution of such technological development in innovative service delivery to citizens; Perera et al. (2014) emphasize the managerial efficiency; Angelidou (2014) approach it based on interdisciplinary inclusion and diverging stakeholder's interests; and Lombardi (2012) connects with the triple helix for knowledge production but neglects the citizens on it.

Cleland (2018) places citizens as the main drivers of the governance practices in smart cities for the development of policies and services. In the same vein goes also Lee and Lee (2014) who propose a citizen-centered typology to be developed by the urbanists and planers based on the user's perspectives. Linders (2012) also considers citizens as partners rather than consumers in the public services and highlights the fact that they must gain empowerment in this regard. Baesens et al. (2016) and Martens (2016) show how the use of big data can provide better performance to public administrators and business managers and at the same time offer the possibility of active participation of citizens.

Despite those valuable contributions, the potential contribution of citizens in better solving and addressing complex governance issues in smart cities is still vague. Although there are some attempts, they are fragmented. Lokers et al. (2016) indicate the complexity of dealing with heterogeneous data of this nature and the absence of trust between the data providers and data users, and Mergel et al. (2016) review the methodological and practical complications in collecting and using those data. Smart city is a multi-agent ecosystem which incorporates all the stakeholders through the technological infrastructure (Angelidou, 2015), and Meijer (2015) considers the citizens as co-producers of the governance. Based on the interplay between good governance, information and telecommunication technology, and citizen participation, this work tries to critically analyze how sustainable are the smart cities themselves by looking at how government uses its mechanisms to create value for citizens taking into consideration the fact that nowadays technological advancement is being a necessity and a priority. To elaborate this, it raises questions like:

What kind of relationship fosters the sustainability of smart cities and how can technology contribute to that?
How government deploys ICT to create and/or constrain opportunities for citizens in the decision-making processes?
What are the similarities and/or difference in participation in different areas, and finally, what is the difference in the planning and implementation process?

The main result of the research is that the sustainability of smart cities requires accountability measures by the governance and not necessarily to become active themselves. It is derived from the special importance of the clear participatory frame for the citizen, and the main recommendation derived is the special consideration to the context-dependent factors in the smart city.

14.2 Literature Review

Nam and Pardo (2011) define smart cities as "use information and information technology to make better decisions to improve the quality of life," but it is sustainable foundation that requires good governance of the information available.

Giffinger et al. (2010), due to dual consideration (technological and human-based) it does to smart city, derives from it different dimensions used to identify empirical characteristics of a city for its "smart" definition. As such, a city to be smart must fulfill from the practical perspective effectively and efficiently dimensions such as transportation, greening, participation, digitalization, growth, and administration. In this work, citizens are the main component of the city to become smarter, as active participant in social and public life and as integral element of any policy and strategy.

The first step in creating a smart city is to incorporate it into an existing urban context within a certain geographic area (Snow et al., 2016). Despite the localization or attachment to the territory, smart city unifies all the resources as a unique combination to the common objective, which interplay with each other and in a separate manner have their own function and role to task for the objectives. Meijer and Bolivar (2016) highlight that in fact citizen participation is among the basic rights and an indicator of the "quality of society" in which they live and further contribute to sustainable development.

According to Bibri and Krogstie (2020), a place is transformed into an intelligent setting once it puts into place creative practices and choices, accompanied by advanced digitalization and innovative know-how. Shortly, a city becomes "smarter" by deploying strategies and having decisions, which are based on data-driven solutions for the enhancement of the functions and operations of all strategies and policies (Zhuhadar et al., 2017). Stakeholders incorporated into smart city eco-system and their active involvement, interaction and reaction is the main driving force to the improvement of the governance, city, and quality of life (Axelsson & Granath, 2018). Smart city utilizes ICT to offer quality service to citizens and increase the standard of living in an effective and efficient operational manner. In this way, policies rely heavily on the bottom-up approach and the urbanization takes place better and cities are better developed (Li et al., 2021; Kandt & Batty, 2021).

14.2.1 Smart City Requires Good Governance for Managing Information

Ruhlandt (2018) clearly states that the literature on smart cities is limited when it comes to a systematic knowledge and various metrics to assess the elements for its governance, which makes the smart city governance a long-lasting objective, especially when it comes to practical implementation of the concept. Smart city governance successfully incorporated ICTs to foster growth, but digital governance of such new way of managing and administering the city is still a question mark (Caragliu et al., 2011; Kitchin, 2015; Samuel et al., 2022). Smart city is conceptualized as an inclusive solution where accurate information deployment to the development of daily operations is believed to reduce the disparities between groups and lower unequal distribution of information and of policies. The phenomenon is contemporaneous and the term is relatively new, but the problem is traditional, lying on the basic function of the government "information management." "One-size-fits-all" approach becomes complicated due to the fact that it is based on big data, and such huge information needs governance to be properly managed. The critical point derives from the renovation of the approach to the processes and the way how the huge information is considered to develop inclusive development for all the citizens (Lee & Kim, 2014).

14.2.2 Good Governance for Citizen Participation Value Creation

Fischer (2006) concludes that (when the concept of smart city did not see such fast development) citizen perception of having influential potential implies to them they are powerful and the public better accepts the policies. This is restated again by Gil-Garcia et al. (2019), who preview that in this way citizens are more willing to be engaged in the decision-making process and daily operations. Kopackova and Komarkova (2020) illustrated that citizen participation transforms the smart city model. Konig (2021) emphasizes that the adaptation of ICT infrastructure would require cities to change also the manner of management and the way how the information collection is going to be translated into value. Quijano et al. (2020) point out that the big data or huge information must be properly processed and filtered to be converted into value, which improves the relationships between stakeholders and makes up considerable portion of decision-making process. Finding the proper mechanism to create value "from citizen for citizens" requires a novelty of the governance and the way it uses information (Micheli et al., 2020). Despite the level of information usage and the way it is processed, by simply transferring the information to the interested parties (Wanger & Eckhoff, 2018) or directly integrating it into the management process (Coletta & Kitchin, 2017), good governance takes place when the information contributes to the improvement.

14.2.3 Citizen Participation and Participatory Technologies

The advantages of utilizing ICT in citizen-government interactions are summed up by Wacquant et al. (2014) as follows "the ever more important role of citizens and closer interactions with government lead to a model of smart government where the relationship goes beyond service improvement and delivery and into areas of decision making, openness, wider societal issues and wider stakeholder networks." Other authors highlight the advantages of electronic decision-making and electronic consultations as a cutting-edge method of fostering trust (Bernardo, 2019; Gil-Garcia et al., 2019). Even so, not all citizens can make use of the many advantages of participatory technologies due to lack of access and knowledge, that is why UN (2018) recommends a combination forms of participation between technological participation and physical one. But, despite the form of participation, the starting point of a successful contribution begins once the government considers the citizens as capable contributors to their governance. Reforgiato Recupero et al. (2016) add that there are required changes needed in the contextual setting to properly engage citizens and ICT deployed to motivate citizen participation. Lastly, cities nowadays are overcrowded, face trafficking problems, long queries are created, sometimes access is not that easy and, as such, efficacy and efficiency are difficult to be achieved which according to Chen et al. (2021) result in unaffordable demand for resources. Du Plessis (2012) concludes that all the factors must be combined and form an interplay, which makes sense only if it is sustainable.

14.2.4 Sustainability of Smart Cities

The shift toward smart cities is considered to contribute to the achievement of the 11th Sustainable Development Goal, which reaches the three pillars of sustainability, economic, social, and environmental aspect through resilient and sustainable city. Global sustainability necessitates various types of initiatives additionally to the city sustainability. There is no single best-established definition in terms of sustainability in the urban scale; nevertheless, there is a commonly used set of characteristics of urban sustainability. Smart city offers strategic solutions to sustainability issues resulting from urbanization (Toli & Murtagh, 2020), but the concrete results of those solutions vary depending on the scope, purpose, and goals, and the works that consider different aspects of it range from economic dimension, social dimension, or a mix of elements from different dimensions (Ahvenniemi et al., 2017; Kourtit et al., 2012; Nam & Pardo, 2011; Bibri & Krogstie, 2017; Ibrahim et al., 2015). Based on Correira et al. (2020) and Yigitcanlar et al. (2019), a city cannot be smart if it has no sustainability as its outmost objective. The most used concept associated with smart city is the increased quality of citizen's life (Clarke et al., 2019; Heitlinger et al., 2019), but little attention is given to environmental dimensions of sustainability.

14.3 Methodology

The study overviews the Albanian capital city context to understand how the nexus is initiated, and development process of it and the main gaps and challenges identified. It is used a mix method to conduct the research. Initially is done a systematic literature review of the interconnected relationship within the nexus so that to derive the final philosophical and strategical aim of the research. The related concepts are explained in a progressive way to go to the ultimate goal, which is to see the functioning in the Albanian context. We want to see the possibility of attaining the desirable future of Tirana as e-sustainable smart city, by applying a back-casting method as explained by Soria-Lara and Banister (2017). To do so, the study takes into analysis different secondary data and documents and developed cases in this regard. The analysis includes different developmental strategies and implementation plans to identify where the Albania stands toward the transformation for becoming a smart city and furthermore a sustainable one. At the second phase, five in-depth interviews were conducted with key experts and representatives from the central and local government dealing with the following issues: 1—governance issue; 2—IT expert; 3—environmental expert; 4—education sector; and 5—citizen engagement expert. The information collected was synthetized and processed accordingly.

14.4 Analysis/Result Interpretation

Harmonically, arrangement of information, data, and technology resulting from an enhanced life and improved city standard makes up the foundation of the smart cities (Johnson et al., 2020). Smart city's sustainability remains questionable, and the critical elements that should be taken care of are the implementation process including the proper coordination of the stakeholders and effective monitoring and intervention (van den Buuse et al., 2021; Van Winden & Van den Buuse, 2017).

The key element for the successful planning and implementation of the nexus application once the information and technology is available is the "contextualization of it," by which we mean the proper adjustment to the territory and to the specific characteristics of the cities (Ruijer et al., 2017). There is a considerable literature considering good governance as the main player of the nexus for the sustainability of the cities. Brutti et al. (2019), Desouza et al. (2020), and Gupta et al. (2020) highlight the problems revealed from the way the information and the data are used by the governments. This problem is present especially in countries where there is lack of democracy and the phenomena of corrupted governments is existent and continuous potential, due to the fact that they may use the information for own purposes orienting the information to negative paths. Additionally, technological infrastructure is one of the enablers of the sustainability when it contributes to lowering the consumption and improving the production, and when all the actors of the city use it for a better efficacy and effective realization of their needs and functions

(Wu & Chen, 2021; Du Plessis, 2012). The use of ICTs in the context of cities for their smart and sustainable development is commonly suggested for all despite the level of development, but this takes a vital role when it comes to underdeveloped countries (Larasati et al., 2021). Digital technologies improve the efficacy of any city despite the diverse development plans and wide range of needs they have. Incorporating sustainability goals on cities' strategies and plans through the incorporation of technology enables the shift of the terms from "smart sustainable city" to "sustainable smart city."

14.4.1 What Kind of Relationship Fosters the Sustainability of Smart Cities?

Different authors define different dimensions of the smart cities to be sustainable. Dewalska-Opitek (2014) integrates to such a city six main components: governance, economy, people, environment, mobility, and the standard of living. Meijer and Bolivar (2016) clearly state that a city to be smarter must go beyond the technology adoption. In the same vine comes Adams et al. (2019), which emphasize that technological interventions are not enough for the sustainability challenges. Together with Murtagh et al. (2018), they suggest that for the sustainability of smart cities also "systemic shifts" are necessary. Sustainability practices incorporated into ICTs, affect the creation of smart city sustainability, and also foster the merger of sustainability goals and city smartness (Repette et al., 2021) and minimize long-term risks, which as Yigitcanlar et al. (2020) highlight technological intensive models may become obsolete very quick. Shehab et al. (2021) relate the sustainability of smart cities with the level of which they contribute to sustainability pillars and to living standard of the cities, and for this, Chen and Zhang (2020) suggest the triple bottom line.

In Albania, there are good improvements in this regard and the main development noticed so far additional to the reforms is the pass from e-governance to the open government. According to experts, the main challenge for the sustainability of Albanian cities is the collaboration between different actors, and this is due to the disparities in the capacities that sometimes are noted when compared between central and local governments of different cities. Another problem in Albanian context is the lack of proper monitoring and evaluation frames. The experts highlight the fact that the pillars of sustainability for developing countries are partly hard to be achieved at once and that is why prioritization is a must there. Proper identification of stakeholders, strictly division of the roles and duties, and identification of the effective matter of their engagement are the key to shift toward sustainable smart city development in Albanian context. Assurance of sustainability of Albanian smart cities must consider especially the social and environmental dimension for proper shelter. In this regard, the good governance should promote informed decision-making on those two main pillars and the main point where the focus should be natural resources conservation and restoration, work safety, and vulnerable group consideration.

14.4.2 How Government Deploys ICT to Create and/or Constrain Opportunities for Citizens in the Decision-Making Processes

A key element in here is the level of complexity when compared between the technology itself and the cities' settings. According to dos Santos (2017) cities, dynamics are much more frequent than the technological systems adoption rate. Khan and Salah (2018) highlight the fact that ICTs are effective tools, but they are subject of security risks, and this may be a hindering factor for the government to fully rely on its decision-making process. Meanwhile, Salah et al. (2019) indicate the fact that technological infrastructures sometimes may have misalignment between each others, which may complicate planning and implementation phases. ICT provides governance with information, which literally means "knowledge" for smart city development. In order to create value, this big data set must be organized in such a manner that it supports all decision-making level and all the persons and groups find themselves included. Janowski (2015) adds to this value the contextualization in terms of urban governance, which is going to result in an enriched and sustainable relationship. Abella et al. (2017) reveal that governments deploy ICT to create a citizen-centered information assessment and participatory decision-making policies. The successful implementation of this happens when there is a balance in consideration between the individuals and the groups and all the governance decisions may be updated and adjusted. Chourabi et al. (2012) emphasize that ICTs deployed by governments must result on an improved level of resource allocation and capacity building to lower the disparities in between the cities.

Regarding the ICT deployment of the Albanian government, the backbone dimension taken into consideration to initiate the back-casting analysis is "connectivity" as fundamental for the technological shift. In this vein, the main indicator data reported from ITU are that during 2020 the level of Internet usage is 72.2% and almost 99% of the population is using 3G and 4G/LTE; broadband per 100 inhabitants is 17.7, fixed telephone 7.8, and mobile phone 91. According to given connectivity is improved, but further data show huge differences between urban and rural areas, which report different costs and entrance level. The increased demand was also pushed by COVID-19 pandemic. Albania has improved a lot in the availability of connectivity and its affordability, but still lower than the other countries in the region. The good thing in here is that Albanian government has supported ICT sector with supporting strategies and policies (National Plan for Sustainable Development of Digital Infrastructure 2020–2025; National Cybersecurity 2020–2025), but the digitalizing process increased the demand for improvements in the digital skills in an environment where disparities are evident and the literacy is high (the basic skills among population is at the level of 21% according to Eurostat), which was further foreseen under the National Education Strategy 2021–2026 separated into different projects with other partners.

The need for digital skills was even more emergent during the COVID-19 pandemic when it comes to education and employment. According to the expert, Albania has much to do regarding the inclusion in ICT of people with disabilities, in both planning and implementation phases, development programs in this regard, and service improvements for them.

One very important point emphasized from them is the fact that all those are matter of time, but Albanian government has to do a lot in building of trust and confidence. It has done considerable work in providing the services to citizens, but the efficiency is again a question mark. "e-Albania" is still the only platform of service delivery, but the level of usage has still space for improvements and the citizen approach toward it is still skeptical.

According to all the experts, citizen participation in the decision-making process through the ICT lack transparency and as a consequence those decisions are not fully accountable. Additionally, they point out that there are two main dimensions that are not explicitly shown in the portal, how is going to be the inclusion of people with disabilities and the way how the environmental issue is going to be addressed. On the policy level, Albania has the new National Waste Management Plan 2020–2025, which aims as a ultimate goal for the transformation toward circular economy, but the main challenge in here is that "nor the system neither the other components are designed to be circular."

14.4.3 What Are the Similarities and/or Difference in Participation Between Different Areas, and Finally, What Is the Difference in the Planning and Implementation Process?

So far, we have considered the nexus as the main interoperability to realize the sustainability of smart cities, but before going to the effectiveness with which the nexus takes place, Neirotti et al. (2014) remind us that smart city depends on the contextual factors and on the urban structures. Urban structure is a broad term that includes the factors from the form of organization to the population profiles and the consecration of the knowledge. In this regard, Marsal (2020) emphasizes that despite the urbanization setting from being urban or rural, the main result of the participation in smart cities must be the creation of innovative solutions coming from spontaneous initiatives. According to them, technology adaptation is the least indicator of the nexus interplay, more importantly for citizen's effective participation in different urban settings is the type of ICT deployed, and for this, they suggest the community-led technologies. Marsal (2018) suggests decentralization of the governance as the main solution to the effective participation on different urban settings. According to

Araral (2020), a city becomes smarter when it focuses on the effectiveness of ICT implementation and general public requirements fulfillment.

Different age groups have different participation patters, and based on demographics, there should be different technological infrastructure deployed for them: Rexhepi et al. (2018) claim that gamification is the main way to approach the youngsters; Lee and Kim (2014) related it to the historical relationship developed between parties, and they tend to participate if they have a positive experience from past participations; Porwal et al. (2016) relates it with the educational dimensions and accomplishment level; and Ayed et al. (2017) add to existing literature the citizen's culture to their participation behavior.

The proper participation of Albanian citizens in different urban settings is foreseen under the Albania Digital Agenda 2022–2026 strategy in the frame of the digital transformation which comes as an updated version of all other existing strategies and has shown special care to minimize social and environmental risks. According to experts, despite the fact of evaluating it as a very good strategy, they highlight the fact that it lacks proper provision in current regulatory base, and it is not enough supported with proper resources and infrastructure. From the other side, considering the fact that in Albania there is considerable difference between urban and rural areas and recent phenomena like earthquake and –COVID-19 disproportionally affected the population, the governance model to be followed has challenges to overpass. The disparities in regions are evident due to the following reasons: e-Albania is just user-centric and lacks pro-activity, and according to IT expert, the infrastructure is outdated and not fit-for-purpose. Different regions within the country are related to different sectors and sector vise details lack specifications. Additionally, human resources also are not equally spread across the regions and efficiency of natural and human resource management differs a lot between the national institutions and local institutions.

14.5 Conclusions and Recommendations

This work tries to review how sustainable are smart cities by assessing the effectiveness of the interplay between the smart city, good governance, and citizen participation, through the incorporation of ICTs as the main mediator of the nexus. Overall, smart cities are modern solutions to the existing urban settings, which imply smarter citizens, smarter technologies, and smarter governance properly adjusted and adopted to the specific characteristics of territories.

Our main conclusion is related to the power of information, and having this power makes the accountability of the decisions doubtful on the way how it is used. In this regard, transparency is a key element that may diminish the ambiguity associated with it, and clear division between the weight each stakeholder has on the decisions, planning, and strategies may result in better management of the expectations. Technological solutions greatly facilitate the processes, but a city cannot become smarter only by this advancement, and for the sustainability of such initiatives, they must address international challenges by giving local solutions.

Regarding the Albanian context, we can say that there is a lack of collaboration between the national and local government; the main pillars of sustainability where good governance should take care are social and environmental dimension of it; the main challenge for the nexus is that the system is designed in the traditional way and it require systemic shift which means it requires re-dimensioning of education, sector vise details, regional disparities minimization, infrastructure update, and proper identification of risks like earthquake and COVID-19.

So far, we could not find any work dealing with the financial dimension of smart cities and if there is self-sustainability regarding this part. For the sustainability of the smart cities, we suggest that city planners should focus more on implementation phase of smart city projects and give special importance to the risks associated with them. Unpredicted consequences should be prevented through a very regular monitoring and evaluation process. Finally, for the sustainability of smart initiatives, contextual factors of smart city development should be adjusted when there is a transfer of knowledge from case to case.

References

Abella, A., Ortiz-de-Urbina-Criado, M., & De-Pablos-Heredero, C. (2015). Information reuse in smart cities' ecosystems. *El Profesional de la Informacion, 24*(6), 838–844.

Abella, A., Ortiz-de-Urbina-Criado, M., & De-Pablos-Heredero, C. (2017). A model for the analysis of data-driven innovation and value generation in smart cities' ecosystems. *Cities, 64*, 47–53.

Adams, D., Adams, K., Ullah, S., & Ullah, F. (2019). Globalisation, governance, accountability and the natural resource 'curse': Implications for socio-economic growth of oil-rich developing countries. *Resources Policy, 61*, 128–140.

Ahvenniemi, H., Huovila, A., Pinto-Seppä, I., & Airaksinen, M. (2017). What are the differences between sustainable and smart cities? *Cities, 60*, 234–245.

Allen, B., Tamindael, L. E., Bickerton, S. H., & Cho, W. (2020). Does citizen coproduction lead to better urban services in smart cities projects? An empirical study on e-participation in a mobile big data platform. *Government Information Quarterly, 37*(1), 101412.

Angelidou, M. (2014). Smart city policies: A spatial approach. *Cities, 41*, S3–S11.

Angelidou, M. (2015). Smart cities: A conjuncture of four forces. *Cities, 47*, 95–106.

Araral, E. (2020). Why do cities adopt smart technologies? Contingency theory and evidence from the United States. *Cities, 106*, 102873.

Axelsson, K., & Granath, M. (2018). Stakeholders' stake and relation to smartness in smart city development: Insights from a Swedish city planning project. *Government Information Quarterly, 35*(4), 693–702.

Ayed, H., Vanderose, B., & Habra, N. (2017). Agile cultural challenges in Europe and Asia: Insights from practitioners. In *Proceedings - 2017 IEEE/ACM 39th international conference on Software Engineering: Software Engineering in Practice Track* (pp. 153–162).

Baesens, B., Bapna, R., Marsden, J. R., Vanthienen, J., & Zhao, J. L. (2016). Transformational issues of big data and analytics in networked business. *MIS Quarterly, 38*(2), 629–631.

Bernardo, M. D. R. M. (2019). Smart city governance: From e-government to smart governance. In *Smart cities and smart spaces: Concepts, methodologies, tools, and applications* (pp. 196–232). IGI Global.

Bibri, S. E., & Krogstie, J. (2017). Smart sustainable cities of the future: An extensive interdisciplinary literature review. *Sustainable Cities and Society, 31*, 183–212.

Bibri, S. E., & Krogstie, J. (2020). The emerging data–driven Smart City and its innovative applied solutions for sustainability: The cases of London and Barcelona. *Energy Informatics, 3*, 1–42.

Brutti, A., Sabbata, P. D., Frascella, A., Gessa, N., Ianniello, R., Novelli, C., et al. (2019). Smart city platform specification: A modular approach to achieve interoperability in smart cities. In *The internet of things for smart urban ecosystems* (pp. 25–50). Springer.

Capdevila, I., & Zarlenga, M. I. (2015). Smart city or smart citizens? The Barcelona case. *Journal of Strategy and Management, 8*(3), 266–282.

Caragliu, A., Del Bo, C., & Nijkamp, P. (2011). Smart cities in Europe. *Journal of Urban Technology, 18*(2), 65–82.

Chen, Y., & Zhang, D. (2020). Evaluation of city sustainability using multi-criteria decision-making considering interaction among criteria in Liaoning province China. *Sustainable Cities and Society, 59*, 102211.

Chen, X., Qin, K., & Wu, L. (2021). Citizen characteristics and their participation in food safety social co-governance: Public health implications. *Frontiers in Public Health, 9*, 772117.

Chourabi, H., Nam, T., Walker, S., Gil-Garcia, J. R., Mellouli, S., Nahon, K., et al. (2012). Understanding smart cities: An integrative framework. In *Proceedings of the 45th Hawaii international conference on System Sciences (HICSS-45)* (pp. 2289–2297). IEEE.

Clarke, R., Heitlinger, S., Light, A., Forlano, L., Foth, M., & DiSalvo, C. (2019). More-than-human participation: Design for sustainable smart city futures. *Interactions, 26*(3), 60–63.

Cleland, B., Wallace, J., & Black, M. (2018). The 'engage' system: Using real-time digital technologies to support citizen-centred design in government. In *User centric egovernment* (pp. 183–201). Springer.

Coletta, C., & Kitchin, R. (2017). Algorithmic governance: Regulating the 'heartbeat' of a city using the Internet of Things. *Big Data & Society, 4*(2), 2053951717742418.

Correia, D. I. O. G. O., Teixeira, L. E. O. N. O. R., & Marques, J. O. Ã. O. (2020). Triangular pyramid trunk: The three axes of the smart city assessment tool. *WIT Transactions on Ecology and the Environment, 241*, 79–90.

Desouza, K. C., Hunter, M., Jacob, B., & Yigitcanlar, T. (2020). Pathways to the making of prosperous smart cities: An exploratory study on the best practice. *Journal of Urban Technology, 27*(3), 3–32.

Dewalska–Opitek, A. (2014). Smart city concept–the citizens' perspective. In *International conference on Transport Systems Telematics* (pp. 331–340). Springer.

Dos Santos, R. P. (2017). On the philosophy of bitcoin/blockchain technology: Is it a chaotic, complex system? *Metaphilosophy, 48*(5), 620–633.

Du Plessis, A. (2012). Climate governance in South African municipalities: Opportunities and obstacles for local government. In *Local climate change law*. Edward Elgar Publishing.

Fischer, F. (2006). Participatory governance as deliberative empowerment: The cultural politics of discursive space. *The American Review of Public Administration, 36*(1), 19–40.

Giffinger, R., Haindlmaier, G., & Kramar, H. (2010). The role of rankings in growing city competition. *Urban Research and Practice, 3*, 299–312. https://doi.org/10.1080/17535069.2010.524420

Gil-Garcia, J. R., Guler, A., Pardo, T. A., & Burke, G. B. (2019). Characterizing the importance of clarity of roles and responsibilities in government inter-organizational collaboration and information sharing initiatives. *Government Information Quarterly, 36*(4), 101393.

Gupta, A., Panagiotopoulos, P., & Bowen, F. (2020). An orchestration approach to smart city data ecosystems. *Technological Forecasting and Social Change, 153*, 119929.

Han, M. J. N., & Kim, M. J. (2021). A critical review of the smart city in relation to citizen adoption towards sustainable smart living. *Habitat International, 108*, 102312.

Heitlinger, S., Bryan-Kinns, N., & Comber, R. (2019, May). The right to the sustainable smart city. In *Proceedings of the 2019 CHI conference on Human Factors in Computing Systems* (pp. 1–13).

Hienerth, C., Keinz, P., & Lettl, C. (2011). Exploring the nature and implementation process of user-centric business models. *Long Range Planning, 44*(5), 344–374.

Ibrahim, M., Adams, C., & El-Zaart, A. (2015). Paving the way to smart sustainable cities: Transformation models and challenges. *JISTEM-Journal of Information Systems and Technology Management, 12*, 559–576.

Janowski, T. (2015). Digital government evolution: From transformation to contextualization. *Government Information Quarterly, 32*(3), 221–236.

Jin, J., Gubbi, J., Marusic, S., & Palaniswami, M. (2014). An information framework for creating a smart city through internet of things. *IEEE Internet of Things Journal, 1*(2), 112–121.

Johnson, P. A., Robinson, P. J., & Philpot, S. (2020). Type, tweet, tap, and pass: How smart city technology is creating a transactional citizen. *Government Information Quarterly, 37*(1), 101414.

Kandt, J., & Batty, M. (2021). Smart cities, big data and urban policy: Towards urban analytics for the long run. *Cities, 109*, 102992.

Khan, M. A., & Salah, K. (2018). IoT security: Review, blockchain solutions, and open challenges. *Future Generation Computer Systems, 82*, 395–411.

Kitchin, R. (2015). The promise and peril of smart cities. *Computers and Law: The Journal of the Society for Computers and Law, 26*(2).

König, P. D. (2021). Citizen-centered data governance in the smart city: From ethics to accountability. *Sustainable Cities and Society, 75*, 103308.

Kopackova, H., & Komarkova, J. (2020). Participatory technologies in smart cities: What citizens want and how to ask them. *Telematics and Informatics, 47*, 101325.

Kourtit, K., Nijkamp, P., & Arribas, D. (2012). Smart cities in perspective–a comparative European study by means of self-organizing maps. *Innovation: The European Journal of Social Science Research, 25*(2), 229–246.

Larasati, A., Jamil, A., & Briandana, R. (2021). Communication strategies in providing good government education through social media: A case study at the Parliament of the Republic of Indonesia. *Psychology and Education, 58*(1), 722–734.

Lee, J., & Kim, S. (2014). Active citizen E-participation in local governance: Do individual social capital and E-participation management matter?. In *Proceedings of the 47th Hawaii international conference on System Sciences* (p. 10).

Lee, J., & Lee, H. (2014). Developing and validating a citizen-centric typology for smart city services. *Government Information Quarterly, 31*, S93–S105.

Li, Z., He, Y., Lu, X., Zhao, H., Zhou, Z., & Cao, Y. (2021). Construction of smart city street landscape big data-driven intelligent system based on Industry 4.0. *Computational Intelligence and Neuroscience*, https://doi.org/10.1155/2021/1716396.

Linders, D. (2012). From e-government to we-government: Defining a typology for citizen coproduction in the age of social media. *Government Information Quarterly, 29*(4), 446–454.

Lokers, R., Knapen, R., Janssen, S., van Randen, Y., & Jansen, J. (2016). Analysis of big data technologies for use in agro-environmental science. *Environmental Modelling & Software, 84*, 494–504.

Lombardi, P., Giordano, S., Farouh, H., & Yousef, W. (2012). Modelling the smart city performance. *Innovation: The European Journal of Social Science Research, 25*(2), 137–149.

Lynn, L. E., Heinrich, C. J., & Hill, C. J. (2000). Studying governance and public management: Challenges and prospects. *Journal of Public Administration Research and Theory, 10*(2), 233–262.

Marsal-Llacuna, M. L. (2018). The standards revolution: Who will first put this new kid on the blockchain? In *Proceedings of the IEEE Xplore, 2017 ITU Kaleidoscope: Challenges for a Data-Driven Society (ITU K)*.

Marsal-Llacuna, M. L. (2020). The people's smart city dashboard (PSCD): Delivering on community-led governance with blockchain. *Technological Forecasting and Social Change, 158*, 120150.

Martens, D., Provost, F., Clark, J., & Junque de Fortuny, E. (2016). Mining massive fine-grained behavior data to improve predictive analytics. *MIS Quarterly, 40*(4), 869–888.

Meijer, A. (2015). E-governance innovation: Barriers and strategies. *Government information quarterly, 32*(2), 198–206.

Meijer, A., & Bolívar, M. P. R. (2016). Governing the smart city: A review of the literature on smart urban governance. *International Review of Administrative Sciences, 82*(2), 392–408.

Meijer, A. J., Gil-Garcia, J. R., & Bolívar, M. P. R. (2016). Smart city research: Contextual conditions, governance models, and public value assessment. *Social Science Computer Review, 34*(6), 647–656.

Mergel, I., Rethemeyer, R. K., & Isett, K. (2016). Big data in urban affairs. *Public Administration Review, 76*(6), 928–937.

Micheli, M., Ponti, M., Craglia, M., & Berti Suman, A. (2020). Emerging models of data governance in the age of datafication. *Big Data & Society, 7*(2), 2053951720948087.

Murtagh, M. J., Blell, M. T., Butters, O. W., Cowley, L., Dove, E. S., Goodman, A., et al. (2018). Better governance, better access: Practising responsible data sharing in the METADAC governance infrastructure. *Human Genomics, 12*, 1–12.

Nam, T., & Pardo, T. A. (2011). Smart city as urban innovation: Focusing on management, policy, and context. In *Proceedings of the 5th international conference on Theory and Practice of Electronic Governance* (pp. 185–194).

Neirotti, P., De Marco, A., & Cagliano, A. C. (2014). Current trends in smart city initiatives: Some stylised facts. *Cities, 38*, 25–36.

Odendaal, N. (2003). Information and communication technology and local governance: Understanding the difference between cities in developed and emerging economies. *Computers, Environment and Urban Systems, 27*, 585–607.

Perera, C., Zaslavsky, A., Christen, P., & Georgakopoulos, D. (2014). Sensing as a service model for smart cities supported by internet of things. *Transactions on Emerging Telecommunications Technologies, 25*(1), 81–93.

Porwol, L., Ojo, A., & Breslin, J. G. (2016). Social software infrastructure for eparticipation. *Government Information Quarterly, 35*(4), S88–S98.

Quijano-Sánchez, L., Cantador, I., Cortés-Cediel, M. E., & Gil, O. (2020). Recommender systems for smart cities. *Information Systems, 92*, 101545.

Razaghi, M., & Finger, M. (2018). Smart governance for smart cities. *Proceedings of the IEEE, 106*(4), 680–689. https://doi.org/10.1109/JPROC.2018.2807784

Reforgiato Recupero, D., Castronovo, M., Consoli, S., Costanzo, T., Gangemi, A., Grasso, L., et al. (2016). An innovative, open, interoperable citizen engagement cloud platform for smart government and users' interaction. *Journal of the Knowledge Economy, 7*, 388–412.

Repette, P., Sabatini-Marques, J., Yigitcanlar, T., Sell, D., & Costa, E. (2021). The evolution of city-as-a-platform: Smart urban development governance with collective knowledge-based platform urbanism. *Land, 10*(1), 33.

Rexhepi, A., Filiposka, S., & Trajkovik, V. (2018). Youth e-participation as a pillar of sustainable societies. *Journal of Cleaner Production, 174*, 114–122.

Ruhlandt, R. W. S. (2018). The governance of smart cities: A systematic literature review. *Cities, 81*, 1–23.

Ruijer, E., Grimmelikhuijsen, S., Hogan, M., Enzerink, S., Ojo, A., & Meijer, A. (2017). Connecting societal issues, users and data. Scenario-based design of open data platforms. *Government Information Quarterly, 34*(3), 470–480.

Salah, K., Rehman, M. H. U., Nizamuddin, N., & Al-Fuqaha, A. (2019). Blockchain for AI: Review and open research challenges. *IEEE Access, 7*, 10127–10149.

Samuel, O., Javaid, N., Alghamdi, T. A., & Kumar, N. (2022). Towards sustainable smart cities: A secure and scalable trading system for residential homes using blockchain and artificial intelligence. *Sustainable Cities and Society, 76*, 103371.

Shehab, M. J., Kassem, I., Kutty, A. A., Kucukvar, M., Onat, N., & Khattab, T. (2021). 5G networks towards smart and sustainable cities: A review of recent developments, applications and future perspectives. *IEEE Access, 10*, 2987–3006.

Snow, C. C., Håkonsson, D. D., & Obel, B. (2016). A smart city is a collaborative community: Lessons from smart Aarhus. *California Management Review, 59*, 92–108.

Soria-Lara, J. A., & Banister, D. (2017). Participatory visioning in transport backcasting studies: Methodological lessons from Andalusia (Spain). *Journal of Transport Geography, 58*, 113–126.

Toli, A. M., & Murtagh, N. (2020). The concept of sustainability in smart city definitions. *Frontiers in Built Environment, 6*, 77.

United Nations Publications (UN). (2018). *Sustainable development goals report 2018*. United Nations Pubns.

van Winden, W., & van den Buuse, D. (2017). Smart city pilot projects: Exploring the dimensions and conditions of scaling up. *Journal of Urban Technology, 24*(4), 51–72.

Van den Buuse, D., van Winden, W., & Schrama, W. (2021). Balancing exploration and exploitation in sustainable urban innovation: An ambidexterity perspective toward smart cities. *Journal of Urban Technology, 28*(1–2), 175–197.

Wacquant, L., Slater, T., & Pereira, V. B. (2014). Territorial stigmatization in action. *Environment and planning A, 46*(6), 1270–1280.

Wagner, I., & Eckhoff, D. (2018). Technical privacy metrics: A systematic survey. *ACM Computing Surveys (CSUR), 51*(3), 1–38.

Wu, Y. J., & Chen, J. C. (2021). A structured method for smart city project selection. *International Journal of Information Management, 56*, 101981.

Yigitcanlar, T., Kamruzzaman, M., Foth, M., Sabatini-Marques, J., da Costa, E., & Ioppolo, G. (2019). Can cities become smart without being sustainable? A systematic review of the literature. *Sustainable Cities and Society, 45*, 348–365.

Yigitcanlar, T., Desouza, K. C., Butler, L., & Roozkhosh, F. (2020). Contributions and risks of artificial intelligence (AI) in building smarter cities: Insights from a systematic review of the literature. *Energies, 13*(6), 1473.

Zanella, A., Bui, N., Castellani, A., Vangelista, L., & Zorzi, M. (2014). Internet of things for smart cities. *IEEE Internet of Things Journal, 1*(1), 22–32.

Zhuhadar, L., Thrasher, E., Marklin, S., & de Pablos, P. O. (2017). The next wave of innovation—Review of smart cities intelligent operation systems. *Computers in Human Behavior, 66*, 273–281.

Chapter 15
Digital Finance Is a Key of European and Global Integration

Otilia Manta

Abstract The current needs of the financial consumer are constantly changing in the context of the digital era, which is why we can appreciate that the future of financial instruments that satisfy these needs is given precisely by the digitalization of financial instruments through technologies, financial innovations and, finally, new models of business in the financial field. In our paper, we propose that, based on the analysis of existing empirical studies in international scientific databases, we highlight those innovative financial solutions based on artificial intelligence, which have contributed to the acceleration of the process regarding innovations in digital financial services, as well as to the development of digital infrastructure related to institutions financial, which from a strategic point of view offers accessibility, reliability, safety and comfort to the final consumer.

Keywords Digital finance · Financial instruments · International agreements

15.1 Introduction

Digital finance has recently been increasingly associated with the concept of "FinTech." For the terms associated with the concepts related to financial innovations to be as clear as possible, at the European level, experts have redefined the concepts and associated different terms, respectively, "FinTech" comes from the association of the terms "technology" and "finance". Moreover, it is important that within these associations we contribute to the sharing and reuse of personal data to offer a wide range of financial services. At the same time, the concept of "digital

---

O. Manta (✉)
Romanian Academy, "Victor Slavescu" Centre for Financial and Monetary Research, Bucharest, Romania
e-mail: otilia.manta@icfm.ro; otilia.manta@rgic.ro

financing" represents financing that uses digitized infrastructures according to European and global regulations related to the digital era.

The evolution both at the financial and technological levels has been analyzed since 1928 with the development of technology and the innovation of the telegraph as a direct instrument for transmitting information of a financial nature, as well as certain data, being otherwise generically called Fintech 1.0. Technology has evolved, and with it, blockchain has also appeared, with direct implications both in finance and in the generation of data blocks with a direct influence on all sectors of activity and even with a direct impact on social life, being called Fintech 5.0 with the period of reference 2014 and 2016. The process of accelerated digitization has led to the development of innovative solutions both in the financial industry and in the IT industry, which makes them currently generate the concept of "open finance," which creates an innovative environment dynamic in the field of financial innovations. At the same time, it is also worth mentioning the dynamics of the robotization of banking institutions" front office activities, which makes artificial intelligence play an active role in defining the current architecture of the global financial market with an impact on the economies of states and implicitly on the users of digital financial services.

15.2 Literature Review

The current financial regulations show us that we are in a new era of finance, namely digital ones, this aspect being due both to the change in the profile of consumers, and especially to the offer of financial products and services adapted to this new era. Moreover, this aspect is also due to the active participation of financial innovators through the development of technologies oriented toward new models of development of financial institutions.

Financial technologies support the current needs of companies and the population, and this aspect is also being accelerated by the COVID-19 pandemic. The online space allows a new digital identity for the consumer, which gives them the possibility to optimize the time of identifying financial offers, as well as financing processes according to their own needs. Along with the basic offer of financial institutions, namely that of financing, there is an online payment service that has seen exponential growth because of the accelerated development of electronic commerce, as well as the development of a new remote work strategy that generates access to these financial services.

Financial technologies in the last period have seen a growing evolution and have helped to facilitate access to loans/financing, including grants managed by management authorities during the COVID-19 pandemic. The infrastructure of financial services has undergone a radical change in the last period, because of the fact that more and more people are using online financial services, activities are performed remotely in some jobs, and we can say that many of the back-office employees in the institution's financial banking, remote access also works.

Europe, by taking major decisions toward the digitization of the economy, should take advantage of its resilience and recovery strategy, so that social and economic damage is limited in this post-pandemic period. Digital technologies are support tools not only for the field of finance, but also for all fields of activity, being essential for the relaunch and modernization of the European economy. All decisions, strategies, regulations, and directives will contribute and enable the member states of the European Union to advance globally as a digital actor.

A key priority established in 2020 at the European level is the date of supporting the transition to digitization through financial instruments, a priority that has been transposed in all areas of activity, including the financial one, which can be found in the states" resilience and recovery plans at the European level. The programs of the EU, and other innovative financial instruments, allow the creation of a flexible framework for the initiation and development of innovative projects in the financial field at the level of member states, and innovative digital technologies involved in the process of online payments remain a priority in terms of innovation and security digital.

It is obvious that these financial innovations will have a direct impact on consumers, natural persons, and legal entities implicitly changing the profile and the business model. Certainly, the decisions at the European and global levels regarding the digitization process will change society at a global level. In terms of financial innovations, the technologies regarding payment services and their integration at the level of the activity sectors, not only of the banking financial institutions but also at the level of all the activity sectors, represent the financial innovation with the greatest impact, which allows everyone to optimize the most of price "time" resources in an efficient and safe framework. Digital payment solutions are indispensable for making payments in stores and on e-commerce platforms, paying money transfers for any payment obligation, regardless of whether it is financial products (loans, insurances, and others) or usual payments for any type of user. The regulatory framework at both European and national levels provides security in the use of this service in terms of "digital payments," as we otherwise identify regulated measures and included in the "EU Retail Payments Strategy," strategy that was published in 2020. As I mentioned before, these decisions to transform economies through the digitization process directly changed both innovations in the financial field and business models at the level of all sectors of activity in the real economy (including the financial sector).

The digital space is a generator of digital innovation, facilitating the development of enterprises. Increasingly, innovation involves new products, processes, or business models that are made possible by digital technologies. While in the beginning they performed only a simple support function, information technology systems, combined with the corresponding software applications directly contribute to the optimization of internal processes at the level of the business environment, as well as at the level of public institutions that opt for such a solution. The digitization process has multiple effects, from optimizing work times to cost efficiency and, finally, increasing the level of productivity and quality through the digitization process.

In the innovative processes, the models are more and more oriented toward the collaborative economy model, which makes the level of innovations in the digital space maintain the accelerated growth rate. The developers of digitized application solutions through the offered solutions allow development adapted to both the current needs of the market and an integrated development based on specialized modules, which makes innovations to be transposed as easily as possible on these specialized modules and with friendly communication interfaces and easy to understand for the end user.

In 2022, numerous FinTech events and rankings were organized at European and international levels (Singapore, USA, India, and others), which confirm that this market has an accelerated dynamism. The traditional financial institutions themselves are in a process of reinvention and re-adaptation in the context of the digital age and associate their activity with the partnership with IT experts. IT companies are becoming more and more oriented toward the financial industry, and the financial industry is more and more involved with IT companies, which makes us confirm that partnership is the basic solution in the sustainable development of the financial market digitized. A major challenge in the digitization process is the management of risks, especially cyber risks, with a direct impact on financial stability and with a direct impact on those active in this market.

As we could see from the elements mentioned above, digitization comes with multiple opportunities, but also with related risks. In terms of opportunities at the European level, one of the most relevant is the one related to the consolidation and integration of the European financial market through the Banking and Monetary Union of Europe, as well as the opportunity to develop new innovative financial instruments to support the programs, managed both in the MFF 2021–2027, and the European Green Agreement, respectively, the programs managed by the European Investment Bank.

Through a regulation of the digital financial sector, we appreciate that this digital financial market can contribute to strengthening convergence and increasing the development capacity of the European economy and implicitly of national economies, as well as to financial stability at the European level.

15.3 Methodology

The methodology is based on empirical research, using tools for synthesis and analysis of the current context of digital finance, open finance, and entrepreneurial finance, as responses to the adaptation of local finance to these technologies that are present at European and global levels, being increasingly innovative and with specific new elements. The basis of the structuring of the work is the synthesis of information from specialized studies of the European Commission, the International Monetary Fund, World Bank projects, specialized reports, and scientific research existing in the specialized literature and identified in the main academic networks (e.g., ResearchGate, Academia.edu, Clarivate, Elsevier, and SSRN). In addition to the innovative financial instruments identified and aimed at limiting the risks generated by these changes on the markets, the existing priorities at the level of the institutions involved in supporting digital financial technologies, the digitization of finances, and open finance are presented, which guide their adaptation policies and strategies, i.e., enforcement solutions through strategic action plans. At the same time, the paper also presents local solutions for the national economy starting from the population"s financial data (relevant derived indicators) through innovative elements presented in the paper. Moreover, the identification and presentation of financial instruments are not only a determination for this paper, but also the starting point for future research on innovative financial instruments intended for the national economy.

15.4 Analysis/Result Interpretation

Among the existing priorities at European level, the four priorities[1] related to the digital transformation of the EU financial sector are relevant, respectively:

- Following digitization, priorities are identified, such as the one related to the fragmentation of the common financial market, which allows users of digital financial services to access financial services both at the European and global levels, thus supporting the expansion of the financing offer for the European business environment by expanding activities in the digital space. Moreover, this cross-border process of digital financial services supports the internationalization process of companies at a global level and with positive elements on product policies (higher quality following the increase in market demands) and with an appropriate price policy (optimized and even lower prices).
- Another priority is the regulatory framework adapted to financial innovations and supporting the needs of users of digital financial services and market efficiency. It is evident that artificial intelligence is increasingly present in the world of finance, and innovative applications are coming to optimize repetitive activities in the industry. However, it is very important that, through regulation, the companies developing such innovative solutions are held responsible and, moreover, that they guarantee the effective and responsible way of use and in direct correlation with the existing values at the European and global levels. Regulatory and supervisory institutions continuously provide direct support for the development of digital and open financial markets but must keep pace with these accelerated financial market innovations. Another priority at the European level in terms of digital finance is the creation of a common space of data and financial information, which can be shared among the member states, but above all can be permanently improved, as so are the details regarding the mechanisms and procedures within the payment services directive, which common space will con-

---

[1] Regulation (EU) no. 910/2014.

tribute to supporting the common sustainable investments of the member states Also, among the priorities, we also find the one related to the risks generated by this digitization (transformation), namely the migration of these risks to different and highly fragmented ecosystems, for example IT providers that are interconnected but do not comply with financial supervision regulations, which makes this aspect have a direct impact on financial stability. Moreover, according to the market mechanisms, it is necessary to maintain the sound principles of the market economy, such as those related to fair competition, adequate and secure distribution channels, and correct mechanisms related to price policy.

- At the same time, at the level of the European Commission, the new financial activities are carefully monitored and supported, thus maintaining specific conditions of fairness both between the current financial institutions, as well as between the new actors entering the financial market and the market.

It is worth noting that the "European Digital Financing Strategy" adopted at the European level by the member states had as its main objective the capitalization of all the opportunities offered by the digitization of the single market and with a direct orientation toward the direct benefits offered to users of digital financial services. Moreover, the functioning of the single market of digital products and services will lead to the improvement on the one hand of the access to these services of those in the industries, but above all to the creation of an access channel to this market for those who are financially excluded, which makes that the European digital financial market becomes more inclusive and closer to the needs of the many financially excluded.[2]

The year 2024 is the year in which the EU member states should have a stable and secure regulatory framework, which will support the development of innovative financial invitation services on the one hand, but above all the digital identity can be used, so that users of digital financial services to access these services in real time and with maximum efficiency. At the same time, in direct alignment with these financial innovations, we appreciate that the supporting regulations of the European financial market, such as the e-IDAS Regulation, should be revised and supplemented so that these digital financial services are characterized by trust and determination in accessing and their use.

The great challenge given by the digitization of finances is given by the cooperation at the European level of all the authorities and in real time, in response to the current challenges generated by the new innovative models, which on the one hand are managed by banking financial institutions, but on the other hand are managed by non-banking institutions, or even through their mix, which generates an increase in the degree of supervision in terms of risks and challenges.[3]

---

[2] Regulation (EU) no. 910/2014.

[3] https://ec.europa.eu/info/departments/structural-reform-support_ro

15.4.1 Support Program for Structural Reforms (PSRS)[4]

Support program of the EU comes to the support of the member states to support the reforms generated by the digitization of finances. At the level of the Commission, in 2018, the FinTech digital finance laboratory of the European Union was established, within which all the institutions and actors involved in the development and support of digital financial innovations were brought together, including the authorization, supervision, and regulation institutions existing at the European level.

The creation of common infrastructure (including common data space) that meets the needs of the development of mechanisms for securing and supervising institutions involved in the development of innovations based on digital financial technologies represents a key priority in the optimal functioning of this digital financial market in the context of the digital era,[5] and with an impact on the increase of digital knowledge of the European societal environment, including the challenge of access to innovative technologies with the effects on the optimization of processes, the increase in security, and supervision at the institutional level. Networking and inter-institutional information and data exchange directly support European financial institutions internally and externally.[6]

The specific elements of digitization at the level of financial institutions trigger certain specific risks and changes, such as the following:

- Elements for strengthening financial stability starting from the well-known principle "same activity, same risk, same rules"
- The specific elements of protecting consumers of financial services and protecting markets
- Operationally strengthening the digital financial market

In order to know the realities of the population to which these innovative measures are applied, we took as an example some indicators derived at the level of Romania, respectively (Fig. 15.1).

Indicator 1: Coefficient of the population"s financial financing capacity (Cdf)

The formula is:

$$Cdf = \frac{CNP}{AFP}$$

---

[4] Idem[13]

[5] https://ec.europa.eu/info/funding-tenders/find-funding/eu-funding-programmes/digital-europe-programme_ro

[6] https://ec.europa.eu/info/law/better-regulation/have-your-say/initiatives/12417-Digital-Services-Act-deepening-the-Internal-Market-and-clarifying-responsibilities-for-digital-services
   https://ec.europa.eu/competition/consultations/open.html

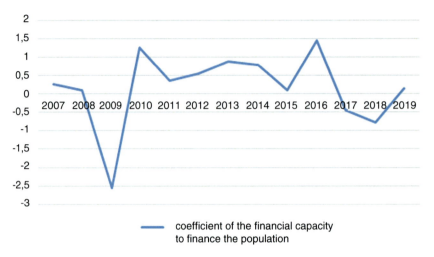

Source: *own processing based on data from the Financial State of Romania project, CCFM,2022*

Fig. 15.1 Cdf indicator during the reference period 2007 and until 2019

In the reference period, it is worth noting that the indicator recorded abnormal values, with the exception of 2009, 2017, and 2018) being influenced by the values of the primary indicators on which the derived indicator depends. The negative values recorded in 2009, namely −2.55%, actually meant a worsening of the population"s financial capacity, as can be seen from the graph and in direct correlation with the other indicators that reflect the financial state of the economy as a whole. It is obvious that in the last period of time, as a result of the multiple crises, the tendency to decrease the financial capacity experienced the same, respectively negative, evolution (Fig. 15.2).

Indicator 2: Financial employment rate of the population (R_{ap})

The formula is:

$$Rap = \frac{DTP}{AFP} \times 100$$

The evolution of this indicator shows periods of growth, respectively, until 2011. After this period follows a period of decrease in the derived financial indicator, with trends close to the value recorded in 2007 (24.72%). In 2019, the indicator reached a value of 25.40%, and the trends are sensitive and follow the downward trend, generated by the degree of prudence of the population during periods of economic crisis. Moreover, we can observe from the evolution of this indicator and based on the calculation formula that the population"s ability to borrow is reduced, what we

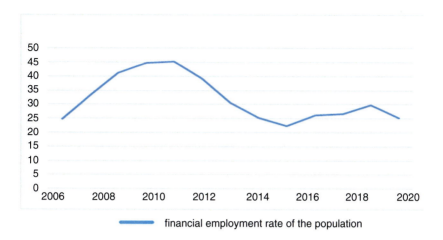

Source: own processing based on data from the Financial State of Romania project, CCFM,2022

Fig. 15.2 Indicator Rap of the population in the reference period

can say is that the population's involvement in economic-financial relations is significantly reduced (Fig. 15.3).

Indicator 3: The rate of financial indebtedness of the population (R_{it})

The formulas are:

$$\text{Rit}(1) = \frac{\text{DTP}}{\text{VDB}} \times 100$$

sau

$$\text{Rit}(2) = \frac{\text{DTP}}{\text{GDP}} \times 100$$

The indebtedness rate, as can be seen from the graph, reflects the actual state of our economy, as well as the economic and financial state of the population. In order to reflect the evolution of the indicator in the reference period, it should be mentioned that this evolution is correlated with the dynamic mode of the indicator related to the saving of (R_{ef}), the rate of interest expenses for the loans committed by the population (R_{cd}), and the financialization rate related to citizens" incomes.

Correlatively, the dynamics of this indicator certify the financial state of the population (savings, consumption, etc.). At the national level, it is very important to adapt innovative financial instruments to the realities of financial indicators that

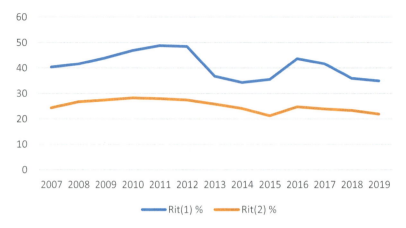

Source: own processing based on data from the Financial State of Romania project, CCFM,2022

Fig. 15.3 Evolution of the Rit derivative indicator during the reference period

reflect the state of the population at a given moment and not to carry out experiments that can affect human lives.

We appreciate the Fintech financial instrument as an innovative solution for the financial market both from an innovative point of view and from the point of view of convergence and competitiveness of financial markets.

Fintech represents the bridge between finance and technology, especially in the context of artificial intelligence between humans and robots involved in the innovative development of the financial market. The European financial sector is more competitive and innovative, as it is oriented towards ensuring the integrity of the EU financial system following the application of the digital financial strategy at the European level (Fig. 15.4).[7]

The digital financial market has reached and will reach very high figures. For example according to Will McCurdy,[8] the total value of embedded finance "will reach $7 trillion" in 2026. Furthermore, business lending will be a key growth area for embedded finance and is expected to grow fivefold over the next five years from just 200 million dollars in 2021 to $1.3 billion by 2026. Another example is FinTech app Mmob, an embedded financial FinTech founded in 2020, which has PensionBee and iwoca as clients, raised £five million sterling in a seed round in March 2022. Modulr, which counts Revolut and financial resilience startup Wagestream as partners, secured a $108 million Series C funding round in the same month to expand the platform"s reach its embedded financing.

---

[7] Report Europena Commission COM(2017)340 final, 26.6.2017.
[8] Press release Will McCurdy, September 15, 2022.

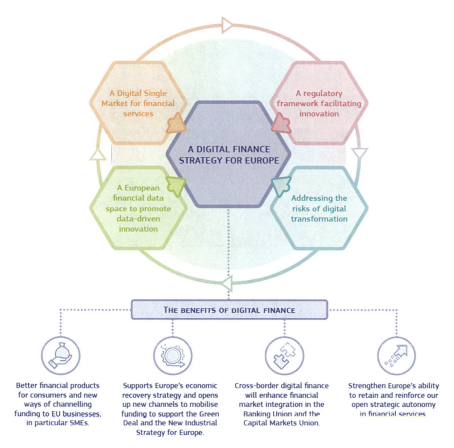

Source: https://ec.europa.eu/

Fig. 15.4 Digital financial strategy at European level

The evolution of purchases of FinTech applications by the main players of the financial market proves to us that this conclusion between finance and technology represents the future of finance. For example, the purchase of a cloud payment technology company by the JPMorgan financial group strengthens its position in the field of payments with innovative "Modernizing Payments" tools, a purchase made in 2022 according to official sources.[9]

Another relevant example is that of the Japanese financial group Mizuho involved in financial innovations in the field of the green bond market in euros, the transaction being 800 million euros, with the main purpose of the integrated green

---

[9] https://finbold.com/jpmorgan-acquires-cloud-payment-tech-firm-to-stay-at-the-forefront-of-payment-innovation/

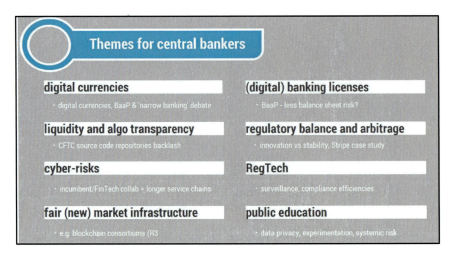

Fig. 15.5 Main themes for central banks

financing of projects, the financial product having the following main characteristics, respectively, maturity on September 5, 2027, and interest rate of 3.490% (Fig. 15.5).[10]

15.4.2 Tech in Finance: Opportunities and Challenges

Regulation of Digital Finance After approximately two years since the launch of the digital financing package by the Commission, we can say that progress has been made in the field of digital finance, especially in the legislative field. However, they are currently subject to major challenges, especially in the context in which innovation in the field of finance is accelerated, and multi-crises make it reach maximum heights. However, the main FinTech trends in 2022 should be noted, respectively:

1. *SWIFT transfers have become real time,* even more as a result of the innovative solutions of the new Fintech generation, payments are safer and faster globally, including using mobile technology.
2. *Biometric authentication.* The "open banking" standard encourages competition and innovation based on service quality. PwC, one of the major auditing and consulting firms, reports that almost 40% of bank clients are willing to share information related to transactions with other financial institutions. Open banking is a government-wide initiative that emerged in the United Kingdom in 2018.

---

[10] https://finbold.com/banking-giant-mizuho-issues-japans-largest-ever-eur-pegged-e800-million-green-bond/

It was proposed by the Competition and Markets Authority with the aim of boosting innovation and competition. At the European level, open banking has become part of PSD2 (Second Payment Services Directive), a directive designed to make payments safer, stimulate innovation, and help banking services adapt to new technologies. Open banking gives customers and businesses greater control over their own finances and the information shared with third parties. It also supports the emergence of new applications and solutions that were not possible before that connect users" finances.
3. *Mobile payments are starting to overtake card or cash payments.* Payments with mobile wallets or the iCard wallet are starting to be used more and more. Globally, mobile payments are forecast to grow from $1.15 billion in 2019 to $3.1 billion in 2024. In Europe, Sweden and Denmark are the top countries that have adopted mobile payments (36% and 41% of mobile payment users and smartphones). The United Kingdom (19%), the Netherlands (20%), Italy (21%), Switzerland (22%), and Norway (25%) are in the middle of the ranking, followed by other countries where mobile payments are used by fewer users: Germany (12%), France, Spain, and Finland (16%, 17%, and 18%).
4. *Biometric Authentication Payments Are Forecast to Grow ten-Fold by 2024,* reaching a total of $2.5 trillion (up from $228 billion in 2019). Biometric debit cards have been tested in Europe. They have a built-in fingerprint reader—the fingerprint is stored when the card is issued, so no one but the holder can use it.

15.5 Conclusions

The emergence of these new innovative technologies on the financial market causes the entire architecture of the financial market to change, and it is very important for our research to keep up with the news and trends in financial technologies, especially in the context where the financial industry is the pillar of support at European level and at global level, of integration, development, well-being, and societal sustainability. Therefore, paying attention to financial innovations, namely innovative companies in digital finance, open finance, and entrepreneurial finance, is a must for us financial researchers. Moreover, there are numerous predictions regarding the future of FinTech and numerous companies that through their activities and solutions are trying to shape the sector and create a new digital finance architecture. Among them, in 2022, the fastest growing FinTech companies are Paidy founded in 2008 and Paidy started as a Japanese payment company, currently has over 6,000,000 users. The year 2021 is characterized by new FinTech transactions, such as the transaction whereby an innovative FinTech company was acquired by the PayPal group for 2.7 billion dollars (USD). Papaya Global founded in 2016, which offers Software as a Service (SaaS) service managed through a platform with Israeli capital and whose main objective is to automate payroll procedures for employees internationally. Another relevant example is that of Grab Financial Group, which in 2018 focused on a new market niche, namely that of digital payments for loans, insurance, and other financial services, reaching in 2021 a value of 300 millions of dollars (USD) of capital raised from the capital market. The blockchain technology is associated with Dapper Labs, a company that was created in 2018 and is involved in the game development market, reaching 550 million dollars (USD) in the capital market. Rapyd and Mollie are FinTechs involved in the development of digital payment services, having raised more than $600 million each from capital market investors. In 2008, Fenergo company developed software products for institutions involved in the financial market, namely the well-known Client Lifecycle Management (CLM) product, by directly involving in the development of its clients" markets, especially in the management of compliance with the regulations in force. It is worth mentioning that they managed to attract more than 600 million dollars in financing from the capital market. The Trade Republic exchange that came into being in 2015 managed to attract in the year the sum of 900 million dollars (USD) from the capital market for the integrated development of the stock exchange platform. Founded in 2018, BharatPe is one of India"s largest FinTech startups, offering app-based payments and card acceptance options to business owners. In 2022, the figures that characterized the company were 1100 employees and the receipt of funding of 545 million USD (USD) from investors to develop new products and services.

According to the Global Banking Benchmark Study 2022, the financial banking industry should orientate its actions to make significant progress following the industry transformation process, i.e., open the team to innovation, innovation that is in line with the needs of customers and develops their ability to access innovative products and services with a direct effect on streamlining processes, through innovative and personalized digital applications applied to each type of customer and according to his specific needs. Therefore, the actions are given by:

(1) Creating rich customer profiles using internal and external data.
(2) Integrating channels to provide a seamless omnichannel experience (holistic approach).
(3) Digitization of core banking systems (banks must replace complex traditional core systems with modern architectures).
(4) The transformation from a product-centric to a customer-centric one.

All these are challenges and drive us to continue our research. Moreover, we appreciate that digital finance, entrepreneurial finance, and open finance will actively contribute to reshaping the present and future architecture of our financial system both nationally, Europeanly and globally. These new innovative financial instruments are concrete research subjects for us, and we appreciate that the results of our research will directly contribute to the creation of new strategies, policies and directives in the field of finance, oriented as much as possible to the needs of society and to the sustainable development of finance.

References

Communication from the Commission to the European Parliament. (2020a). *The Council, the European Economic and Social Committee and the Committee of the Regions.* "Now is Europe's time: repairing the damage caused by the crisis and preparing the future for the new generation", COM (2020) 456 final, 27.5. 2020.

Communication from the Commission to the European Parliament. (2020b). *The Council, the European Economic and Social Committee and the Committee of the Regions.* "A strategy for SMEs for a sustainable and digital Europe", COM (2020) 103, 10.3.2020, https://eur-lex.europa.eu/legal-content/RO/TXT/HTML/?uri=CELEX:52020DC0103&from=EN, https://ec.europa.eu/info/publications/cmu-high-level-forum_en

Communication from the Commission to the European Parliament. (2020c). *The Council, the European Economic and Social Committee and the Committee of the Regions on an EU strategy on retail payments*, COM (2020) 592.

Databases of the National Bank of Romania (from the National Financial Accounts. (2007–2019). and the monthly bulletins from 2007–2020) and the National Institute of Statistics (Statistical Yearbook of Romania, editions 2007–2020, Monthly Statistical Bulletin from December 2007–2019);

Digital Finance Strategy. (2020). https://ec.europa.eu/info/publications/digital-finance-outreach-2020_en

Digital Europe Program. (2020). https://ec.europa.eu/info/funding-tenders/find-funding/eu-funding-programmes/digital-europe-programme_ro

Digital Services Act. (2021). https://ec.europa.eu/info/law/better-regulation/have-your-say/initiatives/12417-Digital-Services-Act-deepening-the-Internal-Market-and-clarifying-responsibilities-for-digital-services;

European Financial Data Space Expert Register. (2022). Report of the Expert Group on European financial data space, 2022, https://finance.ec.europa.eu/system/files/2022-10/2022-10-24-report-on-open-finance_en.pdf

Global Banking Research Report. (2022). https://www.publicissapient.com/industries/financial-services/global-banking-benchmark-study-2022

JPMorgan. (2022). https://finbold.com/jpmorgan-acquires-cloud-payment-tech-firm-to-stay-at-the-forefront-of-payment-innovation/

Mizuho Group. (2022). https://finbold.com/banking-giant-mizuho-issues-japans-largest-ever-eur-pegged-e800-million-green-bond/

Open Finance. (2022). https://ec.europa.eu/competition/consultations/open.html

Press release Will McCurdy. (2022), 15 September 2022.

Regulation (EU) 2022/858 of the European Parliament, (2022), Regulations (EU) no. 600/2014 and (EU) no. 909/2014 and Directive 2014/65/EU, hereinafter referred to as the Regulation on the pilot regime for financial market infrastructures based on DLT or the DLT Regulation.

Regulation (EU) no. 910/2014 on electronic identification and trust services for electronic transactions on the internal market and repealing, (2014), Directive 1999/93/EC, OJ L 257, 28.8.2014, p. 73–114.

Report containing recommendations to the Commission – "Digital finance: emerging risks in crypto-assets – regulatory and supervisory challenges in financial services, institutions and markets", (2020), [2020/2034(INL)], https://oeil.secure.europarl.europa.eu/oeil/popups/ficheprocedure.do?reference=2020/2034(INL)&l=en On 13 December 2019, the Expert Group on Regulatory Obstacles to Financial Innovation, established by the European Commission in June 2018, published its recommendations on how to create an enabling environment for the provision of technology-based financial services.

Report expert group regulatory obstacles financial innovation. (2020). https://ec.europa.eu/info/publications/191113-report-expert-group-regulatory-obstacles-financial-innovation_en

Report from the Commission to the European Parliament. (2017). and the Council on the assessment of money laundering and terrorist financing risks affecting the internal market and linked to cross-border activities. COM (2017)340 final, 26.6.2017.

Structural Reform Support Program. (2020). https://ec.europa.eu/info/departments/structural-reform-support_ro.

Chapter 16
Modeling the Perception of the Business Environment Through the Analysis of Entrepreneurial Opportunities

Ionela Gavrila-Paven and Ruxandra Lazea

Abstract Starting from the hypothesis that perception of the business environment, the entrepreneurial experience, and the field of activity are independent variables influenced by opportunities identified in the market, this chapter aimed to create a development model that reflects these aspects. In order to do that, we have conducted an analysis of specific economic connections and their intensity between the analyzed variables that appear and develop as a result of various influences, which can act with different degrees of intensity in the same or opposite directions. Based on the hypothesis entrepreneurial experience influences the way respondents perceive the opportunities offered by the business environment and can make connections, sometimes very complex. The authors' approach identified the interdependencies between the perception related to the business environment, the entrepreneurial experience, and the field of activity and how the business environment factors influence them. In the second part of the chapter, the authors created a model of these dependencies starting from the hypothesis that there is a linear correlation between these parameters and the specific factors of the business environment that act on the companies.

Keywords Entrepreneurial experience · Business environment · Analysis of entrepreneurial opportunities

I. Gavrila-Paven (✉) · R. Lazea
The 1th December 1918 University of Alba Iulia, Alba Iulia, Romania

16.1 Introduction

Business environment development must respond to the challenges coming from national and international market, supported at the company level by the appropriate endowment in order to create a competitive advantage (Badakhshan et al., 2019; Dumas et al., 2018; Staniewski & Awruk, 2018, 2019, 2021; Staniewski, 2016a, b). The dynamics and intensity of these challenges are supported by technical progress, in general, especially by the current development of the IT sector which is the basis of most transformations, including the labor market (Mat Jusoh et al., 2022; Żebrowska-Suchodolska & Karpio, 2022).

Thus, taking into account the challenges of the business environment, especially the uncertainty that characterizes it, it is very likely that companies will even be forced to change their business models. Updating internal processes in order to obtain further competitive advantages and profitability determines the conversion of business models into more innovative and adaptable ones (Davidsson et al., 2020; Zott & Amit, 2015; Saebi și colab., 2017; Parida și colab., 2019). Thus, the specialized literature brings together a series of studies that start from the static approach of the business model adaptation process, going up to broad and complex approaches regarding the dynamics of the different parameters that characterize the activity of companies and the business environment (Osterwalder & Pigneur, 2010; Climent & Haftor, 2021; Ramdani et al., 2019).

Based on the hypothesis that entrepreneurial experience is an independent variable that has an influence in the identification, analysis, and capitalization of an opportunity identified in the market, a model that reflects these influences was created. The analysis follows the pattern of specific economic analyses where the connections between the variables and their intensity are studied. This is the result of appearance and development of various causes that can act in the same or in opposite direction with different degrees of intensity.

Starting from the hypothesis that the entrepreneurial experience is influenced by the way companies' managers perceive the opportunities offered by the business environment and can make connections the entrepreneurial experience could highlight the categories of opportunities that regional business environment creates, opportunities that determine the appearance, changes or end the interdependence or causality relationships.

The complexity of the interactions between the two variables considered is of a highest importance as they belong to a collective with regional coverage, thus completing the entrepreneurial experience at the center region level, outlined by using a preliminary analysis. Entrepreneurial activity is a very complex one. It includes a number of factors that were identified as being important for the regional level and studied in quantitative research. In the present study, we have considered into study the variables that influence the perception of business environment. To do that, we studied the interdependence relationships between variables and their influence on the decision-making system.

The novelty of this research is represented by creating a new decision-making model in the field of entrepreneurship that can help the managers study the influences in their field of activity and manage the opportunities that can come.

16.2 Methodology

The company is a complex environment, and the analysis of the developed business models depends and will depend on a number of internal and external factors. The complexity of approaches that try to identify models of companies' adaptation to changes in the business environment is very high. The research carried out in this chapter belongs to the category of studies that aim to model the influence of external factors on the development of companies and how they adapt to market changes (Foss & Saebi, 2017, 2018; Lanzolla & Markides, 2021; Massa și colab., 2018; Snihur & Tarzijan, 2018). Understanding how companies operate and adapt to changes in the business environment is one of the challenges of economic researchers in recent years (Brzeziński and Bitkowska, 2022; Cilliers, 2001; Levy, 2000; Simon, 1991; Zott & Amit, 2010; Teece, 2010 Sanaz et al., 2023).

The authors' approach is aimed at identifying the interdependencies between the perception about the business environment, entrepreneurial experience, and the field of activity and how the business environment factors influence them (Ciucan-Rusu et al., 2022; Apostu et al., 2022). Based on the data collected from the questionnaire, the authors extracted the variables that were considered as having an influence on the decision-making process, analyzed them, and after created a model of these dependencies starting from the idea that the existence of a linear correlation between these parameters and specific factors of the business environment influences the decision-making process for the companies that exist on the studied region. The independent variables selected from the analyzed factors used to create the model: (1) introducing new products/services on the market; (2) identifying and penetrating new markets; (3) increasing demand on the market where the company operates; (4) using innovative performance technologies; (5) identifying and accessing funding sources; and (6) developing medium and long-term partnerships.

In order to investigate which variables influence the demand on the market where company operates, considered as being the dependent variable, the authors did first the Pearson correlation coefficient to see the level of influence and second a regression analysis to see if the independent variables (the introduction of new products/services on the market; identifying and entering new markets; increasing demand on the market where the firm operates; the use of innovative performance technologies; identifying and accessing funding sources; developing medium and long-term partnerships) have an influence on the dependent variable.

The statistical method used to analyze the correlation between variables was the Pearson correlation. This method calculates a coefficient that measures and describes the degree of linear association between two normally distributed continuous quantitative variables. This coefficient has values between −1 and 1. A positive value tending to 1 implies that a linear equation describing the relationship between the independent variable and the dependent variable can be determined, and a negative value tending to −1 implies an inverse relationship of causality. A value of 0 or close to 0 implies that there is no linear correlation between the analyzed variables.

The business environment is perceived as challenging by most entrepreneurs, but at the same time, they realize that only those who are flexible and open to adapt to changes in the market have the opportunity to develop and last in the long term on market. Rapid adaptation to changes in the business environment requires the business management to select new approaches and decision-making methods and be flexible to the wishes of customers, use different management methods, and try to capitalize on the opportunities offered and identified at the level of the business environment businesses in which they operate. Business rules control and regulate business processes. By continuously studying and analyzing the business environment in which they operate, entrepreneurs can identify opportunities that they can adapt their activities.

The instrument used to obtain the data presented in the current analysis was the questionnaire built to determine the profile of the entrepreneur from the Centru Region and his assessment of the quality of the business environment in which he operates. The questionnaire was constructed in four parts, where the first part collected the general data of the companies, second part gathered the opinion regarding the regional business environment, the third part asked about strategies, policies, and competitive advantages, and the fourth part investigated aspects regarding the workforce.

In this chapter, according to the main objective of our research, the authors have extracted from the questionnaire only the part that analyzed the business opportunities perceived by the respondents according to their working domain.

16.3 Findings

The first objective of this chapter was to calculate the Pearson correlation coefficient between the variables that are the model's independent variables (Fig. 16.1): (1) the introduction of new products/services on the market; (2) identifying and entering new markets; (3) increasing demand on the market where the firm operates; (4) the use of innovative performance technologies; (5) identifying and accessing funding sources; and (6) developing medium and long-term partnerships. The dependent variable taken into consideration for creating the model is increasing demand in the market where the company operates.

Using the Pearson coefficient to analyze the dependence of the identification of opportunities offered by the regional business environment and their capitalization, viewed as variables influenced by the experience acquired by entrepreneurs, we obtain the data presented in Table 16.1, in which the analysis of correlations between entrepreneurial experience and the typology of business opportunities offered by the regional business environment is captured.

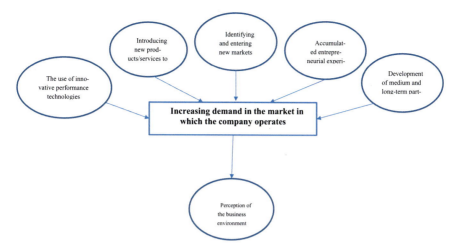

Fig. 16.1 Model of influencing the perception of the business environment by the entrepreneurial experience and the opportunities identified and exploited by entrepreneurs. (Source: Authors' computation, September 2022)

Within the first dimension, namely the entrepreneurial experience, the aim was to identify a direct correlation with the possibility of identifying new products and/or services on the market, the identification and penetration of new markets, the increase in demand on the market where the company operates, the use of innovative performance technologies, identifying and accessing funding sources, and the development of medium and long-term partnerships. The first two factors did not reveal the existence of a correlation, the first significant correlation being observed between the entrepreneurial experience and the increase in demand from the market in which the firm operates. In this case, there is a weak inverse correlation in intensity, and the increase in demand in the market where the firm operates influences the entrepreneurial experience. This result is also perfectly valid in the real business environment, because the fluctuation of the demand for products or services in a certain market entails the continuous adaptation of entrepreneurs, thus broadening their entrepreneurial experience. The second significant correlation is made up of entrepreneurial experience and the use of innovative performance technologies. In this case, the correlation shows the influence of entrepreneurial experience on the use of performing technologies.

The second dimension, the introduction of new products and/or services on the market, registers correlations with the following influencing factors: identifying and penetrating new markets, increasing demand on the market in which the company operates, using innovative performance technologies, identifying and accessing sources of financing, and the development of medium- and long-term partnerships. The most significant correlation (0.757) is obtained in the analysis between the introduction of new products and/or services on the market and the identification and penetration of new markets. These correlations are very strong and express the fact that the introduction of new products and/or services on the market is related,

Table 16.1 Correlations between entrepreneurial experience and the typology of business opportunities offered by the regional environment

Pearson Coefficient	Entrepreneurial experience	Introducing new products/services on the market	Identifying and penetrating new markets	Increasing demand on the market where the company operates	Using innovative performance technologies	Identifying and accessing funding sources	Developing medium and long-term partnerships
Entrepreneurial experience	1	0.059	0.115	−0.293**	0.204**	0.104	0.058
Introducing new products/services on the market		1	0.757*	0.455**	0.530*	0.356**	0.215**
Identifying and penetrating new markets			1	0.583*	0.749*	0.656*	0.581*
Increasing demand on the market where the company operates				1	0.276**	0.376**	0.477**
Using innovative performance technologies					1	0.760*	0.550*
Identifying and accessing funding sources						1	0.750*
Developing medium and long-term partnerships							1

Source: Authors' computation, September 2022
*Correlation is significant at the 0.05 level (1-tailed)
**Correlation is insignificant at the 0.01 level (1-tailed)

most of the time, to the identification and penetration of new markets. This result is perfectly valid because without a continuous process of developing the company's activity on the market it operates in, it is not possible to identify new markets that it can penetrate with its products and services.

The third dimension, namely, the identification and penetration of new markets, registered the most intense correlation with the use of innovative performance technologies. This correlation is direct, of high intensity, with a score of 0.749.

This result is perfectly valid because, in practice, new markets cannot be identified and implicitly penetrated without using state-of-the-art technologies that allow their identification, their analysis, and the discovery of the appropriate method to penetrate that market. In order to identify and penetrate new markets, it must be emphasized that the sources of financing also play an important role. From the results obtained in the table above, it can be seen that this is confirmed by the direct correlation between the previously mentioned items, this correlation registering a score of 0.656. The following significant correlation is recorded between the identification and penetration of new markets and the increase in demand in the market in which the firm operates. It registered a score of 0.583. The fourth dimension, namely the increase in demand on the market in which the company operates, recorded medium-intensity scores with the use of innovative high-performance technologies, the identification and access of funding sources, and the development of medium and long-term partnerships, the latter recorded a correlation of 0.477, and this being the most significant of the scores recorded within this dimension.

The use of innovative high-performance technologies, considered the fifth dimension, recorded significant correlations with the identification and access to funding sources and the development of medium- and long-term partnerships. Of these two scores, the highest level is obtained by the use of innovative high-performance technologies and the identification and access of funding sources, with a value of 0.760. The sixth dimension, identifying and accessing funding sources, registered a significant direct correlation of high intensity, with the development of medium- and long-term partnerships. This correlation recorded a score of 0.750. If we extrapolate the results in the real market, this result is significant because the growth and development of a company on the market are also linked to the capital infusion it has and to which it has access. This infusion of capital can largely come from the conclusion of medium- and long-term partnerships. These partnerships are beneficial for an entrepreneur, because they allow him access to the human, capital, or material resources that the partner company has, facilitating the growth of the entrepreneurial experience and at the same time of the company on the market.

The second objective of this chapter is to see if the independent variables determined changes in the dependent variable. Hence, we ran three linear regressions with bootstrapping on the determinants of the increasing demand in the market the company operates with the help of the statistical software SPSS version 26. Estimated results are presented in Tables 16.2, 16.3 and 16.4.

From Table 16.2, it can be observed that the dependent variable analyzed was influenced by the following independent variables: (1) identifying and entering new

Table 16.2 Linear regression test 1

Model	Unstandardized Coefficients B	Unstandardized Coefficients Std. Error	Standardized Coefficients Beta	t	Sig.	95.0% Confidence Interval for B Lower Bound	95.0% Confidence Interval for B Upper Bound
(Constant)	1.495	.328		4.563	.000	.846	2.144
Identifying and entering new markets	.531	.143	.576	3.706	.000	.247	.814
The use of innovative performance technologies	-.360	.098	-.459	-3.678	.000	-.554	-.166
Development of medium and long term partnerships	.238	.082	.329	2.906	.004	.076	.401

Source: Authors' computation, September 2022
[a]Dependent variable: Increasing demand in the market in which the company operates

Table 16.3 Linear regression test 2

Model	Unstandardized Coefficients B	Unstandardized Coefficients Std. Error	Standardized Coefficients Beta	t	Sig.	95.0% Confidence Interval for B Lower Bound	95.0% Confidence Interval for B Upper Bound
(Constant)	2.550	.322		7.932	.000	1.913	3.187
Introducing new products and services to the market	.485	.079	.474	6.158	.000	.329	.641
Accumulated entrepreneurial experience	-.220	.053	-.320	-4.163	.000	-.325	-.115

Source: Authors' computation, September 2022
[a]Dependent variable: Increasing demand in the market in which the company operates

markets; (2) the use of innovative performance technologies; and (3) developing of medium and long-term partnerships.

Namely, the first explanatory variable had a positive influence on the result, with $b = 0.53$, 95% CI [0.25, 0.81], $t = 3.71$, $p < 0.001$. The influence of the third explanatory variable was also positive, with $b = 0.33$, 95% CI [0.08, 0.4], $t = 2.91$, $p < 0.01$. At the same time, the impact of the second explanatory variable was negative, with $b = -0.46$, 95% CI [−0.55, −0.17], $t = -3.68$, $p < 0.001$.

Table 16.4 Linear regression test 3

Model	Unstandardized Coefficients		Standardized Coefficients	t	Sig.	95.0% Confidence Interval for B	
	B	Std. Error	Beta			Lower Bound	Upper Bound
(Constant)	2.921	.349		8.375	.000	2.231	3.612
Area of activity	-.080	.040	-.166	-1.970	.051	-.159	.000
Identifying and accessing funding sources	.313	.070	.374	4.438	.000	.173	.452

Source: Authors' computation, September 2022
[a]Dependent variable: Increasing demand in the market in which the company operates

The second test was conducted to see if the independent variables, introducing new products and services into the market and accumulated entrepreneurial experience, influence the dependent variables (increasing demand in which the market operates).

From the obtained results, presented in Table 16.4, it can be observed that both independent variables influence the dependent one.

Namely, the first explanatory variable had a positive influence on the result, with $b = 0.48$, 95% CI [0.33, 0.64], $t = 6.16$, $p < 0.001$. The impact of the second explanatory variable was negative, with $b = -0.22$, 95% CI [−0.33, −0.12], $t = -4.16$, $p < 0.001$.

The third test conducted tested the identification and access funding sources and area of activity, both considered independent variables, to see if they exercise an influence on the dependent variable.

The first explanatory variable had no influence on the result, with $b = -0.80$, 95% CI [−1.59, 0.00], $t = -1.97$, $p > 0.001$. The impact of the second explanatory variable was a positive one, with $b = 0.31$, 95% CI [0.17, 0.45], $t = 4.44$, $p < 0.001$. After seeing the test results only, the variable *Identifying and accessing funding sources* influences the demand for the products companies.

After conducting the Pearson correlation test and linear regressions with bootstrapping test, we have identified which independent variables exercise an influence on the dependent one. The authors created the following model that illustrates the influences that occur in the market where the company develops its entire activity and influences the manager's perception regarding the business environment. The model is presented in Fig. 16.1.

16.4 Conclusions

The present analysis offers a series of perspectives on how the opportunities influence and are influenced by the entrepreneurial experience in the business environment, including the entrepreneurs' awareness of the existence of these opportunities on the market. Thus, the perception of the business environment is influenced by the entrepreneurial experience (and to a large extent by the field in which the entrepreneurs operate).

However, the analyzed variables are strongly influenced by the increase in market demand where the company operates and influences it directly. This influence can turn into opportunities for entrepreneurs as key points in the development future possibilities and create new patterns that can be followed by the entrepreneurs in their activities on the market. If the managers consider, the variables presented in the model can identify new opportunities and develop in a more appropriate way their businesses.

In the present research, due to the type of the analyzed variables, logistic correlation could not be performed instead the authors used a linear regression with bootstrapping to test if there are influences of the independent variables on the dependent one. We consider this as a limit to our present research.

For the future, the authors intend to extend the present research to find out what other influences are important for managers. Another limitation of our research is the geographical area, namely the center region area; we consider that we need to extend our research to the other areas to create a better understanding of the factors that influence the perception on the market and influence the decision-making process of the managers. In this chapter, the authors used only a part of the questionnaire to study the perception of business environment; for future research, we intend to expand our research by using the remaining parts of the questionnaire to find out other influences and to conduct more in-depth analysis.

References

Apostu, S. A., Vasile, V., Panait, M., & Sava, V. (2022). Exploring the ecological efficiency as the path to resilience. *Economic Research-Ekonomska Istrazivanja*. https://doi.org/10.1080/1331677X.2022.2108476

Badakhshan, P., Conboy, K., Grisold, T., & vom Brocke. (2019). Agile business process management: A systematic literature review and an integrated framework. *Business Process Management Journal, 26*(6), 1505–1523. https://doi.org/10.1108/BPMJ12-2018-0347

Brzeziński, S., & Bitkowska, A. (2022). Integrated business process management in contemporary enterprises – A challenge or a necessity? *Contemporary Economics, 16*(4), 374–386. https://doi.org/10.5709/ce.1897-9254.488

Cilliers, P. (2001). Boundaries, hierarchies and networks in complex systems. *International Journal of Innovation Management, 5*(02), 135–147.

Ciucan-Rusu, L., Vasile, V., Stefan, D., Comes, C. A., Stefan, A. B., Timus, M., Oltean, A., Bunduchi, E., & Popa, M. A. (2022). Consumers behavior determinants on online local market platforms in COVID-19 pandemic – A probit qualitative analysis. *Mathematics, 10*(22), 4281. https://doi.org/10.3390/math10224281

Climent, R. C., & Haftor, D. M. (2021). Value creation through the evolution of business model themes. *Journal of Business Research, 122*, 353–361.

Davidsson, P., Recker, J., & von Briel, F. (2020). External enablement of new venture creation: A framework. *Academy of Management Perspectives, 34*(3), 311–332.

Dumas, M., La Rosa, M., Mendling, J., & Reijers, H. A. (2018). Introduction to business process management. In M. Dumas, M. La Rosa, J. Mendling, & H. A. Reijers (Eds.), *Fundamentals of business process management* (pp. 1–3). Springer. https://doi.org/10.1007/978-3-662-56509-4_1

Foss, N. J., & Saebi, T. (2017). Fifteen years of research on business model innovation: How far have we come, and where should we go? *Journal of Management, 43*(1), 200–227.

Foss, N. J., & Saebi, T. (2018). Business models and business model innovation: Between wicked and paradigmatic problems. *Long Range Planning, 51*(1), 9–21.

Lanzolla, G., & Markides, C. (2021). A business model view of strategy. *Journal of Management Studies, 58*(2), 540–553.

Levy, D. L. (2000). Applications and limitations of complexity theory in organization. In I. J. Rabin, G. J. Miller, & W. B. Hildreth (Eds.), *Handbook of strategic management* (pp. 67–87). Marcel Dekker, Inc.

Massa, L., Gianluigi, V., & Tucci, C. (2018). Business models and complexity. *Journal of Business Models, 6*(1), 59–71.

Mat Jusoh, Y. H., Azmawaty Abd Razak, S. N., Basirah Wan Mohamad Noor, W. N., Hudayati, A., Puspaningsih, A., & Ahmad Nadzri, F. A. (2022). Audit committee characteristics and timeliness of financial reporting: Social enterprises evidence. *Contemporary Economics, 16*(2). https://doi.org/10.5709/ce.1897-9254.478

Osterwalder, A., & Pigneur, Y. (2010). *Business model generation: A handbook for visionaries, game changers, and challengers, 1*. Wiley.

Parida, V., Sjödin, D., & Reim, W. (2019). Reviewing literature on digitalization, business model innovation, and sustainable industry: Past achievements and future promises. *Sustainability, 11*(2), 391.

Ramdani, B., Binsaif, A., & Boukrami, E. (2019). Business model innovation: A review and research agenda. *New England Journal of Entrepreneurship, 22*(2), 89–108.

Saebi, T., Lien, L., & Foss, N. J. (2017). What drives business model adaptation? The impact of opportunities, threats and strategic orientation. *Long Range Planning, 50*(5), 567–581.

Sanaz Vatankhah, S., Bamshad, V., Altinay, L., & De Vita, G. (2023). Understanding business model development through the lens of complexity theory: Enablers and barriers. *Journal of Business Research, 155*(Part A), 113350. https://doi.org/10.1016/j.jbusres.2022.113350

Simon, H. A. (1991). The architecture of complexity. In G. J. Klir (Ed.), *Facets of systems science* (pp. 457–476). Springer.

Snihur, Y., & Tarzijan, J. (2018). Managing complexity in a multi-business-model organization. *Long Range Planning, 51*(1), 50–63.

Staniewski, M. (2016a). The contribution of business experience and knowledge to successful entrepreneurship. *Journal of Business Research, 69*(11), 5147–5152. https://doi.org/10.1016/j.jbusres.2016.04.095

Staniewski, M. (2016b). *The organisational and psychological predictors of entrepreneurial success* (Pursuit of success). Lambert Academic Publishing.

Staniewski, M., & Awruk, K. (2018). Questionnaire of entrepreneurial success – Report on the initial stage of method construction. *Journal of Business Research, 88*, 437–442. https://doi.org/10.1016/j.jbusres.2017.11.041

Staniewski, M., & Awruk, K. (2019). Entrepreneurial success and achievement motivation – A preliminary report on a validation study of the questionnaire of entrepreneurial success. *Journal of Business Research, 101*, 433–440. https://doi.org/10.1016/j.jbusres.2019.01.073

Staniewski, M., & Awruk, K. (2021). Parental attitudes and entrepreneurial success. *Journal of Business Research, 123*, 538–546. https://doi.org/10.1016/j.jbusres.2020.10.039

Teece, D. J. (2010). Business models, business strategy and innovation. *Long Range Planning, 43*(2–3), 172–194.

Żebrowska-Suchodolska, D., & Karpio, A. (2022). Study of the skills of balanced fund managers in Poland. *Contemporary Economics, 16*(2). https://doi.org/10.5709/ce.1897-9254.474

Zott, & Amit. (2010). Business model design: An activity system perspective. *Long Range Planning, 43*(2–3), 216–226.

Zott, & Amit. (2015). Business model innovation: Toward a process perspective. In J. Zhou (Ed.), *The Oxford handbook of creativity, innovation, and entrepreneurship* (pp. 395–406). The Oxford University Press.

Chapter 17
Circular Economy Performance at Regional Level in European Union

Victor Platon , Simona Frone , Andreea Constantinescu ,
and Sorina Jurist

Abstract Circular economy represents the reuse of products that have reached the end of their life cycle by repairing them or transforming them into recycled raw materials. This way, the consumption of resources and energy needed for the production of new equipment can be diminished and in time waste generation can be reduced. The main objective of this research is to identify a regional hierarchy of the EU member states according to the circular economy indicators. Several relevant monitoring indicators for the circular economy evolution were analyzed, namely generated municipal waste, circular material use rate, packaging recycling rate, biodegradable waste recycling rate, circular economy investment, circular economy innovation, and rate of WEEE recycling. The methodology used includes a literature review, former research outputs analyzed for the objective of this research, and dynamic and comparative statistical analysis on the evolution of relevant indicators at the level of five EU geographical regions. The results of the research highlighted the fact that, at regional level, the circular economy has a fragmented distribution. Consequently, a number of regions, and implicitly the member states that form that region, recorded higher values for some indicators and lower or average values for other indicators.

Keywords Circular economy · Regional change · Circular economy indicators · Statistical dynamic analysis

---

V. Platon · S. Frone · A. Constantinescu (✉) · S. Jurist
Institute of National Economy, Bucharest, Romania

© The Author(s), under exclusive license to Springer Nature Switzerland AG 2024
L. Chivu et al. (eds.), *Constraints and Opportunities in Shaping the Future: New Approaches to Economics and Policy Making*, Springer Proceedings in Business and Economics, https://doi.org/10.1007/978-3-031-47925-0_17

17.1 Introduction

This article represents the preliminary findings of a research work carried out by a collective of researchers within the Institute for National Economy. The research is not finalized, so the research will continue with more elaborate analysis techniques and more indicators of the circular economy topic.

Circular economy is increasingly studied and implemented worldwide nowadays, since helping preserve the natural resources and encouraging reuse and recycle of products at their end-of-life moment (Noja et al., 2022). European Union is one of the main promoters of circular economy concept, creating and implementing policies through all member states.

The main objective proposed by this research paper is to bring some insight regarding the circular economy performance at regional level, throughout the European Union member states using a limited number of indicators. The methodology used was a simple analysis that took into consideration, as main hierarchization criterion, the member states affiliation to five geographical regions within the European Union. The geographical situation has a significant influence on transition to the circular economy model, and this may be observed in the comparative evolution of the selected circular economy indicators.

17.2 Literature Review

There is a consistent background literature on the subject of circular economy, focusing on different indicators from different points of view. Therefore, in this paper, we will only mention briefly some of the latest papers on the subject.

Mihai et al (2018) is an interesting and influential research with insights into the circular economy and renewable energy correlations and developments in the EU is Mihai et al. (2018). Another important research work is by Hysa et al., 2020, who used five major CE indicators to model and measure the effect of circular economy innovation on economic growth. The study strongly confirmed the importance of environmental, economic, and social components of the CE to economic growth and underpins the necessity of innovation in the core of circular economy for EU28.

The authors of the current paper have some previous research on aspects concerning eco-innovation and recycling. One paper focuses on measuring the intensity of influence of innovation on recycling within EU member states. One of the indicators analyzed is the circular material use rate (CMUR). The findings highlight that CMUR, taken as a dependent variable, is highly and positively impacted by Euro area membership— countries belonging to Euro area have +2.3% higher CMUR rate compared with countries that are not yet using Euro as currency (Platon et al., 2022). Another recent paper analyzes the evolution of WEEE within EU member states and how it impacts the implementation of circular economy on regional and national level (Constantinescu et al., 2022). A previous approach of the circular economy indicators highlights the need for better policy and economic instruments in order to create a positive framework at national level (Platon et al., 2020). However, many research papers highlight that there is a lot to improve regarding the waste management in Romania, and it represents a topic of further research (Frone et al., 2020; Constantinescu & Frone, 2015).

In an interesting recent paper, authors revised the circularity of materials under linear and circular models. They examine the recycling of different waste types and present the results for various activity sectors. The results of the research results show that the most important factor affecting the circularity of materials is represented by private investments in recycling, in particular the municipal waste and the WEEE recycling (Burinskiene et al., 2022).

The factors that influence implementation of circular economy innovation by firms in European Union are analyzed in this paper. The analysis stated showed a positive correlation between recycling activity and product redesign (Triguero et al., 2022). Another paper presents strategic directions within EU toward raw material management, with a special approach to circular material use. The authors emphasize the importance of mineral resources management in order to promote circular economy and thus the importance of circular material use (Smol et al., 2020).

The synthesis and importance of business models in implementing and performing the circular economy worldwide are analyzed by Foroozanfar et al. (2022). The most significant drivers are emphasized and discussed for future research.

A recent paper discussed the degree of regulation in the EU WEEE recycling industry. The research highlighted the fact that the impact of competition on the economic performance is rather positive (Favot et al., 2022). Analyzing the recycling situation in EU, a new research used a regression analysis to identify what factors influence most the European waste management policies. Different circular economy indicators (trade in secondary raw materials, circular material use rate, and waste recycling rate) vary, being influenced by general indicators—national GDP, human resources, investments in innovation, and technology (Sultanova et al., 2021).

The objective and findings of our research are closer to the outcomes of a very recent study (Drăgoi et al., 2021). In this study, the results showed that CE within the European Union as aggregate is on the sustainable and circular path of development. Nevertheless, the study did mention that the situation of the member states varies significantly requiring adjustments to be made by national and EU authorities.

17.3 Methodology

The research work that is going to continue took into consideration 28 EU countries for the period 2000–2018 and only seven indicators out of 11 indicators that are included in the circular economy section. At this stage of the research, a simplified methodology was used taking into account only the average values for the seven indicators selected for a period of 19 years. The number of observations is large for each indicator. In theory, we have available a maximum of 532 data points for each indicator. In some cases, when some data are missing, the data available were reduced to 380–400 entries.

As stated before, the EU member states were clustered using the geographical criterion. Countries were clustered in five regions, as follows (see Fig. 17.1):

1. Center region comprises Austria, Czech Republic, Hungary, Poland, Slovakia, Slovenia, and Germany; this group of countries is well known to belong to the Central European cluster.
2. North region comprises Denmark, Estonia, Finland, Leetonia, Lithuania, and Sweden; this region includes mainly Nordic countries and Baltic states.
3. West region comprises Belgium, France, Ireland, Luxembourg, Holland, Portugal, and UK. In the case of Portugal, the fact that Portugal has the time zone aligned with that of UK and not with Spain was considered. As well, in many analyses, southern countries group does not include Portugal but only Mediterranean countries. So, we allocated Portugal to the west region.
4. South region comprises Cyprus, Greece, Italy, Malta, and Spain; all these countries have in commune the Mediterranean Basin.

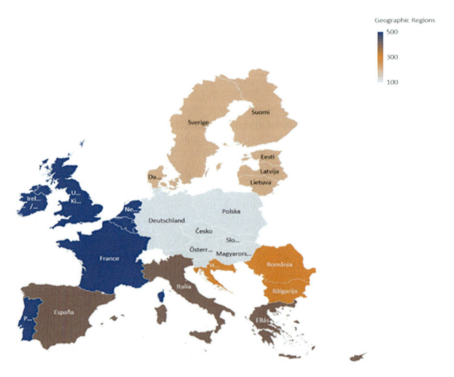

Fig. 17.1 Regional clusterization of EU member states, using geographical criterion. (Source: Authors' own research)

5. Southeast region comprises Bulgaria, Croatia, and Romania; this region includes Balkan countries.

It is important to clarify that UK was included, even if it is no longer a member state, because the analyzed statistical data cover the period 2000–2018, when UK was still part of EU. Nevertheless, it must be stated that indicators analysis covers slightly different periods of time because of the lack of data. Several research methods have been used in this paper, namely desk research, data processing, interrogating available databases, and comparative analysis of data.

As it was said, the methodology is based on data provided by Eurostat database.[1] The indicators of the circular economy taken into account in this preliminary stage were the next:

1. Packaging recycling rate.
2. Municipal waste recycling rate.
3. Biodegradable waste recycling.
4. Circular economy investments.
5. Circular economy innovation (patents).
6. WEEE recycling rate.
7. CMUR—circular material use rate.

The processing method was a simpler one involving only hierarchies of the average values of the indicators selected for this preliminary analysis. A next step of the methodology will be to take into account all indicators describing circular economy and to make use of a more complex processing methods.

17.4 Analysis/Result Interpretation

The indicators chosen to be analyzed are some of the most important ones for circular economy evaluation.

(a) The packaging recycling rate, at regional level, is shown in Fig. 17.2.

The highest average value of the packaging recycling rate is registered by the countries situated in region west of EU (67.1%). The countries in the north and center regions registered almost similar values of the analyzed indicator (61%). The lowest values are recorded in south and southeast region of EU around 56%.

(b) The municipal waste recycling rate is presented in Fig. 17.3.

The highest municipal waste recycling rate is registered by the west region (38.0%).

---

[1] Each indicator has its own detailed explanation at the Eurostat site (https://ec.europa.eu/eurostat/data/database)

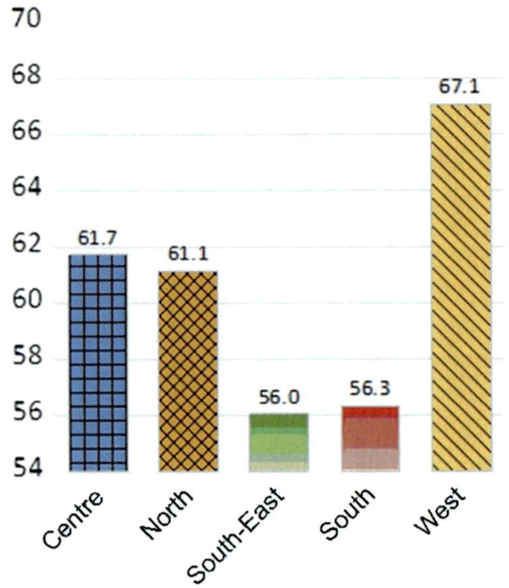

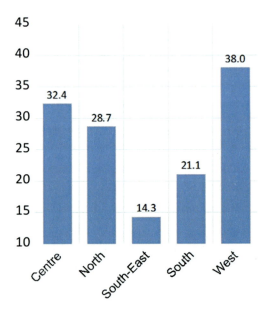

Fig. 17.2 Packaging recycling rate at regional level (%, average of the period 2000–2018). (Source: Authors' own calculations)

Fig. 17.3 Municipal waste recycling rate at regional level (%, average for the period 2000–2018). (Source: Authors' own calculations)

The center region, with a rate of 32.4%, ranks second followed by the north region with 28.7%.

The lowest values are recorded in the south region (21.1%) and the southeast region, with an average rate of only (14.3%).

(c) Figure 17.4 presents the evolution of indicator "biodegradable *waste recycling*." It is expressed in kg/inhabitant and also as an average value for the time period 2000–2018.

The member states located in the west of EU region recycle the largest amount of biodegradable waste (82.9 kg/inhabit.).

In second place, according to the geographical criterion, are the states in the center region, with an average value of 52.9 kg/ inhabit.

The states in the north and south regions of the EU recycle similar amounts of biodegradable waste (46–48 kg/inhabit.), also similar to the European average.

The lowest amounts of biodegradable waste are recycled in the countries in southeast region (15.7 kg/inhabit.)— Romania, Bulgaria, and Croatia.

(d) The next indicator, presented in Fig. 17.5, is circular economy investments, expressed in million Euro and as yearly average for the time period 2000–2018.

The average of circular economy investments for the analyzed period (2000–2018) had the highest value in the west region of EU—11330.3 mil. Euro.

In second place are the countries of the south region, with an average CE investment of 8000 mil. Euro.

In the center region, average values of 5000 million Euros were recorded for investments in the circular economy, in the period 2000–2018.

The north and southeast regions recorded the lowest values for investments in circular economy, in the analyzed period: 1608.5 million Euros in the north region and only 764.4 million Euros in the southeast region.

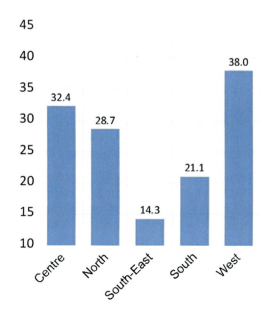

Fig. 17.4 Biodegradable waste recycling, at regional level (kg/inhabit. Average for the period 2000–2018). (Source: Authors' own calculations)

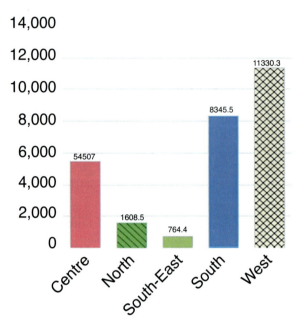

Fig. 17.5 Circular economy investments at regional level (mil. Euro yearly average 2000–2018). (Source: Authors' own calculations)

(e) Another significant indicator for the circular economy implementation at EU level is circular economy innovation, evaluated by the number of registered patents. The evolution, presented in Fig. 17.6, illustrates the average trend for the time period 2001–2016.

The countries in the center region registered, in the analyzed period, the highest number of patents—22.1 patents/year, followed at a long distance by the countries in the west region—12.6 patents/year.

The countries in the south and north regions registered average values of the annual number of patents—7.7 patents/year in the south region and 3.6 patents/year in the north region.

The countries in the southeast region registered, for the analyzed period, the lowest number of circular economy patents, only 1.2 patents/year.

(f) Figure 17.7 presents the evolution of one of the most followed indicators nowadays, namely the recycling of waste of electric and electronic equipment (WEEE). It is expressed in kg per inhabitant, and the figures represent average data for the time period analyzed, 2009–2018.

The north region has the best results with 7.5 kg/inhabit. of WEEE recycled in the analyzed period.

The west region is in second place, with 6.9 kg/inhabit. of recycled WEEE.

The center region with 5.3 kg/inhabit. of recycled WEEE is in third place.

17 Circular Economy Performance at Regional Level in European Union

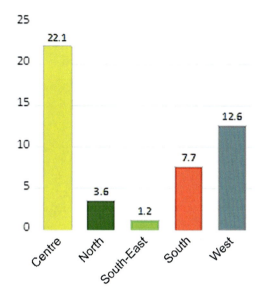

Fig. 17.6 Innovation in circular economy at regional level (number of patents, average for the period 2001–2016). (Source: Authors' own calculations)

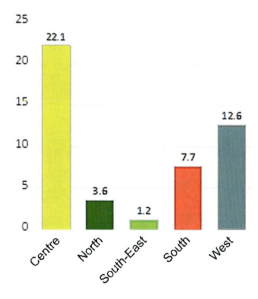

Fig. 17.7 WEEE recycling at regional level (kg/inhabit. Average for the period 2009–2018). (Source: Authors' own calculations)

The south and southeast regions have the lowest (almost similar) levels of WEEE recycling—4.1 kg/inhabit. and 4.2 kg/inhabit.

(g) Fig. 17.8 presents the last and most important indicator for circular economy evolution and circular material use rate. It is analyzed as percentage and also as average for the time period 2010–2020.

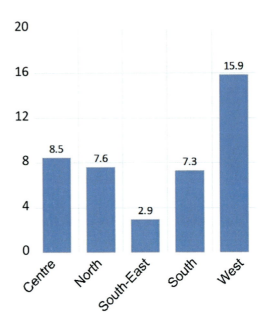

Fig. 17.8 CMUR—circular material use rate, at regional level (%, average for the period 2010–2020). (Source: Authors' own calculations)

Table 17.1 Circular economy indicators in EU at regional level

CE indicator/region	Center	North	Southeast	South	West
Packaging recycling rate (% average 2000–2018)	61.7	61.1	56.0	56.3	67.1
Municipal waste recycling rate (% average 2000–2018)	32.4	28.7	14.3	21.1	38.0
Biodegradable waste recycling (kg/inhabit. average 2000–2018)	52.9	48.6	15.7	45.9	82.9
Circular economy investments (mil. Euro yearly average 2000–2018)	5450.7	1608.5	764.4	8345.6	1130.3
Circular economy innovation (no. of patents 2001–2016 average)	22.1	3.6	1.2	7.7	12.6
WEEE recycling (kg/inhabit. average 2009–2018)	5.3	7.5	4.1	4.2	6.9
CMUR—Circular material use rate (% average 2010–2020)	8.5	7.6	2.9	7.3	15.9

Source: Authors' own research

The west region, which includes the Netherlands and Belgium, has the highest value of the CMUR indicator (15.9%).

In second place is the center region with a CMUR rate of 8.5%.

The north and south regions have average and close values (7.6% and 7.3%).

The lowest value for CMUR evolution is recorded in the southeast region (2.9%).

In the following analyses, Table 17.1 is a compilation of all the analyzed indicators for the five geographical regions in the European Union, according to the proposed methodology.

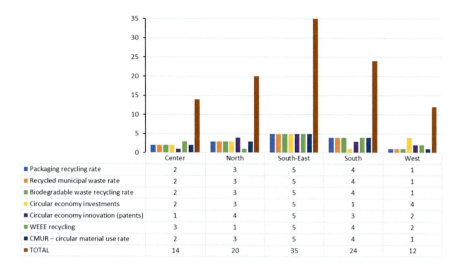

Fig. 17.9 Circular economy indicators in EU hierarchy

Figure 17.9 presents the hierarchical approach of each indicator for the circular economy performance of each region. Each region received a mark (1–5) in accordance with the place in the hierarchy of each indicator. All indicators were considered having equal importance. Simple hierarchies were established, based on the mentioned indicators: 1st place in the hierarchy gets 1 point, and 5th place in the hierarchy gets 5 points. The first in hierarchy are the regions with the lowest number of total points.

First place, with the highest circular economy performance, is occupied by west region (12 points), followed by center region (14 points), in second place. Next places, third and fourth, belong to north and south regions. The last place in this hierarchization, with the poorest circular economy performance, is occupied by southeast region (35 points).

17.5 Conclusions

From the research developed in this chapter, several conclusions may be drafted. Using a simplified methodology and only seven indicators, a picture of the circular economy was outlined.

The main conclusion is that, in the EU, circular economy has a fragmented distribution at regional level. The best performers are the countries from west regions (with 12 ranking points) followed by countries in center region (with 14 points). These two regions have the lowest number of hierarchy points; thus, they have the best values for every indicator analyzed. Regions, north (with 20 ranking points) and south (with 24 points), have mediocre performance in promoting circular economy; they are situated in the middle of the hierarchy.

The southeast region has the last position in every hierarchy of indicators and consequently for the overall ranking (35 points).

Therefore, the most advanced countries in promoting circular economy are in the west of EU, while the east are the feeblest ones. With average performance in CE, there is small difference between northern and southern countries. Their performance is quite similar.

As for the limits and future directions of research, it should be mentioned that, in this analysis, not all CE relevant indicators were taken into account. Consequently, further and recent data should be added, for 2019–2021 period. A new influx of data may change the ranking but not in a significant manner. Therefore, the next research analysis will employ updated information and more advanced methodology.

There is another future research direction that explains what causes this fragmentation. As the legislation regarding CE is consistent across EU member states, there are some ideas to be taken into account: main drivers (eco-investment, eco-innovation), economic instruments for recycling, stable legislative framework, etc.

It is obvious that there is still required a broad range of economic policies and investments for the improvement of circular economy performance. This is mainly needed in the countries located in the southeast and some countries of the south regions of the EU. These are countries also covered by the convergence objective of the Maastricht Treaty.

References

Burinskiene, A., Lingaitiene, O., & Jakubavicius, A. (2022). Core elements affecting the circularity of materials. *Sustainability, 14*(14), 8367; Special Issue Concrete with Recycled and Sustainable Materials) https://doi.org/10.3390/su14148367, https://www.mdpi.com/2071-1050/14/14/8367

Constantinescu, A., & Frone, S. (2015). Ecosystem approach outcomes of a regional metabolism. *Quality–Access to Success, 16*, 56.

Constantinescu, A., Platon, V., Surugiu, M., Frone, S., Antonescu, D., & Mazilescu, R. (2022). The influence of eco-investment on E-waste recycling -Evidence from EU countries, Frontiers in environmental. *Science, 10*, https://www.frontiersin.org/articles/10.3389/fenvs.2022.928955/full

Drăgoi, M. C., Andrei, J. V., & Cvijanovic, D. (2021). Circular economy as a vector for innovative and efficient production and consumption. Analysis on EU's indicators. In C. J. Chiappetta Jabbour & S. A. R. Khan (Eds.), *Sustainable production and consumption systems. Industrial ecology*. Springer. https://doi.org/10.1007/978-981-16-4760-4_12

Favot, M., Grassetti, L., Massarutto, A., & Veit, R. (2022). Regulation and competition in the extended producer responsibility models: Results in the WEEE sector in Europe. *Waste Management, 145*, 60–71. https://doi.org/10.1016/j.wasman.2022.04.027

Frone, D. F., Frone, S., Platon, V., & Constantinescu, A. (2020). Green economy prerequisites of waste management. *Scientific Papers Series Management, Economic Engineering in Agriculture and Rural Development, 20*(4), 211–218.

Foroozanfar, M. H., Imanipour, N., & Sajadi, S. M. (2022). Integrating circular economy strategies and business models: A systematic literature review. *Journal of Entrepreneurship in Emerging Economies, 14*(5), 678–700. https://doi.org/10.1108/JEEE-10-2021-0411

Hysa, E., Kruja, A., Rehman, N. U., & Laurenti, R. (2020). Circular economy innovation and environmental sustainability impact on economic growth: An integrated model for sustainable development. *Sustainability, 12*(12), 4831. https://doi.org/10.3390/su12124831

Mihai, M., Manea, D., Titan, E., & Vasile, V. (2018). Correlations in the European circular economy. *Economic Computation and Economic Cybernetics Studies and Research, 52*, 61–78.

Noja, G. G., Panait, M., Cristea, M., Trif, S. M., & Ponea, C. S. (2022). The impact of energy innovations and environmental performance on the sustainable development of the EU countries in a globalized digital economy. *Frontiers in Environmental Science, Section Environmental Economics and Management, 10.* https://doi.org/10.3389/fenvs.2022.934404

Platon, V., Pavelescu, F. M., Antonescu, D., Frone, S., Constantinescu, A., & Popa, F. (2022). Innovation and recycling-drivers of circular economy in EU. *Frontiers in Environmental Science, 10,* https://www.frontiersin.org/articles/10.3389/fenvs.2022.902651/full

Platon, V., Frone, S., Constantinescu, A., & Jurist, S. (2020). Economic instruments for WEEE recycling in Romania. *LUMEN Proceedings, 14,* 509–523. https://doi.org/10.18662/lumproc/ibmage2020/37

Smol, M., Marcinek, P., Duda, J., & Szołdrowska, D. (2020). Importance of sustainable mineral resource Management in Implementing the circular economy model and the European green Deal strategy. *Resources, 9,* 55. https://doi.org/10.3390/resources9050055, https://www.mdpi.com/2079-9276/9/5/55

Sultanova, D., Maliashova, A., & Gadelshina, S. (2021). Waste management as an element of sustainable development of the circular economy in the European Union. In *International conference on efficient production and processing (ICEPP-2021)* (Vol. 247)., https://www.e3s-conferences.org/articles/e3sconf/pdf/2021/23/e3sconf_icepp21_01007.pdf

Triguero, A., Cuerva, M. C., & Sáez-Martínez, F. J. (2022). Closing the loop through eco-innovation by European firms: Circular economy for sustainable development. *Business Strategy and the Environment, 31*(5), https://onlinelibrary.wiley.com/doi/10.1002/bse.3024

Chapter 18
Bibliometric Analysis of the Evaluation of Interest in Urban Regeneration

Anna-Maria Vasile, Carmen Ghimus, and Mihaela-Georgiana Oprea

Abstract Urban regeneration does not only involve architecture and urban planning projects. The concept is complex and is related to the obligation of collaboration and, necessarily, investments. Urban regeneration starts from context creators and extends to civil society represented by key players and supporters, who represent the personnel that provide education and training at all levels, as well as researchers from all fields of science. The aim of the work is to use digital tools specific to bibliometric analysis in order to evaluate the evolution of interest in urban regeneration and its related key topics over the past three decades. In this sense, to highlight urban regeneration, alongside another subject strictly related to it (development strategy, economic and social impact, economy, education and training, greenhouse gases, local development strategy, quality of life, and urban landscape), Lens, Excel, and VOSviewer were used.

Keywords Lens database · Urban regeneration · Economy · Quality of life · Education and training · Greenhouse gases · Urban landscape · Economic and social impact · Development strategy

---

A.-M. Vasile
School of Advanced Studies, National Institute of Economic Research "Costin C. Kirițes-cu," Romanian Academy, Bucharest, Romania

C. Ghimus · M.-G. Oprea (✉)
National Institute of Economic Research "Costin C. Kirițescu," Romanian Academy, Bucharest, Romania
e-mail: carmen.ghimus@ince.ro; oprea@ince.ro

© The Author(s), under exclusive license to Springer Nature Switzerland AG 2024
L. Chivu et al. (eds.), *Constraints and Opportunities in Shaping the Future: New Approaches to Economics and Policy Making*, Springer Proceedings in Business and Economics, https://doi.org/10.1007/978-3-031-47925-0_18

18.1 Introduction

18.1.1 The Process of Urban Regeneration

Attracting new activities, modernizing infrastructure, improving the environment, and diversifying the social structure are essential components for the development and progress of a community or region. Society's progress was driven by discoveries, inventions, innovations, and social movements, leading to qualitative leaps and new eras.

Over time, the city underwent a process of dynamic growth and advancement, moving from the model of the Greek city, namely the fair city, to that of the Roman city, a conglomeration of settlements subject to the Pax Romana, to that of the commercial city, which had to develop defense strategies, thus centralizing administrative and military functions.

The development and progress of production methods in agriculture, industry, and transportation led to the depopulation of rural areas and the growth of urban populations. This led to a significant shift in population distribution toward urban settlements.

The exchange of manufactured products was developed and generalized, and as a result, cities and peripheral agricultural areas began to "coexist" in an advantageous symbiosis.

The growth of cities has encompassed both industrial and residential areas, making work, mobility, and services essential components of urban life. Industrial areas have been integrated into the expansion of cities, thus acquiring a central position within urban landscapes. As industries undergo restructuring, there is a valuable opportunity to utilize the expansive areas and dormant industrial structures to meet the current and future needs of the population. Integrating these resources into the urban landscape can contribute to an improved and sustainable urban environment.

Industrial zones have become pivotal hubs within urban areas, assuming a central role in shaping the city's dynamics and functionality.

18.1.2 Retrospection and Evolution of Urban Regeneration Process

Urban renewal originated in the late nineteenth century, when major European cities undertook sanitary engineering improvements to address urban health issues. Cities like Paris, Barcelona, London, and Turin underwent extensive demolitions and reconstructions during this period, aiming to create a modernized urban environment with improved air and light. Urban renewal typically involved large-scale demolitions and the replacement of old buildings with new ones, often completely different in form and function.

In contrast to urban decay, urban regeneration processes prioritize new urban development by fostering revitalization and renewal. This shift in urban management focuses on regeneration, governance, and integrated planning tools, rather than solely on expansion and new development. The emphasis is no longer on urban expansion but on the process of urban regeneration and the implementation of strategies such as integrated programs. However, it is crucial to establish a consensus on the precise definition and scope of urban regeneration.

18.1.3 Perspectives on Regeneration Identified Problems

Urban regeneration is a complex phenomenon that lacks comprehensive understanding, requiring fresh perspectives and inspiration from both theory and practice. There is no predefined form or single explanation applicable to all urban contexts, and thus, there are no universally appropriate solutions. The process of urban regeneration should instead be tailored to reflect the unique local characteristics that define each city.

It is evident that local circumstances both limit and support urban regeneration efforts, with constraints that can be overcome through innovative and well-managed actions, even in challenging conditions. Considering the emergence and persistence of urban problems, as well as the evolving nature of theory, practice, and lessons learned from successful or unsuccessful regeneration initiatives, a one-size-fits-all approach is not feasible. The dynamic nature of the regeneration process means that each step and its outcomes depend on the immediate preceding actions, making it difficult to predict with certainty the exact course of action and results.

The necessity for urban regeneration should be viewed as an ongoing process, requiring long-term thinking spanning several generations or political mandates. Consequently, permanent solutions cannot be universally applied since each generation or mandate has its own priorities, perspectives, and available resources when addressing the problems of a specific area.

Thus, to the various priorities, perspectives, and resources of each generation, urban regeneration requires personalized approaches, which take into account the distinctive features of each city. The process is dynamic and unpredictable, requiring continuous efforts over long periods and continuously adapting priorities and resources.

18.2 Literature Review

18.2.1 Evolution of Interest in Urban Regeneration

Urban regeneration is a phenomenon little understood but widely cultivated. More has been done to explain the phenomenon, and this lack of understanding demonstrates the need to provide insights and inspiration, based on advances in both theory and practice.

The process itself takes various forms and actions, depending on the situation at hand. Over the last century, urban improvement and regeneration have played a significant role in shaping cities, starting from the era of the Industrial Revolution up to the present day. The process has drawn the attention of all the social actors, prompting them to perfect the process, the actions, and, of course, the results. An investigation of this period of urban regeneration evolution seems necessary (Table 18.1).

The historical evolution of urban problems and opportunities determines the relationship between physical conditions and social response and influences the contemporary theory and practice of urban regeneration (Roberts et al., 2000).

The changing and the improvement of management of towns and cities, the reconstruction of the model of partnership between social actors involved in the urban policy at all the management and decision levels, have determined the dominant forces of political life, to pay attention to this process.

The diagram illustrates the diverse range of themes and topics encompassed within urban regeneration and highlights its significant outcomes.

18.2.2 Research on Publication Between January 1, 1990, and December 31, 2022

The software tools that we used for our research are Lens and VOSviewer. The first one is a search facility available on the website lens.org, which has the capability to find the patent literature along with any other work published on the Web. We used this search engine to find scholarly works, which have been published from January 1, 1990, to December 31, 2022 (inclusive), and which focus on the subject of urban regeneration, alongside another subject related to it, such as development strategy; economic impact and social impact; economy; education and training; greenhouse gases; local development strategy; quality of life; and urban landscape. After setting the parameters for the research, lens.org created a database file for the articles published between 1990 and 2022 that tackle urban regeneration and each of its related subjects.

Afterward, it was used the VOSviewer software tool, to create the maps based on the discovered network data. Since VOSviewer was developed in the Java programming language, we could then visualize and explore these maps. VOSviewer helped

Table 18.1 Urban regeneration evolution

Period	Developed concepts
Nineteenth century	Great Britain—the first measures and regulations for the preservation of the old urban fabric
Beginning of twentieth century	Great Britain—large-scale reconstruction measures for the destruction caused by the world war
1931	Congress of Athena—First International Congress of Architects and Technicians of Historic Monuments—This document introduced important concepts and principles of conservation: The idea of a common universal heritage The importance of arranging the monuments The principle of integrating new materials
1933	Charter of Athens—IV International Congress for Modern Architecture—with the theme "the functional city" and focused on urbanism and the importance of planning in urban development schemes. It includes a recommendation calling for the destruction of urban slums and the creation of "green areas" in their place, negating any potential heritage value of such areas.
1947	Paris Conference—Marshall Plan
1950	Great Britain—beginning of the post-WWII recovery
1960	Western Europe—regeneration, functional restoration, and textural empowerment (social and economic aspects)
1970	Western Europe—plans for physical renovation taking political, social, and economic aspects into account
1980	Redevelopment, including collaborative reconstruction, improvement, and regeneration (Sharghi et al., 2018)
1990	Preserving history without neglecting historical identities and creating an identity according to present needs
2000	Urban regeneration and focus on sustainability in all aspects with the collaboration of local communities
2001	Sustainable development strategy, which focused on the objectives of protecting the environment and health, as well as combating poverty
2002	The integrated development of Europe structured on balanced regional areas, based on the principles of subsidiarity and reciprocity, competitiveness, cooperation, and solidarity between local and regional authorities
2003	Developing the concept of "coherent city," which assumes a multiple coherence: in the historical evolution, on the social and economic level, on the environmental level, and in the use of the space. Policies aimed at capitalizing on built heritage and reforms in planning and urban design
2004	The promoting of the principle of "more balanced development" or "territorial balance" (in the sense of avoiding territorial imbalances and reducing disparities)
2005	Strategy for Sustainable Community Development, which defines a "sustainable community" as a place where we would like to live and work, today and tomorrow
2006	Kick-off—fight against climate change and committed to a low-carbon, knowledge-based, and resource-efficient economy

(continued)

Table 18.1 (continued)

Period	Developed concepts
2007	The first steps for the polycentric territorial development of the EU, in order to make better use of the resources available in the European regions. An important aspect is the territorial integration of inhabited areas, to promote a balanced territorial organization based on a polycentric European urban structure
2008	Rethinking, preserving the spirit and place of the city, the cultural and historical heritage, establishing the way to exchange good practices, and promoting sustainable and competitive large cities worldwide. The foundations of the "sustainable and cohesive city" are being laid
2009	Territorial cohesion concerns ensuring the harmonious development of all these places and guaranteeing that their citizens are able to benefit to the maximum from the inherent characteristics of these territories, Green Paper of the Commission "Towards a new culture of urban mobility"
2010	Promoting a more resource-efficient, greener, and more competitive economy, the emergence of the concept of integrated urban regeneration
2017	Planning urban expansions, prioritizing the renewal, regeneration and modernization of urban areas, taking into account the planning and management of urban spatial development
2018	Development of measures to support the attractiveness of urban centers and increase their regional/zonal role, by promoting urban regeneration, integrated approach in urban development, strengthening urban-rural and urban-urban relations
2020	Reducing urban sprawl, prioritizing non-renewal and complex regeneration of urban areas, including the redevelopment of abandoned or dilapidated industrial sites
2022	Investments should be targeted at the growth opportunities offered by the green and digital transition to avoid the emergence of new disparities

Source: Information collected from specialized literature

us to determine from the downloaded information a concept to be able to build a quantitative map of a network of terms connected by co-occurrence links. Those terms are the subtopics of urban regeneration and each of its main topics.

Excel was also used to further analyze every database.

18.3 Methodology

In order to improve the amount of material that is accessible and to describe the situation in relation to examples of good behavior and the existing relationships between correspondents, several stages of research methodology have been adopted.

To handle the challenges of record variability, sources, and contextual metadata relevant to the original record, Lens uses the MetaRecord (MeR) paradigm. Lens currently contains records for more than 118 million patents and 208 million scholarly works, representing 95 and 193 affiliation-based countries, respectively.

Additionally, Lens adds more than 313 M publicly released genetic sequences and metadata to its biological data.

These analyses were performed in the following stages.

Stage I: Thematic Documentation

In this phase, the technical documents were analyzed to ascertain the present state of the preexisting scenario. We have set the filters available in Lens, to limit the search to academic publications and a time period from January 1, 1990, to December 31, 2022. The Lens search engine has Boolean operators, allowing users to locate academic publications that include specific terms. The ability to export bibliographic information for more than 1000 documents does, however, necessitate the creation of an account.

Knowing that the comma-separated values (CSV) format is used by Lens to export data and that a plain text file can be accessed with text editors, spreadsheet programs like Excel, or other specialist apps like Google Contracts and Microsoft Outlook, during our research, we have created a CSV bibliographic database file, to import into VOSviewer. A CSV file with the data for each keyword combination (where "and" is the Boolean operator) from 1990 to 2022 was acquired from Lens. Based on the research, a CSV file includes subtopics and additional information that we find during our studies, such as the titles of the publications, as well as a complete list of articles connected to the search query and published within the specified timeframe. Therefore, we could shape the data presented in this paperwork.

Stage II: Qualitative and Quantitative Analysis

At this point, the information used to calculate the number of publications on each combination and the difficulties of urban regeneration were taken into consideration.

As can be seen from these findings in Table 18.2, urban regeneration and economy are the most connected terms, since most scientific works have been written on these two subjects. Because Lens does not allow a user without an account to export data for a number of articles that exceed the 1000 limit, the data on urban regeneration and economy, which turned up 1953 scholarly works in the period between 1990 and 2022, had to be split up. Articles on these two keywords were downloaded from 1990 to 2016 and then downloaded from 2017 to 2022. Data were exported separately, and the two exported data sets were combined in VOSviewer. There were 980 publications in 1990–2016 and 973 publications in 2017–2022.

Stage III: Elaboration of Proposals

The number of publications per year was calculated by transferring the year of each publication from each database to an Excel spreadsheet. A bar chart was then made for each keyword combination in order to identify trends. Excel was also used to calculate the average overall link strength of each data set. The number of publications where two subtopics co-occur together is indicated by the strength of the association. The overall strength of the co-occurrence links between a specific subtopic and other subtopics is referred to as the total link strength. In order to generate a

Table 18.2 Number of publications on every combination of keywords in 1990–2022

Topics	Number of publications including these topics between 1990 and 2022 (inclusive)
"Urban regeneration" and "development strategy"	370
"Urban regeneration" and "economic impact" and "social impact"	90
"Urban regeneration" and "economy"	1953
"Urban regeneration" and "education" and "training"	508
"Urban regeneration" and "greenhouse gases"	108
"Urban regeneration" and "local development strategy"	20
"Urban regeneration" and "quality of life"	741
"Urban regeneration" and "urban landscape"	399

Source: Data obtained from Lens

co-occurrence network map and identify the subtopics that were most pertinent in each situation, every CSV file was imported into VOSviewer.

18.4 Analysis/Result Interpretation

18.4.1 Mapping the Subtopics of a Keyword Combination

On a map made in VOSviewer, the subtopics of a keyword combination are represented in the form of labeled circles known as items, which are sorted into groups known as clusters. The most relevant terms are those whose total link strength has a value above average. Hence, their circles and labels are the biggest. They are also the closest to the center of the map. The links that connect two terms together indicate that the two terms in question appear in the same publication. The thicker these links, the greater the number of publications that share both terms. The strength of association between the terms (the distribution) is highlighted by the distance between the terms on the map.

From VOSviewer, two screenshots of every map have been downloaded. The first screenshot shows a network visualization of the map, where the terms are colored according to the clusters in which they belong. The second screenshot shows an overlay visualization of the map, where the terms are colored in different shades of yellow, green, and blue based on their importance (note that the items do not change position, it is only their colors that are different). The color of the item is closer to yellow if the item is of particular importance. The color of the item is closer to blue if the item is not as relevant. The overlay visualization also includes a

Table 18.3 Number of subtopics and connected subtopics for every combination of keywords

Topics	Number of subtopics	Number of connected subtopics	Number of unconnected subtopics
"Urban regeneration" and "development strategy"	116	101	15
"Urban regeneration" and "economic impact" and "social impact"	45	32	13
"Urban regeneration" and "economy"	469	428	41
"Urban regeneration" and "education" and "training"	334	314	20
"Urban regeneration" and "greenhouse gases"	100	94	6
"Urban regeneration" and "local development strategy"	N/A	N/A	N/A
"Urban regeneration" and "quality of life"	416	412	4
"Urban regeneration" and "urban landscape"	108	97	11

Source: Author's own research based on Lens in VOSviewer

color bar that indicates how colors are attributed to the years in which the most publications with the most relevant terms have been released. The color bar leaves out the years with the fewest number of publications ("few" in relation to the rest of the years).

In addition, VOSviewer counted the number of subtopics for each combination of keywords, as well as the number of subtopics that have at least one co-occurrence link with another.

However, VOSviewer was unable to compute the data on "urban regeneration and local development strategy" due to the scant number of keywords. There must be at least three keywords in order for the program to create a network map.

As shown in Table 18.3, the topic "urban regeneration and economy" has the most subtopics; however, it also has the most unconnected subtopics. The topic "urban regeneration and quality of life," which has the second largest number of subtopics in total, has the least unconnected subtopics.

18.4.2 Urban Regeneration and Economy

As can be seen in Fig. 18.1, out of all the 1953 publications on urban regeneration and economy that have been obtained as a result of the investigations carried out between 1990 and 2022 (32 years), 1504 publications were registered in the last 9 years (over 100 publications per year), so 77% of the total. The interest in urban

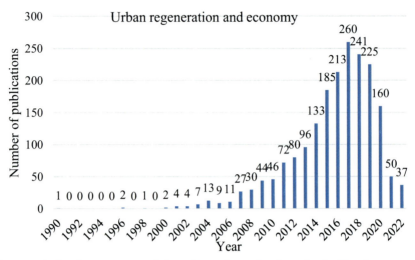

Source: Author's own research based on a Lens database in the Excel program.

Fig. 18.1 Yearly evolution of the number of publications on urban regeneration and economy

regeneration and economy was completely nil from 1991 to 1995 and in the years 1997 and 1999. The number of publications per year increased almost exponentially from 2005 to 2017, whereupon it decreased, dropping abruptly in 2021 and continuing to drop (Fig. 18.2).

In Fig. 18.3, it can be seen that the most relevant subtopics of urban regeneration and economy appeared in the publications released in 2018–2020, those being economic policy, cross-sectional studies, negotiating/psychology, coronavirus infections, age in place, aging, and China. The least relevant appeared in the publications released in 2010–2012, those being animals, poverty, architecture, population density, air pollution/economics, program evaluation, urbanization history, urban health/history, and communicable disease control. With very few publications released prior to 2010 and after 2020 (when compared to the years between 2010 and 2020 inclusive), the intervals 1990–2009 and 2021–2022 were left out altogether.

18.4.3 Urban Regeneration and Quality of Life

As can be seen in Fig. 18.4, the number of publications on urban regeneration and quality of life per year increased almost exponentially, shooting up particularly high in 2017, but starting with 2019 and until 2022, there was a downward trend, in 5 years.

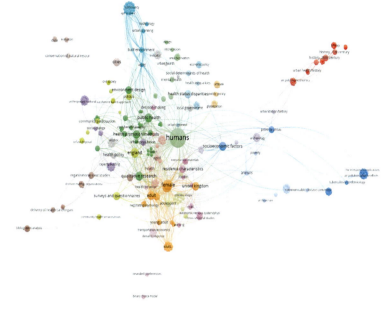

Source: Author's own research based on Lens in VOSviewer.

Fig. 18.2 Network map of the most relevant topics of urban regeneration and economy, sorted by clusters

Figure 18.5 shows that the clusters with the most relevant terms are red and blue. These terms include humans, complexity, air pollution, well-being, health, mental health, research design (red cluster), environment index, city planning, body mass index, and Ireland (blue cluster).

According to Fig. 18.6, the most relevant subtopics of urban regeneration and quality of life appeared in the publications released from 2017 to 2020, while the least relevant appeared in the publications released from 2010 to 2014. The period from 2010 to 2012 focused on mental disorders/epidemiology, employment, while the period from 2013 to 2016 focused on mental health, urban health, health inequalities, and cross-sectional studies. In the last analyzed period, 2017–2020, the focus was on environment design, built environment, age in place, and social determinants of health. Since very few publications were released prior to 2012 and after 2020, the period from 1990 to 2011, as well as the period from 2021 to 2022, was excluded.

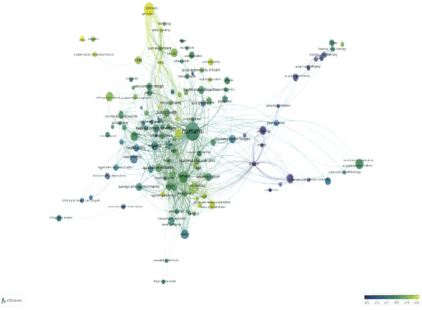

Source: Author's own research based on Lens in VOSviewer.

Fig. 18.3 Network map of the most relevant topics of urban regeneration and economy, sorted by year

Source: Author's own research based on Lens in Excel program.

Fig. 18.4 Yearly evolution of the number of publications on urban regeneration and quality of life

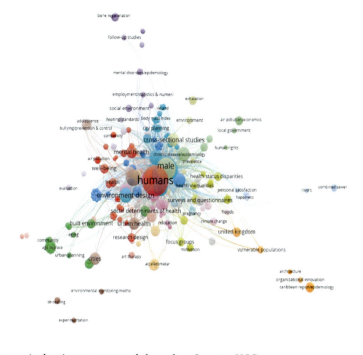

Source: Author's own research based on Lens in VOSviewer.

Fig. 18.5 Network map of the most relevant topics of urban regeneration and quality of life, sorted by clusters

18.4.4 Urban Regeneration and Education and Training

As can be seen in Fig. 18.7, there was little to no interest on urban regeneration and quality of life between 1990 and 2009 (19 years), with only 36 publications that included both terms being registered (which is approximately the number of publications published in 2014). In the period between 2010 and 2020 (10 years), a newfound interest in these two topics was demonstrated through 468 publications. Starting with 2010 and until 2017, the trend remained upward and then decreased sharply, until it suddenly reached 0 in 2022.

As seen in Fig. 18.8, the most important subtopics related to urban regeneration and education and training are humans, health policy, poverty areas (purple clusters), focus groups, housing, and public health (blue clusters).

As shown in Fig. 18.9, the most relevant subtopics of urban regeneration and education and training occurred in the period 2019–2020, while the least relevant occurred in the period 2012–2015. For the period 2012–2015, the studies focused on community health planning, focus groups, organizational case studies, cooperative behavior, developing countries, and personal satisfaction. For the period

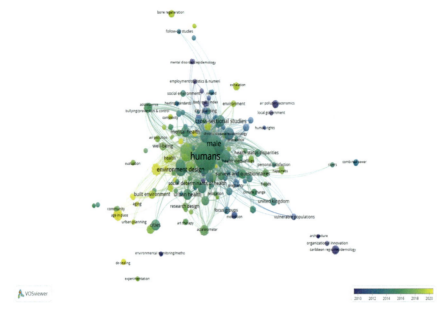

Source: Author's own research based on Lens in VOSviewer.

Fig. 18.6 Network map of the most relevant topics of urban regeneration and quality of life, sorted by year

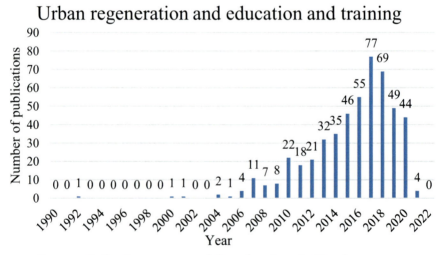

Source: Author's own research based on Lens in Excel program.

Fig. 18.7 Yearly evolution of the number of publications on urban regeneration and education and training

Source: Author's own research based on Lens in VOSviewer.

Fig. 18.8 Network map of the most relevant topics of urban regeneration and education and training, sorted by clusters

2016–2018, the publications had socioeconomic factors, health policy, community health services, urban health, poverty areas, employment, research design, and community health workers as their subject. For the period 2019–2020, interest had decreased for the assimilation of urban regeneration and education and training, the subjects referring to demand-side intervention.

18.4.5 Urban Regeneration and Urban Landscape

Figure 18.10 shows that the number of publications on urban regeneration and urban landscape per year is quite irregular, decreasing and then increasing thrice. The third time, it continued to decrease until it dropped dramatically in 2021. Twice, the same number of scholarly works were published in consecutive years. From 1990 to 2013, the interest in these topics was very low; in 25 years, only 69 publications were registered on this topic.

Figure 18.11 shows that the dark blue cluster, orange cluster, and yellow cluster contain the most relevant terms. The dark blue cluster includes terms such as humans, adult, health promotion/methods, community participation, and community health workers. The orange cluster includes terms such as quality of life, well-being, and built environment. The yellow cluster includes terms such as focus group, investments, and housing.

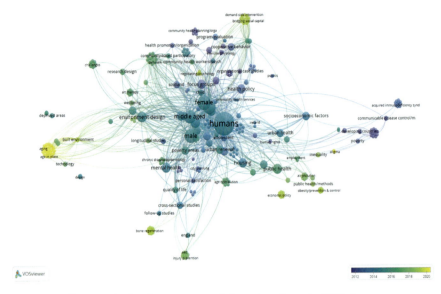

Source: Author's own research based on Lens in VOSviewer.

Fig. 18.9 Network map of the most relevant topics of urban regeneration and education and training, sorted by year

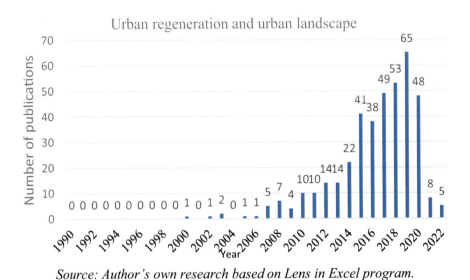

Source: Author's own research based on Lens in Excel program.

Fig. 18.10 Yearly evolution of the number of publications on urban regeneration and urban landscape

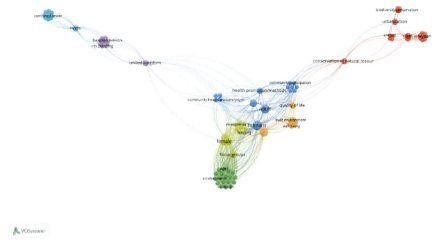

Source: Author's own research based on Lens in VOSviewer.

Fig. 18.11 Network map of the most relevant topics of urban regeneration and urban landscape, sorted by clusters

As shown in Fig. 18.12, the most relevant subtopics of urban regeneration and urban landscape occurred in 2019–2020, while the least relevant occurred in 2014–2015. Between 2014 and 2015, the interest was focused on urban regeneration and combined sewer, rivers, Bayesian networks, city planning, investments, housing, and focus groups. Between 2016 and 2018, the focus was more on community participation, humans, and co-design. By 2019, the interest in urban regeneration and urban landscape was reflected in biodiversity conservation, urbanization, cities and ecosystems.

18.4.6 Urban Regeneration and Development Strategy

Figure 18.13 shows that the number of publications on urban regeneration and development strategy per year is quite uneven, decreasing, and then increasing several times. After briefly dropping in 2018, the trend increased again the following year, with the same number of scholarly works as in 2017, but afterward, it continued to decrease until it dropped dramatically in 2021.

Figure 18.14 shows that the single most relevant term is humans, which belongs to the orange cluster. The orange cluster also includes terms such as Europe and American public health association.

Figure 18.15 shows that the interval 2017–2020 has the most relevant subtopics of urban regeneration and development strategy, while 2005–2013 has the least relevant. The topics presented in the period 2005–2013 were focus groups, governing board, quality of life, and guidelines as topic, and those in the period 2014–2016

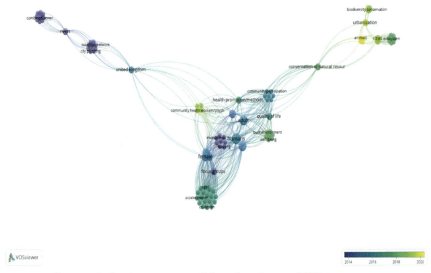

Source: Author's own research based on Lens in VOSviewer.

Fig. 18.12 Network map of the most relevant topics of urban regeneration and urban landscape, sorted by year

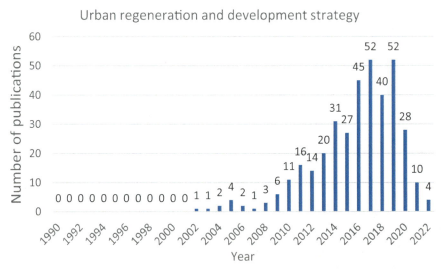

Source: Author's own research based on Lens in Excel program.

Fig. 18.13 Yearly evolution of the number of publications on urban regeneration and development strategy

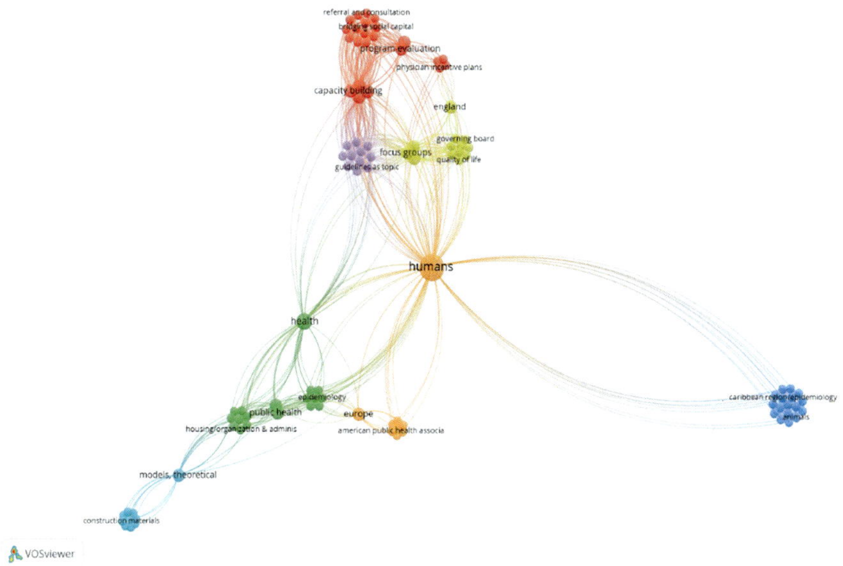

Source: Author's own research based on Lens in VOSviewer

Fig. 18.14 Network map of the most relevant topics of urban regeneration and development strategy, sorted by clusters

were construction materials, models, materials, and capacity building. Between 2017 and 2020, 172 publications had housing/organization and administration, bridging social capital, referral, and consultation as terms of reference.

18.4.7 Urban Regeneration and Greenhouse Gases

As shown in Fig. 18.16, from 1990 to 2011, works related to urban regeneration in correlation to greenhouse gases were near to non-existent. Additionally, from 2006 to 2014, an interest in these two topics combined did not manifest itself, although it was represented by 20 works worldwide, in 9 years. From 2012 onward, interest has increased, but not by much, as the number of publications did not exceed 16 works in 3 years. In addition, the trend was irregular, dropping every now and then until it dramatically decreased in 2021. Starting in 2015 and ending in 2020, the interest remained almost constant, as during that period, a number from 11 to 16 works were being released per year. From 2020 to 2022, only six works were registered.

Figure 18.17 shows that the single most relevant term is humans, which belongs to the blue cluster. The orange cluster also includes terms such as climate change, politics, and economic inequality.

Figure 18.18 shows that the most relevant subtopics of urban regeneration and greenhouse gases occurred in the interval 2018–2019, while the least relevant

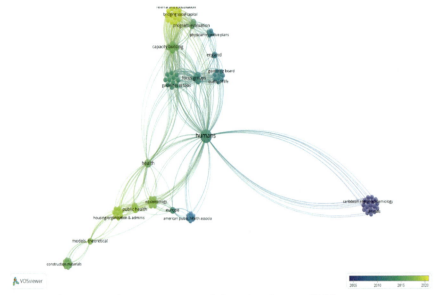

Source: *Author's own research based on Lens in VOSviewer.*

Fig. 18.15 Network map of the most relevant topics of urban regeneration and development strategy, sorted by year

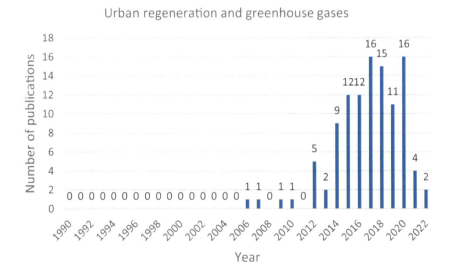

Source: *Author's own research based on Lens in Excel program*

Fig. 18.16 Yearly evolution of the number of publications on urban regeneration and greenhouse gases

18 Bibliometric Analysis of the Evaluation of Interest in Urban Regeneration 233

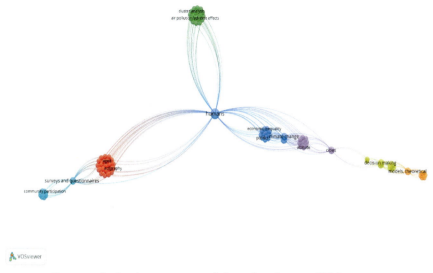

Source: Author's own research based on Lens in VOSviewer.

Fig. 18.17 Network map of the most relevant topics of urban regeneration and greenhouse gases, sorted by clusters

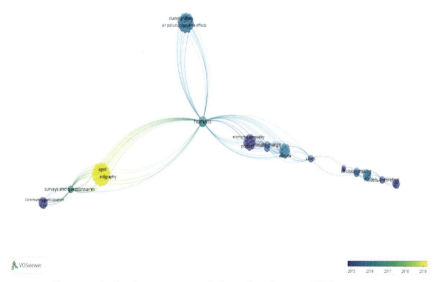

Source: Author's own research based on Lens in VOSviewer.

Fig. 18.18 Network map of the most relevant topics of urban regeneration and greenhouse gases, sorted by year

occurred in 2015–2017. In the period 2015–2017, the most relevant topics were cluster analysis, air pollution and adverse effects, attitude, and decision-making. As of 2018, the topics were attitude, surveys, and questionnaires. A year later, in 2019, the terms were aged and actigraphy.

18.4.8 Urban Regeneration and Economic Impact and Social Impact

Figure 18.19 shows that the keyword combination of urban regeneration and economic and societal impact for the period 1990–2010 did not have an area of interest; only four scientific works were published in those 20 years. However, the number of publications on these three topics increased sharply from 2011 to 2017 (with one small drop in 2016) and then decreased sharply from 2017 to 2022.

Figure 18.20 shows that the single most relevant term is humans, which belongs to the yellow cluster. The yellow cluster also includes terms such as politics and health policy.

As can be seen in Fig. 18.21, it can be seen that the most relevant subtopics of urban regeneration and economic impact and social impact occurred in the 2016–2017 interval, while the least relevant occurred in the 2013–2014 interval. Until 2016, the topics related to urban regeneration and economic and social impacts are only politics and health policy. Around 2017, the trend manifested itself toward social planning, natural environment, socioeconomic factors, regeneration, urban renewal, area-based initiatives, and employment.

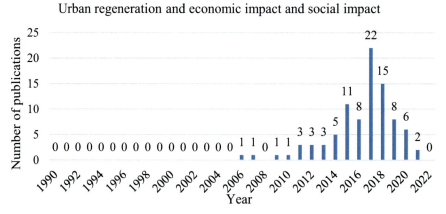

Source: Author's own research based on Lens in Excel program.

Fig. 18.19 Yearly evolution of the number of publications on urban regeneration and economic impact and social impact

Source: Author's own research based on Lens in VOSviewer.

Fig. 18.20 Network map of the most relevant topics of urban regeneration and economic impact and social impact, sorted by clusters

18.4.9 Urban Regeneration and Local Development Strategy

Figure 18.22 shows that, in great contrast to the articles on urban regeneration and development strategy, there are barely any articles on urban regeneration and local development strategy. In total, there are 20 publications containing both of these topics and the biggest number of articles released within 1 year is 3. Three articles have been released both in the year 2013 and in the year 2016.

18.4.10 Connection Between Urban Regeneration and Its Relevant Topics

In order to highlight the connection between urban regeneration and its relevant topics, a visualization of the common subtopics that appeared in all the publications for the period 2010–2020 was realized, as shown in Table 18.4.

In general, the periods where there were little to no publications on any of these topics were 1990–2009 and 2021–2022, with the number almost never exceeding

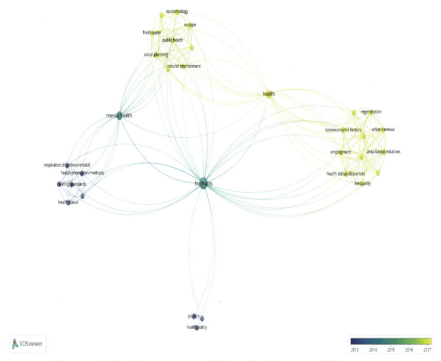

Source: Author's own research based on Lens in VOSviewer.

Fig. 18.21 Network map of the most relevant topics of urban regeneration and economic impact and social impact, sorted by year

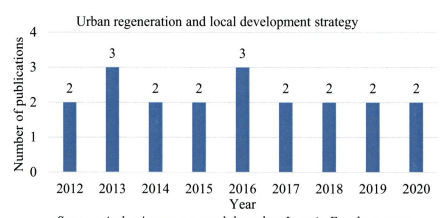

Source: Author's own research based on Lens in Excel program.

Fig. 18.22 Yearly evolution of the number of publications on urban regeneration and local development strategy

Table 18.4 Terms used in the publications related to urban regeneration and associated keywords
Source: Author's own research based on Lens

	2010	2011	2012	2013	2014	2015	2016	2017	2018	2019	2020
history											
20th century											
urban health											
air pollution											
economics											
urbanization											
history architecture											
poverty											
environment design											
disorders/epidemiology											
employment											
mental health											
urban health											
health inequalities											
cross-sectional studies											
built environment											
age in place											
social determinants of health											
community health planning											
focus groups											
organizational case studies											
cooperative behaviour											
developing countries											
personal satisfaction											
socioeconomic factors											
community health services											
health policy											
research design											
community health worker											

(continued)

Tab. 18.4 (continued)

Keyword											
demand-side intervention										■	
combined sewer					■						
rivers					■						
Bayesian networks					■						
city planning					■						
investments					■						
housing					■						
community participation							■				
humans							■				
co design							■				
biodiversity conservation										■	
cities										■	
ecosystems										■	
governing board		■									
quality of life		■									
guidelines as topic		■									
construction materials					■						
models					■						
materials					■						
capacity building					■						
housing/organisation & administration									■		
bridging social capital									■		
referral									■		
consultation									■		
attitude							■				
decision making							■				
surveys								■			
politics				■							
social planning		■									
natural environment		■									
socioeconomic factors		■									
regeneration		■									
urban renewal		■									
area-based initiatives		■									

twenty and thirty. The only exception was the keyword combination "urban regeneration and economy," with over twenty publications since 2007 and with over thirty publications prior to 2022. Furthermore, for every keyword combination, most publications were released in the late 2010s, usually in 2017. In addition, the number of publications often decreased (instead of remaining constant) upon attaining the highest point.

18.5 Conclusions

The graphs presented in this article mark the evolution of the urban regeneration process through time. It is important to note that the evolution of the urban regeneration process is determined by the history, experience, and development of the area in which the urban regeneration process should take place. In time, the interest has changed, as we could see from the strategies and public policies that have been developed. The process itself has to put greater emphasis on the local problems and as such will result in a variation of public policies and planning activities as the time goes by.

The results obtained from the quantitative analysis that has been carried out highlight the following:

- The most reoccurring term among all the databases is "humans," showing that human activity was involved in each case. Other reoccurring terms, in decreasing order of importance, are "female," "male," "adult," "middle-aged," and "health." "Health" is often specified as "public health," "mental health," "health policy," "health status," etc.
- Urban regeneration is of particular interest for the economy and quality of life, the publications presenting common terms (e.g., "air pollution") that have been used since 2010.
- The period 2012–2016 was very fruitful, having publications focused on urban regeneration associated with "economy," "quality of life," "education" and "training," "urban landscape," and "development strategy," with the most used items being economics, urbanization, employment, urban health, community health planning, organizational case studies, personal satisfaction, research design, city planning, construction materials, capacity building, politics, socioeconomic factors, etc.

The expansion of the quantitative analysis and the consideration of the qualitative analysis by using other databases (e.g., Elsevier, Springer, and Wiley Online Library) can be considered as an open problem.

The analysis aims to provide an insight into the reasons behind the decision to take the urban problems into action, and the occurrence and persistence of urban problems are changing the theory and practice of urban regeneration.

References

Roberts, P., Hugh, S., & Rachel, G. (2000). *The evolution, definition and purpose of urban regeneration urban regeneration handbook.* SAGE Publications. Urban Regeneration Second Edition – ISBN-13: 978-1446252628.

Sharghi, A., Jahanzamin, Y., Ghanbaran, A., & Jahanzamin, S. (2018). A study on evolution and development of urban regeneration with emphasis on the cultural approach. *The Turkish Online Journal of Design, Art and Communication – TOJDAC*, 271–284. ISSN: 2146-5193, March 2018, Special Edition.

Chapter 19
Investigating the Impact of COVID-19 Policy Decisions on Economic Growth: Evidence from EU Countries

Cosmin-Octavian Cepoi, Bogdan Andrei Dumitrescu, and Ionel Leonida

Abstract In this chapter, we examine the link between the policy responses to the COVID-19 outbreak and economic growth. Using three key response variables namely containment and health index, overall government response index, and economic support and a sample of 27 EU countries from 2007q1 to 2022q1, we bring strong empirical evidence that the economic recovery was linked to the intensity of the government response. More to the point, the estimates reveal that the higher intensity of support measures, regardless of their type, is leading to an improvement on economic growth and its components in the next quarter. Furthermore, the impact on economic growth is higher when the government increases the intensity of containment and health measures compared to economic measures.

Keywords COVID-19 · Health index · Economic support · EU countries

19.1 Introduction

The spread of the COVID-19 pandemic was an unexpected shock to the global financial system. Unlike other financial turmoil such as the Global Financial Crisis from 2008, the COVID-19 pandemic did not follow the patterns of a classical crisis. However, the damages suffered by the financial markets and the economies worldwide were far more powerful. In Europe, the outbreak of COVID-19 has brought to the media attention the dramatic situations in several countries where the health system was taken by surprise by the pandemic.

In comparison to the GFC of 2008, when the packages of fiscal measures were mostly expansionary, but also restrictive in a few other countries, during the

---

C.-O. Cepoi (✉) · B. A. Dumitrescu · I. Leonida
"Victor Slăvescu" Center for Financial and Monetary Research, Bucharest, Romania
e-mail: bogdan.dumitrescu@fin.ase.ro

COVID-19 pandemic governments applied only packages of expansionary fiscal measures, with direct and immediate impact on the budget of households and companies (Bouabdallah et al., 2020; Fuss et al., 2020). In general, the depth and nature of the COVID-19 crisis, as well as the low efficiency of fiscal stabilizers in such a conjuncture, represent arguments for the use of discretionary fiscal measures at the national level.

In Figs. 19.1 and 19.2, we present the average values for economic support index and containment and health index, both developed by Hale et al. (2020), across UE27 countries in 2020q2.

Against this background, it is of interest to study how these support measures influenced the macroeconomic activity. More specifically, we are interested in investigating to what extent the intensity of the economic support or containment/health measures led to a faster improvement of the main macroeconomic indicators.

The remaining of the chapter is structured as follows: Sect. 19.2 presents the literature review, Sect. 19.3 describes the methodological aspects, the results are in Sect. 19.4, while Sect. 19.5 concludes the chapter.

19.2 Literature Review

The COVID-19 pandemic has brought about unprecedented economic challenges, and the European Union (EU) has been among the hardest-hit regions in the world. In order to mitigate the economic impact of the pandemic, the EU and its member

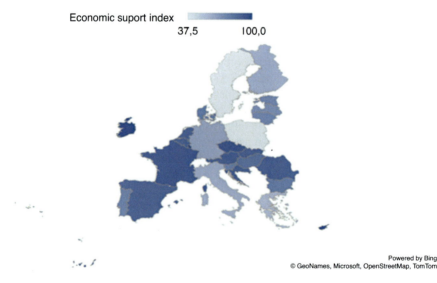

Fig. 19.1 Economic support index. (Source: Own processing)

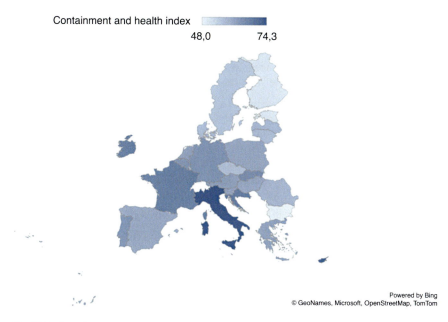

Fig. 19.2 Containment and health index. (Source: Own processing)

states have implemented several measures, some of which were recommended by the International Monetary Fund (IMF).

One of the major challenges facing the EU during the pandemic has been the liquidity squeeze, with businesses struggling to maintain their operations due to reduced cash flows. To address this issue, the EU has implemented liquidity support measures such as access to credit, loan guarantees, and direct grants to affected businesses. The IMF has recommended that such support measures should be targeted to those sectors and small- and medium-sized enterprises (SMEs) that are hardest hit by the pandemic.

Another major challenge facing the EU has been the surge in unemployment resulting from the shutdown and slowed activity in several sectors. The EU and its member states have implemented various measures to support workers who have lost their jobs. Some of the measures unveiled include income support schemes, short-term work schemes, and wage subsidies. To support workers who may be at risk of losing their jobs, the IMF has recommended the implementation of targeted measures that encourage employers to retain their workforce.

Furthermore, the EU has implemented fiscal and monetary measures to support economic activity during the pandemic. Some of the fiscal measures include tax breaks, deferrals, and exemptions, while the monetary measures include interest rate cuts, increased liquidity in the financial sector, and asset purchases. The IMF has recommended that such measures should be implemented in a timely and calibrated manner to support the recovery of the economy.

In conclusion, the EU has implemented various economic measures to mitigate the impact of the COVID-19 pandemic on the economy. The IMF has played a critical role in advising on these measures, and its recommendations highlight the importance of a targeted approach to support those sectors and SMEs that are hardest hit by the pandemic. With this continued support, the EU can hope to recover and transition to a more sustainable and resilient economy in the post-pandemic period.

Up until now, the literature investigating the impact of economic and health measures on some key macroeconomic variables is limited. For example, Guven et al. (2022) have shown that government measures in response to the COVID-19 pandemic positively impacted stock returns. Hoang et al. (2022) have studied the effectiveness of the US government measures including economic support packages and stringent social measures on corporate investment. The conclusions revealed that the government policies in response to COVID-19 and economic supports had a positive impact on corporate investment.

In addition, Gopalakrishnan et al. (2022) show that the government responses to the COVID-19 financial turmoil had a significant impact on debt financing by firms. For example, a one-unit increase in the lockdown stringency leads to a 5.9 pp increase in the propensity for debt financing in the 200q2 and 200q3. Furthermore, Ashraf and Goodell (2021) showed that stringent social distancing policies lead to a decrease in the contemporary GDP growth rate, but at the same time have led to significantly higher GDP growth in the subsequent next quarter.

Finally, Alfano and Ercolano (2022) show that when the level of lockdown became more drastic, however, the economic support measures were not able to completely regain, in the short run, the economic losses due to stringency policies.

19.3 Methodology

One of the most significant challenges faced by the EU during the pandemic was a liquidity crisis, where many businesses experienced a cash crunch due to the decline in economic activity. The EU responded with liquidity support measures that included access to credit, loan guarantees, and direct grants to businesses. These measures helped businesses to stay afloat, and small- and medium-sized enterprises (SMEs) were among the primary beneficiaries. As a result of such measures, there has been an accelerated level of economic growth within the EU.

Furthermore, the EU implemented measures to support consumers in terms of income support schemes, wage subsidies, and short-term work schemes. These measures were introduced to prevent consumer spending from declining significantly and to ensure that an adequate level of consumption growth was preserved. As a result, consumer spending levels remained relatively stable throughout the pandemic.

In terms of investment growth, the EU introduced various measures to support the financial sector and to provide liquidity. Central banks implemented measures such as interest rate cuts, asset purchases, and increased liquidity. The EU also introduced fiscal measures such as tax breaks and deferrals. These measures helped to support investment growth, and there was relatively stable investment in the EU throughout the pandemic.

In this paper, we use quarterly data from 25 EU countries from 2020q1 to 2022q2. The dependent variables are economic growth, consumption growth, and investments growth. All the explanatory variables are stationary and are included in the regression model with one lag. Table 19.1 presents all the variables and their definitions and sources.

Table 19.1 Description of the variables

Variables	Description	
Economic growth (YoY)	The quarterly percentage change in the GDP	Eurostat
Consumption growth (YoY)	The quarterly percentage change in the household consumption	Eurostat
Investments growth (YoY)	The quarterly percentage change in the investments	Eurostat
Inflation (YoY)	The quarterly percentage change in the consumer price index	Eurostat
Unemployment rate	The percentage of the labor force that is without work but available for and seeking employment	Eurostat
Interest rate spread	Business credit interest rate minus bank deposits interest rate	The Global Economy
Building permits (YoY growth)	Authorizations granted by the local authorities before the construction of a new	The Global Economy
Retail sales index (YoY growth)	The quarterly percentage change in the household consumption	The Global Economy
Business confidence survey	It measures, based on surveys the amount of pessimism or optimism that firm managers are feeling about the prospects of their companies	Eurostat
Economic support index	It combines 13 factors of policy response such as workplace closures, school closure policies, contact tracking, travel bans, testing policy, face coverings, and vaccine policy. This index ranges from 0 (weak) to 100 (strong)	The Oxford COVID-19 Government Response Tracker
Containment and health index	This index calculates the relative strength of government policies to support economic agents by providing direct payments related to unemployment, as well as measures for alleviating financial obligations. This index ranges from 0 (weak) to 100 (strong)	The Oxford COVID-19 Government Response Tracker
Government support measures	A composite index capturing both CHI and ESI	The Oxford COVID-19 Government Response Tracker

Source: Authors' own research

19.4 Analysis/Result Interpretation

In Table 19.2, we present the estimation results using a panel data approach with country fixed effects. Significant estimates are in blue. We notice that the evolution of the GDP growth and consumption growth was shaped by the previous evolution of the business cycle indicators (building permits growth, retail sales, and business confidence), in line with Levanon et al. (2015). Basically, the business cycle indicators are the most important variables in estimating the trend that economic growth will follow in the short term. All the variables used in the regressions are stationary based on Levin-Lin-Chu panel unit root test.

Inflation exhibits a negative and robust impact on consumption growth during 2020q1 to 2022q2, an obvious result since a generalized increase in prices will lead to a reduction in consumption, according to economic theory. Furthermore, the higher the inflation rate, the higher the investment growth.

The higher intensity of support measures, regardless of their type, is leading to an improvement on economic growth and its components in the next quarter. The impact on economic growth is higher when the government increases the intensity of containment and health measures compared to economic measures.

Table 19.2 Estimation results (p-values in parentheses)

Variables	Economic Growth (YoY)			Consumption Growth			Investment Growth		
Inflation (YoY)	0.3244 (0.0461)	0.1870 (0.1703)	0.1810 (0.1783)	-1.0492 (0.0000)	-1.1469 (0.000)	-1.1552 (0.0000)	1.9873 (0.0000)	1.8615 (0.0000)	1.8580 (0.0000)
Unemployment rate	-0.9416 (0.0795)	-0.3814 (0.3984)	-0.3246 (0.4666)	0.2939 (0.6417)	0.6845 (0.2514)	0.7486 (0.2045)	-1.2961 (0.0507)	-0.7732 (0.2044)	-0.7270 (0.2317)
Interest rate spread	0.0168 (0.3667)	0.0233 (0.1351)	0.0237 (0.1232)	-0.0220 (0.3900)	-0.0153 (0.5209)	-0.0135 (0.5667)	-0.0058 (0.7595)	0.0001 (0.9944)	0.0004 (0.9836)
Building Permits	0.0547 (0.0007)	0.0356 (0.0086)	0.0352 (0.0085)	0.0836 (0.0000)	0.0690 (0.0001)	0.0676 (0.0001)	0.0885 (0.0000)	0.0712 (0.0001)	0.0711 (0.0001)
Retail sales index	0.3540 (0.0000)	0.2602 (0.0000)	0.2584 (0.0000)	0.1749 (0.0054)	0.0954 (0.1128)	0.0879 (0.1382)	0.3637 (0.0000)	0.2785 (0.0000)	0.2783 (0.0000)
Business confidence	0.0886 (0.0232)	0.1471 (0.0000)	0.1434 (0.0000)	0.1211 (0.0083)	0.1719 (0.0001)	0.1737 (0.0001)	-0.0100 (0.0000)	0.0416 (0.3476)	0.0367 (0.4021)
Economic support index	0.0841 (0.000)			0.0359 (0.0447)			0.0863 (0.0000)		
Gov. response index		0.2307 (0.0000)			0.1492 (0.0000)			0.2220 (0.0000)	
Containment index			0.2415 (0.0000)			0.1645 (0.0000)			0.2301 (0.0000)
Observations	200	200	200	200	200	200	200	200	200
R-squared	0.6513	0.7567	0.7634	0.7910	0.8167	0.8215	0.7696	0.8083	0.8096

Source: Authors' own research

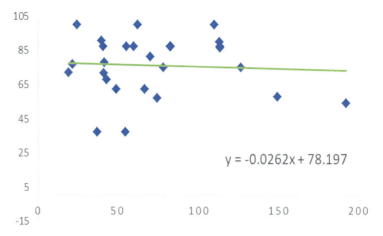

Fig. 19.3 Public debt (x) vs economic support index (y) – 2020q2. (Source: Own processing)

One question arising from these results is the link between economic or health measures and fiscal sustainability.

As we can see in Fig. 19.3, based on a simple linear regression we show that there is a negative relationship between the level of public debt and the intensity of economic support (high indebtedness countries provided less income support to households).

Overall, the economic support measures implemented by the EU during the pandemic have helped to mitigate the impact of the crisis on economic growth, consumption growth, and investment growth. The liquidity support measures helped businesses to stay afloat, consumer support measures prevented a decline in consumer spending, and the introduction of supportive fiscal and monetary policies helped to sustain investment growth. The future remains uncertain, but the measures implemented by the EU provide confidence that they can mitigate further impact from such crises in the future.

19.5 Conclusions

Fiscal budgetary policy supported with all its instruments and resources the maintenance and recovery of economies in most EU countries, with varying degrees of efficiency, heterogeneity being a characteristic of EU countries and fiscal budgetary systems, and after overcoming the crisis, public finances are damaged in many countries and need a reciprocal response from economies, which may come from an increase in voluntary compliance and even from a revision (increasing) of some tax rates.

In this paper, we examine the link between the policy responses to the COVID-19 outbreak and three key macroeconomic variables. Using containment and health index, overall government response index and economic support index and a sample of 27 EU countries during 2007q1 to 2022q1, we bring strong empirical evidence that the economic recovery was linked to the intensity of the government response. More to the point, the estimates reveal that the higher intensity of support measures, regardless of their type, leads to an improvement on economic growth and its components in the next quarter. Even though the results are fresh (the major limitation of the paper is the number of quarters with COVID-19 pandemic information), they provide some novel results with powerful policy implications.

References

Alfano, V., & Ercolano, S. (2022). Stay at home! Governance quality and effectiveness of lockdown. *Social Indicators Research, 159*, 101–123.

Ashraf, B. N., & Goodell, J. W. (2021). COVID-19 social distancing measures and economic growth: Distinguishing short- and long-term effects. *Finance Research Letters, 47*, 102639.

Bouabdallah, O., Checherita-Westphal, C., Freier, M., Muggenthale, P., Müller, G., Nerlich, C., & Sławińska, K. (2020). Automatic fiscal stabilizers in the euro area and the COVID-19 crisis. *Economic Bulletin Articles, 6*(6).

Fuss, J., Whalen, A., & Hill, T. (2020). *Is fiscal stimulus an effective policy response to a recession?* (Fraser Research Bulletin Canada) (pp. 1–15). Fraser Institute.

Gopalakrishnan, B., Jacob, J., & Mohapatra, S. (2022). Covid-19 pandemic and debt financing by firms: Unravelling the channels. *Economic Modelling, 114*, 105929.

Guven, M., Cetinguc, B., Guloglu, B., & Calisir, F. (2022). The effects of daily growth in COVID-19 deaths, cases, and governments' response policies on stock markets of emerging economies. *Research in International Business and Finance, 61*, 101659.

Hale, T., Petherick A., Phillips T., & Webster S. (2020). *Variation in government responses to COVID-19* (Blavatnik Sch. Gov. Work. Pap., 31).

Hoang, K., Mrif A., & Cuong N. (2022). Corporate investment and government policy during the COVID-19 crisis. *International Review of Economics and Finance, 80*, 677–696.

Levanon, G., Manini, J.-C., Ozyildirim, A., Schaitkin, B., & Tanchua, J. (2015). Using financial indicators to predict turning points in the business cycle: The case of the leading economic index for the United States. *International Journal of Forecasting, 31*(2), 426–445.

Chapter 20
The Impact of Pandemic Crisis on Fiscal Sustainability

Ada Cristina Albu

Abstract The pandemic crisis has produced an important transformation of the fiscal framework of European Union states. Thus, the necessity to finance expansionary fiscal policies implemented by governments has resulted in an impressive increase in budgetary deficits and public debts in EU countries. The rise in public indebtedness requires a complete rethinking of the actual fiscal rules. There have been proposed several modifications for the fiscal framework, to consider the high levels of debts and deficits, which cannot be reverted to pre-pandemic values. We will analyze in this paper several proposals to change the actual fiscal rules in a period of low interest rates, which allow the accumulation of further indebtedness. The actual fiscal rules, such as the structural budget balanced rule, the debt rule, or the expenditure rule, are no longer functioning considering the necessity to reach sustainable fiscal positions.

Keywords Fiscal framework · Public debt · Structural budget balanced rule · Expenditure rule · Fiscal regulations

20.1 Introduction

The pandemic crisis has produced an important debate regarding the compliance with the actual fiscal rules in European Union countries. The fiscal framework must be changed to consider the emergence of the crisis and the fact that member states already have high levels of public debt and deficits, which makes the return to pre-pandemic values difficult and requires a different system of fiscal regulations.

A. C. Albu (✉)
National Institute for Economic Research "Costin C. Kirițescu", Romanian Academy, Bucharest, Romania

In 2020, the European Commission activated the escape clause, through which countries are exempted from complying with the Stability and Growth Pact rules regarding debt and deficits, thus allowing member states to borrow in order to provide financing for the programs of support measures during the pandemic crisis.

Fiscal policy has played a very important role during the crisis to support economic recovery, as monetary policy intervention is restrained by the zero lower bound. Fiscal policy was a key instrument in dealing with the negative effects of COVID-19 pandemic and provided the tools for governments to react to smooth output shocks. The macroeconomic stabilization role was supported by the fact that fiscal policy could act to dampen economic contractions by using a significant fiscal stimulus to finance economic recovery.

The impressive fiscal stimulus resulted in a significant accumulation of public debt and deficits in all member states, raising sustainability concerns regarding the evolution of budgetary indicators. European countries already face debt vulnerabilities due to the fact that the global financial crisis and the sovereign debt crisis in the eurozone have resulted in a deterioration of all fiscal indicators. The initiative to implement a common fiscal capacity or a Fiscal Union was resumed during the coronavirus pandemic, when the resilience of the monetary union was effectively tested in the context of relying on national fiscal policies, based on the common fiscal framework (Lane, 2021).

Sustainability of fiscal policy requires the ability of the primary balance to generate future primary surpluses to pay for the debt newly contracted. Thus, public debt is sustainable if governments can generate future surpluses so that countries should be capable to pay their sovereign debts, without entering default or incapacity of payment.

The existence of low interest rates currently represents an advantage for the implementation of expansive fiscal policy, as it allows further buildup in public indebtedness without major sustainability risks. Yet, there are situations when a government cannot roll over the debt, when it is difficult to continue to borrow from the markets. Financial markets can react quite unexpectedly in case a country is regarded as having a liquidity or solvency crisis, and there is always the risk that the rise in sovereign risk premia can entail sovereign default.

The fiscal regulations of the European Union have been established in several treaties, starting with the Maastricht Treaty, the Stability and Growth Pact, Two-Pack or Six-Pack. The limits proposed for public debt – 60% of gross domestic product and deficits – 3% of GDP have been considered as safe thresholds from the perspective of ensuring sustainability of fiscal positions. The accumulation of debt and deficits is strictly monitored by European institutions, in order to return debt and deficits to sustainable trajectories and propose corrections in case budgetary indicators register significant deviations from their main benchmarks.

We utilize in this paper a panel model with fixed effects to analyze the relationship between the Fiscal Rule Index (an indicator calculated at the level of European Union monitoring the actual stance of fiscal regulations) and several budgetary indicators, such as public debt, deficits, interest rates, and inflation rate for countries members of European Union during 1996–2020. The results of the panel model with fixed effects show that public debt, inflation rate, and interest rates have a negative impact on the fiscal rule strength index. Only an increase in deficits will impact positively the fiscal rule index.

Procyclicality is one of the main issues related to fiscal policy when governments cannot create sufficient fiscal space in boom periods to allow the implementation of countercyclical policies during contractions. Pursuing a procyclical fiscal policy is often an important issue from the perspective of economic stabilization, as countercyclical or even a-cyclical fiscal policies are needed to support economies to smooth business cycle fluctuations.

20.2 Literature Review

The actual fiscal rules established within EU Treaties should no longer be regarded as fixed, as they require many modifications to reflect the present economic conditions. Several analyses have shown that the actual fiscal rules no longer comply with the fiscal situations in EU countries. The rules need to be adjusted so that if a rule entails too much fiscal effort (measured by a rise in the primary balance for a 3-year period), then it can be replaced (Giavazzi et al., 2021).

The compliance with fiscal rules is necessary to avoid negative externalities, such as externalities arising from high levels of public debt held by a country or even demand externalities from fiscal policy when interest rates are at the zero lower bound (Constâncio, 2020).

Another proposal by Blanchard et al. (2021) refers to replacing the actual fiscal rules with fiscal standards, based on country-specific evaluations using stochastic debt analysis. Quantitative rules are not enough to cope with country differences; therefore, one should replace them with different non-numerical rules. There is also a proposal toward replacing the present fiscal rules with one expenditure rule, which allows the control of public debt, while deficit can fluctuate due to modifications of revenue.

Afonso and Jalles (2019) investigate using the system GMM the relationship between stock flow adjustments and public debt-to-GDP ratios in 65 countries using data for the period 1985–2014. The results confirm that the reduction in the debt ratio as an effect of enforcing fiscal rules before the crisis was between 1.7% and 4.2% of GDP, while after the global financial crisis, fiscal rules did not contribute to reducing debt. Budgetary deficit responds countercyclically to economic growth, while growth can react positively or negatively to fluctuations of deficit (Taylor et al., 2012).

There is a nonlinear relation between government debt and gross domestic product growth rate in euro-area countries, with a threshold identified at 90–100% of GDP for public debt having a negative impact on growth. There are several channels through which public debt produces an impact on growth ratios: private saving, public investment, total factor productivity, and sovereign long-term nominal and real interest rates (Checherita-Westphal & Rother, 2010).

When public debt exceeds a certain threshold, sustainability concerns become more important than macroeconomic stability. The trade-off stabilization-sustainability becomes more significant during periods of high public debt, when the objective of ensuring macroeconomic stabilization is more difficult to be respected. Non-compliance with EU fiscal rules can lead to pro-cyclicality, while following the fiscal rules can improve the cyclical adjustment (Larch et al., 2020).

There are several fiscal rules that have been established since the formation of European Monetary Union, starting with the Maastricht Treaty. Fiscal rules usually include a debt and deficit rule, and regulations referring to public expenditures and revenues. These rules have been formulated in European treaties and have been revised and improved several times in order to reflect the situations of European member states.

The debt rule establishes a limit of 60% of GDP for the increase in public indebtedness. In case debt exceeds the threshold of 60% of GDP, then it should decrease by 1/20, an adjustment made during a period of 3 years. *The deficit rule* refers to the fact that the general government balance should be less than 3% of gross domestic product. *The structural budget balance* is the budgetary balance without the impact of the economic cycle and one-off measures. The actual expansionary fiscal measures should be followed by consolidation policies, as high budget deficits should be gradually reduced so that not to raise public debt sustainability concerns.

Countries are assigned on an annual basis a medium-term objective, which is established depending on the structural balance: in case of low debt and an increased rate of growth, the structural budget balance could be less than 1% of GDP. In case the structural budget balance is not at MTO, then it should be reduced by 0.5% of GDP per year. *The expenditure rule* refers to the fact that real government expenditures must not increase more than the rate of economic growth if the country structural balance is at its MTO or above.

The actual rules must be reformed for several reasons:

- The rules do not consider the quality of public spending. For instance, public investment is treated the same as current expenditure (Dullien et al., 2020).
- The rules have become extremely difficult to be enforced, as there have been formulated multiple rules, based on complex procedures for application, and this framework has led to excessive difficulty in enforcing the rules. At the same time, both the indicators and the implementing procedures such as ex ante and ex post assessments, preventive and corrective arms, have resulted in a system of rules, which has become increasingly complicated (Carnot et al., 2018).
- Regarding the possibilities to reform the current fiscal rules, there are proposals toward a different set of rules or focus more on market discipline by issuing Eurobonds (Wyplosz, 2019).

The actual fiscal framework had a poor performance in managing trade-offs between stabilizing output and facing fiscal risks, which has led to an excessive fiscal consolidation during boom periods and too little austerity during downturns. The proposal refers to the implementation of risk-based EU-level fiscal rules, meant to achieve a balance between fiscal risks and the size of fiscal consolidation, by using debt sustainability analysis as prepared at the level of the European Commission, European Fiscal Council, and National Fiscal Councils.

EU countries should be divided into high-risk and low-risk fiscal sustainability states, and depending on this, they should prepare their medium-term fiscal plans. High-risk states should implement an expenditure ceiling in line with a zero or positive fiscal balance during a 3- or 5-year projection horizon (Arnold et al., 2022).

Other proposals refer to the establishment of a medium-term debt target, which might serve as an operational anchor for fiscal policy and to draft an expenditure rule based on identifying an expenditure benchmark, which would serve to enhance the countercyclical role of fiscal policy (Alloza et al., 2021).

Another proposal is to enhance the cyclical flexibility of the Stability and Growth Pact, by reforming the cyclical adjustment, which is used as an important tool in budgetary surveillance (Truger, 2020).

There are also proposals for implementation of an expenditure rule, according to which nominal expenditure should not grow faster than long-term national income and that in the group of countries with high debt the expenditure should increase at a slower pace (Beuve et al., 2019).

Second-generation fiscal rules, which have been reformulated after the global financial crisis or sovereign debt crisis, are designed to be more flexible, operational, and easy to be enforced as they have corrected all drawbacks of first-generation fiscal rules. All these changes refer to the fact that rules can correct deviations in an automatic manner, and contain escape clauses and procedures for monitoring and implementing rules, which enforce both fiscal sustainability and macroeconomic stabilization (Bandaogo, 2020).

Fiscal rules can be related to the level of budgetary transparency, in case public budget transparency is not high enough, fiscal rules cannot lead to a better performance of budget deficits. Higher budget transparency makes the achievement of fiscal adjustments more likely (Gootjes & de Haan, 2022).

20.3 Methodology

We will use in this paper a panel data model with fixed and random effects to analyze the relation between the fiscal rule index, public debt, budget deficit, inflation rate, and interest rates in the case of European Union countries. We will utilize an indicator for the Fiscal Rule Strength Index established at the level of the European Commission, in order to provide a measure for fiscal regulations. The Fiscal Rule Index is measured taking into account several characteristics, such as legal base, binding character, institutions, which monitor enforcement, correction mechanism, and resilience toward shocks. The calculus for the fiscal index is based on weighted averages obtained for the main components of the indicator, with values ranging between 0 and 1. An index for fiscal rules is important from the prospect of ensuring both a measure of resilience toward negative output shocks and an instrument for assessing the actual fiscal stance in European Union countries.

We have chosen for the panel regression the main macroeconomic variables, which might influence the dynamics of fiscal rules, such as public debt, government deficit, interest rates paid for debt, and inflation rate. Data are extracted from Eurostat database. We utilize gross public debt annual data expressed as percentage of gross domestic product at current prices and for net lending/borrowing annual data, as percentage of GDP. For interest rates paid for public debt, we use data referring to bond yields (EMU convergence criteria), on an annual basis, expressed in percentages. Inflation rate (harmonized index of consumer prices) is expressed as annual average rates. The data are extracted for all European Union member states, spanning the period 1996–2020.

We will employ a panel data model in order to discern the influence of the main fiscal aggregates on the fiscal rules strength index. Our analysis should provide a measure of how the fiscal index is influenced by the other variables included in the panel model.

$$\text{FiscRuleIndex}_{it} = \alpha + \beta PD_{it} + \gamma \text{Def}_{it} + \delta \text{Inflat}_{it} + \varepsilon \text{Intrate}_{it} + \mu_i + \omega_{it}$$

where FiscRuleIndex$_{it}$ is the dependent variable, while PD_{it} represents public debt, Def$_{it}$ is budget deficit, Inflat$_{it}$ is the inflation rate, Intrate$_{it}$ is the interest rate, and μ_i represents country fixed effects, while ω_{it} is the error term.

A fixed effects model analyzes group differences in intercepts, relying on the assumption of the same slopes and variance in all entities, while a random-effects model estimates variance for groups, based on the same intercept and slopes (Park, 2003).

The model will allow to discern which are the main effects produced on the fiscal rule index by a one-unit increase in the endogenous variables. Analyzing the main determinants of the fiscal rule index is important from the perspective of improving the performance of fiscal regulations in order to ensure sustainable fiscal positions.

20.4 Analysis/Result Interpretation

We estimate fixed-effects and random-effects panel data models for the main variables analyzed using data for European Union countries. The results of the Hausman test confirm the choice of fixed-effects over random-effects model. The regressions run for countries members of the European Union confirm the presence of a negative effect produced on the fiscal rule strength index whenever public debt, interest rate, and inflation increase. Thus, in case inflation registers a one-percent increase, there is a decline in fiscal rule index of −0.06%, which shows that any rise in inflation rate has a negative effect on fiscal regulations. When interest rates increase by 1%, then the fiscal rule index will decrease by 0.05 percentage points, which demonstrates that rises of interest rates will negatively impact fiscal regulations. Any sudden rise of interest rates can produce important perturbations on financial markets, which affects the trajectory of public debt and also the sustainability of the main budgetary positions. The same negative effect can be identified in the relation between a rise in public debt of 1% and a subsequent decline in the fiscal rule index of −0.05 percentage points. Public debt is a determinant factor for ensuring macroeconomic stability and any rise in debt must be strictly monitored as it can trigger significant effects on the other budgetary indicators. Any increase in debt can raise short-term and long-term sustainability concerns. In the present environment of high public indebtedness, the issue of debt reduction is very difficult to be implemented as governments resort to borrowing to finance economic expansions. Henceforth, any increase in public debt, inflation, or interest rates will negatively impact the evolution of the fiscal rule index, which shows it is important to monitor the dynamics of macroeconomic indicators, especially during crisis so as not to affect significantly the fiscal rule index.

At the same time, there is a positive effect of an increase in deficit on the fiscal rule index. In case deficits rise by one-percentage point, this will contribute to an increase in the fiscal rules index of 0.01 percentage points. These results confirm that there is a strong relationship between the main fiscal variables which are taken into consideration when analyzing the fiscal stance and the dynamics of the fiscal rule strength index. In Fig. 20.1, we have presented the relations between the Fiscal Rule Index and the budgetary variables analyzed within the panel model with fixed effects.

20.5 Conclusions

The change in the fiscal framework of European Union countries is very important in the actual context of the economic crisis following the COVID-19 pandemic. The high levels of public debts and deficits, accumulated since the onset of the crisis, can no longer be reduced to the pre-pandemic values, and it is important to identify new fiscal regulations, which can ensure the preservation of public debt sustainability.

We have shown in this paper that fiscal policy plays a significant role in ensuring macroeconomic stabilization, especially during the pandemic crisis. The role of fiscal policy is more important considering the limitations of monetary policy intervention, which is restrained by the zero lower bound. Countercyclical fiscal policy contributed to economic stabilization, reducing asymmetric shocks to gross domestic product.

The actual fiscal regulations implemented at the European level are no longer functional because the rules were established during a period of low public debts and deficits, while the rise in public indebtedness due to past crisis requires the elaboration of different fiscal rules. At the same time, the actual fiscal framework is considered very difficult to be implemented, since there are too many fiscal regulations, which must be simplified, transforming the rules to make them more operational and more effective in order to ensure fiscal sustainability.

We have presented in this paper several recent proposals toward rethinking the actual fiscal framework for European Union countries, as rules must be adapted to

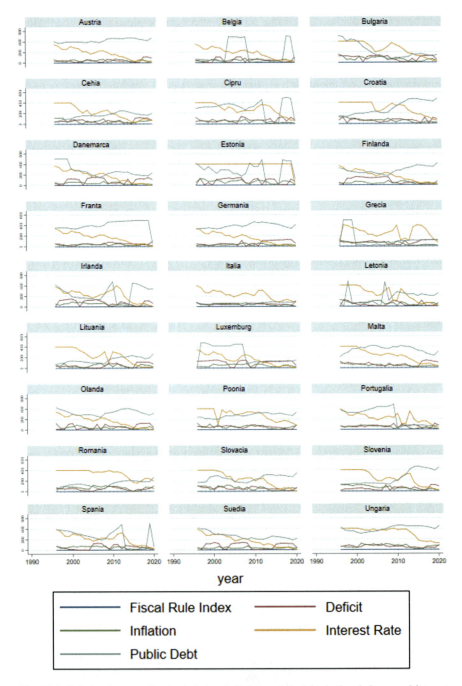

Fig. 20.1 Relation between fiscal rule index, inflation, public debt, budget balance and interest rates, and European Union countries. (Source: Author's research)

the new economic conditions. While many authors advocate the preservation of a single expenditure rule, which could replace the actual rules, it seems that it is difficult to identify new ceilings for the main budgetary aggregates that should reflect the present economic environment. The pandemic has produced an impressive rise in public debt levels in all countries, and establishing different thresholds within a complex debt sustainability analysis might prove very complicated.

We have also tried to investigate the relation between the main fiscal variables, such as public debt, deficits, interest rates, or inflation rate and the fiscal rule index, an indicator established in order to assess the actual fiscal stance. The fiscal rule index seems to be negatively influenced by the evolution of debt, interest rates, and inflation, while deficits have a positive effect on the fiscal rule index. Yet, more extensive research into this field in order to properly identify the determinants of the fiscal index is needed. A comparison with other fiscal unions might prove useful from the perspective of further investigating the behavior of the fiscal rule index and different fiscal regulations in response to the past pandemic crisis.

Using countercyclical fiscal policy to stabilize the economy and ensure public debt sustainability remains a challenge for EU governments, especially in the actual context of recession and deep economic transformations. A common fiscal capacity could ensure more coordination at the level of national fiscal policies, allowing thus to use fiscal policy as an instrument to react to negative output shocks.

References

Afonso, A., & Jalles, J. T. (2019). *Stock flow adjustments in sovereign debt dynamics: The role of fiscal frameworks*. Working Papers REM 2019/66, ISEG – Lisbon School of Economics and Management, REM, Universidade de Lisboa.

Alloza, M., Andrés, J., Burriel, P., Kataryniuk, I., Pérez, J. J. & Vega, J. L. (2021). *The reform of the European Union's fiscal governance framework in a new macroeconomic environment*. Bank of Spain Occasional Paper Series 2121.

Arnold, N. G., Balakrishnan, R., Barkbu, B. B., Davoodi, H. R., Lagerborg, A., Lam, W. R., Medas, P. A., Otten, J., Rabier, L., Roehler, C., Shahmoradi, A., Spector, M., Weber, S., & Zettelmeyer, J. (2022). *Reforming the EU fiscal framework: Strengthening the fiscal rules and institutions*. International Monetary Fund.

Bandaogo, M. S. (2020). *Fiscal rules in times of crisis*. World Bank Research & Policy Briefs.

Beuve, J., Darvas, Z., Delpeuch, S., Martin, P., & Ragot, X. (2019, Summer). *Simple rules for better fiscal policies in Europe*. ifo DICE Report II 2019 (vol. 17).

Blanchard, O., Leandro, A., & Zettelmeyer, J. (2021). *Redesigning EU fiscal rules: From rules to standards*. Peterson Institute for International Economics Working Paper 21-1.

Carnot, N., Deroose, S., Mourre, G., & Pench, L. R. (2018). *EU fiscal rules: Root causes of its complexity*. VoxEU.org.

Checherita-Westphal, C., & Rother, P. (2010). *The impact of high and growing government debt on economic growth: An empirical investigation for the euro area* (ECB working paper, no. 1237). European Central Bank (ECB).

Constâncio, V. (2020). The return of fiscal policy and the euro area fiscal rule. *Comparative Economic Studies, 62*, 358–372.

Dullien, S., Paetz, C., Watt, A., & Watzka, S. (2020). *Proposals for a reform of the EU's fiscal rules and economic governance* (IMK Report, No. 159e, Hans-Böckler-Stiftung). Institut für Makroökonomie und Konjunkturforschung (IMK).

Giavazzi, F., Guerrieri, V., Lorenzoni, G., & Weymuller, C. H. (2021). *Revising the European fiscal framework*. Retrieved from: https://www.governo.it/sites/governo.it/files/documenti/documenti/Notizie-allegati/Reform_SGP.pdf

Gootjes, B., & de Haan, J. (2022). Do fiscal rules need budget transparency to be effective? *European Journal of Political Economy, 75*, 102210.

Lane, P. R. (2021). The resilience of the euro. *Journal of Economic Perspectives, 35*(2), 3–22.

Larch, M., Orseau, E., & van der Wielen, W. (2020). *Do EU fiscal rules support or hinder countercyclical fiscal policy?* (CESifo working paper, no. 8659). Center for Economic Studies and Ifo Institute (CESifo).

Park, H. M. (2003). *Linear regression models for panel data using SAS, Stata, LIMDEP, and SPSS*. University Information Technology Services Center for Statistical and Mathematical Computing Indiana University.

Taylor, L., Proan, C. R., de Carvalho, L., & Barbosa, N. (2012). Fiscal deficits, economic growth, and government debt in the USA. *Cambridge Journal of Economics, 36*, 189–204.

Truger, A. (2020). Reforming EU fiscal rules: More leeway, investment orientation and democratic coordination. *Intereconomics, 55*(5), 277–281.

Wyplosz, C. (2019, Summer). *Fiscal discipline in the eurozone: Don't fix it, change it*. ifo DICE Report II 2019 (vol. 17).

Chapter 21
Stock Market Reactions to ESG Dynamics: A European Banking Perspective

Iulia Lupu and Adina Criste

Abstract The actions taken worldwide to combat the effects of climate change have boosted the analysis of related economic risks in the financial sector on the three components: environment, social, and governance (ESG). ESG scores calculated by specialized providers for listed companies are increasingly taken into account, in addition to economic and financial ones, demonstrating the importance of these factors for the financial system. Some studies show that from the investors' point of view, pursuing ESG objectives positively limits legal and reputational risks, firm performance, and the perception of firms' risk profiles. These factors help reduce the risk premium and cost of capital, benefiting financial performance. Based on these findings, we considered investigating the reaction of listed European banks' returns to ESG value changes. The analysis covers the stock prices of all banks traded on stock exchanges from Europe, considering the analysis of daily frequencies between 2010 and 2021. We collected data on the values of ESG components for all these companies and created a database with all moments when changes in these values took place. Further, we run an event study analysis of the impact of these modifications on the dynamics of stock market log returns for the sample of banks. Our objective is to quantify investors' reactions to these changes and document differences in responses to increased versus decreased values of ESG.

Keywords ESG · Stock market · Banking sector · Event study

I. Lupu (✉) · A. Criste
"Victor Slăvescu" Centre for Financial and Monetary Research, Bucharest, Romania
e-mail: iulia_lupu@icfm.ro

21.1 Introduction

Although the environment, social, and governance (ESG) concept has older roots, in its current meaning, it was launched in 2004 in a United Nations report (United Nations, 2004). Its development took place over time, and recently, the foundations are being laid, and a new business model is being promoted.

ESG goals have become a symbol for responsible investing and capture information not found in standard financial reporting. This process involves consistent evaluation, monitoring, or reporting efforts. Research that looked at 141 journals in the Scopus database for the period 2001–2021 points out that since 2017, the number of articles published in the ESG field has almost doubled yearly (Sachini et al., 2022).

The actions taken worldwide to combat climate change effects have intensified the financial sector's analysis of related economic risks on the environment, social, and governance components.

ESG scores calculated by specialist providers for listed companies are increasingly taken into account, in addition to other economic and financial aspects, demonstrating the importance of these factors for the financial system.

Analyzing the reaction of capital markets to ESG dynamics is important because these factors represent one of the biggest challenges for the economy and society today and influence stock prices.

The purpose of the study carried out in this paper was to investigate the reaction of the calculated share returns for banks listed on European stock exchanges to changes in the dynamics of ESG scores using the event-study methodology.

The first objective was to measure investor reactions to changes in ESG scores, and the second is to test whether there is a difference between market responses to increased versus decreased ESG scores.

21.2 Literature Review

As the latest United Nations report notices, the period until 2030 is essential for global warming diminishing, a context that may impact all ESG constituents; furthermore, a new concern is emerging regarding social aspects (Shukla et al., 2022).

From a financial perspective, specifically from the capital markets, a recent report of the European Securities and Markets Authority (ESMA) on the efficiency and costs regarding investment items in the European Union for the year 2020 states that those with a specified strategy for ESG outperformed the non-ESG financial products (ESMA, 2022). As a result, the increase in ESG-related financial products occurred through the appearance of new funds and by the insertion of ESG features in the available funds' strategy. Concomitantly, the ESG factors were included in the new banking regulatory packages at the European and national levels. Bruno and Lagasio (2021) synthesized them. Moreover, results have been presented in the economic literature showing that a good ESG performance enhances banks' resilience in tumultuous periods (Chiaramonte et al., 2021), and better ESG performance protects against contagion (Cerqueti et al., 2021) and is related to financial stability (Lupu et al., 2022).

The economic literature on ESG in the banking sector has developed significantly in recent years. Until recently, it was considered a minor player in pollution problems. Before 2015, the environment was included in the social dimension, as noted by Galletta et al. (2022) in the bibliometric study carried out for the period 1986–2021, for 271 publications included in the Web of Science in which subjects related to the performance of ESG in the banking sector are studied.

Research that uses the proposed methodology (event study) is carried out by Wang et al. (2022) to measure the reaction of the US capital market to the introduction of legislation requiring companies to report ESG performance using specific measurement standards to be finalized by the Securities and Exchange Commission. On the one hand, this new mandatory reporting of non-financial information is seen as a benefit for the company, investors, and society as a whole. Still, on the other hand, it involves some additional costs for businesses. A considerable adverse response of -1.1% was observed for the entire sample of banks, which persisted for 5 days. Industrial or carbon-intensive companies are more sensitive, and those with higher ESG scores had an attenuated adverse reaction. A similar methodology was employed to capture the link between the news related to macroeconomic growth and the stock market reaction (Lupu & Dumitrescu, 2010).

The importance of ESG for the banking system, demonstrated by the increased interest in academic research and institutional reports and regulations, and the previous use of the event study in the field of ESG, motivates our research proposal. We also consider the lack of studies that analyzes the reaction of capital markets to the dynamics of ESG factors in the European banking sector.

21.3 Methodology

To carry out the analysis, we used the prices of the shares of the European banks included in the STOXX Europe 600 index, with daily frequency. We calculated the ESG score values for these banks according to the Refinitiv methodology (Refinitiv, 2022).

Each pillar (E, S, and G) has in its composition several elements that receive scores based on the performance of the analyzed company; they have different weights in the score's computation for the pillar in question. From the ten categories, three are considered for the environmental pillar: resource use, emissions, and innovation. The social pillar contains four different classes, equivalent to the largest number of elements considered, for which a corresponding weight is attached: labor, human rights, community, and product responsibility. The governance pillar refers to management issues, shareholder-related aspects, and corporate social responsibility conduct.

When calculating the final ESG score for a company, each pillar receives a weight that takes different values for each industry minus the governance score, whose weight remains the same. According to the Refinitiv methodology, for the banking sector, the relative importance of the three pillars is distributed as follows: 14.4% corresponds to the environmental aspect, 49.6% to the account of social component, and the remainder of 36% is assigned to the governance elements. Final scores range from 0 to 100, with 100 reflecting the highest level of ESG performance.

The analyzed period is 2010–2021, and the data source is the Datastream Refinitiv platform. After eliminating the companies for which data were unavailable for the entire analyzed period, 81 European banks remained in the study sample.

The first step consisted of calculating the ESG values based on the E, S, and G components (for all companies) and identifying the times when these values occurred.

Subsequently, we conducted an event study to determine the influence of these changes in the dynamics associated with the stock returns of the European banks in the considered sample. The event study is based on calibrating a market model (respectively, a single index model, following the capital asset pricing model) for 100 days before the event window.

Therefore, for this time frame, we fit the following model

$$R\_(i,t) - r\_f = \beta\_i \times (R\_M - r\_f)$$

where $R\_(i,t)$ is the log-return at moment t for each individual stock i and r_f is the risk-free asset, while R_M is the log-return of the market index. The model is used to generate forecasts for the event window (the time frame around the event), but we test the significance of β_i coefficients for each event and individual asset. The difference between these forecasts and the actual values (abnormal returns) and the cumulated differences (cumulative abnormal returns) are tested for statistical significance using the standard errors of the residuals for the fitted values.

The index used to calibrate this model is the STOXX 600 index, and the estimation was made for the logarithmic returns computed for the index and the European banks in the sample.

Based on the estimates and the values of the returns of the stock market index for the period around the event (the window −5/+10 days around the event (considered position 0), predictions were made for the returns of each bank's shares for this period.

The difference between the realized values of the logarithmic returns for the analyzed banks, on the one hand, and the predicted returns using the model described above, on the other hand, constitute abnormal returns.

The statistical significance of these returns is equivalent to the validation of the hypothesis that the event determined the manifestation of significant reactions on the part of investors because the new dynamics of returns deviate significantly from the predicted values. Also, the study of the statistical significance of the cumulative abnormal returns provides information about the event's impact on the transactions made on the stock market by investors interested in the banking companies under analysis.

Investor reactions to these changes were quantified to establish differences in market responses, and differences in response to increased versus decreased ESG scores were examined.

21.4 Analysis/Result Interpretation

For the 81 European banks, the situations in which changes occur were identified, separated into six levels: lower/higher than zero ESG score units, lower/higher by at least one ESG score unit, lower/higher by at least two ESG score units, lower/higher by at least three ESG score units, lower/higher by at least four ESG score units, and lower/higher by at least five ESG score units.

For each combination of event and bank in our sample, we fitted the single index model and tested the significance of the β_i coefficient. The model produced significant coefficients in all situations, and we analyzed the significance of the abnormal returns.

In Table 21.1, we can see more positive than negative changes, which can be interpreted as an evolution of ESG's performance in banking.

As we increase the level of difference in ESG score (number of units), the number of changes becomes more petite (except for the category of smaller/larger changes with at least five ESG score units where all changes exceeding five units are included).

Figure 21.1 shows the changes identified for positive events, while Fig. 21.2 exposes those for the negative events, represented as a percentage for each

Table 21.1 ESG score changes for European banks' models

Changes	No. of positive events (increase)	No. of negative events (decrease)
Less than/greater than 0 ESG score units	361	262
Smaller/larger by at least 1 ESG score unit	298	207
Lower/higher by at least 2 ESG score units	243	159
Smaller/larger by at least 3 ESG score units	189	115
Lower/higher by at least 4 ESG score units	154	76
Smaller/larger by at least 5 ESG score units	134	55

Source: Authors' research

Fig. 21.1 ESG score changes—number of positive events (increases), graphic breakdown. (Source: Authors' research)

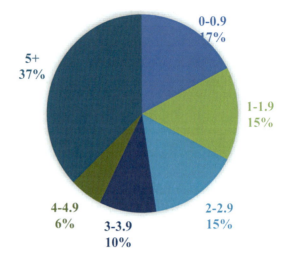

Fig. 21.2 ESG score changes—number of negative events (decreases), graphic breakdown. (Source: Authors' research)

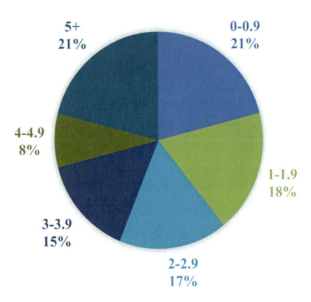

considered interval. Significant changes (more than 5 ESG units) represent 37% of all positive changes, much more numerous than negative ones, representing 21% of all negative events. The range 4–4.9 has the lowest weight for positive events (6% of total positive events) and for negative events (8% of total negative events).

The impact on European bank stock returns is plotted in the figures below. The quantified implications of changes in the ESG scores lower/higher than zero units are shown in Fig. 21.3. We observe that for negative events, the returns stay longer in the negative side and later recover and reach the end of the investigation window at values similar to those observed for positive events.

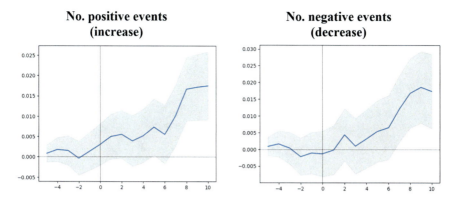

Fig. 21.3 Impact on European bank stock returns for ESG score changes below/above 0 units. (Source: Authors' research)

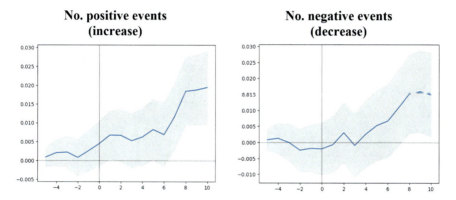

Fig. 21.4 Impact on European bank stock returns for ESG score changes below/above 1 unit. (Source: Authors' research)

The calculated impact for smaller/larger changes by at least one unit is represented in Fig. 21.4. Cumulative abnormal returns remain on the negative side for a more extended period for negative events. The increase until the end of the window is less compared to the situation observed for positive events.

A similar situation can be seen in Fig. 21.5 for score changes of at least two units.

As the score gap increases, for negative events, in addition to returns staying longer in the negative zone, we can see that returns increase much less.

Thus, in Fig. 21.6, we can observe the evolution of returns for score differences of at least three score units. In comparison, in Fig. 21.7, the impact on European bank stock returns for lower/higher ESG score changes in at least four units is plotted.

In Fig. 21.8, the difference in impact for score changes greater than five units is most noticeable. Cumulative abnormal returns remain negative until the fifth day

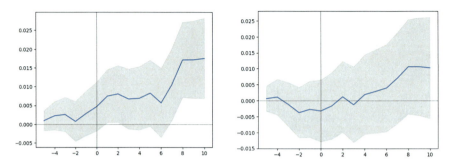

Fig. 21.5 Impact on European bank stock returns for ESG score changes below/above two units. (Source: Authors' research)

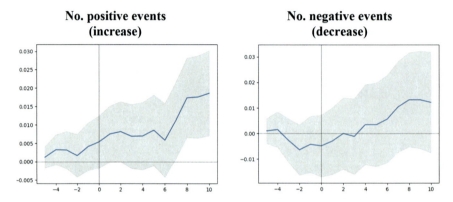

Fig. 21.6 Impact on European bank stock returns for ESG score changes below/above three units. (Source: Authors' research)

after the event. After that, increases are modest and do not reach the level corresponding to positive events.

Overall, we observe that the extensive amplitude changes are more numerous in the case of positive events, thus marking an improvement in the performance of ESG in banking.

For negative events, cumulative abnormal returns remain in the negative range for several days. The more significant the score difference, the increase in cumulative abnormal returns becomes very small for negative events compared to positive ones.

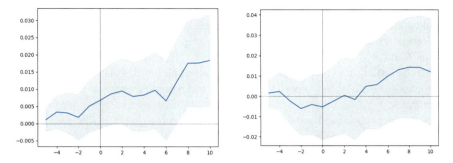

Fig. 21.7 Impact on European bank stock returns for ESG score changes below/above four units. (Source: Authors' research)

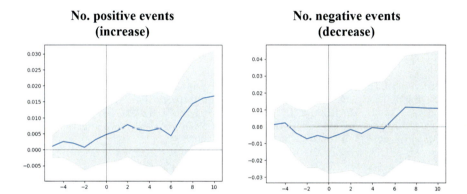

Fig. 21.8 Impact on European bank stock returns for ESG score changes smaller/larger by at least five units. (Source: Authors' research)

21.5 Conclusions

The first objective stated in this article was to measure investor reactions to changes in ESG scores. Our results display more positive changes compared with negative ones, which can be accounted for a good evolution of ESG's performance in banking.

On the other side, we intended to explore if there is a differentiation between investors' responses for increased versus decreased ESG scores. Empirical results confirm that in the case of negative events (decreased ESG scores), the effects are more potent and last longer, demonstrating the need to integrate ESG factors into financial decisions. Awareness of the importance of ESG factors sheds new light on financial markets, opening up new opportunities and challenges.

The obtained results are significant under the conditions that the new banking regulations directly consider the ESG factors. European regulations, periodically improved, entitle the European Banking Authority to assess the ESG risks for this sector. Considering this new framework, our results may display economic policy implications for financial entities and regulators' management and strategy design.

Recent advances in measuring ESG factors are intended to mitigate the discrepancies found by Berg et al. (2022) and Billio et al. (2021), which are associated with research limitations and difficulties. Globally, global regulations are being announced to unify the reporting side and make things easier to classify and interpret.

A new approach has been developing in the economic literature in recent years. It has the effect of a reconsideration of corporate governance through the proposal of Hart and Zingales (2017), who propose the pursuit of maximizing the welfare of shareholders and not the market value of shares. This perspective encourages the development of ESG objectives and their better financial integration and opens new levels of research for analyzing the new welfare-ESG relationship.

References

Berg, F., Kölbel, J. F., & Rigobon, R. (2022). Aggregate confusion: The divergence of ESG ratings. *Review of Finance, 26*(6), 1315–1344. https://doi.org/10.1093/ROF/RFAC033

Billio, M., Costola, M., Hristova, I., Latino, C., & Pelizzon, L. (2021). Inside the ESG ratings: (Dis)agreement and performance. *Corporate Social Responsibility and Environmental Management, 28*(5), 1426–1445. https://doi.org/10.1002/CSR.2177

Bruno, M., & Lagasio, V. (2021). An overview of the european policies on ESG in the banking sector. *Sustainability, 13*(22), 12641. https://doi.org/10.3390/SU132212641

Cerqueti, R., Ciciretti, R., Dalò, A., & Nicolosi, M. (2021). ESG investing: A chance to reduce systemic risk. *Journal of Financial Stability, 54*, 100887. https://doi.org/10.1016/J.JFS.2021.100887

Chiaramonte, L., Dreassi, A., Girardone, C., & Piserà, S. (2021). Do ESG strategies enhance bank stability during financial turmoil? *Evidence from Europe, 28*(12), 1173–1211. https://doi.org/10.1080/1351847X.2021.1964556

ESMA. (2022). *ESMA annual statistical report. Performance and costs of retail investment products in the EU*. https://www.esma.europa.eu/document/esma-annual-statistical-report-performance-and-costs-retail-investment-products-in-eu-2022

Galletta, S., Mazzù, S., & Naciti, V. (2022). A bibliometric analysis of ESG performance in the banking industry: From the current status to future directions. *Research in International Business and Finance, 62*. https://doi.org/10.1016/J.RIBAF.2022.101684

Hart, O., & Zingales, L. (2017). Companies should maximise shareholder welfare not market value. *Journal of Law, Finance, and Accounting, 2*(2).

Lupu, I., & Dumitrescu, D. G. (2010). Stock market reaction to news on macroeconomic growth. An event study analysis at the Bucharest stock exchange. *Transformations in Business and Economics, 9*(1 SUPPL. A), 361–376.

Lupu, I., Hurduzeu, G., & Lupu, R. (2022). How is the ESG reflected in European financial stability? *Sustainability, 14*(16), 10287. https://doi.org/10.3390/SU141610287

Refinitiv. (2022). *Environmental, Social and Governance (ESG) Scores from Refinitiv*.

Sachini, S., Senadheera, R., Gregory, J., Rinklebe, M., Farrukh, J. H., Rhee, Y., Sik, O., Senadheera, S. S., Gregory, R., Rinklebe, J., Farrukh, M., Rhee, J. H., & Ok, Y. S. (2022). The development of research on environmental, social, and governance (ESG): A bibliometric analysis. Sustainable. *Environment, 8*(1). https://doi.org/10.1080/27658511.2022.2125869

Shukla, P. R., Skea, J., Slade, R., Khourdajie, A. Al, Diemen, R. van, McCollum, D., Pathak, M., Some, S., Vyas, P., Fradera, R., Belkacemi, M., Hasija, A., Lisboa, G., Luz, S., & Malley, J., (eds.). (2022). IPCC *climate change 2022: Mitigation of climate change*. Contribution of working group III to the sixth assessment report of the intergovernmental panel on climate change. https://doi.org/10.17159/sajs.2022/14690

United Nations. (2004). *Who cares wins. Connecting financial markets to a changing world*.

Wang, J., Hu, X., & Zhong, A. (2022). Stock market reaction to mandatory ESG disclosure. *Finance Research Letters, 103402*. https://doi.org/10.1016/J.FRL.2022.103402

Chapter 22
The Efficiency of Futures Markets on Cryptocurrencies

Radu Lupu and Catalina Maria Popa

Abstract From the launch of Bitcoin till the present moment, cryptocurrency market had expanded continuously, gaining more and more influence over the global economy with each passing year. Yet, the events of 2020 marked a new phase for the cryptocurrency ecosystem, which has experienced a significant increase in size and complexity. The third halving cycle that led to an increase in cryptocurrency prices, the beginning of pandemic, and afterward inflation and economic uncertainty made Bitcoin an attractive asset for both retail and institutional investors. Although the liquidity of the cryptocurrency assets increased, their volatile nature is still persistent, causing mixed views on its status. While crypto-enthusiasts are perceiving it as a worthwhile investment with novel economic properties, the more skeptic participants consider it only a speculative asset with a transitory presence. The absence of a consensus on this topic has attracted the interest of the academic community, which aims to analyze whether cryptocurrencies display economic properties. A keystone characteristic for considering cryptocurrency an economic asset is the lack of price manipulation. In this respect, numerous papers have investigated the efficiency of the cryptocurrency market. Even though the results are mixed, a large body of studies indicate that the efficiency of the crypto-assets market varies, increasing from period to period. However, most of the papers focus on testing information efficiency only on the spot market. Thus, the objective of this study is to analyze whether the futures cryptocurrency market is efficient. In this regard, the futures prices for Bitcoin from 2018 to 2022 are used. On them, a battery of tests is applied, which investigate several statistical properties that can assess the efficiency hypothesis. Furthermore, under the assumption of efficient market hypothesis the spot and future prices are supposed to move together. In the contrary case, the

---

R. Lupu (✉)
Bucharest University of Economic Studies, Bucharest, Romania
e-mail: radu.lupu@rei.ase.ro

C. M. Popa
Bucharest University of Economic Studies, Bucharest, Romania

Institute for Economic Forecasting, Romanian Academy, Bucharest, Romania

© The Author(s), under exclusive license to Springer Nature Switzerland AG 2024
L. Chivu et al. (eds.), *Constraints and Opportunities in Shaping the Future: New Approaches to Economics and Policy Making*, Springer Proceedings in Business and Economics, https://doi.org/10.1007/978-3-031-47925-0_22

efficient market hypothesis is rejected. Thus, the property is evaluated from a double perspective by using statistical tests and evaluating the relation between the spot and the future price.

Keywords Cryptocurrency market · Cryptocurrency efficiency · Bitcoin · Efficient market hypothesis · Spot market · Futures market · Cointegration test

22.1 Introduction

Over the years, the impact of the cryptocurrency market on the global economy has increased. The debate concerning whether cryptocurrency has the potential to change the monetary and financial system has raised the attention of the regulatory institutions. Their main concerns target the financial stability and the risk that the investors are exposing to. Under this context, the study of the economic properties of the crypto-coins is mandatory for understanding their comportment and the risks associated with it. For deciding if the cryptocurrencies are more than a speculative asset, the efficiency of the cryptocurrency market was highly studied in the literature. Yet, an exceedingly number of papers have investigated the efficient market hypothesis on spot level, neglecting the futures market. The aim of this paper was to fill this gap, by applying two methods. First, a battery of tests was applied on Bitcoin future prices, which investigates the statistical properties needed to confirm EMH. Secondly, the Engle-Granger co-integration test was applied for studying if the spot and futures prices move together.

22.2 Literature Review

In the last years, the popularity of cryptocurrencies has considerably increased both among retail and institutional investors. Their increased participation and the strengthened role of the cryptocurrency in world's economy raised the question of whether the crypto-coins are more than a speculative asset or not. This dilemma raised the attention of the research community whose aim is to analyze whether the cryptocurrency displays some economic properties, similarly to other financial assets. Thus, a large body of studies that concern this topic have emerged. The investigated properties concern the volatile nature of the crypto coins (Baur, 2018; Katsiampa et al., 2019; Bouri et al., 2019a), their safe-haven capabilities (Corbet et al., 2018, 2020), bubbles (Bouri et al., 2019b; Bubbles and crashes in cryptocurrencies: Interdependence, 2022), and herding behavior (Bouri et al., 2019c; Mnif et al., 2020).

Another studied property is the efficiency of the crypto-market. Introduced by Fama (1970), the efficient market hypothesis infers that financial assets display all the information available, which makes them impossible to be consistently predicted. The incapacity of price manipulation under EMH would change the perspective over the cryptocurrency market, possibly implying that is stable and mature enough to invest in. On the contrary, the invalidation of EMH would suggest a speculative character. These implications motivate the large number of studies developed in this area. However, the results are still mixed. On one hand, some scholars reject EMH on cryptocurrency market (Vidal-Tomás et al., 2019; Jiang, 2018). On the other hand, other studies show that the efficiency of the cryptocurrency market fluctuates in time, becoming more efficient over the years (Urquhart, 2016). Although many factors have been considered when the efficiency was studied (comparing the efficiency of different exchanges, at different time frequencies, between different cryptocurrencies), many studies have targeted the spot market, neglecting the futures market.

Introduced by Chicago Mercantile Exchange in 2017, the futures contracts on Bitcoin have represented a milestone moment for the cryptocurrency market. Later, the contracts were launched for other currencies as well, like Ethereum, Polygon, Cardano, and Tezos. The presence of futures contracts issued through a standardized process supported by CME represents a vote of confidence for the cryptocurrency market. In this respect, several studies analyze the impact of future introductions on the market. Shaen Corbet (2018) suggests that the volatility spiked after the introduction of Bitcoin futures. Kochling et al. (2018) show that the efficiency of the spot cryptocurrency market showed signs of improvement after the introduction of Bitcoin. Godinh (2020) argues that Bitcoin futures may be a proper instrument for hedging. Other studies discussed the price discovery of Bitcoin (Fassas et al., 2019; BurcuKapara, 2019; Corbet et al., 2019). Yet, the efficiency of the cryptocurrency futures market was not frequently discussed by the academic community. The aim of this study was to complete this gap.

22.3 Methodology

In respect to the scope of this paper, the efficiency of the cryptocurrency futures market was analyzed using two approaches.

Firstly, the literature indicates that the returns respect certain statistical properties if the market is efficient. For testing this assumption, a battery of tests was applied. Secondly, under EMH the spot and future prices are presumed to move together. Thus, the Engle-Granger cointegration test was used.

In respect to the first approach, the historical CME Futures Daily Roll Index prices of Bitcoin have been used. The index is a gauge for the return that stems from rolling a long position in two Bitcoin futures contracts that have the closest maturity and are traded on the Chicago Mercantile Exchange. This indicator in developed with the purpose to capture the performance of Bitcoin futures market within a day. The analyzed period was from December 18, 2017, when the futures contracts for Bitcoin were introduced to November 18, 2022. During this period, several events, such as the beginning of the pandemic, the economic uncertainty generated by it, and the third halving cycle of Bitcoin, have significantly impacted the cryptocurrency market. To investigate the impact of these milestone moments over the efficiency of the futures market, the data were divided into three subsets named base period (December 18, 2017-November 20, 2020), ATH 1 (November 30, 2020-November 10, 2021), ATH 2 (November 11, 2021-November 18, 2022). The periods were selected based on the newest all time high of Bitcoin which, after the third halving cycle, was first hit on November 30, 2020, and lastly achieved on November 11, 2021. Thus, ATH 1 set is marked by an ascending trend (a bull period), while ATH 2 is mostly characterized by a descending trend (the beginning of the bear period). The dynamic is depicted in Fig. 22.1.

For all the periods, the Bitcoin futures prices were transformed in logarithmic returns by applying the formula: $r_t = \ln(P_t/P_{t-1})$, where P_t represents the price at the moment t, P_{t-1} represents the price at $t-1$, and r_t represents the return at moment t. The efficiency was analyzed by applying six statistical tests proposed by (Urquhart, 2016) Under EMH, the returns cannot be autocorrelated to assure that the future returns cannot be predicted based on the past ones. To evaluate this property, the Ljung-Box test (Ljung & Box, 1978) was applied. The statistics is defined by the formula:

$$\text{(a)}\ Q_k = n(n+2)\sum_{j=1}^{k}\frac{c_j^2}{n-j} \qquad (22.1)$$

where the sample size is depicted by n, the number of lags tested is captured by k, and the sample autocorrelation at lag j is expressed by c_j^2.

Another property is the independence of returns, which was investigated by applying the Runs test (Wald & Wolfowitz, 1940) and the Bartels test (Bartels, 1982). The Runs test presumes that any element of a sequence is independent and is computed by the formula:

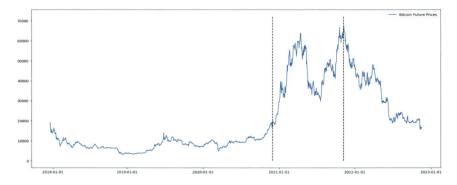

Fig. 22.1 BTC Future Prices Dynamic—Sampling. (Source: Author's calculations)

$$(b)\; Z = \frac{R - \mu_R}{\sigma_R} \qquad (22.2)$$

where R is used to represent the number of runs, μ_R stands for the expectation for the number of runs, which is captured by the formula: $\mu_R = \frac{2N_+ N_-}{N} + 1$ and σ_R depict the standard deviations expressed as $\sigma_R = \sqrt{\frac{2N_+ N_- (2N_+ N_- - N_+ - N_-)}{(N_+ N_-)^2 (N_+ + N_- - 1)}}$. N_+, N_- are the count of positive and negative elements contained in a sequence. The second test applied for evaluating the independence property is defined by the formula:

$$(c)\; RVN = \frac{\sum_{i=1}^{T-1}(R_i - R_{i+1})^2}{\sum_{i=1}^{T}(R_i - \bar{R})^2} \qquad (22.3)$$

where the rank for the ith observation in a sequence of T observations is depicted by R_i. Given that the size of the sample exceeds 100 in both cases ($T > 100$), the p-value was approximated by using the formula $\sim N\left(2, \frac{20}{5T+7}\right)$.

Besides the lack of autocorrelation and the property of independence, the returns have to follow a random walk process under EMH. To evaluate this property, the variance ratio test (Lo & MacKinley, 1988) was used, whose null hypothesis states that the returns follow a random walk. The test is computed as:

$$(d)\; Z^*(q) = \frac{\sqrt{nq}\, VR(q)}{\sqrt{\hat{\Theta}(q)}} \sim N(0,1) \qquad (22.4)$$

where n denotes the count of observations, q stands for the number of lags, VR is the variance ratio, and $\widehat{\theta(q)}$ depicts the heteroscedasticity estimator of $\theta(q)$.

For investigating whether the returns are serial dependent, the BDS test (Broock, 1996), whose null hypothesis states the returns are independently identically distributed, was applied. The test is defined as:

$$C_{m,T}(\epsilon) = T^{1/2} \frac{\left[C_T(\epsilon) - C_1(\epsilon)^m\right]}{\sigma_{m,\tau}(\epsilon)} \qquad (22.5)$$

where $C_{m,T}(\epsilon)$ represents the correlation integral, m the embedding dimension, τ designates the time delay, ϵ is the threshold distance indicator, and σ represents the variance.

For analyzing whether the returns present long-term memory, the rescaled Hurst Exponent (Taylor, 1971) was applied. The statistics is computed as:

$$\text{(e)} \quad E\left[\frac{R(n)}{S(n)}\right] = Cn^H, \text{ as } n \to \infty \qquad (22.6)$$

where we consider $R(n)$ to be the range of the first n cumulative standard deviations, we use $S(n)$ to represent the standard deviation, and we employ C for a constant and n to capture the span.

The second approach started from the assumptions that the spot and future prices move together. To test this assumption, Engle-Granger test (Engle, 1987) is applied, which assumes that the time series do not drift apart. In this respect, two data sets have been used. The first one was the historical spot prices of Bitcoin, and the second one was the historical futures prices. Both of the series had daily frequency and were analyzed between December 18, 2017, to January 14, 2022. On this, the Engle-Granger co-integration test was used, whose null hypothesis assumes that the time series are not co-integrated. The test is expressed mathematically as:

$$S_t = \alpha + \beta F_{t-i} + \epsilon_t \qquad (22.7)$$

where S_t represents the spot price at moment t and F_{t-i} denotes the future price at moment $t - i$.

22.4 Analysis/Result Interpretation

Figures 22.2, 22.3, and 22.4 depict the dynamic in time of the p-values corresponding to each efficiency test. According to the results presented in Fig. 22.2, the Ljung-Box test tends to be constant and above the significance level (0.05) for all the periods, meaning that returns tend to not be autocorrelated. Moreover, the variance ratio test varies along the periods, but in most of the cases, the values exceed the level of significance, implying that returns are following a random walk process.

However, during ATH 1 period the market tends to be less efficient according to both tests. The Runs and Bartels tests exhibited in Fig. 22.3 are also fluctuating in time, although in most of the cases the p-values are beyond the level of significance, suggesting that the returns tend to be independent.

Similarly, to the previous tests, Runs and Bartels' corresponding p-values display a lower level of efficiency during ATH 1 period. The BDS test is depicted in Fig. 22.4. Although the p-values vary in time, there are no major differences between data sets. The majority of the p-values are above the significance level inferring that the returns are independently identically distributed most of the time.

The Hurst exponent is displayed in Fig. 22.5. For all three samples, the rescaled Hurst is under 0.5, indicating an anti-persistent behavior. This mean-reverting tendency implies that a period of decrease will be followed by a period of increase and the other way around. Otherwise the future returns tend to go toward a long-term mean.

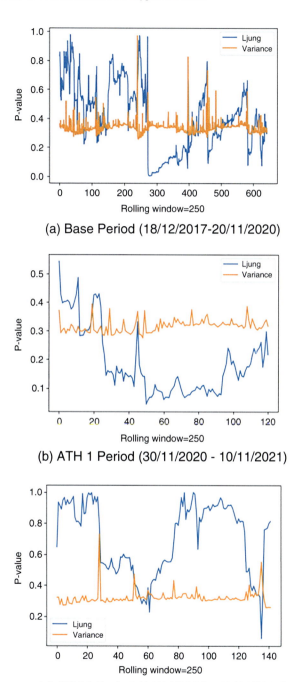

Fig. 22.2 *P*-values of Ljung-Box test and variance ratio test. (**a**) Base period (18/12/2017–20/11/2020). (**b**) ATH 1 Period (30/11/2020–10/11/2021). (**c**) ATH 2 period (11/11/2021–18/11/2022)

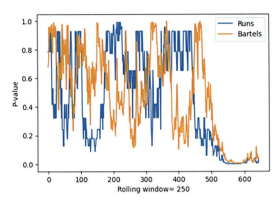

(f) Base Period (18/12/2017-20/11/2020)

5

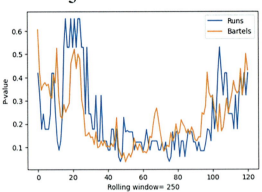

(g) ATH 1 (30/11/2020 – 10/11/2021)

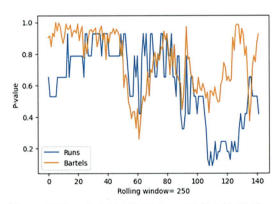

(h) ATH 2 (12/11/2021 – 18/11/2022)

Fig. 22.3 *P*-values of Runs and Bartels test. (**a**) Base Period (18/12/2017–20/11/2020). (**b**) ATH 1 (30/11/2020–10/11/2021). (**c**) ATH 2 (12/11/2021–18/11/2022). (Source: Author's calculations)

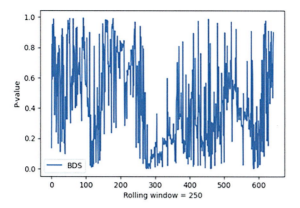

(a) Base Period (18/12/2017-20/11/2020)

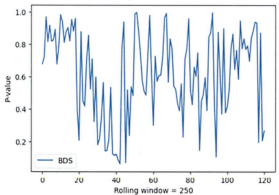

(b) ATH 1 (30/11/2020 – 10/11/2021)

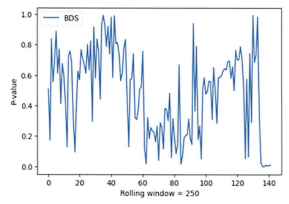

(c) ATH 2 (11/11/2021 – 18/11/2022)

Fig. 22.4 *P*-values of BDS Test. (**a**) Base period (18/12/2017–20/11/2020). (**b**) ATH 1 (30/11/2020–10/11/2021). (**c**) ATH 2 (11/11/2021–18/11/2022). (Source: Author's calculations)

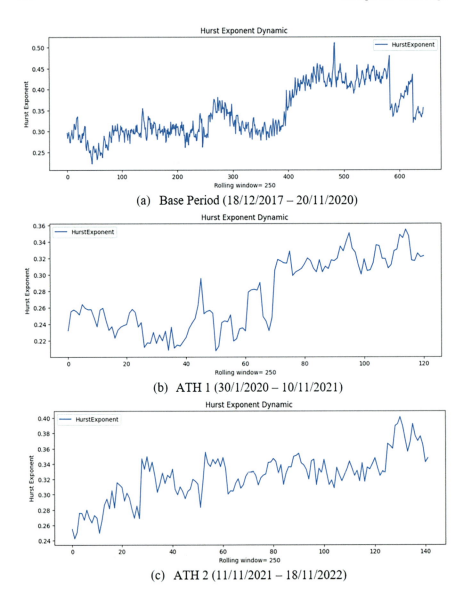

Fig. 22.5 Hurst exponent. (**a**) Base period (18/12/2017–20/11/2020). (**b**) ATH 1 (30/1/2020–10/11/2021). (**c**) ATH 2 (11/11/2021–18/11/2022). (Source: Author's calculations)

Overall, the cryptocurrency future market tends to be efficient, yet the level of efficiency tends to decrease during the ATH 1, having even some short moments of inefficiency. The fact that this behavior is displayed during ATH 1 may suggest that the market tends to be more predictable when is on an ascending trend, with investors expecting the prices to further increase.

Nevertheless, the tendency of the cryptocurrency futures market to be efficient is supported by the Engle-Granger test, whose null hypothesis that states that the time series are not co-integrated has been rejected. Thus, future prices are an indicator for the future spot prices. In other words, the EMH assumptions are validated, and the future prices are the best indicator of spot prices.

22.5 Conclusions

The efficiency of the cryptocurrency market is necessary to be studied in order to understand if the prices are manipulated or not. Thus, a large body of studies emerged. However, most of them have analyzed the efficiency on the spot market, neglecting the futures market. In this respect, the scope of this chapter was to investigate whether the cryptocurrency market is efficient using two approaches. Firstly, a battery of tests was applied on CME Daily Bitcoin Futures prices between December 18, 2017, and November 20, 2020. The data were divided in three sets, cut based on the all-time high dates. Overall, the tests indicate that the cryptocurrency futures market tends to be efficient, although during ATH 1 the level of efficiency decreased. This might suggest that during the ascending periods, the market leans to be more predictable, possibly due to the over-optimistic expectations of the investors. Secondly, the Engle-Granger co-integration test was used on Bitcoin spot prices and futures prices from December 18, 2017, to January 14, 2022. The test indicated that the spot and future prices are co-integrated, which implies that the spot and future prices do not deviate from one another. This result sustains the efficiency of the cryptocurrency futures market. Further studies may consider the usage of different cryptocurrencies at a more detailed frequency (hourly, minute). This approach may extend the knowledge on this topic, providing an exhaustive view.

References

Bartels, R. (1982). The rank version of von Neumann's ratio test for randomness. *Journal of the American Statistical Association, 77*, 40.
Baur, D. G. (2018). Asymmetric volatility in cryptocurrencies. *Economics Letters, 173*, 148.
Bouri, E., et al. (2019a). Trading volume and the predictability of return and volatility in the cryptocurrency market. *Finance Research Letters, 29*, 340.
Bouri, E., et al. (2019b). Co-explosivity in the cryptocurrency market. *Finance Research Letters, 29*, 178.
Bouri, E., et al. (2019c). Herding behaviour in cryptocurrencies. *Finance Research Letters, 29*, 216.
Brock, W. A. (1996). A test for independence based on the correlation dimension. *Econometric reviews, 15*, 197.
Bubbles and Crashes in Cryptocurrencies: Interdependence, c. o. (2022). Bubbles and crashes in cryptocurrencies: Interdependence, contagion, or asset rotation? *Finance Research Letters*.
BurcuKapara, J. (2019). An analysis of price discovery between Bitcoinfutures and spotmarkets. *Economics Letters*.

Corbet, S., et al. (2018). Exploring the dynamic relationships between cryptocurrencies and other financial assets. *Economics Letters, 165*, 28.

Corbet, S., et al. (2019). *Investigating the dynamics between price volatility, price discovery, and criminality in cryptocurrency markets.*

Corbet, S., et al. (2020). Any port in a storm: Cryptocurrency safe-havens during the COVID-19 pandemic. *Economics Letters, 194*, 109377.

Engle, R. F. (1987). Co-integration and error correction: Representation, estimation, and testing. *Econometrica: Journal of the Econometric Society.*

Fama, E. (1970). Efficient capital markets: A review of theory and empirical work. *The Journal of Finance, 25*, 383.

Fassas, A., et al. (2019). Price discovery in Bitcoin futures. *Research in International Business and Finance.*

Godinh, S. (2020). Bitcoin futures: An effective tool for hedging cryptocurrencies. *Finance Research Letters, 33*, 101230.

Jiang, Y. H. (2018). Time-varying long-term memory in Bitcoin market. *Finance Research Letters, 25*, 280.

Katsiampa, P., et al. (2019). High frequency volatility co-movements in cryptocurrency markets. *Journal of International Financial Markets, Institutions and Money, 62*, 35.

Kochling, G., Muller, J., & Posch, P. (2018). Does the introduction of futures improve the efficiency of Bitcoin? *Finance Research Letters, 30*, 367.

Ljung, G., & Box, E. (1978). On a measure of lack of fit in time series models. *Biometrika, 65*, 297.

Lo, A., & MacKinley, A. (1988). Stock market prices do not follow random walks: Evidence from a simple specification test. *The Review of Financial Studies, 1*, 41.

Mnif, E., et al. (2020). How the cryptocurrency market has performed during COVID 19? A multifractal analysis. *Finance Research Letter, 36*, 101647.

Shaen Corbet, B. L. (2018). Bitcoin futures—What use are they? *Economics Letters.*

Taylor, J. C. (1971). The hydrogen-atom locations in the α and β forms of uranyl hydroxide. *Acta Crystallographica Section B: Structural Crystallography and Crystal Chemistry, 27*, 2018.

Urquhart, A. (2016). The inefficiency of Bitcoin. *Economic Letters, 148*, 80.

Vidal-Tomás, I., et al. (2019). Weak efficiency of the cryptocurrency market: A market portfolio approach. *Applied Economics Letter, 26*, 1627.

Wald, A., & Wolfowitz, J. (1940). On a test whether two samples are from the same population. *The Annals of Mathematical Statistics, 11*, 147.

Chapter 23
The Impact of Climate Change on Revenues from Environmental Taxes and Expenses for Environmental Protection in the EU for 2010–2020

Alina Georgeta Ailincă and Gabriela Cornelia Piciu

Abstract In the last decades, climate change has been treated more and more frequently in the literature, as its consequences multiply. However, specific local, regional, or global studies are still needed to discern the particular aspects of climate change and the most effective ways to mitigate it. Therefore, through an econometric analysis, the article aims to address a set of indicators of climate change and highlight their impact on the evolution of taxes and national environmental expenses, in EU member countries, for the period 2010–2020. The work reveals the need to increase the efficiency of taxation and environmental expenses, through a better involvement of the governments of the EU states.

Keywords Climate change · Effect · Environmental taxation · Efficiency

JEL Classification H23 · Q51 · Q53 · H21

23.1 Introduction

In addition to the current risks and challenges, climate changes also bring into question the difficulty of identifying and measuring their impact on macroeconomic variables and the economy in general.

Also, the effects can be mixed, positive, and negative at the same time; for example, global warming can lead to the improvement of the climate for the introduction into agricultural culture of some types of plants considered exotic, until recently, and on the other hand through the loss of some species considered autochthonous, but which no longer face these climate and temperature challenges. For this reason, commensuration in time (how much time is needed to adapt) and in space (what

A. G. Ailincă (✉) · G. C. Piciu
"Victor Slăvescu" Centre for Financial and Monetary Research, Bucharest, Romania

area will be most affected) translated from an economic point of view can prove difficult.

The objective of the study was to find out if a series of indicators that show the state of the environment affects environmental taxation. The perspective is interesting for the literature precisely for this reason, thus inverting the classical concept that taxation affects the environment and less environmental elements are so strong that they can substantially change the perspective on environmental taxation.

In this sense, the article brings into discussion the ability of some environmental indicators to reflect their impact on the environmental tax income and public spending for ecological protection.

23.2 Literature Review

In specialized literature, the problem of negative environmental externalities resulting from pollution from economic processes was treated for the first time by Pigou (1920) in his work *Economics of well-being*. He showed that these market weaknesses must be corrected through state intervention, environmental taxes, and regulations in this area.

The purpose for which environmental taxes were created is not only to bring income to the state budget (like any tax collected), but to correct the behavior of the consumer, in our case, that of the polluter. In Chen et al. (2017) it is pointed out the clear effects of the carbon tax, thus the emission reduction effects and the energy saving of the carbon tax surpasses that of the energy tax under the equivalent tax revenue with even fewer significant negative impacts upon the economy, contributing to the capital transfer towards non-energy intensive industries. It should be noted also that carbon taxes will restrain economic growth and curb carbon emissions, but the effects will continuously decrease with the enhancement of carbon taxes (Xu et al., 2014; Hu and Zhou, 2014; Sundar et al., 2016). However, discussions about the direction of the influences and the variables involved persist. For example, in Fan et al. (2006)'s study it is stated that it is rather the growth in consumption than the number of people leading CO_2 emissions to increase and that energy efficiency reductions is most harmfully effect of CO_2 emissions within the high-income panel in the long-run and short-run.

The impact of environmental taxes on CO_2 emissions in EU member states is also studied by Aydin and Esen (2018) who find that, after exceeding a threshold level, the effect of environmental taxes on CO_2 emissions changes insignificantly. In the paper of Agostini et al. (1992) underlines that energy-saving or inter-fuel substitution processes, that result from the introduction of environmental taxation, stabilize emissions at the level of a single domain, and only if high tax rates are assumed. Also, as solutions, there are mentioned that there are to be recommended country-specific coordinated environmental policies where international coordination ought to concern environmental targets rather than instruments. Equally, the application of the carbon tax could require the application of a compensation method from the state, because there are studies that mention that the economic objectives cannot be met simultaneously with the environmental ones (Gemechu et al., 2014). In this context, the argumentation of multiple economic dividends regarding environmental taxes remains unclear (Goulder, 1995).

However, Xu and Long (2014) show that taxes will limit economic growth and reduce carbon emissions, but with increases, their effects continuously decline.

Despite the fact that the decarbonization that will be achieved in order to mitigate climate change will erode the tax base, it is urgently necessary to find the balance between the sustainability objectives and the revenues collected at the state budget from the imposition of taxes.

According to Terjanika and Pubule (2022), in their study of the EU economy, they discovered that the biggest obstacle to reducing CO_2 emissions, which constitute the causes of climate change, is a combination of several factors: the high complexity of processes, the lack of knowledge, and the high level of expenditure. However, a series of solutions can be envisioned, by supporting areas with an impact on the reduction of carbon emissions. Thus, in the work of Bezić et al. (2022), for the period 2012–2019, for the EU27 countries, it is emphasized that human capital, innovation activity, industrial structure and development and institutional framework correlate negatively with CO_2 emission levels contribute significantly to the reduction in CO_2 emissions.

This review of specialized literature leads to the conclusion that the benefits of fiscal measures to mitigate climate change can exceed the costs of imposing and collecting environmental taxes. The specialized literature presents limits, generally dealing with specific elements of the environment and on the other hand of environmental taxation, generally underlining the limits of environmental taxation. The current study, although brief, reverses the perspective, the environmental elements are becoming more and more pressing, and these, in one form or another, are reflected in environmental taxation. For this reason, beyond the limits of this econometric study (which is punctual—only a few aspects captured by some indicators—and local—only at the EU28 level), it tries to point out the clear idea that environmental problems (generated or not by people) can it influences much more dramatically the reality in which we live, and, from this perspective, also the environmental taxation.

23.3 Methodology

The analysis refers to the relation of tax and expenses Eurostat indicators in correlation with some Eurostat environmental ones. The EU28 area (EU27 and United Kingdom) and the 2010–2020 are the period of the study. The data structure is panel data for all EU28 countries (308 observations). The method used is the estimates for the smallest ordinary squares.

First, in order to identify the link between the evolution of taxation and environmental indicators, this research will select the Eurostat indicators (treated also by other studies, e.g., Rincón-Moreno et al., 2021): EnvTaxRev—Environmental tax revenues (percentage of total revenues from taxes and social contributions (excluding imputed social contributions, Eurostat code [TEN00141]), NExpendEP—national expenditure on environmental protection by institutional sector (percentage of gross domestic product or GDP), GHG—greenhouse gas emissions by source sector (source: EEA) (thousands of tons); CRELCIC (an original combined indicator)—Climate economic losses to which it was added the contribution to the $ 100 billion international commitment on climate spending (EUR million); Gen waste—generation of waste, except for major mineral waste on domestic material consumption (percentage); Recycl.Rate—the recycling rate of all waste, except major mineral waste (percentage); and Share renewable—share of renewable energy in gross final energy consumption (percentage) (Eurostat code: [SDG_07_40]). The climate economic losses by country are estimated by the authors by extrapolating information to the EU level. The international contribution is available statistically from the year 2014, and it was added as a value to the indicator of economic loss from the climate.

In the results section, this paper will present the statistics of the model, the correlation matrix for the panel data, and two regression equations (one for income tax and the other for environmental protection expenses) that explain the connection between the chosen variables. Thus, the regression equations generally look in the form: EnvTaxRev = f (EnvTaxRev (t-1), GHG, CRELCIC, Gen waste, Recycl.Rate, Share renewable)

$$NExpendEP = f(NExpendEP(t-1), GHG, CRELCIC, Gen\ waste, Recycl.Rate, Share\ renewable)$$

The detailed description is presented in the results section.

The prudence in the interpretation of the results must be specified from the beginning on the basis of the need to adjust the initial data through interpolation, extrapolation, and proxy; therefore, the follow-up over time on a more extensive series of data can increase the reliability of the results obtained. Also, although they are not highlighted in the text, a series of additional tests, regarding serial correlation of residuals, heteroskedasticity tests, Johansen test and ADF test (Durbin & Watson, 1951; Bai and Carrion-i-Silvestre, 2009; Hansen, 1999; Maddala and Wu, 1999) were performed to confirm the correctness of the model.

23.4 Analysis/Result Interpretation

This investigation starts in our analysis from the statistical description of the indicators used in the regression model for panel data at EU28 level (e.g., minimum, mean, maximum, median, standard deviation, kurtosis, and skewness—shown in Table 23.1).

Table 23.1 Statistical situation regarding the model

Obs:308	ENVTAXREV	NEXPENDEP	GHG	GEN_WASTE	CRELCIC	RECYCL_RATE	SHARE_RENEWABLE
Mean	7.388258	1.927483	144496.9	12.32708	778.6866	49.40052	19.57479
Median	7.387500	1.900000	59292.04	10.17500	241.6977	51.00000	16.70050
Maximum	11.75000	3.500000	921074.0	35.80000	10433.59	87.00000	60.12400
Minimum	3.620000	0.600000	1831.960	3.700000	9.158630	10.00000	0.979000
Std. dev.	1.740492	0.611701	199617.0	6.665762	1645.746	16.33359	11.56848
Skewness	0.129079	0.324692	2.056194	1.590208	3.911517	−0.069868	0.916397
Kurtosis	2.182745	2.967363	7.005523	5.135543	19.06122	2.440474	3.571351
Jarque-Bera	9.426738	5.425497	422.9347	188.3368	4095.921	4.268330	47.29817
Prob.	0.008974	0.066354	0.00000	0.000000	0.000000	0.118345	0.00000
Sum	2275.584	593.66354	44505046	3796.742	239835.5	15215.36	6029.035
Sum Sq. Dev.	929.9988	114.8728	1.22E+13	13640.74	8.32E+08	81903.37	41085.75

Source: Author processing in EViews 12; Eurostat

Table 23.2 Pearson's correlation matrix between environmental independent and dependent variables and at EU28 level

	EnvTaxRev	NExpendEP
EnvTaxRev	1	
NExpendEP	−0.09180	1
GHG	−0.34953	−0.00293
CRELCIC	−0.40258	0.00689
Gen waste	0.01927	0.31426
Recycl.Rate	−0.35036	0.30456
Share renewable	−0.01253	0.14797

Source: Author processing in Excel data analysis; Eurostat data

The normal distribution is usually shown by the closeness of the mean and median of the variable's values of the data, so with some exceptions, this paper can generally conclude that the mean and median have almost similar values. Thus, mostly, this research could say that the data follow a normal distribution according to the literature.

To be in a position to see the relationship's intensity and direction, the Pearson correlation matrix is usually used. To outline the model, this investigation first makes global correlations at the EU28 with panel data average level. The matrix is presented in simplified form only to evidence the EnvTaxRev and NExpendEP with the environmental explanatory variables (Table 23.2).

Thus, it can be observed that the correlation matrix coefficients appear to be below 0.75, which usually indicates that no multicorrelation exists among the variables. The evolution of Environmental Taxes Revenues has a negative sign with almost all explanatory variables (except generation of waste) and the strongest with the climate economic losses and contribution to the $ 100 billion international commitment on climate spending (CRELCIC). This trend can be explained by the fact that at the EU 28 level, according to Eurostat data, revenues from environmental taxes decreased starting from 2016, and even more steeply starting from 2019, until 2020, while the trends of the waste recycling rate and the share of renewable energy were slightly increasing.

Also, the national expenditure on environmental protection by institutional sector (percentage of gross domestic product or GDP), (NExpendEP) is positively correlated with all selected indicators (except, GHG). The NExpendEP strongest correlations are with the generation of waste and with recycling rate. At the moment when, on a constant basis, the expenses regarding the environment will correlate more strongly with the recycling rate than with the generation of waste, this paper can say that the transition from the linear model to the circular economy (Janik & Szafraniec, 2019) has been successfully achieved.

Thus, in order to be able to detect causality, this paper constructs a series of regression equations of the form:

Table 23.3 Results of the regression equation for the EU28 to explain the link between EnvTaxRev and GHG, CRELCIC, Gen waste, Recycling Rate, and Share renewable for the period 2010–2020

Method: Least Squares			
Sample (adjusted): 2308			
Included observations: 307	**Dependent Variable: ENVTAXREV**		
R-squared	0.801998	Mean dep. var.	7.386265
Adjusted R-squared	0.798038	Akaike inf crit.	2.371932
F-statistic	202.5229	Schwarz crit.	2.456909
Prob.(F-statistic)	0.000000	Hannan-Quinn crit.	2.405914
Sum sqrd. resid.	184.0671	Durbin-Watson stat.	1.998137
Variable	**Coefficient**	**t-Statistic**	**Prob.**
C	1.662735	4.969454	0.0000
ENVTAXREV(−1)	0.833092	28.35343	0.0000
GHG	−1.87E-07	−0.491841	0.6232
CRELCIC	−7.39E-05	−1.677113	0.0946
GEN_WASTE	0.010792	1.527119	0.1278
RECYCL_RATE	−0.008103	−2.739952	0.0065
SHARE_RENEWABLE	−0.004395	−1.046930	0.2960

Source: Authors' processing in EViews 12. Eurostat data. Methodological details also in the study Akaike (1976), Schwarz (1978).

Table 23.4 Results of the regression equation for the EU28 to explain the link between NExpendEP and GHG, CRELCIC, Gen waste, Recycling Rate, and Share renewable for the period 2010–2020

Method: least squares			
Sample (adjusted): 2308			
Included observations: 307	**Dependent variable: NEXPENDEP**		
R-squared	0.805544	Mean dep. var.	1.929038
Adjusted R-squared	0.802313	Akaike inf crit.	0.254403
S.E. of regression	0.272147	Schwarz crit.	0.327240
Log likelihood	−33.05081	Hannan-Quinn crit.	0.283530
Sum sqrd. resid.	22.29328	Durbin-Watson stat.	1.997687
Variable	**Coefficient**	**t-Statistic**	**Prob.**
NEXPENDEP(−1)	0.858718	31.23222	0.0000
GHG	−1.08E-07	−0.825618	0.4097
CRELCIC	7.52E-06	0.503386	0.6151
GEN_WASTE	0.0006702	2.677589	0.0078
RECYCL_RATE	0.002697	3.037258	0.0026
SHARE_RENEWABLE	0.003214	2.419906	0.0161

Source: Authors' processing in EViews 12. Eurostat data

$$\text{EnvTaxRev} = \alpha 0 + \alpha 1 \text{EnvTaxRev}(t-1) + \alpha 2 \text{GHG} + \alpha 3 \text{CRELCIC} \\ + \alpha 4 \text{Gen waste} + \alpha 5 \text{Recycl.Rate} + \alpha 6 \text{Share renewable} + \varepsilon \quad (23.1)$$

Table 23.5 Results of the Granger causality test results for selected environmental indicators for the period 2010–2020

Pairwise Granger causality tests		
Sample: 1308, Date:11/14/22, Time:10:08		
Lags: 2		
Obs.: 306		
Null Hypothesis:	**F-Statistic**	**Prob.**
CRELCIC does not Granger cause NEXPENDEP	3.79011	0.0237
CRELCIC does not Granger cause GHG	4.30873	0.0143
GHG does not Granger cause CRELCIC	20.6829	4.E-09

Source: Author processing in EViews 12; Eurostat data; data for prob. under 5%. Methodological details in the study of Granger (1969).

$$\text{NExpendEP} = \alpha 0 + \alpha 1 \text{NExpendEP}(t-1) + \alpha 2 \text{GHG} + \alpha 3 \text{CRELCIC} + \alpha 4 \text{Gen waste} + \alpha 5 \text{Recycl.Rate} + \alpha 6 \text{Share renewable} + \varepsilon \quad (23.2)$$

where αi and i with values between 0 and 6 are the coefficients of the for the constant and EnvTaxRev (−1), NExpendEP (−1), GHG, CRELCIC, Gen waste, Recycl. Rate, Share renewable are the independent variables explained above, and ε is the error term.

According to the explanatory variables, the results of the regression models are revealed in Tables 23.3 and 23.4.

It can be noted that, in general, the coefficients of the variables are different from zero but some of them are not substantial (e.g., Recycl.Rate and Share renewable). The *p*-value or the associated probability is below the threshold of 0.05 only for recycling rate.

Thus, only for this indicator the null hypothesis H0 can be rejected, proposing him for the model. The R-square value is big (0.801998) also the adjusted R-square (0.798038) for the proposed equation, so this research emphasizes that the variability of the endogenous variable is largely determined by exogenous factors of the model.

In Table 23.4, in this investigation, it can be noted that the national expenditure for environmental protection (NExpendEP) has a R-square value of 0.805544 and also a similar high adjusted R-square for the proposed equation (0.802313). Thus, in this investigation, it can be said that the variability of the endogenous variable is largely determined by exogenous factors of the model.

The *p*-value or the associated probability is below the threshold of 0.05 for Gen Waste, Recycle Rate, and Share renewable. Thus, for those indicators the null hypothesis H0 can be rejected, proposing those indicators for the model.

Also, based on some tests, in this paper it is constructed a Granger causality test. The results are presented only for the variables with a probability under 0.05.

In Table 23.5, the values under the 0.05 probability for the Granger causality test are fulfilled for NexpendEP, which is Granger caused by CRELCIC, CRELCIC, which is Granger caused by GHG, and also GHG is Granger caused by CRELCIC.

23.5 Conclusions

The paper presents the impact on environmental tax revenues and national expenses of some environmental indicators. Environmental indicators can surprise in their evolution benefits that far exceed the scope of concrete well-being from the increase in receipts to the state budget, or the reduction in losses in the case of public expenditure. Cleaner air, less waste, and lower consumption of raw materials are all benefits that translate into public health and more resources for the future production process.

The results show basically that the recycling rate is a relatively good explanatory variable for the evolution of environmental tax revenues, while generation of waste, the recycling rate, and share of renewable are satisfactory explanatory variables for the evolution of national expenditure on environmental protection by institutional sector.

Thus, the analysis connects with the economic literature on the impact on taxation evolution of environmental indicators. The framework proposed in this study presents a systematic perspective and is intended to cover all environmental taxation in all activities and sectors of the economy, so that the results of its evaluation can support the consistent development of environmental protection.

The relevance of such an approach resides in a panel data model with general coverage of all EU28 GHG emissions.

The proposed analysis improves and supports the design of environmental fiscal policies, not only by identifying areas and activities that can bring the most benefits but also by comparing them with national carbon budgets.

Acknowledgments The article is a partial capitalization of the project of the year 2022: "The Potential of The Circular Economy For Climate Change Mitigation" ("POTENȚIALUL ECONOMIEI CIRCULARE DE ATENUARE A SCHIMBĂRILOR CLIMATICE"), Gabriela Piciu (coord.), project that it is realized in the framework of "Victor Slăvescu" Centre for Financial and Monetary Research, NIER, RA. The capitalization of the article is mostly from chapter 4.

References

Agostini, P., Botteon, M., & Carraro, C. (1992). A carbon tax to reduce CO2 emissions in Europe. *Energy Economics, 14*(4), 279–290.
Akaike, H. (1976). An information criterion (AIC). *Mathematical Sciences, 14*(153), 5–9.
Aydin, C., & Esen, Ö. (2018). Reducing CO2 emissions in the EU member states: Do environmental taxes work? *Journal of Environmental Planning and Management, 61*(13), 2396–2420.
Bai, J., & Carrion-i-Silvestre, J. L. (2009). Structural changes, common stochastic trends, and unit roots in panel data. *Review of Economic Studies, 76*(2), 471–501.
Bezić, H., Mance, D., & Balaž, D. (2022). Panel evidence from EU countries on CO2 emission indicators during the fourth industrial revolution. *Sustainability, 14*(19), 12554. https://doi.org/10.3390/su141912554

Chen, W., Zhou, J. F., Li, S. Y., & Li, Y. C. (2017). Effects of an energy tax (carbon tax) on energy saving and emission reduction in Guangdong province-based on a CGE model. *Sustainability, 9*(5), 681–704.

Durbin, J., & Watson, G. S. (1951). Testing for serial correlation in least squares regression, II. *Biometrika, 38*(1–2), 159–179. https://doi.org/10.1093/biomet/38.1-2.159.JSTOR2332325

Fan, Y., Liu, L. C., Wu, G., & Wei, Y. M. (2006). Analyzing impact factors of CO2 emissions using the STIRPAT model. *Environmental Impact Assessment Revie, 26*(4), 377–395.

Gemechu, E. D., Butnar, I., Llop, M., & Castells, F. (2014). Economic and environmental effects of CO2 taxation: An input-output analysis for Spain. *Journal of Environmental Planning and Management, 57*(5), 751–768.

Goulder, L. H. (1995). Environmental taxation and the double dividend: A reader's guide. *International Tax and Public Finance, 2*(2), 157–183.

Granger, C. W. J. (1969). Investigating causal relations by econometric models and cross-spectral methods. *Econometrica, 37*(3), 424–438. https://doi.org/10.2307/1912791.JSTOR1912791

Hansen, B. E. (1999). Threshold effects in non-dynamic panels: Estimation, testing, and inference. *Journal of Econometrics, 93*, 345–368.

Hu, H., & Zhou, W. (2014). The impact of carbon tax policy on the carbon emission reduction and profit. *International Journal of Smart Home, 8*(5), 175–184.

Janik, A., & Szafraniec, M. (2019). Circular economy performance of EMAS organizations in Poland based on an analysis of environmental statements. *Multidisciplinary Aspects of Production Engineering, 2*(1), 536–547. https://doi.org/10.2478/mape-2019-0054

Maddala, G. S., & Wu, S. (1999). A comparative study of unit root tests with panel data and a new simple test. *Oxford Bulletin of Economics and Statistic, 61*, 631–652.

Pigou, A. C. (1920). *The economics of welfare. 4th edition 1938.* Weidenfeld and Nicolson.

Rincón-Moreno, J., Ormazábal, M., Álvarez, M. J., & Jaca, C. (2021). Advancing circular economy performance indicators and their application in Spanish companies. *Journal of Cleaner Production, 279*, 123605.

Schwarz, G. (1978). Estimating the dimension of a model. *The Annals of Statistics, 6*(2), 461–464. https://doi.org/10.1214/aos/1176344136

Sundar, S., Mishra, A. K., & Naresh, R. (2016). Effect of environmental tax on carbon dioxide emission: A mathematical model. *American Journal of Applied Mathematics and Statistic, 4*(1), 16–23.

Terjanika, V., & Pubule, J. (2022). Barriers and driving factors for sustainable development of CO2 valorisation. *Sustainability, 14*(9), 5054. https://doi.org/10.3390/su14095054

Xu, S. C., & Long, R. Y. (2014). Empirical research on the effects of carbon taxes on economy and carbon emissions in China. *Environmental Engineering and Management Journal, 2014*(13), 1071–1078.

Xu, S. C., He, Z. X., & Long, R. Y. (2014). Factors that influence carbon emissions due to energy consumption in China: Decomposition analysis using LMDI. *Applied Energy, 127*, 182–193.

Chapter 24
Recovery of Critical Metals from Mine Tailings

Alina Butu ⓘ, Paula V. Morais ⓘ, Marian Butu ⓘ, Sorin Avram ⓘ, and Steliana Rodino ⓘ

Abstract The availability of primary resources correlated with waste production from exploration and mining activities will remain a need to satisfy the growing global demand for raw materials. The present research started with the idea that tailings and wastes from mining can be considered mineral reserves. The project aimed to increase the efficiency of resources through the recycling of residues and their integration into a circular economy concept. Special emphasis is placed on processing mine tailings to turn them into a valuable source of secondary raw materials. This is an important step toward sustainability and reducing the negative impact on the environment. This chapter presents the objectives targeted by the REVIVING research project. Therefore, the aim was to obtain improved models for efficiently recycling metals from residues in selected case study mines, based, for the first time, on the manipulation of the microbiome existing within autochthonous tailings, using molecular data to promote the bioleaching bacterial populations, and innovative hydrometallurgy, using negative pressure. The study aimed to cover the entire cycle of obtaining metals, from secondary sources to the production of a marketable product. It also aimed to enable the efficient recycling of tailings and reduce the residues generated by the mining process, thus contributing to the reconnection of raw materials to society. The ultimate goal of the project was to find alternative sources of critical metals, as these are vulnerable to disruption of supply because their core source is restricted to just one or two regions of the world, and they are difficult to substitute within the specific technologies that use them, being vital raw materials in various new and green emerging industrial processes.

A. Butu · M. Butu · S. Rodino (✉)
National Institute of Research and Development for Biological Sciences, Bucharest, Romania

P. V. Morais
University of Coimbra, Department of Life Sciences, Coimbra, Portugal

S. Avram
National Institute of Economic Research "Costin C. Kirițescu," Romanian Academy, Bucharest, Romania

Keywords Critical metals · Recovery · Bioleaching · Natural resources · Circular economy

24.1 Introduction

Critical materials support the ability of the industrial economy to adapt to digital and green technologies. There are studies reporting that we are undoubtedly moving from the dependence on oil to another dependence on other materials that are gaining importance and on other suppliers. Over time, the same happened with gas and coal.

At the same time, this paradigm change gives rise to geopolitics that is no less challenging than the one that had to be managed while approaching the fossil fuels.

In Europe, the term "critical raw materials" first appeared in a 2011 report by the European Commission. It is a list that includes about 15 so-called critical raw materials: agricultural and especially minerals and metals. Indeed, in 2010, there was a Chinese embargo on rare earths: China informally blocked its exports of rare earths to Japan and the United States. This lasted 6 months. European countries then realized their dependence on China and sought to take stock of the risks of supply disruption to which they had subjected themselves by depending on only a handful of producing countries. In brief, these raw materials are both indispensable and not so obvious to access.

This list is updated every 3 years (2014, 2017, and 2020). In September 2020, the European Commission announced a list of 30 critical raw materials. There are agricultural materials such as natural rubber but also minerals, ore such as graphite, some very abundant in the earth's crust such as silicon (it takes a lot for solar panels), and strategic and rare metals (indium, bismuth, rare earths, and lithium) (Table 24.1, Fig. 24.1).

In this context, there are a series of metals that are becoming totally indispensable to daily activities and probably even more so in the future, especially with regard to the energy transition. First of all, this chapter answers several questions

Table 24.1 List of critical materials – 2020

Antimony	Gallium	Natural rubber	Tungsten
Baryte	Germanium	Niobium	Vanadium
Beryllium	Hafnium	Platinum group metals	Bauxite
Bismuth	Heavy rare earth elements	Phosphate rock	Lithium
Borate	Light rare earth elements	Phosphorus	Titanium
Cobalt	Indium	Scandium	Strontium
Coking coal	Magnesium	Silicon metal	
Fluorspar	Natural graphite	Tantalum	

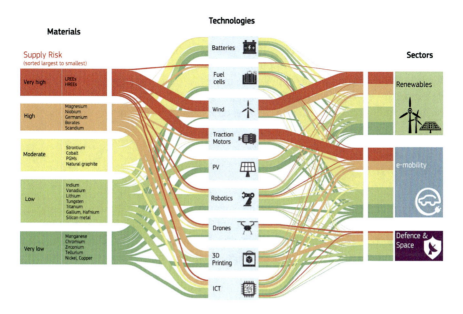

Fig. 24.1 Supply risk of critical raw materials according to the EU critical assessment in 2020. (Source: European Commission (2020b))

regarding the criticality of materials: What are these critical raw materials? How did they become critical, and how are they indispensable to us? Where are the sources of critical metals? What is the difference between rare metals or strategic metals, and critical metals?

24.2 Literature Review

Even if there are several years now since this criticality movement has taken place in Europe, and not only, the terms of rare, strategic and critical metals continue to be rather vague for the general public. The term "critical" is sometimes either attributed to geology domain, or to economic dimension, or to planetary availability of resources.

24.2.1 Rare Metals

Rare metals are elements that are less abundant or less accessible in the earth's crust. This might be due to their low ability to concentrate on deposits. This is the case of indium, cobalt, or antimony. Lanthanides are a group of fifteen metals, also known as rare earths, included in the rare metals category. Contrary to what their name suggests, rare earths are not uncommon. They are characterized by a low presence of their deposits, meaning natural concentrations in economically exploitable levels. Rare earths are essential components of magnetic, optical, and electronic devices and are of particular importance in the defense and aerospace industries. The properties that enhance their choice as raw materials are related to lightness, resistance, energy storage, thermal resistance, magnetic properties, and optics.

24.2.2 Strategic Metals

Generally, inclusion of an element in the category of strategic resources is due to its capacity of being essential to the economy of a state, or region, in specific areas of development, which are strategic for security, defense, or energy policy. In the same way, it can also be a question of strategic resource, more specifically, strategic metal, for a business or a sector, such as aeronautics, defense, automotive, optics, electronics, nuclear energy, and photovoltaics.

24.2.3 Critical Metals

According to the literature, a specific metal becomes critical when a supply difficulty of this metal can lead to undesirable effects both at economic and industrial scales. Generally, the criticality of a mineral substance is assessed along two axes plot: the risks weighing on supply volume and the economic importance that mirrors the vulnerability to a possible shortage, or even a disruption of supply, resulting in a surge in prices.

The risk may include geological, technical, geographical, economic, and geopolitical risks.

A critical metal is a metal that can be rare for geological reasons and that is strategic for our modern economies (solar panels, wind turbines, and electric car engines). Given the concentration of their production in certain areas of the world, with countries holding the majority of production, there are risks of supply disruption (Fig. 24.2).

To summarize, critical metals are metals associated with tensions on supplies, both on the supply and demand sides.

It becomes thus obvious that, in a competitive environment, the objective of any state is to ensure stable supply, to increase its strategic autonomy, and to reduce dependence on imports for such resources.

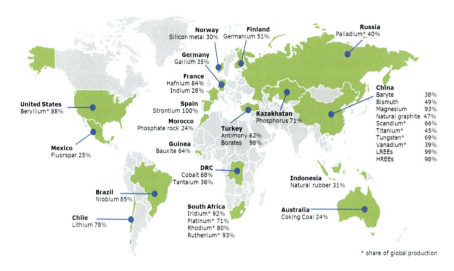

Fig. 24.2 Countries accounting for the largest share of the EU supply of CRMs. (Source: https://ec.europa.eu/growth/sectors/raw-materials/areas-specific-interest/critical-raw-materials_en)

24.2.3.1 Recovery of Critical Elements

As we move toward a more digital, connected, and greener world, we find ourselves having to manage and become aware of new challenges, including procurement.

A series of changes between global supply and demand patterns lies beneath today's massive developments. To strengthen the competitiveness of the European industry, an important number of challenges arise when it comes to both access to raw materials and encouraging their efficient use and recycling, in line with a low-carbon, resource-efficient renewed strategy (EC, 2020a, b). Due to the increasing green-technology needs, chemolithoautotrophic and chemoorganoheterotrophic microorganisms are intensively used to recover the heavy metals and critical metals from various secondary solid wastes such as mining waste: tailings, sludge, slag, and fly ash (Srichandan et al., 2019; Mikoda et al., 2019), and waste electrical and electronic equipment (WEEE): batteries, coin cells, magnets, printed circuit boards, displays, and memory drives (Naseri et al., 2019; Auerbach et al., 2019; Işıldar et al., 2019).

The microbial biorecovery of waste materials such as metallurgical waste (tailings dams) must be seen in today's society as having a major technological impact, not only through offering a green recycling strategy due to the reduced use of chemicals and lower carbon emissions but also through involving increased efficiency of the resource management and financial metrics. Tailings dams contain crushed rock and processing fluids that remain after the metals of economic importance are extracted and stored in dammed impoundments. The rate of mine waste production accelerated in step with the increases in the human population. The estimated worldwide production rate is 350×10^9 t year^{-1} (Vallero & Blight, 2019). The magnitude of annual tailings production should at least make us think that managing such an amount of waste is tremendously critical for the environment and consecutively dangerous for our health.

Chemolithotrophs are known to employ atmospheric carbon dioxide as a carbon source and inorganic compounds such as ferrous iron, elemental sulfur, and/or reduced sulfur compounds as an energy source (Işıldar et al., 2019). Most chemolithoautotrophs were reported to have a high tolerance for heavy metal toxicity (Levett et al., 2021), which makes them the most widely studied group of microorganisms based on bacterial leaching basic scientific research.

Tungsten was included on the list of Critical Raw Materials Initiative since 2011 (EC, 2017), as a strategic metal. Tungsten is mainly used as cemented carbides in machine tools that are well collected at the end of life. Despite the high recycling input rate (64%) (EC, 2017), it can be observed that tungsten's commodity price recorded an increasing trend in the last two decades, proportional to its increasing demand in industries such as construction, manufacturing, and high-tech applications (USGS, 2019).

One way of innovating raw material supply reliance consists of using gravimetric methods to recover the metal (e.g., tungsten recovery was 50%), which can be implemented on-site, and magnetic separation to allow further concentration (e.g., tungsten was concentrated 12.6 times more) (Tunsu et al., 2019). The result of these techniques can be achieved after a preliminary combined analysis of geostatistics, topographical survey, and geochemical data, to construct the reprocessing circuits of the tailings (Figueiredo et al., 2019). The other way of innovating raw material supply is inspired by a biotechnological principle: Microorganisms represent the point from which the critical metal recovery can be achieved and developed. Unlike the physical recovery methods previously presented, which comprise large amounts of power supply and technical support, the recovery methods using microbial bioleaching involve fewer costs, as the microbes are naturally available. This eco-friendly approach encourages sustainable perspectives for the future, gaining popularity in the scientific community.

From all the three pillars of sustainability point of view (economic, social, and environmental), the recovery of critical elements from any secondary source (including mine tailings, electronic waste, and industrial residues) could be beneficial from circular economy perspective, closing the loop on raw materials and reducing the environmental footprint of emerging electronic technologies. The potential recovery of critical metals from alternative sources such as mine waste and drainage, residues of phosphogypsum, and U-mine tailing is a subject of interest worldwide (Costis et al., 2020).

Due to the large volumes generated annually and the significant residual levels of strategic metals, mine tailings represent an interesting secondary source. This promising research project aimed to enhance the strategic elements contained in tailings from inactive mines, while reducing their contaminant load. Two key methodologies may be used, and these are the metallurgical approach and the agri-mine approach. The metallurgical process includes the use of mineralogical separation processes for the extraction and concentration of interest minerals. The other involves the use of specific plant species with the potential to accumulate target metals and extract them from the discharges.

24.3 Conclusions

The explosion of new technologies will continue to generate increased needs and highlights the challenges of regionalization of supply chains.

At this moment, many states are assessing opportunities to secure and diversify their supply of critical metals, including extraction from secondary sources such as mine tailings, and this is why research and innovation in this direction are of maximum importance.

However, it is still needed an in-depth and reliable investigation of mine tailings for a detailed characterization related to possible amounts of critical materials that might still be extracted. The same applies to any kind of materials considered industrial wastes.

Acknowledgments This work was supported by a grant from the Ministry of Research, Innovation and Digitization, CNCS/CCCDI–UEFISCDI, project number 181/2020 within PNCDI III.

References

Auerbach, R., Bokelmann, K., Stauber, R., Gutfleisch, O., Schnell, S., & Ratering, S. (2019). Critical raw materials – advanced recycling technologies and processes: Recycling of rare earth metals out of end of life magnets by bioleaching with various bacteria as an example of an intelligent recycling strategy. *Minerals Engineering, 134*(April), 104–117.

Costis, S., Mueller, K. K., Coudert, L., Neculita, C. M., Reynier, N., & Blais, J. (2020). Recovery potential of rare earth elements from mining and industrial residues: A review and cases studies. *Journal of Geochemical Exploration*. https://doi.org/10.1016/j.gexplo.2020.106699

European Commission. (2017). Communication from the Commission to The European Parliament, The Council, The European Economic and Social Committee and The Committee of The Regions on the 2017 List of Critical Raw Materials for the EU. Brussels.

European Commission. (2020a). *Critical raw materials resilience: Charting a path towards greater security and sustainability.* Communication from the Commission to the European Parliament, the Council, the European Economic and Social Committee and the Committee of the Regions, COM (2020) 474 Final; European Commission.

European Commission. (2020b). *Critical materials for strategic technologies and sectors in the EU – A foresight study.*

Figueiredo, J., Vila, M. C., Góis, J., Biju, B., Futuro, A., Martins, D., Dinis, M. L., & Fiúza, A. (2019). Bi-level depth assessment of an abandoned tailings dam aiming its reprocessing for recovery of valuable metals. *Minerals Engineering, 133*(March), 1–9.

Işıldar, A., Hullebusch, E. D., Lenz, M., Laing, G. D., Marra, A., Cesaro, A., Panda, S., Akcil, A., Kucuker, M. A., & Kuchta, K. (2019). Biotechnological strategies for the recovery of valuable and critical raw materials from Waste Electrical and Electronic Equipment (WEEE) – A review. *Journal of Hazardous Materials, 362*(January), 467–481.

Levett, A., Gleeson, S. A., & Kallmeyera, J. (2021). From exploration to remediation: A microbial perspective for innovation in mining. *Earth-Science Reviews, 216*, 103563.

Mikoda, B., Potysz, A., & Kmiecik, E. (2019). Bacterial leaching of critical metal values from Polish copper metallurgical slags using Acidithiobacillus Thiooxidans. *Journal of Environmental Management, 236*(April), 436–445.

Naseri, T., Bahaloo-Horeh, N., & Mousavi, S. M. (2019). Environmentally friendly recovery of valuable metals from spent coin cells through two-step bioleaching using Acidithiobacillus thiooxidans. *Journal of Environmental Management, 235*(April), 357–367.

Srichandan, H., Ranjan, K. M., Parhi, P. K., & Mishra, S. (2019). Bioleaching approach for extraction of metal values from secondary solid wastes: A critical review. *Hydrometallurgy, 189*(November), 105122.

Tunsu, C., Menard, Y., Eriksen, D. Ø., Ekberg, C., & Petranikova, M. (2019). Recovery of critical materials from mine tailings: A comparative study of the solvent extraction of rare earths using acidic, solvating and mixed extractant systems. *Journal of Cleaner Production, 218*, 425–437.

USGS. (2019). *Tungsten Statistics and Information.* https://www.usgs.gov/centers/nmic/tungsten-statistics-and-information

Vallero, D. A., & Blight, G. (2019). Mine waste: A brief overview of origins, quantities, and methods of storage. In *Waste* (pp. 129–151). Elsevier.

Chapter 25
The Geopolitics of Resources: The Critical Minerals

Cristian Marius Moisoiu

Abstract In the context of COVID-19 pandemic and restrictions on mobility, the interruptions on the global supply chains generated a steep problem for all economies. To this, other challenges like the trade war between USA and China, the natural disasters, and the recent military conflict in Ukraine have added new blockages of supply with raw materials and intermediary goods, which impacted an accelerated escalation of prices for essential products.

The high-tech fields with high value added contain rare goods, which require predictability of supply and affordable costs. Either we talk about the green transition, the digitalization or, so to speak, the fourth industrial revolution, these processes envisage products with high-tech input. No transformational process could be realized in energy, manufacturing, or the economy, as a whole, if the access to basic resources remains restricted.

This chapter analyzes the global access to critical minerals, which are in demand for producing future technologies, with a particular view on the USA–China relationship and the competition for mineral resources. In the context of the new national security strategy of the USA, it is relevant to observe how the largest economy in the world considers increasing access to these minerals, what are their advantages and vulnerabilities with which they might confront in the global competitiveness race, and which are the opportunities that this field is providing.

Keywords Geopolitics · Mineral resources · International competitiveness · Industrial revolution · Industrial policy

---

C. M. Moisoiu (✉)
Institute for World Economy, Romanian Academy, Bucharest, Romania
e-mail: cmoisoiu@iem.ro

© The Author(s), under exclusive license to Springer Nature Switzerland AG 2024
L. Chivu et al. (eds.), *Constraints and Opportunities in Shaping the Future: New Approaches to Economics and Policy Making*, Springer Proceedings in Business and Economics, https://doi.org/10.1007/978-3-031-47925-0_25

25.1 Introduction

Access to mineral resources was always a critical issue for industries and national economies. As long as the economic activity was strictly dependent on raw materials, acquiring the necessary inputs had become vital for fulfilling production and developing new products. But starting with the first industrial revolution, the equipment and products have increased in complexity, together with the boost of demand and trade for those products in the large Western markets. The access to mineral resources, including rare minerals, became a game changer and a matter of national security. Whether the powerful economies disposed of large deposits inland or made it possible to acquire resources from offshore that determined, on a large scale, the volume of production, of the international trade and, hereafter, their economic growth. But not always the required minerals were easy to be found or extracted, as for many of them either the deposits were limited in amounts or isolated and costly, or it was not always easy to cooperate with the owners of resources when matters of rivalry and competition intervened in between the economic powers. This latter fact led to conflicts or even wars.

Nowadays, the recent trends and evolutions show that while the topics of disputes have changed, the geopolitical approaches remain unaltered. Who are the actual subjects of rivalry? The most powerful economies in the world: the USA, China, the European Union, Japan, India, Russia, and some other less powerful, but relevant, competitors. What are the topics of dispute now? The technologies required to win the global race for a new industrial revolution. What does the new industrial revolution mean? As the identified megatrends require (European Commission, 2018), the commitment of the states of the world on two directions is increasingly demanded, among the others: digitalization and decarbonization of human systems (Muench, 2022). This strategic vision, though, relies on innovation, respectively, enabling a wide range of advanced technologies embedded with minerals that have specific properties.

In the context of the COVID-19 pandemic and mobility restrictions, disruptions in global supply chains have been a pressing issue for all economies. Added to this have been the trade war of the USA with China, natural disasters, and, more recently, the military conflict in Ukraine, which is causing new bottlenecks in the supply of raw materials and an accelerated rise in the prices of some essential commodities, amid increasing dependence on imports in last decades (USGS, 2021).

The year 2021 was marked by the effects of the COVID-19 pandemic, which involved the imposition of restrictions on the transport of goods and people. The quarantine measures imposed in different countries of the world, in periods of intensification of the contagion wave, have caused blockages in the international trade in goods, which has been reflected in interruptions or decreases in production in downstream industries. In addition, port activity has been affected by business interruptions or agglomerations in port services. The largest US, EU, or China ports have suffered long periods of disruptions or logistical bottlenecks.

On the other hand, 2021 and 2022 experienced an intensification of economic activities, compared to the pandemic year 2020, determined by the efforts to recover and supported by periods of easing the restrictions. The consumption of materials and minerals increased compared to 2020 in the lucrative sectors, especially commercial construction, steel production, automotive, and transport.

This chapter analyzes the global access to critical minerals, which are in demand for producing future technologies, with a particular view on the US–China relationship. In the context of the new national security strategy of USA, it is relevant to observe how the largest economy in the world considers increasing access to these minerals, what are their advantages and vulnerabilities with which they might confront in the global competitiveness race and technological progress, and which are the opportunities that this field is providing.

25.2 Literature Review

25.2.1 *The Geopolitics of Resources*

Some authors define geopolitics as the struggle of geographical entities with international and global dimensions to gain political advantages (Flint, 2022). Geopolitics focuses on the balance of power and tensions among nations (Yergin, 2020). But with a narrower view, it was stated that geopolitics only belongs, as a prerequisite, to global powers and superpowers, and it describes their political games and actions in their attempt to wield power. But there are different kinds of power to talk about: It is the power provided by the economy, military, and geography, on the one hand, and it is the power given by the resources that shape the future (Yergin, 2020).

In Wallerstein's model of geopolitics, not trade is the main cause of conflict, but the battle over who controls the new technologies that will lead to further economic growth (Wallerstein, 1979).

As regards the topics for the geopolitical debate, Le Billon stated that the resource conflicts are determined by their geographical location, being either concentrated in points (i.e., oil, gold, or gas) or diffused (i.e., iron, timber, and cropland) and by the ability of rebel or non-state forces "to harvest" the resources and put them on the market (Le Billon, 2005). So, for Le Billon, when a point resource is located in the proximity of the center of power, it is more likely that it will provoke rebellions or coup d'etat in order to control it. If it is distant from the center of power, at a distant border, for instance, then it will lead to secessionist attempts. A diffused resource that is proximate could probably lead to a mass rebellion or peasants uprising to overthrow the existing government, while if the diffused resource is distant, it mostly provokes "warlordism," the use of violence to control the region. In that sense, wars can be related to resources differently in different countries (Le Billon, 2005).

As oil was the main resource that provoked conflicts during the twentieth century, theoreticians have referred mostly to this resource when discussing geopolitics of the access to resources. At the beginning of XIX-th century, Mackinder elaborated the heartland theory stating that whoever controls Eastern Europe, controlled the heartland and whoever controlled the Heartland, could easily gain control of the World Island. And this was due to the fact that Eastern Europe was a key position of the pivot area that gave access to control the World island. In the context of oil predominance as a key resource in the global economy, Harvey provided a parallel of the heartland theory arguing that "the pivot area" was replaced by the "oil spigot", so that "whoever controls the Middle East controls the global oil spigot and whoever controls the global oil spigot can control the global economy" (Harvey, 2003). From that point of view, the political actions of the USA and the Soviet Union in the Middle East during the Cold War or of the USA in Iraq, Iran, and Syria, in competition with China's Belt and Road Initiative, after the Cold War, were regarded as well as a struggle to control the oil resources (Flint, 2022).

On the other hand, the transition to new energy sources that require renewable technologies has diminished the role of oil as a key resource in the past 10 years and that will continue to fall, even if it will not vanish. As attention moves toward new sources of energy and the states engage in climate change policies, we are in the making of a new geopolitical map of energy supply and demand (Yergin, 2020). This also can be related to the decreasing relevance of OPEC (The Organization of Petroleum Exporting Countries), the cartel controlling the amount of oil production, and its price on the global market (Flint, 2022).

The high-tech areas that are being discussed more and more intensively in the current period, related to digitalization and decarbonization, are areas that contain rare products and materials with a high added value. Whether it is the ecological transition, whether it is digitalization, or, put it more broadly, the fourth industrial revolution, they target products with a high technological content.

It is clear that the green transition could not be achieved without access to "green" technologies. Among the technologies most often referred to, renewable technologies for the production of clean energy or for increasing energy efficiency include solar or photovoltaic panels, wind turbines, electric cars, batteries and accumulators for electric cars, heat pumps, smart meters, hydrogen fuel cells, biofuels, technologies for environmental protection, smart meters of air quality, and water and soil.

On the other side, with the digitalization of industries, the economy and society in general, technologies represent new equipment and applications in the field of information and communication: mobile technologies, smartphones, supercomputers, environmentally friendly and intelligent home appliances, sensors for the Internet of things and for vehicles, nanotechnologies, biotechnologies, robotics and automation, telecommunications satellites, aerospace equipment and systems, lasers and medical equipment, military equipment for defense and security, and so on.

The question arises as to how the necessary structural changes could be achieved in industries or in the economy, whether access to resources still remains restricted or within the reach of natural or economic monopolies, in authoritarian or rival states. The production of innovative technologies requires sine qua nonaccess to a range of critical mineral resources.

25.2.2 The Critical Mineral Resources

As regards the nature and classification of critical minerals, in this chapter, we will use the definition that the US authorities have provided. Critical minerals have been defined by the USA in the renewed Energy Act as *"the minerals essential to the economic or national security, which have a supply chain that can suffer disruptions, have a key role in the production of goods, and, in their absence, there are significant consequences on the economic or national security [...]"* (USDI, USGS, 2022). In order to classify minerals as critical minerals, USGS[1] used a methodology of assessment of the risk of supply that considers the concentration of production in countries that may become unwilling to supply, the rate of dependence on imports, and the relevance of the supplied industry for the national economy (USGS, 2021).

In addition, a quantitative risk threshold has also been established, based on objective criteria, up to which minerals are recommended to be included in the list of critical minerals. Of the 54 analyzed minerals, 36 were within the threshold of risk minerals (Table 25.1). A particular case is that of uranium, which was not included in the list, the reason being its inclusion by law in the category of fuels (USGS, 2021).

A classification of minerals by their main utilization for high-tech production is difficult to realize, due to their specific characteristics. This is an important issue for this research, as it would be useful to assess the risk of a mineral shortage and its geopolitical implications if a mineral can be tracked on the value chains of the

Table 25.1 List of critical minerals of USA by supply risk criterion, 2022

1. Gallium	11. Iridium	21. Vanadium	31. Barite
2. Niobium	12. Praseodymium	22. Tin	32. Indium
3. Cobalt	13. Cerium	23. Magnesium	33. Samarium
4. Neodymium	14. Lanthanum	24. Germanium	34. Manganese
5. Ruthenium	15. Bismuth	25. Palladium	35. Lithium
6. Radium	16. Yttrium	26. Titanium	36. Tellurium.
7. Dysprosium	17. Antimony	27. Zinc	Recommended:
8. Aluminum	18. Tantalum	28. Graphite	37. Beryllium
9. Fluorine	19. Hafnium	29. Chromium	38. Nickel
10. Platinum	20. Tungsten	30. Arsenic	39. Zirconium

Source: (USGS, 2021)

---

[1] United States Geological Survey (USGS) is the public agency for science, under the Department of Interior, that provide science about the natural hazards, water, energy, minerals, and other natural resources, the health of ecosystems and environment, and the impacts of climate and land-use change.

envisaged technologies. Most critical minerals, but especially rare metals, have many applications in various high-tech and clean industries and many industrial processes require specific weights of the very pure metal or alloys. Some elements have the same properties as others and could be substituted in case of blockages of supply, but not always with the same efficacy, as regarding costs or yields.

25.3 Methodology

The paper uses quantitative analysis and the description of policy papers in the researched area, based on existing data at the national level, in order to fulfill a qualitative analysis from a geopolitical point of view.

A case study is also elaborated, about one specific mineral with an important role in high-tech industry, to highlight the degree of existing complexity and the relevance of security of supply with key resources. The case study aims to provide an insight into the risks and vulnerabilities that may arise if the technological competition between the great powers intensifies.

25.3.1 USA vs. China: A New Cold War with a Track on Resources

25.3.1.1 China, Not Only the "Workshop of the World" but Also "the Ore of the World"

As the existing data show, China is the world's leading producer of rare minerals. China holds the highest weight of production for a number of 15 minerals, plus 17 rare earth metals, from the extended list of critical minerals (Fig. 25.1). More than this, China is expanding its influence and control overseas using offensive diplomacy and the Belt and Road Initiative in the regions that are proven rich in resources, like Africa, the Middle East, Latin America, and Central Asia. It is well known case of cobalt, a mineral used for aircraft engines and batteries for electric cars that it is mostly extracted in Congo by a Chinese company (Davie, 2022).

By integrating the supply chain, from extraction down to primary processing, advanced technology production, and development, China seems to intend to monopolize the global production of some high-tech industries. This might confer China with the highest comparative advantage in a global competition for a new industrial revolution and the highest market share.

Besides the existing reserves, China still has the competitive advantage of an emergent economy and the low labor cost and the demographic premium that makes mining extraction of resources profitable.

It is not to be neglected that, in recent years, the Chinese government has introduced stricter rules on environmental protection, which has led to an increase in the

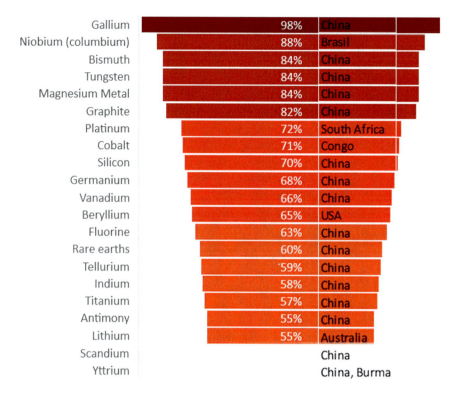

Source: author's compilation, based on (USGS, 2021)

Fig. 25.1 Main country producer of critical minerals and the percentage of world production, 2021ᵉ Note: e-estimates. In the case of scandium and yttrium, data are not available, but there are many signals that indicate China as a main producer of these rare earths

cost of production for mining companies. In addition, the economic boom that China is experiencing since decades was also reflected in the significant increase in wages. These factors have therefore led to an escalation in commodity prices, which has also been reflected in international commodity markets.

25.3.2 USA Dependence on Imports from China

During their history, the USA had a strong tradition in the extraction and processing of mineral resources. Until the 1980s, the USA was world leader in ore extraction and the processing of rare minerals. Since the 2000s, however, the USA has turned into a country dependent on imports of critical minerals, reaching a level of almost total dependence on imports, especially from China. Industrial activity on the upstream links, from extraction to the primary and secondary processing of minerals, has drastically diminished, as a result of the globalization and relocation of industries to countries with cheaper labor.

Between 2015 and 2018, China supplied the USA with 80% of imports of rare earths and metals. In addition, US imports from other regions were derived from Chinese production. After the start of the trade war between the two major powers, U.S. imports of rare earths and metals from China are diminishing. This had two effects: the increase in the purchase prices of the raw materials needed for the American high-tech industries and the decrease in the security of supply of the necessary quantities. In some cases, consumption volumes have decreased over the past few years. In the meantime, actions have been started to encourage domestic production, to discover new deposits and to extend exploitation licenses (Nakano, 2021).

An important comparative advantage for the US economy and the prospects for future technologies is that they have both reserves and domestic production for a considerable number of critical minerals, from the list of those at risk of supply (15 minerals, plus rare earth ore, except for yttrium and scandium), without having 100% covered the necessary consumption for any of the elements. The USA produces metals, metal alloys, and superior alloys, among which the productions of aluminum, nickel, beryllium, zinc, metal magnesium, platinum, palladium, and zirconium and in a smaller proportion of titanium, cobalt, and rare earths stand out. The USA is the world's leading producer of beryllium. In the case of non-fuel industrial minerals, there is a significant production of barite, silicon, bauxite, and lithium.

On the other hand, the USA is dependent 100% on imports for 14 minerals, plus some others for which there is no registered production, but there is a capacity of recycling and recovery. For other 15 critical minerals, the USA had a net import reliance greater than 50% of the apparent consumption The main suppliers for U.S. imports in 2021 were China and Canada (USDI, USGS, 2022).

A second strong point is that the USA has improved in secondary production from recovered or recycled materials with a strategic goal of innovating in this industry. For 9 critical minerals, there is this capacity, which complements the primary one, especially for aluminum, nickel, beryllium, magnesium, zinc, and platinum metals.

From the analysis, it results that, in general, in the activity of mining of critical minerals, but also of secondary production, very few companies are involved. This indicates an extremely high concentration of production, which at the same time constitutes an additional supply risk in the long term. The level of concentration of activity is determined by various factors, including the specialization of industrial and labor and the concentration of resources in a small number of deposits. On the other hand, globalization and the relocation of industrial activity to other countries have left their mark on the American extractive sector. The extractive industry and the primary or intermediate processing industry have become industries with low added value; as a result, many companies have exited the market.

25 The Geopolitics of Resources: The Critical Minerals

The critical minerals with a significant role in the technologies of the future for which the USA has demonstrated reserves but have a modest production at present are silicon, lithium, beryllium, aluminum, palladium and platinum, nickel, chromium, cobalt, zinc, and vanadium.

In the case of rare earths, the USA has ore reserves, from which it also extracts a relatively modest production, but which is exported, in order to separate the metals and compounds used in downstream industries. *The USA imports most of the required volumes for domestic consumption of rare earth metals, especially from China.*

As for the US dependence on imports of critical minerals from China, there is a high dependence on a number of four elements: antimony, gallium, arsenic, and bismuth, plus a very high dependence on rare earths, including the 15 lanthanides and yttrium. A moderate dependence can be reported in the case of eight other elements (see Fig. 25.2).

As a strategic relevance in high-tech industries, gallium and yttrium, along with the other metals from rare earths, are the critical minerals with the most important role in the list of minerals at risk of supply to the USA.

The industrial applications in which these materials are essential are among the most advanced: semiconductors, optical devices, medical equipment, military, industrial, telecommunications equipment, computers, hard disks, screens, LED, laser diodes, electric car motors, aircraft engines, wind turbines, sensors for cars and aircraft, sensors for the Internet of things, radars, measuring instruments, etc.

For 15 critical minerals, the US import dependency rate is high or very high, but the main sources of import are other than China. Among the critical elements for the leading industries, noteworthy would be metals that have particular importance in

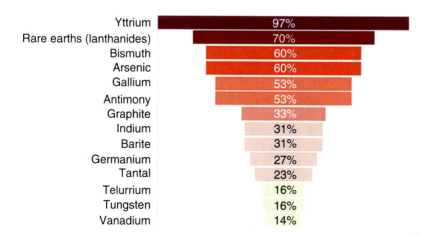

Source: author's compilation, based on (USDI, USGS, 2022)

Fig. 25.2 Import dependency rate of critical minerals from China, as a percentage of US consumption, 2021

the manufacture of metal alloys and superior alloys, from which medical, aerospace, military, industrial, energy, transport, and telecommunications equipment are produced. These are vanadium, niobium, tellurium, titanium, chromium, cobalt, platinum, magnesium, nickel, and aluminum.

25.3.3 USA–China Trade War

The year 2010 was a turning point in addressing US public policies in the area of security of critical mineral supply. That year, China imposed an embargo on the export of rare earths to Japan, which led to an escalation in the prices of these minerals in global markets. Acknowledging the growing relevance of critical minerals to the national economy, the US administration has gradually adopted an increasingly active policy, both to boost domestic production and secure supply chains. Critical minerals have evolved from a supply problem for the economy to a matter of national security. A strategy on critical materials was developed in 2010. This was followed by successive decisions, during the Trump administration (2017–2020), to support the national industry dedicated to the sector, on the links affected upstream and on those of intermediate processing. Trump administration established a trade tariff for imports of critical minerals from China, in order to reduce dependence on imports from this country.

In 2019, the Energy Resources Governance Initiative was launched, which proposes an integrated approach of demand for critical minerals, the growth of renewable energy sectors, resource management, and building governance capacities connected to resource-rich countries worldwide. However, the federal strategy has not paid much attention to critical minerals and their contribution to climate action. This theme became a priority for the Biden administration, which was committed to achieving carbon neutrality by mid-century, implying an acceleration of electrification and the spread of clean technologies throughout the American economy (The White House, 2022).

In its recent national security strategy, the US affirms its intention to launch a broad industrial policy, which will *"kick off public investment in strategic sectors and supply chains, including emerging and critical technologies."* Among the strategic sectors, semiconductors, advanced computers, state-of-the-art communications, clean energy, and biotechnologies are mentioned in particular. In these areas, the security strategy establishes the need for public investment in research and development and in securing supply chains (The White House, 2022).

In order to secure critical mineral supply chains, the US administration has taken a number of public policy measures: (a) widening of the domestic production base, by exploring and identifying new mineral deposits and by conferring new exploitation licenses and supporting industrial production; (b) encouraging academics to carry out research and development projects to support the production, recovery, and recycling of critical minerals vital for the transition to sustainable energy; and (c) diversification of supply chains, to reduce import dependency from China by stepping up international cooperation with close partners in all regions of the world, but especially with resource-rich countries that do not present adversity toward the USA.

In the following section, it presents a study case of gallium, as it might be a relevant case of how the risk of supply reverberates on the national economy in times of disruptions and global disarray.

Box 25.1 Case Study: Gallium

Gallium is a by-product of bauxite and zinc extraction, respectively. Its relevance is given by the semiconductor properties. In arsenic alloy (GaAs), gallium is used in the manufacture of semiconductor wafers from integrated circuits and not only. GaN (gallium-nitrogen) alloy has much better semiconductor properties than SiC (silicon-carbon) wafers. That is why they form the basis for the 5G telecommunications industry (Emilio, 2021).

China is the world's leading producer of gallium (420 t/year or 98% of global production, with a production capacity estimated at 650 t/year, accounting for 84% of the world's production capacity). Other producing countries include Japan, South Korea, Russia, and Ukraine (which stopped the production in the last 3 years). The main manufacturers of secondary processing of refined gallium are China, Japan, Slovakia, and the USA (USDI, USGS, 2022).

USA was totally dependent on imports, mostly from China. Since 2019, USA' imports from China have been in drastic decline. Amid the trade war with China, the USA imposed very high tariffs on gallium imports, which reached 25% in 2019. In 2019, China supplied America with 60% of its gallium import volume, followed by Germany, UK, and Taiwan. In 2021, the volume of US imports increased by 140%, compared with 2020, but from Canada, Japan, and Singapore, despite the escalation of commodity prices on global markets. The price of Chinese gallium increased by 146% in 2021, compared to the beginning of 2020.

The lower access to gallium for U.S. industry is reflected by the gradual decline in consumption in the economy. If in 2016, the USA consumed 18,100 kg of gallium metal, in 2021, the consumption was only 16,000 kg. As well, the volume of imported wafers decreased from 1290 tons to 270 tons, in the same period of time. It is to be noticed here that China's Huawei is the largest world producer of 5G telecom stations, and it plans to maintain its largest share in the 5G global market.

The effects were soon to appear, the US production in downstream industries, which depend on semiconductors being affected: ICT, automotive, aerospace, military, and so on. The semiconductor crisis has led to higher prices of electronic products on the global market, but also to an increase in the waiting time for existing orders in most manufacturers.

Source: Author's compilation

25.4 Conclusions

Global challenges have become increasingly acute, for all the economies of the world. In the context of the COVID-19 pandemic and mobility restrictions, disruptions in global supply chains have been a pressing issue for developed, high-tech economies.

In the case of some critical minerals, essential in high-tech production, such as gallium or yttrium, there is a huge concentration of resources and global production. This can constitute a great vulnerability, in terms of economic security and national security, for developed countries. Both the USA and the European Union have developed strategies on critical minerals in order to increase the security of supply and reduce dependence on imports. The USA is trying, through dedicated public policies, to diversify sources of import, to expand the base of exploitation of rare earths and metals in its territory, and to intensify research and development activities, to develop substitutes for critical materials, or to develop the recovery and recycling of minerals from industrial processes.

In the case of gallium, an essential element in the production of semiconductor wafers, but also of appliances for the defense, aerospace, telecommunications, or medicine industries, there is a quasi-total dependence on China, the country that dominates the global production of this critical mineral. For the time being, it seems that China is gaining a good position on the global market for 5G technologies, by integrating the upstream and downstream value chains in high-tech industries and profiting its monopoly position over some critical minerals.

It is to be noted, though, that the resource new world map is incomplete, due to the lack of physical records, the lack of exploration and exploitation technologies, and the lack of access to data and high protectionism.

This research could be further developed with an improved assessment of the risk of supply with critical minerals for national economies taking into consideration a more elaborated model of integration of minerals in the value chains for various high-tech and clean industries that will shape the future.

Certainly, the geopolitics of resources are shifting from fossil fuels to critical minerals, without which no process of transforming the economy and reaching a sustainable economy with access to renewable sources of energy can be achieved.

References

Davie, M. (2022, 2 24). *Blood Cobalt*. Retrieved from ABC : https://www.abc.net.au/news/2022-02-24/cobalt-mining-in-the-congo-green-energy/100802588

Emilio, M. D. (2021). *GaN power semiconductors target 5G applications*. Retrieved from Electronic Products: https://www.electronicproducts.com/gan-power-semiconductors-target-5g-applications/

European Commission. (2018). *14 Megatrends*. Competence Center on Foresight. Retrieved from https://knowledge4policy.ec.europa.eu/sites/default/files/megatrends_hub_booklet_-_web.pdf

Flint, C. (2022). *Introduction to geopolitics, Fourth Edition*. Routledge.
Harvey, D. (2003). *The new imperialism*. Oxford University Press.
Le Billon, P. (2005). The geography of 'resource wars'. In C. Flint (Ed.), *The geography of war and peace* (pp. 217–241). Oxford University Press.
Mackinder, H. J. (1904). The geographical pivot of history. *The Geographical Journal, 23*(4), 421–437.
Muench, S. S. (2022). *Towards a green and digital future*. Publications Office of the European Union. ISBN 978-92-76-52452-6, https://doi.org/10.2760/54, JRC129319.
Nakano, J. (2021). *The geopolitics of critical minerals supply chains*. Center for Strategic and International Studies.
The White House. (2022). *National Security Strategy*. The White House. Retrieved from https://www.whitehouse.gov/wp-content/uploads/2022/10/Biden-Harris-Administrations-National-Security-Strategy-10.2022.pdf
USDI, USGS. (2022). *Mineral commodity summaries 2022*. USGS. Retrieved from https://pubs.usgs.gov/periodicals/mcs2022/mcs2022.pdf
USGS. (2021). *USGS critical minerals review*. USGS.
Wallerstein, I. (1979). *The capitalist world-economy*. Cambridge University Press.
Yergin, D. (2020). *The new map: Energy, climate, and the clash of nations*. Penguin Press.

Chapter 26
The Critical Mineral Rush: Lithium and Cobalt – A Canadian Perspective

Daniel Bulin

Abstract Critical minerals are essential for the transition to clean and green energy and for the development of new technologies. Although lists of critical minerals may vary from country to country based on national priorities, there is generally overlap in a number of key resources. The definition of critical minerals serves to prioritize and guide investment, support projects and supply chains, and overall transition to the new economy. As the energy transition and industries of the future rely on essential minerals and forecasts show a significant increase in demand that current supply cannot meet, building supply chains is an important priority for any major economy. In addition, geopolitical uncertainties and conflicts that are intensifying or frozen increase the risks related to mineral resources and critical metals, so governments are obliged to assess their own vulnerabilities and capabilities. The current list of critical minerals in the Canadian strategy includes 31 minerals, but six of them require special attention (in alphabetical order): cobalt, copper, graphite, lithium, nickel, and rare earths. This paper proposes an analysis of the two critical minerals, lithium and cobalt, highlighting Canada's strengths and weaknesses, as well as risks and opportunities.

Keywords Critical minerals · Lithium · Cobalt · Key minerals trade · Value chain

26.1 Introduction

The key characteristics that lead to a mineral resource being classified as critical are: (1) has few or no substitute products; (2) is a strategic commodity for specific industries and is limited in scope (defined by acute or critical need); (3) is geographically concentrated, in terms of extraction on the one hand, but also in terms of the location of processing on the other (Canada Government, 2022).

D. Bulin (✉)
Institute for World Economy, Romanian Academy, Bucharest, Romania

Critical minerals, like all resources classified as critical, are subject to periodic evaluation, creating dynamics over time that depend on supply and demand, new technologies, and the need for change. The utility of critical minerals lists is to prioritize and guide investment, support projects and supply chains, and overall transition to the new economy. Although critical minerals lists may vary from country to country based on national priorities and criteria, there is generally overlap in a number of key resources.

What are critical minerals for Canada? According to the National Strategy, to be considered "critical" in Canada, a mineral resource must be essential for economic security, necessary for transition to low-carbon economy and strategically important for Canada's partners (Canada Government, 2022).

Currently, Canada's list of essential minerals includes 31 resources and the list is reviewed every 3 years and revised as necessary after consultation with industry experts and local professionals. Its benefit is that it provides predictability to national strategies in this area, as well as to other stakeholders, such as developers, investors, and also Canada's trading partners.

Canadian experts prioritized the minerals on the list, taking into account the urgent need to build supply chains, emphasizing the need to focus efforts on six key minerals: cobalt, copper, graphite, lithium, nickel, and rare earths (Canada Government, 2022). Their selection is based on their benefits for economic growth, but also on the impact they have on the labor market, especially on the opportunities they offer for employment of local people throughout the value chain, especially in the fields of environmentally friendly and clean technologies, information and communication technologies, etc.

At a second level, other minerals are named (in alphabetical order)—gallium, germanium, magnesium, niobium, scandium, tellurium, titanium, vanadium, and zinc—whose acceleration of production and processing is seen as necessary for Canada and its partners to create and stabilize some strategic industrial value chains. Areas where Canada and its partners can add value through increased extraction and processing of these critical minerals include military optics, semiconductors, prosthetics, ultrasonic devices, solar panels, and wind turbines.

In another category, Canada's strategy in this area also aims to strengthen its position as a producer of potassium, uranium, and aluminum (Government of Canada, 2022). These resources are critical in the green economy (energy, low-carbon emissions) as well as in other sectors such as health care, real estate (green buildings), and food safety, while strengthening Canada's position in trade relations and its strategic place in key commodity markets around the world.

26.2 Literature Review

Su and Hu (2022) argue that critical minerals have become the focus of global competition among major world powers. Based on the fact that countries have different ways of accessing and trading critical mineral resources, Zhu et al. (2022) examined the importance of the critical minerals trade network for renewable energy. Bubar and Syed (2022) note that the security of value chain supply has become a major concern for many governments given the disruption of global supply chains caused by COVID-19, and geopolitical concerns about the security of supply of critical minerals have increased given China's control over many of these supply chains. Wang and Yuan (2022) show that China, the United States, and the European Union have a high degree of overlap in some strategic minerals, and both the United States and other Western European countries are trying to establish a supply chain for critical minerals independent of China.

Gulley et al. (2018) show that resource conflicts have often focused on fossil fuels in the past and that international trade will continue to be severely affected in the future if the supply of these resources is seen as threatened or insufficient to meet growing demand. The transition to a new economy is creating geopolitical tensions over energy security, and as critical minerals become one of its most important components, a new global competition for access to these resources is emerging. In this context, Kakişim (2021) analyzes global competition in critical minerals in trade and production. Moreover, Kalantzakos (2020) shows that new trends (e.g., decarbonization, fourth industrial revolution) have created hotbeds of conflict and that securing access to these commodities in the face of accelerating economic upheavals will have an impact and help determine the balance of power in the years ahead. In addition, Zhai and Hu (2021) show that these changes create unpredictable challenges and risks in global resource allocation, and argue that public policies related to mineral resources need to be adjusted, especially with regard to mineral resource security and international resource competition.

Marshall (2021) provides an analysis of the resilience of critical minerals supply chains, based on increasing geopolitical uncertainty and the need to assess the vulnerability of economies. In a recent report, Simas et al. (2022) examine the challenge of mineral availability from different perspectives and put some questions in discussion, such as what does a responsible supply of minerals mean for the green transition? (Simas et al., 2022). Heffron (2020) brings to the discussion a different approach of an ethical nature from the field of social justice—starting from the challenges of economic crises and the need to distribute resources, the author argues that a balance is needed in the market for key minerals, where revenues and profits should be distributed equitably across value and supply chains.

Heredia et al. (2020) addressed the lithium importance for the energy transition to a low-carbon economy. Zhou et al. (2014) highlight the main challenges for the lithium industry—the high concentration level of production, the need to improve extraction technology, and the need to increase the safety of lithium-ion batteries. Christmann et al. (2015) analyzed the factors underlying the current supply-demand balance for lithium and outlined a perspective for long-term market development, particularly through the lens of sustainable development, highlighting the importance of policy decisions, governance, and scientific innovation. In another study, Egbue and Long (2012) conducted a comprehensive literature review on global EV battery supply chains and highlighted potential issues in lithium safety, supply, and production.

In an analysis of changes in the cobalt market from the 1970s to 2018, Campbell (2020) concluded that it is characterized by frequent supply crises and high cyclicality. Sun et al. (2022) point out the main problem regarding cobalt—the geographical concentration of supply. The results of Shi et al. (2022) show that most of the world's economies are involved in only one or two stages of the cobalt industrial chain, while some economies (such as China, the United States, Germany, the United Kingdom, and Spain) have global influence and play an important systemic role in global supply.

Based on the increasing dependence on imports and the associated risk of disruption in the supply of these commodities from third countries, Lewicka et al. (2021) highlighted the need to promote domestic production and proposed a number of measures to reduce dependence on imports for the specific case of the EU. Ali et al. (2018) emphasized that Paris Agreement will require adaptation to new "green technologies" on an unprecedented scale, leading to a supply problem for mineral raw materials. Gadd et al. (2022) believe that Canada is economically well-positioned to become a major supplier of some critical minerals because of its expertise in the exploration and mining industry.

26.3 Methodology

Based on the three categories of critical resources and the additional classification from the strategy proposed by Canadian experts (prioritization, investment acceleration, consolidation), we will focus on the two priority elements. The analysis will cover brief aspects of their exploitation, especially in terms of future technologies, production capacities, Canada's access—direct and indirect—to resources, the current status of projects and partnerships, trade, market conditions and prices, supply risks, highlighting Canada's situation, its strengths and weaknesses, risks and opportunities, but also the position of China, a strong competitor in each of the selected critical commodity markets.

The method used is documentary analysis, based on secondary data, and the main sources are government projects and strategies (Canada, regions), statistical databases (national, OEC—the observatory of economic complexity, United States Geological Survey), studies, and articles.

26.4 Analysis/Results Interpretation

26.4.1 Priority Critical Mineral Analysis for Canada: Lithium

Description and Use As a soft metal with the lowest density of all that reacts strongly with water, lithium is an important resource for clean energy production. According to the Canadian government, in 2020, most of the world's lithium was

Source: author, based by Ontario Mining Association (2022)

Fig. 26.1 Lithium value chain. (Source: Author, based by Ontario Mining Association, 2022)

used in the manufacture of batteries (71%), with a significant (but much smaller) share going to ceramics and glass products (Government of Canada, 2022) (Fig. 26.1).

Production Australia is the world leader in lithium production, concentrating more than half of the estimated global total in five mines. Chile, Argentina, and China share the rest of the world's production. The latest data for 2021 show that the cumulative shares of Australia (55%, 55,000 tons) and Chile account for more than 4/5 of total world production. If the share of China (14%) is added, there is a strong concentration of this resource in only a few countries. Chile has the largest share of reserves (almost 42%), but so does Australia (26%). China (1.5 million, 7% of total reserves) but also Argentina (2.2 million, 10%) complete the quartet of four countries that currently hold virtually the world's lithium resources (Table 26.1).

Despite the fact that lithium deposits are concentrated in South America (Argentina, Bolivia, Chile), according to the USGS, lithium potential is better distributed, many different countries have proven lithium resources (U.S. Geological Survey, 2022a).

26.4.1.1 Canada's Access to Resources

Canadian government statistics indicate that lithium production will be limited in 2014–2019 and insignificant in 2020. At that time, there were a number of projects aimed at switching extraction technologies from traditional mining to unconventional sources (salts from oil fields, industrial wastewater) in different regions of the country—Ontario, Quebec, Alberta, Manitoba, and Saskatchewan (Government of Canada, 2022). The same sources assume an estimated potential of about 2.9 million tons of lithium resources, including existing reserves, but the development of new generation projects could significantly increase the projections.

In recent years, a series of events have upset the lithium market in Canada. First, the Quebec lithium mine ceased operations after prices fell in international markets, largely due to the doubling of global production. In addition, North American Lithium ceased production in 2019 and was acquired by Sayona Québec in 2021. However, an opportunity could arise from the new owners' plans to restart not only the mine, but also other projects in the region, including the construction of a lithium hydroxide refinery. Another troubled project, Nemaska Lithium, achieved initial results at its Whabouchi mine in Quebec in 2017, but ceased production in 2019

Table 26.1 Lithium production and reserves in 2021 worldwide, in thousands of tons and percentage

Country	Production (thousand tons)	% Production in total	Reserves (thousand tons)	% Reserves in total
Australia	55,000	55%	5,700,000	25.9%
Chile	*26,000*	*26%*	*9,200,000*	*41.8%*
China	14,000	14%	1,500,000	6.8%
Total	**100,000**	**100%**	**22,000,000**	**100%**

Source: Author processing, U.S. Geological Survey (2022a)
Note: The table shows the production and reserves of the leading countries (production 2021), China and Canada

and was acquired by Pallinghurst Group in partnership with the Quebec government in 2020. Again, future plans—restarting the mine at full capacity and building lithium hydroxide refineries in Bécancour, Quebec—could create new opportunities.

As of today, there are 21 lithium projects in Canada, of which 20 are active and 11 are at an advanced stage, concentrated in five regions: Quebec (five in advanced stage, three in exploration), Ontario (three in advanced stage, two in exploration), Manitoba (one in advanced stage, two in exploration), Saskatchewan (one in advanced stage), Alberta (two in advanced stage, of which only one is active, two others in exploration).

Abroad, Canadian-based companies own a number of projects in South American countries and the United States. Lithium Chile Inc. is a Canadian company that owns exploration and development projects in Chile—Lithium Chile has the world's largest high-grade lithium reserves in Chile and in Argentina, as well as other prospective properties for gold, silver, and copper. The company presents itself on its official website as the largest owner of lithium salt mines after Chile and the SQM company, with a portfolio of 14 projects, including (Mining Watch Canada, 2022): (1) Laguna Blanca—early-stage exploration property covering the Chilean sector of the Laguna Blanca salar-lagoon complex (Lithium Chile, n.d.); (2) Coipasa Project—an early-stage exploration property covering the southwestern sector of the Salar de Coipasa Basin (Lithium Chile, 2021); and (3) Salar de Arizaro—with 33,846 hectares covering portions of the western and eastern parts of the Salar de Arizaro in Salta province, one of the largest known salt lakes in the world (Lithium Chile, 2021). One weakness, however, is that Lithium Chile has an investor from China, Chengxin Lithium, the second largest lithium processor in the Asian country.

In Brazil, Sigma Lithium Resources owns properties in the state of Minas Gerais, in the municipalities of Araçuaí and Itinga, focusing on the 100% owned Grota do Cirilo Project, the largest hard rock lithium deposit in the Americas (Sigma Lithium, n.d.). Also in South America are the Laguna Caro, Antofalla Nord, and Antofalla Sud projects, owned by Lithium Energi Exploration (Reuters, n.d.).

In the United States, Nevada Sunrise Metals Corp. is worth noting, a Vancouver-based resource exploration company with 100% interests in the Gemini Lithium, Jackson Wash Lithium, and Coronado VMS projects, as well as parts of the Kinsley

Mountain Gold Project (20%) and the Lovelock Mine and Treasure Box Copper-Cobalt projects (15% each) (Nevada Sunrise, n.d.).

Access to lithium deposits is far less, about a quarter of the world's lithium resources, leaving the Asian country vulnerable in the medium term, experts say, despite its high dependence on Chinese supply chains, because it must rely on supplies from other countries (fDi Intelligence, 2022). China's most important advance in securing its lithium needs is access to Chile's state-owned reserves: In 2019, Chilean regulators approved a $4.1 billion deal in which China's Tianqi acquired a 24 percent stake in Chile's SQM, which is involved in extracting lithium from the Atacama salt pan (Global Americans, 2021).

Recently, China announced additional transactions in South America and Africa (fDi Intelligence, 2022): (1) On July 11, 2022, Ganfeng Lithium, a supplier to Tesla, entered into an agreement to acquire the Lithea mining group with projects in Argentina for $962 million; (2) Sinomine Group acquired Bikita Minerals in Zimbabwe, Africa's only lithium-producing mine, in January 2021; and (3) Premier African Minerals announced on June 23, 2022, will supply spodumene concentrate from its Zulu lithium mine in Zimbabwe to China.

Other Chinese projects in the lithium processing market reinforce its dominant position (Mining Technology, 2021a): (1) Jiangxi Ganfeng is the largest lithium (metal) producer in the world. The company owns lithium deposits in Australia, Argentina, and Mexico and (2) Tianqi Lithium owns projects in Australia, China, and Chile.

26.4.1.2 Trade

- Statistical data published by the Canadian government show that exports of lithium carbonate amounted to 13.5 tons in 2019, while they were insignificant in 2020 (Government of Canada, 2022). In contrast, Canada exported 86 tons of lithium oxide and hydroxide in 2020, but this level also decreased compared to 41 thousand tons in 2019 and 97 thousand tons in 2018. This trend is attributed to the discontinuation of lithium mines in Whabouchi and Quebec (North), due to the decline in world prices for the compounds of this element (carbonate, oxide, hydroxide).
- In contrast, Canada is a net importer of lithium, with imports totaling $161 million in 2020, and imports of lithium and lithium products came almost exclusively (91%) from four countries—Chile, China, Russia, and the United States.
- To get a clearer picture of Canadian trade relations for this product group, we also look at statistics provided by the OEC (2022a): Canada exported only $46.1 thousand worth of lithium carbonates in 2020, mainly to India ($45.2 thousand); also in 2020, Canada imported $5.66 million worth of lithium carbonates, with the main import markets being the United States ($1.58 million), Chile ($1.39 million), China ($943 thousand), but also EU countries—Slovenia ($754 thousand) and Austria ($398 thousand).

- As for China's position (OEC, 2022b), it is the third largest exporter of lithium carbonates in the world (in 2020, the total value was $60.4 million), with the main destinations being South Korea ($31.1 million), Japan ($20.3 million), the United States ($2.26 million), Australia ($1.06 million), and, as mentioned, Canada ($943 million). In 2020, China imported $230 million worth of lithium carbonate, making it the world's second largest importer of lithium carbonate, mainly from Chile ($161 million), Argentina ($56.1 million), South Korea ($9.75 million), but also from the Netherlands ($1.95 million), or Japan ($765 million).

26.4.1.3 Market Conditions and Supply Risks

China is a world leader in processing lithium for battery production, and as lithium supply security has become a top priority for technology companies around the world, a feature of supply chains is the formation of strategic alliances between technology and exploration companies to ensure a reliable and diversified supply (U.S. Geological Survey, 2022a). According to Benchmark Mineral Intelligence, the growth of electric vehicles will account for more than 90% of lithium demand by 2030 (CNBC, 2022).

Lithium prices increased significantly in 2021, reaching record highs due to strong demand in the electric vehicle market, and this trend is expected to continue in the near future. In the short term, prices could also react quickly to signs of supply shortages but could stabilize in the medium to long term as new projects come online and begin production. In both the short and medium to long term, carbon emission reduction programs will drive demand for lithium. However, the future generation of substitutes for lithium-ion batteries, such as solid-state batteries, may reduce demand in the future (Ontario Mining Association, 2022).

26.4.2 Priority Critical Mineral Analysis for Canada: Cobalt

Description and Use Cobalt is a ferromagnetic element that forms many compounds, stable in air and resistant to water, sensitive to dilute acids, with a high melting point and wear resistance and good conductive properties (Matmatch, n.d.). Globally, cobalt is mainly used for electrodes in rechargeable batteries (USGS, n.d.) (Fig. 26.2).

Global cobalt production from mines and refineries reached record levels in 2021. The DR Congo is the world's top source of cobalt, accounting for over 70%, and China is the world's largest consumer of cobalt, with the rechargeable battery industry accounting for more than 80% of consumption (U.S. Geological Survey, 2022b). As Congo accounts for 70% of cobalt production (mining), the remaining 30% is decentralized; other producing countries include Russia, Australia, and the Philippines. In terms of reserves, Australia's share (1.4 million, 18.4%) is worth noting (Table 26.2).

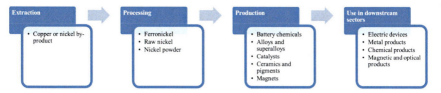

Source: author, based by Ontario Mining Association (2022)

Fig. 26.2 Cobalt value chain

Table 26.2 Global cobalt production and reserves in 2021, in thousands of tons and percentage

Country	Production (thousand tons)	% Production in total	Reserves (thousand tons)	% Reserves in total
RD Congo	120	70,6%	3500	46%
Russia	7,6	4,5%	250	3,3%
Canada	*4,3*	*2,5%*	*220*	*2,9%*
China	*2,2*	*1,3%*	*80*	*1%*
Total	**170**	**100%**	**7600**	**100%**

Source: Author processing, U.S. Geological Survey (2022b)
Note: the table shows the production and reserves of the leading countries (production 2021), China and Canada

26.4.2.1 Canada's Access to Resources

In 2021, Canada produced about 2.5% of the world's cobalt, with its reserves accounting for nearly 3% of the global total. Canada's cobalt production is concentrated in a few regions: Quebec (35%), Newfoundland and Labrador (35%), Ontario (25%), with the remainder in Manitoba (Statista, 2021).

It is important to note that there are few pure cobalt producers in Canada. Most Canadian cobalt companies are primarily nickel or silver producers where cobalt is a by-product (Liew, 2022).

- Sherritt International is a large cobalt producer that produced nearly 40% of Canada's cobalt in 2020; Canada Silver Cobalt is another large Canadian cobalt producer.
- Vale, based in the United States, produces cobalt along with other minerals, and its main production facility is located in Moa, Cuba; some of the raw material produced is refined in Canada.
- Wheaton is a company that buys some or all of the metal produced by the mines/mining companies it finances, usually at a discount, and although only a small portion of its revenue comes from cobalt (about 4%), the amount of cobalt it receives from the producers it has access to is significant.

- Electra owns the first sustainable battery materials park in North America, and as cobalt is central to the development of this project, the company has commissioned a battery cobalt sulfate plant (with local extraction) as the first stage in the development of an electric vehicle supply chain.
- Nickel 28 focuses on the most valuable and expensive battery metals—nickel and cobalt—and is well-positioned to produce both, owning for example the Ramu Nickel-Cobalt Project.
- Canada's cobalt deposits could prove a valuable resource for producers of clean energy technologies that would reduce dependence on supply chains. Major multinational mining companies Glencore and Vale operate significant projects in Canada, including the Voisey's Bay, Raglan, Thompson, and Fraser mines (NS Energy, 2021).

Another opportunity for Canada could be the new projects and partnerships that have been completed in recent years—the investment in First Cobalt Corp.'s Ontario refinery, the new supply agreement with Glencore plc and a partnership with a unit of China Molybdenum Ltd. (Newswire.ca, 2021).

The biggest threat to the cobalt market is China's control over Congolese resources (GlobalEDGE, 2022). The main Congolese mines under Chinese ownership (Mining Technology, 2021b): (1) Sicomines copper-cobalt mine—open pit in Katanga, owned by China Railway Group; (2) Tenke Fungurume Mine—open pit in Katanga, owned by China Molybdenum (mine to operate until 2052); (3) Kamoya Mine (Katanga), owned by Wanbao Mining; and (4) Ruashi Mine (Katanga), owned by Jinchuan Group, with mining horizon until 2029.

26.4.2.2 Trade

- Canada was the global second largest exporter of cobalt in 2020, with a total value of $300 million directed to five main destinations: Norway ($73.9 million), the United States ($70.4 million), China ($51.4 million), Japan ($26.8 million), and the Netherlands ($19.5 million). Imports amounted up to $37.4 million in 2020, supplied mainly by the U.S. market ($17.4 million); other sources of imports were Germany ($4.4 million), Madagascar ($3.88 million), Switzerland ($3.12 million), and Belgium ($2.81 million) (OEC, 2022c).
- China is the world's largest importer of cobalt, with an estimated $2.6 billion in 2020, with the largest share coming from DR Congo ($2.06 billion), with major source markets including Malaysia ($89 million), Australia ($69.5 million), Canada ($51.4 million), and Japan ($34.8 million). As a net importer, China exported only $73.4 million, with rather small exports to the Netherlands ($12.9 million), Japan ($12.8 million), South Korea ($8.31 million), Germany ($7.27 million), and the United States ($4.98 million) (OEC, 2022d).

26.4.2.3 Market Conditions and Supply Risks

As explained earlier, cobalt is a commodity that is virtually controlled by only two countries: DR Congo (70% of resources, supplier) and China (owns about 80% of DRC's industrial cobalt mines) (GlobalEDGE, 2022).

Recent indications suggest that China Molybdenum and other major Chinese mining companies may be gradually required by law to withdraw from the management of cobalt mines in the DRC, and this change could not only support the economy of the African nation but also lead to lower cobalt prices on the global market and weaken the current bargaining power of Chinese companies (GlobalEDGE, 2022).

Cobalt prices fluctuate depending on the material traded (metal powder, chemicals, cathodes) and have been very volatile over the past 5 years. In 2021, the price increased and reached 70 thousand dollars per ton. According to the forecasts, the price of cobalt raw materials is expected to remain relatively constant at about 50 thousand dollars per ton, but under certain conditions, it could exceed 80 thousand dollars per ton (Ontario Mining Association, 2022).

Demand for cobalt will increase as more electric cars are sold, especially in Europe where governments are encouraging sales through special programs. Cobalt is the most expensive component of lithium-ion batteries, accounting for about a quarter of their total cost (Liew, 2022). Recent forecasts by the World Economic Forum's Global Battery Alliance indicate that demand for cobalt for use in batteries will quadruple by 2030 (Council on Foreign Relations, 2020).

26.5 Conclusions

Australia, the market leader in lithium, is considered a stable supplier, so the supply chain risk is considered rather low. However, it should be kept in mind that lithium is of increasing economic importance given the growing demand for lithium from battery manufacturers and the limited substitution options. China's strong position in trade, as well as in production and available resources, remains a significant threat alongside Canada as a net importer. In addition, there are the risks of business interruptions, strong competition, and recent price developments. The concentrated production in Australia, and the resources and high potential in South America, and the active projects, many of which are at an advanced stage, are aspects that can mitigate the risks and turn into opportunities in the medium and long term.

Cobalt reserves are heavily concentrated in Congo and are processed in China. European countries and the United States may experience disruptions in the cobalt supply chain given the growing demand from new tech-based industries (electrical, automotive, aerospace) (Ontario Mining Association, 2022). Although China and Canada are major players in international markets and their domestic production is rather small, the dominant position of the Asian country is maintained by the China-Congo relationship. Since Canada imports little, the announced projects could represent a major opportunity in the medium to long term.

References

Ali, S., Toledano, P., Maennling, N., Hoffman, N., & Aganga, L. (2018). *Resourcing green technologies through smart mineral enterprise development: A case analysis of cobalt*. Available at SSRN 3669838.

Bubar, D. S., & Syed, Z. (2022). *Critical minerals supply chains between Canada and the indo-Pacific*.

Campbell, G. A. (2020). The cobalt market revisited. *Mineral Economics, 33*(1), 21–28.

Canada Government. (2022). Canada's critical minerals strategy: Discussion paper. Opportunities from exploration to recycling: Powering the green and digital economy for Canada and the world, available at: https://www.canada.ca/en/campaign/critical-minerals-in-canada/canada-critical-minerals-strategy-discussion-paper.html

Christmann, P., Gloaguen, E., Labbé, J. F., Melleton, J., & Piantone, P. (2015). Global lithium resources and sustainability issues. In *Lithium process chemistry* (pp. 1–40). Elsevier.

CNBC. (2022). *How the U.S. fell behind in lithium, the 'white gold' of electric vehicles*, Available at: https://www.cnbc.com/2022/01/15/how-the-us-fell-way-behind-in-lithium-white-gold-for-evs.html

Council on Foreign Relations. (2020). *Why Cobalt Mining in the DRC Needs Urgent Attention*, Available at: https://www.cfr.org/blog/why-cobalt-mining-drc-needs-urgent-attention

Egbue, O., & Long, S. (2012). Critical issues in the supply chain of lithium for electric vehicle batteries. *Engineering Management Journal, 24*(3), 52–62.

Fdi Intelligence (2022). *Chinese companies expanding footprint in global lithium mines*, Available at: https://www.fdiintelligence.com/content/feature/chinese-companies-expanding-footprint-in-global-lithium-mines-81261

Gadd, M. G., Lawley, C. J., Corriveau, L., Houlé, M., Peter, J. M., Plouffe, A., Potter, E., Sappin, A.-A., Pilote, J.-L., Marquis, G., & Lebel, D. (2022). *Public geoscience solutions for diversifying Canada's critical mineral production* (p. 526). Geological Society, London, Special Publications.

Global Americans. (2021). *Chinese advances in Chile*, Available at: https://theglobalamericans.org/2021/03/chinese-advances-in-chile/

GlobalEDGE. (2022). *Congo's Cobalt Controversy*, Available at: https://globaledge.msu.edu/blog/post/57136/congos-cobalt-controversy

Gulley, A. L., Nassar, N. T., & Xun, S. (2018). China, the United States, and competition for resources that enable emerging technologies. *Proceedings of the National Academy of Sciences, 115*(16), 4111–4115.

Heffron, R. J. (2020). The role of justice in developing critical minerals. *The Extractive Industries and Society, 7*(3), 855–863.

Heredia, F., Martinez, A. L., & Surraco Urtubey, V. (2020). The importance of lithium for achieving a low-carbon future: Overview of the lithium extraction in the 'Lithium Triangle'. *Journal of Energy & Natural Resources Law, 38*(3), 213–236.

Kakişim, C. (2021). New energy geopolitics shaped by energy transition: The energy balance for rare earth elements and critical minerals. *Avrasya Etüdleri, 60*, 5–28.

Kalantzakos, S. (2020). The race for critical minerals in an era of geopolitical realignments. *The International Spectator, 55*(3), 1–16.

Lewicka, E., Guzik, K., & Galos, K. (2021). On the possibilities of critical raw materials production from the EU's primary sources. *Resources, 10*(5), 50.

Liew, C. (2022). 10 Best Cobalt Stocks in Canada (Nov 2022), Available at: https://wealthawesome.com/best-cobalt-stocks-in-canada/

Lithium Chile. (2021). *Coipasa Project. Executive Summary Report*, Available at: https://lithiumchile.ca/wp-content/uploads/2022/06/Coipasa-2021-Exec-Summary_web.pdf y

Lithium Chile. (n.d.). *Salar de Arizaro*, Available at: https://lithiumchile.ca/salar-de-arizaro/

Marshall, B. (2021). *Building supply chain resiliency of critical minerals*.

Matmatch. (n.d.). *Cobalt: Properties, production, and applications*, Available at: https://matmatch.com/learn/material/cobalt

Mining Technology. (2021a). *Top 5 largest lithium mining companies in the world*, Available at: https://www.mining-technology.com/analysis/top-5-largest-lithium-companies/

Mining Technology. (2021b). *World's ten largest cobalt mines in 2020*, Available at: https://www.mining-technology.com/marketdata/ten-largest-cobalts-mines-2020-2/

Mining Watch Canada. (2022). *Canadian lithium investments in Chile: Extractivism and conflict*, Available at: https://miningwatch.ca/sites/default/files/2022-03-04_canadian_mining_investments_in_chile.pdf

Nevada Sunrise. (n.d.). *Nevada: the right place, the right time*, Available at: https://nevadasunrise.ca/

Newswire.ca. (2021). Canadian government makes joint $10 million investment in cobalt refinery adjoining the Teledyne and Glencore Bucke property, Available at: https://www.newswire.ca/news-releases/canadian-government-makes-joint-10-million-investment-in-cobalt-refinery-adjoining-the-teledyne-and-glencore-bucke-property-846604971.html

NS Energy. (2021). *Profiling the six largest cobalt reserves in the world by country*, Available at: https://www.nsenergybusiness.com/features/largest-cobalt-reserves-country/

OEC. (2022a). *Lithium carbonates in Canada, database* Available at: https://oec.world/en/profile/bilateral-product/lithium-carbonates/reporter/can

OEC. (2022b). *Lithium carbonates in China, database* Available at: https://oec.world/en/profile/bilateral-product/lithium-carbonates/reporter/chn

OEC. (2022c). *Cobalt in Canada, database* Available at: https://oec.world/en/profile/bilateral-product/cobalt/reporter/can

OEC. (2022d). *Cobalt in China, database* Available at: https://oec.world/en/profile/bilateral-product/cobalt/reporter/chn

Ontario Mining Association. (2022). *Critical Minerals Analysis*, Available at: https://oma.on.ca/en/ontario-mining/2022_OMA_Mineral_Profiles.pdf

Reuters. (n.d.). Lithium Energi Exploration Inc, Available at: https://www.reuters.com/markets/companies/LEXI.V/

Shi, Q., Sun, X., Xu, M., & Wang, M. (2022). The multiplex network structure of global cobalt industry chain. *Resources Policy, 76*, 102555.

Sigma Lithium. (n.d.). *Our project*, Available at: https://www.sigmalithiumresources.com/project/

Simas, M., Rocha Aponte, F., & Wiebe, K. S. (2022). *The future is circular-circular economy and critical minerals for the green transition*.

Statista. (2021). *Production of cobalt in Canada by province 2020*, Available at: https://www.statista.com/statistics/434662/estimate-of-cobalt-production-in-canada-by-province/

Su, Y., & Hu, D. (2022). Global dynamics and reflections on critical minerals. In *E3S web of conferences* (Vol. 352, p. 03045). EDP Sciences.

Sun, X., Shi, Q., & Hao, X. (2022). Supply crisis propagation in the global cobalt trade network. *Resources, Conservation and Recycling, 179*, 106035.

U.S. Geological Survey. (2022a). *Lithium*. Mineral Commodity Summaries, January 2022, Available at: https://pubs.usgs.gov/periodicals/mcs2022/mcs2022-lithium.pdf

U.S. Geological Survey. (2022b). *Cobalt*. Mineral Commodity Summaries, January 2022, Available at: https://pubs.usgs.gov/periodicals/mcs2022/mcs2022-cobalt.pdf

USGS. (n.d.). *Cobalt statistics and information*, National Minerals Information Center, Available at: https://www.usgs.gov/centers/national-minerals-information-center/cobalt-statistics-and-information

Wang, A., & Yuan, X. (2022). Security of China's strategic and critical minerals under background of great power competition. *Bulletin of Chinese Academy of Sciences (Chinese Version), 37*(11), 1550–1559.

Zhai, M. G., & Hu, B. (2021). Thinking to state security, international competition and national strategy of mineral resources. *Journal of Earth Sciences and Environment, 43*(1), 1–11.

Zhou, P., Tang, J. R., & Zhang, T. (2014). Supply and demand prospect of global lithium resources and some suggestions. *Geological Bulletin of China, 33*(10), 1532–1538.

Zhu, X., Ding, Q., & Chen, J. (2022). How does critical mineral trade pattern affect renewable energy development? The mediating role of renewable energy technological progress. *Energy Economics, 112*, 106164.

Chapter 27
How Romania May Benefit from the Natural Gas Resources' Offshore Exploitation of the Black Sea Romanian Continental Shelf?

Marius Bulearcă

Abstract The age of natural gas is not over, and it won't be over any time soon. With significant reserves of natural gas, Romania can become an important player in this market, if it knows how to play this card. In this respect, Romania has an extraordinary chance that few countries in Europe have: its own natural gas resources and, above all, the significant deposits discovered in the Black Sea continental shelf. Therefore, these huge natural gas reserves call for important investments in the Black Sea in the coming years. For these reasons, the paper examines and analyzes both the natural gas resources and the great benefits these investments may induce in Romania. If the domestic consumption remains at the present level, Romania may be independent of Russian gas and even export up to a quarter of the gas production, and this represents the great opportunity given by such projects. In the article, this impact is quantified by analyzing the volume of investments, including capital and operational expenditures. In addition, employment, revenues to the state budget, and macroeconomic indicators have multiple impacts on the Romanian economy. Concerning the spillover effects in the economy of investments from the Black Sea, the paper demonstrates that the development of offshore natural gas projects from the Romanian continental shelf will create new opportunities for other Romanian industries as well, contributing to their return to the level of past achievements or the development of new products and services for the economy.

Keywords Black Sea · Offshore exploitation projects · Natural gas · Continental shelf · Benefits

---

M. Bulearcă (✉)
Centre of Industry and Services Economics, National Institute for Economic Research "Costin C. Kiritescu" of the Romanian Academy, Bucharest, Romania

27.1 Introduction

The use of natural gas will continue into this decade. The natural gas industry is transforming itself through complex innovation processes to successfully face the energy transition and contribute to the goal of achieving climate neutrality. One of the future technologies with which natural gas can play a significant role in making the transition from fossil fuels to green ones is hydrogen technology. Romania has large reserves of natural gas and, above all, the significant deposits discovered in the Black Sea and thus can become a significant player in the hydrogen market.

In the context of the new European regulations under the umbrella of the Green Deal, which emphasizes green energy, this window of opportunity could close for us faster than we would like.

27.2 Literature Review

Black Sea Deep Offshore Exploration

The Euxine Point is considered to have a potential comparable to that of the North Sea, the most important region in terms of energy in Europe. This potential has not yet been confirmed as under 100 exploration wells were drilled so far and important deposits being discovered only in the Romanian Neptune block (Moroșanu, 2012). All the states bordering the Black Sea have exploration projects, the most advanced being Romania, Turkey, and, to some extent, Bulgaria (Fig. 27.1).

At the same time, recently, the geopolitical risk has increased a lot as a result of the events in Crimea in 2014 and after the start of the war in Ukraine in 2022.

Despite the high hydrocarbon potential of the region, the exploration activity of the last 5 years is less intense than expected, probably because of the risks associated (Anastasiu, 2019). According to Schlumberger data, it currently operates exploration wells only in the deep waters of Romania and Turkey, and a few in the shallow waters of Bulgaria (Schlumberger, 2021).

In the public debate in our country, a great emphasis was placed on the deposits in Romania's exclusive economic zone, and the debate was accompanied by great enthusiasm. The recent situation in Turkey regarding explorations in the Black Sea is, however, an example of the call to realism.

The Case of Romania

The Romanian offshore area covers 22,000 square kilometers, with over 1000 meters depths. This entire area has a diverse size of perimeters (Fig. 27.2), some of which are concessioned by the holders for exploration, development, and exploitation activities.

Thus, in 1975, the first marine drilling platform was installed off the Black Sea. Initially, the Ovidiu East well no. 1 was located in an area where the water had a depth of 84 meters. This platform was meant to cooperate in waters up to 90 meters depths and waves as high as 12 meters. The well was dug to a depth of 5006 meters,

27 How Romania May Benefit from the Natural Gas Resources' Offshore Exploitation... 331

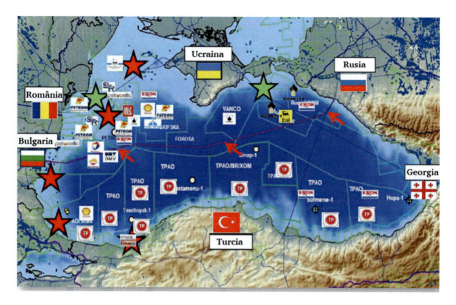

Fig. 27.1 Offshore exploration projects in the Black Sea. (Source: Rystad Energy, 2018)

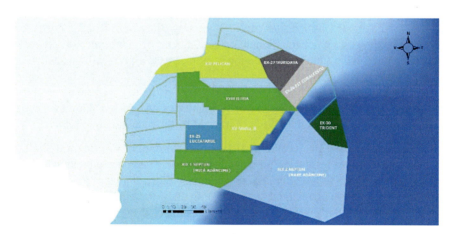

Fig. 27.2 Romanian exploration, development, and exploitation perimeters in the Black Sea. (Source: OMV, 2022)

from where it collected samples rich in geological information, which led to the first oil production in the Black Sea in 1987.

A second drilling was carried out in the XV Midia perimeter, the result being negative. Thus, a third location was chosen, in the XVIII Istria perimeter. Called Lebăda, the field is located in shallow waters of 50 meters deep, at 80 km NE of Constanța, and important crude oil deposits were found here.

As a result of these efforts, some of the exploration activities carried out in the last 30 years have resulted in hydrocarbon discoveries, the most important being the following: the Lebăda East fields (in production since 1987), Lebăda West (in production since 1993), Sinoe (in production since 1999, with the Gloria platform), Pescăruș (in production since 2003), and Delta (in production since 2009). Since their commissioning, these fields totaled 185 million barrels of crude oil, eight million barrels of condensate, and 48 billion cubic meters (bcm) of natural gas. After their long-time exploitation, some reserves are almost exhausted (for crude oil and condensate), while the remaining ones (for natural gas) reach about 6 bcm (OMV, 2021).

On the other hand, both in the perimeters mentioned above and in other perimeters, a significant number of wells were drilled, but they were not successful.

Considering the prospects of the current onshore fields (drastically decreasing potential), combined with those of the constantly high crude oil and natural gas consumption, it follows that in the absence of other options, Romania may be a net importer, as a great share of natural gas demand will be supplied by imports. Therefore, to safeguard energy security and to be a regional hub, the entire upstream sector must upgrade.

Thus, three alternatives were identified: the discovery of new onshore reserves of crude oil and gas; extraction by hydraulic fracturing; and exploitation of oil and gas proven reserves in the Black Sea, for it may play a major role in the European Union.

Among the three identified alternatives, exploiting Black Sea oil and gas reserves seems to be the best choice for Romania regarding energy independence and additional revenues to the state budget and job creation (these aspects will be dealt with in the following paragraphs).

In conclusion, deep offshore exploitations are essential to cover the demand for oil and gas in future. Such projects involve high costs and risks and are long-term investments. Moreover, their viability is affected by the reduction in oil prices.

Offshore Exploration Projects in the Black Sea Romanian Continental Shelf

Romania is the oldest oil and gas producer in the world, with an exploitation history of over a century, but today, after periods of intensive exploitation of these deposits, onshore production is in a natural decline. Fortunately, the offshore deposits in the continental shelf of the Black Sea are very promising, so they could bring Romania to the status of Norway. It depends on our authorities what we will do with these deposits: "they be either a bonanza (a treasure) or a Fata Morgana (a beautiful dream)" (Gaz de Romania, 2021).

In the last three years, there has been a wave of enthusiasm, optimism, and certainty in Romanian society regarding the potential of deep offshore natural gas in Romania's exclusive economic zone from the Black Sea. Not far from 7 to 8 years ago, the same optimism was manifested toward the exploitation of shale gas. But after the departure of those from Chevron, there was "a deafening silence."

Therefore, the next paragraphs will give a detailed analysis of the most important offshore exploration projects in the Black Sea Romanian continental shelf.

Fig. 27.3 Location for the Ana and Doina natural gas fields in the XV Midia Block (Source: BSOG, 2019)

27.2.1 Midia Natural Gas Development Project

Two significant discoveries were made in the XV Midia B perimeter, Doina (in 1995), and Ana (in 2008) (see Fig. 27.3), totaling 9.5 bcm of natural gas reserves. In the beginning, the Black Sea Oil & Gas Company (BSOG), as the operator of this project, had planned to start gas production from the Ana and Doina fields in the first quarter of 2021, but in November 2021, this deadline was postponed to June 2022 for the supply of the first gas production. Two significant discoveries were made in the XV Midia B perimeter, Doina (in 1995), and Ana (in 2008) (see Fig. 27.3), amounting 9.5 bcm of natural gas reserves.

Previously, however, on September 22, 2021, through a press release (BSOG, 2021), BSOG officials announced that they had installed the Ana platform for natural gas production, representing the first of this kind commissioned in Romania since 1990 (*Midia Natural Gas Development Project,* known as the "MGD Project"). The platform was successfully installed approximately 120 km from the shore, on the Ana field, in waters with a depth of 70 meters (BSOG, 2022a).

As a result, on Wednesday, June 15, 2022, BSOG and its concession partners (Petro Ventures Resources and Gas Plus Dacia) announced (BSOG, 2022b) the start of gas production from the Midia Gas Development and the introduction of the first gases into the National Transport System (SNTGN) (Transgaz, 2022).

With an estimated reserve of around 10 bcm of natural gas, the expected annual production is 1 bcm, which is equivalent to 10% of Romania's gas consumption (Romgaz, 2022). Since a few years ago, half of the production is already accounted for by the French from ENGIE, which distributes and supplies gas throughout the southern half of the country. Putting this project into operation represents an important step that was taken toward supplying Romania with Romanian gas. The MGD project is now 70% completed.

This project in the Black Sea continental shelf is proof of the great chance Romania has to gain independence in terms of natural gas and therefore to reduce its reliance on imported gas (mainly from Russia, supplied by GAZPOM).

Moreover, the implementation and development of the MGD Project allow other natural gas deposits to be discovered in the Black Sea Romanian continental shelf by other concessionaires, aiming at the use of natural gas as a transition fuel toward green energy production.

27.2.2 Neptune Deep Offshore Project

Despite a relatively long history of offshore production in shallow waters, the first deep discovery in the Black Sea was made no earlier than 2012. But how did it get here?

In 2008, OMV Petrom and ExxonMobil established a joint venture to explore the Neptune block in the deep-sea area of the Black Sea, in a perimeter covering about 7500 square kilometers, where water depths vary between 100 and 1700 meters (OMV, 2016).

Thus, in March 2012, the two partners announced the discovery of recoverable resources estimated between 42 and 84 bcm of natural gas in the XIX 2 Neptune (Deep) perimeter. This is why the Neptune Deep project represents OMV Petrom's long-term development commitment (OMV, 2022). In this sense, Neptune Deep stands now as a great opportunity for the company.

During 2008–2016, exploration and evaluation activities were carried out in the Neptune Deep block. In 2012, the exploration well Domino 1, the first exploration well in the deep area in Romania's territorial waters, identified natural gas reserves. Later, in January 2016, the explorations of the Romanian deepwater sector of the Black Sea were completed, and a successful test of one well was also recorded on the Domino structure.

On December 21, 2018, the Romanian Government approved the extension of the exploration licenses for Block XIX Neptune (Black Sea, Offshore). Thus, once the production activity starts in the Neptune Deep perimeter, provided commercial viability is confirmed, the regional expansion will represent an important way of capitalizing on the natural gas from the offshore area of the Black Sea.

The investments made only in the period 2008–2016 exceeded $1.5 billion, of which 50% were made by OMV Petrom.

Unfortunately, as early as July 2019, ExxonMobil announced to its Romanian partner the intention to sell 50% company's share in the Neptune Deep perimeter, aiming at getting out from Romania (ExxonMobil, 2019). This decision to abandon the Black Sea project was a result of the hostile offshore legislation at the time, which was seen as unacceptable both because of the high taxation and the imposition of cumbersome approval procedures.

At the same time, ExxonMobil also announced the discovery of huge hydrocarbon deposits in other areas, including Cyprus, where the gas reserve in the Glaucus perimeter is three times bigger than that of the Black Sea, and decided to concentrate its financial resources on projects where the company's analysts forecast more secure revenues.

Except for the Americans from BSOG, no other firm with a license in the Black Sea has made the final decision to start gas production in the Black Sea. Eight years after the first gas discoveries, the fields are unexploited and several investors are leaving. Even OMV Petrom stated that it may take the final decision to invest in the Neptune Deep Project only in 2023, depending on the legislative changes in Romania (amending the offshore law, first of all) and the market situation.

Hence, on March 30, 2021, Romgaz submitted a binding offer to take over the Romanian subsidiary of ExxonMobil, an offer initially not made public. On June 17, 2021, the two companies signed an Exclusivity Agreement by which the seller granted Romgaz an exclusivity right for 4 months, until October 15, 2021; later, the deadline was extended until November 15, 2021 (Romgaz, 2021).

In the end, on Friday, December 10, 2021, for 1.060 billion euros, Romgaz shareholders approved the takeover of the American stake from ExxonMobil in the Neptune Deep gas exploitation project from the Black Sea, as stated in a press release of the company published on the Bucharest Stock Exchange (BVB) (Romgaz, 2021). The purchase price can be adjusted positively by no more than ten million dollars.

Romgaz shareholders also approved the contracting of a 325 million euro loan to cover part of the purchase amount. At the same time, it was initially estimated that the transaction between Romgaz and ExxonMobil would be completed in the first quarter of 2022.

The consulting company Rystad estimates (Oil & Gas Journal, 2022) that, with Romgaz as a new partner in the project, a final investment decision may be adopted in 2023, while production may begin at the end of 2026 or early in 2027. As a result, starting from a production of 8.7 bcm of natural gas in 2020, according to a Romgaz report [Romgaz, 2021], Romania may get to 14–15 bcm of natural gas per year in the period 2027–2029, after starting production in Neptune Deep and the other offshore perimeters. With a consumption of about 10 to 12 bcm of natural gas per year, *Romania may gain its independence from Russian gas and even export almost a quarter of its domestic production, and this represents the huge benefit of involving in such a giant offshore project!*

There are, however, risks that this transaction brings to the company's activity. The main nine risks vary from the decrease in dividends due to shareholders, exchange rate, the reduced possibility to focus on other investments, including those related to decarbonization, the instability of the fiscal framework, the uncertainty of a final investment decision, and up to the risk that Romgaz will not receive on time the money for the gas delivered to the thermal power plants (CETs)—which has also happened in the past.

As part of the new consortium that will be formed in the development of the Neptune Deep Project, OMV Petrom has announced that it will act as the Operator of the Neptune Deep perimeter, exploiting gas from the Black Sea (Veit, 2021), as ExxonMobil accepted Romgaz's offer. The position of operator of the project is an essential one, and Romgaz expressed its desire to take over the operation, but in the end, the two companies came to the conclusion that OMV Petrom has more experience.

However, operating an offshore production project is extremely complicated compared to onshore projects due to special conditions (Allen, 2019). It is recognized that Romgaz has no experience in this respect, while OMV Petrom is involved in such projects in Bulgaria and, recently, in Georgia, without having experience in deep offshore exploitations. The company operating the project leads the operations, i.e., the preparation of the drilling campaign, logistics, and possible interventions.

The potential development of the discovered resources (if they prove to be commercially viable) will involve additional investments of several billion dollars. In this respect, several variables must be taken into account: endogenous factors (such as gas volumes to be handled, concept of production methods, and exploitation costs) and exogenous factors (such as fiscal and legal framework and changes in the natural gas market—natural gas price, potential buyers, and network transport) (Beattie, 2021).

If commercial viability is confirmed, the Neptune Deep Project will contribute substantially to achieve the 100% reserve replacement rate goal at OMV Petrom and, at the same time, will help Romania increase its energy security.

27.3 Benefits of Implementing Offshore Projects in the Black Sea

The application of policies to exploit the oil and gas reserves discovered in the Black Sea Basin, similar to those applied in the North Sea by countries such as Norway, Great Britain, the Netherlands, Denmark, or Germany (to a lesser extent), gives Romania the potential to become one of the most important natural gas producing areas in the European Union (Iuga, 2015).

Moreover, these natural gas resources if proven commercially viable can help Romania to ensure a sustainable energy supply to achieve long-term decarbonization targets and to develop the national infrastructure or other industries with high added value, such as chemistry and petrochemicals.

Impact analyzes generally consider pilot projects for offshore hydrocarbon exploitations from the Black Sea starting from the characteristics of the deposits discovered by the companies that have carried out geological surveys in this area (OMV Petrom SA and Exxon Mobil Exploration & Production Romania Ltd., for the Neptune Deep perimeter, or BSOG and Lukoil, Pan Atlantic, and Romgaz, also for the continental platform of Romania—all three for gas fields).

This impact can be quantified, on the one hand, by *the investment volume*, which includes capital expenditures (decommissioning costs also) and operational expenditures (Kaiser & Snyder, 2018).

At the same time, *employment, revenues to the state budget, and macroeconomic indicators* (such as GDP and balance of payments) can be considered, on the other hand, as measures having multiple impacts (direct, indirect, and induced) on the Romanian economy, also included in the impact study (RRU, 2004; Stantec, 2012; Deloitte, 2017).

In offshore projects, the cost may be affected by several factors (OCD, 2010) including water depth, well depth, field size, exploitation platform's distance from the shore, and also pressures and temperatures in the field. According to some estimates (Kaiser, 2019b), between 40% and 50% of the capital expenditure corresponds to drilling and completion work, out of which almost half of drilling and completion costs are related to facility leasing, while the remainder is allocated to equipment, logistics, engineering services, and consumables (Dudău, 2014)

For major offshore projects, up to 80% of drilling and completion costs heavily depend on time (Kreutzer, 2018). Hence, if the time to complete the work may be shortened, this will help to significantly reduce costs (Brun et al., 2020). Moreover, the drilling itself consumes a greater share of the well's total costs in offshore projects than in onshore ones (Hossain, 2020).

Thus, *the cumulative value of investments* in offshore natural gas exploration, development, and production was estimated (Deloitte, 2018) at $22.2 billion, of which $15.7 billion will represent capital expenditure (CAPEX) and 6.5 $ billion will represent operational expenditures (OPEX). Of the total investments, a share of 63% will be spent in the Romanian economy, out of which 54% for CAPEX and 82% for OPEX.

These investments may support over 30,500 employees per year during the entire period, thus leading to the generation of *additional cumulative revenues* of $26 billion to the state budget, as well as an additional cumulative contribution of $71.3 billion to the production of goods and services between 2020 and 2040.

All in one, it results that every $1 billion spent on offshore natural gas projects may lead to the following:

- The job creation of about 2200 full-time jobs between 2020 and 2040;
- The cumulative increase in revenues to the national budget of about $2 billion between 2020 and 2040;
- The cumulative GDP growth of $3 billion between 2020 and 2040.

Investment volume can be also estimated by measuring CAPEX and OPEX for the exploration, development, and production phases over the total span of a project

(Lioudis, 2021). Capital expenditure also takes into account decommissioning costs at the end of a project (Kaiser, 2019a).

Moreover, important expenses may be incurred in the development and production operation, representing over 74% of the overall coming investments. Under these conditions, *the share of investments made in the Romanian economy will represent 63% of the total future expenses.*

Moreover, it is estimated that between 2020 and 2040 (Deloitte, 2018), offshore projects will involve, on average, more than 700 employees each year, for the entire period. The creation of these new jobs can indirectly support over 22,500 jobs provided by the concessionaires' suppliers of goods and services. Also, the impact that expenses of concessionaires' employees, but also of suppliers may have, will lead to the support of another about 7200 jobs in various other industries and sectors of activity.

Moreover, as previously mentioned, the Black Sea developments will contribute an additional $71.3 billion to Romania's production of goods and services and jobs equivalent to more than 700,000 work years, many of which are paid above the national average.

The fees and taxes from the concessionaires' offshore projects will contribute significantly to Romania's national budget. For the period 2020–2040, the total revenues to the state budget generated as a result of offshore exploitations may reach $26 billion (of which over $5.5 billion in the form of royalties), most of the tax contributions coming from paying profit tax and social security contributions (Iuga & Dudău, 2018).

These estimated results do not include the income that the Romanian state, as a shareholder in companies operating in offshore projects (e.g., OMV Petrom or Romgaz), could obtain additionally from the dividends distributed to their shareholders and the impact of the state's expenses from the distribution of these dividends.

The direct impact of offshore projects on revenues to the state budget, resulting from tax contributions, may rise up to $12 billion. These contributions mainly consist of royalties and profit tax that concessionaires have to pay.

The indirect impact may rise to over $10 billion and consists mainly of social security contributions, income tax paid by individuals, and taxes on products (VAT and excises). Additionally, it can propagate in the economy an *induced impact* by expenses incurred by direct employees and supplier employees. These contributions will amount to $3.7 billion and represent, mainly, contributions to social security and taxes on products (VAT and excises).

Moreover, the amount of $26 billion represents the cumulative revenues to the state budget, paid by concessionaires following the development of offshore projects between 2020 and 2040 (Deloitte, 2018), in the conditions in which it is estimated that *$1 spent in Romania in the framework of offshore projects will generate revenues to the state budget of $1.9.*

The multiplier effect is another issue that must be considered to calculate the impact on GDP. As it was calculated, for GDP the multiplier is 3 to 1; i.e., *for $1 spent on Black Sea projects, $3 of GDP may be generated in the Romanian* *economy.* Moreover, if the entire analyzed period is taken into account, the highest impact on the production of goods and services is the development and production operation stages.

27.4 Conclusions

At the end of the analysis, concerning *the economic spillover effects of offshore investments from the Black Sea,* we must emphasize that the development of these projects should create new opportunities for other Romanian industries as well, contributing to their return to previous economic performance levels or to the development of new products and services for the economy.

In this respect, the centralizing data given in Table 27.1 reflect the use of natural gas as fuel and raw material for certain industries and various products with major contributions to any developed economy.

As such, the substantial development of upstream activities in the Black Sea presents significant opportunities for economic growth, as well-paid jobs and foreign direct investments may bring Romania multiple competitive advantages over other countries in the region, but also over other EU member states with a similar level of development.

In conclusion, large-scale investment and implementation of upstream projects in the Black Sea Romanian continental shelf can undoubtedly bring sustained growth in the economy, with multiple impacts (direct, indirect, and induced) on job creation, state budget revenues, and production of goods and services, thus significantly contributing to the country's economic well-being, its energy security, and the transition to a low-carbon economy.

Table 27.1 Spillover effects of offshore investments on the Romanian economy between 2020 and 2040

Indicator	UM	Value
Cumulative investments in the midstream, downstream, and other industries	Billion $	8,9
Average number of employees over the entire period in the midstream, downstream, and other industries	Number	41,995
Revenues to the state budget generated in the midstream, downstream, and other industries	Billion $	18.3
Production of aggregated goods and services generated in the midstream, downstream, and other industries	Billion $	98.9

Source: Own calculations

References

Allen, B. (2019, November 30). *How offshore oil and gas production benefits the economy and the environment*. Backgrounder – The Heritage Foundation.

Anastasiu, N. (2019, Aprilie 12). *Hydrocarbons in the Black Sea - between challenges and risks*. Academica.

Beattie, A. (2021, June 25). *The economics of oil extraction*. Investopedia.

Brun, A., Aerts, G. & Jerkø, M. (2020, May). *How to achieve 50% reduction in offshore drilling costs. Oil & Gas Practice*. McKinsey Company.

BSOG. (2019). Midia gas development project additional environmental and social information and assessment report. Document Number: MGD-E-EERM-EN-REP4–004-D1, 16 April. Retrieved from https://www.bstdb.org/Additional-ESIA-English.pdf

BSOG. (2021). Black sea oil & gas completes the installation of the Ana gas production platform in the Black Sea. Bucharest, Romania, 22 September. Retrieved from https://www.blackseaog.com/black-sea-oil-gas-completes-the-installation-of-the-ana-gas-production-platform-in-the-black-sea/

BSOG. (2022a). *The Midia Gas Development Project*. Retrieved from https://www.blackseaog.com/midia-gas-development/

BSOG. (2022b). *Black sea oil & gas first gas from the MGD project*. Bucharest, Romania, 15 June. Retrieved from https://www.blackseaog.com/black-sea-oil-gas-delivers-first-gas-from-the-mgd-project/

Deloitte. (2017, April 23). An overview on royalties and similar taxes. The upstream sector of oil and natural gas in Europe.

Deloitte. (2018, May). The contribution of Black Sea oil & gas projects to the development of the Romanian economy.

Dudău, R. (2014). *The oil and gas industry in Romania: Tradition and strategic opportunity*. Energy Policy Group.

ExxonMobil. (2019). 2019 Analyst Meeting.

Gaz de România (2021, March 29). Natural gas deposits in the Black Sea: Bonanza or fata morgana?.

Hossain, M. E. (2020, September). Drilling costs estimation for hydrocarbon Wells. *Journal for Sustainable Energy Engineering, 3*(1).

Iuga, V. (2015, June). *The challenges of deep offshore mining. The situation of the Black Sea*. Energy Policy Group.

Iuga, V., & Dudău, R. (2018, September 15). *Risks, taxation, investment decisions in the offshore oil and gas sector. Black Sea and Romania*. Oil and Gas Employers' Federation.

Kaiser, M. J. (2019a). *Decommissioning forecasting and operating cost estimation*. Gulf Professional Publishing.

Kaiser, M. J. (2019b). Modelling the time and cost to drill an offshore well. *Energy*.

Kaiser, M. J., & Snyder, B. (2018). Capital investment and operational decision making in the offshore contract drilling industry. *The Engineering Economist, 58*(1).

Kreutzer, D. (2018). *The economic case for drilling oil reserves, environment*. The Heritage Foundation.

Lioudis, N. (2021, July 21). How do average costs compare among various oil drilling rigs?. *Investopedia*.

Moroșanu, I. (2012). The hydrocarbon potential of the Romanian Black Sea continental plateau. *Romanian Journal of Earth Sciences, Second Edition, 86*.

Offshore Center Denmark – OCD. (2010). *Offshore Book, an introduction to the offshore industry*.

Oil & Gas Journal. (2022). Romgaz to buy ExxonMobil Romanian affiliate for $1 billion, May 9. Retrieved from https://www.ogj.com/general-interest/article/14276589/ogj-newsletter

Royal Roads University – RRU. (2004). *British Columbia offshore oil and gas*. Socio-Economic Issue Papers.

Rystad Energy (2018, May 1). Global offshore industry looks ready to turn the corner toward growth. *Offshore*.

Schlumberger. (2021). Schlumberger Annual Report 2021, 27 January. Retrieved from https://www.annualreports.com/HostedData/AnnualReports/PDF/NYSE_SLB_2021.pdf

SN OMV Petrom SA. (2016-2021). Annual Report, 2016–2021.

SN OMV Petrom SA. (2022). OMV Group Report January–September and Q3 2022, October 28.

SNGN Romgaz SA. (2016–2021). Annual Report, 2016-2021.

SNGN Romgaz SA. (2022, November 16). ROMGAZ 9M/Q3 2022 results - group overview.

SNTGN Transgaz SA. (2022). Development Plan for the National Gas Transmission System 2021–2030, January 2nd.

Stantec. (2012, June 5). Socio-economic benefits from petroleum industry activity in Newfoundland and Labrador, 2008–2010. *Petroleum Research*.

Veit, Ch. (2021, July 11). OMV Petrom targeting regional growth in the Black Sea area. *Energy Industry Review*.

Chapter 28
Application of Machine Learning Techniques in Natural Gas Price Modeling. Analyses, Comparisons, and Predictions for Romania

Stelian Stancu, Alexandru Isaic-Maniu, Constanța-Nicoleta Bodea, Mihai Sabin Muscalu, and Denisa Elena Bălă

Abstract The current global energy crisis is an important topic, which emphasizes the need to study the natural gas market, with appropriate modeling methods, for a proper substantiation of the public policies. The specialized literature is generous in terms of the analyses carried out on the electricity market, but the natural gas market is not a subject fully exploited by researchers; therefore, this article represents an important contribution to knowledge in the field. This article analyses the natural gas market in Romania between November 2016 and September 2022, using data collected daily, representing the weighted average daily price of natural gas. The research is carried out with the help of advanced machine learning methods, namely, a series of basic algorithms (models), but also three categories of ensemble learning methods (bagging, boosting, and stacking). It was found that the price of natural gas in Romania can be estimated with high accuracy, using decision tree (DT) algorithms or with the help of artificial neural networks (ANNs). However, ensemble learning-based modeling proves to be the best estimation method, characterized by reduced prediction errors compared to basic models.

S. Stancu · C.-N. Bodea (✉)
Informatics and Economic Cybernetics Department, Bucharest University of Economic Studies, Bucharest, Romania

Centre for Industry and Services Economics, "Costin C. Kiritescu" National Institute for Economic Research, Romanian Academy, Bucharest, Romania
e-mail: bodea@ase.ro

A. Isaic-Maniu · M. S. Muscalu
Centre for Industry and Services Economics, "Costin C. Kiritescu" National Institute for Economic Research, Romanian Academy, Bucharest, Romania
e-mail: alexandru.isaic@csie.ase.ro

D. E. Bălă
Bucharest University of Economic Studies, Bucharest, Romania
e-mail: baladenisa16@stud.ase.ro

© The Author(s), under exclusive license to Springer Nature Switzerland AG 2024
L. Chivu et al. (eds.), *Constraints and Opportunities in Shaping the Future: New Approaches to Economics and Policy Making*, Springer Proceedings in Business and Economics, https://doi.org/10.1007/978-3-031-47925-0_28

Keywords Natural gas market · Price prediction · Commodity price shock · Machine learning · Ensemble modeling · Python environment

28.1 Introduction

Natural gas represents one of the main sources of energy globally and plays a key role in social and economic development. It is considered an energy source with the potential to reduce environmental problems. Romania has an important energy advantage compared to other countries, benefiting from the exploitation of natural gas, which provides a good part of the resource requirements, and having a history of over a century regarding the exploitation of these deposits.

The studies related to the price of natural gas are still not so numerous, compared to those aimed at the consumption of natural gas. Classical econometric techniques represent the main means of analyzing the evolution of natural gas prices. Numerous machine learning techniques have been designed to facilitate the modeling and interpretation of data, and their applications prove useful in the most varied fields. In recent years, with the rapid development of various industries, the demand for energy has increased proportionally, which has also determined the increase in the prices of energy sources.

The identification of appropriate models for forecasting the price of natural gas could thus prove to be a suitable solution for both governments and investors, who can use these models as tools based on which to base their different policies and possibly reduce their risks. The data provided by ANRE indicate that Romania ranks first when it comes to the size of the natural gas market in Central Europe. Moreover, Romania was the first country to introduce the use of natural gas in the industrial field.

The structure of the article is as follows: At the beginning, a study of the specialized literature was carried out. The following section is dedicated to the exposition of the methods and data used in the research. Afterward, the results of the research are presented, and the work ending with the main conclusions and the bibliographic sources is used.

28.2 Literature Review

The price of natural gas is a debated topic in specialized literature, considering that after oil and coal, natural gas is the third most used energy commodity (Čeperić et al., 2017). The price of natural gas is influenced by several external factors, represented by geopolitical events, economic shocks, or oil price fluctuations. Price bubbles are reported on the markets of the European Union, the USA, and Asia. (Shi & Shen, 2021). Natural gas price movements have implications for market players, whether they are consumers, producers, distributors, or investors.

Analyzing the specialized literature, it is noted that forecasting the price and consumption of natural gas are topics of interest for researchers (Zhou et al., 2020; Qiao et al., 2020; Liu et al., 2021). Machine learning algorithms have become increasingly popular as natural gas price forecasting methods, including support vector machines or artificial neural networks (Chen et al., 2004).

Salehnia et al. (2013) focus on natural gas price using artificial neural networks, dynamic local linear regression (DLLR), and local linear regression (LLR) using the Gamma test. The obtained results indicate the high performance of artificial neural networks compared to the other two methods.

The comparison between traditional econometric methods and machine learning techniques is addressed by Herrera et al. (2019) in an analysis regarding the price of natural gas and oil. They highlight the increased accuracy of machine learning models compared to established econometric models. Wang et al. (2020) propose the construction of hybrid models for the purpose of forecasting the price of natural gas.

Su et al. (2019) also apply machine learning methods for natural gas price forecasting. The applied models include regression based on Gaussian processes (GBM), support vector machines (SVM), gradient boosting machine (GBM), and artificial neural networks (ANNs). Their results indicate an increased performance of ANN compared to other methods. The indicators regarding the prediction errors (MAE, MSE, and RMSE) record the lowest values in the case of the ANN application, while the regression based on Gaussian processes performs the worst in terms of forecasting. SVM is also a model that provides good results in forecasting the price of natural gas.

Another analysis was performed by Zhang and Hamori (2020), which researches the US market also using machine learning models. ANN, SVM, decision trees, XGBoost, and logistic regression algorithms are compared. The results reveal the superiority of the XGBoost algorithm compared to the other methods considered. The price of natural gas is investigated by Jiang et al. (2021), based on a variational decomposition model. The predictions made are proved to be more stable and more rigorous.

The UK and US natural gas markets are researched by Pavićević and Popović (2022), who propose a maximal overlap discrete wavelet transform (MODWT) decomposition technique, combined with an ensemble machine learning algorithm. It is noticeable in both countries the existence of persistent trends. The price forecast is tracked over two time horizons, a horizon prior to the COVID-19 pandemic and a horizon framed during the pandemic period. The accuracy of the prediction is superior in the pre-pandemic stage in the case of the UK, while in the case of the USA, the prediction results are better during the pandemic. Therefore, the authors indicate that the COVID-19 pandemic cannot be identified as a key driver of future natural gas prices.

Ensemble models improve predictions by building superior, accurate, and robust models starting from several base models. Zhao et al. (2017) use such an approach, based on the bagging method with the help of which the price of electricity is forecast using multiple ANN models. Bhatia et al. (2020) use bagging aggregation to improve the accuracy of electricity price forecasting.

28.3 Methodology

Prior to the construction of the machine learning models, the data standardization procedure was completed, so that all the values in the considered dataset were brought into the range [0,1], with the help of the MinMaxScaler function from the scikit-learn library in the Python environment. The data on which this research is based were collected from the website of the National Natural Gas Transport Company and represent time series collected with a daily periodicity regarding the weighted average price of natural gas, further represented by means of the notation y_i. The analyzed time horizon is between November 1, 2016, and September 30, 2022, which led to a number of 2159 observations.

28.3.1 Linear Regression (LR)

The equation of the regression line can be expressed as follows:

$$Y = \beta_0 + \beta_1 X + \varepsilon \tag{28.1}$$

where

Y represents the target variable (dependent variable).
X represents an explanatory vector variable (independent variable).
β_0 represents the free term (the intercept).
β_1 represents the vector of the estimated coefficients of the explanatory variables
ε represents the prediction error (noise).

28.3.2 Support Vector Machines (SVMs)

The class of machine learning algorithms dedicated to supervised learning also includes the SVM algorithm, used both in classification problems and in regression problems.

We consider the following set of form:

$$\theta = \{(y_1, x_1), (y_2, x_2), \ldots, (y_i, x_i), \ldots (y_n, x_n)\} \epsilon\, Y \times X \tag{28.2}$$

where y_i represents a vector in space R^n, and x_i can take the values -1 or 1, designating the class in which each shape point is assigned y_i.

The SVM-type classifier seeks to identify a hyperplane that separates the two classes. Such a separating hyperplane is expressed as follows:

$$\langle w, y \rangle + b = \sum_{i=1}^{N} w_i y_i + b = 0 \qquad (28.3)$$

where

w represents the normal vector that establishes the orientation of the hyperplane.
b represents the bias.

The SVM-type model must identify the vector associated with the weights, $w = (w_1, w_2, \ldots, w_n)$ and b—hyperplane bias.

The hyperplane of the form $(w; b)$ is associated with the following function on the basis of which to define the separation of entities into classes:

$$h_{w,b}(y) = \operatorname{sgn}\{<w,y> + b\} = \begin{cases} +1, \text{if } \langle w, y \rangle + b > 0 \\ 0, \text{if } \langle w, y \rangle + b = 0 \\ -1, \text{if } \langle w, y \rangle + b < 0 \end{cases} \qquad (28.4)$$

28.3.3 Decision Tree (DT)

Decision tree is also part of the supervised learning algorithms, allowing predictions to be made. Regression trees follow recursive binary partitioning, so that the dataset is repeatedly divided into partitions, which in turn will be divided into smaller and smaller partitions.

28.3.4 Artificial Neural Networks (ANNs)

The simplest feedforward neural network model with a single output neuron (the simple perceptron) can be expressed as follows: whether $u_1, u_2, u_3, \ldots, u_j, \ldots, u_m$ a series of m values of input type. Each input will be assigned a weight $w_1, w_2, w_3, \ldots, w_m$, and a variable z is calculated (combination function) by summing the inputs $u_1, u_2, u_3, \ldots, u_m$ multiplied by the weights $w_1, w_2, w_3, \ldots, w_m$.

$$z = u_1 w_1 + u_2 w_2 + u_3 w_3 + \ldots + u_j w_j + \ldots + u_m w_m = \sum_{j=1}^{m} u_j w_j \qquad (28.5)$$

The output is calculated in the form of an activation (transfer) function of the form:

$$y = f(z) = \sum_{i=1}^{m} u_j w_j \quad (28.6)$$

In the case of the present analysis, the output is a vector and is calculated in the form of an activation (transfer) function of the form:

$$y_i = f(z_i) = \sum_{j=1}^{m} u_j w_{ji} \quad (28.7)$$

where $i = \overline{1, N}$ (and $N = 2159$, in this study).

28.3.5 Ensemble Learning Methods

Ensemble learning is a machine learning modeling technique that usually involves obtaining a prediction model with superior performance, starting from a series of basic models. In other words, ensemble learning aims to define a precise and robust prediction model, based on weaker models (*"weak learners"*).

Three categories of ensemble learning methods are considered the most important, namely bagging, boosting, and stacking. The bagging (or bootstrap aggregating)-type classifier is a meta-algorithm that estimates a series of basic models in relation to random subsamples of the initial dataset and performs an aggregation of the predictions made toward a final prediction, considered more accurate and robust.

Starting from the initial dataset, a number of M subsamples are obtained through the bootstrap random sampling technique, used in training the individual models. The prediction obtained based on the bagging-type method can be formalized as follows:

- For each subsample $i = \overline{1, M}$, the output is calculated, and therefore, the output at the bagging level is of the form:

$$y_{Bagging}^{M}(x) = \frac{1}{M} \sum_{i=1}^{M} y_i(x) \quad (28.8)$$

where $y_i(x)$ represents the output at the subsample level i.

In the case of classification problems, the result of the prediction is represented by the average probability of the observations belonging to a certain class, while in the context of regression, the prediction calculated as the average value of the individual predictions is obtained.

Boosting is an ensemble learning method that works on the same principle as bagging. Among the most used boosting models are AdaBoost (adaptive boosting), gradient boosting machine (GBM), or extreme gradient boosting (XGBoost). In this work, the gradient boosting machine method was used, a generalization of AdaBoost. The relation that defines the mean-squared error is given by the form:

$$\text{MSE} = \frac{1}{N}\sum_{i=1}^{N}(y_i - \hat{y}_i)^2 \qquad (28.9)$$

where

$\hat{y}_i$ represents the predicted value.
y_i represents the observed (actual) value.
N represents the number of observations.

For $j = \overline{1, K}$ is calculated as follows:

$$\hat{y}_{i,j+1} = \hat{y}_{i,j} + h_{i,j} = y_i \text{ sau } h_{i,j} = y_i - \hat{y}_{i,j} \qquad (28.10)$$

The aim is to minimize the loss function L_{MSE} defined as follows:

$$\min_{\hat{y}_i} L_{\text{MSE}} = \frac{1}{N}\sum_{i=1}^{N}(y_i - \hat{y}_i)^2 \qquad (28.11)$$

From the first order conditions (FOC) of the minimization problem, the results are given as:

$$\frac{\partial L_{\text{MSE}}}{\partial \hat{y}_i} = 0. \text{It results } \frac{2}{N}\sum_{i=1}^{N}(y_i - \hat{y}_i) = \frac{2}{N}h_{i,j} \qquad (28.12)$$

The third ensemble learning method is stacking, in which weak but heterogeneous algorithms are trained. They are aggregated into a meta-model that will provide the final predictions. The present study used the SVM, linear regression, and artificial neural networks as basic models, and the random forest model was selected as the meta-algorithm.

The predictions made by the basic models serve as inputs for the meta-algorithm, based on which the final predictions are returned. Performance evaluation of the considered Machine LearningMachine Learning models for this research, as the quality of the modeling was evaluated with the help of three indicators, namely: the coefficient of determination (R^2), mean absolute error (MAE) and respectively the mean squared error (MSE).

The coefficient of determination indicates the proportion in which the variance of the dependent variable (the target variable) is explained by means of the independent variables.

$$R^2 = 1 - \frac{\sum_{i=1}^{N}(y_i - \hat{y}_i)^2}{\sum_{i=1}^{N}(y_i - \overline{y})^2} \qquad (28.13)$$

where

$\hat{y}_i$ represents the predicted value of y_i.
$\bar{y}$ represents the average value of the variable y.

The mean absolute error (MAE) is defined according to the relationship:

$$\text{MAE} = \frac{1}{N}\sum_{i=1}^{N}|y_i - \hat{y}_i| \qquad (28.14)$$

The mean-squared error (MSE) indicates how close the points in a dataset are to the regression line:

$$\text{MSE} = \frac{1}{N}\sum_{i=1}^{N}(y_i - \hat{y}_i)^2 \qquad (28.15)$$

The root-mean-square error is calculated according to the formula:

$$\text{RMSE} = \sqrt{\frac{\sum_{i=1}^{N}(y_i - \hat{y}_i)^2}{N}} \qquad (28.16)$$

28.4 Analysis/Result Interpretation

The present analysis is focused on the price of natural gas in Romania, it is modeled with the help of machine learning methods, namely a series of basic models, as well as through ensemble learning. The performance of these models was evaluated according to the coefficient of determination (R^2), mean absolute error (MAS), mean-squared error (MSE), and the root-mean-square error (RMSE).

For a better understanding of the dataset, previously the associated descriptive statistics were highlighted. We find that the dataset consists of a total of 2159 observations. On average, at the level of Romania, the price of natural gas registered 143.7 lei/MWh in the period November 2016-September 2022

The minimum price in the analyzed period reached 26.5 lei/MWh, while the maximum of the period was 1175 lei/MWh. It is noted that the maximum price reached was more than eight times higher compared to the average of the analyzed period. If we refer to the minimum price corresponding to the analyzed horizon, the maximum value is approximately 45 times higher than the minimum price.

Therefore, the weighted average daily price of natural gas was characterized by significant movements, especially in the last two years, out of the approximately six analyzed (Fig. 28.1).

The daily evolution regarding the average price of natural gas in Romania can be appreciated according to the graph in Fig. 28.2. The trend is predominantly upward, but what is noteworthy is the fact that starting with 2021, the price of natural gas suffered several shocks represented by increases and decreases sudden, successive.

Mean	143.717964
Standard Error	2.99147042
Median	81.9
Mode	7
Standard Deviation	138.998794
Sample Variance	19320.6649
Kurtosis	5.94957547
Skewness	2.31101559
Range	1149.2
Minimum	26.5
Maximum	1175.7
Sum	310287.085
Count	215

Fig. 28.1 Statistics on natural gas prices. (Processing by the authors, using the data: Transgaz and OPCOM)

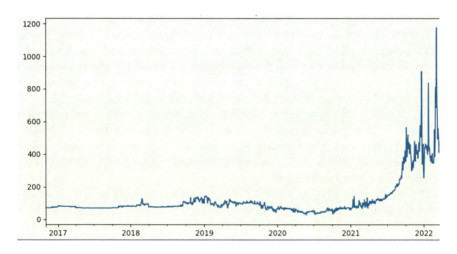

Fig. 28.2 Daily natural gas price series. (Processing by the authors, using the data: Transgaz and OPCOM)

The maximum of the analyzed value is recorded in 2022, exceeding the threshold of 1175 lei/MWh. Before 2021, price variations were quite low.

According to the histogram graph in Fig. 28.3, we can appreciate the distribution of observations from the analyzed dataset. In principle, the gas price came close to the average of the analyzed period, but the asymmetry to the right also indicates the numerous situations in which the daily price exceeded the recorded average values.

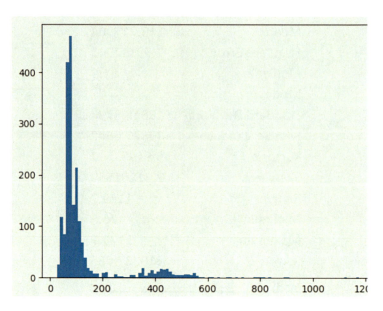

Fig. 28.3 Histogram of gas price. (Processing by the authors, using the data: Transgaz and OPCOM)

A common aspect in building machine learning models is that of dividing the dataset into two subsamples. One subset of the data is dedicated to training (learning) the model, while the second subset is dedicated to testing (validating) the model. For the models considered in this research, 80% of the observations were included in the training set, while the remaining 20% constituted the test set, the distribution of the observations in the two subsamples being done randomly.

In Table 28.1, the estimation results of the considered machine learning models are shown. Four metrics were selected to be able to make comparisons regarding the accuracy/performance of the models. More precisely, we refer to the coefficient of determination (R^2), mean absolute error (MAE), mean-squared error (MSE), and the root-mean-square error (RMSE).

The results shown below show the accuracy of the forecast made on the subsample dedicated to testing (validation). First, the performance of the basic machine learning models can be observed, namely the DT, ANN, SVM, and LR models. The last three lines of Table 28.1 are dedicated to highlight the measures regarding the accuracy of the ensemble models.

It is noted that among the basic models, the best performance corresponds to the decision tree (DT) model, for which the accuracy/performance indicators record the best values. The determination coefficient is high, while the error metrics are the lowest. In second place are the artificial neural networks, with high performance as well. Among the basic models, the worst prediction in terms of accuracy/performance is made with the help of the linear regression model.

Table 28.1 Coefficient of determination and measures of errors obtained

Model	R^2	MAE	MSE	RMSE
Base machine learning models				
Decision tree (DT)	0.878	0.019	0.003	0.054
Artificial neural networks (ANNs)	0.853	0.02	0.004	0.063
Support vector machines (SVMs)	0.803	0.038	0.005	0.070
Linear regression (LR)	0.761	0.055	0.016	0.126
Ensemble machine learning models				
Bagging model	0.891	0.015	0.012	0.109
Boosting model	0.899	0.011	0.01	0.1
Stacking model	0.912	0.009	0.008	0.089

Processing by the authors, using the data: Transgaz and OPCOM

Once the predictions have been made using the basic models, the problem arises researching the performance of ensemble learning models, identified in Table 28.1 as bagging model, boosting model, and stacking model. The ensemble models were designed on the following principle. The bagging model was based on the estimation of 100 decision trees, using 100 distinct subsamples generated using the bootstrapping technique. The decision trees were selected as a result of the individual performance achieved. In the present case, the coefficient of determination increases from 0.878 corresponding to the basic model to 0.891 in the case of ensemble modeling. In the case of ensemble learning from the boosting category, the gradient boosting model algorithm using decision trees was considered, its performance also being high. The MAE and MSE indicators register low values, which is desirable for a more accurate prediction.

The stacked model (stacking type) is still the best performing model, considering the considered accuracy/performance indicators. This model was built using artificial neural networks, support vector machines, and linear regression as basic models, while the decision tree algorithm was selected as a meta-algorithm to build the ensemble.

To highlight the impact of the number of iterations on the evolution of forecast errors, we will consider the decision tree-type model (whose individual performance was the highest), and we will further present, through Fig. 28.4, how the forecast errors change as the number of iterations increases. Note the inverse relationship between the number of iterations considered and the values associated with the forecasting error, both in the case of the training set and in the case of the test set, for the decision tree-type algorithm. As the number of iterations increases, the prediction errors decrease considerably, and the two curves tend to get closer and take on similar shapes.

Once we have analyzed the performance of the basic models as well as the performance of the ensemble models, the problem arises of making some predictions regarding the price of natural gas at the level of Romania, the target time horizon being between October 2022 and the end of December 2022. Thus, the ensemble learning model based on stacking is one of the bases on which the predictions were made (see Fig. 28.5).

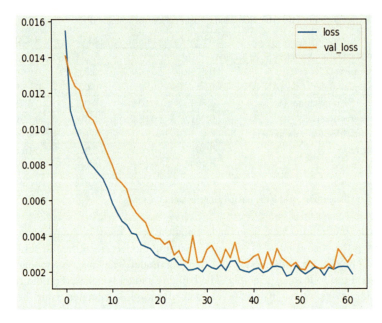

Fig. 28.4 Prediction errors in case of decision tree models. (Processing by the authors, using the data: Transgaz and OPCOM)

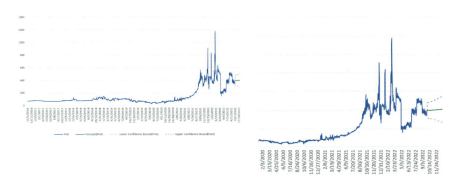

Fig. 28.5 Forecasting the price of natural gas in Romania using the model based on stacking. (Processing by the authors, using the data: Transgaz and OPCOM)

In the last three months of 2022, according to the predictions made, it is expected that in Romania, the average price of natural gas will stabilize. The estimates obtained based on the ensemble learning model indicate average monthly values of the average weighted daily price of approximately 421.2 lei/MWh in October, approximately 365.6 lei/MWh in November, and 436.5/MWh in December, 2022 The prediction was made assuming unchanged current economic, geopolitical, and environmental conditions.

28.5 Conclusions

The price of natural gas is a topic of major interest, considering the importance of this resource in most of the economic activities carried out worldwide. Conducting research by forecasting natural gas prices helps to optimize decision-making processes. Until now, the evolution of the price of natural gas has been explored mainly with the help of conventional econometric models, while advanced methods based on automatic learning have not been applied on a large scale.

The article makes a contribution to the specialized literature by analyzing the evolution of the price of natural gas in Romania and proposing the use of machine learning techniques in an attempt to model, estimate, and analyze the price of this energy source over a time horizon between November 1, 2016, and September 30, 2022, subsequently making a prediction regarding the weighted average price of natural gas in the period October 1, 2022-December 31, 2022. At the level of Romania, there is a sharp increase in the price of natural gas starting with the last quarter of 2021. Using the environment of Python programming, several machine learning models were used, namely decision trees, ANN, SVM, and classic linear regression model. Also, the research took into consideration of ensemble-type learning models.

The results of the research indicated that at the level of Romania, machine learning algorithms represent a reasonable method of predicting the price of natural gas. The metrics considered for evaluating the accuracy of the prediction ranked the decision tree algorithm as the best model, closely followed by ANN and SVM. These conclusions align with the results of other studies in the field (Zhang & Hamori, 2020; Pavićević & Popović, 2022). The construction of ensemble models represented a way of improving the quality of the prediction, considering the determined accuracy indicators. The aggregation of the basic models determines the reduction of prediction errors, regardless of the ensemble learning method that is used, in the present case, the stacking aggregation. According to the predictions made based on the stacking model, the weighted average price of natural gas in Romania is expected to stabilize until the end of 2022 and the beginning of 2023.

As a future direction of research, the development of "assembly of assemblies"-type models can be considered, in which several stacking-type models are aggregated.

References

Bhatia, K., Mittal, R., Tripathi, M. M., et al. (2020). A multi-phase ensemble model for long term hourly load forecasting. In *2020 IEEE 7th international conference on industrial engineering and applications (ICIEA)* (pp. 592–598). IEEE.

Čeperić, E., Žiković, S., & Čeperić, V. (2017). Short-term forecasting of natural gas prices using machine learning and feature selection algorithms. *Energy, 140*, 893–900.

Chen, B.-J., Chang, M.-W., & Lin, C.-J. (2004). Load forecasting using support vector machines: A study on EUNITE competition 2001. *IEEE Transactions on Power Systems, 19*(4), 1821–1830.

Herrera, G. P., Constantino, M., Tabak, B. M., Pistori, H., Su, J.-J., & Naranpanawa, A. (2019). Long-term forecast of energy commodities price using machine learning. *Energy, 179*, 214–221. https://doi.org/10.1016/j.energy.2019.04.077

Liu, C., Wu, W. Z., Xie, W., Zhang, T., & Zhang, J. (2021). Forecasting natural gas consumption of China by using a novel fractional grey model with time power term. *Energy Reports, 7*, 788–797.

OPCOM. (2022). Retrieved from OPCOM: https://www.opcom.ro/pp/home.php

Pavićević, M., & Popović, T. (2022). Forecasting day-ahead electricity metrics with artificial neural networks. *Sensors, 22*(3), 1051.

Qiao, W., Yang, Z., Kang, Z., & Pan, Z. (2020). Short-term natural gas consumption prediction based on Volterra adaptive filter and improved whale optimization algorithm. *Engineering Applications of Artificial Intelligence, 87*, 103323.

Salehnia, N., Falahi, M. A., Seifi, A., & Mahdavi Adeli, M. H. (2013). Forecasting natural gas spot prices with nonlinear modeling using Gamma test analysis. *Journal of Natural Gas Science and Engineering, 14*, 238–249.

Shi, X., & Shen, Y. (2021). Macroeconomic uncertainty and natural gas prices: Revisiting the Asian Premium. *Energy Economics, 94*.

Su, M., Zhang, Z., Zhu, Y., Zha, D., & Wen, W. (2019). Data driven natural gas spot price prediction models using machine learning methods. *Energies, 12*(9), 1680.

Transgaz. (2022). Retrieved from Transgaz: https://www.transgaz.ro/

Wang, J., Lei, C., & Guo M. (2020). Daily natural gas price forecasting by a weighted hybrid data-driven model. *Journal of Petroleum Science and Engineering, 192*, 107240. https://doi.org/10.1016/j.petrol.2020.107240

Zhang, W., & Hamori, S. (2020). Do machine learning techniques and dynamic methods help forecast US natural gas crises? *Energies, 13*(9), 2371.

Zhao, Z., Wang, C., Nokleby, M. & Miller, C. J.. (2017). *Improving short-term electricity price forecasting using day-ahead LMP with ARIMA models.* 2017 IEEE Power & Energy Society General Meeting, pp. 1–5.

Zhou, W., Wu, X., Ding, S., & Pan, J. (2020). Application of a novel discrete grey model for forecasting natural gas consumption: A case study of Jiangsu Province in China. *Energy, Elsevier, 200*, 117443.

Chapter 29
Recent Developments of Medium Technology Activities Specific to the Romanian Manufacturing Industry in the Context of the COVID-19 Pandemic and the War in Ukraine

Andrei Silviu Dospinescu

Abstract The Romanian manufacturing industry was affected by two consecutive shocks in the form of the COVID-19 pandemic and the war in Ukraine. A number of factors, including global value chain disruptions and the increased volatility of domestic and foreign demand, have contributed to the output contraction of the manufacturing industry during the pandemic. The war in Ukraine generated a second shock to the economy, particularly to industry. The significant increase in prices, especially for energy, has led to increased production costs, negatively impacting the industry. In this context, the paper analyzes the dynamics of production in medium technology activities specific to the manufacturing industry in Romania and compares the dynamics in Romania with the main economies in the region and with the EU average. The paper also estimates two autoregressive vector models that allow for the econometric analysis of the impact on the medium technology activities of two shocks, one represented by the pandemic and the other by the significant increase in industrial producer prices. The econometrical results are consistent with the statistical data on the production dynamics during the pandemic and capture the high impact of the pandemic shock on manufacturing. The analysis of the impact of the industrial producer prices shock on medium-technology activities reflects the impact of the disinflationary trends during the pandemic period, especially the second and third quarters of 2020, as well as the strong inflationary shock generated by the war in Ukraine.

Keywords Manufacturing industry · Medium technology activities · Exogenous shock · VAR model · Impulse response function

---

A. S. Dospinescu (✉)
Centre for Industry and Services Economics, National Institute for Economic Research, "Costin C. Kiritescu," Romanian Academy, Bucharest, Romania

© The Author(s), under exclusive license to Springer Nature Switzerland AG 2024
L. Chivu et al. (eds.), *Constraints and Opportunities in Shaping the Future: New Approaches to Economics and Policy Making*, Springer Proceedings in Business and Economics, https://doi.org/10.1007/978-3-031-47925-0_29

29.1 Introduction

The economic shock induced by COVID-19 led to a strong global recession in 2020. The easing of health restrictions, as well as the increased ability of economies to adapt to the new conditions imposed by the health crisis, allowed the global economy to recover in 2021. However, the shock induced by COVID-19 is proving to be more persistent on the supply side. A number of factors, such as global value chain disruptions and increases in commodity and energy prices, are more persistent than originally thought.

The war in Ukraine generated a second shock to the economy and industry in particular. The significant increase in energy prices has led to increased production costs with a negative impact on the industry.

In this context, this paper analyzes the dynamics of production in medium technology activities specific to the manufacturing industry in Romania and compares the dynamics recorded in the case of Romania with the main economies in the region and with the EU average.

Two autoregressive vector models are estimated to capture the impact on medium technology activities of two shocks, one represented by the pandemic and the other by the significant increase in industrial production prices.

This paper contributes to the debate on the impact of COVID-19 on the economy. In the context of high economic, health, and geopolitical uncertainty, the paper also investigates the economic impact of possible price shocks on medium technology activities specific to the manufacturing industry.

29.2 Literature Review

The economic crisis induced by COVID-19 has revealed a series of vulnerabilities at the level of the European and global economy. Industrial activity registered a strong contraction against the background of a constellation of factors, among which we list the impact of global value chain disruptions, the sharp increases in raw material prices, and the increased volatility of domestic and foreign demand. A number of recent studies have investigated the economic turmoil induced by COVID-19. Saurav et al. (2020) highlighted the significant increase in the penetration of digital technologies and the diversification of suppliers and production in 2020, which allowed the increased resilience of industry and partially counteracted the impact of COVID-19 on industry. Baldwin and Freeman (2020) and Bonadio et al. (2020) highlighted the significant impact of COVID-19 on global value chains. Hayakawa and Mukunoki (2021) analyzed the impact on international trade and indicated a significant reduction in trade volumes amid the restrictions generated by COVID-19. Dorn (2020) and Prades and Casas (2020) identified a strong link between the type and intensity of sanitary restrictions and economic performance. Maarten de Vet et al. (2021) investigated the impact of COVID-19 on EU industries and concluded that the impact is not homogeneous. Low-and medium technology activities were more strongly affected by COVID-19, while high technology activities and those that allowed a faster transition to a flexible, remote work schedule were less affected by COVID-19.

29.3 Methodology

Autoregressive models are frequently used in economics to capture the impact of economic shocks, including in the analysis of the impact induced by COVID-19 (Sims, 1980; Hamilton, 1994; Castellini, 2020; Bobeica and Hartwig, 2021).

Vector autoregression (VAR) is a statistical model that allows the analysis of the relationships between economic variables without introducing a priori assumptions about the causal relationship between these variables. Mathematically, the model is described as follows:

$$y_t = c + A_1 y_{t-1} + A_2 y_{t-2} + \cdots + A_p y_{t-p} + e_t, \qquad (29.1)$$

where Y represents a vector of analyzed variables, $t-i$ represents the number of lags used, and e represents a vector of errors with mean 0 and finite variance.

In this paper, two autoregressive vector models are estimated, allowing for the econometric analysis of the impact on medium technology activities of two shocks, one represented by the pandemic and the other by the significant increase in industrial production prices.

29.4 Analysis/Result Interpretation

Romania's economy returned to the level prior to the shock induced by COVID-19 in the fourth quarter of 2021, after experiencing the strongest quarterly contraction since 1995, of 10.1%, in the second quarter of 2020. The reduced level of health restrictions in 2021 supported the services sector, which grew by 9.4% in 2021 after contracting by 6.4% in 2020. Accommodations and food service saw a record contraction of 65.2% in the second quarter of 2020. Statistical data indicate a return of services to the pre-COVID-19 level starting in the third quarter of 2021. Amid the reduction in international trade and the induced shock to global value chains, industrial production contracted by 4.5% in 2020, while manufacturing contracted by 4.4%. Supported by the economic recovery, industry grew by 5% in 2021, while manufacturing grew by 6.4%. The impact of the war in Ukraine was felt in 2022, with industry contracting in the first half of the year amid a significant increase in energy prices. The contraction was particularly felt in the second quarter of 2022, with industry contracting by 3.1% and manufacturing by 3.6% (see Fig. 29.1).

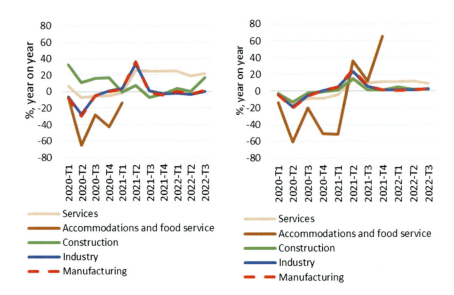

Fig. 29.1 Impact of COVID-19 on sectoral output (percentage change, year on year) (**a**) Romania. (**b**) UE27
Source: Eurostat
Legend: Index calculated on the basis of production at constant prices in 2015

What significantly differentiates Romania from the EU 27 average is the dynamics of the construction sector, especially in 2020. Against the background of the reduction of investment opportunities simultaneously with the quantitative easing and the reduction of interest rates, there was a reallocation of investments toward construction. Additionally, a series of factors specific to Romania supported the dynamics of the sector. The return of Romanians working abroad, a good part of them in the construction sector, led to a strong increase in the labor supply. At the same time, the construction market in Romania experienced a positive dynamic prior to the crisis induced by COVID-19 with a series of ongoing projects in large urban centers. In this context, the construction sector grew by 12.5% in Q2, 2020. At the EU 27 level, construction contracted by 13.7% in the same analyzed period. In 2021, the construction sector picked up in the EU 27 countries registering on average a positive dynamic of 4.5%. In Romania, construction has stagnated, with the dynamics of the sector even negative in the third quarter of 2021. However, it can be observed (see Fig. 29.1) that production in the construction sector is experiencing a revival in 2022, especially in the third quarter.

The manufacturing industry activities most affected by the economic shock induced by COVID-19 were those of medium technology. In this sense, the most affected activities were the manufacture of motor vehicles, trailers, semi-trailers, and other transport equipment and the manufacture of machinery and equipment n.e.c. The production in the first-mentioned activity contracted by 53.5% in Q2, 2020, and registered an increase of 96.8% in the second quarter of 2021, reflecting a combination of the economic recovery and the base statistical effect. Production

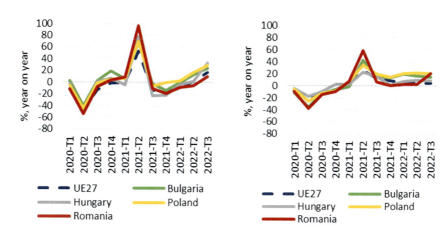

Fig. 29.2 Impact of COVID-19 on industrial output (percentage change, year on year). (**a**) MMAC*. (**b**) MMOTOR*
Source: Eurostat
Legend: Index calculated on the basis of production at constant prices in 2015
*See footnote 1 for the acronyms

in the second-mentioned activity contracted by 37.1% in Q2, 2020 and grew by 59% in Q2, 2021 (see Fig. 29.2). Both activities are more resilient than manufacturing as a whole to the shock induced by the war in Ukraine, registering significant output increases in the third quarter of 2022.

The paper built two VAR models that included the following variables: (a) production dynamics in the manufacturing industry and in medium technology activities and (b) the producer prices in manufacturing. The models were estimated based on monthly data covering the period from January 2019 to July 2022 (Eurostat, 2022a, b). A VAR-type model was initially estimated in which all medium technology activities were included. Different functional forms of the model were tested without identifying a model that passed the statistical tests specific to VAR models. This led to the grouping of activities according to the production response to the pandemic shock. In this vein, two models were estimated.[1] The first model included the equations from 2 to 5, and the second model the equations 6 and 7.

The consistency of results was ensured by running a series of specific tests for both models. Stationarity was tested using the Dickey-Fuller (ADF) test. The production dynamics series were stationary in level and the price index stationary in the first difference. The selection of the optimal number of lags was made using the five criteria available in EViews. The criteria indicated an optimal mode of lag 1 for the

---

[1] M—production dynamics in manufacturing; MCHEM—production dynamics in manufacture of chemicals and chemical products; MCOKE—production dynamics in manufacture of coke and refined petroleum products; MRUB—production dynamics in manufacture of rubber and plastic products and other nonmetallic mineral products; MMET—production dynamics in manufacture of basic metals and fabricated metal products, except machinery and equipment, MMOTOR—production dynamics in manufacture of machinery and equipment n.e.c.; MMAC—production dynamics in manufacture of motor vehicles, trailers, semi-trailers, and other transport equipment; and MPR—producer prices in manufacturing.

first model and lag 2 for the second. The stationarity of the system was tested using the AR root table, and it was observed that all the roots of the VAR system are inside the unit circle. The LM test of autocorrelation was used to investigate whether there is residual serial correlation in the model, and the presence of first-order autocorrelation was not identified. The F-test was significant at 5% and 10% levels of significance, respectively, for both VAR models used in the analysis of the impulse response functions.

$$MCHEM = -0.15^*MCHEM(-1) + 0.10^*MCOKE(-1) - 1.29^*MRUB(-1) - 0.30^*MMET(-1) + 1.03^*M(-1) - 0.08^*D(MPR(-1)) + 0.71$$
$$[F\ statistic = 1.21] \tag{29.2}$$

$$MCOKE = 0.02^*MCHEM(-1) - 0.02^*MCOKE(-1) - 0.63^*MRUB(-1) - 0.94^*MMET(-1) + 0.74^*M(-1) + 0.003^*D(MPR(-1)) + 0.85$$
$$[F\ statistic = 0.7] \tag{29.3}$$

$$MRUB = 0.19^*MCHEM(-1) - 0.05^*MCOKE(-1) - 1.26^*MRUB(-1) - 0.46^*MMET(-1) + 1.28^*M(-1) + 0.003^*D(MPR(-1)) + 0.46$$
$$[F\ statistic = 3.22] \tag{29.4}$$

$$MMET = -0.07^*MCHEM(-1) + 0.11^*MCOKE(-1) - 0.34^*MRUB(-1) - 0.56^*MMET(-1) + 0.64^*M(-1) - 0.014^*D(MPR(-1)) - 0.40$$
$$[F\ statistic = 2.08] \tag{29.5}$$

$$MMOTOR = 0.76^*MMOTOR(-1) + 1.094^*MMOTOR(-2) - 1.17^*MMAC(-1) + 0.28^*MMAC(-2) - 1.80527375903^*M(-1) - 2.84^*M(-2) + 0.25^*D(MPR(-1)) + 0.03^*D(MPR(-2)) - 2.18$$
$$[F\ statistic = 2.26] \tag{29.6}$$

$$MMAC = 0.40^*MMOTOR(-1) + 0.192^*MMOTOR(-2) - 0.83^*MMAC(-1) - 0.357^*MMAC(-2) + 0.139^*M(-1) - 0.001^*M(-2) + 0.09^*D(MPR(-1)) + 0.06^*D(MPR(-2)) - 0.69$$
$$[F\ statistic = 4.85] \tag{29.7}$$

The results of the statistical data analysis indicated a high impact of the pandemic shock on medium technology activities. The econometrical results reflect the historical data, in the sense that the impact of a shock in production is higher in the case of the manufacture of motor vehicles, trailers, semi-trailers, and other transport equipment and the manufacture of machinery and equipment n.e.c. and reflects the significant contraction of demand in 2020, in the context of health restrictions with

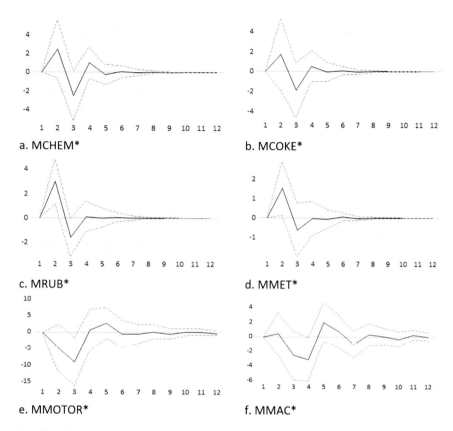

Fig. 29.3 Response of medium technology activities to a shock to the manufacturing industry output
Source: Author's calculations using EViews 12
Legend: The shock response function measures the impact of a shock equal to a standard deviation of the residues of the regression equation specific to the manufacturing industry. The shock response is monitored for 12 periods equivalent to 12 months
*See footnote 1 for the acronyms

a high impact on mobility. It can be seen that the impact is absorbed in 3-4 periods, and the statistical confidence interval is reduced. This result is consistent with the economic revival in 2021, which led to increased demand for the abovementioned activities (see Fig. 29.3).

The response of the activity manufacture of coke and refined petroleum products to a shock in the manufacturing industry is positive, but the statistical confidence interval is large in the first periods and includes the value 0. This indicates the reduced statistical confidence in the positive response of the analyzed activity. The result is consistent with the increased volatility recorded in the analyzed activity. The same large statistical confidence interval in the first periods is observed for Fig. 29.3a, d and is consistent with the increased volatility and uncertainty at the beginning of the pandemic.

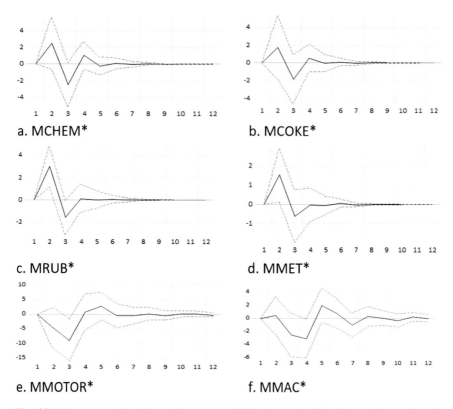

Fig. 29.4 Response of medium technology activities to a shock in the producer prices in manufacturing
Source: Author's calculations using EViews 12
Legend: The shock response function measures the impact of a shock equal to a standard deviation of the residues of the regression equation specific to the manufacturing industry. The shock response is monitored for 12 periods equivalent to 12 months
*See footnote 1 for the acronyms

The analysis of the impact of the inflationary shock on medium technology activities is inconclusive. The analyzed period captures the deflationary impact of the pandemic on prices and the strong inflationary impact induced by the war. This leads to a high uncertainty of the response of the analyzed activities to a price shock (see Fig. 29.4).

It can be seen that the confidence interval contains the value zero in all but one case. The deflationary shock during the pandemic was positively correlated with the drop in output. The subsequent increase in prices coincided with the economic recovery and growth in aggregate demand leading to the results obtained in Fig. 29.4. In this sense, most of the historical data analyzed illustrate an increase in production concurrent with the increase in prices. For a better identification of the impact of the inflationary shock generated by the war, a longer period of time is needed after the outbreak of the war in Ukraine.

29.5 Conclusions

Industrial activity registered a strong contraction against the background of a constellation of factors, among which we list the impact of global value chain disruptions, the sharp increases in raw material prices, and the increased volatility of domestic and foreign demand.

Romania's economy returned to the level prior to the shock induced by COVID-19 in the fourth quarter of 2021, after experiencing the strongest quarterly contraction since 1995, of 10.1%, in the second quarter of 2020. Against the background of the economic recovery, industry increased by 5% in 2021, while manufacturing grew by 6.4%. Among the activities specific to the medium technology manufacturing industry, the strongest economic recovery was recorded for the industrial activities that benefited significantly from the lifting of the COVID-19 restrictions, mainly related to mobility.

The analysis of the inflationary shock reflected the deflationary impact of the pandemic and the strong inflationary impact generated by the war. The disinflationary pressures during the pandemic were positively correlated with the decrease in production, while the economic recovery and the revival of the aggregate demand were approximately synchronous with the price increases. In this context, the impact of the inflationary shock on aggregate demand has not been fully propagated yet. A longer period of time is needed since the start of the war in Ukraine for a better identification of the impact of the inflationary shock suggesting the utility of the econometric analysis in a future study.

References

Baldwin, R., & Freeman, R. (2020). *Supply chain contagion waves: Thinking ahead on manufacturing contagion and reinfection from the COVID concussion*. VoxEU.org, April.

Bobeica, E., & Hartwig, B. (2021). *The COVID-19 shock and challenges for time series models* (ECB Working Paper Series No. 2558).

Bonadio, B, Z Huo, A Levchenko, & N Pandalai-Nayar (2020). *Global supply chains in the pandemic* (NBER Working Paper No. 27224).

Castellini, M., Donadelli, M. & Gufler, I. (2020). On the impact of COVID-19 related uncertainty. *A New World Post COVID-19* (31 July 2020). https://doi.org/10.30687/978-88-6969-442-4/016

Dorn, F. (2020). *The economic costs of the coronavirus shutdown for selected European countries: A scenario calculation* (EconPol Policy Brief, No. 21).

Eurostat. (2022a). *High-tech classification of manufacturing industries*. https://ec.europa.eu/eurostat/statistics-explained/index.php?title=Glossary:High-tech_classification_of_manufacturing_industries

Eurostat. (2022b). *Eurostat database*. http://ec.europa.eu/eurostat/data/database

Hamilton, J. D. (1994). *Time series analysis*. Princeton University Press.

Hayakawa, K., & Mukunoki, H. (2021). Impacts of Covid-19 on global value chains. *Development Economics*. https://doi.org/10.1111/dpr.12539

Maarten de Vet J., Nigohosyan, D., Núñez Ferrer, J., Gross, A.K., Kuehl, S. and M. Flickenschild (2021). *Impacts of the COVID-19 pandemic on EU industries*. European Commission. https://www.europarl.europa.eu/RegData/etudes/STUD/2021/662903/IPOL_STU(2021)662903_EN.pdf

Prades Illanes, E., & Tello Casas, P.. (2020). The heterogeneous economic impact of Covid-19 among Euro Area Countries and Regions. *Economic Bulletin,* No. 2, Banco de España.

Saurav, A., Kusek, P., & Kuo, R. (2020). *The impact of COVID-19 on foreign investors: Early evidence from a global pulse survey.* World Bank, Washington, DC. https://hdl.handle.net/10986/33774

Sims, C. (1980). Macroeconomics and reality. *Econometrica, 48*(1), 1–48.

Chapter 30
Characterization of the Main Changes in the Natural Gas Market in Romania on the Context of Current Energy Crisis

Alexandru Isaic-Maniu, Stelian Stancu, Constanța-Nicoleta Bodea, Mihai Sabin Muscalu, and Denisa Elena Bălă

Abstract The current studies on the European Union natural gas market highlight the high demand for natural gas, despite efforts to achieve the transition to a low-carbon energy system. At the same time, world natural gas production is still dominated by countries from the Middle East region, the Russian Federation, and the USA.

The article presents the main results of statistical research aimed at changes on the natural gas market in Romania, highlighting the impact of the COVID-19 pandemic and presenting some initiatives to reduce dependence, especially on natural gas supplies from the Russian Federation.

The natural gas market in Romania is analyzed from the perspective of natural gas demand, natural gas import and export, domestic production, infrastructure, and price evolution. Also, the impact of the changes on the world natural gas market on the Romanian economy was evaluated and recommendations were formulated for the implementation of measures to mitigate the negative effects of the increase in natural gas prices on the evolution of macroeconomic indicators, under the conditions of harmonization with European Union policies in the field.

A. Isaic-Maniu · M. S. Muscalu
Centre for Industry and Services Economics, "Costin C. Kiritescu" National Institute for Economic Research, Romanian Academy, Bucharest, Romania
e-mail: alexandru.isaic@csie.ase.ro

S. Stancu · C.-N. Bodea (✉)
Centre for Industry and Services Economics, "Costin C. Kiritescu" National Institute for Economic Research, Romanian Academy, Bucharest, Romania

Informatics and Economic Cybernetics Department, Bucharest University of Economic Studies, Bucharest, Romania
e-mail: bodea@ase.ro

D. E. Bălă
Bucharest University of Economic Studies, Bucharest, Romania
e-mail: baladenisa16@stud.ase.ro

© The Author(s), under exclusive license to Springer Nature Switzerland AG 2024
L. Chivu et al. (eds.), *Constraints and Opportunities in Shaping the Future: New Approaches to Economics and Policy Making*, Springer Proceedings in Business and Economics, https://doi.org/10.1007/978-3-031-47925-0_30

Keywords Natural gas reserves · Transport networks · European gas market · Liquefied gases · Competitive pressure

30.1 Introduction

The COVID-19 pandemic generated the biggest contraction of the global economy since the Great Economic Crisis, but in the first months of 2020, the advent of vaccines led to the gradual restoration of market confidence and the gradual resumption of production. Another effect was a temporary drop in global energy demand.

In Europe, the long-term transition from coal to natural gas and in the future to hydrogen and other renewable sources, as well as dependence on gas imports, especially from the Russian Federation, have led to a serious energy crisis across the continent. This crisis reveals, in fact, the accentuation, in the long term, of the dependence of European markets on natural gas imports. The dominant position of the Russian Federation in the European supply of natural gas presented a threat to energy security for European countries and for the EU in general. For several months, natural gas and energy prices have set new records, and companies have rushed to cover the part of gas demand not covered by long-term contracts on the spot market. With limited capacity to quickly replace natural gas, European countries now face, because of high energy prices, the prospect of slowing or reversing the much-anticipated economic recovery after the COVID-19 pandemic.

The evolution of the pandemic and measures taken to limit the spread of the virus and support from policies to mitigate the economic impact of the pandemic were the main determinants of the trend of economic recovery worldwide. After reaching a low level in the second quarter of 2020 due to containment measures, the global economy began to recover in the third quarter, as the pandemic and restrictive measures recorded a moderation in the incidence of infection of the population. During the last quarter of 2020, the re-introduction of strict measures to limit the spread of the pandemic in some developed economies slowed down GDP growth considerably.

In Romania, the pandemic caused the first annual economic decrease in the last decade of −3.9%, compared to 2019. Despite the increase in average income, the GDP decrease was determined by the consumption reduction by −2.7%. Estimates indicated a return to economic growth in 2021, between 3.8% in 2021, and 4.2% in 2022 (European Commission, 2021a, b, c) and 4.3% (CNP, 2021).

Compared to the quarterly growth, the GDP experienced a steep drop, of 11.8%, in the second quarter of the year, resuming its growth in the third and fourth quarters, with 5.6% and 4.8%, respectively. In nominal terms, Romania's Gross Domestic Product was 1,053,881 million lei in 2020, a slight decrease compared to the level of 2019 (1,053,884 in 2019).

Romania's international trade also experienced a negative evolution in 2020, a year in which exports were 62.17 billion euros, down 9.9% compared to 2019, and imports 80.56 billion euros, down by − 6.6% compared to the previous year.

This sharper drop in exports compared to imports led to a deepening of the trade balance deficit, up to 18.38 billion euros. The situation was reflected in the significant increase in general consolidated budget deficit, which reached 9.2% of GDP and after it had reached 4.4% of GDP in 2019. In the future, large infrastructure works, both road and railway, will generate new jobs and local value chains, in which Romanian companies can easily integrate. The projects advanced by the public authorities indicate a major consolidation of public investments toward infrastructure, made through the National Resilience and Recovery Plan (PNRR).

The national economy will benefit from around five billion euros annually for the next 6 years (2021–2026), a level similar to the foreign direct investments annually attracted by Romania.

Priority will be given to investments in transport, health, digitalization, education, and employment. The actions in the green zone will also have funds to ensure a just transition to a carbon-free economy, where the European objective is to reduce CO_2 emissions by at least 55% by 2030 and by 100% by 2050 and create new opportunities for the Romanian economy.

The new industrial strategy of the European Union reconfigures European industry industrial ecosystems, covering a wide spectrum of economic activities (digital, low-carbon industries, health, agri-food, healthcare, renewable energy, aerospace and defense, mobility and automotive, construction, electronics, textiles, retail, tourism, creative and cultural industries). The integration of Romanian companies into the European industrial ecosystems will generate new opportunities for the local economy, and Romania's administrative capacity will be put to the test for accessing the over 75 billion euros allocated in the next 6–7 years.

The economic recovery has put a major strain on the current energy system, triggering major price increases in the natural gas, coal, and electricity markets. With all the progress made in promoting renewable energy sources, the year 2021 forced a significant return to the use of coal and oil.

Displayed equations are centered and set on a separate line.

$$x + y = z \qquad (30.1)$$

30.2 Literature Review

Most of the papers related to the natural gas market are of two types: One is represented by the papers published by specialized energy entities and includes estimation of natural gas production and consumption (BP, 2022; BSOG, 2022; GTS, 2022; GOGC, 2021) Another important type of literature regarding the natural gas market is represented by the academic scientific literature.

Estimation of the market supply (Wang et al., 2013, 2017; Höök & Tang, 2013) applied in the demand prediction most of the time does not consider the constraints generated by the depletion of the fossil resources and the increase in production. In

BP (2022), three scenarios were defined to explore the energy transition toward 2050: accelerated, net zero, and new momentum scenarios. By means of these scenarios, a large range of possible outcomes during the next years are explored.

Long-term production of natural gas in several countries has been studied by different authors (Söderbergh et al., 2009; Lin & Wang, 2012; Patzek et al., 2013).

Salmachi and Yarmohammadtooski (2015) studied the coal production. Wang et al. (2018) estimated the growth of China's production based on unconventional gas resources. From the perspective of applied models, three model types became largely applied, meaning Hubbert's model, Brecha's linear model (Brecha, 2008), and the supply-demand model for geological resources (Mohr et al., 2015). For non-renewable resources, such as natural gas, the usual production dynamic follows the following pattern: an increase and a first peak production and then a production decline due to resource depletion (Wang et al., 2017). In the long term, the production curve has a bell shape (Saraiva et al., 2014). Other types of estimation models are the system dynamic (Tang et al., 2010; Kiani & Pourfakhraei, 2010). Mohr et al. (2015) included other perspectives to analyze unconventional gas resources. It is well accepted the fact that unconventional gas resource extraction was significantly accelerated since the "shale revolution" in the USA. Several studies suggested that unconventional gas resources will develop in the future (Medlock, 2012).

30.3 Methodology

Considering the flow of the production and publication of statistical data, the references will refer to the years 2020–2021 and, where possible, partial data from 2022, and the entire approach assumed as stages:

- Consulting the information available on the pages of international bodies.
- The data extracted from official sources, both those published by the INS and those from Eurostat publications, were harmonized and organized as a coherent database for processing.
- Data pre-processing, which involved the systematization of data extracted from different sources and grouping, as far as possible, into homogeneous categories.
- Processing the database and calculating some relevant indicators to obtain a picture of the gas market in Romania.
- Formulation of conclusions based on the interpretation of the calculated indicators.

The activities that are the subject of this study are detailed in the national economy classification system (CAEN-Rev2), as follows: CAEN 062: natural gas extraction (which also includes gas desulfurization), CAEN 352 and CAEN 3521: gas production, and CAEN 3522 and CAEN 3523: marketing of gaseous fuels through pipelines.

30.4 Analysis/Result Interpretation

The natural gas industry has a long history in Romania, for more than 110 years. It is in third place in Europe regarding natural gas production, being an important member of the Energy Community Treaty since 2005, prior to joining the EU and participating in the European energy market through PEGAS. Romania's offshore gas reserves are the fifth largest in Europe.

In Romania, the main operators in the field of natural gas are the following:

- There is limited competition on natural gas production, with only two main producers: OMV Petrom and Romgaz, contributing 95% of the total domestic gas production. The situation is different in the natural gas supply and distribution sector, where 36 companies have regular activities.
- Compania Națională Transgaz S.A. operates in the field of transport, which is the national TSO (Transport and System Operator) with majority state capital (Transgaz-2020), which has a network consisting of 13,381 km of pipes and connections.
- Two trading platforms are operational in Romania: BRM (private operator, since 1992) and OPCOM (state operator).
- Two operators operate in the field of storage: Depogaz Ploiesti and Depomureș-Târgu Mureș. Depogaz owns five underground storage units with a total capacity of 30.1213 TWh.

The gas transport network consists mainly of:

- Trans-Balkan corridor, including two main natural gas pipelines starting in Russian Federation and passing through Ukraine, Moldova, Romania, and Bulgaria.
- Pipeline (T1)—Transit 1 ends in Bulgaria.
- Pipeline (T2)—Transit 2 crosses Bulgaria, Turkey, Greece, and North Macedonia.

30.4.1 Structure of the Natural Gas Market

The market is strongly focused on both the manufacturing and distribution segments. The 10 producers and their market shares are as follows: Romgaz: 53.66%, OMV Petrom: 44.44%, Stratum Energy Romania: 0.64%, Amromco Energy: 0.43%, Serinus Energy Romania: 0.33%, Mazarine Energy Romania: 0.18%, Dacian Petroleum: 0.16%, Hunt Oil Company: 0.08%, Foraj Sonde: 0.06%, and Raffles Energy: 0.02%. The main supplier, Romgaz, far exceeds the 20% limit from which it is estimated that a concentrated market begins, and the first three competitors together hold more than 98% of the market, which leads to the same conclusion. The Herfindahl-Hirschman (HH) index was established for the domestic production market and calculated according to the formula:

$$HH = g_1^2 + g_2^2 + \ldots + g_n^2$$

where g_i is the market share of producer i. The HH indicator had the calculated value of 5186.041, a value that exceeds 2000, that is, the limit above which a high concentration in the market is considered.

Concentration/diversification can also be measured by the entropy indicator, which for a system composed of k elements with the probabilities $p = [p_1, \ldots, p_k]$, with $p_i \geq 0$ and $\sum_{i=1}^{k} p_i = 1$, is calculated as follows:

$$\mathbf{H}(\mathbf{p}) = -\sum_{i=1}^{k} p_i \cdot \ln(p_i) = 2.7598$$

with values in the range of values: $[0; \ln k]$. The calculated entropy also indicates a high concentration of the natural gas market in Romania.

30.4.2 Price Evolution

In the context of the disruptions that occurred at the level of suppliers, prices influenced the dynamics of industrial activity in the euro area, and the slowdown in the latter part of 2021 largely reflects the contraction of the German manufacturing sector. In the Eurozone, industrial production was on average about 2.5% below trend in the last 6 months of 2021. The new wave of Omicron and the war in Ukraine generated new uncertainties, including in the gas market. The rise in gas and crude oil prices was initially supported on the demand side by the recovery of the Chinese economy, and later by the relaunch of the economies of developed countries in Europe.

It should be noted that the increasing trend of prices, but also equalization with the level practiced in the EU, so if in the second semester of 2016 the unit price in Romania was equal to 64.1% of the average recorded in the EU, and in the first semester of 2021, this it reached 98.7%, a fact that was reflected in the price criteria of industrial products and then found in consumer prices.

For household consumption, the gap was much higher; thus the unit price in 2016 semester 2 was 0.0167 euro/kilowatt-hour representing 35.5% of the European level, and in 2021, it represented 64.9% of the European average.

30.4.3 Modeling the Connection Between Energy Consumption and Economic Performance

It was considered to highlight the regression link between the economic results and different influencing factors. Following a process of successive tests, the link between macroeconomic results measured by GDP (expressed in market prices) and the dynamics of industry turnover (VIT) and final energy consumption (FEC, expressed in ktoe, 1 toe) was recognized as having statistical significance = 41,868 gigajoules), through a linear multiple regression model of the form:

$$Y_{GDP} = \beta_0 + \beta_1(VIT) + \beta_2(FEC) + \xi$$

In a first phase, the intensity of the correlation (through Pearson coefficients) between the considered variables was determined, and the results confirmed the option, as follows:

Correl GDP-VIT	0,976218
Correl GDP-FEC	0,144538
Correl VIT-FEC	0,07767

The link is particularly strong between GDP and industry turnover, and the regression model through the particularly high value of the coefficient of determination R^2 explains the variation of GDP (details in Fig. 30.1).

30.4.4 The Degree of Energy Independence

The degree of energy independence was oscillating and decreased in level after 1992. Thus, it was 72% in 1992, differentiated by category, as follows: for coal 68.7%, 51.3% for crude oil and 82, 9% for methane gas, and in 2020, the general level was 69.5%, with more energetic differences: 73.9%, only 32.2% for crude oil,

SUMMARY OUTPUT

Regression Statistics	
Multiple R	0,9786
R Square	0,9578
Adjusted R Square	0,9517
Standard Error	56792,8720
Observations	17,0000

ANOVA

	df	SS	MS	F	Significance F
Regression	2,0000	1023692945216,6700	511846472608,3350	158,6909	0,0000
Residual	14,0000	45156024396,1383	3225430314,0099		
Total	16,0000	1068848969612,8100			

	Coefficients	Standard Error	t Stat	P-value	Lower 95%	Upper 95%
Intercept	-555785,1859	370442,4584	-1,5003	0,1557	-1350305,2392	238734,8675
Value index of turnover in ir	8161,2543	463,1854	17,6198	0,0000	7167,8204	9154,6882
Final energy consumption (k	20,4338	16,2862	1,2547	0,2301	-14,4967	55,3643

Fig. 30.1 Regression model validation statistics

and 76.3% for natural gas. The values of the degree of natural gas independence in the interval 1992–2020 are presented below. The descriptive statistics elements of the series indicate a mean of 79.6% and a variance of 60.7%. The skewness and skewness coefficients suggest a skewed but relatively homogeneous distribution of the 29 values.

After successive tests (using the test $\chi^2_{\alpha,k-c}$), the Wakeby distribution was validated (Johnson et al., 1994, pp. 46) at various values of the decision risk (10, 5, 2.5, and 1%), and five parameters with its quantile function (Figs. 30.2 and 30.3) were defined as follows:

$$W(p) = \xi + \frac{\alpha}{\beta}\left(1-(1-p)^{\beta}\right) - \frac{\gamma}{\delta}\left(1-(1-p)^{\delta}\right)$$

with parameters:

$$\alpha = 42.659;\ \beta = 3.8319;\ \gamma = 6.4194;\ \delta = -0.05631;\ \xi = 64.718$$

The plot of the likelihood function reflects the reduced degree of high values (of the degree of independence) and the accelerated decrease at lower values.

					Statistic	Value	Percentile	Value
82.9	74.8	74.1	79.9	86.4	Sample Size	29	Min	65.7
82.0	81.5	69.0	78.0	88.6	Range	32.7	5%	67.2
79.9	80.2	65.7	80.3	86.1	Mean	79.624	10%	69
75.1	81.8	70.6	87.8	89.6	Variance	60.673	25% (Q1)	74.4
70.9	77.9	72.0	93.6	76.3	Std. Deviation	7.7893	50% (Median)	79.9
74.7	68.7	84.2	98.4		Std. Error	1.4464	90%	89.6
$f(x) = \dfrac{(1-F(x))^{(\delta+1)}}{\alpha t + \gamma}$					Skewness	0.36803	95%	96
					Excess Kurtosis	-0.0616	Max	98.4

Source: INS, *Tempo-online, the matrix* IND121A

Fig. 30.2 Statistics regarding the testing of the energy independence indicator series

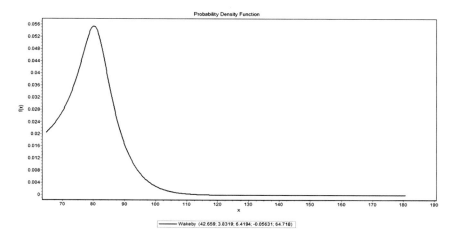

Fig. 30.3 Wakeby frequency function graph—f (42.66; 3.83; 6.42; −0.056; 64.72)

30.5 Conclusions

The current energy crisis highlights the need for a common energy security policy at the European level. The strong volatility on the energy markets manifested in recent years is not accidental, but is the result of the way the energy systems are structured in each of the European countries, when short-term efficiency criteria were taken into account, i.e., by ignoring interconnection markets and ensuring the necessary balance in a competitive market.

Natural gas is also a marginal fuel in that natural gas prices often drive electricity prices. Historically, natural gas markets have been primarily regional rather than global because they are more difficult to store and transport, and liquefaction for transport is not only expensive but also energy intensive. The technical infrastructure associated with natural gas requires large investments and requires the conclusion of long-term contracts.

A characteristic that appeared more prominently in the last decade is represented by the increase in the size, not only regional, but also global, of the natural gas market.

Over the past decade, the global volume of natural gas trade has increased by more than 60%, and of this growth, the USA has provided over a third, becoming the third largest world exporter. Another new feature of the energy market is that natural gas prices are now decoupled from oil prices.

The vigorous recovery of economies in the post-COVID-19 period has put great pressure on energy systems, generating significant price increases in the natural gas, coal, and electricity markets. With all the progress made in the expansion of renewable energy sources, the year 2021 saw a significant return of the use of coal and oil in the economy.

In all national economies, but also at the European Union level, measures were taken to mitigate the effects of the increase in natural gas prices, as a necessity generated by the increase in energy prices and the serious impact of these increases on household budgets. Among the immediate measures to protect consumers and businesses, many of which also worked during the pandemic and have been reactivated (C.E. Energy prices 2021), such as:

- Providing emergency support for consumers affected by energy poverty, through different means, such as vouchers or partial compensation of bills.
- Authorization of the temporary postponement of invoice due dates.
- Taking protective measures to avoid disconnection from the gas network.
- Temporary reductions in the levels of fees and taxes for vulnerable households.
- Support schemes for companies, in compliance with EU rules on state aid.
- Facilitating wider access to contracts for the purchase of energy from renewable sources and supporting them through financial measures.

At the same time, following the explosion of energy prices, there was also a particularly strong deterioration of the standard of living of large categories of the population, if we take into account the level of the minimum wage in the economy and the high proportion of employees working for this level of wages, and, similarly, there is a high share of pensioners who have incomes in the area of the minimum subsistence basket, which is why a new set of measures would be possible and urgently needed, such as:

- Making changes in the energy tax system, because in the last 10–15 years the degree of energy independence of the economy has decreased, increasing imports, and the additional excise tax on energy, which is a slightly elastic product from a household's budget, a product related to civilized conditions of life, is not an appropriate procedure. in the current context. Currently, Romania has become dependent on imports, it needs new development of production capacities, and thus, the current fiscal system must necessarily be adapted.
- Another important element where an intervention would be useful is the cogeneration tax, in fact, a subsidizing mechanism for thermal energy consumers, through the participation of all electricity consumers.
- The introduction for a limited period of time of some thresholds for the profit margin at the level of suppliers and energy producers, which will lead to a reduction in the selling prices of natural gas.
- The introduction of changes in the Vulnerable Consumer Law in such a way as to expand the scope, considering the impact of inflation that has generated an increase in the number of vulnerable individuals and families, including by introducing some quantitative, objective indicators for the designation of individuals, and households in energy poverty.

References

BP. (2022, February). *BP energy outlook 2040*.
Brecha, R. J. (2008). Emission scenarios in the face of fossil-fuel peaking. *Energy Policy, 36*, 3492–3504.
BSOG. (2022). https://www.blackseaog.com/ro/acasa/
CAEN-Rev2. https://coduricaen.info/
CNP. (2021). *Comisia Națională de Strategie și Prognoză, Prognoza de iarnă 2021*. http://www.cnp.ro/user/repository/prognoze/Prognoza_iarna_proiect_buget_2021.pdf
Comisia Europeană. (2021a). *Energy community*. Energy Community Procedural Acts. https://www.energy-community.org/legal/procedural-acts.html
Comisia Europeană. (2021b). *Energy prices*. https://multimedia.europarl.europa.eu/en/package/energy-prices_20304
Comisia Europeană. (2021c). *Prognoza economică de iarnă 2021*. https://ec.europa.eu/economy_finance/forecasts/2021/winter/ecfin_forecast_winter_2021_ro_en.pdf
GOGC. (2021). *JSC georgian oil and gas corporation GOGC*. https://www.gogc.ge/en/article/georgia-takes-key-step-to-establish-gas-exchange/539/
GTS. (2022). *Gas transmission system operator of Ukraine*. https://tsoua.com/en/about-us/#
Höök, M., & Tang, X. (2013). Depletion of fossil fuels and anthropogenic climate change—A review. *Energy Policy, 52*, 797–809.
Johnson, N. L., et al. (1994). *Continuous univariate distributions* (Vol. 2). Wiley.
Kiani, B., & Pourfakhraei, M. A. (2010). A system dynamic model for production and consumption policy in Iran oil and gas sector. *Energy Policy, 38*(12), 7764–7774.
Lin, B., & Wang, T. (2012). Forecasting natural gas supply in China: Production peak and import trends. *Energy Policy, 49*, 225–233.
Medlock, K. B., III. (2012). Modeling the implications of expanded US shale gas production. *Energy Strategy Reviews, 1*(1), 33–41.
Mohr, S. H., et al. (2015). Projection of world fossil fuels by country. *Fuel, 141*, 120–135.
Patzek, T. W., Male, F., & Marder, M. P. (2013). Gas production in the Barnett Shale obeys a simple scaling theory. *Proceedings of the National Academy of Sciences of the United States of America, 110*, 19731–19736.
Salmachi, A., & Yarmohammadtooski, Z. (2015). Production data analysis of coalbed methane wells to estimate the time required to reach to peak of gas production. *International Journal of Coal Geology, 141*, 33–41.
Saraiva, T. A., et al. (2014). Forecasting Brazil's crude oil production using a multi-Hubbert model variant. *Fuel, 115*, 24–31.
Söderbergh, B., Jakobsson, K., & Aleklett, K. (2009). European energy security: The future of Norwegian natural gas production. *Energy Policy, 37*(12), 5037–5055.
Tang, X., et al. (2010). Forecast of oil reserves and production in Daqing oilfield of China. *Energy, 35*(7), 3097–3102.
Wang, Q., et al. (2018). Forecasting US shale gas monthly production using a hybrid ARIMA and metabolic nonlinear grey model. *Energy, 160*, 378–387.
Wang, J., Feng, L., Tang, X., & Bentley, Y. (2013). The implications of fossil fuel supply constraints on climate change projections: A supply-side analysis. *Futures, 86*, 58–72.
Wang, J., et al. (2017). The implications of fossil fuel supply constraints on climate change projections: A supply-side analysis. *Futures, 86*, 58–72.

Chapter 31
Solutions for the Adoption of a Real Sustainable Mobility System

Frantz Daniel Fistung

Abstract Sustainable transport, developed on the basis of the general concept of sustainable development, has in recent decades become increasingly important for socioeconomic development strategies. In this context, many researchers, economists, politicians, or interest groups have tried to define, first, and subsequently implement the concept of sustainable transport and implicitly the policies and instruments specific to this approach. However, the results were not great. Therefore, this paper aims to present briefly the elements (instruments, economic policies, legislations, etc.) that can support the development of a sustainable transport system. The paper begins by briefly presenting the defining elements of the concept of sustainable transport and the practices (legislative, technical, etc.) existing so far. The analyses carried out show, in particular, that, so far, policy in the field has, for the most part, been aimed at encouraging the use of less polluting means of transport, but, in my opinion, the most important instrument, namely a substantial reduction in demand for transport, has been excluded. That reduction must certainly be made in line with the coverage of mobility needs but, at the same time, the reduction of the areas of land occupied by transport infrastructure and the development of social policies to combat the negative effects of transport. Using the key elements of the transport demand function, the study also presents some potential elements to be found in a concrete strategy to develop sustainable mobility. In this context, the document presents many examples of good practices and concrete proposals to support the real implementation of a sustainable transport system.

Keywords Sustainable transport · Transport demand · Transport infrastructures · Green vehicles · Integrated ecology

F. D. Fistung (✉)
Centre for Industry and Services Economy of the National Institute of Economic Research "Costin C. Kirițescu," Romanian Academy, Bucharest, Romania

31.1 Introduction

Mobility will increase, but the transport sector is at a crossroads. As Constantin Necula states, "from any previous stage you also have something to inherit correctly and effectively" (Necula & Dobos, 2022). Therefore, even if, at the moment, the transport system is facing major challenges, the previous accumulations, both technologically and administrative strategically, make us look optimistically toward successfully overcoming the current situations. Among the most important influences on the future evolution of the transport system, we mention only the still very high dependence of vehicles on the use of hydrocarbons, with adverse environmental consequences, regardless of the increase in consumption efficiency levels; the continuous increase of land occupied by transport infrastructures, at the expense of other economic activities possible and even necessary to be developed on these premises (especially agricultural areas); and the orientation, in recent years, toward the sharp replacement of vehicles on the market with electric ones, which will lead to higher energy consumption and the shift of environmental pollution poles from the hauliers' area to that of electricity producers, which is not a just solution, in our view.

31.2 Literature Review

Analyses and models related to the development of sustainable transport have grown, but since 1987 the concept of sustainable development was launched, according to the Brundtland Report (UN, 1987). Since then, many international specialists have sought to define, first, the concept of sustainable transport and subsequently to establish tools and policies for the practical implementation of such a system.

Most of the views on sustainable transport were, however, descriptive and rather general. For example, Kågeson in 1994 highlighted that sustainable transport policies can only be sustainable when addressing the basic needs of today's mobility, the environment and resources for the future, and health hazards such as local short-term pollution (Zuidgeest et al., 2000). Camagni in 1998, emphasizes "process" and change. Therefore, he states that a certain "type of process" is needed for definitions. Such an algorithm is described by Deen and Skinner in 1994. Akinyemi and Zuidgeest (Zuidgeest et al., 2000) discuss a sustainably developed transport system in 2000, i.e., a transport system that meets people's needs, equating mobility with accessibility and safety within available or accessible environmental, financial, and social resources. Since 2000, almost all researchers have tried to impose certain criteria for assessing the sustainability of transport projects and policies (Kraus & Proff, 2021). In Romania, the analysis of sustainable transport has been done much less, and there are only few research groups that have investigated and are still investigating this field today.

31.3 Methodology

The present work is carried out in two main directions of analysis. The first is the brief presentation of the concept of sustainable transport and the characteristic elements and policies to support the implementation of this concept. In the second direction, the main one, it is envisaged to present concrete solutions to support sustainable transport. In doing so, an analysis of the influence factors that can and may even change the direction and intensity of specific transport policies is carried out. Important, from this perspective, is the multicriterial analysis of the evolution of specific factors such as fuel prices, occupancy of areas with transport infrastructures, and increasing the social dimension as a potential applicant of the transport activity. In order to highlight concrete solutions to support the development of sustainable transport, the paper highlights the main influence factors that compete in the success or failure of a correct policy for the development of sustainable transport. Among these, the best solution, in the opinion of the authors, will be highlighted, namely to reduce the demand for transport. At the same time, examples of good practices will be presented, at national and international levels, but also trends for the future, related to sustainable development policies. In this paper was used the information presented in the most important but also recent research studies in the field, developed worldwide, an important focus being placed on those made by European researchers.

31.3.1 Influences of Transport Developments on the Environment and Economic Activity

The need to introduce the principles of the concept of sustainable development also for transport has become increasingly necessary in recent years for many reasons.

One of these is caused by the competition in land areas between transport infrastructure and agricultural land, which has intensified. So far, transport has won the "battle" over agricultural areas, especially in industrialized countries, where transport activities are much more intense. Millions of hectares of agricultural land have been redistributed to road transport, largely. This means that every vehicle in the United States (USA), for example, has about 0.07 ha of land. Thus, for every five vehicles that increased the national fleet, a field the size of American football was covered with asphalt, being redirected from agricultural sectors to transport infrastructure. Moreover, the well-drained land, useful to farms, was paved, with priority, being ideal for the construction of roadways. In fact, the USA, with its 214 million vehicles registered at the beginning of the third millennium, had paved 6.3 million kilometers of roads, to surround the Earth 157 times by the equator (Brown, 2001). Therefore, the conflict between machinery and agricultural land is "paid" by wetlands and rice croplands in countries where hunger is present everywhere. The result of this conflict in China and India, for example, two countries that together account for 38% of the world's population, is likely to affect everyone's food supply security.

The global population grew very much and fast, estimating that by the end of 2022, the world's population will exceed eight billion, with a geographically unbalanced growth rate (the Asian area, with almost half of the world's population will be increasingly crowded, with increasingly severe consequences, at social and economic levels). In fact, the United Nations estimates that around 8.6 billion people will live on the planet in 2030, and by 2050, it will reach about 9.8 billion people, an increase of more than 27% in three decades (UN, 2022). As the population grows, more transport services will be needed.

In the last 10–12 years, the global gross domestic product (GDP) has grown permanently, until the COVID-19 pandemic started to exceed the increase in transport energy consumption.

Global oil demand has started to decline since 2016, with this trend increasing since 2020, as the pandemic has affected not only oil demand but also prices. The beginning of 2022, amid the war in Ukraine, halted this trend and recorded an accelerated increase in transport fuel prices due to distortions produced on the specific market by the reduction of Russian exports of petroleum products.

Global air travel increased by 4.2% from 2018 to 2019. At the end of July 2019, about 225,000 aircraft were active in a single day, the largest daily aircraft movement ever recorded.

Global demand for public transport increased by 4% per annum between 2012 and 2017. Transport via buses, trams, trolleybuses, metros, and urban rail trains has expanded, differently in almost all regions, with bus systems growing in Europe and urban rail transport becoming more widespread in Oceania.

In these circumstances, solutions must be found and adopted quickly to reduce global demand for transport, while meeting essential mobility needs and supporting fair views on social and environmental protection policies.

The adoption of policies for the sustainable development of transport systems, however, does not mean immediate and total lifestyle changes. Measures to reduce mobility or limit the purchase of vehicles (especially cars) are not necessarily necessary. The most important objective is that any desire for mobility, which generates negative effects on environmental and health factors, is met at the same time as the adoption of measures to mitigate these effects.

In these demarches, the European Commission's Green Charter on Supply Security of November 2000 noted the important role of transport in increasing energy demand and CO_2 emissions. At that time, transport accounted for 26% of total emissions from activities in the EU. For 2010, there was an estimated 40% increase compared to 1990 in this type of emissions caused by transport. But the reality was completely different.

In 2020, according to (EUROSTAT, 2022) transport was responsible for 11% of all greenhouse gases produced in the EU this year (strongly influenced by the health pandemic).

31.3.2 Sustainable Mobility Between Desire and Necessity

Three ways of action can be used to achieve sustainable mobility, namely:

- Decrease in transport demand.
- Predominant use of green transport systems (vehicles, infrastructures, logistics, etc.)
- Development of a policy with a mix of the two types of actions.

Obviously, the third solution is the ideal one.

The decrease in demand for transport can only be achieved through actions to reduce its specific components.

However, the general microeconomic theory of demand is not applicable to transport. This is mainly due to the obvious differences between transport activity and any other economic activity.

Thus, the demand for transport is a secondary demand, which means that the transport is intermediate consumption compared to a final one, at the destination, of a different kind. Secondly, the quality of the service offered is of particular importance in the demand for transport (e.g., speed and speed of travel). Thirdly, in the process of choosing a mode of transport, there is a much more important random component than in other forms of consumption (Kanafi, 1983).

The demand for transport may vary when the transport volume (number of passengers or quantity of cargo) or the distance over which this volume is carried differs.

Demand, in terms of volume, structure, and level of consumer requirements, changes from one period or another, thus having a dynamic character. The main factors on which demand dynamics depend are needs, income, and price.

The law of demand expresses the relationship between demand and price, in which demand evolves in the opposite direction of price.

The most important factors of transport demand are as follows:

- From a demographic perspective: the number of persons (residents, employees, and visitors), the employment rate, income, age, lifestyle, and the preferences.
- From the perspectives of economic activities: number of jobs, the type of economic activity, the volume of transportable goods, and tourism.
- Transport options: walking, riding a bicycle, public transport, transport in partnership (ridesharing), taxi service, teleworking, and transport services for delivery to a predefined address.
- From a land use perspective: density, potential for use as transport infrastructure, connectivity, design of infrastructure networks, and proximity to transport flow generating centers (economic, educational knots, etc.).
- Management of demand: prioritizing the use of transport networks, price reforms, promotion campaigns, detailed and comprehensive information to users of transport services, and creating the conditions for proper intermodal competition.
- From a price perspective: the level of fuel prices and related taxes, the level of transport insurance (correct determination of the statistical value of life indicator),

internalization of external costs, labor costs, and the level of total social costs expressed in the formula:

$$C_g = P + vt + aC + bS + cE \tag{31.1}$$

where

P = Transport fare
t = Transport time
V = The individual monetary value attributed to time
C = Indicator of comfort conditions
S = Safety condition indicator
E = Indicator of external effects on environmental and health factors (noise, pollution, trepidation, etc.)
a, b, c = Parameters corresponding to comfort, safety, and external effects.

In these circumstances, we can say that the demand for transport has the following peculiarities:

- It is derived
- It is different from the notion of traffic
- It is strongly influenced by the quality of service as a parameter of supply
- The elasticity of transport demand must also be analyzed according to the generalized cost containing particular terms (individual monetary unit value) and indicators of comfort, safety, and environmental conditions.

Therefore, in the case of transport, we consider that demand is a function of the form:

$$Ct = f(Pt, \text{CAt}) \tag{31.2}$$

Or, more specifically:

$$\text{CAt} = f\left[(Vt, Dt, Tt)/Pt\right] \tag{31.3}$$

where

Ct = Demand for transport
Pt = Transport price
CAt = Specific characteristics of consignments
Dt = Transport distance
Tt = Transport time
Vt = Transport volume (goods and passengers)

It is obvious that transport demand decreases by increasing prices and increases with the increase of specific transport factors (volume and distance). At the international level, transport demand is measured by the size of freight and passengers.

From all these considerations, it is clear that solutions need to be found to decrease transport demand (to reduce the natural degradation of environmental factors) by decreasing distances or transport volumes.

Among the less agreed methods is the one aimed at increasing transport prices. Unfortunately, this is happening today, for reasons totally different from ecological principles. More specifically, the price of transport is higher, even if more environmentally friendly vehicles are used (one example is the cost of transporting goods by rail, higher than that of road, over the same distance), which is contrary to the objective pursued, of reducing the negative effects on the environment and human health. This situation needs to be remedied, and an immediate solution would be to require all carriers to pay all social transport costs, including external transport costs (mostly indirectly subsidized, especially in the case of road transport).

The use of environmentally friendly transport systems is an action that has been gaining momentum in recent years, especially with regard to motor vehicles. In this case, electric vehicles are becoming more and more widespread, but unfortunately, only part of the problem is solved globally. Thus, if pollution levels in congested areas can decrease significantly, the level of pollution in electricity generation sources (the main source of electric battery vehicles) will increase.

In this context, the solution of electric vehicles must be considered as a good one for areas with high road traffic intensity, but in order to balance the environmental balance it is necessary to accelerate the uptake of a large share of transport demand by more environmentally friendly modes (multimodal transport, rail, etc.).

The European Commission has also proposed a series of measures to improve transport systems in line with the principles of sustainable development.

As a member of the European Union (EU), Romania will have to continue the process of harmonizing the national strategic framework with the main components of the sustainable transport policy strategy (Table 31.1).

Energy efficiency should aim at meeting transport demand while adopting technical solutions to significantly reduce energy consumption, especially those based on hydrocarbons. In this respect, in the coming years, the specific energy consumption relative to vehicles (number of passengers-km) and cargo volume (ton-km) should be reduced by at least 10% compared to 2000 levels, while achieving a gradual reduction of up to 20% by 2030. For these purposes, consideration should be given to the use of alternative, environmentally friendly fuels as compared to conventional fuels, in line with the objectives of the European Union. At the same time, the share of electric vehicles in the total specific transport fleets should be increased.

For the near future, in order to achieve this objective, at the community level, according to VIRTA's estimates, there are three possible scenarios (VIRTA, 2022):

- By 2030, the global stock of electric vehicles (with the exception of the two/three wheels) would reach almost 200 million vehicles representing about 10% of the global fleet of vehicles.
- Under a more ambitious scenario, 270 million electric vehicles will be roaming by 2030 and the share of electric vehicles in the global vehicle stock will reach 14%.

Table 31.1 Key components of a strategic framework for sustainable transport policies

Common policies	Priorities for Romania	Impact	Barriers
Building of the Trans-European Transport Network (TEN-T)	Modernization and development of the transport network of national and European interest (TEN-T)	High and increasing costs of investment in maintenance and operation	Economic uncertainty
Improving road safety	Balanced development of conventional infrastructures throughout the country	Stimulating long-term demand for transport	Insufficient investment resources and reduced direct efficiency in their use
Revitalization of railways	Increasing safety conditions	Modest modal change in the short and medium term and substantial long-term effects	Difficulty in identifying priorities in the construction of infrastructure
Promoting shipping (as an economic alternative to road transport)	Coordination with territorial and urban planning policies	Increasing the use of public passenger transport	Negative effects on the environment
Supporting multimodal transport	Increasing the competitiveness of transport companies	Fostering the competitiveness of the whole national economy and companies at the European level by including in their decisions the total impacts and costs of the transport system	Low international competitiveness of national companies operating in Europe (limited intermodal capacity)
Improving energy efficiency	Support and stimulate cooperation between operators		Divergence from European policies
Development of high-quality urban transport	Improving the energy efficiency of the transport system	Increasing the efficiency of intermodal transport	Difficulty in delivering on the commitments of transport policies
Use of intelligent transport systems to reduce pollution and clean and increase the efficiency of activity	Internalization of external costs		Reduced real capacity for implementation and control of the new rules
Adopt a policy on effective charging for transport and recognition of users' rights and obligations	Technological improvements in vehicles		Limited ability to influence international policy measures
			Social benefits concentrated only in specific groups
			The need for parallel development of complementary measures in other sectoral policies
			The existence of disproportionate local expectations regarding the legal opportunities for infrastructure development

- By 2050, the global stock of electric vehicles is expected to reach 350 million units, and its share is expected to rise to 20% by 2030.

Worldwide, there are many strategies and policies to support sustainable transport, some of which are implemented, but unfortunately many remain only in the phase of proposals, theories, and debates. Some of them are promising.

For example, in mid-2022 in Germany, the world's first fleet was inaugurated, with rail trainsets based on the fueling of hydrogen engines. The fleet of 14 trains, supplied by the French group Alstom in Lower Saxony, runs on a 100-kilometer route connecting the towns of Cuxhaven, Bremerhaven, Bremervorde, and Buxtehude, located a short distance from Hamburg (Maciucă, 2022).

The new fleet, which cost 93 million euros, replacing diesel traction along the route will reduce air pollution by around 4400 tons of CO_2 each year. The experiment started this year is expected to be rapidly expanded, so that in about 10 years, in Germany, between 2500 and 3000 diesel trains will be able to be replaced by hydrogen trains.

In fact, by the 2035s, about 15–20% of the European regional rail market will be able to operate on hydrogen. Hydrogen trains are particularly efficient for small regional lines, where the cost of a transition to electric gaskets would be too high in relation to the cost-effectiveness of the links.

However, it is not only rail transport that aims to use hydrogen mobility solutions in the future but also the entire transport sector, including road and air, as well as heavy industry, in particular steel and chemistry, relies on this technology to reduce its CO_2 emissions.

Romania is also interested in the purchase of hydrogen train gaskets for the renewal and modernization of the current national fleet. Unfortunately, in the last 15 years, in Romania, there has been no public procurement of new rolling stock intended for public passenger rail transport, the public-owned rail passenger transport operator has not acquired and does not have in the active fleet a sufficient number of rolling stock to serve the traveling public, and privately-owned rail passenger transport operators, which entered the Romanian rail market, have acquired only secondhand rolling stock, with a considerable seniority, which no longer meets the European quality and safety requirements. The authorities argue that the introduction of hydrogen fuel cell electric traction trucks is not a solution to cancel electrification programs in Romania, but only an environmentally friendly alternative to diesel traction transport on unelectrified lines. The public rail network in Romania was, at the level of 2021, about 10.500 km long, of which 64% were unelectrified, with electric traction in the "classic" catenary-pantograph supply system not possible.

Therefore, in July 2022, the Romanian authorities approved the purchase of 12 hydrogen trains as part of a pilot project to test green trains.

The 12 hydrogen trains cost 174 million euros, but the maintenance, repairs, and supply of hydrogen, for a period of 30 years, cost almost one billion euros (Podaru, 2022). In the National Recovery and Resilience Plan (PNRR), in addition to financing the acquisition of the 12 hydrogen trains, it is also foreseen to restore/renew two train lines on the relationships: Bucharest—Pitesti and Resita—the will.

From a financial point of view, however, it is a question mark if we notice that, again, the purchase of trains in Romania is made at a higher price than in other Western countries, much more economically potent. Thus, the examples presented above show that a hydrogen train purchased in Germany (the year 2022) costs about EUR 6.65 million, while Romania, in the same year and for the same type of train liner, foresees a price of EUR 14.5 million, which is more than double that of Germany.

However, the financial effort is worthwhile because the replacement of diesel and electric traction based on hydrogen fuel cells reduces transport pollution by an equivalent of more than EUR 600,000 per year, which means 18,348 tons CO_2/year and 306 tons NO_x/year less in the atmosphere, contributing to the objectives of European and national strategies to achieve the net-zero pollution effect in 2050.

A real development of a sustainable mobility system calls for the adoption of certain measures, the most important ones aiming at:

- Decrease in demand for nonessential transport.
- Adoption (choice) of non-fossil fuel vehicles.
- Internalization of external costs.
- Shift from car use to more environmentally friendly systems (e.g., car sharing).
- Increased use of public transport, cycling (or other equivalent vehicles), or on foot.
- Obtain the greatest possible support (political and public) in support of sustainable transport, technological innovations, and/or laws and regulations in this field.

31.4 Analysis/Result Interpretation

In line with the principle of sustainable development, transport policies must aim at real measures to increase the efficiency of this field of activity, so as to simultaneously meet the demand for mobility, social fairness, and environmental protection. In this paper was proposed a complex mechanism for achieving this goal consisting of a combination of measures aimed at reducing transport demand concomitantly with the widespread use of new, clean technologies for transport vehicles. However, these elements are linked to general economic policies, which, in my view, need to be fundamentally changed toward an integral ecology. From this perspective, political decisions play a major role, technologically being much simpler to achieve. This means that, in the future, the creation of a real sustainable transport system must be supported by society as a whole, through appropriate campaigns that influence political and economic decision-makers.

31.5 Conclusions

Transport caused, in the last decades, more problems than advantages. But, as Francis Dobos said, "we are not called to resist evil but to create good, to be proactive and not to avoid obstacles" (Necula & Dobos, 2022). Therefore, humanity has reacted positively and began to put into practice solutions to remedy negative situations, created by an increasingly remaining mobility system following the demands of the development of today's human society. The achievements, shy, at first, have been added, permanently, new elements, so that in recent years we can see a greater global involvement for the swift and efficient implementation of the sustainable transport system.

The constant change in prices of classical fuels (hydrocarbon-based) and also major events such as sanitary pandemics or military conflicts have accelerated the development of tools, techniques, and technologies to support sustainable transport. Undeniably, the most obvious and agreed solutions concerned the use of vehicles using alternative fuels and less pollutants. As an example, the electric car industry experienced a real development boom in just a few years.

However, it is not only this solution that needs to be supported in order to properly develop a sustainable transport system. Among the elements to be considered, the most important is to reduce the demand for transport. This clearly needs to be done, at the same time, with policies that fully meet the need for mobility. In support of this approach, some examples of good practices are presented in the paper, but in principle, the whole approach should be considered as an action aimed at a paradigm shift.

The new paradigm must have at its core the vision of the development of integral ecology. According to Petrini, "we cannot resolutely address the enormous issues of care to save the environment if we do not put them in close connection with social and economic inequality" (Petrini, 2020). In this equation, sustainable transport occupies an important place because it connects the social and economic side and can influence the increase or decrease in the standard of living and the value of biodiversity. However, given the increased speed of implementation of less polluting transport policies in recent years, we can say that sustainable transport can become a reality in the near future. The final result, as in any other approach, depends not only on the level of development of each area but mainly on the choices of politicians or more clearly stated by their interests. At national and international levels, no matter how many strategies or projects to support the implementation of a sustainable transport system, they will not be able to be put into practice without the right policy decisions. This must be understood by the decision-makers and act accordingly.

References

Brown, L. R. (2001). *Pavement is replacing the world's croplands.* https://grist.org/article/rice/

Eurostat. (2022). *Greenhouse gas emission statistics—Air emissions accounts.* https://ec.europa.eu/eurostat/statistics-explained/index.php?title=Greenhouse_gas_emission_statistics_-_air_emissions_accounts#Analysis_by_economic_activity

Kanafi, A. (1983). *Transportation demand analysis.* Mc Graw Hill. ISBN: 0070332711.

Kraus, L., & Proff, H. (2021). *Sustainable urban criteria and measurements—Systematic literature assessment.* https://duepublico2.uni-due.de/servlets/MCRFileNodeServlet/duepublico_derivate_00074497/sustainability_13_07113_Kraus_Proff_2021.pdf

Necula, C., & Doboș, F. (2022). *Reconciliation with yourself* (Bookzone, Ed.). ISBN 978-606-9639-05-4.

Petrini, C. (2020). Earth of the future (Rao, Ed.). ISBN 978-606-006-535-7.

Podaru, M. (2022). *Hydrogen trains in Romania: The government approves the acquisition of 12 hydrogen trains, an investment of over EUR 1 billion.* https://economedia.ro/trenuri-cu-hidrogen-in-romania-guvernul-aproba-achizitia-a-12-trenuri-cu-hidrogen-investitie-de-peste-un-miliard-de-euro.html#.YwyAJnZBxPZ

UN (2022). World population prospects: The 2017 revision. https://www.un.org/en/desa/world-population-projected-reach-98-billion-2050-and-112-billion-2100

Virta (The Electric Vehicle Charging Platform). (2022). *Sustainability policy.* https://www.virta.global/hubfs/Sustainability%20Policy%20Virta%202022%20EN.pdf

Zuidgeest, M. H. P, Witbreuk, M. J. G., & van Maarseveen, M. F. A. M. (2000). *Sustainable transport: A pragmatic review.* https://ris.utwente.nl/ws/portalfiles/portal/5538770/34+Zuidgeest.pdf

Chapter 32
Industrial Policies Regarding R&D Activities and Their Effects on Economic Performance

Alexandra-Ioana Lazăr

Abstract Industrial policies are aimed at ensuring a favorable framework for industrial competitiveness and especially aim at exploiting the industrial potential of the innovation policy, a concept interpreted differently from one country to another. The objectives of the innovation policy derive from the need to promptly respond to problems, constituting a condition of economic vitality, productivity growth, and the adoption of such a policy supported by the allocation of financial, material, and human resources will allow the identification and successful application of the most appropriate solutions.

Keywords R&D sector · Competitiveness · Innovation policy

32.1 Introduction

According to Article 173 of the Treaty on the Functioning of the European Union (TFEU), industrial policy aims to ensure the conditions – framework favorable to industrial competitiveness and the adaptation of industry to structural changes. It also favors SME development and the cooperation between them, as well as the exploitation of the industrial potential of R&D policies.

Innovation policy that is closely linked to other European Union policies aims to transform R&D results into high-quality products and services to maintain competitiveness.

The European Commission defines industrial policy as a policy that considers the effective and coherent application of all policies that influence the structural adjustment of industry, in order to promote competitiveness (European Commission, 1994).

A.-I. Lazăr (✉)
National Institute for Economic Research "Costin C. Kirițescu", Bucharest, Romania
e-mail: alexandra.lazar@ince.ro

In the European Union, the emergence of the concept of industrial policy was favored by the implementation of an industrial policy at the level of the member countries and by some policy actions to be followed within the entire European Union.

32.2 Literature Review

Some specialized papers highlight the particularly important role of the state in a knowledge-based economy, as demonstrated by the successful industrial policies of the USA, Finland, Germany, and France (Cohen, 2006).

A successful industrial policy focused on economic activities at the European, national, and local levels would approach current macroeconomic, industrial, innovation, cohesion, and environmental issues, which would significantly contribute to the recovery of developing countries (Pianta, 2014).

Although there is a complementary relationship between business, education, and government spending on R&D, industrial policies tend to work in opposite directions. In this context, to solve this paradox, increasing the innovation capacity of the regions, implementing industrial policy by increasing investments in R&D activities become imperatively necessary (Oughton et al., 2002).

A coherent industrial policy is not a policy in which the government applies Pigouvian taxes, but a policy of strategic collaboration between the private sector and the government (Rodrik, 2004).

In 2005, the European Commission proposed an integrated approach to industrial policy through a program that provided sectoral and cross-sectoral initiatives. The approach proved to be successful and the results were favorable. The program enjoyed the support of both the European Parliament and the member countries and, as a result, it was proposed to maintain it.

The Communication Industrial Policy: Increasing Competitiveness, adopted by the European Commission in October 2011, pointed out the importance of developing coherent policies in order to increase sustainable industrial competitiveness and targeted, in particular, the key areas where sustained efforts are needed: the innovativeness of industries, the environment economic, SME, single market.

European Commission Communication – A stronger European industry for economic growth and recovery – Update of the communication on industrial policy, 2012 - highlights the importance of investments in innovation (advanced technologies for non-polluting production, essential generic technologies, bio-products, a sustainable policy for industry, construction and raw materials, ecological vehicles and boats, smart networks).

Also, the importance of human resources and skills, access to financing, and improving market conditions in order to promote the competitiveness of the industry was highlighted.

Europe 2020 – A European strategy for smart, sustainable, and inclusive growth proposed seven initiatives, four of which are particularly important for increasing the competitiveness of EU industry: an innovation union, a digital agenda for

Europe, an integrated industrial policy for an era of globalization, and new skills for new jobs.

In the Innovation Scoreboard, 2020, based on the evaluations carried out, the European Commission placed Romania in the category of modest innovators, with results below the European Union average.

In the current conditions, for Romania, the problem of specialization based on competitive advantage is determined by the need to reduce existing unfavorable gaps, which implies, among other things, the identification and successful application of the most suitable solutions capable of ensuring the successful confrontation of international competition.

32.3 Analysis/Results Interpretation

Romania's industrial policy.

In the context of the aspects presented, the main coordinates of Romania's industrial policy regarding CD&I activities must, in our opinion, be the following:

- Increasing the share of expenses for R&D in GDP, especially for ensuring/modernizing the infrastructure indispensable for the stimulation of creative acts, the practical transposition of their results and their dissemination over a wide area, at the national and international level.
- Due to chronic underfunding, the objectives of the National R&D Strategy could not be fully fulfilled. Apart from the imperative requirement to substantially increase the funds allocated from the state budget, we believe that it is also necessary to take additional measures regarding the diversification of funding sources by increasing private and foreign ones (those that come from participation in the managed and financed Framework Projects by the European Union).
- Increasing the international visibility of the CD&I sector by intensifying the participation of specialists from universities and research institutes in various European projects and programs. Creating a favorable framework for the confirmation of universities and institutes as centers of excellence at the European level and their association with the European network will favor establishing scientific partnerships with research centers, universities and prestigious companies in the country and abroad.
- The development and application of the industrial policy through "bottom up" mechanisms, which refers to the process of conception and implementing the respective policy carried out with the involvement of agents from the public and private sector, research units from the academic and university environment and non-governmental organizations with concerns in the field.
- The mechanism involves information providing, forecasts and suggestions by economic agents and research units, their analysis by the government, and the outline of coordinates and paths of action for the application of industrial policy.

- The specific instruments used for the application of the industrial policy, respectively, the instruments of direct intervention (subsidies, public orders, etc.) and indirect intervention, must be focused on improving the quality of the factors (facilitating access to financing, offering specialized services, stimulating R&D and the training of the workforce, the creation and consolidation of industrial agglomerations – clusters and local networks – networks of companies, banks, academic, and university research units).
- Intensification of intangible investments to increase the competitiveness of R&D activities and the dissemination of their results, in workforce training and in intellectual services (consultancy, expertise, benchmarking studies, etc.).
- Worldwide experience has shown that ensuring sustainable competitive growth is conditioned by the nature of the resources involved in the economic development process. It is obvious that the preponderance of intangible factors provides a much more solid basis for the sustainable growth of competitiveness (innovative, managerial, organizational, marketing, technological know-how assimilation capacity, workforce qualification level, organizational culture). The promotion of intangible investments in the field of R&D implies, in addition to the directions of action mentioned above, also ensuring a closer relationship between the industry and the system of science and technology.
- It also directs R&D activities more rigorously towards satisfying the requirements of the socio-economic environment and promotes active quality policies.
- The development of scientific and technological parks is able to ensure the attraction of foreign investments, the improvement of product competitiveness, the improvement of the professional skills of employees, and the generation of highly qualified jobs.

These structures will support the development of companies and generate poles of sustainable development based on the promotion of applied research and technology transfer.

Increasing the volume of technical, economic, managerial, marketing, etc. consulting services offered by teams of specialists from the university environment will provide more credibility, prestige on the market, access to resources and information, high quality services and solving with the greatest promptness of problems, which gives additional chances of success.

Identifying the appropriate courses of action requires knowing the influencing factors of R&D activities and their effects on the economic and financial performance of companies.

32.4 Conclusions

In the context of these expected coordinates of the industrial policy and in order to ensure success in the market, we believe that the efforts of Romanian companies must be directed in the following directions:

- Consolidation of the R&D function
- The lack of this function in most Romanian industrial companies drastically reduces their innovative potential and leads to an increase in production costs, because these companies are forced to turn to specialized R&D units to obtain technological solutions
- Increasing the attractiveness of R&D activities for young graduates by ensuring professional development prospects, optimizing the R&D infrastructure and working conditions. Stimulating personal initiative and effort by giving material and moral rewards can ensure the mobilization of employees to achieve R&D objectives.
- Increasing the human potential of the R&D activity through the priority integration of people with the appropriate training and experience, with creative capacity, who manage to make better use of their professional training. In the current conditions, in a good part of Romanian companies where the culture of quality is missing, the selection process should be carried out through procedures based on rigorous criteria and financial resources that allow the entry and maintenance of specialists in the R&D sector, respectively, the elimination of non-performing employees.
- Intensification of continuous training and improvement, of continuous training of personnel from research and development activities, an essential condition for keeping them permanently connected to scientific and technological progress. Such a direction to follow is all the more necessary since numerous studies and surveys have highlighted the reality that most domestic companies have drastically reduced the budget allocated to staff training, in general, and to those in R&D activities, in particular. It is also necessary to increase concerns regarding the provision of training programs (training, improvement, and continuous learning) taking into account the long duration of their preparation and that of the manifestation of the effects of participation in these programs.
- The modernization and diversification of information services, in the conditions of the accelerated development of communication techniques, ensure access to information in real time and reduce the duration of the scientific approach for up-to-date knowledge of scientific and technological achievements.
- The modern organization of information services means digitization, using equipment and applications that allow storing the necessary data and using them operatively according to the specific requirements of the work to be performed or the decisions to be made. Through digitization, they can ensure the necessary data for effective management at all organizational structural levels, for the adoption of decisions under conditions of certainty and those under conditions of risk.
- Designing an action plan that ensures the effective transition based on which to effectively move from the implemented strategy proven unsuccessful as a result of the occurrence of unforeseen events, to a new strategy. An environment in constant transformation can cause a change in the market demand for a new good/service that no longer coincides with the forecasts that were the basis for

the development of the existing strategy, the design of an action plan for its change presupposes the identification of some strategic alternatives from which to opt for the best.
- Intensification of partnerships with industrial companies, aimed at strengthening the respective company's position on the national and international markets by increasing the degree of competitiveness of its products/services. Considering the risks involved in R&D activities and the reduced ability of many firms to solve all the technological problems raised by the production process and costs on their own, most of these firms are interested in partnerships with others in the same industry, which can provide them with faster access to markets, technologies, and increased learning opportunities.

References

Cohen, E. (2006). *Theoretical foundations of industrial policy* (EIB Papers, ISSN 0257-7755, Vol. 11, Iss. 1, pp. 84–106). European Investment Bank (EIB), Luxembourg.

Commission of the European Communities. (2005). *Communication from the Commission: Implementing the community lisbon programme: A policy framework to strengthen EU manufacturing – Towards a more integrated approach for industrial policy, COM (2005) 474 final, Brussels*. Retrieved from http://www.europarl.europa.eu/RegData/docs_autres_institutions/commission_europeenne/com/2005/0474/COM_COM(2005)0474_EN.pdf

Commission of the European Communities. (2011). *Comunicare a Comisiei: Politica industrială: Creșterea competitivității, COM (2011) 642 final, Brussels*. Retrieved from https://eur-lex.europa.eu/legal-content/ro/TXT/PDF/?uri=CELEX:52011DC0642&from=ro

European Commission. (1994). *An industrial competitiveness policy for the European Union, COM (94) 319 final*.

Oughton, C., Landabaso, M., & Morgan, K. (2002). The regional innovation paradox: Innovation policy and industrial policy. *The Journal of Technology Transfer, 27*, 97–110. https://doi.org/10.1023/A:1013104805703

Pianta, M. (2014). An industrial policy for Europe. *Seoul Journal of Economics, 27*(3), 277–305. Retrieved from SSRN https://ssrn.com/abstract=2530344

Rodrik, D. (2004). *Industrial policy for the twenty-first century*. Retrieved from SSRN https://ssrn.com/abstract=666808

Chapter 33
Study Regarding the Use of Mobile Phones in Romania

Vanesa Madalina Vargas ⓘ and Cosmin Alexandru Teodorescu

Abstract The development of the IT&C environment has provided opportunities regarding the way data is collected, stored, created, and managed, both at the individual and organizational level. People prefer mobility for devices they use. Therefore, computing systems have benefited from a constant stream of technological development. Mainframe computers were succeeded by minicomputers, which led to personal computers and then to mobile devices. The benefits of mobile technology include innovation, flexible work opportunities, higher-quality work, and better cross-border collaboration and communication. However, managing the security of the data contained within these devices remains a challenge. Smartphones are the most widely used means in this regard, both for personal and work purposes. As their prevalence has increased, smartphones have become more prone to cyberattacks and are associated with an increasing level of security risks. The present study aims to analyze the current state of the number of mobile phone users in Romania, both from the perspective of individual users and companies that offer their employees the opportunity to have a work phone. Another aspect that this paper examines is the evolution of smartphone users and mobile Internet connectivity. This chapter represents the baseline for the development of a complex research that aims to build directions towards preventing and detecting intrusions associated with specific mobile environments cyberattacks.

Keywords Smartphone evolution · Cybersecurity · Mobile · iOS · Android · Cyberattacks

---

V. M. Vargas (✉)
Institute for Economic Forecasting, Romanian Academy, Bucharest, Romania

Bucharest University of Economic Studies, Bucharest, Romania
e-mail: vanesa.vargas@fabiz.ase.ro

C. A. Teodorescu
Bucharest University of Economic Studies, Bucharest, Romania

33.1 Introduction

Smartphones are ubiquitous in modern society and have transformed the way we communicate, access information, and interact with the world around us. Over the past few decades, the introduction of mobile devices has completely changed our lives, making communication easier than ever. Social media allows us to always stay in touch with our friends and millions of other people, no matter where we are. The only thing we need is a smartphone that can access the internet. Nowadays, we use our mobile phones frequently for communication as well as accessing a wide range of apps that might facilitate our daily life. It is worth mentioning that some of these apps have been optimized for mobile app stores so that it will be easier for us to find them. We can read books, listen to music, shop online, snap pictures, watch films, play games, create and edit documents, even obtain medical advice, and do a lot more with just our mobile devices. As a result, individuals are using their phones for longer and longer periods of time.

Smartphones have become an integral part of daily life for many people around the world, and Romania is no exception. In recent years, the use of smartphones in Romania has increased significantly, with more and more people relying on these devices for communication, information access, and a variety of other purposes. Smartphones are also used for accessing the internet and obtaining information, whether for work or personal use. In addition, smartphones are increasingly being used for entertainment, with people using them to watch videos, listen to music, and play games.

The widespread adoption of smartphones in Romania has had several impacts on society. On the positive side, they have made it easier for people to stay connected and informed and have provided access to a wide range of services and information that was not previously available. However, there are also concerns about the potential negative effects of smartphone use, including distraction.

This article will explore the use of smartphones in Romania and its evolution, what are the important characteristics when buying a new mobile device, the use of smartphones for work purposes, and any challenges or concerns that have arisen as a result of their widespread adoption.

33.2 Literature Review

These days, the instable and changeable conditions of the business environment, forced organizations intensely to be entrepreneurial and agile, especially with the emergence of the Internet and its advanced tools (Bataineh et al., 2015). The spread of innovative mobile devices, such as smartphones, tablets, and PDAs, was capable of providing multisided and highly targeted interactive advertising messages, even inside games. Because smartphones and related technologies have become so ingrained in our lives, most businesses tend to use mobile platforms to target their clients (Apergis, 2019). Furthermore, the fast-growing mobile gaming has increased the demand of mobile games as a marketing medium (Newzoo, 2012). Therefore, there is an increased desire from both researchers and practitioners to become informed about new developments.

Although the first computers were created in the twentieth century, it was the twenty-first century that saw the rapid rise of digitalization (Juhász et al., 2022). The total number of smartphone users has considerably increased over the years mainly due to the advent of new operating systems and proliferation of new applications (Martins et al., 2017). According to recent data provided by Statista (2023a), the number of smartphone subscription worldwide in 2021 was 6.2 billion with a potential forecast of 7.2 billion by 2025. The smartphone penetration rate in Europe is now at 77,64%, while in Romania, it is at 74% (Statista, 2023b). With increasing internet penetration, the average time spent on such devices has also increased to 3 h and 41 min while 1 in 5 smartphone users worldwide spends upwards of 4.5 h on average on their phones every day (Datareportal, 2022a, b). However, 68% of individuals in the EU ordered or bought goods or services over the internet for private use in 2022, up from 54% in 2017 (Eurostat, 2023).

Additionally, the phenomenal expansion of smartphones has attracted academic interest, particularly in relation to the factors that influence smartphone brand choice (Lee et al., 2013; Yeh et al., 2016). Numerous studies have examined factors that impact brand communication, such as social media and advertising (Martins et al., 2019); factors affecting brand communication (Esmaeilpour et al., 2017), or factors affecting users' personal experiences with the product (Hossain et al., 2018). However, some authors studied elements like the product's functional and symbolic value dimensions (Hung et al., 2011) or the brand image of the product (Lee, 2015). Everyone needs to be digitally competent because it offers significant benefits and lack of it can result in several dangers (Ala-Mutka, 2011; Cimini et al., 2021).

33.3 Methodology

The present study aims to analyse the current state of the number of mobile phone users in Romania, both from the perspective of individual users and companies that offer their employees the opportunity to have a work phone. Another aspect examined in this paper is the evolution of smartphone users and the connectivity of the mobile Internet.

To achieve our aim, we used the rational method of the analytic synthetic process, in which we break down the idea of using a mobile device into smaller, simpler parts to better understand it. This method is often used in the natural and social sciences to analyze and understand the components that make up a particular system or phenomenon and to study how these components interact with each other to produce the overall behavior or properties of the system. The purpose of the analytical approach is to analyze the Eurostat data available for member states of the European Union and highlight these data for Romania. Using data visualization, we created graphics to make the information contained in a complex database like Eurostat sets more easily understandable and interpretable. Data visualization is an important tool in data analysis, helping to uncover patterns, trends, and insights that might not be immediately obvious when looking at raw data. The goal of the synthetic process is to explain the created data visualization by interpretation.

This paper represents the baseline for the development of a complex research that aims to build directions towards preventing and detecting intrusions associated with specific mobile environments cyberattacks.

33.4 Analysis/Results Interpretation

Smartphones and tablets are less of a luxury and more of a necessity in today's connected world. Connecting to the Internet whenever and wherever we are is increasingly vital in our daily lives. Whether it is to avoid missing important emails, stay up to date with the news, or locate our way when we get lost, being online is a necessity. Mobile Internet is a version of the larger Internet that has been shrunk to fit the screen size of a phone's web browser. A cellular network is one that supports mobile devices. A "cell" is a group of related geographic locations in a cellular network that connects to the Internet even via satellites. A transmitting tower is located in the middle of each cell, via which digital radio waves are used to broadcast and receive data.

The upward evolution of the number of individuals with internet access through the smartphone is obvious as more and more people feel the need to use their phones for buying products or services online, use ride-sharing apps or to use the digital public services as paying taxes and fees remotely. Moreover, the migration of the population from rural to urban areas is one of the proofs that people will need a mobile device with Internet access, as seen in Fig. 33.1.

Regarding the significance of sustainability factors in IT equipment purchases, according to Table 33.1, in 2022, 66% of EU citizens saw pricing as a key factor when making their mobile or smartphone purchase. Hard drive or processor speed (54%) was ranked as the second-most significant attribute, followed by energy efficiency (22%), eco-design (13%), the ability to prolong life (9%), a manufacturer's or seller's take-back program (7%), and none of these characteristics (6%). In the EU, 5% of people claimed that they had never purchased a smartphone or a mobile device.

According to Eurostat data, different age groups utilize different types of internet access devices (Fig. 33.2). When it comes to mobile phones, the proportion of users between the ages of 16 and 24 and 55–74 differs by over 50%.

Due to the fact that desktop computers are used on average significantly less frequently than mobile devices among various age groups, the biggest variation in desktop computer usage is just 16%. The usage of smartphones and mobile devices to access the internet climbed by 12% among persons aged 55–74 and by 9% overall

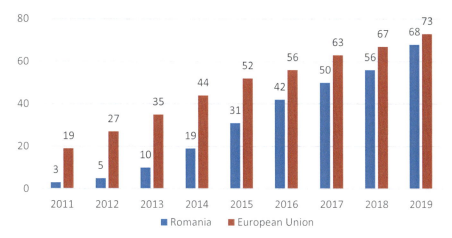

Fig. 33.1 Individuals – mobile internet access; Percentage of all individuals. (Source: Authors own research based on Eurostat data)

in 2018, according to data. The current situation differs greatly amongst EU member states. For instance, there are no appreciable disparities across age groups in Sweden or Denmark. On the other side, smartphone internet connectivity is four times more common among 16–34-year-olds in Bulgaria, Greece, and Romania than it is among 55–74-year-olds. It is sometimes asserted that women have less access to emerging technology than males. However, this also differs according on a person's age, level of education or place of origin.

According to Fig. 33.3, there is a clear increase both at the European and Romanian levels in the percentage of employed persons that are provided with a portable device that allows internet connection via mobile networks, for business purposes. However, it varies widely depending on the industry, company size, and location. In some industries, such as technology and finance, it is common for employees to be provided with a portable device for business use, while in other industries, it may be less common. Additionally, larger companies are more likely to provide these devices to their employees than smaller ones, and employees in urban areas may be more likely to have access to these devices than those in rural areas. Given the fact that Romania attracted more and more investors and created an IT hub, especially in the Western part of the country, the higher number of mobile devices used for business purposes and provided by the employer is a certainty. Figure 33.3 (right) also shows that in 2021 the percentage of Romanian enterprises providing such a device reached the same level as the European Union average.

Table 33.1 Important characteristics when buying a mobile or a smartphone 2022 (% of individuals)

Country	Price	Hard drive/ processor speed	Energy efficiency	Eco-design	Possibility of extending the life span	Take-back-scheme by manufacturer or seller	None of these characteristics	Have never bought a smartphone
EU	65.71	53.63	21.75	12.53	8.94	6.7	5.64	4.59
Belgium	68.28	52.96	–	8.9	4.81	3.94	–	2.73
Bulgaria	61.98	42.79	7.99	4.00	4.5	2.4	4.05	5.52
Denmark	59.81	52.05	26.63	12.44	5.08	12.73	8.83	8.16
Germany	58.86	44.95	18.01	8.56	8.5	4.8	8.84	5.88
Estonia	62.91	63.01	24.11	18.49	10.35	12.83	5.61	5.15
Greece	66.6	56.8	23.84	19.1	27.99	9.24	1.61	7.39
France	73.05	55.31	18.11	13.03	5.54	7.07	5.47	2.88
Cyprus	79.34	65.23	43.45	38.7	39.04	34.66	3.66	0.45
Latvia	61.35	52.33	18.53	18.3	6.83	12.28	5.87	7.89
Lithuania	68.07	52.85	25.34	20.45	13.16	13.12	3.75	5.09
Luxembourg	63.22	52.88	26.26	12.09	10.6	7.85	11.03	3.68
Hungary	64.22	44.73	23.83	12.06	11.83	10.28	6.36	3.48
Malta	74.41	69.19	45.5	43.21	27.63	23.54	2.43	0.45
Netherlands	69.01	80.83	21.5	8.48	4.9	4.47	3.4	0.62
Austria	70.81	69.89	42.81	61.97	22.37	20.07	1.83	8.38
Poland	63.67	56.26	17.95	8.9	7.36	5.04	3.58	3.78
Portugal	71.72	66.3	40.52	24.58	20.97	16.37	1.85	4.39
Romania	**65.17**	**41.37**	**17.96**	**7.64**	**12.69**	**4.13**	**2.24**	**8.61**
Slovenia	61.83	60.2	16.24	12.4	10.19	8.31	4.75	3.45
Slovakia	70.12	55.3	17.39	11.53	5.66	4.4	5.32	1.71
Finland	71.05	61.63	12.85	16.1	3.07	5.35	6.01	2.63
Sweden	66.26	58.13	66.26	10.1	3.13	4.52	9.64	4.11
Norway	72.7	73.59	37.03	30.52	20.41	23.93	2.96	6.08

Source: Own research based on Eurostat data

Fig. 33.2 Use of the internet on a mobile phone or smart phone by age group (%). (Source: Authors own research based on Eurostat data)

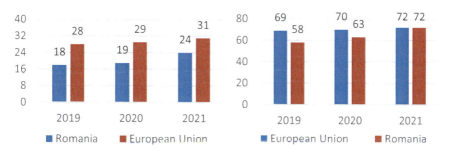

Fig. 33.3 Provide the employed persons with a portable device that allows internet connection via mobile telephone networks, for business purpose: Percentage of total employment (left) vs percentage of enterprises (right). (Source: Authors own research based on Eurostat data)

33.5 Conclusions

The evolution of the smartphone has had a significant impact on modern society. Since the introduction of the first smartphone in 1992 (Andrew, 2019), these devices have become an integral part of daily life for billions of people around the world. One of the key reasons for the rapid adoption of smartphones is the wide range of functionality they offer. In addition to making phone calls and sending text messages, smartphones can be used for tasks such as browsing the internet, checking email, creating and editing documents, streaming music and video, and much more. This versatility has made them a necessary tool for both personal and professional use.

The development of mobile apps has also played a major role in the success of smartphones. These small software programs allow users to perform a wide variety of tasks, from ordering food to tracking workouts and even managing finances. The availability of a vast app ecosystem has made smartphones even more useful and has helped drive their widespread adoption.

Another important factor in the evolution of smartphones is the rapid advancement of technology. Each new generation of smartphones has brought with it significant improvements in processing power, battery life, and other key features. This has allowed smartphones to become increasingly powerful and capable of handling more complex tasks.

Overall, the evolution of the smartphone has had a profound impact on the way we communicate, work, and live. These devices have become an indispensable part of modern life and will likely continue to evolve and shape the world in new and exciting ways in the future.

References

Ala-Mutka, K. (2011). *Mapping digital competence: Towards a conceptual understanding*. European Commission Joint Research Centre Luxembourg.

Andrew, O. (2019). *The history and evolution of the smartphone: 1992–2018*. Text Messaging Service for Small Business [Online]. Available https://www.textrequest.com/blog/history-evolution-smartphone/

Apergis, E. (2019). Who is tech savvy? Exploring the adoption of smartphones and tablets: An empirical investigation. *The Journal of High Technology Management Research, 30*(2), 100351.

Bataineh, A., Alhadid, A., Al-abdallah, G., Alfalah, T., Falah, J., & Idris, M. (2015). The role of information technology capabilities in capitalizing market agility in jordanian telecommunications sector. *International Journal of Academic Research in Business and Social Sciences, 5*(8), 90–101.

Cimini, C., Adrodegari, F., Paschou, T., Rondini, A., & Pezzotta, G. (2021). Digital servitisation and competence development: A case-study research. *CIRP Journal of Manufacturing Science and Technology, 32*, 447–460. https://doi.org/10.1016/j.cirpj.2020.12.005

Datareportal. (2022a). *Digital 2022 local country headlines*. Available online https://datareportal.com/reports/digital-2022-local-country-headlines

Datareportal. (2022b). *Digital 2022 global overview*. Available online https://datareportal.com/reports/digital-2022-global-overview-report

Esmaeilpour, M., Sayadi, A., & Mirzaei, M. (2017). Investigating the impact of service quality dimensions on reputation and brand trust. *International Journal of Business and Economic Sciences Applied Research, 10*(3), 7–17.

Eurostat. (2023). *Digital economy and society statistics – Households and individuals*. Available online https://ec.europa.eu/eurostat/statistics-explained/index.php?title=Digital_economy_and_society_statistics_-_households_and_individuals

Hossain, M. S., Zhou, X., & Rahman, M. F. (2018). Examining the impact of QR codes on purchase intention and customer satisfaction on the basis of perceived flow. *International Journal of Engineering Business Management, 10*, 1847979018812323.

Hung, K., Huiling Chen, A., Peng, N., Hackley, C., Amy Tiwsakul, R., & Chou, C. (2011). Antecedents of luxury brand purchase intention. *The Journal of Product and Brand Management, 20*(6), 457–467.

Juhász, T., Kálmán, B., Tóth, A., & Horváth, A. (2022). Digital competence development in a few countries of the European Union. *Management & Marketing Challenges for the Knowledge Society, 18*(2), 178–192. https://doi.org/10.2478/mmcks-2022-0010

Lee, S. Y. (2015). Interpersonal influence on online game choices. *Computers in Human Behavior, 45*, 129–136.

Lee, J., Lee, D., Moon, J., & Park, M.-C. (2013). Factors affecting the perceived usability of the mobile web portal services: Comparing simplicity with consistency. *Information Technology and Management, 14*, 43–57. https://doi.org/10.1007/s10799-012-0143-8

Martins, J., Alves, J., Cabral, J., Tavares, A., & Pinto, S. (2017). μ RTZVisor: a secure and safe real-time hypervisor. *Electronics, 6*(4), 93.

Martins, J., Costa, C., Oliveira, T., Gonçalves, R., & Branco, F. (2019). How smartphone advertising influences consumers' purchase intention. *Journal of Business Research, 94*, 378–387.

Newzoo. (2012). *Mobile games trend report.* Available at: Cited 28 September 2012.

Statista. (2023a). *Number of smartphone subscriptions worldwide from 2016 to 2021, with forecasts from 2022 to 2027.* Available online https://www.statista.com/statistics/330695/number-of-smartphone-users-worldwide/

Statista. (2023b). *Forecast of the smartphone user penetration rate in Romania from 2015 to 2025.* Available online https://www.statista.com/statistics/568223/predicted-smartphone-user-penetration-rate-in-romania/

Yeh, C.-H., Wang, Y.-S., & Yieh, K. (2016). Predicting smartphone brand loyalty: Consumer value and consumer-brand identification perspectives. *International Journal of Information Management, 36*(3), 245–257., ISSN 0268-4012. https://doi.org/10.1016/j.ijinfomgt.2015.11.013

Chapter 34
The Impact of Energy Crisis on the Vegetable Sector in Romania

Cornelia Alboiu

Abstract The Covid-19 pandemic spread throughout the world, followed by the crisis of rising energy and gas prices, and their immediate consequences tend to have disruptive effects on food security, in Romania's vegetable sector inclusively. The purpose of the chapter is to estimate the effects of energy and fertilizer price changes on producer and consumer prices and the degree of threat to food security in the vegetable sector, including the presentation of several scenarios regarding the change in production costs and vegetable farm net income. Total specific costs, costs of agricultural inputs including energy and fertilizers, farmgate and consumer prices, and related volatility coefficients are among the indicators used for this purpose. The results of the scenarios used reveal that there is a significant impact on producer and consumer prices, but also on the net farm income. At the same time, the results reveal an adaptation of farmers to this crisis by adjusting the use and application of agricultural inputs or cultivated areas. This adaptation of vegetable farmers to crises increases the food insecurity in this sector, which has been confronted with many other vulnerabilities over the years.

Keywords Energy crises · Impact · Scenarios · Horticultural sector

34.1 Introduction

Agricultural production is sensitive to changes in energy and gas prices, either through energy consumed directly or through inputs that depend on the energy price, such as chemical fertilizers and crop protection products. Energy prices that farmers have to face, as well as the evolution of oil and natural gas markets affect the production decision of farmers in the vegetable sector. The oil price has increased in 2022 by 200% since the spring of 2020, while that of gas by 30% in the second

---

C. Alboiu (✉)
Institute of Agricultural Economics, Romanian Academy, Bucharest, Romania

© The Author(s), under exclusive license to Springer Nature Switzerland AG 2024
L. Chivu et al. (eds.), *Constraints and Opportunities in Shaping the Future: New Approaches to Economics and Policy Making*, Springer Proceedings in Business and Economics, https://doi.org/10.1007/978-3-031-47925-0_34

quarter of that year only. The current moment is full of uncertainties. In fact, for more than 30 years, the Romanian vegetable market has been a market full of uncertainties, primarily due to the poor organization of producers and the weak contractual system. The vegetable sector in Romania is going through a difficult period and many producers risk disappearing from the market.

In this entire unfavourable context, it is worth noting the appearance of a new actor on the scene: climate change. Climate change also has an important effect on vegetable production (Parajuly et al., 2019). The analysis in this chapter focuses on relatively short-term adjustments in production, cultivated areas, prices, production value, and net farm income in response to higher energy and gas costs.

Vegetable production uses large amounts of energy, either directly by burning fuels or indirectly by using energy to produce agricultural inputs, especially chemical fertilizers and crop protection products. In the period 2015–2020, energy expenses increased significantly, mainly expenses for chemical fertilizers. Vegetable growing is a sector with relatively high energy consumption due to the specificity and requirements of certain vegetable species, especially if they are produced in the cold season. Therefore, vegetable production is sensitive to changes in energy and gas prices. The current energy crisis further deepens the vulnerabilities of the vegetable sector that seem insurmountable for over 30 years.

The current analysis refers to the period 2015–2020, but it should be emphasized that in the last decade, the total areas cultivated with vegetables decreased from 263 thousand ha in 2010 to 228 thousand ha in 2019 (−14%), the same negative trend being noticed in the total production of vegetables, which decreased from 3864 thousand tons to 3529 thousand tons (−18%). The main reason for this situation is the reduced ability of farmers to associate, less than 1% of farmers are members in a cooperative or producer group, together with meteorological changes, with trends of extreme weather events. Romania has over 400,000 vegetable farms, accounting for 26% of the total number of vegetable farms in the EU, with a low level of market organization.

34.2 Literature Review

According to an article published in the Financial Times (September, 2022), across the EU, farmers and food producers have warned of shortages and significant price rises for a wide range of staples this winter, calling for government support to cope with rising energy costs. Thus, several associations have announced that their members have already started to close their operations and reduce their production, demanding that the food chain not be included in the European energy rationalization plans. Pekka Pesonen, representative of Copa-Cogeca, showed that Europeans will face rising prices and shortages, especially in the fruit and vegetable sector. "It is something unprecedented. No one expected such a thing and did not anticipate the consequences". Farmers said that the increase in input prices has greatly accelerated in recent months. Many vegetable growers are already reducing their cultivated areas for the next harvest. Sweden's largest tomato grower has announced that it will not plant anything during the winter because it cannot afford the electricity cost. Some greenhouses in the Netherlands, the world's second-largest agricultural exporter by value after the US, are also closing.

According to a Reuters article (September, 2022), a producer group in the Netherlands estimates that up to 40% of its 3000 members have financial problems. This could mean less fruit, vegetables, and flowers in European supermarkets and relocating production to warmer countries. In the UK, heated greenhouse production, such as cucumbers and peppers, will halve current levels due to high energy prices. According to another European association, it is shown that the cultivated areas will depend very much on the extremely tough price negotiations with the supermarkets.

34.3 Methodology

For this study, FADN (Farm Accounting Data Network) and NIS (National Institute for Statics) tempo online data were used for the period 2015–2021. For prices, data starting with the second quarter of 2020 up to the second quarter of 2022 were used. The analysis is interesting not only in terms of the impact of the energy crisis on the sector but also in the context of the Farm to Fork Strategy. Thus, since its publication in May 2020, when its objectives were clearly stated, namely to reduce nutrient losses by at least 50%, to maintain soil quality and reduce fertilizer use by at least 20% by the year 2030, there has been a growing interest to analyse the actual use of fertilizers. The FADN database was set up to monitor farm income and business activities and collect information on the cost and quantities of fertilizers used in all EU countries. This allows capturing the use and importance of the economic costs that energy and fertilizers can represent for farms, especially in the context of the current energy and natural gas crisis. The main indicators used for this study are: total specific costs (euro), seed costs (euro), chemical fertilizers (euro) and by types in q, other specific costs (euro), energy costs, total production value (euro), farm gate and consumer prices.

The analysis of producer and consumer prices and the related volatility coefficients for the main vegetable species was carried out for the period 2020–2022. Food security and the impact on consumers were highlighted through the evolution of prices for the main types of vegetables. In this study, several scenarios were also used to study the impact of the increase in energy and input prices in the vegetable sector on production, production value, production costs, and net income at the farm level.

Thus, the objective of the paper is to estimate the impact of the increase in electricity and fertilizer prices on variable production costs at farm level, on farm production and net income. Implications for market adjustments and the impact on food security in this sector are also discussed.

34.4 Analysis/Results Interpretation

In order to analyse the impact of the increase in energy and gas prices, this section will present the evolution of prices of the main inputs used in the vegetable sector as well as their impact on the evolution of the sector in the short and medium term (Fig. 34.1).

Total input costs sum up specific costs, farm overheads, depreciation, and external factors. They also include amounts related to the use of production obtained on the holding as inputs for agricultural activity. They do not include agricultural taxes and other taxes.

The evolution of the main specific costs of the vegetable sector is presented in Fig. 34.2. They registered significant increases in the period 2016–2020, mainly for seeds and plants (+43%), followed by chemical fertilizers (+32%) and pesticides (+49%). Regarding the structure of specific costs, according to the calculations presented in Table 34.1, in 2020, the largest weight is held by the expenses for seeds and plants (52%), followed by the expenses for chemical fertilizers (21%) and for crop protection products (20%) (Table 34.1).

In order to observe the share of other production expenses, Table 34.2 shows the structure of variable costs by category of expenses.

Thus, regrouping the costs by variable expenses, in the year 2020, the paid salaries expenses had the largest weight (24%), followed by seed and plant costs (23%) and energy costs (16%). Chemical fertilizer expenses accounted for 10% and crop protection expenses 9%. The calculations in Table 34.2 reveal that the paid salaries expenses had the highest increase in 2020 compared to 2015, by +30%, followed by fertilizer expenses, by +21%. On the other hand, the energy expenses decreased by 15%, mainly due to the increase in the share of paid salaries.

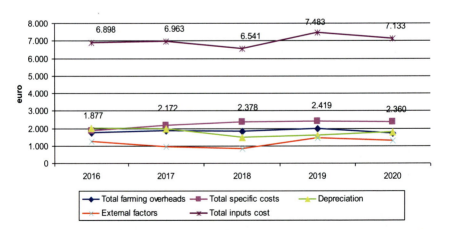

Fig. 34.1 Evolution of total input expenses (euros) by component category. (Source: FADN database, 2022)

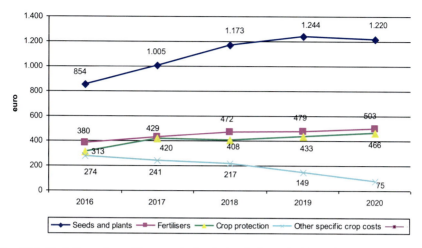

Fig. 34.2 Evolution of specific costs in horticultural farms in Romania (euros). (Source: FADN database, 2022)

Table 34.1 Structure of total specific costs %

	Seeds and plants	Fertilizers	Other specific costs	Feed for grazing livestock	Feed for pigs & poultry	Other livestock-specific costs	Total specific costs for OGA	Crop protection
2015	45.1	17.9	13.5	0.3	0.5	0.1	0.8	21.8
2016	45.5	20.3	14.6	0.4	2.1	0.2	0.3	16.7
2017	46.3	19.8	11.1	0.2	2.9	0.2	0.2	19.3
2018	49.3	19.8	9.1	0.5	3.7	0.4	0.1	17.2
2019	51.4	19.8	6.2	0.6	3.8	0.2	0.0	17.9
2020	52.1	**21.2**	3.2	1.1	2.1	0.0	0.0	**20.1**

Source: FADN (2022)

In order to see the evolution of the expenses for chemical fertilizers and pesticides in the period 2015–2020, from Fig. 34.3, it can be seen that even before the significant increase in the price of gas, the costs of chemical fertilizers and crop protection products had already registered increasing trends.

Thus, the evolution of expenses for chemical fertilizers and crop protection products had an increasing trend, by 36.7% and 3.8% respectively higher in 2020 compared to 2015. In 2020 compared to 2018, expenses for chemical fertilizers increased by 6.6% and 14.2% respectively for crop protection products. Some member states, including Romania, started collecting N-P-K data from 2014, and most of them communicated this data to the Commission starting from the accounting year 2016. From 2017 onwards, data on N-P-K quantities (nitrogen, phosphorus, and potassium) are compulsorily reported by all member states. This is why, in the chart below, no data is available for the years 2015 and 2016 (Fig. 34.4).

Table 34.2 Structure of variable costs %

	Wages paid	Costs for equip. and buildings	Energy costs	Contractual work	Other direct costs with inputs	Seeds and plants	Fertilizers	Other specific crop cost	Crop protection costs	%
2015	18	10	19	5	4	20	8	6	10	100
2016	18	10	21	5	5	20	9	6	7	100
2017	17	10	22	4	3	21	9	5	9	100
2018	15	8	21	5	4	24	10	4	8	100
2019	25	8	18	5	3	22	8	3	8	100
2020	**24**	9	**16**	5	3	**23**	10	1	**9**	100
2020/2015%	**30**	**−11**	**−17**	**−4**	**−21**	**17**	**21**	**−76**	**−8**	**0**

Source: FADN (2022)

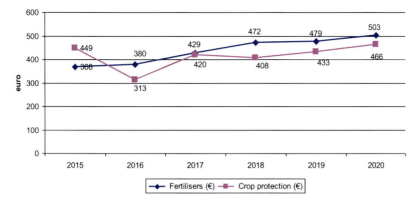

Fig. 34.3 Evolution of expenses for chemical fertilizers and crop protection products. (Source: FADN database, 2022)

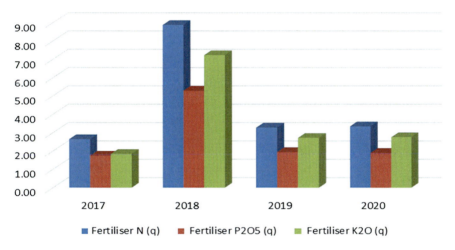

Fig. 34.4 The amount of chemical fertilizers applied per hectare in the vegetable sector of Romania. (Source: FADN database, 2022)

As regards the amounts of chemical fertilizers applied per hectare, these decreased dramatically in 2020 compared to 2018, being reduced by more than half. On the other hand, fertilizer costs have increased, which means, by logical reasoning, that vegetable producers have reduced chemical fertilizer application rates per hectare, basically adapting to a crisis situation.

Overall, in the horticultural sector, there is a decreasing trend of general expenses in 2020, both compared to 2019 and 2015. The trend is determined by the decrease in energy expenses by −19% in 2020 compared to 2018, but also the slightly smaller decrease of other expenses such as contractual work expenses, costs of equipment and buildings or other direct costs of agricultural inputs.

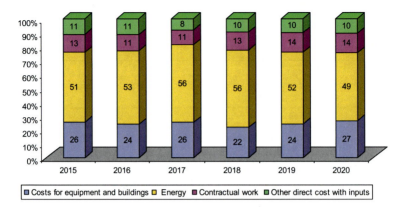

Fig. 34.5 Share of expenses for equipment and buildings, energy, contractual work and other direct input costs in total overheads %. (Source: FADN database, 2022)

From Fig. 34.5, it can be noticed that the share of the costs of equipment and buildings increased slightly in 2020 compared to 2015, from 26% to 27%, while the share of energy costs decreased slightly from 51% to 49%.

To assess the impact of the increase in electricity prices on vegetable production, the best way is to estimate the share of energy expenses in the value of horticultural production. According to the calculations presented in Fig. 34.6, the share of energy expenses in the value of horticultural production was 16% in 2020, reaching the maximum level in 2017, which was 18%.

Given these negative aspects that affect the vegetable farm activity, the increase in the prices of energy and fuel for heating, important in the case of greenhouses and plastic tunnels, leads to an accumulation of negative effects, which can further contribute to diminishing the competitiveness of this sector and its capability to provide food security.

Impact on Prices

To show the impact on vegetable prices, volatility coefficients were calculated in order to see the variation of prices over the period 2020–2022 (monthly and quarterly). The coefficient of volatility was calculated as a ratio between standard deviation and the mean. Farmgate prices showed an upward trend in 2020–2022. The largest increase is noticed for peppers (+48.6%), followed by field cucumbers (+22.8%) and field tomatoes (+19.6%) in the second quarter of 2022, compared to the second quarter of 2020 (Table 34.3).

The prices of vegetables in Romania have traditionally had very high volatilities compared to the price of vegetables in other EU countries. However, the period Q2 2020- Q2 2022, marked by a significant increase in the prices of energy and other agricultural inputs, contributed even more to this volatility increase. *Farmgate price volatility* increased significantly in 2021 compared to 2020. For example, the monthly volatility coefficient for field-grown tomatoes was 21.5%, while in 2020, the monthly volatility coefficient was 7. 6%. The quarterly volatility coefficient for

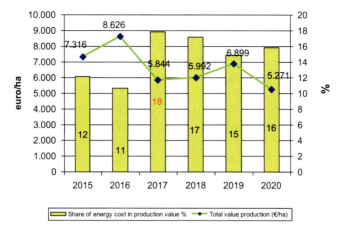

Fig. 34.6 Evolution of the value of horticultural production (euros/ha) and the share of energy expenses in the production value (%). (Source: FADN database, 2022)

Table 34.3 Average, standard deviation, and volatility coefficient of farmgate prices for various vegetable species during Q2 2020–Q2 2022

	Average 2nd Q 2020 – 2nd Q 2022	Standard deviation	Quarterly volatility coefficient 2nd Q 2020 – 2nd Q2022	Monthly volatility coefficient 2020	Monthly volatility coefficient 2021
Field tomatoes	3.1	0.5	16%	7.6%	21.5%
Field cucumber	2.6	0.5	19%	12.7%	27.2%
Peppers	3.4	1.2	35%	20.4%	13.7%

Source: Author's own calculations

the period between Q2 2022 and Q2 2020 was the highest for peppers (35%), followed by field-grown cucumbers (19%) and field-grown tomatoes (16%). The calculations reveal the fact that farmgate prices have increased a lot, registering important fluctuations. In addition to the energy crisis that led to the increase in input prices, a low degree of production contracting and a weak level of producers' organization have created greater difficulties for vegetable producers to negotiate better prices with intermediaries or retailers, in order to be able to offset the increase in production costs.

The evolution of vegetable prices at the consumer level also recorded an important upward trend, being very volatile from one quarter to another. Apparently, consumer prices were higher than farmgate prices, suggesting that a great part of these increases were passed on to consumers, while producers struggled with weak bargaining power in relation to intermediaries/retailers. Furthermore, to the extent that consumer demand for vegetables has remained at least constant, short- and medium-term price changes/increases show that the overall impact on the retail price of vegetables is very high. The growth margin was transferred to consumers, with intermediaries benefiting the most from this situation. These statements are also supported by the calculation of the quarterly volatility coefficient of vegetable prices sold in open markets, which show very high volatility for eggplants (31.9%), peppers (25.5%) and tomatoes grown in the field (21.8%) (Table 34.4).

Due to the fact that consumer demand for vegetables is relatively inelastic and does not change much with price changes (Huang, 1993), much of the price increases in 2021 were passed to consumers. The result was the largest increase in the consumer price index for fresh vegetables and canned vegetables in recent years, +13% in June 2022 compared to December 2021 and + 14% June 2022 compared to June 2021.

Scenario Regarding the Impact of Gas and Energy Price Increase on Production

Fuels used for tractors, generators, and irrigation pumps, including fuels used for heating greenhouses and plastic tunnels, are included in the FADN database in the energy cost category and represented 16% in the structure of variable costs and 49% in the structure of direct costs. For this analysis, fertilizer application rates per hectare were assumed to decrease by 2%. According to the calculations carried out in this analysis, in the short term, immediately, in this period marked by a strong energy crisis, vegetable growers seem to have adjusted their application methods and quantities of chemical fertilizers used, and also the cultivated areas and species.

In addition, electricity is needed on these farms to run irrigation pumps, and in some cases (especially for those few farmers who also have storage facilities), lighting and sorting and packaging equipment. The cost of electricity is the largest component of utilities expenses besides irrigation water. In the medium and long term, however, this adaptability by reducing the areas or the amounts of fertilizers used per hectare can lead to an increase in food insecurity.

By contrast, overall vegetable input prices rose by about 48% in 2020 from 2015, and by 4% in 2020 from 2018, largely due to a fast increase in gas prices, which contributed to higher fertilizer and pesticide prices, including seeds and plants. A similar response, but with a smaller impact on output, is likely in the energy price

Table 34.4 Average, standard deviation, and volatility coefficient of prices for various types of vegetables during period Q2 2020–Q2 2022

	Average	Standard deviation	Quarterly volatility coefficient 2nd Q 2020 – 2nd Q2022
Autumn cabbages	2.5	0.4	16.0%
Field tomatoes	5.5	1.2	21.8%
Field cucumbers	4.4	0.8	18.2%
Dry onions	3.5	0.4	11.4%
Peppers	5.1	1.3	25.5%
Eggplants	4.7	1.5	31.9%

Source: Author's own calculations

change scenarios, especially since the magnitude of the energy cost impact is significant (Table 34.5).

According to the calculation for the scenario with changes in energy prices, it is noticed that the annual impact on production is important and increases as the prices of the two inputs increase. Production will continue to decline as prices further increase in the near future, further threatening food security in the sector.

Scenario Regarding the Impact on Total Production Expenses/ Agricultural Inputs

The higher fertilizers and electricity prices had a negative impact on total input expenditure, in the vegetable sector, of −5% in the short term and −2% in the medium term, assuming declining fertilizer use rates and energy used. For this analysis, it was assumed that fertilizer application rates per hectare will decrease in both the short and medium term. In the long term, however, growers will likely continue to adjust application methods, amounts, or the type of species grown in response to rising fertilizer prices. On the other hand, in the conditions in which yields are anyway very low compared to the EU average, the food security of the sector is threatened.

Impact on the production costs in the horticultural sector is presented in Table 34.6.

Scenarios Regarding the Average Annual Impact on Agricultural Income

Based on scenarios calculations, the net farm income decreases on average by -1862-1854 euros (by −26% in the short term and −7% in the medium term), according to the calculations made in the two scenarios. This change is primarily due to higher production expenses, which are not offset by higher revenue due to lower production and higher production costs. The net income at the farm level decreases significantly in the case of both scenarios both in the short term and in the medium term, by 26% and 7%, respectively (Table 34.7).

Longer-Term Adjustments to Higher Energy Prices in the Romanian Vegetable Sector

In case energy prices continue to increase in the coming years, beyond the short- and medium-term focus of this paper, for example, further increases in gas and energy prices, this will lead to further adjustments in the horticultural sector taking place in the longer term because increases in electricity, gas and crude oil prices can lead to higher production costs and prices of phosphate and potash fertilizers and

Table 34.5 Average annual percentage impact on production

	Smaller price change scenario		Larger price change scenario	
	Energy price	Production	Energy price	Production
Field-grown vegetables	+25	−0,5	+30	−0.8
Vegetables in greenhouses and plastic tunnels	+20	−2	+35	−2.5
Vegetables in kitchen gardens	+15	−3,5	+25	−4

Source: Author's own calculations

Table 34.6 Average annual impact on production costs

	Short-term price change scenario		Medium-term price change scenario	
	euro	%	euro	%
Fertilizers	503	+4.7	533	5.9
Energy	834	−22	802	−3.8
Labour	1242	−13.5	1150	−7.4
Total production costs	7133	−4.9	6980	−2.14

Source: Author's own calculation

Table 34.7 Average annual impact on net vegetable farm income

	Short-term price change scenario		Medium-term price change scenario	
	euros	%	euros	%
Production value	5271	−30%	5126	−2.7
Total production costs	7133	−4%	6980	−0.4
Net income	−1862	−25,9%	−1854	−7.4

Source: Author's own calculations

nitrogen fertilizers (Huang, 2009), threating food security (Morrison and Sarris, 2016). At the same time, according to Monforti-Ferrario and Pinedo (2015), several opportunities for renewable energy are available to farmers including re-use in agriculture and re co-production in the farm systems to cope with these threats.

The decline of cultivated areas as well as the change in the use of inputs related to gas and energy represents options that will continue. This could include using less fertilizer, including redirecting its use more efficiently. In addition, energy consumption per unit of production in the horticultural sector is likely to continue its decline in the coming years. Some of these trends could lead to the development of new technologies and spur investment, but the declining financial strength of farmers calls this option into question. Investments made with support from farmers in the central or northern part of the continent, who are facing similar problems due to rising energy and gas prices, would be possible. However, long-term adjustments to higher energy prices in the vegetable sector will follow the same dynamics as seen in the short-term results. In response to higher production costs, cultivated areas will continue to decrease, with a significant diminution of the number of cultivated species, leading to further increases in consumer prices.

34.5 Conclusions

Based on the results presented in this paper, it can be concluded that the impact of the increase in gas and energy prices is very high, the cultivated areas registering decreases both for vegetables grown in the field and for those grown in greenhouses and plastic tunnels.

Due to the reduction in the inputs used, production has also experienced significant decline, leading to rising and highly volatile selling prices. The prices of vegetables sold in open markets to consumers as well as of processed vegetables will continue to increase, reflecting increases related to energy costs in the marketing chain with higher growth rates than prices at the farm level. This trend calls into question the ability of the sector to ensure food security, given that the sector cannot cover vegetable consumption from its own production anyway. The scenarios suggest that, both in the short and medium term, under the conditions of maintaining these increases in input prices, the decline will continue both in terms of the evolution of production and its value, with a negative impact on the net income at the farm level.

References

Huang, K. S. (1993). *A complete system of U.S. demand for food*. U.S. Department of Agriculture, Economic Research Service, TB-1821, September.

Huang, W. (2009). *Factors contributing to the recent increase in U.S. fertilizer prices, 2002-08*. U.S. Department of Agriculture, Economic Research Service, AR-33.

Morrison, J., & Sarris, A. (2016). Food staple market volatility and food security in eastern and southern Africa: What role for intra-regional trade and market policy? In *Africa's Progress in regional and global economic integration-towards transformative regional integration*. Food and Agricultural Organization (FAO).

Monforti-Ferrario, F., & Pinedo, P. I. (2015). *Energy use in the EU food sector: State of play and opportunities for improvement*. Joint Research Centre, Science and Policy Report.

Parajuly, R., Thoma, G., & Matlock, D. (2019). Environmental sustainability of fruit and vegetable production supply chains in the face of climate change: A review. *Science of the Total Environment, 650*(2), 2863–2879.

*** CE, EU Agricultural and Farm Economics Briefs No 19l, 2021 Fertiliser input estimates in farms. An overview of costs and quantities of the main fertilizer components used in the EU farms based on FADN data.

*** F&V market situation, https://ec.europa.eu/info/sites/default/files/food-farming-fisheries/farming/documents/fruit-and-vegetables-market-situation-report-2021-03_en.pdf

*** https://www.researchandmarkets.com/reports/5156412/world-vegetables-primary-market-analysis#relc0-4828911

*** https://www.ft.com/content/2853f30e-211d-40eb-80e1-618e27358a2c

*** https://www.reuters.com/world/europe/europes-vegetable-farmers-warn-shortages-energy-crisis-bites-2022-09-22/

*** FAO (2020). The State of Food Security and Nutrition in the World. http://www.fao.org/faostat/en/#home

*** NIS; tempo on line.

*** FADN database

Chapter 35
Assessment of Pesticide and Fertilizer Consumption and Its Effects on Agricultural Output in Romanian Farms

Cecilia Alexandri, Bianca Pauna, Corina Saman, and Lucian Luca

Abstract The requirements of the European Green Deal on climate and environment have been included in the two strategies launched in 2020, namely, the Farm to Fork Strategy and the Biodiversity Strategy. The aim is to design a healthy, fair, and environmentally friendly agri-food system by 2030. According to these strategies, the EU wants to reduce the dependence of agricultural production on pesticides, antibiotics and on the overuse of chemical fertilizers, in conjunction with the increase in organically cultivated areas and set aside areas. The aim of the study is to assess the pesticide and fertilizer consumption by Romanian farms and to analyse their effects on agricultural output. The study uses the FADN data from 2016, 2017 and 2018.

The paper estimates a Cobb-Douglas production function for crop farms in Romania using the control function method with the capital as a state variable and labour as a free variable. Farms were divided into four groups according to size, and for each group, a production function was estimated.

An analysis of the use of crop protection and fertilizers depending on the size of the farm showed that in Romania, the smallest farms are the ones that make the most intensive use of both fertilizers and crop protection and might be most affected by the requirements. The estimation of the production function showed that the small farms have the highest elasticity of fertilizers with respect to the output, more than double in comparison to the next farm group. The elasticity of crop protection is also largest for the small farms, but very large farms and medium farms have also large elasticities.

C. Alexandri · C. Saman (✉) · L. Luca
Institute of Agricultural Economics, Bucharest, Romania
e-mail: cecilia@eadr.ro; csaman@eadr.ro; luca@eadr.ro

B. Pauna
Center for Macroeconomic Modelling, National Institute of Economic Research, Bucharest, Romania

Keywords Productivity · European Green Deal · Crop farms · Romania

35.1 Introduction

The chapter aims to analyse the effect that the Green Deal strategy will have on the Romanian crop farms. The European Commission adopted the Green Deal strategy with the aim of transforming Europe into "the first climate neutral continent by becoming a modern, resource efficient economy". At the centre of the Green Deal is the Farm to Fork strategy which aims to reform the agricultural system into an environmentally friendly, equitable system by 2030. The environment part of the strategy is achieved via a reduction in pesticides, antibiotics, chemical fertilisers, an increase in organic production, and a reduction in agricultural land with the aim of increasing bio-diversity. In figures, the strategy can by summarized as follows by 2030 the agricultural industry should reduce the use of pesticides by 50%, the use of fertilisers by 20%, reduce the loss of soil nutrients by 50%, increase the set-aside area to 10%.

The reduction of chemical fertilizers is important because of the adverse effects of using too much (reduction of soil fertility, negative impact on the environment, etc.) which could be offset by the use of animal manure, biochar, biofertilizers (He et al., 2015; Watts et al. al., 2010; Zhao et al., 2014) and improved nitrogen management. However, in the short term, there are negative impacts on crop yields, and advanced management practices are difficult to implement in a short time, especially on small farms. Also, along with the efficiency of nutrient use, crop productivity must also be taken into account (Panhwar et al., 2019) as the principal goal is sustainable development of agriculture.

In our paper, we use the FADN database for 3 years (2016–2018) and estimate a production function for crop farms in Romania. We are concentrating on assessing the impact of reducing chemical inputs, namely, fertilisers and crop protection, since they can be easily quantifiable and the records of the expenses are included in the database.

The present article is an extension of Alexandri et al. (2022). In the previous article, we estimated a basic production function, where the inputs included were labour, assets, fertilisers and crop protection, and we have computed elasticities for each. In our current article, we have extended the model to include other farm characteristics, like land, a diversity index which captures the diversity of the crops produced by the farm, a dummy variable for the altitude of the farm, dummy variables for different crops, the demand conditions of the market at which farms have access to, quantified by an aggregate price index.

35.2 Literature Review

The data used is a panel consisting of crop farms from Romanian FADN database from 2016 to 2018. We limit our analysis only to one specialization out of the eight which are declared in FADN due to the heterogeneity of the production process which might give misleading results if farms of different types were included. The database collects information on agricultural land, paid, unpaid labour, different measures of capital (assets, machinery and equipment), output in quantity and monetary value and other inputs like seeds and plants, fertilisers, pesticides, subsidies, liabilities, location, etc. We have no information regarding the human capital of the farmers and their families and on the manufacturing activity of the farms, if they have any.

In our analysis, we have divided the farms into four groups depending on the size of the utilised agricultural land as follows, the first group consists of small farms with less than 10 hectares of land, the second group consists of medium farms with land in the interval 10–100 hectares, the third category consists of large farms with land in the interval of 100 and 500 hectares, and the fourth category consists of very large farms with utilised agricultural land of above 500 hectares.

Farms Characteristics

The database contains, in general, the same farms from year to year, but some of them drop out of the survey probably due to the fact they went out of business or due to the change in the conditions for inclusion, in 2018, the number of small farms dropped significantly (almost by half) when the FADN raised the threshold of farms included from above 2000 Euro standard output to 4000 Euro standard output.

Table 35.1 presents the distribution of farms according to the classes described above. There are enough farms in each size category, which gives confidence to the estimated elasticities.

The regional distribution of farms is presented in Table 35.2. All regions, with the exception of Bucharest-Ilfov, are sufficiently covered by farms from FADN. Since the last region covers mostly the capital, and the Ilfov is quite small in comparison, the fact that the number of farms in this region is so small is not a surprise.

Table 35.3 presents the average fertilisers per land for different sized farms and years. The figures show that per hectare the small farms spend the most for fertilisers, and the results are true for all years. We cannot say for sure that small farms use

Table 35.1 Number of farms in different class sizes

Size/year	2016	2017	2018	Total
Small	886	862	480	2228
Medium	908	948	976	2832
Large	783	829	771	2383
Very large	413	408	364	1185
Total	2990	3047	2591	8628

Source: Authors' computations

Table 35.2 Regional distribution of farms

Region/year	2016	2017	2018
Nord-Est	432	431	359
Sud-Est	606	620	515
Sud-Muntenia	621	667	597
Sud-vest-Oltenia	300	313	265
Vest	330	329	278
Nord-vest	366	361	289
Centru	290	267	239
Bucuresti-Ilfov	45	59	49
Total	2990	3047	2591

Source: Authors' computations

Table 35.3 Average fertilisers per hectare (Euro)

Size/year	2016	2017	2018
Small	121.08	112.98	125.54
Medium	100.5	91.47	89.5
Large	99.35	90.81	92.03
Very large	106.78	91.33	94.29
Total	107.17	97.36	97.6

Source: Authors' computations

more fertilisers, since larger farms buying larger quantities are able to negotiate a better price in comparison to small farms. For the medium, large, and very large farms, there is a tendency for the expenditure to decrease. We cannot infer from this that farms are reducing their fertiliser consumption, since there is also the price that shows into the figures. It might be that there was a decrease in the prices in the analysed interval.

In order to understand the tendency in fertiliser consumption by farms by year, we have used the information pertaining the quantities of N, P_2O_5, and K_2O that farms utilise by year, data which is not polluted by the evolution of prices and price differentials depending on the size of the farm.

Figure 35.1 shows there is clear tendency for the increase in the quantity of fertilisers used the line for the year 2018 is always above the line for the year 2016. Also, the small farms use more fertilisations than the rest of the farms, this might be because of an absence of technology but also due to less quality in the seeds used (Table 35.4).

The findings from fertilisers are almost consistent with the use of crop protection. In this case, the small farms are also consumers of crop protection, and there is a tendency, with the exception of medium farms for expenses for crop protection to increase in time.

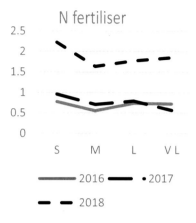
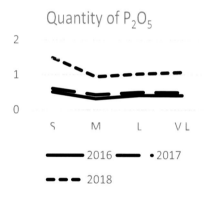
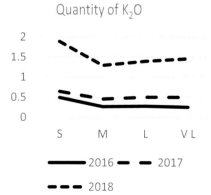

Fig. 35.1 Quantity of different components of fertilisers by size and year. (Source: Authors' computations)

Table 35.4 Average crop protection per hectare (Euro)

	2016	2017	2018
Small	97.69	84.84	109.68
Medium	60.47	55.42	58.17
Large	52.87	53.06	56.23
Very large	57.44	57.95	61.96
Total	69.09	63.44	67.67

Source: Authors' computations

35.3 Methodology

We estimate a Cobb-Douglas production function using control functions to address the simultaneity of inputs and productivity. This approach is based on Olley and Pakes (1996), Levinsohn and Petrin (2003) contributions that assume that productivity is a function of input demand determined by inverting an increasing function of some variable (investment for OP, intermediate inputs for LP) on productivity shocks for a fixed level of capital.

In our approach, the level of crop protection is monotonically increasing in the productivity shock conditioning on capital and then inverting this control function, we get a proxy for the productivity. We follow the approach of OP/LP using the Wooldridge (2009) methodology:

The variables are as follows:

(i) x_{it} state variables that are not affected by productivity shocks at time t because they were already subject to the choice at a previous time t-k: usually capital, in our approach is valoarea echipamentelor (lmachinery) și terenul utilizat exprimat în numarul de hectare cultivate (lland);
(ii) free variables w_{it} that are affected by the productivity shocks: usually labor inputs, in our approach is total labour input of holding expressed in annual work units (totallb, SE010) and valoarea semințelor utilizate (ltseeds);
(iii) control variables:

- fertilizers (fert, SE295) is the value (€) of purchased fertilizers and soil improvers,
- a variable (agreg_price) that expresses the aggregated prices resulting from the database; the reason for the introduction of this variable depends on the fact that in the database most of the variables are expressed in terms of value, not quantity;
- a variable (div) that expresses the diversity of cultures;
- variable (altitude) that differentiates farms by altitude;
- variable (organic) that differentiates farms according to the type of organic or non-organic crop;
- dummy variables that take the value 1 if there is a culture of a certain type. We included dummies for barley, maize, rapeseed, sunflower, soybeans and wheat;

(iv) a proxy variable for productivity: crop protection (cropprot, SE300) that represents plant protection products, traps and baits, bird scarers, anti-hail shells, frost protection, etc. (excluding those used for forests).

The model:

$$y_{it} = \alpha + \beta w_{it} + x_{it}\gamma + \omega_{it} + \eta_{it}$$
$$\log(A_{it}) = \alpha + \varepsilon_{it}$$
$$\varepsilon_{it} = \omega_{it} + \eta_{it}$$
$$\Phi_{it}(i_{it}, x_{it}) = x_{it}\gamma + h(i_{it}, x_{it}) = x_{it}\gamma + \omega_{it}, \quad (35.1)$$

where y_{it} is the output, ω_{it} is an unobservable variable representing the productivity shock that is proxied by a function $\omega_{it} = h(i_{it}, x_{it})$, which is the inverse function of the demand of some input iit (in our approach the level of crop protection).

We include dummy variables to control for production heterogeneity due to regional and annual differences in farm output.

The estimation method uses the approach of Wooldridge (2009).

35.4 Analysis/Results Interpretation

The European Green Deal strategy stipulated the need to reduce chemical inputs, namely, fertilisers and crop protection. The question we intend to pose is how important are the chemical inputs in terms of crop production in Romania, and the extend that the reduction due to European Green Deal strategy will have on different size farms in the short run. We have estimated a different model for each size, small, medium, large, and very large.

The present article is an extension of Alexandri et al. (2022). In the previous article, we have estimated a basic production function, where the inputs included were labour, assets, fertilisers and crop protection, and we have computed elasticities for each. In our current article, we have extended the model to include other important farm characteristics. The results are presented in Table 35.5. The variables are transformed in logarithms, so the coefficients are elasticities.

The variables included in the model are variables related to the inputs used by the farm, like total labour (paid and unpaid) expressed as working units, the agricultural land, the value of the seeds, the value of the fertilisers and soil improvers, the value of the crop protection products. To quantify the farms' capital, we have used the variable machinery and equipment which consists of tractors, motor cultivators, lorries, vans, cars and major and minor farming equipment, which are owned by the farm. We have included an index of diversity computed as an Herfindahl-Hirshman index, based on the information regarding the different crops' production:

Table 35.5 Average elasticities of the inputs

	Small farms	Medium farms	Large farms	Very large farms
Total labour	**0.115**	**0.114**	**0.033**	**0.072**
Seeds	**0.261**	**0.337**	**0.391**	**0.589**
Machinery	**0.093**	**0.07**	**0.027**	0.02
Land	**0.379**	**0.548**	**0.646**	**0.41**
Fertilisers	**0.061**	**0.025**	**0.017**	0.017
Price	0.82	**0.66**	0.229	0.036
Region1	**−3.357**	**−2.127**	9.989	**−2.877**
Region2	−0.723	**1.647**	**−3.623**	**−4.713**
Region3	**−0.228**	**−0.151**	0.039	0.117
Region4	0.012	**0.008**	**−0.004**	−0.001
Region5	0.025	−0.012	0.008	−0.011
Region6	0.001	0.009	0.001	−0.002
Region7	0.256	0.645	−0.151	0.047
Region8	0.004	−0.042	−0.012	0.01
Year 2016	−0.108	−0.03	0.02	0.004
Year 2017	0.044	**−0.269**	−0.019	**−0.208**
Year 2018	0.012	**0.019**	−0.006	0.009
HHI (1/diversity)	**0.612**	0.073	−2.378	0.357
Altitude	0.097	−0.023	0.164	**−0.179**
Organic	**−0.178**	0.056	−0.022	**0.311**
Barley	**0.688**	0.036	0.719	−0.032
Maize	0.027	−0.021	−0.034	**−0.202**
Rapeseed	−0.005	**−0.128**	0.194	**0.517**
Sunflower	−0.002	0.005	0.001	0.026
Soybeans	−0.017	**0.033**	0.006	−0.012
Wheat	0	**0.001**	0.001	0.001
Crop protection	0.25	0.209	0.179	0.215

Source: Authors' computations
Note: the marked values (bold) represent coefficients corresponding to statistically significant variables

$$\text{HHI} = \frac{1}{\text{diversity}} = \sum_{i=1}^{n} \left(\frac{x_i}{X}\right)^2$$

where x_i is the output of crop i, n is the number of crops cultivated by the farm, and

$$\sum_{i=1}^{n} x_i = X$$

The highest value for the HHI can be 1, which means that the farm is specialized, and has the lowest possible diversity. As HHI decreases, the diversity of crop production increases.

We have included also dummies for different crops, in order to analyse whether in the period under consideration, some crops were associated with higher production. In order to control for different soil quality, we included a variable for the region of the country (there are eight regions in Romania), as well as a variable for the altitude, which takes the value 1 if the farm is in a higher location.

The impact of total labour on crop production is positive irrespective of the size of the farm, but for small and medium farms, the effect is larger. The size of the land is also an important determinant on the production. The higher the farm the larger the elasticity, with the exception of very large farms where there are indications of diminishing returns. There seems to be scope to increase production by dividing the very large farms into somewhat smaller entities, either large or medium-sized farms.

The effect of the capital is positive and significant with the exception of very large farms. The effect of capital is largest for small farms, probably due to the fact that they are less capital intensive their access to credit is restricted.

There is some evidence that different-sized farms fare better in some regions as opposed to other regions, but it might be due to certain weather conditions that happened into a certain region. That is also true with respect to the year dummy.

The altitude variable decreases output especially in the case of very large farms. Organic farming is non-efficient for small farms, but efficient for very large farms, but this effect could be due to the fact that there are very few organic farms in the database. Diversifying production is not an option for farms, especially in the case of small ones, which seemed to benefit from specialization.

With respect to specific crops, barley is a good crop for small farms, while rapeseeds is for large and very large farms, but these findings might originate due to some weather conditions in the analysed years, or some market particularities in the 3 years.

The seeds are a very important input as well, becoming more important with the increase in the size of the farm. The coefficients for fertilisers are positive, but significant only for small farms, which are the farms which use significantly more fertilisers per hectare than other size farms. The crop protection input has also a positive influence on production, and again the coefficient is larger for small farms, and smallest for large farms.

35.5 Conclusions

We estimated the short-run effect of reducing fertilizers and crop protection materials on productivity depending on the size of the farm. However, the amount of fertilizers used doesn't reflect the quality of nitrogen management as the level of nitrogen inputs used efficiently by crops depends on the quality of soil, irrigation, and climatic conditions (Abreu et al., 1993; Li et al., 2009; Waqas et al., 2020). The data limitation allow us to account for such factors only using dummy variables for region and year.

The estimations show that the impact of reducing the use of crop protection materials and fertilizers is larger for small farms. Also highlights, as expected, the smaller role of labor for large and very large farms which is consistent with the fact that this input is of a significantly lower level for these farms. The elasticity of capital is significantly higher for small and medium farms, which expresses the fact that the increase of capital for these farms is very important, as they are poorly capitalized.

The results seem to suggest that the small farms would lose the most by the provisions introduced by the Green Deal strategy and since they do not appear to benefit from organic farming they would be the losers from the Green Deal in Romania.

Acknowledgements This chapter is a result of a research theme of the Institute of Agricultural Economics (The impact of the European Green Deal targets on Romanian farms"), financed by Romanian Academy, and LIFT project (Low-Input Farming and Territories – Integrating knowledge for improving ecosystem-based farming") funding from the European Union's Horizon 2020 research and innovation programme under grant agreement No 770747.

References

Abreu, J. P. D. M. E., Flores, I., De Abreu, F. M. G., et al. (1993). Nitrogen uptake in relation to water availability in wheat. *Plant and Soil, 154*, 89–96. https://doi.org/10.1007/BF00011076

Alexandri, C., Saman, C., Pauna, B., & Luca, L. (2022). Will Romanian crop farms be affected differently by low-input farming? *Agricultural Economics and Rural Development, 19*(2), 155–164.

He, Y. T., Zhang, W. J., Xu, M. G., Tong, X. G., Sun, F. X., Wang, J. Z., Huang, S. M., & He, X. H. (2015). Long-term combined chemical and manure fertilizations increase soil organic carbon and total nitrogen in aggregate fractions at three typical cropland soils in China. *Science of the Total Environment, 532*, 635–644.

Levinsohn, J., & Petrin, A. (2003). Estimating production functions using inputs to control for unobservables. *Review of Economic Studies, 70*, 317–341.

Li, S.-X., Wang, Z.-H., Malhi, S. S., Li, S., Gao, Y.-J., & Tian, X.-H. (2009). Chapter 7: Nutrient and water management effects on crop production, and nutrient and water use efficiency in dryland areas of China. *Advances in Agronomy, 102*, 223–265. https://doi.org/10.1016/S0065-2113(09)01007-4

Olley, G. S., & Pakes, A. (1996). The dynamics of productivity in the telecommunications equipment industry. *Econometrica, 64*, 1263–1297.

Panhwar, Q. A., Ali, A., Naher, U. A., & Memon, M. Y. (2019). Fertilizer management strategies for enhancing nutrient use efficiency and sustainable wheat production. In *Organic farming* (pp. 17–39). Woodhead Publishing.

Waqas, M. A., Li, Y., Smith, P., Wang, X., Ashraf, M. N., Noor, M. A., Amou, M., Shi, S., Zhu, Y., Li, J., Wan, Y., Qin, X., Gao, Q., & Liu, S. (2020). The influence of nutrient management on soil organic carbon storage, crop production, and yield stability varies under different climates. *Journal of Cleaner Production, 268*, 121922. https://doi.org/10.1016/j.jclepro.2020.121922

Watts, D. B., Torbert, H. A., Feng, Y., & Prior, S. A. (2010). Soil microbial community dynamics as influenced by composted dairy manure, soil properties, and landscape position. *Soil Science, 175*(10), 474–486.

Wooldridge, J. M. (2009). On estimating firm-level production functions using proxy variables to control for unobservables. *Economics Letters, 104*, 112–114.

Zhao, S., He, P., Qiu, S., Jia, L., Liu, M., Jin, J., & Johnston, A. M. (2014). Long-term effects of potassium fertilization and straw return on soil potassium levels and crop yields in north-Central China. *Field Crops Research, 169*, 116–122.

Chapter 36
Identifying the Determining Factors of the Adoption of Ecological Practices by Dairy Farms in Suceava County, Romania

Mihai Alexandru Chițea, Marioara Rusu, Violeta Florian, Lorena Florentina Chițea, Elisabeta Roșu, Monica Mihaela Tudor, Sorinel Ionel Bucur, Lucian Luca, Iuliana Ionel, Ioan Sebastian Brumă, Lucian Tanasă, Codrin Dinu Vasiliu, and Gabriel Simion

Abstract The present paper aims to identify the main factors for the adoption of ecological practices by dairy farmers from Dornelor Basin, Suceava county. In the last decade, this topic has received increased attention from the academic sector, in order to better understand the determining factors that can lead to a transition to ecological farming practices, as part of the efforts to protect biodiversity in agricultural landscapes. The main results highlight that the decision to adopt ecological farming practices is based on a mix of economic, social, institutional, and behavioural factors, closely related to farmers' self-identity, experience, motivation and social context in which they carry out their activity. Some studies indicate that the best method to support this transition to more sustainable practices is to influence farmers' motivation and behaviour, while other studies focus on a broader approach that calls for social, economic, technological, and institutional changes at the level of different actors (farmers, supply chain, natural resource management, etc.). In this context, the present study uses a large-scale survey implemented on 52 dairy cow farms in the Dornelor Basin, in order to analyse the main factors for the

---

M. A. Chițea (✉) · M. Rusu · V. Florian · L. F. Chițea · E. Roșu · M. M. Tudor · S. I. Bucur · L. Luca · I. Ionel
Institute of Agricultural Economics, Romanian Academy, Bucharest, Romania

I. S. Brumă
Mountain Economy Center CE-MONT, Romanian Academy, Bucharest, Romania

L. Tanasă · C. D. Vasiliu
Institute of Economic and Social Research "Gh. Zane", Romanian Academy, Iași Branch, Bucharest, Romania

G. Simion
University of Bucharest, Bucharest, Romania

© The Author(s), under exclusive license to Springer Nature Switzerland AG 2024
L. Chivu et al. (eds.), *Constraints and Opportunities in Shaping the Future: New Approaches to Economics and Policy Making*, Springer Proceedings in Business and Economics, https://doi.org/10.1007/978-3-031-47925-0_36

adoption of ecological practices. The questionnaire used for data collection specifically sought to find out farmers' opinions regarding different elements, of personal, institutional, and motivational nature. Data were processed using the SPSS software, standard statistical methods and non-parametric tests. The preliminary results indicate that in the case of dairy farms from the Dornelor Basin, the main factors that influence the decision to adopt ecological practices are related to individual motivation (mainly personal/family issues), social norms (e.g., their identification as farmers and belonging to the farming community), and certain economic and environmental benefits (such as high profitability and biodiversity improvement).

Keywords Ecological farming practices · Dairy farms

36.1 Introduction

In the recent decades, at the European level, an increase of concerns for the sustainability of farming systems has been noticed, both from the academic sector and from different European institutions with regulatory role in this field, starting from the need to identify new methods/technologies to limit the negative effects on the environment, mainly in terms of biodiversity and agricultural landscapes. From the perspective of European policies, the development of agro-environmental schemes was the most used tool in this field, which provided financial support to farmers who developed a specific environmental protection behaviour.

On the other hand, in the academic sector, efforts have been directed both to the identification of new farming methods/technologies and practices to ensure the protection of the environment, and to the evaluation of factors that determine the adoption of ecological practices by European farmers. In the latter case, the approach includes many aspects related both to farmers' personal domain (motivation, expectations, belonging to the farming community, etc.) and to the economic domain (benefits, constraints, influence of supply chain and buyers, etc.).

In this context, the aim of the study was to identify the factors that determine the adoption of ecological practices by dairy farmers in the Dornelor Basin, Suceava county, on the basis of a field survey conducted in this area.

The main working hypotheses are the following:

- Personal elements and social norms are important factors in the decision to adopt ecological farming practices.
- The economic benefits associated with the transition to ecological practices can support farmers' decision in the study area.

36.2 Literature Review

The ever-increasing pressure on the agri-food sector, to cope with the growing demand, at the European level, has recently brought to the core of debates the need to protect agricultural landscapes, as an essential condition for preserving biodiversity. The changes that have taken place at this level can increase the degradation of land resources and represent a threat to agro-diversity. An alternative solution to intensive farming is the shift to agro-ecological practices, which can contribute to maintaining and even improving biodiversity (Schoonhoven & Runhaar, 2018). The directions on which attention regarding the sustainability of different agricultural systems concentrates, namely, the advancements in environmentally friendly technologies/practices, can be approached by farmers and support improved productivity (Pretty, 2008). However, the need to better understand/identify the factors that explain the adoption of agro-ecological practices by farmers is equally important, both personal (behaviour, motivation), economic (benefits, constraints), as well as institutional and social factors.

In this context, the studies and research in this field can be grouped into several categories, depending on the nature of investigated factors, which can determine the adoption of practices/technologies based on ecological principles:

- Studies that focus on aspects related to motivation/behaviour/self-identity: an example in this sense is the report elaborated in LIFT HORIZON 2020 Project – "Low input farming and territories", whose conceptual framework brings to the foreground a behavioural approach centred on attitudes, values, perception, and self-identity, associated to farmers (Hansson et al., 2019). At the same time, elements referring to the decision-making environment in which farmers operate (farm characteristics and farming activities, specific policies) are also considered, together with issues related to supply chain, institutional conditions and perception of consumers' attitude and demand for organic products. Another study brings into focus the factors associated with farmers' goal to adopt some agro-environmental financial aid free measures (van Dijk et al., 2016). Results highlight the importance of attitude, perception of social standards, and personal skills as significant factors related to farmers' goal to adopt/apply agro-environmental measures, without these being supported by financial benefits. Overall, authors consider that farmer's self-identity is the determining factor in this case. With regard to behavioural and motivational elements, de Snoo et al. (2013) embrace the idea that farmland conservation/protection represents a social change that should seek to influence the motivation and behaviour of individual farmers. For this purpose, the authors propose the involvement of several branches of social sciences (sociology, anthropology, economics, psychology) in the conservation/protection process, in order to achieve effective communication in terms of natural values, shaping of social norms and identity. Another approach is presented by Greiner et al. (2009) who, on the basis of a survey of 94 farmers, identified a clear correlation between motivation and attitude towards risk and

the adoption of best management practices, conservation practices aimed at reducing diffuse pollution from agricultural activities.
- Studies based on multidisciplinary approaches: for example, Pretty J., (2008), in a study on agriculture sustainability, advocates the need to develop new approaches that include biological and ecological processes in agri-food production, minimise the use of non-renewable resources, effectively use farmers' knowledge and skills and the collective ability of people to work together to solve common problems related to agricultural activities and natural resources. Duru et al. (2015) support agricultural systems based on biodiversity as a substitute for cost-effectiveness ones but highlight that such a transition might be difficult in certain areas where intensive farming is highly developed. Therefore, the authors consider that the adoption and development of biodiversity-based agriculture rests on actions that require changes at the level of different actors with various interests and opinions. Schoonhoven & Runhaar (2018) propose an integrated framework to explain farmers' decision to adopt agro-ecological practices, which includes both the conditions that promote adoption and the elements that support or hinder this process. The elements are grouped into four clusters from the economic, social, informational, and political fields. The results show that farmers' rationality is based on their personal perspective and context. The barriers perceived by farmers can represent a starting point for the identification of certain structural factors, which in turn can support the development of interventions such as increasing the perception and demand of agro-ecological products and agro-ecology integration in agricultural education/training.
- Studies addressing economic factors (benefits/barriers): in this sense, one example brings to attention the tendency of the academic environment to focus mainly on processes and less on results, expressing the benefits in such a manner that is not always relevant for farmers. This process creates a distance between researchers and farmers, at the level of perceived benefits of ecological intensification (Kleijn et al., 2019). According to the authors, these shortcomings could be overcome if the studies on ecological intensification addressed the relevant issues for farmers, like potential benefits and costs. Therefore, the probable cost of ecological intensification appears as an integrated component necessary to research activities. Another study, elaborated by Brown et al. (2019), who investigated the adoption of CAP measures strengthening biodiversity and ecosystem services by farmers, argues that, at the national level, the actions that are relevant to farmers are more likely to be chosen over those that support biodiversity. At the same time, at the farm level, farmers had the tendency to opt for actions that maximize yields, do not call for major management changes and involve fewer constraints on the long term.

These are a few examples of studies and research works that aimed to identify the determining factors of the adoption of environment-friendly practices by farmers that can contribute to reaching the objectives of biodiversity protection and improvement at the European level. In this context, the approach of the present study uses a mix of elements referring to farmers' behaviour and motivation, social norms, information sources and the benefits and constraints associated to the adoption of ecological practices.

36.3 Methodology

The present study aims to identify the determinants of farmers' adoption or ecological farming practices, based on a field survey conducted on 52 dairy farms in the Dornelor Basin, Suceava county, Romania (Fig. 36.1).

The questionnaire on which the field survey was based was developed within the European Union's research project Horizon 2020 LIFT – *Low-input farming and territories*, being adapted to the specificity of each study area where it has been implemented, in Romania's case inclusively.[1]

The questionnaire was intended to collect farmers' opinions regarding different elements, of personal, institutional, and motivational nature that influence the adoption of ecological practices in the study area. The collected data were centralised in a database created using the SPPS software. Data were processed, taking into consideration their nature, i.e., ordinal data (Likert scale – which falls into the category of ordinal measurement instruments, where the categories of answers "have a rank

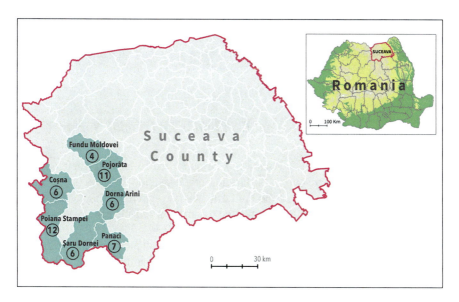

Fig. 36.1 Study area in Romania (number of questionnaires/communes). (Source: authors' processing based on the field survey data)

---

[1] Tzouramani, I. et al. (2019). Deliverable D2.2 – LIFT Large-scale farmer survey questionnaire, 2019, available at: https://www.lift-h2020.eu/deliverable-d2-2-lift-large-scale-farmer-survey-questionnaire

order, but the intervals between them cannot be considered equal" (Jamieson, 2004), using specific methods such as frequencies/percentages, median, contingency tables).

36.4 Analysis/Results Interpretation

The section of the questionnaire dedicated to the determinants of the adoption of ecological practices by farmers included 18 questions, each of them containing several statements to be evaluated by participants, grouped into three categories, according to their nature: personal, institutional, and motivational. The first two questions, however, sought to assess the relationship and interaction between farmers and buyers with regard to farming practices, from farmers' personal perspective (Fig. 36.2).

Participants' answers with regard to their interaction with those to whom they sell their products reveal the existence of an information/debate process with reference to the environmental and social benefits, as well as a constant evaluation, by buyers, of the farming practices used. At the same time, farmers had rather a neutral opinion regarding both the possibility of buyers restricting their ability to practice a greener agriculture and the low interest of these in the farming practices used by farmers.

Referring to their personal relationships with the buyers of their products, farmers evaluate positively the aspects related to the existence of a partnership; however, in the case of trust/equity/long-term relationship, a neutral attitude of participants in this questionnaire can be noticed.

36.4.1 Informal Institutional Conditions and Social Norms

In this section, the questions addressed to farmers tried to find out their opinion regarding the information sources on farming practices, how other people see the use of ecological practices, perception of farmers in the area regarding the adoption of these practices, as well as aspects related to farmer's self-identity, belonging to the farming community and the multiplier effect at its level.

The most important information sources of farmers are the family, other farmers, printed press/radio/TV as well as online sources (social platforms inclusively). At the same time, there is an obvious reticence of farmers with regard to the information disseminated by agricultural consultancy/extension bodies, by environmental advisors, as well as by representatives of input suppliers (Fig. 36.3).

At the same time, however, when it comes to association forms (cooperatives, farmer organizations, associations of farmland owners) and non-governmental organizations/certification bodies, these are not a main information source for farmers, the interactions with these being quite limited, most farmers not being affiliated to

	Do you discuss your farming practices with the buyers of your products?					
	Strongly disagree	Disagree	Neither agree or disagree	Agree	Strongly agree	Median *
I discuss the environmental and social benefits of my faring practices with those who buy my products	9.6%	7.7%	25.0%	30.8%	26.9%	4
My farming practices are regularly assessed against environmental and/or social farming practices standards by those who buy my products	9.6%	3.8%	26.9%	25.0%	34.6%	4
The requirements of those who buy my products restrict my ability to farm using more ecological farming practices	23.1%	11.5%	21.2%	30.8%	13.5%	3
The buyers of my products have little interest in the farming practices that I use	15.4%	9.6%	36.5%	23.1%	15.4%	3
How would you describe your relationship with the buyers of your paroducts?						
Our relationship is truthful and frank	5.8%	5.8%	40.4%	9.6%	38.5%	3
Our relationship is fair and equal	25.0%	19.2%	25.0%	3.8%	26.9%	3
We have a long-term relationship	7.7%	5.8%	38.5%	13.5%	34.6%	3
We have a partnership	17.3%	7.7%	19.2%	21.2%	34.6%	4

Source: authors' processing of field survey data

Fig. 36.2 Interactions/relationship between farmers and buyers
*****Likert scale, from 1 to 5, where 1, strongly disagree and 5, strongly agree**

such organizations. The farmers who participated in this survey consider that in the study area, there is recognition of the importance of using ecological practices by those involved in farming activities, with obvious environmental benefits.

How often do you consult the following sources of information to ge id eas for farming practices?						
	At least monthly	Several times per year	Once a year	Less than once a year	Never	Median
Family and friends	63.5%	25.0%	3.8%	1.9%	5.8%	1
Agricultural advisors	9.6%	11.5%	7.7%	19.2%	51.9%	5
Environmental advisors	3.8%	1.9%	21.2%	13.5%	59.6%	5
Supplier representatives	2.0%	3.9%	9.8%	7.8%	76.5%	5
Buyer representatives	5.8%	11.5%	23.1%	17.3%	42.3%	4
Open days. demonstration activites training	5.8%	15.4%	13.5%	13.5%	51.9%	5
Other farmers	21.2%	53.8%	13.5%	7.7%	3.8%	2
Press/Radio/TV	44.2%	28.8%	9.6%	3.8%	13.5%	2
Internet. including social media	40.4%	28.8%	1.9%	3.8%	25.0%	2

Fig. 36.3 Main information sources. (Source: authors' processing of field survey data)
*Likert scale, from 1 to 5, where 1, at least monthly and 5, never

Furthermore, more than 70% of respondents rather agree that this is a current practice of farmers in the area, by their adoption of at least one farming practice that is very similar to ecological ones.

Referring to aspects related to self-identity and belonging to the farming community in the area, participants strongly agree on the importance of their identification as farmers, as well as on the existence of a strong feeling of belonging to the farming community, which is also a very important factor for them (Fig. 36.4).

A similar agreement is manifested in: (1) personal projection, identification as ecological farmer, (2) assimilation of ecological farming, as an intrinsic part of respondents, (3) effects that overall changes have on personal life (at the level of farmers' situation), (4) importance of understanding farm ecology as fundamental to agriculture.

As regards the multiplying effect at the level of farming community, most participants considered that the important factors in supporting the decision on farmers' agricultural practices are the following: identification of a certain practice at the level of other farms in the area, large-scale use on similar farms and the innovating character of the practice.

To what extent do you agree with the following statement about farmers and farming?						
	Strongly disagree	Disagree	Neither agree or disagree	Agree	Strongly agree	Median *
Being a farmer is an important reflection of who I am	5.8%	1.9%	23.1%	21.4%	48.1%	4
What happens to farmers as a whole will have an effect on what happens in my life	11.5%	1.9%	21.2%	23.1%	42.3%	4
I have a strong sense on belonging to the farming community	1.9%	1.9%	28.8%	26.9%	40.4%	4
I see myself as a farmer who prioritises the environment	-	-	17.3%	25.0%	57.7%	5
Understanding the ecology of the farm is what farming is about	3.8%	-	23.1%	25.0%	48.1%	4
Faarming in a way that preserves the environment is part of who I am	5.8%	1.9%	15.4%	28.8%	48.1%	4

Fig. 36.4 Identity, community, ecology. (Source: authors' processing of field survey data)
*Likert scale, from 1 to 5, where 1, strongly disagree and 5, strongly agree

36.4.2 Individual Motivational Factors

In this section, the questions addressed to farmers tried to find farmers' opinions referring to their personal objectives, the relationship between the ecological practices and farm production, management style and farmers' change/adaptive capability.

Regardless of the category in which the objectives are found (agricultural activity, recognition by the community or personal/family aspects), these were considered important by participants (Fig. 36.5).

The objectives that stand out, by the significant share of (important and very important) answers, are those from the sphere of personal life, such as being fit and healthy, providing a satisfying lifestyle and helping (financially) the next generation. To a very large extent, farming in a way that improves the environment, enhancing land quality and producing high-quality products are also very important objectives for the farmers in the study area.

In general, the objectives that farmers consider easy to achieve at the farm level are related to their own farming experience and the farming experience in the

	How important are the following objectives to you?						
	Not at all important	Unimportant	Neither important nor unimportant	Important	Very important	Median	*
Producing high quality products	1.9%	-	9.6%	11.5%	76.9%	5	
Being fit and healthy	1.9%	-	3.8%	5.8%	88.5%	5	
Providing a satisfying lifestyle	1.9%	-	3.8%	25.0%	69.2%	5	
Farming in a way that enhances the environment	2.0%	-	7.8%	27.5%	62.7%	5	
Improving the condition of the land	1.9%	-	5.8%	23.1%	69.2%	5	
Helping (financially) the next generation	1.9%	-	5.8%	15.4%	76.9%	5	

Fig. 36.5 Personal and professional objectives. (Source: authors' processing of field survey data)
*Likert scale, from 1 to 5, where 1, not at all important and 5, very important

investigated area. These refer to the improvement of soil quality, use of alternatives to chemical farm inputs (fertilizers, pesticides, and herbicides) as well as the recycling of a greater amount of biomass. At the same time, the integration of different agro-ecosystems within the farming activities and maintaining or creating habitats for wild species seem to be rather achievable objectives in the study area.

From the perspective of professional training, the possibilities to have access to information and advisory services related to organic farming and the complexity level in terms of understanding and easy use of ecological practices, farmers largely agree on the possibility of developing this sector in the study area, in the next period. Most farmers consider that they are prepared to use ecological farming practices, have the ability to achieve their set goals, have access to advice and support for farming ecologically, that there are opportunities to shift to organic farming and, last but not least, that the farming practices that comply with ecological principles are easy to understand and use.

36.4.3 Benefits, Triggering Factors and Barriers

As regards the influence of adopting ecological farming practices on aspects referring to farm economy, environment and necessary labour resources, most participants consider that farm profitability and biodiversity would largely benefit from adopting these practices. However, the farmers who participated in the survey consider that the following would not be affected by an eventual transition to ecological practices: farm production, labour requirements for the farm, ability to meet current and future support payment requirements, ability to meet farming objectives, time spent working on the farm, soil fertility, farms's dependence on external inputs, intensity of seasonal peaks of work during the year, physical nature of work and mental workload.

The most important aspects for farmers who participated in the survey, in terms of changing the farming practices, are mainly grouped, on the basis of the cumulated value of answers "important" and "very important", into two categories: economic/meeting standards and environmental. In the category of economic aspects, the most important are the ability to meet product quality and safety standards, the market rewards, the availability of necessary skilled labour and the cost of adopting practices. As regards the environment, the most important for farmers are the ability to cope with climate change and to cope with pests and diseases. Besides these two categories, another aspect that met the majority of farmers' options is related to personal projection, namely, challenge and personal interest.

Farmers' experience with regard to the changes of farming practices adopted in the past highlights two important categories of aspects that have influenced this process: economic aspects and personal/family aspects. From the first category, in farmers' opinion, the most important factor considered was the changes in the prices of products, followed by the financial difficulties of farm, availability of skilled labour, changes in the regulations on farming activities, as well as access to new (domestic or export) markets. At the personal/family level, farm succession planning and farm inheritance represented important factors considered by farmers in supporting the decision to change the farming practices of the past.

36.5 Conclusions

At the level of the study area, behaviours compatible with the requirements of ecological agriculture are manifested, both from the perspective of farming activities and of the personal projection of farmers, through the use of practices that can be assimilated to ecological practices, and also through farmers' strong ties to the natural and social environment in which they operate. All these create a favourable framework to farming ecologically in the area in the next period.

The analysis reveals the existence of a mix of factors that can influence the adoption of ecological practices by dairy farms, among which the most important of which refer (without creating a hierarchy) to aspects related to institutional conditions and social norms (expectations from the society, recognition of the importance of using ecological farming practices, farmer identity and sense of belonging to the farming community, multiplying effect at community level), individual/identity factors (from the sphere of personal life, related to health, ensuring a satisfactory standard of living and support for the next generation, and also the necessary knowledge and training to practice organic farming) and benefits/constraints (increased profitability, market rewards, cost of adoption). To sum up, the determining factors of the adoption of ecological practices by dairy farmers in the Dornelor Basin are clustered around elements from personal, economic, professional and social contexts.

Acknowledgements This research study was carried out within the LIFT project – "Low-Input Farming and Territories. Integrating knowledge for improving ecosystem-based farming" that received funding from the European Union's Horizon 2020 Research and Innovation Programme under Grant Agreement no. 770747, May 2018 – April 2022.

References

Brown, C., Kovacs, E. K., Zinngrebe, Y., Albizua, A., Galanaki, A., Grammatikopoulou, I., Herzon, I., Marquardt, D., McCraken, D., Olsson, J., & Villamayor-Tomas, S. (2019). *Understanding farmer uptake of measures that support biodiversity and ecosystem services in the Common Agricultural Policy (CAP)*. Report prepared by an EKLIPSE Expert Working Group. Centre for Ecology & Hydrology.

de Snoo, G, R., Herzon, I., Staats, H., Burton, R. J. F., Schindler, S., Van Dijk, J., Lokhorst, A. M., Bullock, J. M., Lobley, M., Wrbka, T., Schwarz, G., & Musters, C. J. M. (2013). Towards effective nature conservation on farmland: Making farmers matter. *Conservation Letters, 6*, 66–72.

Duru, M., Therond, O., & Fares, M. (2015). Designing agroecological transitions – A review. *Agronomy for Sustainable Development, 35*(4), 1–21.

Greiner, R., Patterson, L., & Miller, O. (2009). Motivations, risk perceptions and adoption of conservation practices by farmers. *Agricultural Systems, 99*(2–3), 86–104.

Hansson, H., Thompson, B., Manevska-Tasevska, G., Toma, L., Leduc, G., & Vranken, L. (2019). *Drivers of farmers' up-take of ecological approaches – A conceptual framework with a behavioural focus*. Deliverable D2.1, Project H2020 Lift. https://publications.slu.se/?file=publ/show&id=100106

Jamieson, S. (2004). Likert scales: How to (ab)use them? *Medical Education, 38*(12), 1217–1218.

Kleijn, D., Bommarco, R., Fijen, T. P. M., Garibaldi, L. A., Potts, S. G., & van der Putten, W. H. (2019). Ecological intensification: Bridging the gap between science and practice. *Trends in Ecology & Evolution, 34*(2), 154–166.

van Dijk W, F. A., Lokhorst, A. M., Berendse, F., & de Snoo, G, R. (2016). Factors underlying farmers' intentions to perform unsubsidised agri-environmental measures. *Land Use Policy, 59*, 207–216.

Pretty, J. (2008). Agricultural sustainability: Concepts, principles and evidence. *Philosophical Transactions of The Royal Society B Biological Sciences, 363*, 447–465.

Schoonhoven, Y., & Runhaar, H. (2018). Conditions for the adoption of agro-ecological farming practices: A holistic framework illustrated with the case of almond farming in Andalusia. *International Journal of Agricultural Sustainability, 16*(6), 442–454.

Chapter 37
Pollution and Value Added in Agriculture: Evidence from the Biggest Agricultural Producers in the European Union

Mihaela Simionescu

Abstract Agricultural pollution might have many sources, but the consequences could refer to direct and downstream effects. The impact of pollution on climate change has intensified the research in this field. This paper proposes a revised Environmental Kuznets Curve (EKC) adapted to agriculture by considering value added in this sector instead of GDP. The results using CCEMG estimator for the biggest agricultural producers in the EU (France, Germany, Spain, Italy, Romania, Poland, Greece, the Netherlands, Denmark, and Hungary) in the period 2009–2020 could support policy measures to reduce pollution. The inverted-N pattern and the positive impact of energy consumption and employment in agriculture suggest that more efforts are necessary to reduce GHG emissions in this sector by promoting green technology, renewable energy, and qualified labour force to use advanced technology in agriculture.

Keywords Pollution · GHG emissions · Agriculture · Value added in agriculture · Energy consumption

37.1 Introduction

The EU agenda promotes the climate change mitigation through pollution reduction that might be explained by economic development in a world with high competition on various markets. The growth-pollution nexus has been the topic of many papers based on the hypothesis that economic development is a real threat for the environment if GHG emissions are not reduced (Simionescu, 2021a, p. 60881). Pollution minimization is one of the paths for achieving sustainable development in the EU. The GHG emissions have to reduce by 40%–60% until 2040 and by 80% until

---

M. Simionescu (✉)
Institute for Economic Forecasting, Bucharest, Romania
e-mail: mihaela.simionescu@ipe.ro

© The Author(s), under exclusive license to Springer Nature Switzerland AG 2024
L. Chivu et al. (eds.), *Constraints and Opportunities in Shaping the Future: New Approaches to Economics and Policy Making*, Springer Proceedings in Business and Economics, https://doi.org/10.1007/978-3-031-47925-0_37

2050 with respect to the value registered in 1990 (Heinrichs & Markewitz, 2015, p. 2541). Net GHG emissions should arrive to the zero level by 2050 due to climate procedures, reforestation, green technologies, and decoupling (Qin et al., 2021, p. 215).

The goals of the Paris Agreement could be achieved by promoting absolute decoupling rather than relative decoupling (Zeng et al., 2022, p. 2). The absolute decoupling promotes the specific decrease in GHG emissions when growth is achieved, but the concept of relative decoupling supposes a less value the for rate of growth in the case of pollution with respect to output rate as Haberl et al. (2020), p. 2) wrote.

Few targets have been established for total GHG emissions, but specific measures on sectors should be implemented. Even of industry is the main source of pollution, the GHG emissions from agriculture have been grown fast lately (Tongwane & Moeletsi, 2018, p. 124). The increasing food demand will contribute to pollution growth in the next year and policy proposals to reduce GHG emissions in agriculture are necessary. The previous studies have focused on overall pollution, but the separate analysis of agricultural sector should not be neglected. In this context, the literature gap covered by this paper refers to the assessment of the impact of growth on pollution in the 10 biggest agricultural producers from EU in the period 2009–2020. The results are the support for policy recommendations to decrease GHG emissions from agriculture in these states to promote sustainable development.

After this brief introduction, important findings from the literature are reported on growth-pollution nexus in agriculture. The next sections present the methodological framework, empirical findings, and conclusions.

37.2 Literature Review

The economic growth-pollution nexus has made the subject of Environmental Kuznets Curve (EKC) formalization that initially included only variables related to environmental degradation and income per capita (Stern, 2004, p. 1419). In the first stages of growth, the pollution increases, but in the long-run, it reduces due to environmental improvement supported by higher income per capita. From the mathematical point of view, the indicator used as proxy for environmental degradation represents an inverse U connection for per capita output. Our case uses log-GHG emissions that are represented in dependence with square log of output. The EKC concept has been introduced by Grossman and Krueger (1991, p. 1) to evaluate the environmental impact of NAFTA.

GHGs include CO_2, methane known as CH_4 and N_2O written as nitrous oxide that grow fast in the air and cause global climate change. In most of the cases, CO_2 is used as proxy for pollution and only a few papers employed the level of GHG emissions. In one study of Ali and others (2021, p. 4531), various proxies for pollution were used in the EKC framework for OIC countries during 1991–2018: total GHG emissions, but also the levels of CO_2, N_2O, CH_4, and ecological footprint. The inverted-U pattern was supported for all groups of OIC countries when indicators like ecological footprint, CO_2, CH_4 are explained. On the other hand, the U pattern was confirmed in the case of OIC and in poor ones when N_2O was explained.

There are few studies explaining GHG emissions in the EU countries. For example, the inverted-U pattern was obtained by analyzing 20 EU countries in the period 1995–2011 (Lapinskienė et al., 2015, p. 1109). The inverted U connection was also confirmed for 27 EU countries, excepting Malta in the period 1995–2015 when GHG emissions were used as proxy for pollution (Baležentis et al., 2019, p. 215). For the EU-27 states, various forms of EKC were discovered, but the inverse U is figured out in few zones (Jesus Lopez-Menendez et al., 2014, p. 368). Using GHG emissions in period 1985–2018, Mohammed and others (2021, p. 1) have shown that long-run economic growth has the capacity to improve the environment in Hungary.

Despite the results for overall GHG emissions, there are even less studies focusing only on the pollution from the agricultural sector. Pradhan et al. (2019, p. 1) showed that 25% of total GHG emissions came from the agricultural sector. For example, Simionescu (2021a, p. 60881) showed an inverted N connection when explaining pollution in agriculture in some CEEs (Romania, Poland, Czech Republic, Bulgaria, Hungary, and Slovakia) in the period 1990–2019. For few EU new member states, Simionescu (2021b, p. 1767) obtained an N-shaped pattern in the period 1990–2019 for pollution in agriculture using dynamic and panel threshold models.

The basic form of EKC is extended by adding control variables. One of the most employed control variable is the energy consumption. Previous findings from the literature confirm the role of energy consumption in the intensification of pollution in various countries: 22 EU states in 1995–2014 (Lapinskienė et al., 2017, p. 1109), 16 EU states from 1990 to 2008 (Boluk & Mert, 2014, p. 439), the EU new member states in the period 1992–2010 (see he reference Kasman & Duman from 2015, p. 97), in CEEs in the period 1980–2002 (Atici, 2009, p. 1903) and in the interval 1996–2015 (Lazăr et al., 2019, p. 1121) and, in Romania, Hungary, Bulgaria, and Albania in the period 1980–2006 (Ozturk & Acaravci, 2010, p. 3220). The role of human capital in achieving pollution should not be neglected. The increase in employment might generate more GHG emissions, if green technology is not employed.

Given this concise presentation of few studies from the literature, these research hypotheses are formulated using GHG emissions as a proxy for pollution given the European directives that refer to this indicator. The analysis is focused only the impact of economic growth on pollution in the top 10 agricultural producers from EU in the period 2009–2020. Control variables are attended to the EKC model by considering energy consumption in agriculture and employment in this sector. The energy use and employment are expected to have a positive contribution to pollution.

37.3 Methodology

The EU agriculture accounts for 10% of the total GHG emissions. Even if the energy sector is the major source of pollution, GHG emissions from agriculture might have multiple negative consequences in terms of food safety.

The paper employs panel data for the 10 biggest EU agricultural producers covering the period 2009–2020: Denmark, France, Germany, Italy, Netherlands, Spain, Poland, Greece, Romania, and Hungary. The variables used in the econometric models are represented as follows:

- GHG emissions in agriculture that shows trends in these polluted gasses by agriculture, using the estimation recommended by the UNFCCC, and the Decision 525/2013/EC.
- Employment in agricultural sector shows people with jobs in agriculture, fishing, hunting, forestry, being computed as percent of total employment;
- Value added in agriculture that represents net output coming from agriculture considering that intermediate inputs are excluded.
- Final energy use by agriculture/forestry per hectare of agricultural surface that is computed as sum of the energy supplied to agriculture for all energy use.

The data for GHG emissions and specific final energy use are provided by the Eurostat, while data sets for value added in agriculture and employment in agriculture were taken from the World Bank database. Our data series are transformed into natural log to have interpretations as elasticities and the variables are named GHG, VAA, employment in agriculture, energy consumption in agriculture.

The literature does not show a consensus regarding the formalization of EKC, but a general class of EKC is considered in this paper. The dependent variable should reflect the indicator measuring the level of pollution, GHG emissions in agriculture in this case. A third-order polynomial is considered to show the relationship between GHG emissions and value added in agriculture. The original form of EKC is modified by replacing GDP with value added in agriculture that is considered better proxy for growth since the analysis refers only to agricultural sector.

The standard EKC is given as follows:

$$GHG_{it} = \alpha_i + \beta_1 \bullet GDP_{it} + \beta_2 \bullet GDP_{it}^2 + \beta_3 \bullet GDP_{it}^3 + e_{it}$$

where GHG is the greenhouse gas emissions (in natural logarithm)

GDP refers to domestic product (in natural logarithm)
X is the vector of specific control indicators
α_i is the country-fixed effect
$\beta_1, \beta_2, \beta_3$ are the coefficients
e_{it} is the innovation
Specific indexes: t – year, i – country

An extended specification of EKC considers additional explanatory variables in a vector X (vector of control variables):

$$GHG_{it} = \alpha_i + \beta_1 \bullet GDP_{it} + \beta_2 \bullet GDP_{it}^2 + \beta_3 \bullet GDP_{it}^3 + +\gamma \bullet X_{it} + e_{it}$$

where γ is the coefficient.

The modified EKC proposed in this paper is written as follows:

$$GHG_{it} = \alpha_i + \beta_1 \bullet VAA_{it} + \beta_2 \bullet VAA_{it}^2 + \beta_3 \bullet VAA_{it}^3 + e_{it}$$

where VAA is the value added in agriculture (in natural logarithm).

When employment in agriculture (denoted by employment) and energy consumption in agriculture (denoted by ec) are considered as control variables, the EKC becomes:

$$GHG_{it} = \alpha_i + \beta_1 \bullet VAA_{it} + \beta_2 \bullet VAA_{it}^2 + \beta_3 \bullet VAA_{it}^3 + \beta_4 \bullet employment_{it} + \beta_5 \bullet ec_{it} + e_{it}$$

where β_4, β_5 are the coefficients.

Preliminary tests are necessary before establishing the type of the panel data model. These tests are used to check for existence of cross-sectional independence, potential presence of heterogeneity, the existence or not of unit root in the series, and potential cointegration connection.

Cross-sectional dependence might be the effect of correlations between pollution levels of states in the sample knowing the competition between countries to produce more using agricultural input. The same argument might explain the cross-sectional dependence with respect to value added in agriculture.

In this particular case, Pesaran's (2004) approach is employed in the case of cross-sectional dependence since it is not affected by sample size in case of small periods and few countries. The null assumption considers independence between countries:

$$H_0 : \rho_{ij} = \rho_{ji} = cor(e_{it}, e_{jt}) = 0, i \neq j$$

$$H_1 : \rho_{ij} = \rho_{ji} \neq 0, \text{ for some } i \neq j$$

where ρ_{ij} is the pair-wise correlation coefficient of the errors

$$\rho_{ij} = \rho_{ji} = \frac{\sum_{t=1}^{T} e_{it} \bullet e_{jt}}{\sqrt{\sum_{t=1}^{T} e_{it}^2} \bullet \sqrt{\sum_{t=1}^{T} e_{jt}^2}}$$

The CD statistic of Pesaran's (2004) test for unbalanced panels is used:

$$CD = \sqrt{\frac{2}{N(N-1)}} \bullet \sum_{i=1}^{N-1}\sum_{j=i+1}^{N} \sqrt{T_{ij}} \bullet \hat{\rho}_{ij}$$

where T_{ij} is the number of common observations between the particular states i and j

$$\hat{\rho}_{ij} = \hat{\rho}_{ji} = \frac{\sum_{t\in T_i \cap T_j}(\hat{e}_{it}-\bar{e}_i)(\hat{e}_{jt}-\bar{e}_j)}{\sqrt{\sum_{t\in T_i \cap T_j}(\hat{e}_{it}-\bar{e}_i)^2} \bullet \sqrt{\sum_{t\in T_i \cap T_j}(\hat{e}_{jt}-\bar{e}_j)^2}}$$

$$\bar{e}_i = \frac{\sum_{t\in T_i \cap T_j}(\hat{e}_{it})}{\#(T_i \cap T_j)}$$

Slope heterogeneity should be checked using Pesaran and Yamagata (2008) test.

$$\tilde{S} = \sum_{i=1}^{N}\left(\hat{\beta}_i - \tilde{\beta}_{WFE}\right)' \frac{X_i' I_t X_i}{\tilde{\sigma}_i^2}\left(\hat{\beta}_i - \tilde{\beta}_{WFE}\right)$$

where I_t is the identity matrix

$\tilde{\sigma}_i^2$ is the estimate of dispersion
$\hat{\beta}_i$ is the OLS estimator based for each i
$\tilde{\beta}_{WFE}$ is the weighted fixed effect pooled estimator

The standardized variance ($\hat{\Delta}$) and biased-adjusted variance ($\bar{\Delta}_{adj}$) are computed as follows:

$$\hat{\Delta} = \sqrt{N} \bullet \frac{N^{-1}\tilde{S}-k}{\sqrt{2k}}$$

$$\bar{\Delta}_{adj} = \sqrt{N} \bullet \frac{N^{-1}\tilde{S}-E(\bar{z}_{it})}{\sqrt{\text{var}(\bar{z}_{it})}}$$

$$E(\bar{z}_{it}) = k, \text{var}(\bar{z}_{it}) = \frac{2k(T-k-1)}{T+1}$$

The second-generation tests employed to check for the existence of unit root (e.g., cross-sectionally augmented Dickey-Fuller (CADF)) should be applied in case of dependence. The CADF statistic uses the relationship as follows:

$$\Delta Y_{i,t} = \alpha_i + \beta_i Y_{i,t-1} + \gamma_i \bar{Y}_{t-1} + \delta_i \Delta \bar{Y}_{i,t} + e_{it}$$

$$\bar{Y}_{t-1} = \frac{1}{N}\sum_{i=1}^{N} Y_{i,t-1}$$

$$\Delta \bar{Y}_{i,t} = \frac{1}{N}\sum_{i=1}^{N} \Delta Y_{i,t}$$

The cointegration relationship between various panel data series is verified by applying the Westerlund test that presents robustness to dependence in cross-sections. In the end, the CCEMG approach is employed to include the non-observed common effects that present non-homogenous factor loadings (f_t):

$$Y_{it} = \alpha_i + \beta_i X_{it} + \gamma_i \bar{Y}_{it} + \delta_i \bar{X}_{it} + c_i f_t + \varepsilon_{it}$$

where

Y_{it} is the dependent variable
X_{it} are the exogenous variables
α_i is the constant
β_i is the country-specific slope
γ_i, δ_i, c_i are the coefficients
f_t is the unobserved common factor
ε_{it} are shocks

37.4 Analysis/Results Interpretation

According to statistics in Table 37.1, we have the growth of GHG emissions that ranges between 1.791759 and 4.273364. The maximum growth was seen in 2020 in Denmark, while the lowest value was observed in 2010 in Germany. The latter also registered the minimum growth of value added in agriculture in 2009, while Denmark obtained the highest increase in value added in agriculture in 2009. The relative range of energy consumption is higher than the relative range of the other indicators which suggests significant discrepancies between countries in terms of energy use.

Table 37.1 Descriptive statistics (2009–2020)

Variable (series in natural logarithm)	Mean	Standard deviation	Minimum value	Maximum value
GHG	2.331273	0.3740086	1.791759	3.273364
VAA	23.27883	0.8569866	21.55182	24.39104
Employment in agriculture	1.572088	0.8643575	0.1906204	3.43431
Energy consumption in agriculture	5.046458	1.069645	3.174715	7.678766

Source: Author's own calculations

Table 37.2 Preliminary tests results

Indicator (data series in natural log)	CD-test stat.	p-value	$\overline{\Delta}_{adj}$	p-value
GHG	19.95	0.000	−1.362	0.173
VAA	1.21	0.226	0.422	0.673
Employment in agriculture	4.23	0.000	1.483	0.138
Energy consumption in agriculture	2.25	0.025	2.414	0.016

Source: Author's results from Stata 15

Table 37.3 CADF test results

Indicator (data series in natural log)	Initial series		Series once differentiated	
	1 lag	2 lags	1 lag	2 lags
GHG	0.622 (0.733)	8.530 (0.9)	4.696* (<0.01)	3.544* (<0.01)
VAA	−2.030** (0.021)	8.890 (0.9)	−2.965* (<0.01)	−2.754* (0.002)
Employment in agriculture	3.432 (0.9)	8.167 (0.9)	−2.686* (0.004)	3.756* (<0.01)
Energy consumption in agriculture	−1.889** (0.029)	9.967 (0.9)	−6.503* (<0.01)	3.988* (<0.01)

Source: Author's results from Stata 15
*indicates significance at 10% level and **shows significance at 5% level

According to Table 37.2, the cross-sectional dependence is supported for GHG emissions, employment in agriculture and energy consumption in agriculture at 5% level of significance. Moreover, slope heterogeneity was confirmed for energy consumption in agriculture at the same significance value.

Given the dependence in sections, CADF test is used in two variants: equation augmented with 1 and 2lags, since the test varies with the number of lags. This equation includes constant and trend for initial data and only intercept for series differenced once. Table 37.3 indicates stationary data only in the first difference (0.05 level of significance).

Given that series are I(1), the cointegration is checked using the Westerlund test for data in level. This test has the advantage that provides reliable results under cross-sectional dependence. Table 37.4 indicates that in most of the cases, cointegration is supported for the analyzed variables.

Under cointegration, the DOLS/ FMOLS approach could be used, but this method can generate biased results without consistency if cross-sectional dependence was detected (Adeneye et al. 2021). This limitation is solved by the CCEMG method. The results in Table 37.5 suggest an N-inverted pattern while explaining the GHG emissions in agriculture. As expected, more employment and energy consumption in agriculture contribute to pollution in the 10 biggest agricultural producers from EU.

Table 37.4 The results of Westerlund cointegration test

Statistics	Cointegration between GHG and	
	VAA	VAA, employment and energy consumption in agriculture
Gt	−1.3361 (0.0908)	2.8625 (0.0021)
Ga	10.0032 (0.0000)	16.3518 (0.0000)
Pt	−1.9095 (0.0281)	0.3514 (0.3627)
Pa	5.7324 (0.0000)	9.0110 (0.0000)

Source: Author's results from Stata 15, *p*-values in brackets

Table 37.5 The results of CCEMG estimators

Variable	Coefficients (*p*-values in brackets)	
VAA	−0.1211966 (0.000)	−0.2238763 (0.000)
VAA^2	0.0632263 (0.000)	0.300126 (0.000)
VAA^3	−0.0016709 (0.000)	−0.0084509 (0.000)
Employment in agriculture	–	0.2319644 (0.000)
Energy consumption in agriculture	–	0.1905077 (0.000)
Constant	−10.8152 (0.000)	−52.18078 (0.000)
Cross-section averaged regressors for		
GHG emissions	0.9288355 (0.000)	1.305094 (0.001)
VAA	−1.9646373 (0.0877)	−2.546679 (0.098)
VAA^2	0.2919172 (0.0247)	1.284852 (0.043)
VAA^3	−0.0086138 (0.0244)	−0.0367965 (0.043)
Employment in agriculture	–	0.2554696 (0.041)
Energy consumption in agriculture	–	0.3103393 (0.096)

Source: Author's results from Stata 15

The N form was previously obtained by Simionescu (2021a) that explained GHG emissions in agriculture based on value added in this sector in Poland. Moreover, Lazăr et al. (2019) identified the same pattern while explaining the carbon dioxide in more CEEs. The energy consumption in agriculture has the capacity to accelerate the environmental degradation and more initiatives should be undertaken in the analyzed countries to reduce the traditional energy consumption and use more renewable energy. In addition, more environmental regulations on pollution could reduce energy consumption in agriculture. More employment in agriculture also enhances GHG emissions which suggest it is necessary to employ more people that know to use friendly-environmental technology.

37.5 Conclusions

This paper brings contribution in EKC research by considering a new version of this model adapted for agricultural sector. The GHG emissions in agriculture are explained based on value added in this sector and by control variables like energy consumption and employment in agriculture. An inverted-N pattern was identified which suggest that more efforts are necessary to reduce pollution in the 10 biggest agricultural producers from the EU. On the other hand, renewable energy should be promoted more and the human capital working in this sector should know to use new green technology.

Besides these results, the study presents few limitations. For example, the analysis is limited only to 10 EU countries with the highest agricultural production in 2020 and only one method has been employed. In a future study, more methods should be applied for robustness (mean group estimator, augmented mean group estimator, etc.) and the analysis should be extended to more EU countries.

References

Adeneye, Y. B., Jaaffar, A. H., Ooi, C. A., & Ooi, S. K. (2021). Nexus between carbon emissions, energy consumption, urbanization and economic growth in Asia: Evidence from common correlated effects mean group estimator (CCEMG). *Frontiers in Energy Research, 8*, 610577.

Ali, S., Yusop, Z., Kaliappan, S. R., & Chin, L. (2021). Trade-environment nexus in OIC countries: Fresh insights from environmental Kuznets curve using GHG emissions and ecological footprint. *Environmental Science and Pollution Research, 28*(4), 4531–4548.

Atici, C. (2009). Pollution without subsidy? What is the environmental performance index overlooking? *Ecological Economics, 68*(7), 1903–1907.

Baležentis, T., Streimikiene, D., Zhang, T., & Liobikiene, G. (2019). The role of bioenergy in greenhouse gas emission reduction in EU countries: An environmental Kuznets curve modelling. *Resources, Conservation and Recycling, 142*, 225–231.

Bölük, G., & Mert, M. (2014). Fossil & renewable energy consumption, GHGs (greenhouse gases) and economic growth: Evidence from a panel of EU (European Union) countries. *Energy, 74*, 439–446.

Grossman, G. M., & Krueger, A. B. (1991). *Environmental impacts of a north American free trade agreement.* Working Paper No. 3914.

Haberl, H., Wiedenhofer, D., Virág, D., Kalt, G., Plank, B., Brockway, P., et al. (2020). A systematic review of the evidence on decoupling of GDP, resource use and GHG emissions, part II: Synthesizing the insights. *Environmental Research Letters, 15*(6), 065003.

Heinrichs, H. U., & Markewitz, P. (2015). A coal phase-out in Germany–clean, efficient and affordable? *Energy Procedia, 75*, 2541–2547.

Kasman, A., & Duman, Y. S. (2015). CO_2 emissions, economic growth, energy consumption, trade and urbanization in new EU member and candidate countries: A panel data analysis. *Economic Modelling, 44*, 97–103.

Lapinskienė, G., Peleckis, K., & Radavičius, M. (2015). Economic development and greenhouse gas emissions in the European Union countries. *Journal of Business Economics and Management, 16*(6), 1109–1123.

Lapinskienė, G., Peleckis, K., & Nedelko, Z. (2017). Testing environmental Kuznets curve hypothesis: The role of enterprise's sustainability and other factors on GHG in European countries. *Journal of Business Economics and Management, 18*(1), 54–67.

Lazăr, D., Minea, A., & Purcel, A. A. (2019). Pollution and economic growth: Evidence from central and eastern European countries. *Energy Economics, 81*, 1121–1131.

López-Menéndez, A. J., Pérez, R., & Moreno, B. (2014). Environmental costs and renewable energy: Re-visiting the environmental Kuznets curve. *Journal of Environmental Management, 145*, 368–373.

Mohammed, S., Gill, A. R., Alsafadi, K., Hijazi, O., Yadav, K. K., Hasan, M. A., et al. (2021). An overview of greenhouse gases emissions in Hungary. *Journal of Cleaner Production, 314*, 127865.

Ozturk, I., & Acaravci, A. (2010). CO_2 emissions, energy consumption and economic growth in Turkey. *Renewable and Sustainable Energy Reviews, 14*(9), 3220–3225.

Pradhan, B. B., Chaichaloempreecha, A., & Limmeechokchai, B. (2019). GHG mitigation in agriculture, forestry and other land use (AFOLU) sector in Thailand. *Carbon Balance and Management, 14*(1), 1–17.

Qin, Z., Griscom, B., Huang, Y., Yuan, W., Chen, X., Dong, W., et al. (2021). Delayed impact of natural climate solutions. *Global Change Biology, 27*(2), 215–217.

Simionescu, M. (2021a). Revised environmental Kuznets curve in CEE countries. Evidence from panel threshold models for economic sectors. *Environmental Science and Pollution Research, 28*(43), 60881–60899.

Simionescu, M. (2021b). The nexus between economic development and pollution in the European Union new member states. The role of renewable energy consumption. *Renewable Energy, 179*, 1767–1780.

Stern, D. I. (2004). The rise and fall of the environmental Kuznets curve. *World Development, 32*(8), 1419–1439.

Tongwane, M. I., & Moeletsi, M. E. (2018). A review of greenhouse gas emissions from the agriculture sector in Africa. *Agricultural Systems, 166*, 124–134.

Zeng, L., Ye, A., & Lin, W. (2022). Deepening decoupling for sustainable development: Evidence from threshold model. *Energy Efficiency, 15*(5), 1–11.

Chapter 38
Strategies for Bioeconomy in Central and Eastern Europe: BIOEAST Initiative and BIOEASTsUP Project

Dan-Marius Voicilas ⓘ

Abstract The concept of bioeconomy is relatively new in the world. As a consequence, the strategies and policies in economy have changed toward bioeconomy. They follow the goals fixed by the concept. The study presents the concept, BIOEAST Initiative and BIOEASTsUP Project. Based on the information available, it is presented the level of development of the strategies, in the European Union (EU) countries, with special focus on Central and South Eastern member states. The study highlights the opportunities, threats, challenges the countries have, using the findings from BIOEAST and BIOEASTsUP and the links between them. To reach the objectives proposed, statistical data available on the official web pages of the European Commission (EC), documents elaborated by EU institutions, and texts and analyses from initiative and project were used. For better understanding of the initiative and the project, it is presented the role the project has, to help the achievement of the objectives established in bioeconomy, when the BIOEASTS was created for countries from Central and South East of EU. The results of the study reflect the benefits of the strategies. They open new opportunities for member states and eliminate the main issues appeared in economy in the last decades. By initiative and project, the creation of the strategies in accordance with EU regulations is important and useful in the future, especially if we have in view the EU funds available in this field. Obviously, in Europe, especially for EU member states, bioeconomy will become more and more important and will play strategic role at the national level.

Keywords Bioeconomy concept · EU Bioeconomy · CEE countries · BIOEAST Initiative · BIOEASTsUP Project

---

D.-M. Voicilas, Assoc. prof. Ph.D (✉)
Institute of Agricultural Economics, Romanian Academy, Bucharest, Romania
e-mail: voicilas@eadr.ro

© The Author(s), under exclusive license to Springer Nature Switzerland AG 2024
L. Chivu et al. (eds.), *Constraints and Opportunities in Shaping the Future: New Approaches to Economics and Policy Making*, Springer Proceedings in Business and Economics, https://doi.org/10.1007/978-3-031-47925-0_38

38.1 Introduction

Naturally, we wonder why bioeconomy is so important lately. Statistical data and analyses performed in the field give us, easily, the answer to this question. For example, at the EU level, if we analyse some basic indicators for the bioeconomy, we see (Fig. 38.1) how many resources it entails and how many effects it produces, such as jobs, turnover, or added value.

In the case of the presented indicators, the majority share in the bioeconomy field has agriculture and the food and beverage industry. In addition, important and high-weight activities are in the field of wood, furniture, and paper and also, plastics, rubber, pharmaceuticals, and chemicals. Almost 18 million employees are involved in bioeconomy in EU. The turnover is huge and the value added is more than 650 billion Euros. The remarkably high statistical values of these economic activities are strong arguments for treating the bioeconomy seriously and for developing dedicated strategies at national level and plans for future activities at the regional level. We predict that the bioeconomy will develop in the near future because the potential is big for all EU members. Obvious, the CEE countries have their personal contribution at the EU level. These are the arguments why we consider this study and the implementation of the national strategies as useful. The BIOEAST Initiative and BIOEASTsUP Project have in view this objective.

38.2 Literature Review

Bioeconomy has many definitions. The experts in the field did not elaborate a unanimous accepted definition. For instance, there is a definition from European Commission (see EC, 2012), a definition from BIOEAST Initiative (see http://bioeast.eu), from USA (see White House, 2012), from different organisations in the bioeconomy field, like associations, clusters, and other initiatives (see https://youmatter.world/en/definition/bioeconomy-definition/). Also, there are definitions elaborated by Romanian authors, like Orboi et al., 2017, or Voicilas, 2021 (see Box 38.1).

> **Box 38.1: Definition of Bioeconomy Elaborated by Author (Voicilas, 2021)**
> A complex system composed of Earth resources and their anthropic and natural transformation processes, which belong to biology and contribute to the economic, social and cultural development of people in a sustainable way, based on knowledge, forethought and empathy.

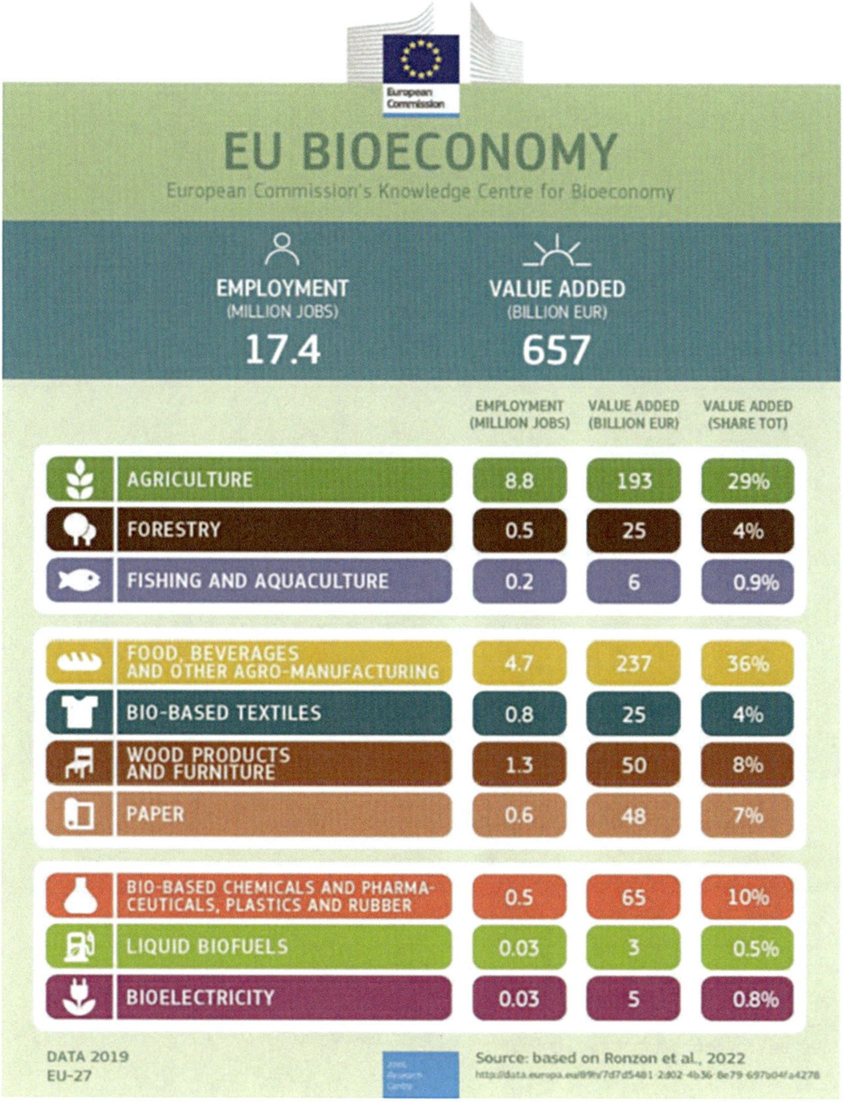

Fig. 38.1 Indicators of the bioeconomy in the EU. (Source: EC, Based on Ronzon et al., 2022, JRC)

From our research, the term bioeconomy was used for the first time by Grigore Antipa, a Romanian scientist, in an article published in 1933, in a Romanian Academy publication (see Fig. 38.2). Other famous scientists that use the term in their work were Jiri Zeman, Nicolae Georgescu-Roegen, Juan Enriquez Cabot, or Rodrigo Martinez (Birner, 2018). Later, after 2000, an important role in promoting the bioeconomy concept had Christian Patermann, a lawyer and the founding

Fig. 38.2 Grigore Antipa's publication, 1933. (Source: Sustainable Development Department-Romanian Government, personal collection)

member of the first German Bio-economics Advisory Committee, also the Programme Director for Biotechnology, Agriculture and Food from European Commission, presently, important advisor for BIOEAST Initiative.

Nowadays, many institutions and scientist work in this field, in the world. In Romania, there is no specialised institution in bioeconomy but there are other institutions that have research in this field, like institutes of the Romanian Academy, research centres from universities or the Department of Sustainable Development of the Romanian Government.

38.3 Methodology

The purpose of this article is to provide an overview of bioeconomy and its strategies currently being developed in CEE countries. This article aims to introduce the concept of bioeconomy and the development of bioeconomy strategies in CEE countries. They initiated a government partnership called the BIOEAST Initiative and collaborated to create and apply for research projects, like BIOEASTsUP, one of its first "product".

To accomplish the objectives of this study, thorough research was conducted. This included an extensive literature review, textual analysis of studies and documents related to the topic, and comparisons between the analysed states. The BIOEAST Initiative, BIOEASTsUP Project, official documents of the European Commission, and other European institutions with attribution in this field, as well as national documents of the CEE member states, were examined and used as sources of information.

38.4 Analysis/Results Interpretation

38.4.1 Bioeconomy Strategy in Europe

At the EU level, the bioeconomy was developed after 2000 and the first bioeconomy strategy was elaborated in 2012.

Later, in 2017, the EC considered it necessary to assess the effects of this strategy at the EU level, to see the stage of development of national bioeconomies in the member states and to align the objectives of the bioeconomy strategy with sustainable development goals. The results of the evaluation highlighted the need to develop an update strategy, and thus, a new official EC document was elaborated. It was adopted in 2018.

It proposes three main areas of action upon which actions are based (EC, 2018): investments in bio-based sectors; the implementation of the national bioeconomies; and ecological limits of the implementation.

In the EU, there are four groups of countries with different levels of development of the bioeconomy strategy (Fig. 38.3). According to data from 2022 (April), EU member states that already have a national strategy are Latvia, Finland, Germany, France, the Netherlands, Ireland, Portugal, Spain, Italy, and Austria (https://knowledge4policy.ec.europa.eu/visualisation/bioeconomy-different-countries_en).

There is a second group of countries that has strategies under development, like Lithuania, Sweden, Poland, Slovakia, Czech Rep., Hungary, and Croatia. The third group of countries that has "Other policy initiatives dedicated to the bioeconomy" is: Estonia, Denmark, Belgium, Romania, Bulgaria, and Slovenia. Other EU countries have "Other related strategies at national level", like Greece, Cyprus, Malta, and Luxemburg. Among countries from Western and Central Europe, that are not

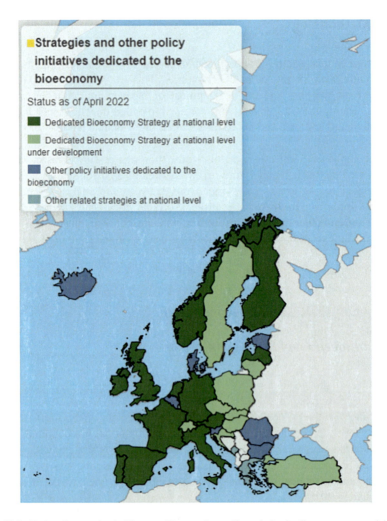

Fig. 38.3 National strategies in Europe. (Source: https://knowledge4policy.ec.europa.eu/visualisation/bioeconomy-different-countries_en)

EU members, Norway and U.K. have national strategy and Switzerland has strategy under development. Also, Island has other policies and initiatives for bioeconomy and Montenegro has different other strategies with bioeconomy connections". There are no other data for the rest of the European countries on the official web page of EC, except Turkey which has a national strategy under development.

From 27 EU member states, only 17 have national strategies or strategies under development. We see that, the process of the creation of a national strategy is not easy, and after 10 years since the first EU Bioeconomy strategy still 10 EU countries do not have national strategy. Only Latvia has a bioeconomy strategy in CEE. Six other countries have strategies in elaboration (Hungary, Slovakia, Czech Rep.,

Poland, Lithuania, and Croatia), and the remaining countries have other types of policy and strategies, relevant for bioeconomy.

38.4.2 BIOEAST

BIOEAST is a political engagement signed by EU members from CEE. However, 11 countries joined the agreement, which officially born after a few years of negotiations in 2014. They are Visegrad countries, plus Baltic countries, plus South-East EU countries like Romania, Bulgaria, Croatia, and Slovenia (Fig. 38.4). They look to formulate 2030 vision for bioeconomy, in line with EU Bioeconomy Strategy.

Only ministries are eligible for membership.

For a sustainable bioeconomy, BIOEAST provides a special framework on research and innovation, with strategic role.

The initiative promotes the inclusive growth of the countries, maintain or enhance environmental sustainability, creates jobs in rural areas (especially), with high value-added, through the use of knowledge and collaborative efforts, to develop a circular economy based on bioeconomy. The mission is to help CEE countries to harness their potential and realize their vision towards 2030 by providing the following opportunities (http://bioeast.eu):

- Sustainable growth in biomass production to become a leading producer of globally competitive quality food and feed
- Zero waste processing of existing biomass
- Inclusive, innovative, climate-friendly growth models in rural, in a dynamic way

The scope of BIOEAST is:

- A strategic way of thinking
- Food and feed with high quality
- Stimulation in rural by industrialisation

There are general goals set to address the challenges of achieving the overall mission:

- Strategize
- Collaboration and development of policies based on evidence
- Identification of the challenges that are common and validation for research areas that are common
- Provide evidences
- Improve the skills
- Synergy development
- Better visibility

The main activities planned are as follows:

- Preparation of intergovernmental joint declaration at ministerial level

Fig. 38.4 BIOEAST countries. (Source: http://bioeast.eu)

- A common research and innovation agenda
- Advice for strategic policies and position papers
- To that end, a mobilisation of the research institutions, government, practitioners, NGOs, and citizens (stakeholders) is necessary. In this way, they achieve the goals proposed, thus defining his BIOEAST Hub across the country as a network that brings together stakeholders to support their mobilisation.

The structure is shown in Fig. 38.5. The board has Secretary general and national contact points. At the beginning, at the macro-regional level, there were five thematic working groups (TWGs), like food systems, forestry, agroecology, bioenergy,

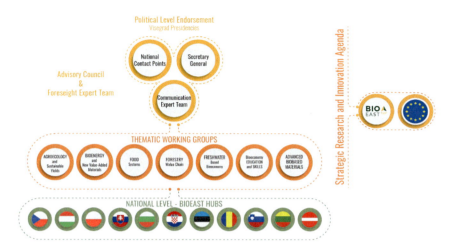

Fig. 38.5 BIOEAST' structure. (Source: http://bioeast.eu)

and freshwater, and the scope was to guide the board in these fields. Later, other two TWG were established: bioeconomy education and bio-based materials.

Also, an expert panel was established as an advisory board to support the initiative. The objective is two-fold: not only to furnish national policymakers with guidance, but also to pinpoint the particular difficulties that macro-regions could encounter, and assist in the development of BIOEAST's Strategic Research and Innovation Agenda (SRIA). Foresight exercise, which is periodically planed, supports the BIOEAST countries in developing their sustainable bioeconomies. Experts and the reports show the future prospects of the macro-regional bioeconomy (2030–2050) by examining the details, specific needs, and developments of the macro-regional bioeconomy, into a wider EU and global context, with possible scenarios. They want to raise awareness of the challenges to national policy development, improve policy frameworks on long-term, underlining challenges and providing advices on the development of SRIA.

The web page of the initiative has details about the bodies which are involved in this partnership, and the TWGs selected at the macro-regional level. An important section is dedicated to the "Stakeholder platform". It is a common platform for all 11 countries, that wants to gather all stakeholders from the partners under one umbrella, based on the platforms developed at the national level by members. The stakeholders are from academia and research, policy makers and administration, business (small and large), other entities like NGOs, associations, foundations, etc. Another important section of the web page is the project BIOEASTsUP, one of the main achievements of the initiative, Horizon 2020 project (RUR-2019-1 call), financed by EC for the period 2019–2022/2023.

38.4.3 BIOEASTsUP

BIOEASTsUP was started in 2019. Its main objective was to help BIOEAST to implement its 2030 vision and action plan. The structure of the project was created similar with the initiative and the connections are shown in Fig. 38.6.

In order to assist the execution of country-wide strategies, mobilize research, innovation, and create chains with value-added in bioeconomy through stakeholder engagement, BIOEASTsUP offers coordinated actions and incorporated moves. This measure creates a framework and capacity for an evidence-based policy-based approach that is systematic, particularly in rural areas, for a sustainable circular bioeconomy.

The Romanian Academy, by the Institute of Agricultural Economics, is one of the members of the consortium that has 21 partners. Beside BIOEAST countries, in this project participate Germany and Finland. Other institutions which support the project are ministries (26), different associations, chambers of commerce/industrial, centres for innovation, private/state research organisations, and NGOs.

Under the aegis of the bioeconomy, BIOEASTsUP is creating a community-based platform with the purpose of connecting with the larger community at the Member State level in order to accomplish the EU's circularity and sustainability goals. This scope provides a vision document and action plan for implementing the BIOEAST Initiative by bringing together macro-regional collaboration of stakeholders, from consortium, academic institutions, governmental bodies, and national

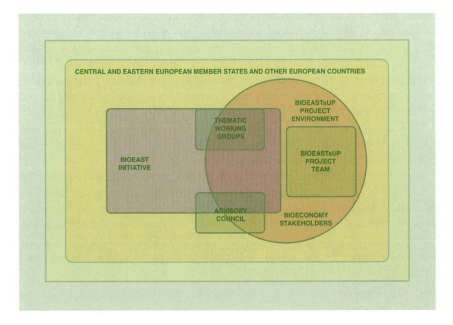

Fig. 38.6 Connections between initiative and project. (Source: BIOEASTsUP Project)

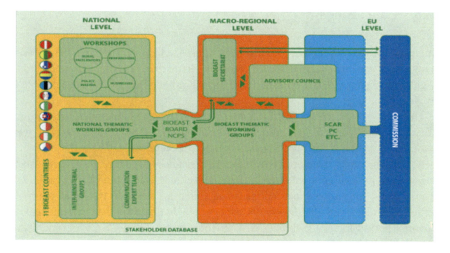

Fig. 38.7 Project' activities. (Source: BIOEASTsUP Project)

administrations, with help from partners with national bioeconomy strategy, like Germany and Finland.

The project has specific objectives (https://bioeast.eu/bioeastsup/):

- Stimulate strategic thinking at national level and transnational developments
- Stress the importance of multi-stakeholder approaches in the creation of the new value chains
- Develop a unified SRIA
- Special and strong support for the initiative and SRIA, at macro-regional level
- Promote evidence for policymakers
- Raise the visibility

The activities planned are presented in Fig. 38.7:

- Operational: integration and streamlining of BIOEASTsUP and BIOEAST
- Policy: building a strategic framework for bioeconomy at national level and SRIA at macro-regional level
- Support: for BIOEAST

The work of BIOEASTSUP aims to improve institutions, build capacity, and support evidence for decision makers. The activities are directly influenced by the BIOEAST's and its stakeholders' existing institutional framework and their identified demands. By fostering ownership and ensuring that stakeholder demands and desired objectives are satisfied, this will promote long-term sustainability, development, and embedding of BIOEAST activities past the project's completion. A bottom-up methodology is used in the project.

38.5 Conclusions

CEE countries are late in their process of building the national strategies. There are many challenges that CEE states are currently facing, like research and innovation stagnation; stagnation in bio-based value chains; governance gridlock; social apathy; financial barriers.

The study shows the threats that may hinder the plans the member states from CEE have. The political commitment and will are the most significant ones we found. They can be powerful obstacles to strategy development.

At the same time, there are favourable circumstances for national strategies and action plans to develop more quickly. First, stakeholders are interested in building them. Second, the national institutions engaged in these activities were real, open to participation, and well qualified in terms of people. In that case, the future financial planning period for EU members will, in some ways, force CEE's EU member states to develop strategies more quickly.

The opportunities they have for investments, in research or others, and support from Brussels officials are strong arguments for rapid and solid development of the national strategies with BIOEAST Initiative help. The CEE countries can recover de differences that appeared in the development of the strategies compared to countries from Western EU.

Other findings of the study show that the Ministry of Agriculture has the main role in the development of the national strategies, in all countries. This is a proof of the importance of the agriculture and food industry for bioeconomy.

The BIOEAST Initiative is also a joint action of all countries from CEE. We believe that the initiative is an important structure that will help CEE countries develop and implement the strategies, at the national level, and together to the development of the bioeconomy in macro-region. As a consequence, the financial benefits will come, like the development of new research projects, or the development of new business based on the programs from financial programming period 2021–2027 and the next. It is obvious that the nations in the macro-region must prioritized absorbing EU money by programs/projects in this field.

In conclusion, the BIOEASTsUP Project has had important contributions in developing the national strategies in CEE, helps the initiative to reach the objectives and creates links between the actors involved in bioeconomy field.

Acknowledgements

References

Antipa, G. (1933). *La biosociologie et la bioeconomie de la Mer Noire*. Bulletin de la section scientifique, Romanian Academy (Sustainable Development Department-Romanian Government, personal collection).

Birner, R. (2018). Bioeconomy concepts. In I. Lewandowski (Ed.), *Bioeconomy, Hans-Ruthenberg-Institute, Social and Institutional Change in Agricultural Development*. University of Hohenheim.

European Commission. (2012). *Innovating for sustainable growth-a bioeconomy for Europe, Directorate-General for Research and Innovation.*, ISBN 978-92-79-25376-8,. Publications Office of the European Union. https://doi.org/10.2777/6462

European Commission. (2018). A sustainable bioeconomy for Europe: strengthening the connection between economy, society and the environment-updated Bioeconomy Strategy, European Commission, Directorate-General for Research and Innovation Unit F – Bioeconomy, Print ISBN 978-92-79-94145-0 doi: 10.2777/478385 KI-04-18-806-EN-C, PDF ISBN 978-92-79-94144-3 doi:10.2777/792130 KI-04-18-806-EN-N, Brussels, Belgium, https://ec.europa.eu/research/bioeconomy/pdf/ ec_bioeconomy_strategy_2018.pdf (10.09.2020).

European Commission, Based on Ronzon et al. (2022). JRC.

http://bioeast.eu

http://bioeast.eu/bioeastsup/

https://knowledge4policy.ec.europa.eu/visualisation/bioeconomy-different-countries_en

https://youmatter.world/en/definition/bioeconomy-definition/

Orboi, M.D. et al. (2017). www.spasb.ro/index.php/spasb/article/download/2404/pdf

Voicilas, D. M. (2021). *Perspectives for bioeconomy strategy in Romania*. AERD Journal, Year XVIII, No.2, IEA, Ed. Academiei Române, ISSN 1841-0375.

White House, (2012). National Bioeconomy Blueprint.

Chapter 39
Are Census Socioeconomic Variables a Consistent Tool for Analyzing Human Resources Sustainability on Romania's Labor Market?

Raluca Mazilescu ⬤, Valentina Vasile ⬤, Ana-Maria Ciuhu ⬤, and Marius-Răzvan Surugiu ⬤

Abstract Censuses ensure obtaining important data on some indicators of the labor market, as they observe the entire population of the national territory, in its smallest subdivisions. Multiple difficulties regarding the harmonization of census data provided by the EU member states emerged at the level of the European Union. However, solutions have gradually been identified and implemented for ensuring data comparability between countries. Among the EU states, there has been a growing tendency to move from the traditional organization of census to an approach based totally or partially (for the time being) on administrative sources. Using a combined census (survey data combined with administrative registers) is considered as a tool for statistical information consolidation. Another interesting trend, which arose in the context of the expansion of ICT technologies, was the digitalization of the census data collection system, considered as a factor with an impact on the respondents' compliance degree. Best practices regarding online self-enumeration in the EU countries were analyzed. For Romania, the main characteristics of self-enumeration were highlighted, along with the changes made in Romania's census questionnaire, with a focus on labor market indicators.

Keywords Population Census · Labor Market · EU-27

R. Mazilescu (✉) · V. Vasile · M.-R. Surugiu
Institute of National Economy, Bucharest, Romania

A.-M. Ciuhu
Institute of National Economy, Bucharest, Romania

National Institute of Statistics, Bucharest, Romania

39.1 Introduction

Population and housing censuses (PHC) in each country are organized by national statistical offices, starting from the principles and recommendations at the international level. In some situations, the traditional method of collecting data for censuses, i.e., directly from the population, was added to the one consisting in the use of administrative sources. Sometimes they are used together. In other states, the traditional census method is aborted when the administrative sources manage to become sufficiently comprehensive and well-integrated into a coherent system.

At the level of the European Union, various challenges in terms of harmonizing the data provided by the member states appeared and, with the possibility of ensuring their comparability between countries. Such challenges were felt with increased intensity especially following the enlargement stages of 2004 and 2007, when 12 new member states, with very different statistical systems, joined the European Union. In an attempt to overcome these problems, an important step in the field of designing PHC was the approval of Regulation 763/2008 (EP, 2008), which stipulated, among other things, the obligation of member states to provide a standardized set of data specific to this field, at the national and regional level (NUTS 1, 2, and 3 levels from the Common Nomenclature of Territorial Statistical Units) and local (LAU 2 level – communes, municipalities and cities). The respective data were to be obtained following the introduction of certain themes in the questionnaires used for PHC in EU.

The purpose of this paper is to create an image regarding census socioeconomic variables and to analyze their relationship with the labor market indicators. The paper is structured as follows: in the following section, a review of literature is performed; Sect. 39.3 discusses the methodology, Sect. 39.4 presents the mains results, while the last section concludes the paper.

39.2 Literature Review

The population census is an important statistical tool in permanent modernization. Thus, the data are collected with a decennial frequency, representing a comprehensive research/survey on the entire population, presenting definite informational advantages compared to sample surveys, such as the Labor Force Survey, Household Budget Survey, etc. The indicators are completed by expanding the information base and diversifying the aspects tracked by reporting - from indicators specific to the demographic area to indicators of the population's economy, which involves components/indicators with economic and social implications - regarding education, presence on the labor market, and the degree of access of social policy tools. Thus, there is a convergence with similar surveys from the EU and international area, with some differences, some being significant, regarding the detailing of the indicators on demographic attributes of the population, with the declaration of some aspects regarding ethnicity, nationality, social status, etc. It is thus important to increase the correlation between the survey indicators and the administrative data, to avoid double reporting, this being facilitated by the digitalization of the data collection.

A PHC is usually carried out every 10 years and it is the only statistical survey that covers the entire national territory, including its smallest subdivisions (INS, 2011). It aims acquiring important information regarding indicators such as: the size of the resident population; the demographic profile (age group, sex, and territorial distribution); socioeconomic structure (active and inactive population), but also the number and main characteristics of housing units (surface area, existence/type of spaces intended for certain functions (bathroom, kitchen/kitchenette, etc.), which ultimately outline the living conditions).

The practice of counting the population has existed since ancient times, arising to respond to the need of the administrative structures of states/empires to obtain useful information for their proper functioning. Initially, only certain segments of the population were targeted, such as the number of taxpayers, the pool of population suitable to serve in the army or for forced labor (slaves). From a historical perspective, along with the development of the states, the population counting underwent an extensive process of transformation, refinement, up to the forms used in the modern period. While in the first censuses, the main goal was to highlight the number of people who lived in a territory, gradually, a tendency to increase the number of data collected in the censuses was observed, as a result of the diversification of the needs of different categories of users. In this context, the topics addressed in the censuses began to go beyond the demographic sphere, to also include economic and social aspects. Currently, the census is a valuable tool, widely used worldwide. It is important to stress out that some indicators highlighted during PHCs are also mentioned in some global development strategies, such as the 2030 Agenda. Consequently, monitoring the level of achievement of the targets/indicators will be possible (also) by using PHC data.

As global interdependencies among nations grew, there emerged initial efforts to standardize the methods used for gathering and analyzing statistical data, especially in relation to PHC, to guarantee international data comparability. According to international recommendations (UN, 1958, 2017), in the process of developing the questionnaire used in the population and housing censuses, two categories of aspects should be considered. On the one hand, a questionnaire should include topics of general interest to all countries (core topics), which later allow international comparisons. On the other hand, there may also be topics that respond to the needs of statistical data that exist on a national/regional/local level.

In Romania, the first population census that met the main criteria required for such a survey took place in 1838, in Wallachia (INS, 2023a). Another landmark in the history of national censuses is the census of 1859–1860, the first census that aimed to investigate the demographic and socioeconomic situation in the United Principalities. After the fall of communism, the process of modernizing Romanian statistics was initiated, so that in 1992, a census was organized that marked the transition to the decennial model of conducting PHCs.

The 12th round of the Romanian census, respectively, PHC 2011, represented a landmark, being the first organized after Romania's accession to the European Union. After the enlargement waves of 2004 and 2007, when 10 plus two countries joined the EU, the conduct of the first post-accession census, respectively, 2011 round of PHC in the new Member States was prepared by adopting methodological changes to ensure alignment with the framework of population censuses in the EU. Starting from the moment of accession to the EU, the implementation of all the requirements of the Community acquis became mandatory for the respective countries, including in the field of statistical practice, and especially in the field of conducting PHC.

Important changes were also adopted in the 13th edition of the Romanian census – 2021 PHC which represented a paradigm shift, through the following three new elements:

- Digitalization of data collection by using CAPI and CAWI methods.
- Launching the method of collecting data from administrative sources - for now at a limited level.
- Introducing the possibility of self-enumeration – an important step for increasing the degree of digitalization and, implicitly, for reducing the costs of collecting, transporting and storing printed questionnaires.
- The implementation of the latest European methodological changes regarding the PHCs implementation framework, namely the introduction of reporting at grid level (1 square km) for a series of 13 indicators.

The use of data from administrative sources is of particular importance because census data are collected only once every ten years, and on the other hand, the Quarterly Household Labor Force Survey (AMIGO) is conducted on a sample basis. In contrast to these two methods, administrative sources can feed into a database from which indicators can be produced periodically (with a higher frequency than once every 10 years). At the institutional level, the use of administrative sources is a priority axis for Romanian statistics, because it allows the exploitation of already recorded information (practically, the costs of data collection are reduced, when they already exist). Moreover, by using administrative sources, greater correctness and completeness of the collected data is ensured. The trend at the European level is the exclusive use of administrative sources for the production of census-type indicators.

The population census is a robust source of population data. In other words, census data validates a certain resident population, on the basis of which later population data can be recalculated. For example, for the period 2002–2011, the number of the resident population on January 1 was recalculated, to ensure comparability with the final results of the 2011 PHC (INS, 2023b). Another consequence is the recalculation of the employed population from the Quarterly Household Labor Force Survey (AMIGO), because the update of the resident population entails the modification of the survey estimates, in the process of expanding the survey results. Thus, starting from 2004, the survey data were re-estimated based on the resident population recalculated/calculated under conditions of comparability with the PHC 2011 results.

In the most recent list of UN recommendations on the choice of topics that can be included in a population census questionnaire (UN, 2017), the core topics were divided into several categories, with the aim of highlighting the main characteristics of each people enumerated, according to several thematic coordinates: geographical characteristics; internal and international migration; household and family; demographic profile and social characteristics; fertility and mortality; education; economic profile and participation in agriculture. In addition to the basic topics, the questionnaire used for PHC may also include additional topics, when the situation at the national level makes such an approach necessary.

The main framework for conducting the 2020 World PHC Program was agreed in 2015, establishing, among other things, that between 2015 and 2024, UN member states will organize at least one PHC, which can ensure data comparability at the international level (UN, 2015a). Moreover, the collected data should be used to quantify the progress made in the implementation of the post-2015 development agenda (UN, 2015b). The most recent four rounds took place as follows: the 1990 round – in which member states had to organize the census between 1985 and 1994; the 2000 round (with the census taking place in the period 1995–2004); round 2010 (2005–2014) and round 2020 (2015–2024).

The interest in the analysis of the census data and, in particular, in the aspects related to the methodology applied and the comparability of the data has continuously increased. For example, the works published in the WoS database regarding the methodology of the population census indicate that, of the total, from 1975 until now (end of July 2023 of 27,687 papers), only 4.5% of them addressed aspects related to the methodology. As we get closer to the present and with the growing interest in enriching data and refining the content of information on several categories of characteristics (not only demographic, but also economic activity, incomes, mobility, education, social, living conditions, geographical distribution, etc.), but also the need for comparability between countries and the correlation of information with administrative data, the improvement of the questionnaire and the methodology of application and correlation of the data made the share of scientific works analyzing the methodology to increase. For the period 1991 to the present, we identify a share of studies that also analyze methodological aspects of 4.8% (of a total 25,760), and if we consider only the last rounds of changes, respectively, from 2011 to the present, the share increases to 5.1% (of 17,334 scientific works). The distribution by year of the works published in WoS is presented in the following graph (Fig. 39.1).

Various thematic approach can be found in the literature that analyze aspects such as: the pros and cons of conducting national censuses, the census as an information source in public policy-making, evolution and evaluation of the modern census, the relevance of the traditional census, reasons for abandoning the conventional census and the alternatives, population redistribution across metropolitan regions, and population disaggregation on the building level based on outdated census data. Most recent papers focused on new methodologies for (self-) enumeration that have

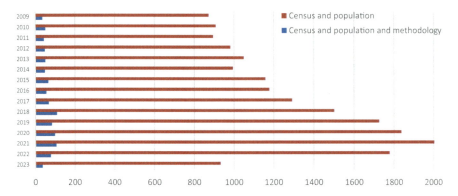

Fig. 39.1 Paper published in WoS with the topic related on population census methodology, from the year 1991. (Source: WoS database, queried by thematic keywords on July 30, 2023)

the potential to reduce cost and improve quality, including geo-location of the households (Depsky et al., 2022), sampling (Burakauskaite & Ciginas, 2023), digitalization and data protection (Giessing & Nordholt, 2017), just to mention several related thematic aspects. Generally, national censuses are characterized by high costs and are organized after long periods of time. Boyle and Dorling (2004) discuss their necessity, as well as the advantages and disadvantages of carrying them out and question their importance. Valente (2010) analyzes the situation in various countries that have moved away from traditional census practice in favor of alternative forms, often relying on the use of population registers, as well as a mixed technique that combines registers and other sources, such as the surveys. White (2009) examines the situation in the UK and the significant developments in census design, outlining the main methodological changes that have been introduced since the 2001 census, with the main aim of producing and reporting the most accurate estimate of the resident population.

Coleman (2013) discusses the context of the census, reasons for abandoning the conventional census and possible alternatives, considering the situation in different countries. Baffour et al. (2013) point out that a national census provides important information about a country's population, but its necessity has been questioned on grounds of financial austerity and the widespread availability of alternative sources of information about the population. The authors review how the modern census emerged and how it has evolved to meet these challenges, quality indicators and user needs being important. Also, the authors provide reflections on the future of the census within the national statistical infrastructure.

Killick et al. (2016) provide an assessment of the national census as a source of information, with reference to its use in policy making, highlighting the fact that, although the value of the census is recognized, policy makers do not consider it to be a tool for targeting the development and implementation of policies, this situation being evident due to the lack of knowledge of the changes proposed in the census and the rare use of available data. Rontos et al. (2020) analyze population redistribution in metropolitan regions, taking into account changes over time in the spatial distribution of population. The authors highlighted how the ratio of present to resident population is growing faster in urban areas than in rural areas. The analysis indicates that the ratio of present to resident population reflects the intense suburbanization, causing population redistribution and settlement dispersion over larger areas.

Durr (2021) discusses the definitions of the census and the methodologies used, focusing on the costs involved, the technology used, the role of international organizations and the challenges faced due to the COVID-19 pandemic. Pajares et al. (2021) propose a new approach to population disaggregation, updating census data and disaggregating the population at the building access level. The authors use a population estimate for new development areas, combined with a mapping process to update census data.

39.3 Methodology

We analyzed the type of census carried out in the last period in the EU countries. The best practices for online self-enumeration within the EU-27 member states were examined. The major features of self-enumeration in Romania were highlighted, along with the recent adjustments made to the census questionnaire, which targeted some indicators of the labor market.

The information used in the analysis was obtained mainly from the websites of the national statistical offices of the EU member states, but also from other relevant sources.

39.4 Analysis/Results Interpretation

39.4.1 Harmonization of the Survey Databases with the Administrative Ones – A Tool for Statistical Information Consolidation

When discussing the complementarity of survey data with administrative information, we could list various multiple advantages, such as: the possibility of performing an integrated analysis with other databases that manage economic and social variables; offering the possibility of a better substantiation of policies at the national level; ensuring better evidence of the territorial dispersion of the population, allowing a more accurate analysis of the dynamics of some demographic phenomena (internal mobility and external mobility), economic (workforce potential, employment indicators, identification of regional asymmetry by groups/categories of population with vulnerabilities, at risk, etc.), and social (maps of the distribution of the population by socio-demographic attributes - the existence of social enclaves, household organization models by geographical areas, differences in incomes, and in demographic behavior (birth rate, life expectancy at birth, survival rate after 60 years, long-term unemployment, etc.).

Harmonization of survey databases with administrative ones is an important process that aims to integrate the collected data from different sources. This harmonization allows the combination and enrichment of information from surveys, which collect data directly from individuals or households, with administrative data, which are collected by government agencies or organizations for administrative purposes. The important aspects of this harmonization process refer to elements such as:

- Data integration: The harmonization process involves the integration of data from surveys and administrative sources, using indicators such as names or addresses.
- Data consistency: It is essential to standardize the variables used to ensure consistency and comparability.
- Data cleaning: Surveys and administrative data often contain errors, missing values, or inconsistencies. The harmonization process involves cleaning the data to correct such problems.
- Confidentiality: Harmonizing survey and administrative data requires handling sensitive information while respecting privacy rules. It is important to ensure that data protection regulations are respected. Harmonizing survey and administrative databases allow researchers and decision makers to leverage both data sources by combining survey information with administrative data. By addressing the challenges presented, the harmonization process can lead to an increase in data quality, to improved perspectives and to the adoption of informed decisions.

Table 39.1 The census types developed within the 2020 Round in the EU-27 member states.

As illustrated in Fig. 39.2, in the 2020 Round of the Population and Housing Census conducted in the EU-27, the most common approach to producing census data was based on administrative registers that hold various relevant information on

Table 39.1 The 2020 Round by census type: EU-27

The 2020 round by census type	EU member states[a]	Number of member states
Combined	Czech Republic, Germany, Hungary, Italy, Luxembourg, Poland, Romania, Slovakia	8
Register-based	Austria, Belgium, Denmark, Estonia, Finland, Ireland, Latvia, Lithuania, Netherlands, Slovenia, Spain, Sweden	12
Rolling	France	1
Traditional	Bulgaria, Croatia, Cyprus, Greece, Malta, Portugal	6

Source: Authors' interpretation based on Global Census Tracker, 2023 data
Note: [a]The majority of the EU member states have carried out population and housing censuses every 10 years. In France and Italy, censuses are conducted every year, while in Ireland, it is conducted every five years

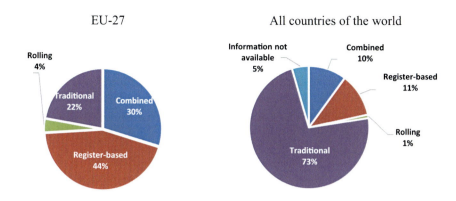

Fig. 39.2 The 2020 Round by census type: EU-27 vs world. (Source: authors' interpretation based on Global Census Tracker, 2023 data)

the subjects researched. The majority of the EU member states (twelve states, over 44%, respectively) used administrative sources for producing census data. The second most used approach was a combination of data collected based on surveys/full field enumeration and data from administrative sources (eight EU member states, representing around 30% of the total).

In other words, almost three-quarters of the EU-27 states (20) used in the 2020 Round administrative sources to produce the census data, either exclusively or in combination with other approaches. At the same time, worldwide, the traditional approach was preferred by 73% of the countries for which information was available. For comparison, among the EU-27 states, only six carried out a traditional census, based on a questionnaire completed by the respondents or by the enumerators, irrespective of the procedure used for gathering the data. At the global level, the share of states that carried out a combined census is three times lower than in the EU-27, while the share of countries where administrative registers were used to produce census data is four times lower than in the EU-27.

39.4.2 Digitalization of the Census Data Collection System – A Factor with an Impact on the Respondent's Compliance Degree

Best practices regarding online self-enumeration in various EU states. During the 2011 round of PHC, there were important differences between the Member States that used field enumeration of the entire population (without using administrative registers). In Greece, for example, only questionnaires printed on paper were used during the interviews with enumerators (UN, 2013). At the same time, in

Luxembourg, the method applied was self-enumeration using paper-based questionnaires, so there was no need for enumerators. In Portugal, half of the population self-enumerated by completing printed questionnaires, while the other half used the online questionnaire. In Cyprus, the entire population was enumerated by computer-assisted interviewing. Of the nine EU countries that used the enumeration of the entire population, supported by registers, used as a framework/control, in four member states, the data were collected only by self-enumeration, either using printed questionnaires (most responses), or questionnaires completed online. Regarding the latter method, its share varied between 7% in Slovakia and 33% in Italy. In Romania and Malta, all questionnaires were completed during interviews with enumerators, using a paper-based questionnaire. In Ireland, self-enumeration based on printed questionnaires was used exclusively. For EU countries that used the combined enumeration method (registers and field enumeration), the share of questionnaires completed in an interview by using electronic devices was highest in Latvia (59%), followed by Estonia (almost a third of responses) and Poland (over a fifth of responses), while in Spain only 10% of responses were collected by this method. Online self-enumeration was preferred by the majority of the reviewed population in Estonia (67% of all responses), reaching a double share than in Latvia and Lithuania – around one third of responses. At the same time, in Germany, online self-enumeration was very unpopular (only 5% of responses), the self-enumeration by using a printed questionnaire being preferred instead (30%) or an interview with an enumerator, with answers recorded in a printed questionnaire (15%).

As far as concerns the 2021 round of PHC, it is interesting to note that, among the EU member states that used self-enumeration, there are significant differences in the self-enumeration rate, for example: Bulgaria (34%), Croatia (40%), Slovakia (86%) and Portugal (99.3%) (Fig. 39.3). During 2021 Round, Romania had a self-enumeration rate of 46.8%.

In Hungary, online self-enumeration was introduced during the round 2011 of the PHC (Hungarian Central Statistical Office, 2011). The newly introduced method did not gain much popularity among the population, ranking second (18.6%), compared to the share of responses gathered by interviews with enumerators (65% of the total). The share of online self-enumeration rose to 63% during PHC-2021 (actually implemented in 2022). In order to boost self-enumeration, contests were organized with five daily prizes worth 100,000 forints each (Hungarian Central Statistical Office, 2022), in which people who had completed the online questionnaire had the right to participate.

In Bulgaria, online self-enumeration was also introduced in PHC 2011, and the share of the population that used this method rose to over 40%.

In the Czech Republic, the rate of online self-enumeration during PHC 2021 was extremely high, namely, around 90% (Czech Statistical Office, 2021).

In the 2011 round of PHC in Lithuania, the possibility of self-enumeration of the population via the Internet was introduced (Statistics Lithuania, a). The 2021 round of the Lithuanian PHC was carried out on the basis of administrative data from the main national registers and information systems.

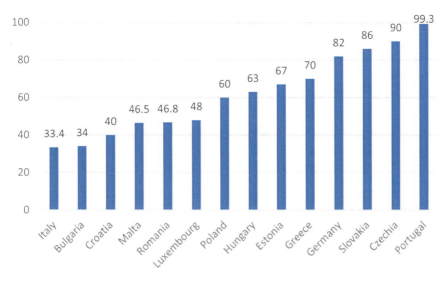

Fig. 39.3 Self-enumeration rate – PHC – 2021/2022 round, in some EU member states (%). (Source: authors' contribution, based on various sources, mainly national statistics offices)

In Slovakia, the 2011 census round was the first to introduce a choice between completing the questionnaire on paper and completing an electronic questionnaire. Later, it was decided to abandon the questionnaires on paper, so that the 2021 round was the first in which a completely electronic census took place.

Self-enumeration in Romania. Digitalization is a current necessity, with implementation gaps in countries. Self-enumeration is a new practice for Romania, but already in place for many EU states. For the 2021 round of the Romanian PHC (actually carried out in 2022), some changes were made to the methodology, compared to the one used in the previous round (2011). These changes appeared primarily as a result of the application of the new regulations at the European level regarding the conduct of censuses. These are Regulation 2018/1799 on the establishment of a temporary direct statistical action for the dissemination of selected themes of the 2021 population and housing census, Regulation 2017/881 on the modalities and structure of quality reports, as well as the technical format for data transmission, Regulation 2017/712 on establishing the reference year and the program of statistical data and metadata on the population and housing census, and Regulation 2017/543. However, other changes in the methodology were determined by the establishment of new priorities at the national level, which emphasized, for example, elements specific to the concept of sustainable development, such as those related to the energy transition towards a green economy. Regarding the digitalization aspects, on the one hand, the new type of data collection represented an important step in increasing the degree of digitalization of the census. On the other hand, however, the only question from PHC 2011 that referred to the topic of digitalization, namely, the use of the Internet by individuals, was no longer found in the 2021 questionnaire.

In 2021, compared to the previous round, some changes appeared in the methodology, determined by the changes at the national level. Thus, elements specific to the concept of sustainable development were brought to the fore, such as those related to the energy transition towards a green economy. On the digitalization component, on the one hand, the new type of data collection represented an important step in increasing the degree of digitalization of the census. On the other hand, however, the only question from 2011 that touched on the topic of digitalization, namely, the use of the Internet by individuals, is no longer included in the 2021 questionnaire.

It should also be mentioned that one of the reasons that led to the adoption of some changes in the questionnaire used was the desire to simplify the response burden of the population, as well as the work of the enumerators. In Romania, due to the overwhelming interest from the population in self-enumeration, the initial deadline of May 15, 2022, was extended. This high demand led to congestion on the online platform, causing it to be inaccessible on certain days. Moreover, in the days close to the initial deadline, the daily number of completed questionnaires increased almost 3 times, compared to the beginning of the self-enumeration period (INS, 2022).

The national average of self-enumeration was 46.8%, and the counties that exceeded the average are Bistrita-Năsăud (47.2%), Dâmbovița (47.6%), Brăila (47.7%), Argeș and Galati (48.1%), Prahova (48.4%), Vâlcea (49.4%), Arad (50.6%), Sibiu (51.3%), Gorj (51.5%), Sălaj (52.2%), Cluj (52.3%), Satu Mare (52.6%), Mureș and Bihor (55.5%), Botoșani (55.8%), Teleorman (56.6%), Brașov (59.4%), Covasna (62.5%), and Harghita (65.2%). Among the counties that recorded the lowest rates of self-enumeration, we mention: Dolj (35.5%), Iași (35.8%), and Giurgiu (36.9%). In Bucharest, the degree of self-enumeration was 44.9% of the resident population. We specify that the previously mentioned percentages are those related to the validated questionnaires (complete from the point of view of data integrity and which were taken into the final database of the PHC).

For respondents, the main advantages arising from the self-enumeration process are: avoiding home visits by enumerators; data could be provided by one person (usually the head of the household) for all household members; each person has the freedom to manage his time completing the census questionnaire. At the same time, from the organizer's perspective, data collection costs are reduced. Every employee who self-enumerated was granted a day off as a reward from their employer. This provision was included in GEO no. 19/2020 regarding the organization and conduct of the population and housing census in Romania in 2021. The day off was granted based on the proof of self-enumeration generated on the online platform (https://dovrec.insse.ro/).

If we consider the dynamics of the digital transformation of the society, both business and households, and increased level of connectivity using internet by the population, on the one hand, and the methodological improvements of the PHC regarding digital self-enumeration, on the other hand, the main issue related to the recorded rate of online responses to PHC is why it is so low, considering the fact that, according to Eurostat data, the average rate of internet use is over 90% at the EU level.

An analysis to identify the factors or constraints that determined this behavior of EU citizens indicates that digitization (by owning equipment and access to the Internet) is only a facilitator, to which is also added the opening of states to improve participation methods / to fill out the questionnaire. The problems that arise for increasing the degree of compliance in participating in the survey by digital self-enumeration for the future rounds (EU, 2022) are related to three categories of limitations, namely: (a) one related to the methodology of application and the way of implementing the application of the questionnaire, and here we have in mind: the use of user-friendly applications, which allow the correct and easy filling; the prior completion of some information already held by the authorities, obtained from administrative data, in order to reduce the response time to the questionnaire and the verification costs; (b) the second challenge is given by the level of digital skills of the respondents, at least at a basic level, which allows the correct completion of the questionnaire, and, at the same time, access to the methodological explanations for clarification, considering that not all internet users have basic digital skills; (c) the third, and the most important post, from the perspective of supporting the overall development of e-government, is related to the trust of the population in public authorities and the facilities offered for online interaction and efficiency/individual satisfaction (satisfactory as problem-solving related to authorities, which allows saving time for the citizen and ensures confidence regarding the use of personal data and the security of databases).

From the analysis carried out regarding these previously mentioned aspects, based on the data available from the EUROSTAT database, for the year 2021, we have identified, on the one hand, that the use of the Internet in the interaction with the public authority largely depends on the level of digital education and much less than the access and use of the Internet (fig.39.4) and, on the other hand, it is strongly influenced by the trust of the population in the authorities and in public institutions, which, in recent years, has decreased in the vast majority of states (Edelman, 2023).

39.4.3 Changes in Romania's Census Questionnaire – Focus on Labor Market Indicators

Several census indicators are related to the labor market. These indicators provide insights into various aspects of employment, unemployment, occupation, and income: employment status is providing information on the number of employed individuals and helps in understanding the overall labor force participation rate; occupation of individuals helps identify the distribution of workers across different job categories; educational attainment data is closely related to the labor market and

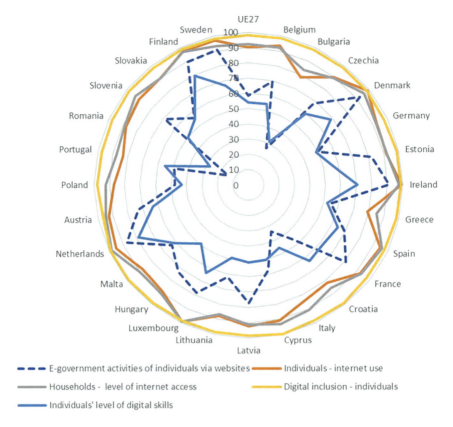

Fig. 39.4 Factors potentially influencing the self-enumeration, year 2021, EU member states. (Source: Eurostat database, [ISOC_CIEGI_AC$DEFAULTVIEW]; [ISOC_CI_IFP_IU__custom_7196947]; [ISOC_CI_IN_H__custom_7196903]; [ISOC_BDEK_DI__custom_7197254]; [ISOC_SK_DSKL_I21$DEFAULTVIEW])

reveals the educational qualifications of individuals, which is crucial for understanding the skill levels of the workforce; employment by age, gender, and ethnicity data allows for the analysis of labor market participation and employment outcomes by demographic characteristics and helps identify disparities and inequalities in employment opportunities across different groups; self-employment and entrepreneurship data shed light on the prevalence of small businesses and the overall entrepreneurial landscape in an area. These are just a few examples of census indicators that are relevant to the labor market. The availability and specificity of these indicators may vary depending on the country and the particular census conducted.

The census questionnaires used in Romania for the last two rounds (2011 and 2021/2022) were analyzed, for highlighting the most important changes.

The 2021 census questionnaire, in the section on enumeration of persons, the economic characteristics module was reconfigured. Insertion of question P11 (asking if the person worked at least one hour for wages or other income in week 22–28

November 2021) was carried out to implement the new definition of employment (data on employment is also collected through the Quarterly Household Labor Force Survey - AMIGO, but this is only carried out at the level of a representative sample). Also, questions P11a (asking if the person was actively looking for work), P11b (asking if the person could have started work during the period), as well as P12 (regarding the reason why the person did not work during the period) were introduced in order to support the gathering of relevant information. Thus, question 30 of the questionnaire dedicated to persons (P) of PHC 2011 disappeared as such from the new questionnaire, but its components were taken over in several other questions from PHC 2021 (P11, P11a-b, P12, P12a).

The possibility of selecting the appropriate option from the Classification of Occupations in Romania (COR) was introduced to the question regarding occupation (P14). Previously (PHC 2011), the answer was passed freely, to be then coded, according to COR. The professional status question (P15) is similar to its counterpart in the PHC 2011 questionnaire – [(P)(33)], except that a new answer option has been created by merging two of the existing options in the PHC 2011 questionnaire In the question regarding the place of work (P16), the full name of the unit is no longer requested (as in PHC 2011 – question 34.1), but only the main activity of the unit (P16a), which was also found in the old questionnaire (question 34.2).

The question regarding the geographical location of the workplace, which captures the mobility component within the workplace, was maintained, but not as a stand-alone question (as in PHC 2011 – question 35), but was integrated into question P16, as a sub-component P16b. A new answer option was added, namely: "without a fixed job (within Romania or in another country)". The question regarding the type of sector in which the person works – [(P)36] from the questionnaire used for PHC 2011, is no longer found in the new questionnaire, because the respective information emerges from the answer to question P16a.

The questions addressed to the unemployed (37 and 38 of the PHC 2011 questionnaire) were also removed from the new questionnaire, considering that the respective information is produced periodically in the unemployment statistics. Also in this module, a new question was introduced that captures the self-consumption component of the population. Thus, question P17 from PHC 2021 refers to the use of at least 50% for own consumption of products obtained from agricultural activity on one's own account.

39.5 Conclusions

The modernization of the statistical survey regarding the population census included the following main components:

- Completing and adapting the indicator system to the information needs for demographic, economic, and social statistical analyses.

- Increasing the number of statistical variables with socioeconomic content, which allowed thematic analyses associated with the labor market and social policies.
- Complementarity with administrative data and an increase in the correlation of indicators.
- The possibility of providing, in the period between the moments of application of the survey, some annual data on the indicators of the total population, better calibrated with the real demographic dynamics.
- Methodological development and modernization of the system for collecting information from respondents:
  - Digitalization of the collection system from the perspective of field operators.
  - Facilitating self-enumeration through a digital platform accessible to respondents.
  - Complex and faster processing of collected data.
  - Facilitating the digital dissemination of census results for database users, for thematic analyses and substantiation studies of demographic, education, labor market and social policies.

From the respondent's perspective, the social impact focused on aspects such as increasing the level of knowledge of the utility of the survey, for individual and group benefits and easing the compliance procedure through self-enumeration.

From a broad historical perspective, while, in the first censuses, the main aim was to highlight the number of people from the reference population, gradually, there was a tendency to increase the number of data collected in the censuses, against the background of the diversification of needs shown by different categories of users. In this context, the subjects addressed in the censuses began to go beyond the strictly demographic sphere, including also aspects of an economic and social nature. In the current context, the census continues to have a high degree of relevance, as it represents one of the primary data sources (at the national and administrative-territorial level) used in the policy-making process regarding socio-economic development, increasing social inclusion and ensuring a sustainable development from the point of view of the environment.

Along with the increase in the number of subjects/themes included in the census questionnaire, there has also been a diversification of data collection methods. In addition to the traditional method of completing the questionnaire, i.e. in a face-to-face interview with an enumerator, in an increasing number of countries, the resident population can self-enumerate using paper-printed questionnaires which can then be sent by post, or, more recently, the self-enumeration can be done online. Also, there was a tendency to increase accessibility, by translating the questionnaire into several languages of the minorities living on the territory of a state, and, in some cases, by implementing measures to facilitate the filling in of the census questionnaire by people who have certain deficiencies (sight, hearing). There are some states that have given up conducting censuses in their traditional form (with filling in questionnaires – in the classical or online method), choosing instead to use administrative sources.

At the international level, there are a number of principles and recommendations in the field of conducting population and housing censuses, which have been developed with the aim of ensuring comparability of data between countries. The selection of subjects/themes included in the questionnaire for the census is carried out, first of all, in close connection with the purpose of this large-scale statistical research, namely the provision of statistical data according to the needs that exist on a national/regional/local level. However, in the process of designing such a questionnaire, states usually also consider the UN recommendations, so as to ensure comparability of data between different countries of the world.

Over time, at the level of the European Union, there have been challenges in terms of harmonizing the data provided by the various member states. Such challenges were felt with increased intensity especially following the enlargement waves of 2004 and 2007, when twelve new member states, with very different statistical systems, joined the European Union. In an attempt to overcome these problems, an important step towards harmonization in the field of the population and housing census was the approval of Regulation 763/2008, which stipulated, among other things, the obligation of the member states to provide a standardized set of data specific to this field, at national level, regional (NUTS 1, NUTS 2 and NUTS 3 levels of the Common Nomenclature of territorial statistical units) and local (municipalities and cities). In this context, unlike the previous population and housing censuses conducted in the EU member states, the 2011 round stood out for the fact that it was the first organized on the basis of a common legislation, thus ensuring a better comparability of the data. Another novelty was the creation of a website dedicated to the dissemination of the census results of all member states (EU Census Hub).

References

Baffour, B., King, T., & Valente, P. (2013). The modern census: evolution, examples and evaluation. *International Statistical Review / Revue Internationale de Statistique, 81*(3), 407–425. https://www.jstor.org/stable/43299644. Last accessed 18 Aug 2023

Boyle, P., & Dorling, D. (2004). The 2001 UK census: remarkable resource or bygone legacy of the "pencil and paper era"? *Area, 36*(2), 101–110. https://doi.org/10.1111/j.0004-0894.2004.00207.x. Last accessed 18 Aug 2023

Burakauskaite, I., & Ciginas, A. (2023). An approach to integrating a non-probability sample in the population census. *Mathematics, 11*, 1782. https://doi.org/10.3390/math11081782

Coleman, D. (2013). The twilight of the census. *Population and Development Review, 38*, 334–351. http://www.jstor.org/stable/23655303, Last accessed 18 Aug 2023

Czech Statistical Office: The Census ends today, you have the last chance to get counted – Press Release, 11 May 2021 (2021). https://www.czso.cz/csu/czso/the-census-ends-today-you-have-the-last-chance-to-get-counted. Last accessed 18 Aug 2023

Depsky, N. J., Cushing, L., & Morello-Frosch, R. (2022). High-resolution gridded estimates of population sociodemographics from the 2020 census in California. *PLoS One, 17*(7), e0270746. https://doi.org/10.1371/journal.pone.0270746

Durr, J. M. (2021). Population and Housing Censuses: An overdue and old-fashioned instrument or still a modern, severely needed and steadfast tool? *Statistical Journal of the IAOS, 37*(2), 713–716. https://doi.org/10.3233/SJI-210818

Edelman. (2023) Edelman Trust Barometer, 2021, https://www.edelman.com/sites/g/files/aatuss191/files/2021-03/2021%20Edelman%20Trust%20Barometer.pdf and 2023 https://www.edelman.be/sites/g/files/aatuss331/files/2023-03/2023%20Edelman%20Trust%20Barometer%20Global%20Report%20Region_EUROPE_FINAL_WEBSITE.pdf

EP. (2008). The European Parliament and The Council: Regulation (EC) No 763/2008 of the European Parliament and of the Council of 9 July 2008 on population and housing censuses (2008), https://eur-lex.europa.eu/legal-content/EN/TXT/PDF/?uri=CELEX:32008R0763&from=EN. Last accessed 18 Aug 2023

Giessing, S., & Nordholt, E. S. (2017). *Recommendations for best practices to protect grid data (D3.4) in Package 3 Development and testing of the recommendations; identification of best practices*. Harmonised protection of census data in the ESS. https://cros-legacy.ec.europa.eu/system/files/recommendations_for_the_protection_of_grid_data.pdf

Global Census Tracker. (2023). https://experience.arcgis.com/experience/6c3954186a17429b84fe518af72aa674/page/Page/?views=Census-Methods. Last accessed 18 Aug 2023

Hungarian Central Statistical Office: About the 2011 Census (2011). https://www.ksh.hu/nepszamlalas/answer_options_menu. Last accessed 18 Aug 2023

Hungarian Central Statistical Office: About the 2022 Census (2022). https://nepszamlalas2022.ksh.hu/en/census-2022. Last accessed 10 Jan 2023

INS. (2011). Manualul personalului de recensământ, pentru RPL 2011 [Census Staff Handbook for the 2011 PHC] (2011). https://www.recensamantromania.ro/wp-content/uploads/2021/11/manual-rpl_pag-1-32.pdf; https://www.recensamantromania.ro/wp-content/uploads/2021/11/manual-rpl_pag33-59.pdf; https://www.recensamantromania.ro/wp-content/uploads/2021/11/manual-rpl_pag60-93.pdf; https://www.recensamantromania.ro/wp-content/uploads/2021/11/manual-rpl_pag94-121.pdf

INS. (2022). Comunicat de presă [Press release], 13 mai 2022 (2022). https://www.recensamantromania.ro/wp-content/uploads/2022/05/2022_05_13_cp-autorecenzare.docx. Last accessed 10 Jan 2023

INS. (2023a). Lista recensămintelor populației din România [List of population censuses in Romania], https://www.recensamantromania.ro/istoric-rpl/. Last accessed 18 Aug 2023

INS. (2023b). Tempo Online database, http://statistici.insse.ro:8077/tempo-online/#/pages/tables/insse-table. Last accessed 10 Jan 2023

Killick, L., Hall, H., Duff, A. S., & Deakin, M. (2016). The census as an information source in public policy-making. *Journal of Information Science, 42*(3), 386–395. https://doi.org/10.1177/0165551516628471

Pajares, E., Muñoz Nieto, R., Meng, L., & Wulfhorst, G. (2021). Population disaggregation on the building level based on outdated census data. *ISPRS International Journal of Geo-Information, 10*(10), 662. https://doi.org/10.3390/ijgi10100662

Rontos, K., Colantoni, A., Salvati, L., Mosconi, E. M., & Morera, A. G. (2020). Resident or present? Population census data tell you more about suburbanization. *Land, 9*(10), 383. https://doi.org/10.3390/land9100383

Statistics Lithuania, a. (n.d.). *Population and Housing Census*, https://osp.stat.gov.lt/gyventoju-ir-bustu-surasymai1. Last accessed 18 Aug 2023

UN. (1958). Principles and recommendations for national population censuses. ST /STAT / SER.M/27, Statistical Office of the United Nations, New York (1958), https://unstats.un.org/unsd/demographic-social/Standards-and-Methods/files/Principles_and_Recommendations/Population-and-Housing-Censuses/Series_M27-E.pdf. Last accessed 18 Aug 2023

UN. (2013). United Nations, Economic and Social Council: Census methodology: Key results the UNECE Survey on National Census Practices, and first proposals about the CES Recommendations for the 2020 census round (2013), https://unece.org/fileadmin/DAM/stats/documents/ece/ces/ge.41/2013/census_meeting/3_E_x_15_Aug_WEB_revised_map.pdf. Last accessed 18 Aug 2023

UN. (2015a). UN Economic and Social Council, Statistical Commission: Report on the forty-sixth session (3–6 March 2015) E/2015/24-E/CN.3/2015/40 (2015), https://unstats.un.org/unsd/statcom/46th-session/documents/statcom-2015-46th-report-E.pdf. Last accessed 18 Aug 2023

UN. (2015b). UN Economic and Social Council: Resolution adopted by the Economic and Social Council on 10 June 2015 [on the recommendation of the Statistical Commission (E/2015/24)], 2015/10. 2020 World Population and Housing Census Programme (2015). https://unstats.un.org/unsd/demographic/sources/census/iccc/docs/UN_E-RES-2015-10.pdf. Last accessed 18 Aug 2023

UN. (2017). Principles and Recommendations for Population and Housing Censuses, Revision 3, ST/ESA/STAT/SER.M/67/Rev.3 (2017). Department of Economic and Social Affairs Statistics Division, United Nations Publication, https://unstats.un.org/unsd/demographic-social/Standards-and-Methods/files/Principles_and_Recommendations/Population-and-Housing-Censuses/Series_M67rev3-E.pdf. Last accessed 18 Aug 2023

UNFPA. (2022). The future of population and housing censuses: prospects for the 2030 census round and beyond, Working paper 5, Septembr 2022 https://unece.org/sites/default/files/2022-09/WP5_UNFPA_CangianoJongstra_ENG.pdf

Valente, P. (2010). Comment la population est-elle recensée dans les pays européens en 2010? *Population & Sociétés, 5*(467), 1–4. https://www.ined.fr/fichier/s_rubrique/19135/467.fr.pdf. Last accessed 18 Aug 2023

White, I. (2009). The 2011 Census taking shape: methodological and technological developments. *Population Trends, 136*, 64–72.

Chapter 40
Montanology and Current Challenges at European and Global Level

Radu Rey and Otilia Manta

Abstract Starting from the definition given by Professor Radu Rey, respectively, montanology is the multi-, inter- and transdisciplinary scientific discipline, which aims to study economic-ecological-social phenomena in mountain areas, and which characterizes human-nature relations within the systems mountains. Moreover, this science aims to conceptualize and promote ways (methods, tools and techniques) that lead to the optimization and development of mountain systems as a whole. In addition, montanology integrates multidisciplinary knowledge in the following related fields such as: agriculture, animal husbandry, human ecology, geoecology and pedology, biology, demography and ethnography, human and animal psychology, architecture, construction and building materials, elements of forestry and geology, beekeeping, fish farming, economy, organization and operation of the private mountain household, as well as other specific systems, mountain systematization, mountain design, specific ergonomics, small industry and crafts, tourism and agrotourism, health education, nature. Similarly to the above, material resources (mineral, plant and animal), energy resources (unconventional), legislation and legal relations, other useful knowledge specific to mountains, human resources – tradition and culture are also integrated.

Keywords Mountainology · Mountain economy · Sustainable development

40.1 Introduction

In our research we start the scientific approach from the key milestones in the history of the Mountain Partnership (Alberton et al., 2017): 1992 is the year that stands out for the UN Earth Summit organized in Rio and attended by world leaders who supported this item on the agenda of the UN Agenda 21.

In the following year, 1993, the event is marked by which the FAO Agency involved in the creation of the Mountain Partnership is designated to manage Chap. 13 intended for the mountain within the UN Agenda 21.

The period of consultations on the issue of the mountain dates from 1994 to 1996 at the level of government representatives from the participating states at the level of Europe, Africa, Asia, and Latin America.

However, 1995 is the year in which, based on international consultations, the Mountain Forum was established in Lima, Peru. And in 1998, through the resolution of 130 states present in the UN General Assembly, the international year of the mountain was supported. The succession of events on the mountain support policy continued, and 2002 was the year in which the Mountain Partnership received the rank of Type II partnership and the sustainable mountain development plan was supported at the global level. Moreover, we must mention that Italy was not only the initiating state, but also a state permanently involved in supporting the mountain at a global level, which is why in 2003, it organized the first global meeting in Merano, at which time the interim secretariat was also defined of the mountain, continued thematic initiatives during 2004 at Curso in Peru, and in 2005, the FAO Agency established the secretariat that will manage the Mountain Partnership. During the years 2008, 2010, and 2011, international conferences were organized in Condesan (Latin America), Central Asia, and in Lucerne (Switzerland) and developed hubs with direct implications on the mountain.

Known as Rio+20, the UN Conference for Sustainable Development generated the strategic document supporting the sustainable development of mountains, a reference document that we still find today in international reference strategies and programs. Moreover, they are also found in three of the sustainable objectives, respectively, 6.6, 15.1, and 15.4.

According to the 2022 UN Report, mountains are ecosystems of strategic importance and cover one-third of the globe's land surface, the importance being vital for sustaining societal balance and for the safety and security of the population living in these areas. Rather, it is the mountains that support the balance of planetary biodiversity. International institutions (World Bank, 2017) draw attention to the vulnerabilities generated by climate change on these mountain areas with their entire ecosystem. At the same time, also within this Support Report, the adverse conditions for the development of activities by mountain communities are mentioned, these being estimated at 1.1 billion citizens (approx. 15% of the total population of the globe). Therefore, in all the supporting literature of the UN, we have identified reports, programs and strategies that come to sustainably support local communities in mountainous areas at a global level. The most distant times, mountains have represented not only a protective wall, but a good resource for the balance of the ecosystem. Moreover, because of the inclusion of mountains in the UN Agenda as a priority, a global awareness campaign was launched, as well as an understanding of the mountain ecosystem, as well as the importance of mountains at the global level, being sources of resources for multiple services and activities that they offer, especially in the context of the vulnerabilities to which mountain communities and ecosystems are subject. It is worth noting that in the last period they have seen an increase, being debated at the global and regional level through the multiple important meetings held by scientists, government institutions and agencies and other key actors involved. Among the specific results, we can mention the UN declaration of 1998, as well as the one in 2002 when it was designated the "International Year of Mountains" (Alberton et al., 2017), on which multiple activities were organized both scientific, especially applicative recognition of the important values of the many and their importance in the sustainable development of humanity at a global level.

Another remarkable event from the year 2002 is that of the Summit in Johannesburg, on which occasion the MONTAN Partnership was born at the international level, with the main objective of supporting the sustainable development of the mountain area at the international level, an initiative that was supported by the government decision-makers of Italy and Switzerland, as well as the FAO, which is also the main UN agency that supports mountains at an international level. The "Mountain Partnership" (MP) is a "Type II" partnership, which according to the UN framework represents an alliance at a transnational level, based on the volunteering of mountain actors (governments, civil society, governmental organizations, and agencies, as well as private institutions) and which support collaboration to promote all the specificities and objectives of the mountains. The FAO institution is, was, and will remain the institution designated to manage the secretariat of the Mountain Partnership and to support through specific programs this global objective with direct implications on societal safety and security at the international level. Note that the first paragraph of a section or subsection is not indented. The first paragraph that follows a table, figure, equation, etc., does not have an indent, either. Subsequent paragraphs, however, are indented.

40.2 Literature Review

In specialized scientific literature we can mention the fact that alongside the most relevant work "Mountaineering: The Freedom of the Hills" and which work is considered the "bible" of mountaineering and offers a wide range of information on techniques, equipment and safety in the mountain environment, there are other magazines and Scientific Journals. In the latter are scientific articles published in fields such as mountain geology, alpine ecology, or mountain climatology. Journals such as "Journal of Applied Meteorology and Climatology" or "Arctic, Antarctic, and

Alpine Research" can be an important source of documentation for specialists in the field of montanology.

"The Mountain Encyclopedia: An A to Z Compendium of Over 2,300 Terms, Concepts, Ideas, and People" (Frederic H. et al, 2005), this encyclopedia provides a comprehensive overview of mountain terms and concepts. Moreover, the works of famous explorers and climbers in which the adventures and personal experiences of explorers such as Reinhold Messner, Sir Edmund Hillary or Jon Krakauer are described can provide a captivating insight into the mountain world.

"The Eight-Thousanders: A Moutaineer's Multiple Quest" (Voiland A, 2013) is a work that explores the history and stories of those who have reached the world's highest peaks, also known as "eight-thousanders", and who includes bibliographic references such as: (Dech, S. et al, 2005), (Sale, R. et al, 2012), (Searle, M., 2013).

The literature of mountaineering is rich primarily through scientific articles on the discoveries of experts in their adventures in mountain communities.

40.3 Methodology

The methodology is based on empirical research, using tools for synthesis and analysis of the current context of the economy specific to the mountains, as responses to the adaptation of local economies to the climate changes that are present in the mountain ranges, including the Carpathians. The basis of the structuring of the work is the synthesis of information from specialized studies of the UN, of the European Commission, projects of the World Bank, specialized reports and scientific research existing in the specialized literature and identified in the main academic networks (ResearchGate, Academia.edu, Clarivate, Elsevier, SSRN, e.g.). In addition to the measures identified and oriented to limit the key risks identified, the existing priorities at the level of the institutions involved in supporting the mountain economy and which orient their adaptation policies and strategies, i.e., application solutions through strategic action plans, are presented. At the same time, the paper also presents local solutions for the mountain economy at the national level through innovative elements presented by the authors of the paper. Moreover, the identification and presentation of innovative financial instruments supporting the mountain economy at the European level is a priority of our work.

40.4 Analysis/Results Interpretation

First of all, in our work, we appreciate that the 2022 UN Report represents a priority that should be translated into strategies and action plans at the local level, given the fact that within it the results and activities for the "joint action" function were presented. One of the priorities of the joint actions was *to develop communities by identifying practical application solutions to the problems faced by the communities in the mountain areas* (for example, it is important for the communities in the mountain areas to adapt to all the elements generated by climate change, more to prepare programs and plans to manage the risks generated by these changes; another example, it is caused by the depopulation of the towns in the mountain areas and implicitly the phenomenon of migration), and through direct communication with the representatives of the mountain partnership in the territory, all these problems can be properly managed through support programs that meet their specific needs. Another result directly oriented to the activities fulfilling the function of *"knowledge management and communication"* and which was supported both in the UN Report and in the key strategies applied was given by "developing and implementing a clear and comprehensive structured strategy forMountain Partnership".

It is worth noting that, along with the results mentioned above, the activities directly connected to the *"capacity development and technology transfer"* function presented in the above-mentioned report, constituted the starting point in the promotion and development of the "Development Strategy curriculum Sustainable Mountain for target groups identified according to the analysis of needs and the creation of channels to capitalize on these with the experiences and initiatives at the community level in the Mountain Partnership members and beyond".

The function mentioned in the *"mobilization of resources"* report is a pillar supporting the results of activities and strategies in the mountain area and according to which the results are directly connected through the platforms to the donors involved in directly supporting the Mountain Partnership.

Sustainable mountain development according to the Report of the UN Secretary-General, 22 July 2022. All the challenges generated by the current crises have a direct impact on local communities and the ecosystem, which is why sustainability support programs with a direct impact on the inclusion and convergence of vulnerable mountain areas are promoted globally. Moreover, the support strategies are doubled by the action and financing programs that, based on the directions of action, the proposed activities and the result indicators, support this phenomenon of inclusion at the level of mountain communities. *Sustainable mountain development according to the Report of the UN Secretary-General, 22 July 2022.*

Poverty, conflict, inequality, as well as access to basic minimum services (education, health, and infrastructure), limit the resilience and attitude of citizens to shocks, the results leading to the phenomenon of depopulation of mountain areas (Boțanić et al., 2010).

Activities in mountain areas are limited, the most active sector being tourism and agritourism, these destinations attract approximately 20% of the total number of tourists globally (Calaciura, & Spinelli, 2008). However, most of the time through uncontrolled industrial development, the ecosystem and biodiversity suffer through this improper exploitation (refer to the Declaration on the impact of the climate on tourism from Glasgow). *The 2030 Agenda for Sustainable Development and mountain areas globally* (Fig. 40.1).

The objectives set out in the UN 2030 Agenda are in line with the sustainable development of the mountain area and are found in all the current programs and strategies of the European Commission. The lack of localized and disaggregated

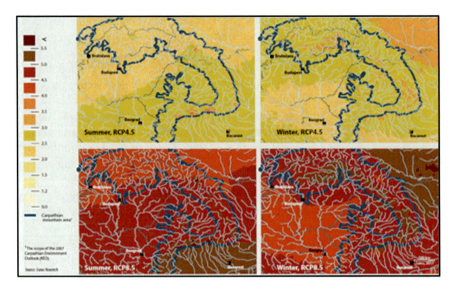

Fig. 40.1 Predictions of average temperature values (including related scenarios). (Source: Eurac Research, 2017)

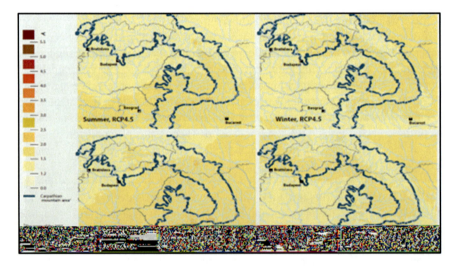

Fig. 40.2 Scenarios regarding changes in average temperature values. (Source: Eurac Research, 2017)

mountain data directly influences programs, action plans, and policies in the sustainable development of mountains (Fig. 40.2).

One of the most urgent current problems is given by the crisis generated by climate change, with direct effects on the ecosystems in the mountain areas, as well as on the safety and food security of the local communities related to the mountains, as well as on the biodiversity of this completely affected and impacted areas directly on the landscapes.

Global warming of more than 1.5 °C causes changes in the ecosystem to radically change the current situation of mountain areas, as well as biodiversity, and the risks generated by this crisis become a problem with a multiplying effect at the societal level.

In 2022, the reanalysis of the issue of ecosystems in mountain areas was carried out according to the document on mountains in the context of climate change and were examined by experts involved in the integrated research activity of mountains, respectively, the effects and impact that climate change has on communities in mountain areas. The Italian experts involved in the strategic program on mountains generated multiple studies and research that became valuable sources for GEO Mountains (Fig. 40.3).

In 2019, the Summit of the World Meteorological Organization was organized which, in addition to the action plan, also generated a work agenda regarding support, risk assessment and their limitation, so that sustainable mountain development is actively supported (Barcza et al., 2013).

Within the International Partnership on Mountains, studies were generated on the state of ecosystems and mountain biodiversity (Borsa et al., 2009), as well as interdisciplinary studies on the evaluation of the impact generated by these changes (Bardarsja et al., 2013).

These international initiative groups support the identification of technological solutions through specialized platforms, such as PLANETech, as well as Andorra Research + Innovation.

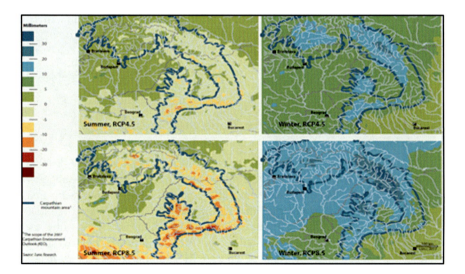

Fig. 40.3 Estimated fluctuations of average monthly values of temperatures. (Source: Eurac Research, 2017)

At the level of mountain communities, themes with a direct effect on the mountain economy and on communities in mountain areas have been identified, such as:

1. The COVID-19 pandemic had a major impact on mountain communities, and the decision-makers proposed support programs regarding both the response during the pandemic period and post-pandemic recovery programs.
2. Mountain communities are affected by the phenomenon of depopulation (migration), as well as due to the development of industries (such as, for example, tourism) with an effect on the urbanization process.
3. Social inclusion and the creation of support programs for social protection, gender equality, as well as the optimal management of resources at the local level.
4. The promotion of mountains with a direct effect on strengthening capacities, increasing skills and continuing professional training based on the concept of long-life-learning.
5. The reconstruction and adaptation of the current conditions of the agri-food networks in the mountain areas, all the more since they are the pillars of supporting well-being at the local level (Borsa et al., 2009) and create the framework for the sustainable development of local entrepreneurs. Moreover, the support financing programs are built according to the analyzes of local needs and with result indicators corresponding to the current situations, so from the point of view of the challenges, but especially of the reconfiguration of local needs with all the related specificities. In Romania, products from the mountain area have the European and national label, in the year 2022 there were approximately 3375 products registered as a mountain product. This approach started as early as 2008 (Carpathian Convention, 2008).
6. A major priority is given to tourism in the mountain area, especially after its reconfirmation following the COVID-19 pandemic, the approaches being adapted to the challenges both in terms of preferences, but especially in terms of the balance of natural resources. This aspect was also supported and promoted at the UNWTO event in 2021 when the international mountain day was celebrated (Fig. 40.4).

40.5 Financing Related to the Mountain Economy

Green financing is the new innovative tool that supports the sustainable development of local communities in mountain areas. Moreover, this financial support is designed not only to limit the risks to which the communities in the mountain areas are subjected, but especially to develop them in the current context and to create financial instruments that are not limited only to short-term needs but to be also oriented towards long-term strategic objectives, such as infrastructure investment projects. The Green Fund, for example, allocated 1.7 billion dollars for 29 investment projects in countries with strategic mountainous areas.

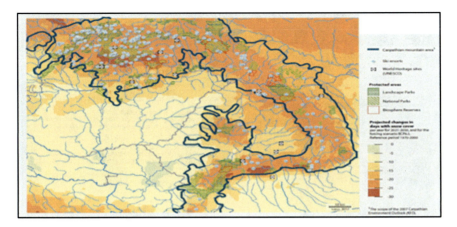

Fig. 40.4 Tourism and climate change. (Source: Eurac Rsearch Carpathian Network of Protected Areas, 2017)

The Mountain Partnership generates, through its action plans and according to the adopted strategies, supporting funding instruments (including grants) to support local communities in mountainous areas, thus contributing to both the resilience and the convergence of the areas, as it was supported throughout history to support biodiversity in the mountains (Carpathian Convention, 2014). The author Prof. univ. dr. Radu Rey, President of the Romanian Mountain Forum, presents a "VISION" OF MOUNTAIN DEVELOPMENT – SUSTAINABLE – HORIZON 2040, IN AN AGRO-COOPERATIVE MICRO-REGIONAL SYSTEM (Fig. 40.5).

The project can ensure the application of the "Mountain Law" no. 197/2018 according to the guidelines of the European Green Pact, Horizon 2050 and rapidly imposes a "reform" aimed at 4.89 million people (21.97% of the total), of which two million in family farms. It contributes to mitigating the socioeconomic consequences generated by the pandemic, facilitates access to diversified supply chains, contributing to the creation of strategic reserves of essential goods and the recovery of the non-polluting sustainable mountain economy.

After 32 years of experience (1990–2022) and case studies, it has been demonstrated that in the case of mountain areas in Romania, where small- and medium-sized family farms dominate, the capitalist, employer system, focused on maximum profit, without temporary measures from on the part of the state, it generated a state of degradation of a large agro-zoo-alimentary, mountain economy, partly irrecoverable, with large phenomena of the youth of the over 3500 mountain villages leaving the agricultural occupation, with migration to cities and abroad, no tendency to return.

A major consequence is the discontinuity of traditional family farms, due to the aging of farmers physically and psychologically adapted to harsh natural conditions and "mountain type" social life – a population specialized in raising animals, which cannot be replaced by ANYONE.

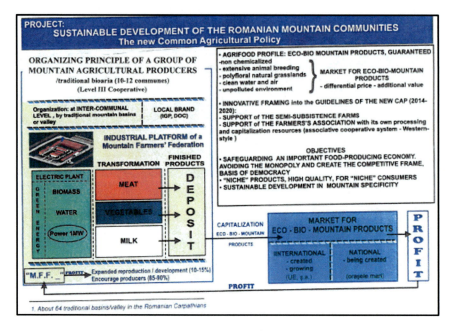

Fig. 40.5 The sustainable development of mountain communities in Romania project. (Source: author's own concept Prof. univ. dr. Radu Rey, President of the Romanian Mountain Forum)

As a consequence, the decrease in the Romanian mountains (in 2022, compared to 2020) of cattle herds by 50–60% and of sheep by over 80% in many areas and implicitly the reduction of organic fertilizers – essentially necessary – with the effect of degradation extremely serious of the valuable biodiversity of the natural, fodder flora, from the mountain pastures and hayfields, a multi-century creation of the cooperation between MOUNTAIN MAN and NATURE, with the use of "good practices" perpetuated annually. There are little hopes of recovery, with the guarantee of economic and social sustainability, in the conditions of sec. XXI.

- Degradation/wilding of mountain meadows occurs insidiously, unevenly, on thousands of small areas that become, in a few years (7–8), tens of thousands of hectares, and restoring the floral structure with a significant percentage of protein plants would take years, with too high costs and dependent on four inseparable factors: MAN (farmer) – ANIMALS – ORGANIC FERTILIZERS – NATURAL MULTIFLORA OF MOUNTAIN MEADOWS. Small mountain farms produce protein food (milk, meat, etc.), with recyclable energy, minimal oil consumption, in a circular economy system, adapted, under "ZERO chemical" conditions, the result being "mountain products" agro-food, with high biological value, guaranteed for the health of consumers.
- Necessary, reparative interventions, through "mountain policies" adapting to regional specificities, able to stop mountain depopulation and the disintegration of small/medium mountain farms, become imperative and urgent – through com-

plex, motivating measures, expected both from entities with major financial potential and from the governments of affected mountain countries.

Through great efforts, European and national, through the achieved "pilot" objectives, it has been radically demonstrated that the only sustainable and still possible logical alternative is the transition to the mountain agri-food cooperative system.

Description of the intervention:

1. EU/EC Regulations 1151/2012 and 665/2014 regarding the high-quality "mountain product"
2. "Mountain Law" no. 197/2018 and subsequent laws
3. Practical, successful experiences, carried out in 3 representative mountain microzones: Mountain agricultural cooperative from Sângiorz-Băi, Bistrița-Năsăud county; The cooperative from Șaru Dornei commune; the "Dornelor basin" microregion, Suceava county; Intercommunity association "Tara de Piatră" – Apuseni Mountains.

Interventions from the author's personal point of view: the three proposed pilot areas were discussed and agreed with the World Bank (Commissioner Franz Fishler) in 2019, at the Ministry of Agriculture. They correspond to three types of mountain conditions and traditions. Expectations: The proposed micro-regions include elements of research-innovation and experimentation. The results will create multiplication effects through the proposed solution, in the entire mountain area of Romania, with utility in other mountain areas of emerging EU countries, at Horizon 2040–2050, with the necessary regional adaptations.

The *main objectives* pursued within the project are the organization of the associative-cooperative system for the superior valorization of the agro-food "mountain products". Moreover, we appreciate:

1. A single cooperative at communal level that collects and semi-industrializes raw materials, mountain products, quality guaranteed: milk, meat, and vegetable products.
2. Creation of an Agricultural-Mountain Intercooperative Association at the mountain micro-region level.

At this level, an "industrial park" is created (reasons to reduce general expenses), with three factories (which become the "locomotives" of development):

1. Dairy products factory (hard and fresh cheeses).
2. Slaughterhouse with butchery and for by-products.
3. Factory of vegetable products (forest fruits, cultivated fruits, concentrates for juices, medicinal plants, jams and compotes, teas, candy, alcoholic beverages). Warehouse, with three cells: dairy, sausages, vegetables – "mountain products", guaranteed, with domestic and export valorization, with prices covering the restrictions and intense efforts required to produce the raw material in mountain conditions.

The final goal of the proposed project is to ensure incentive prices for raw materials and support, respectively through the recovery of the animal breeding activity, the effort and motivation of the own farmers, an aspect that must be supported by both the European Union and the Romanian state.

Expected effects of the project are conservation of the valuable biodiversity of the mountain meadows (organic fertilizers), local workforce for small industries, forestry activities, construction, conservation of valuable traditional ("good practices") and cultural heritage, and an economic-social stability/sustainability. Furthermore, the implementation of the proposed project could be a concrete first step for the implementation of the multi-year strategy envisaged by the European Green Deal (Green Deal), Horizon 2040–2050.

40.6 Conclusions

Partnerships were and are the most frequently used solution in the sustainability of mountain areas both on a social and economic level, as that is how the Mountain Partnership was created in 2002 and with permanent and direct implications in identifying solutions for direct problems of mountains globally (Bartholy et al., 2013). At the level of 2022, the number of members who are part of this strategic alliance has reached 454 and within which both governmental and non-governmental institutions, such as the private environment and civil society, are present. From our point of view, we appreciate that these alliances are extremely necessary both at international and national level, but especially locally, given the fact that local specificities differ from one mountainous area to another, and the implications must be as more concrete and closer to local needs.

Representatives of government institutions are permanently involved in participating in various regional summits, such as the one organized in 2020 for the Himalayan Mountains, with global warming as the main topic on the agenda (Chovancova et al., 2013). Even more, as in every event, the priorities of mountain areas are directly related to the objectives of sustainability, which makes this partnership even more foreign at the level of the international communities (UN, 2022). Another example of strategic partnership was the one achieved in the Andes Mountains, an event supported by a close political-technical collaboration (UNEP, 2014). At the same time, it should be mentioned that during these meetings directly oriented towards the pragmatism of strategic partnerships, documents, strategies, thematic programs, and dissemination tools are generated, including communication web portals (EEA, 2016a, b; Niewiadomski, 2017).

At the national level, partnerships help to identify specific solutions with concrete elements regarding the balanced development of communities in mountainous areas, raising the level of competitiveness of businesses in these areas, and finally, maintaining and preserving the biodiversity of the Carpathians, given that the global challenges they become local challenges and solutions must be identified according to these local specificities (Antofie et al., 2015). Moreover, the programs and funding instruments allocated by the European Commission at the national level, we appreciate that they are extremely useful and support this community, and the cooperation with central and local government institutions helps to orient these resources as strategically as possible to those prioritized local needs (Arany et al., 2013). Complementary funding programs can also be identified within the UN (based on strategic documents and support programs) and managed through specialized agencies, and which can gather the resources necessary to meet local investment and sustainability needs (UNDP, 2017) and with optimal use of natural resources at the local level (Boțanić, 2010). The partnerships as we mentioned, on the one hand, we refer to the strategic documents adopted by international institutions, central and local government institutions, but also through specific actions such as those related to the knowledge and involvement of partners from university and research centers in this mechanism of knowledge (Central European University, 2008); the development of support mechanisms and tools for the sustainable development of the mountain area; limiting the risks in the mountain area and creating strategic plans regarding the limitation of these risks; solutions regarding the conservation of the ecosystem (Pellissier et al., 2013) and in some mountain areas even their restoration (Borsa et al., 2009); the mix of activity and knowledge between traditional and elements generated by current technologies as tools to optimize local activities (Werners et al., 2014b); the promotion of strategic and integrated projects (for example, the pilot project supported by Acad. Prof. univ. dr. Radu Rey and which is mentioned in our paper); equal opportunities and gender, as well as encouraging the young population towards mountain entrepreneurship; the development of innovative financial instruments such as Mutal Intervention Funds both for the sustainable development of mountain communities and for financial intervention in case of impact phenomena.

Therefore, the associative forms both for the current problems of the local communities in the mountain areas, but also for the joint development of economic activities generating profit, we appreciate that it is the solution to maintain a sustainable mountain ecosystem. Our work also has limitations, such as the presentation of an econometric model of the development of mountain areas at the national level, but these limitations become challenges to determine us to continue our research in the mountain areas so necessary to maintain the societal balance at the national level and at global level (the mountain being the one that generates this global societal balance) (UN, 2016). Development of innovative financial instruments at the level of local communities in mountain areas. Supporting the mountain economy through support funding programs of the EU Hydrogen Bank and the European Investment Fund. From a personal point of view, we appreciate the fact that open financing can be a supporting tool for projects at the European level for the sustainable development of the mountain economy.

As a conclusion, we appreciate that the inter-institutional strategic partnership represents the key solution regarding the sustainable development of the mountain economy at the national and global level.

References

Alberton, M., Andresen, M., Citadino, F., Egerer, H., Fritsch, U., Götsch, H., Hoffmann, C., Klemm, J., Mitrofanenko, A., Musco, E., Noellenburg, N., Pettita, M., Renner, K., & Zebisch, M. (2017). *Outlook on climate change adaptation in the Carpathian mountains*. United Nations Environment Programme, GRID-Arendal and Eurac Research, Nairobi, Vienna, Arendal and Bolzano. www.unep.org, www.grida.no, www.eurac.edu

Antofie, T., Naumann, G., Spinoni, J., & Vogt, J. (2015). Estimating the water needed to end the drought or reduce the drought severity in the Carpathian region. *Hydrology and Earth System Sciences, 19*, 177–193.

Arany, I., Kondor, A., Orosz, B., Köpataki, É., Adriansens, V., Lambert, S., & Szalai, S. (2013). *Insights in costs and benefits of forest, wetlands and non-agricultural grassland* (Final Report for SR 4 Task 3). CaprathCC, report to European commision – DG Environment. REC – The Regional Environment Center For Central Eastern Europe, ARCADIS, INCDPM, INHGA, ARTELIA. Budapest.

Barcza, Z., Bodea, L., Csoka, G., Dodor, L., Galvánek, D., György, D., Hidy, D., Hlásny, T., et al. (2013). *In-depth study on the impacts of climate change threats on ecosystems* (Final report – Module SR2). CarpathCC, report to European Commission – DG Environment http://carpathcc.eu/node/35. REC – The Regional Environmental Center For Central Eastern Europe, AQUAPROFIT, INCDPM, CAR HAS, ARTELIA, Budapest, HU.

Bardarsja, G., Raev, I., Stankunavicius, G., Stakenas, V., Vilhar, U., Kutnar, L., Buksha, I., Buksha, M., Pyvovar, T., & Pasternak, V. (2013). *Assessment of drought impact on forests (act.5.2)*. OUTPUT 3/Milestone 4: Adaption measures for the forests to mitigate negative effects of the drought. Integrated Drought Management Programme in Central and Eastern Europe. Global Water Partnership.

Bartholy, J., Borka, G., Csabragi Sleizne, A., Hatvani, I.G., Kis-Kovacs, G., Kovacevic, T., Molnar, M., Molnar, S., Pongracz, R., Takacs, T., Somogyi, Z., & Toth Naarne, Z. (2013). *6th national communication to the UNFCCC*. Republic of Hungary. https://unfccc.int/files/national_reports/annex_i_natcom/submitted_natcom/application/pdf/nc6-final_hun[1].pdf

Borsa, M., Chifelea, C., Egerer, H., Gal, Z., Glowacki, W., Halas, M., Hopfgartner, V., Illes, I., Niewiadomski, Z., Ptacek, P., & Wiederwald, D. (2009). *VASICA: Visions and strategies in the Carpathian area*. The Carpathian Project, UNEP, Vienna.

Boțanić, et al. (2010). *Initial national communication of the Republic of Serbia under the United Nations Framework Convention of Climate Change*. Ministry of Environment and Spatial Planning Serbia, Belgrade.

Calaciura, B., & Spinelli, O. (2008). *Management of natura 2000 habitats*. Semi-natural dry grasslands (Festuco-Brometalia). Technical Report 12/24.

Carpathian Convention. (2008). Sustainable and integrated water/river basin management – Article 6 of the Carpathian Convention, para. 5. Dec. COP 2/3.

Carpathian Convention. (2011). Protocol on sustainable tourism to the Framework Convention on the Protection and Sustainable Development of the Carpathians. Bratislava, 27 May 2011, in force 29 April 2013.

Carpathian Convention. (2014). Strategic agenda on adaptation to climate change in the Carpathian Region, Dec. COP4/10.

Central European University. (2008). *Impacts of and adaptation to climate change in the Danube-Carpathian region*. Department of Environmental Sciences and Policy, Central European University, Budapest.

Chovancova, L., Gnida, M., Balaz, P., Veres, I., Malatinska, L., Zvara, M., Fratricova, H., Greguska, B., Zemko, M., Nejedlik, P., Stastny, P., Skoda, P., Lapin, M., Balajka, J., & Mraz, M. (2013). *The sixth national communication of the Slovak Republic on Climate Change under the United Nations Framework Convention on Climate Change and Kyoto Protocol*. Ministry of Environment of the Slovak Republic, Slovak Hydrometeorological Institute, Bratislava.

Council of Ministers Poland. (2015). Resolution No. 213 of the Council of Ministers.

Dech, S., Messner, R., Glaser, R. and Martin, R. (2005). Mountains from Space (New York: Harry N. Abrams, Inc.)
EEA. (2016a). *Climate-ADAPT-Sharing adaption information across Europe*. European Climate Adaptation Platform: Poland. European Environment Agency. http://climate-adapt.eea.europa.eu/countries-regions/countries/poland/index_html
EEA. (2016b). *Climate-ADAPT-Sharing adaption information across Europe*. European Climate Adaptation Platform: Romania. European Environment Agency. http://climate-adapt.eea.europa.eu/countries-regions/countries/romania
EEA. (2016c). *Climate-ADAPT-Sharing adaption information across Europe*. European Climate Adaptation Platform: Hungary. European Environment Agency. http://climateadapt.eea.europa.eu/countries-regions/countries/hungary
Eurac Research (2017): Activity Report 2016/17. Esperia printing, Trento.
Frederic, H., Robert, H., & Jamling, T. N. (2005). The Mountain Encyclopedia: An A to Z Compendium of Over 2,300 Terms, Concepts, Ideas, and People, Publisher Taylor Trade Publishing, ISBN-10: 158979161
Niewiadomski, Z. (2017). *World heritage and sustainable tourism in the Carpathians*. Background document. UN Environment, Vienna Programme Office – Secretariat of the Carpathian Convention, Vienna.
Nuppenau, E. A., Waldhardt, R., & Solovyeva, I. (2011). Biodiversity and transition pathways to sustainable agriculture: Implications for interdisciplinary research in the Carpathian Mountains. In B. Knowles (Ed.), *Mountain hay meadows: Hotspots of biodiversity and traditional culture*. Society of Biology.
Pellissier, L., Anzini, M., Maiorano, L., Dubuis, A., Pottier, J., Vittoz, P., & Guisan, A. (2013). Spatial predictions of land-use transitions and associated threats to biodiversity. The case of forest regrowth in mountain grasslands. *Applied Vegetation Science, 16*, 227–236.
Sale, R., Jurgalski, E., and Rodway, G. (2012). On Top of the World: The New Millennium, Gloucestershire: Snowfinch Publishing.
Searle, M., (2013). Colliding Continents: A Geological Exploration of the Himalaya, Karakoram, and Tibet, (New York: Oxford University Press.
The Mountaineers (10 October 2010). Mountaineering: The Freedom of the Hills (50th Anniversary Edition). Vol. 8th Ed. Mountaineers Books. ISBN 978-1-59485-137-7.
UN. (1992). *AGENDA 21*. Konferenz der Vereinten Nationen für Umwelt und Entwicklung. Rio de Janeiro. http://www.un.org/Depts/german/conf/agenda21/agenda_21.pdf
UN. (2012). *Environmental performance reviews*. Romania. Second review. United Nations, New York, Geneva.
UN. (2015). *Serbia environmental performance reviews*. Third review. United Nations Publication, Geneva.
UN. (2016). *Climate change resilience: An opportunity for reducing inequalities*. World Economic and Social Survey. United Nations, New York. https://wess.un.org/wp-content/uploads/2016/06/WESS_2016_Report.pdf
UN. (2022). Raportul Secretarului General "Dezvoltare montană durabilă", 74/227.
UNDP. (2017). *National capacity self-assessments*. Available at http://www.undp.org/content/undp/en/home/ourwork/environmentandenergy/strategic_themes/integrating_environmentintodevelopment/cdes/ncsa.html
UNEP. (2014). *Fourth meeting of the conference of the parties to the Framework Convention on the Protection and Sustainable Development of the Carpathians*. Strategic Agenda on Adaptation to Climate Change in the Carpathian Region. UNEP/CC/COP4/DOC12/REV1.
Voiland, A. (2013). The Eight-Thousanders: A Moutaineer's Multiple Quest, NASA Earth Observatory, The Eight-Thousanders (nasa.gov)
Werners, S., Bos, E., Civic, K., Hlásny, T., Hulea, O., Jones-Walters, L., Köpataki, E., Kovbasko, A., Moors, E., Nieuwenhuis, D., Vande Velde, I., Zingstra, H., & Zsuffa, I. (2014a). *Climate change vulnerability and ecosystem-based adaptation measures in the Carpathian region*. Final Report. Integrated assessment of vulnerability of environmental resources and

ecosystem-based adaptation measures. Wageningen, Alterra Wageningen UR (University & Research Centre).

Werners, S., Bos, E., Civic, K., Hlásny, T., Hulea, O., Jones-Walters, L., Kőpataki, E., Kovbasko, A., Moors, E., Nieuwenhuis, D., van de Velde, I., Zingstra, H., & Zsuffa, I. (2014b). *Climate change vulnerability and ecosystem-base d adaptation measures in the Carpathian region.* CARPIVA Final Report. Integrated assessment of vulnerability of environmental resources and ecosystem-based adaptation measures. Wageningen, Alterra Wageningen UR (University & Research centre). Alterra report 2572. 132 pp. 37 fig. 14 tab. 111 ref.

World Bank. (2017, April). *World development indicators database.* http://databank.worldbank.org/data/download/GDP.pdf. Accessed 23 Aug 2017.

Chapter 41
Relevant Methods for Reducing the Phenomenon of Food Waste in the HORECA Sector in the Romanian Mountain Regions

Daniela Antonescu and Ioan Surdu

Abstract Food waste is a generalized process that affects both the environment and resources (natural, financial, sanitary, etc.). The negative effects are felt both at the individual level (household budget) and at the society level, being difficult to combat. From the quantitative and qualitative analyses, it was observed that food waste at the household level represents over 50% of its total volume, although food waste is produced throughout the supply chain. Some economic sectors, by the nature of their activities, have a greater predilection to waste food, such as the HoReCa sector or large stores. Advanced solutions for diminishing the food waste take on different forms of manifestation, from awareness of the phenomenon itself to the sizing of portions, the promotion of good practices, innovative packaging, etc. Considering the aforementioned, this article seeks to contribute to a better knowledge of the phenomenon of food waste and to identify some viable solution by which this phenomenon can be combated.

Keywords Food waste · HoReCa · Sustainable development · Natural resources

41.1 Introduction

The process of food waste affects both the environment and resources (natural, financial, sanitary, etc.). The negative effects are felt both at the individual level (household budget) and at the societal level, and they are difficult to combat.

Studies have shown that food waste at the household level represents over 50% of the total volume, although food waste is produced throughout the supply chain. It is also observed that some economic sectors, by the nature of their activities, have a greater predilection to waste food (e.g., HoReCa, large retail stores, etc.). Solutions

---

D. Antonescu (✉) · I. Surdu
Center of Mountain Economy, Vatra Dornei, Romania

to reduce this phenomenon take different forms of tackling, from awareness of the phenomenon itself to rethinking portions, promoting good practices, innovative packaging, etc.

Considering the above-mentioned situation, this article aims to review a number of conceptual and practical approaches to food waste. The analysis aims, in particular, to evaluate food waste in the HoReCa sector. Furthermore, an effective way to reduce the waste phenomenon is proposed, with the help of smart packaging.

41.2 Literature Review

According to the Explanatory Dictionary of the Romanian language, waste represents the reckless use of material or monetary goods, an immeasurable expense, but also a destruction, ruin, shattering, having as a synonym wasting. Different things can be wasted, from material things to money or immaterial aspects (e.g., time).

Waste can be caused by certain defects (caused by: incomplete specifications, lack of training, poor process control, improper maintenance of equipment etc.); costs: associated: cost of waste, quarantined stock, re-inspection, rescheduling and loss of capacity, customer satisfaction; overproduction (the most expensive form of waste) which generates other wastes, such as: large number of employees, extra costs in storage and transport due to excess stock; causes: wrong sales forecasts, full capacity production to maximize machine/personnel utilization, overcoming problems caused by fluctuating peak orders, optimal production lot (lowest total cost). To these, food waste can be added caused by waiting time (poor flow of materials and/or components, production in large batches, capacity bottlenecks, machine downtimes, material shortages, long production changeover times, lack of a production plan, etc.), over-processing or improper processing, inefficient transportation (waste is caused by: inadequate transportation equipment/techniques, misplacement of machinery, management of large batches, long distances between processes), etc.

In a series of specialized studies carried out by FAO, food waste represents a global phenomenon to reduce the mass of edible food. The food loses during the production, post-harvest and processing level in the food supply chain, till to the end of the food chain (retail and final consumption) and referring to trader behaviour (Parfitt et al., 2010).

According to the FUSION-EU project, food waste can, at some point, turn into "edible products, intended for human consumption", this being defined as "food or parts of food resulting from the entire production chain, which can be recovered or processed". This includes: raw or cooked food thrown into the trash, food scraps resulting in all stages of the preparation meal in the household and waste food resulting from manufacturing, distribution, retail and service process, products in the form of shells of vegetables, eggs, meat side dishes and excess ingredients or cooked and discarded food, but also bones, carcasses, organs, edible, and inedible food scraps (Chirsanova & Calcatiniuc, 2021).

Globally, the composition of food waste is different from one state to another, regions or nations, being correlated, in particular, with the level of economic and social development (Cánovas et al., 2018). Thus, in middle- and high-income countries, food is wasted, even if it still corresponds consumption at household level (the significant food losses occur early in the supply chain). In lower-income countries, losses occur mainly in the early stages of the food supply chain (less food at the consumer level) (Belletti & Marescotti, 2020).

Around 40% of food waste occurs after harvest in developing countries and in developed over 40%. Supermarket promotions encourage food waste (discounted products can be bought even if they are not necessarily needed).

Although the amount of waste (of food) is increasing, currently, there is no overall perspective on its situation and evolution, both in the European Union and in Romania, due to as a result of the non-existence of statistical data and information. According to estimates, the sources of food waste are similar between European countries, the only identified differentiation being given by the specifics of the product (its properties).

Regarding the evaluation of the phenomenon of food waste, there is still no common methodology. However, based on the existing information in the specialized literature, there are a number of criteria and indicators that can be used to develop policies and strategies to prevent food waste (De Laurentiis et al., 2020).

The evaluation methods that can be taken into account must be based on the life cycle of the products and on the relevant principles of Circular Economy (Aschemann-Witzel et al., 2017).

41.3 Methodology

The methodology used in the paper consists in the analysis of statistical data and their interpretation in the sense of identifying a global assessment of food waste in the HoReCa sector in Romania and presenting the results of some international projects that support and promote innovative packaging, as one of the most effective methods of preventing waste feeding.

41.4 Analysis/Results Interpretation

General estimates made at the national level show that around 73% of restaurants face food waste, and 30% is represented by prepared meals. Furthermore, between 5% and 15% of food cooked in restaurants is thrown away, and 50% of food thrown away is about to expire. However, it was discovered that 55% of operators had already implemented measures (e.g., donated to staff, donated to animals, stocked short term, invested in storage area or prepared only to order).

Food waste in the HoReCa sector was evaluated in various specialized studies carried out at the national level,[1] the results being mainly questionnaires and interviews. Therefore, this paper proposes an assessment of food waste in the HoReCa sector in the mountain area, based on the specific indicators existing in the national statistics and in Eurostat. Thus, a first indicator is related to the number of one-night and 3-night trips. Taking in account Eurostat data, the number of one-night trips to mountain agro-pensions in Romania was, in 2019, 19.4 million trips, and the number of those who stayed 1–3 nights was 11.14 million trips. For both indicators, an upward trend can be observed compared to 2014. Therefore, there is a clear tendency to develop this sector, and implicitly also an increase in the phenomenon of food waste, corresponding to a greater number of tourists. Other analysed indicators are those from the national statistics (NIS), which show the evolution of the HoReCa sector in the mountain area. According to NIS data, the tourist capacity of mountain areas (year 2021) was 2492 tourist accommodation structures, which represents 27.25% of the total at the national level. About 52.85% of the total are agro-tourist guesthouses, followed by tourist guesthouses (17.47%), tourist villas (8.47%), and hotels (7.95%). Most are three stars and are agro-tourist guesthouses. There are 66,374 accommodation places in the tourist accommodation structures in the mountain area (with an average of 27 places per tourist unit). About 32% of places are in agritourism guesthouses, followed by hotels (26.58%) (Antonescu et al., 2022).

The mountain tourist structures had an average degree of occupancy in 2021 of 42.5%, the most sought after/occupied being hotels (52.8%), followed by tourist villas (36.5%). Mountain agro-tourist guesthouses had an occupancy rate of 23.1%, while tourist guesthouses were occupied in proportion to 26.2%.

Taking into account the information presented previously, the most food waste is produced in hotels in the mountain area (95.8 tons annual maximum and 57 tons minimum), followed by agro-tourist guesthouses (36 tons maximum and 21 tons minimum, for the analysed period of time).

According to estimates, the units in the total HoReCa sector show that there are more than 250,000 tons of food waste thrown into the landfill annually (12%–15% of total). Compared to the total value estimated for the HoReCa sector, the food waste in the mountain area has a relatively small size, it represents 0.014% of the estimated 250,000 tons (the maximum value of the waste in the mountain area).

In conclusion, starting from these general estimates, it is obvious to the authors that a real assessment of the quantities of food waste in Romania is necessary, which takes into account each sector of activity separately. Moreover, a standardization of the amount of waste for each sector is necessary, so that the estimate is as close as possible to the real situation.

---

[1] Study on food waste in the local HoReCa industry, carried out by Edenred Romania, in partnership with the Employers' Organization of Hotels and Restaurants in Romania (HORA) and Mastercard, April–August 2022, on a sample of 97 food establishments.

41.4.1 Model for Combating Food Waste through Innovative Packaging

The packaging process is vital in maintaining the quality and safety of food, but also to extending the life of the food and reducing food waste. However, packaging represents a product with a short life cycle; therefore, its incorrect management can lead to negative effects on the environment. Also, the food waste affects the environment and causes unwanted additional costs.

Packaging has a direct link to the circular economy (Williams et al., 2012). From a circular economy perspective, the food chain includes three important stages: food production, food consumption, and food waste generation, including food surplus management.

Currently, the food journey "from farm to consumer" shows the need for the new packaging systems that reduce the food waste. Some forms of packaging, such as reusable boxes and pallets, offer a solution that minimizes product handling. Food and packaging have a unique relationship. By using food packaging correctly, household food waste can be minimized and the environmental burden caused by food overproduction would be eased.

Many specialized studies show that packaging is an interesting and attractive topic because people have become more aware of packaging waste than food waste, underestimating the amount of food waste produced.

The form and nature of pack is considerate one of the most studied methods of reducing food waste. For example, the shift to single-serving formats in certain food categories may result in more packaging per unit mass of food, and the generation potential is reduced. It becomes essential to recognize and investigate the trade-offs between packaging consumption and food waste in order to produce the best environmental outcome (Wikström et al., 2014).

In practice, the type of packaging is selected according to the packaged product (Crenna et al. 2019):

- Bags, satchels, sacks for grain, seeds, sugar, and bakery products
- Bottles and flasks for bottling pasteurized milk, deformable tubes for mustard, mayonnaise, purees, tomato paste, etc.
- Small capacity container for certain products (yoghurt, creams, fresh cheese, ice cream, mayonnaise, etc.)
- Drums and barrels for the transport of milk and dairy products (cream, fresh cheese, ice cream, etc.)
- Trays for fish, pieces of meat, vegetables, and fruits

These types of packaging must comply with certain specific quality conditions for the entire duration of both transport and the life of the food products, their quality deteriorates, thus affecting people's health and generating important material and financial losses.

A survey-based estimate showed that packaging-related food loss/waste contributes 20–25% to the total amount of household food waste (Table 41.1).

Table 41.1 Types of food waste caused by packaging damage

Stage		Types of food waste caused by packaging damage
Food in the supply chain	Post-harvest handling and storage	Product damage caused by contaminants, sharp edges or chips from storage containers
	Processing and packaging	Filling process; difficulties Sealing difficulties; Marketing difficulties
	Distribution	Inappropriate packaging material, poor stability, damage to the barcodes on the packaging
Food in households		Packaging difficult to open; Packaging difficult to empty; Improper package size

Source: https://iba-riscuriambalaje.ro/wp-content/uploads/2020/09/Strategie_risipa_final.pdf

Table 41.2 The packing and the smart technology

Improved packaging properties (mechanical, thermal, barrier, etc.)
The quality of biodegradability
A type of active packaging that helps to extend the life of product
Smart packaging follow the connection with the environment
Bioactive compounds to keep the product fresh (for example, vegetable oils)
Packaging to warn of the approaching expiration date
Packaging with nano sensors, to indicate the quality of food, the amount of micro-organisms
Product information: Nano-barcode, product authenticity

Source: Love Food Hate Waste (2018) A–Z of food storage

According to the European Regulation 450/2009, the main design criteria of an ideal package are: zero toxicity, easy handling, adequate mechanical strength, firm closing characteristics (such as resealing), moisture control, and appropriate labelling. The main benefits of reducing food waste by using innovative packaging are (Caldeira et al. 2019):

- Savings in money by reducing over-purchasing and waste disposal costs; tax benefits through food donation
- Reducing pollution
- Supports efforts to reduce hunger and poverty and reduce health problems

The food packaging technology has a permanent evolving process. Table 41.2 presents the smart and innovative technologies to prevent food waste, from the perspective of packaging,

The role of the pack must change from a passive one (a simple container that protects the contents from moisture, air, microbes, vibrations, shocks, etc.) to an active one (interacting with the product). In these conditions, nanotechnology can be an innovative tool for the development of active food packaging. An example is the Nano Pack project (https://www.nanopack.eu/). Nano Pack films are able to extend the life of bread without additives till 20 days.

High barrier packaging materials (plastics and metallized films) can be used because they provide an important mechanical barrier and are resistant to environmental factors (water, pathogens, etc.) (Study on Food Waste in the Local HoReCa Industry, Carried Out by Edenred Romania 2022).

Another project that can be mentioned is RefuCoat[2] (financed by EU funds), which proposes the development of two new models of bio-based packaging for food:

(1) A fully recyclable active packaging for metallized foils (that used in packs for cereals, crisps, salty snacks etc.)
(2) A fully biodegradable package for chicken products.

An innovative packaging model follow YPACK program of EU[3] (2017). The project develops a fully recyclable and fully biodegradable packaging. The related pack film forms a passive barrier and has active antimicrobial properties, able to prolongue the life of products.[4]

Materials that are considered derived from non-renewable resources are the following: composite material from aluminium foil, from polyethylene and/or polypropylene paper, polypropylene - PP, polyvinyl chloride - PVC, polystyrene - PS, etc. Stopping this waste is done with the help of legislation. Therefore, in Romania, there is Law no. 87/2018 concerning the management of waste. The law prohibits the sale of certain categories of plastic bags (thin plastic bags with handles 50 microns thick). But to reduce the whole phenomenon an ecological tax is necessary.[5]

In order to align national legislation with European objectives in the field, the minimum rates of recycling/utilization of packaging waste in Romania will be increased by 5% (January 1, 2025, respectively, January 1, 2030).

Conclusions In conclusion, the reduction of food waste in Romania must start today, given the potentially positive effects it can generate, as follows:

- Economic and social effects – according to the Institute of Food Bioresources, the relationship between the national level of food waste and existing financial resources is confirmed.
- The effects on the environment (reducing food losses have an positive effect upon land, water, energy, raw materials and the environment, and, implicitly, to the reduction of CO_2 emissions and pollution).
- Reduced costs at the level of companies - by complying with the measures to make economic operators responsible and the hierarchy for reducing food waste, the costs related to the collection of biodegradable waste are reduced, by reducing the quantities, and a part of the food will be recovered through donation, recovery through composting or their transformation into biogas.

---

[2] https://www.refucoat.eu/

[3] https://www.ypack.eu/

[4] https://www.ypack.eu/

[5] 2 fees are paid for plastic bags, regardless of whether they have a handle or not. The first tax is 0.15 lei/pc + VAT and is called the ecotax. The second fee is the packaging fee, which is also 2 lei/kg, as with classic packaging (source: https://www.pungi-biodegradabile.com/2019/10/25/ce-taxe-se-achita-pentru-ambalaje-si-pungi)

At the HoReCa field, there are many ways to reduce food waste, of which here are the most relevant:

(1) Carrying out a food waste audit and perfecting the food waste strategy in tourist guesthouses
(2) Using food waste patterns
(3) Limiting the number of menu options or reducing their quantity
(4) Communicating with suppliers about seasonal produce and purchasing and menu planning
(5) Management of stock in refrigerators, warehouses, and freezers
(6) Using attractive beautiful crockery and cutlery to enhance the presentation and enjoyment of food
(7) Educating about why reducing food waste is important to any business
(8) The presence of suitable storage containers and jars so that food can be stored safely
(9) Labeling and storing food in accordance with food safety guidelines
(10) The food containers and innovative packaging
(11) Selective collection of food waste

Taking into account the fact that sustainable development objective 12 (SDG 12) aims a 50% drop in food waste (in retail and consumer stage), but also to diminish food waste throughout the supply chain, in Romania, there is an urgent need to collect separate and estimate the phenomenon of food waste as close as possible to real.

A national strategy for the prevention of waste and food waste is necessary, in parallel with a more accurate estimate of the phenomenon itself, because it burdens the waste management systems and pollute the environment, not to mention the ethical potential of this reduction (there are people who are at the bottom line of subsistence).

References

Antonescu, D., Apetrei, M., & Surdu, I. (2022). *The dimension of food waste phenomena in Romania. Case-study: Agro-mountain pensions* (pp. 561–574). 30 Years of Inspiring Academic Economic Research – From the Transition to Market Economy to the Interlinked Crises of 21st Century, Sciendo. https://doi.org/10.2478/9788366675261-039

Aschemann-Witzel, J., de Hooge, I. E., Rohm, H., Normann, A., Bossle, M. B., Grønhøj, A., & Oostindjer, M. (2017). Key characteristics and success factors of supply chain initiatives tackling consumer-related food waste – A multiple case study. *Journal of Cleaner Production, 155*, 33–45. https://doi.org/10.1016/j.jclepro.2016.11.173

Belletti, G., & Marescotti, A. (2020). *Short food supply chains for promoting local food on local markets*. United Nations Industrial Development Organization (UNIDO).

Caldeira, C., De Laurentiis, V., & Sala, S. (2019). *Assessment of food waste prevention actions: Development of an evaluation framework to assess the performance of food waste prevention actions, EUR 29901 EN*. Office of the European Union, . ISBN 978-92-76-12388-0JRC118276. https://doi.org/10.2760/9773.2019

Cánovas, C. A., Bernstad Saraiva, A., & Arruda, E. F. (2018). Structured evaluation of food loss and waste prevention and avoidable impacts: A simplified method. *Waste Management & Research, 36*(8), 698–707. https://doi.org/10.1177/0734242x18778779

Chirsanova, A., & Calcatiniuc, D. (2021). The impact of food waste and ways to minimize it. *Journal of Social Sciences, IV*, 128–139. https://doi.org/10.52326/jss.utm.2021.4(1).15

Crenna, E., Sinkko, T., & Sala, S. (2019). Biodiversity impacts due to food consumption in Europe. *Journal of Cleaner Production, 227*, 378–391. https://doi.org/10.1016/j.jclepro.2019.04.054

De Laurentiis, V., Caldeira, C., & Sala, S. (2020). No time to waste: Assessing the performance of food waste prevention actions. *Resources, Conservation and Recycling, 161*, 104946.

https://www.fao.org/3/mb060e/mb060e.pdf

https://iba-riscuriambalaje.ro/wp-content/uploads/2020/09/Strategie_risipa_final.pdf

https://www.pungi-biodegradabile.com/2019/10/25/ce-taxe-se-achita-pentru-ambalaje-si-pungi

https://www.refucoat.eu/

https://www.ypack.eu/

Love Food Hate Waste. (2018). A–Z of food storage,

Parfitt, J., Barthel, M., & Macnaughton, S. (2010). Food waste within food supply chains: Quantification and potential for change to 2050. *Philosophical Transactions of the Royal Society B, 365*, 3065–3081. https://doi.org/10.1098/rstb.2010.0126

Study on Food Waste in the Local HoReCa Industry, Carried Out by Edenred Romania, in partnership with the Employers' Organization of Hotels and Restaurants in Romania (HORA) and Mastercard, April–August 2022, on a sample of 97 food establishments.

Wikström, F., Williams, H., Verghese, K., & Clune, S. (2014). The influence of packaging attributes on consumer behaviour in food-packaging life cycle assessment studies - a neglected topic. *Journal of Cleaner Production, 73*, 100–108. https://doi.org/10.1016/j.jclepro.2013.10.042

Williams, H., Wikström, F., Otterbring, T., et al. (2012). Reasons for household food waste with special attention to packaging. *Journal of Cleaner Production, 24*, 141–148. https://doi.org/10.1016/j.jclepro.2011.11.044

Chapter 42
Study on Demographics and Tourism as the Main Economic Activity in the Dornelor Country

Niculina Onesifereanu, Dănuț Gîțan, and Mioara Bocanici

Abstract The current economic and social context generated by the COVID-19 pandemic has made the post-pandemic tourist more attracted by the safety, food, and environmental health in which they choose to spend their leisure time, but also by the desire for authentic experiences. The Dorna Country manages to harmoniously combine all these elements. Among non-agricultural activities, rural tourism, agrotourism, and ecotourism have seen significant development in recent times. These activities play an important role in the economic development of the Dorna Country and, implicitly, in increasing the income of the inhabitants. The tourists' choice to spend their leisure time in the mountain localities of the Dorna Country determines the support for the entrepreneurial spirit of the inhabitants for the establishment and development of businesses specific to tourism services. The local products consumed by tourists in tourist accommodation units, originating mostly from their own households and from the Dorna Country area, represent an element of cultural and traditional identity specific to local gastronomy. The Dorna Country offers valuable natural tourist attractions, enhanced by the mountain scenery, based on which a wide range of forms of tourism can be developed.

Keywords Tourism · Safety · Demographics · Economic growth · Mountain

42.1 Introduction

The Dorna Country is a mountain area with fairy-tale landscapes where traditions, culture and people's kindness are at home. Taleb Rifai, Secretary General of the World Tourism Organisation, says "Europe is moving towards eco-tourism, towards nature. Romania has a strategy and a vision that is heading in the right direction

---

N. Onesifereanu (✉) · D. Gîțan · M. BOCANICI
Mountain Economy Centre, Vatra Dornei, Romania

© The Author(s), under exclusive license to Springer Nature Switzerland AG 2024
L. Chivu et al. (eds.), *Constraints and Opportunities in Shaping the Future: New Approaches to Economics and Policy Making*, Springer Proceedings in Business and Economics, https://doi.org/10.1007/978-3-031-47925-0_42

when it focuses on the Carpathians and the Delta" and that tourists are tending to turn away from traditional seaside destinations and to find alternative destinations.

Indeed, we must focus on the Carpathians because these mountains of Romania, as University Professor Radu Rey PhD points out, constitute a defined geographical, economic and social entity, with specific relief, climate, natural and social-cultural heritage, an identity recognized in Europe and in the world.

Tourism is integrated into medium- and long-term economic development strategies with the aim to create and offer work opportunities for the population, to support local and national production and to valorise it as well as to improve or to build a modern communications and transport infrastructure that will improve the level of culture and education of the people, to answer the need to improve the knowledge and skills of staff involved in tourism activity, to diversify the local economy, to create opportunities for new partnerships, to attract foreign tourists interested in economy, culture, history; to preserve traditions, culture and identity, etc. Given the complexity of the implications of tourism activity, including in rural areas, with appropriate funding, it can take the form of a real industry.

The main objective of rural tourism is the revitalisation and development of Romania's villages by creating new jobs in rural areas for various categories of employees, therefore financing it becomes a necessary condition.

The development of rural tourism can directly benefit rural communities, where wages are below the population average.

Rural tourism includes a set of entrepreneurial structures, generating important economic and social benefits, operating in a balanced, integrated and sustainable way, which justifies the interest in its development as an economic branch.

Financing rural tourism can eliminate or mitigate the shortcomings faced by this sector (small number of accommodation structures in rural areas, lack of a regulatory framework for tourism development, lack of information about the value of the heritage tourism area and its use, lack of investment in rural infrastructure to encourage the flow of investment in tourism enterprises, improvement of tourism infrastructure, etc.), the specificity of strategic financing being the functionality of this factor of economic development.

Rural tourism has the effect of increasing economic and social development in the area where it is practised and creates interdependence between production, consumption, and social activities.

Even if it offers seasonal or part-time jobs, at a modest wage level, the tourist activity becomes an opportunity for the local population to benefit from additional income and even to follow further training and/or retraining courses that contribute to their personal development. In rural areas, part-time and seasonal jobs seem to be more justifiable than in urban areas because people are usually engaged in personal agricultural activities for themselves and their families which do not allow them to work full time and overtime.

Tourism activities in the countryside require substantial medium and long-term investment, energy, time and money, which must be balanced with the willingness of tourists interested in the countryside but also in comfort, to spend considerable amounts of money on holidays in agri-pensions. Although a tourism industry is emerging in the countryside, the activities carried out must not become overly commercial so as not to undermine the dominant traditional element which is the main factor in the appeal of the countryside.

42.2 Literature Review

A particular geographical unit, the Dornelor Depression is framed by the Suhard Massif and the Călimani Mountains to the north and south, narrowing towards the east, towards the Zugrenilor Gorge, formed between the Giumalău and Pietrosu Massifs, and opening wide to the west.

In the Romanian geographical literature, the depression is also called Dornelor Country, meaning the depression proper and the surrounding mountain range, up to where the economic field extends.

The size of the localities is very different, we have very small communes such as Ciocănești (8290 ha), Iacobeni (9461 ha), medium-sized communes: Șaru Dornei (18,014 ha), Poiana Ștampei (18,076 ha) and very large localities such as Broșteni (42,440 ha) or Cârlibaba (27,148 ha). One explanation for the small size of some administrative-territorial units is the division that took place in 2003 of Iacobeni commune into Iacobeni and Ciocănești communes, respectively, Dorna Candrenilor into Dorna Candrenilor and Coșna.

The share of the areas of the localities in Dornelor Country in the total area of the basin varies between 3.74% Ciocănești commune (the smallest locality) and 19.16% Broșteni town (the largest locality in the area).

The Dornelor Country represents 26% of the area of Suceava County.

The way of living is an aspect to which the inhabitants of Țara Dornelor pay particular attention, the houses are becoming more and more attractive and are the pride of every householder in the area. In general, the houses respect a certain local architecture combining tradition and modernity, a particular situation being found in Ciocănești commune, where a decorative element called the girdle can be seen on almost all the houses of the locality (Fig. 42.1).

Lately, special attention has been paid to increasing the comfort of these houses through specific fittings: water supply, bathroom, kitchen facilities, which makes them more attractive to visitors.

The Dorna Country represents 0.63% of the total area of the Oriental Carpathians. Within the boundaries of this area there are 10 communes and two urban centres as shown in Table 42.1.

Population evolution is one of the most discussed issues when referring to rural areas. Although the decline in the rural population seemed to be a natural phenomenon until 10–15 years ago, and has accompanied the modernization of society in all countries, there are nevertheless situations where the population decline has exceeded the tolerable limits of the demographic system and the demographic balance has been altered.

Fig. 42.1 House from Ciocăneşti commune

Table 42.1 Population of the ATUs in the Dornel Country – pandemic year 2020

No.	Name of locality	Administrative-territorial unit	Population
1.	Vatra Dornei	Municipality	16.731
2.	Broşteni	Town	6.392
3.	Ciocăneşti	Commune	1447
4.	Cîrlibaba	Commune	1950
5.	Şaru Dornei	Commune	4169
6.	Panaci	Commune	2275
7.	Dorna Arini	Commune	2933
8.	Iacobeni	Commune	2078
9.	Dorna Candrenilor	Commune	3113
10.	Poiana Stampei	Commune	2293
11.	Crucea	Commune	2032
12.	Coşna	Commune	1482

Source: National Institute of Statistics, Tempo database
Authors' own research

In the graphical representation below, we can see a slight demographic increase in the communes of Dorna Candrenilor and Poiana Stampei during the period analysed. The distance between these two communes and the municipality of Bistrita makes it easier for the population to commute to jobs in the neighbouring county. There are three large water bottling plants in the communes of Dorna Candrenilor and Panaci, and a fourth in the municipality of Vatra Dornei. These provide jobs for the inhabitants of the whole area of the Dornelor Country. In terms of the number of inhabitants, the commune of Șaru Dornei ranks first, followed by Dorna Candrenilor and Dorna Arini. In terms of the number of inhabitants, Ciocănești comes in last.

The distances from Vatra Dornei municipality to the two communes (Dorna Candrenilor and Poiana Stampei) with a growing population are relatively small (Fig. 42.2).

From the data presented in the graph above, it appears that the population of the Dornelor Country area is decreasing alarmingly in each administrative territorial unit.

This decrease in the population of the Dornelor Country is determined by factors such as a decreasing birth rate, an increasing death rate, but also due to the migration of the population towards more developed towns in the county, or in neighboring counties.

After the closure of mining enterprises in the Dorna area, which occurred mainly between 1991 and 1996, enterprises that had made an important contribution to the employment of a large percentage of the working population in areas such as agriculture and tourism.

The tourism sector has provided a generous source of jobs in recent years in Dornelor Country, given the large number of investments in tourist and agro-tourism guesthouses, most of which have been possible accessing European funds for tourism infrastructure.

Agrotourism is a relatively recent concept, which refers to the various forms of tourism directly related to agricultural activities and/or to buildings with agricultural purposes, roles and functions. This specific form of rural tourism is based on providing accommodation, meals, leisure, and other complementary services within the farm.

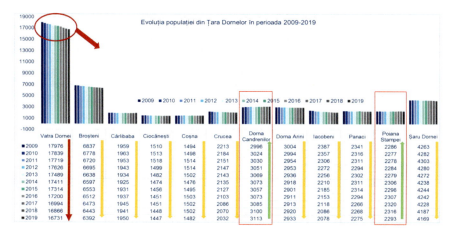

Fig. 42.2 Evolution of Dornelor Country population between 2009 and 2019. (Source: National Institute of Statistics, Tempo database, processed data)

Agrotourism is aimed at those who love nature, cultural-historical values, traditions and customs present in the countryside.

It is also important to underline that tourists have the opportunity to consume fresh food obtained in natural conditions and with high biological value.

Agrotourism is a means to fully exploit the rural environment with its agricultural, tourist, human, and techno-economic potential, with features that differentiate it from standard tourism, namely: the tourist activity takes place in the countryside, where the following are essential: the quality of the guesthouse and tourist reception services, the natural and cultural environment, as well as the authenticity of the tourist products; the tourism offer is authentic, differentiated, multiple in its diversity, organized and run by farmers, therefore by the people of the village; it is an economic activity complementary to farming. It is aimed at the low-income population who want to spend their leisure time on holidays or weekends in the picturesque landscape of the countryside, with cultural and educational activities; it avoids the large tourist agglomerations on the seaside or in bathing or mountain resorts; it is a "diffuse" type of tourism because of the specific nature of its diversified and widely spread offer; therefore, apparently, it does not cause major damage to the natural environment but a certain "ecological threshold" must be taken into account; it is not compatible with mass tourism.

The economic potential of the Dornelor Country is based on the area's resources, namely: forestry resources, dominated by conifers (about 32% of the county's forestry resources are found in the Dornelor Country); natural grassland resources, which can help develop livestock farming, especially cattle; resources of useful mineral substances (manganese, sulphur, iron, uranium, and other substances); mineral water resources, used for therapeutic purposes in internal or external cleansing, in the Vatra Dornei resort, or bottled.

Furthermore, tourist services (accommodation, services, etc.) do not carry additional indirect costs, overheads, commissions, etc., which would increase their costs. Agri-tourism policies should encourage the advantages of rural tourism, in terms of tax relief, tax reduction, resulting in the overall reduction and maintaining of prices, with the effect of retaining customers; the development of the agri-tourism sector implicitly leads tourists to get to know the cultural traditions, landscape and historical values of the countryside.

However, the landscapes and the traditional local culture are not enough in themselves to develop agritourism. Only 0.1% of our country's economy comes from rural tourism and agritourism, which shows that the development of road infrastructure, investment in continuing vocational training and staff training to provide attractive tourist services and customer safety are elements that contribute to the development of this form of tourism.

It has been and it is still necessary to set up more local cooperatives with rural tourism products – attractions, accommodation, and activities – to attract visitors' attention to certain areas of the country. There is also a need to develop more tourism products/programs that do not include accommodation in order to offer tourists a wider range of attractive tourism products.

The evolution of the number of active economic agents in Țara Dornelor, registered in the Trade Registry, in the period 2009–2019, for each administrative territorial unit: there is a slight increase in the number of these agents for all the ATUs of Țara Dornelor, especially in Șaru Dornei commune (Fig. 42.3).

Considering the potential of the area in terms of geography and environmental quality, as well as the tourism potential, the number of economic agents in the Dornelor area is significantly small. We can see that since 2011 a slight recovery in their number has begun, after the great economic crisis of 2008 that affected all sectors of the economy.

There is a numerical evolution of the economic agents for each ATU in Dornelor Country. This is due to the increasing number of farmers accessing European agricultural and non-agricultural funds through the National Rural Development Program.

In recent years, agritourism has undergone a strong development as a variant of rural tourism, which allows for the obtaining of income complementary to farming, by setting up accommodation capacities on the farm and valorising the agricultural products obtained through this activity. Such agro-tourism farms have appeared in almost all rural localities in the Dornelor Basin. A special case is the Ciocănești commune, declared a museum commune, where there is a veritable explosion of agritourism houses.

The Dorna region has a wide range of elements that contribute to the development and maintenance of the quality of tourist products: natural landscapes, traditions, the practice of tourist sports, specific local gastronomy based on high-quality local products: milk and dairy products; products of the sheepfold: cheese, sheep's milk, balm, lamb in the rut; forest products, etc.

Specific local experiences that encourage tourists to return: active recreation; the feeling of security that the area offers, peace and tranquillity; natural, healthy food; a sense of oneself, a return to one's ancestral roots; knowledge of local customs.

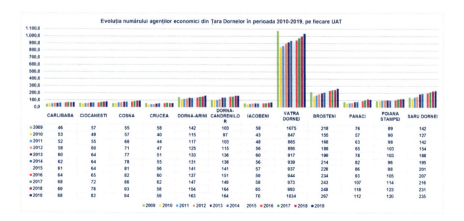

Fig. 42.3 The evolution of the economic agents in Dornelor Country between 2009 and 2019 for each ATU. (Source: National Institute of Statistics, Tempo database, processed data)

42.3 Methodology

The research methods used for this study are: the observation method, the content analysis method. In carrying out the present research, we used the processing and analysis of the existing statistical data.

42.4 Analysis/Results Interpretation

The economy of the Dorna Country is typically mountainous, based on the exploitation of its available resources: agro-zootechnical, agro-tourism, spa, and landscape.

Among the non-agricultural activities, rural tourism, agrotourism, and ecotourism have experienced a significant development in recent times, with the number of tourist structures and leisure facilities in the Dornelor Country showing an increasing trend. Agritourism aims to strengthen the economic capacity of rural households to offer agritourism services. For foreign tourists who spend their holidays in agritourism guesthouses, agri-tourism can be a form of "domestic" export of agri-food products.

The tourists' choice to spend their leisure time in the mountain villages of the Dorna Country determines the support of the inhabitants' entrepreneurial spirit for setting up and investing in local tourism businesses. The local gastronomy is based on products obtained from local raw materials, specific to the area of the Dorna Country.

The Dorna Country offers valuable natural tourist attractions, highlighted by mountain hiking trails, which can be used to develop a wide range of forms of tourism. These are to be found in nature reserves that are valuable from a touristic point of view.

What are the specific elements that attract to this area? What is it that the tourist choosing the Dornelor Country identifies with?

Family tourism, as a component of the local economy, has gained importance in the summer of 2020 as opposed to business tourism. The tourism sector in the Dorna Country registered growth in 2021 in terms of tourist facilities coverage, offering accommodation, recreational and outdoor leisure facilities, while local gastronomy was also in high demand, with local products and cuisine being nationally recognized.

The orientation towards agritourism, due to the immense potential of the area. There are a large number of newly established guesthouses. A very important role has been played by the National Rural Development Programme 2007–2014 and 2014–2020 in supporting this type of economic activity, which the current beneficiaries have accessed.

The legislative factor offers opportunities for diversification of economic activities in the area, through the Mountain Law and the laws for the higher valorisation of agricultural products specific to the mountain area. The abandonment of traditional agricultural activities and the disappearance of the area's specific multi-activity due to the closure of important economic branches such as mining is of note.

42.5 Conclusions

The new tourist profile is based on safety, health, peace, and tranquility of the place where they choose to spend their leisure time, food safety, and health, but also on the desire for authentic experiences, and the Dorna Country manages to harmoniously combine all these elements.

The fact that most of the food consumed in agritourism comes from the region's own production means that there is a high level of profitability in agritourism and the prices of agritourism services are below those of other forms of tourism.

"SWEET BUCOVINA WITH CREAM" is the description offered by the regretted Radu Anton ROMAN, describing it this way and at the same time addressing an invite to this unmissable region:

Tales and legends, my friends, do not belong anywhere else than Bucovina. I'm telling you this as an elite area expert that I am. Where would the charmed prince better guard his garden with golden apples else than in a green valley, near a small monastery and a lively creek? Where else would the bears and legend characters find their "salads" other than next to the storytale pastoral multicolor village, spread onto flowering hills, with poetic paths?

- Come to Bucovina! You will find yourselves at home, the locals are more familiar with tourists than the TV lover with soap opera. You will discover the cow civilization as far as eating cream with cream and you will find out what it means to go through five-six courses at a meal, until you feel like exploding.
- It is a huge loss for a real collector not to mark in his priceless record a bowl of cabbage meat rolls with cream, a pork stew with cream, some cheese pies with cream and some mushroom soup… with cream!"

References

Davies, T., & Cahill, S. (2000, March). Environmental implications of the tourism industry. In *Resources of the future* (Paper 00-14).

European Regional Committee. (2019). *Project for approval – Macroregional strategy for the Carpathian area.* The 137th session, 4 and 5 December 2019.

Ghinea, D. (2018). *The geographical encyclopedia of Romania, 4th edition, completed and updated, Toronto.* http://www.bjdb.ro/docs/egr.pdf

Government Decision no. 558 of 4 August 2017 regarding the approval of the Program for the development of investments in tourism – The masterplan for tourism investment and the eligibility criteria for the tourism investment projects.

Haller, A. P. (2010). Attracting foreign tourists in the Romanian rural area following the economical liberalisation. In *The Romanian rural tourism in the sustainable development context. Present and perspectives* (Vol. XX, pp. 19–128). Tehnopress Publishing House.

Ministry of Entrepreneurship and Tourism. *The list of classified tourist accommodation structures with food serving facilities.* Available at http://turism.gov.ro/web/autorizareturism/.

National Institute of Statistics. *The TEMPO database.* Available at http://statistici.insse.ro/shop/

Nistoreanu, P. (2010). *Sustainable management for the rural communities and the tourism.* ASE Publishing House.

Otiman, P. I. (2005). The sustainable rural development of Romania in the context of European integration (II). *Academica Magazine, no. 44.*

Rey, R., & Ionașcu, G. (2008). *Strategy for a sustainable development of the mountain area in Romania, promoted by the Romanian Mountain Forum.*

Stoian, E. (2005). *Quality management in agrotourism and public food, notes.* USAMV.

The integrated strategy for urban development 2016. Available at http://www.vatradornei.ro/index.php/informatii-publice/strategia-integrata-de-dezvoltare-urbana

The National Plan for Rural Development 2014–2020.

The strategy for socio-economic development of the Vatra Dornei municipality for the horizon 2014–2020. Available at http://www.vatra-dornei.ro/Documente/Strategie_dezvoltare_2014-2020.pdf

Chapter 43
Conclusions and Follow-Ups

Luminița Chivu, George Georgescu, and Jean Vasile Andrei

Abstract The aim of the International Conference ESPERA, initiated in 2013 by the National Institute for Economic Research "Costin C. Kirițescu" (NIER) of the Romanian Academy, is to present and evaluate the economic scientific research portfolio and to argue and substantiate the Romanian development strategies – including European and global best practices. The 9th edition of the Conference, ESPERA 2022, had the theme: "Constraints and opportunities in shaping the future. New approaches to economics and policy making". The Conference agenda includes in the Plenary Session, as guests of honour, scientific personalities from the Romanian Academy and prestigious international institutions, containing approximately 140 papers, structured into 15 parallel sessions, with more than 300 authors from 14 countries. The international event was launched as a thought-provoking exercise for researchers and was organized in such a way as to provide an academic platform for debates, covering the broadest approaches, enabling an interactive exchange of ideas and the latest results and findings, including those emerged in economic science arising from both fundamental and empirical researches and promoting evidence-based policy making new vision under multiple crisis circumstances.

Keywords International scientific event · Romanian academy · Fundamental and empirical economic research · Academic debating platform · Evidence–based policy making

It was a special privilege and a great pleasure for the National Institute for Economic Research "Costin C. Kirițescu", Romanian Academy, Romania, and its partners to welcome the participants to the 9th edition of the International Conference

L. Chivu (✉) · G. Georgescu · J. V. Andrei
National Institute for Economic Research "Costin C. Kirițescu", Romanian Academy, Bucharest, Romania
e-mail: chivu@ince.ro

© The Author(s), under exclusive license to Springer Nature Switzerland AG 2024
L. Chivu et al. (eds.), *Constraints and Opportunities in Shaping the Future: New Approaches to Economics and Policy Making*, Springer Proceedings in Business and Economics, https://doi.org/10.1007/978-3-031-47925-0_43

"Economic Scientific Research – Theoretical, Empirical and Practical Approaches", ESPERA 2022.

The aim of the International Conference ESPERA, initiated in 2013 by the National Institute for Economic Research "Costin C. Kirițescu" (NIER), is to present and evaluate the economic scientific research portfolio and to argue and substantiate the Romanian development strategies – including European and global best practices. The 9th edition of the Conference had the theme: Constraints and opportunities in shaping the future. New approaches to economics and policy making.

The Conference was intended as a thought-provoking exercise for researchers and it is organized in such a way as to provide an academic platform for debates, covering the broadest approaches, enabling an interactive exchange of ideas and the latest results and findings, including those emerged in economic science arising from both fundamental and empirical researches and promoting evidence-based policy making new vision under multiple crisis circumstances.

The contributions and views expressed, on a meritorious and wide-ranging level will be disseminated, as in previous years, in a volume – Proceedings of the International Conference ESPERA 2022 – that will be submitted to EBSCO and also for evaluation and inclusion in Conference Proceedings Citation Index by Clarivate, Web of Science.

The conference agenda includes approximately 140 papers, structured into 15 sessions, with a number of more than 300 authors from 14 countries.

First of all, we want to address special thanks to:

- Our international and national partners for being traditionally with us
- To our guests of honour from the Romanian Academy and abroad who accepted the invitation to participate at the ESPERA conference
- To the sessions` moderators and reviewers for their work performed every year from the first call for papers to the publishing proceedings volumes
- To all the participants because they are confident of the potential and scientific level of the international conference ESPERA and keep it alive!

The first part of the ESPERA 2022 plenary session was dedicated to Speeches and messages.

We were honored with the presence of Academician Ioan Dumitrache, General Secretary of the Romanian Academy. The Romanian Academy, thanks to the prestigious scientific results of the academicians and researchers from more than 70 institutes in its research network, stands first in the SCIMAGO ranking for Romania in 2022, and in top 500 academic and research-related institutions in the world.

The extraordinary potential for interdisciplinary research has been proved recently, during the COVID pandemic, when in May 2020, more than 30 studies elaborated by the researchers in the fields of economic, social, and medical sciences regarding the impact of the pandemic have been posted on the Romanian Academy website.

Under the coordination of Mr. Secretary General, a cycle of debates was organized, with the participation of researchers and specialists from all fields, focusing the post-pandemic evolution of the Romanian economy and society, the results of which were sent to the general public and decision-makers.

On behalf of the institute, we had the special pleasure of having with us the Deputy General Director, Professor Valeriu Ioan – Franc, Corresponding Member of the Romanian Academy.

Valeriu Ioan-Franc is also corresponding member of the Real Academia de Ciencias Económicas y Financieras of the Institute of Spain, member of the European Academy of Management and Business Economics and member of its Executive Council, Madrid; member of the Barcelona Economics Network and of the Academic Council of the Association of Economics Faculties from Romania.

Professor Valeriu Ion-Franc is the head of the Centre for Economic Information and Documentation and Editor-in-chief of our institute publications. He also has a prodigious scientific activity with more than 30 books and 150 articles, editorial and publishing in economics.

In the second part of the plenary session they were, Honorary Keynote Speakers.

First, Dr. Mile Vasić which is full professor, former ambassador and diplomat, manager and consultant with experience in teaching, consulting, managing various systems, in the for-profit, non-profit and public sectors, with a strategic and focused approach to planning and establishing creative strategies for optimization internal business, and encouraging employee satisfaction.

His Excellency is current President of the European Marketing and Management Association, founded in 2007, an institution that has gained international prestige through performance and high-quality scientific results.

The opportunity offered to our institute, in 2021, to become a member of this association has opened up important ways for international scientific collaboration developments, exchange of ideas, keeping in permanent contact with the latest scientific results and achievements of partners, with the events organized by them, contributing at the same time to the increase in the international visibility of our research results and opening new opportunities for collaboration within various projects, including those regarding PhD students and young researchers.

Professor Mile Vasic presented his plenary paper with the title: "New global challenges and the necessity to rethink cooperation among academia, business and policy makers!"

The second plenary paper, with the title "The impact of disruptive digital technologies on the knowledge economy and education strategies" was presented by Mr. David Wortley, Bournemouth University, United Kingdom.

Mr. David Wortley is a Fellow of the Royal Society of Arts with a career which has embraced the converging and emerging technologies of telecommunications, computing, digital media and community informatics and the creative industries. He is an entrepreneur and innovator with a passion for applying technology to social and economic development.

David recently supported De Montfort University in Leicester as a Research Fellow in the Art, Design and Humanities Faculty. He was also Founding Director of the Serious Games Institute at Coventry University and was responsible for the development of the Institute as a global thought leader on the application of immersive technologies to social and economic issues such as education, health, commerce and climate change.

Professor Ahmet Niyazi Özker deliver the presentation entitled "New approaches of post-2015 economic growth-oriented policies in Turkey: the actual position of macro variables"

Dr. Ahmet Niyazi Özker is professor at the Department of Economics, Bandirma Onyedi Eylül Üniversitesi, Turkey and is specialized in Macroeconomics, Financial Economics and Monetary Economics. He is member of the board of directors of the Institute of Economic Development and Social Researches – IKSAD, Turkey.

This year, on August 26–27, IKSAD, in Bucharest, our institute and RebResNet, have organized "VI-International European Conference on Interdisciplinary Scientific Research" which was a good opportunity to gather, meet friends and open new scientific collaboration relationships, to exchange opinions, to take the pulse of advances in specific theoretical, empirical and applied scientific research in our field.

This conference had an impressive number of papers, more than 250, with a number of over 500 authors from 41 countries, on an extremely wide range of subjects, including economics, sociology, linguistics, medicine, engineering etc. Thank you!

Dr. Felix Puime Guillén is associate professor at University of A Coruña, Department of Business, Faculty of Economics and Business, Spain. He has a degree in Economic and Business Administration from the University of Santiago de Compostela. Doctor in Business Administration and Management from the University of Vigo. Professor of Business Schools in Spain, other countries from Europe and Latin America.

Author of numerous publications in specialized financial journals, invited speaker at national and international scientific conferences. He has more than 32 years of experience in the business in the field of corporate finance, both nationally and internationally.

Professor Felix Puime Guillén is also, starting with November this year, associate researcher to the Center for Renewable Energies and Energy Efficiency, part of our institute.

Professor presented the paper "Renewable Hydrogen as the key sustainable solution for the decarbonization of the economy".

The next plenary presentation, with the title: "Stock model analysis and inference based on stochastic processes" had as authors professor Vlad Ştefan Barbu, from Laboratory of Mathematics Raphaël Salem, University of Rouen-Normandy, France, Professor Guglielmo D'Amico, University "G. d'Annunzio", Chieti – Pescara, Italy and Research Fellow Riccardo de Blasis, University Politecnica delle Marche, Italy.

We have the pleasure to tell you that Vlad Ştefan Barbu, starting with November this year, became associate researcher to the Center for Demographic Researches, part of our institute.

Among its scientific responsibilities, we mention vice-president of the Romanian Society of Applied and Industrial Mathematics, member of the National Council for

Statistics and Forecast of Higher Education, Ministry of Education and guidance of master's and doctoral students, of research engineers.

With more than sixty scientific publications, the professor's articles have accumulated over a thousand citations over time.

I would like to address special thanks to INCE General Deputy Director Mr. George Georgescu for his constant scientific support and efforts to make this event possible. And only those who have not organized an international conference do not understand the complexity and difficulty of such an approach. Thank you for your professional work!

An important contribution to this Conference was made by Professor Jean-Vasile Andrei, Scientific coordinator, Center for Research on Renewable Energy and Energy Efficiency. His significant experience in organizing large-scale international events was of real benefit to us. Thank you!

Special thanks to Senior Researcher Carmen Adriana Gheorghe, coordinator of the conference organizing committee, who was with us constantly and also to researchers Oprea Mihaela and Vlădescu Mihaela and Professor Dan Mateescu.

We continue to rely on your scientific, logistical, technical, administrative support to bring this important event to a successful conclusion.

Index

A

Agriculture, 134, 216, 424, 438, 440, 442, 445, 447–456, 460, 462, 470, 477, 503, 523
Analysis of entrepreneurial opportunities, 190–198

B

Banking sector, 263, 264
Benefits, 11–13, 15, 19, 20, 24, 26, 27, 44, 46, 49, 52, 53, 59, 92, 93, 95, 103–106, 118, 140, 178, 220, 318, 332–341, 388, 401, 431, 432, 436–441, 445, 446, 470, 488, 514, 520, 533
Bioeast initiative, 460, 462, 463, 468, 470
BioeastsUp project, 460–470
Bioeconomy concept, 461
Bioleaching, 300
Birth rate, 84–86, 94–96, 480, 523
Bitcoin, 274–276, 278, 283
Black Sea, 332–334, 336–341
Broadband infrastructure, 150, 153
Business environment, 141, 146, 175, 177, 190–193, 197, 198, 400
Business integrity, 24–29, 35, 36

C

CEE countries, 460, 463, 465, 470
Children, 12, 85–88, 90–96, 100, 107
Circular economy, 46, 47, 166, 202, 203, 205, 207–212, 290, 300, 465, 502, 511, 513

Circular economy indicators, 202–203, 210, 211
Citizen participation, 159–162, 166, 167
Climate change, 149, 219, 233, 262, 285, 287, 306, 410, 445, 447, 448, 494, 496–499, 532
Cobalt, 296, 297, 308, 310–312, 320, 323–327
Cointegration test, 75–77, 80, 275, 455
Competitiveness, 2, 13, 58, 113, 139, 140, 144, 149, 150, 182, 219, 299, 305, 388, 393, 394, 396, 398, 416, 504
Competitive pressure, 58
Continental shelf, 334, 336, 341
COVID-19, 101, 147, 148, 167, 174, 243–250, 360–363, 367, 479, 500
COVID-19 pandemic, 41, 44, 48, 101, 148, 165, 166, 174, 243, 244, 246, 250, 252, 257, 304, 314, 347, 360–367, 370, 384, 479, 500
Critical metals, 296–301
Critical minerals, 304–314, 317–327
Crop farms, 424, 425
Cryptocurrency efficiency, 274–283
Cryptocurrency market, 274–276, 283
Cyberattacks, 402
Cybersecurity, 28, 41, 149, 154, 165

D

Dairy farms, 436–446
Demographics, 2, 84, 85, 87, 92–96, 100, 110, 127, 167, 308, 385, 474, 475, 477, 479, 480, 486–488, 519–527, 532

© The Editor(s) (if applicable) and The Author(s), under exclusive license to Springer Nature Switzerland AG 2024
L. Chivu et al. (eds.), *Constraints and Opportunities in Shaping the Future: New Approaches to Economics and Policy Making*, Springer Proceedings in Business and Economics, https://doi.org/10.1007/978-3-031-47925-0

Demography, 2, 100, 308, 385, 474, 475, 477, 479
Determinants of adoption, 436
Development strategy, 2, 4, 140, 218, 222, 223, 231, 233, 234, 237, 238, 241, 475, 497, 520
Digital finance, 173, 176, 177, 179, 184, 185
Digitalization, 40, 147–154, 160, 304, 306, 371, 401, 475, 476, 478, 481–485, 488

E

Ecological farming practices, 436, 439, 444–446
E-commerce, 150–152, 175
Economic and social impact, 148, 218, 236–238
Economic growth, 73, 74, 84, 105, 124–128, 130, 132, 134–136, 139, 158, 202, 247–250, 253, 254, 287, 304, 305, 318, 341, 370, 449
Economic growth trajectory, 126–128, 131–136
Economics, 3, 8, 40, 58, 73, 93, 100, 110, 124, 139, 148, 162, 175, 190, 203, 224, 361, 437, 447, 460, 474, 502, 509, 520, 530
Economic support, 244, 246, 247, 249
Economy, 1, 8, 40, 58, 100, 124, 139, 149, 164, 175, 203, 219, 245, 259, 262, 274, 285, 296, 305, 318, 339, 360, 370, 388, 394, 424, 445, 474, 496, 520, 531
Education, 1, 4, 53, 72–74, 85, 86, 92–94, 100, 102, 103, 105, 133, 140, 143, 144, 163, 166, 168, 222, 223, 227–230, 241, 371, 394, 403, 438, 467, 474, 477, 485, 488, 497, 520, 531–533
Education and training, 100, 218, 227–229
Effect, 26, 60, 73, 86, 103, 112, 143, 151, 175, 202, 236, 248, 252, 262, 285, 298, 304, 340, 362, 370, 384, 396, 400, 410, 424, 436, 451, 460, 499, 509, 520
Efficiency, 43, 45, 47, 49, 51, 59–64, 66, 159, 162, 166, 167, 175, 177, 178, 244, 249, 262, 274–276, 278, 280, 282, 283, 299, 306, 377, 382, 387, 388, 390, 402, 404, 424, 485, 533
Efficient market hypothesis, 274
Employee resourcing, 110–112
Employee trust, 26–27, 36
Energy consumption, 46, 288, 382, 384, 387, 410, 420, 449–451, 453–456
Energy crisis, 377, 409–421
Ensemble modeling, 355
Entrepreneurial experience, 190–193, 195, 197, 198
Environmental taxation, 286, 287, 293
Environment, social and governance (ESG), 28, 262–270
Ethics, 17–20, 24, 26–28, 35
EU-27, 25, 362, 479–481
EU Bioeconomy, 464, 465
EU countries, 35, 203, 248–250, 253, 255, 323, 411, 416, 449, 456, 463–465, 479, 482, 503
European gas market, 372, 374
European Green Deal, 429, 504
Event study, 262–264
Expenditure rule, 253–255, 259
Expenditures, 74, 139–146, 254, 255, 287, 288, 290, 292, 293, 339, 340, 419, 426

F

Fertility, 84–89, 91, 93, 94, 411, 424, 445, 477
Financial instruments, 148, 175–177, 181, 182, 496, 500, 505
Fiscal framework, 251, 252, 254, 257, 338
Fiscal regulations, 251, 252, 255–257, 259
Food waste, 509–516
Futures market, 274–276, 281, 283

G

GDP per capita, 150–153
Geopolitics, 296, 305–307, 314
GHG emissions, 293, 447–450, 453–455
Good governance, 150, 158–168
Greenhouse gases, 218, 222, 223, 233, 235, 384, 450
Green vehicles, 389

H

Health index, 245, 247, 249–250
HoReCa, 509–512, 516
Horticultural sector, 415, 419, 420
Human-Centric, 42, 45, 47, 52
Human resource, 3, 18, 21, 45, 58, 60, 61, 67, 110–114, 118, 167, 203, 394, 480
Human resource development, 58–67
Human resource investment, 58

I

Impact, 26, 41, 59, 80, 84, 100, 113, 124, 139, 148, 174, 196, 202, 222, 244, 253, 262, 274, 285, 299, 307, 318, 339, 355, 360, 370, 388, 400, 411, 424, 448, 488, 497, 530
Impulse response function, 364

Index 535

Industrial policy, 146, 312, 393–396
Industrial revolution, 40–42, 46, 51, 52, 124, 125, 135, 304, 306, 308, 319
Industry 4.0, 40–46, 48, 49, 52
Industry 5.0, 40–53
Inequalities, 8, 101, 107, 153, 158, 225, 233, 391, 486, 497
Information and communication technologies (ICT), 51, 140, 158–168, 313, 318
Integrated ecology, 390
International competitiveness, 388

J
Job duration, 29, 32, 35

K
Kendall's tau-b correlation, 25
Key minerals trade, 318, 319

L
Labour force, 100, 103, 110, 111, 113, 247, 474, 476, 485, 487
Labour market, 44, 46, 86, 103–105, 110–119, 133, 190, 318, 474, 479, 480, 485, 486, 488
Large family, 84–96
Lens database, 224
Lithium, 296, 310, 311, 319–325, 327

M
Machine learning, 346–357
Manufacturing industry, 46, 134, 360, 362, 363, 365–367
Medium technology activities, 360, 361, 363–366
Mineral resources, 203, 304, 307, 309, 317–319
Mobile, 104, 105, 165, 184, 185, 306, 400–406
Moral, 8–15, 24, 25, 397
Mountain, 4, 323, 494–505, 512, 519–521, 524, 526
Mountain economy, 2, 496, 500, 501, 505

N
Natural gas, 332, 334–339, 341, 346–348, 352, 353, 355–357, 370–373, 376–378, 411
Natural gas market, 338, 346, 347, 371, 374, 377, 409
Natural gas reserves, 335, 336
Natural resources, 2, 46, 165, 202, 438, 500, 505

O
Offshore exploitation projects, 332–341

P
Pollution, 46, 47, 224, 225, 236, 241, 263, 286, 382, 386–390, 438, 447–451, 454–456, 514, 515
Population Censuses, 474–478, 487
Price prediction, 356
Primary sector, 125, 126, 129–131, 133–135
Productivity, 24–26, 40, 44, 46, 49, 59, 61, 140, 175, 253, 424, 428, 429, 431, 437
Public debt, 249, 251–259
Public management, 18–20
Public organisations, 17–21
Public service motivation, 18–21
Python environment, 348

Q
Quality of life, 2, 4, 19, 73, 140, 158, 160, 218, 222–225, 227–229, 231, 241

R
R&D sector, 139, 142, 397
Recovery, 95, 147–150, 153, 154, 175, 219, 245, 249, 250, 252, 299–301, 310, 312, 314, 361, 362, 366, 367, 370, 371, 374, 377, 394, 500–502, 504, 515, 525
Recovery and Resilience Facility, 147, 149, 150
Recruiting, 110, 113, 119
Recruitment methods, 110–120
Regional change, 202–212
Research, 1, 8, 18, 25, 41, 59, 72, 87, 103, 111, 140, 149, 159, 176, 190, 202, 218, 247, 259, 262, 274, 287, 300, 307, 346, 382, 395, 402, 437, 449, 461, 474, 496, 526, 530
Resilience, 41, 44, 47–53, 147–150, 153, 154, 175, 182, 252, 255, 263, 319, 360, 497, 501
Romania, 1–5, 12, 14, 84, 85, 87–96, 100–107, 123–136, 141–143, 145, 146, 148, 150, 152, 153, 179, 203, 205, 207, 332–341, 346, 352, 354–357, 360–362, 367, 370–374, 376, 378, 382, 387–390, 395, 400, 401, 403, 404, 410, 413, 415, 416, 424, 429, 431, 432, 439, 449, 450, 462, 463, 465, 474–489, 500–503, 511, 512, 515, 516, 519, 520, 529–531

S

Safety, 2, 27, 28, 46, 51, 60, 165, 318, 319, 382, 386, 388, 389, 445, 450, 494, 495, 498, 513, 516, 524, 527
Scenarios, 2, 85, 221, 372, 387, 411, 418–421, 467, 498
School population, 99–107
Science, 2, 4, 5, 8, 11, 12, 14, 15, 73, 139, 142, 396, 401, 437, 530
Short economic cycles, 124–126, 130, 131
Skills, 25, 30, 31, 35, 46, 48–50, 52, 53, 60, 103, 110, 112, 149, 153, 154, 165, 166, 394–396, 437, 438, 465, 485, 486, 500, 520
Smart city, 158–168
Smartphone evolution, 400, 401, 405, 406
Spot market, 275, 283, 370
Stock market, 263–265
Structural budget balanced rule, 254
Sustainability, 41, 43, 44, 46–49, 52, 53, 149, 158–168, 185, 219, 249, 252, 254–257, 259, 287, 300, 382, 402, 436–438, 465, 468, 469, 483, 497, 502, 504, 505
Sustainable development, 1, 4, 24, 47, 107, 158, 160, 162, 164, 165, 176, 219, 319, 382–384, 387, 390, 396, 424, 447, 448, 462, 463, 483, 484, 488, 494, 495, 497, 498, 500, 502, 505, 516
Sustainable transport, 382, 383, 387–391

T

Tourism, 371, 385, 497, 500, 501, 519–527
Training, 4, 25–31, 35, 36, 46, 50, 51, 53, 58–67, 100, 103, 142, 149, 154, 222, 223, 227–230, 241, 350, 354, 355, 396, 397, 438, 444, 446, 500, 510, 520, 524
Transport demand, 385–387, 390
Transport infrastructures, 382, 383, 385, 520
Transport networks, 373, 385, 388

U

Urban landscape, 216, 218, 222, 223, 229–232, 241
Urban regeneration, 216–241

V

Value added in agriculture, 450, 451, 453
Value chain, 307, 314, 318, 319, 321, 325, 360, 361, 367, 371, 469, 470
Vector autoregression (VAR) model, 75, 77, 363, 364
Vocational training, 30, 524

Printed in the United States
by Baker & Taylor Publisher Services